English Composition and Grammar

BENCHMARK EDITION

Fourth Course

English Composition and Grammar

BENCHMARK EDITION

John E. Warriner

Fourth Course

 Harcourt Brace Jovanovich, Publishers

Orlando   San Diego   Chicago   Dallas

THE SERIES:

English Composition and Grammar: Introductory Course
English Composition and Grammar: First Course
English Composition and Grammar: Second Course
English Composition and Grammar: Third Course
English Composition and Grammar: Fourth Course
English Composition and Grammar: Fifth Course
English Composition and Grammar: Complete Course
Annotated Teacher's Edition and Teacher's Resource Book for each above title.

CORRELATED SERIES:

English Workshop: Introductory Course
English Workshop: First Course
English Workshop: Second Course
English Workshop: Third Course
English Workshop: Fourth Course
English Workshop: Fifth Course
English Workshop: Review Course

Composition: Models and Exercises, First Course
Composition: Models and Exercises, Second Course
Composition: Models and Exercises, Third Course
Composition: Models and Exercises, Fourth Course
Composition: Models and Exercises, Fifth Course
Advanced Composition: A Book of Models for Writing, Complete Course

Vocabulary Workshop: Introductory Course
Vocabulary Workshop: First Course
Vocabulary Workshop: Second Course
Vocabulary Workshop: Third Course
Vocabulary Workshop: Fourth Course
Vocabulary Workshop: Fifth Course
Vocabulary Workshop: Complete Course

John E. Warriner taught English for thirty-two years in junior and senior high schools and in college. He is chief author of the *English Composition and Grammar* series, coauthor of the *English Workshop* series, general editor of the *Composition: Models and Exercises* series, and editor of *Short Stories: Characters in Conflict.* His coauthors have all been active in English education.

For permission to reprint copyrighted material, grateful acknowledgment is made to the following sources:

Joseph Alper: From "Biology and Mental Illness" by Joseph Alper in *The Atlantic Monthly,* December 1983.

Elizabeth Barnett, Literary Executor of the Estate of Norma Millay Ellis: "God's World" by Edna St. Vincent Millay from *Collected Poems.* Copyright © 1913, 1940 by Edna St. Vincent Millay. Published by Harper & Row, Publishers, Inc.

The Boston Globe Newspaper Company/Washington Post Writers Group: From "Eleanor Roosevelt, a Heroine for All Seasons, All People" by Ellen Goodman in the *Boston Globe.* © 1984 by The Boston Globe Newspaper Company/Washington Post Writers Group.

Commonweal Foundation: From "The Right to Remain Indian" by Robert A. Hecht in *Commonweal,* March 30, 1979. © 1979 by Commonweal Publishing Company.

Delacorte Press/Seymour Lawrence: From "Who Am I This Time?" in *Welcome to the Monkey House* by Kurt Vonnegut, Jr. Copyright © 1961 by Kurt Vonnegut, Jr. Originally published in *The Saturday Evening Post.*

Annie Dillard and her agent, Blanche C. Gregory, Inc.: From "Heaven and Earth in Jest" by Annie Dillard in *Harper's* Magazine, October 1973. Copyright © 1974 by Annie Dillard.

Doubleday & Company, Inc.: From *Nothing to Fear* by Fraser Kent. Copyright © 1977 by Fraser Kent.

The Dramatic Publishing Company: Dramatization by Perry Clark based upon the book *The Homecoming* by Earl Hamner, Jr. © MCMLXXVI by Earl Hamner, Jr. All rights reserved. Printed in the United States of America.

Farrar, Straus & Giroux, Inc.: From *The Summer of the Great Grandmother* by Madeleine L'Engle. Copyright © 1974 by Crosswicks, Ltd.

Harcourt Brace Jovanovich, Inc.: From *Economics: Principles and Policy* by William J. Baumol and Alan S. Blinder. Copyright © 1979 by Harcourt Brace Jovanovich, Inc. From *The Origins and Development of the English Language,* Third Edition by Thomas Pyles and John Algeo. Copyright © 1982 by Harcourt Brace Jovanovich, Inc. Abridged from *Adventures in American Literature,* Heritage Edition Revised. Copyright © 1985 by Harcourt Brace Jovanovich, Inc.

Harper & Row, Publishers, Inc.: From pp. 99–100 in *Blood and Grits* by Harry Crews. Copyright © 1975 by Harry Crews. From *Stride Toward Freedom* (Titled: "Nonviolent Resistance") by Martin Luther King, Jr. Copyright © 1958 by Martin Luther King, Jr. Text of "Carving a Wooden Egg for Practice" from *HOW TO MAKE WHIRLIGIGS AND WHIMMY DIDDLES and Other American Folkcraft Objects* by Florence H. Pettit. Copyright © 1972 by Florence H. Pettit.

Harper & Row, Publishers, Inc. and Olwyn Hughes: From "The Mirror" in *Crossing the Waters* by Sylvia Plath. Copyright © 1963, 1971 by Ted Hughes. Originally published in *The New Yorker.* Published in Great Britain by Faber and Faber, Ltd., London.

A. M. Heath & Company Limited, Ruth Prawar Jhabvala, John Murray Ltd., and Russell and Volkening, Inc.: From *Heat and Dust* by Ruth Prawar Jhabvala.

The Hogarth Press: From *Cider with Rosie (The Edge of Day)* by Laurie Lee. Copyright © 1959 by Laurie Lee.

Richard Hopper: From "Why It's Called a Turkey" by Richard Hopper in *American Heritage,* October/November 1984.

Houghton Mifflin Company: From *Let Us Now Praise Famous Men* by James Agee and Walker Evans. Copyright 1939, 1940 by James Agee; copyright 1941 by James Agee and Walker Evans; copyright © renewed 1969 by Mia Fritsch Agee. Entry "president" from *The American Heritage Dictionary of the English Language.* © 1980 by Houghton Mifflin Company.

Alfred A. Knopf, Inc.: From "Prelude" in *The Short Stories of Katherine Mansfield* by Katherine Mansfield. Copyright 1920 by Alfred A. Knopf, Inc.; renewed 1948 by J. Middleton Murry.

Little, Brown and Company: From *An Unfinished Woman* by Lillian Hellman. Published by Little, Brown and Company.

Edmund G. Love and his agent, Blanche C. Gregory, Inc.: From *The Situation in Flushing* by Edmund G. Love. Copyright © 1965 by Edmund G. Love.

PHOTO CREDITS:

Printed in the United States of America

ISBN 0-15-311734-6

To the Student

The reason English is a required subject in almost all schools is that nothing in your education is more important than learning how to express yourself well. You may know a vast amount about a subject, but if you are unable to communicate what you know, you are severely limited. No matter how valuable your ideas may be, they will not be very useful if you cannot express them clearly and convincingly. Language is the means by which people communicate. In your part of the world, it is English, a remarkably rich and flexible language. By learning how your language functions and by practicing language skills, you can acquire the competence necessary to express adequately what you know and what you think.

You have two guides to help you in your study of English. One is your teacher; the other is your textbook. This textbook is designed to help you improve your ability to use English. It will show you how the English sentence works, how words are combined in sentences, and how the parts of sentences may best be arranged for clear communication. You will learn the difference between sentences which are strong and clear and smooth, and sentences which are weak and confusing and awkward. You will learn to plan and organize units of writing much larger than the sentence. You will learn to use standard English, the kind of English that is most widely considered acceptable. The more you put to use the things you learn from this book—in other words, the more you practice the skills explained here—the greater will be your command of English.

Do not limit your use of this book to the times when you are given an assignment in the book. Learn to use the book as a reference book in which you can look up answers to questions that arise when you are writing something for an assignment in any of your courses. As you become familiar with the contents and arrangement of the book, you will know where to look for specific kinds of information. By using the index, you can quickly find answers to questions about grammar and standard usage, punctuation, capital letters, sentence structure, spelling, outlining, letter writing, and many other matters. By using the book in this way, you are actually teaching yourself, which is a very good way to learn.

J.W.

CONTENTS

2. Writing Paragraphs

3. Writing Four Types of Paragraphs   75
PARAGRAPHS FOR DIFFERENT PURPOSES

4. Writing Expository Compositions

5. Writing Expository Compositions   142

SPECIFIC EXPOSITORY WRITING ASSIGNMENTS

6. Writing Persuasive Compositions   157

BUILDING AN ARGUMENT

7. Writing Narration and Description 188

STORIES; CHARACTER AND BIOGRAPHICAL SKETCHES

8. Writing a Research Paper   231

RESEARCH, WRITING, DOCUMENTATION

Picture the Possibilities: IDEAS FOR WRITING IW1

Part Two: COMPOSITION:
Writing and Revising Sentences

Part Three: TOOLS FOR WRITING AND REVISING

GRAMMAR

13. The Parts of Speech   331
THEIR IDENTIFICATION AND FUNCTION

27. Punctuation   608

APOSTROPHES, HYPHENS,
DASHES, PARENTHESES

28. Spelling   624

IMPROVING YOUR SPELLING

Part Four: RESOURCES FOR WRITING AND STUDYING

29. The Library   647

ACCESS TO INFORMATION

Part Five: SPEAKING AND LISTENING

33. Speaking and Listening   721
SKILLS AND STRATEGIES

34. Understanding Mass Media   747
ELECTRONIC AND PRINT

Index   761

PART ONE

COMPOSITION:
The Writing Process

CHAPTER 1

Writing and Thinking
THE WRITING PROCESS

Writing is an ongoing, recursive process, not a single action. Whether writing a paragraph or an essay, you must pass through many stages before you finish: thinking, planning, evaluating, making decisions, making changes. In this chapter, you will learn about and practice the stages of the writing process.

THE WRITING PROCESS

PREWRITING—Identifying your purpose and audience; choosing and limiting a subject; considering attitude and tone; and gathering, classifying, and ordering information

WRITING A FIRST DRAFT—Expressing your ideas in sentences and paragraphs

EVALUATING—Judging the content, organization, and style of a draft

REVISING—Improving the content, organization, and style

PROOFREADING—Checking the revised version to correct errors in grammar, usage, and mechanics

WRITING THE FINAL VERSION—Preparing a final version and proofreading it

PREWRITING

Prewriting, the first stage in the writing process, is a time for thinking and planning. During this stage you must answer important questions: Why am I writing? For whom am I writing? What will I write about? What will I say? How will I say it?

THE WRITER'S PURPOSE

1a. Have in mind a clear purpose for writing.

Every piece of writing has a purpose, and most writing has one of four basic purposes: to tell a story, to inform or explain, to describe, or to persuade. Even when more than one of these purposes is present, a single purpose usually guides the writing. In an essay about the history of the Statue of Liberty, for example, you may describe your first sight of the statue, but your main purpose is to give information. Considering your purpose is an important part of prewriting.

Techniques for Prewriting. Consider your main purpose for writing. Is it

- Narrative: To tell a story?   An essay about a shopping trip
- Expository: To explain   A paragraph defining genes
  or inform?
- Descriptive: To describe?   A letter describing your room
- Persuasive: To persuade?   A brochure encouraging
      organ donations

EXERCISE 1. Identifying Purposes for Writing.   Identify your purpose for writing about the following topics. (Some items may have more than one purpose.)

1. Why the legal drinking age should be twenty-one
2. The earliest history of your community
3. What your best friend looks like
4. What happened when your tent collapsed during the middle of the night on a recent camping trip

5. Why people who live in apartments should (or should not) be allowed to have dogs or cats

EXERCISE 2. Identifying Purposes for Writing. Determine the writer's purpose in each of the following paragraphs.

1. According to the National Centers for Disease Control, lung cancer will soon become the leading cause of all cancer deaths among women. Until now, fewer women than men have suffered from lung cancer because fewer women smoked. The epidemic of lung cancer among women is especially tragic because, according to the National Centers for Disease Control, it is preventable: Approximately eighty-five percent of all lung cancer cases are directly caused by cigarette smoking. In recent years women have been striving for equal rights with men. Let's not make that equality extend to lung cancer. If you are already smoking cigarettes, it's not too late to stop. If you have not yet started, stay smart—and don't!

2. When the frame of a tall building is complete, construction workers hold a ceremony called "topping out." A fir tree (sometimes a flag) is hoisted to the building's top to signal that the framework is complete. During the 1930's this custom was known in New York City as a "roof-tree raising" or "roof-bush raising." Most builders believe that the custom originated in Scandinavia and dates back as far as A.D. 700. According to Scandinavian mythology, spirits lived within each tree. The topping-out ceremony was an attempt to appease the anger of the tree spirits for having chopped down trees for lumber. In Norway today the topping-out ceremony takes place for the building of homes as well as public buildings.

CRITICAL THINKING:
Analyzing How Purpose Affects Writing

Analysis is the critical thinking skill by which you break a whole into smaller parts and determine the parts' relationships. Purpose is just one part of writing, but it affects both content and language. Analyzing purpose during prewriting helps you choose specific details and a writing style.

Consider how purpose affects a paragraph about a bicycle trip. If your purpose is to inform, you will include specific details about planning a route and will write in fairly formal language.

EXAMPLE   The preparation for any bicycle tour—and the fun—begins with planning a route. The first source of information is a good motoring atlas, like Rand McNally's. It indicates the location and size of settlements, classifies highways and points out landmarks and other places of interest that might be worth a visit. Upon request, local chambers of commerce will furnish brochures about particular areas and calendars of local events.

GWEN BALLARD

However, if you are telling a story, you will use less formal language and choose amusing details or events.

EXAMPLE   When my brother Larry persuaded me to join him on a two-day bicycle trip, I should have known better. I had been used to bicycling back and forth to school (about two miles each way), but I'd never really bicycled for a long distance. Also, my bike is an old clunker—a heavy five-speed that seems to have only two speeds no matter what I do. We set out one Saturday morning before dawn. Larry zipped along in the dark on his ten-speed, while I pedaled furiously to keep him in sight. I yelled at him to slow down, but he either ignored me or pretended not to hear. If I'd had any sense at all, I'd have turned back and missed the weekend's disasters; but somehow I was into "proving" myself, so I kept on pedaling madly.

Persuasion and description also combine different details and language. To persuade, you use formal, concise language; you present opinions, reasons, and evidence. To describe, you use less formal language; you include concrete, sensory details and vivid images.

Techniques for Prewriting. Consider how your purpose will affect the language and details you choose for your writing.

PURPOSE:	LANGUAGE:	DETAILS:
• To tell a story	Informal	Important events, interesting details (often descriptive)
• To inform	Formal	Specific facts and examples
• To describe	Informal	Concrete, vivid, sensory details
• To persuade	Formal	Precise opinions, reasons, and evidence

EXERCISE 3. Analyzing How Purpose Affects Writing.   Each of the following numbered items identifies a topic and two purposes for writing about it. Decide how each purpose would affect the piece of writing. For each purpose, indicate what specific aspect of the topic you would write about. Then list three details you would include in your writing and indicate whether you would use formal or informal language. Be prepared to discuss your answers.

1. *Topic:* Baking bread
   Purpose: a. To inform   b. To tell a story
2. *Topic*: Registering to vote
   Purpose: a. To inform   b. To persuade
3. *Topic:* Designing the car of the future
   Purpose: a. To describe   b. To inform
4. *Topic:* Forming a Neighborhood Watch club
   Purpose: a. To tell a story   b. To persuade

THE WRITER'S AUDIENCE

1b. Identify the audience for whom you are writing.

You always write for an audience—a particular reader or readers. Audiences vary widely in age, background, knowledge, interests, opinions, and feelings. Like purpose, audience affects both the content and language of your writing: you will not write the same way for all people. If your topic is the dangers of fad dieting, for example, you will write differently for a group of overweight teen-agers, for members of a health class, and for parents of dieters.

EXERCISE 4. Identifying Purpose and Audience.   List at least five pieces of writing that you have read during the past few weeks. (You might include articles in magazines and newspapers, instructions and directions, and novels.) Identify the main purpose and the intended audience for each piece of writing.

CRITICAL THINKING:
Analyzing How Audience Affects Writing

Always think about your audience as you plan your writing, for they help you decide what you can and should say. The author of the following paragraphs was writing for an audience of educated adult readers:

> One of the country's leading authorities on hieroglyphics received a $128,000 award in February to pursue any work he chose over the next five years. "It's really a shock—still a little hard to comprehend," said the recipient, 18-year-old David Stuart of Silver Spring, Md.
>
> Mr. Stuart became interested in hieroglyphics—or "glyph," as the cognoscenti sometimes call them—at 8, when he accompanied his father, George, an archaeologist, to the Yucatán Peninsula. In February, the youth became the youngest person to win a MacArthur Foundation award.
>
> "It hasn't really changed things in the short run," he says. "Right now I'm working on a book on hieroglyphic writing—Maya stuff." He doubts it will be a best seller, although it is aimed at "a very general audience."
>
> "I suppose I know about roughly the state of knowledge on it now," he says of Mayan hieroglyphics, but he observes that "no one is really able yet" to interpret the glyphs fully. There is no Rosetta Stone to unravel the Mayan puzzle, he says, adding, "I'm working slowly to break little pieces here and there."
>
> RICHARD HAITCH

If you rewrote this same information for an audience of ten-year-olds, you would give background information (what hieroglyphics are, what an archaeologist does, where and when the Mayan culture existed), explain references (the Rosetta Stone), and simplify sentence length and vocabulary (*cognoscenti, comprehend*).

As you analyze audience, you will also consider purpose, for the two are closely related. In persuasive writing, for example, readers' beliefs and feelings are particularly important.

Techniques for Prewriting. To determine how your audience will affect your writing, ask yourself the following questions:

- Who is the audience? Friends? Acquaintances? Strangers? A combination of these groups?
- What does the audience already know about the topic?
- What background or technical information must I supply?
- What language and style are most appropriate for the audience: simple or complex words and sentences, casual or formal presentation?
- Does the audience have any strong feelings about the topic that could affect my writing?

EXERCISE 5. Analyzing an Audience. Read the following paragraphs carefully; then answer the questions.

Qin Shi Huangdi was a man in a hurry. In 221 B.C., while the king of Qin, he conquered the six other feudal states of China, becoming its first emperor and the ruler of what he and his people regarded as the civilized world. His reign lasted fifteen years, but its impact on his country cannot be exaggerated. He standardized China's written language, its monetary system, and even the width of the axles on its carts.

A ruthless and oppressive dictator, he immediately embarked on several of the most ambitious public works in ancient times. He consolidated and extended the various sections of the Great Wall. According to records from the time, he had constructed at the city of Xian a mausoleum for himself, studded with precious stones that represented the sun, the moon, and the stars. The mausoleum was so large that more than 700,000 people spent thirty-six years building it. It was ransacked shortly after his death and has not yet been excavated.

Apart from his role in the construction of the Great Wall, Qin's most stunning known achievement is perhaps the massive group of vaults filled with terra-cotta bodyguards who were destined to serve their ruler in his afterlife.

1. What is the writer's purpose in this article?
2. How do vocabulary, sentence length, and details enable you to determine who the intended audience is?
3. What background information does the audience already seem to have about the topic?
4. List at least five words that would have to be defined or replaced if this article were intended for an audience of second-graders.
5. Which of the following items would you give background information about if your audience were a group of fifth-graders? Be prepared to explain your answer.
   a. Feudal states   b. The axles on carts   c. The Great Wall of China

EXERCISE 6. Analyzing the Effect of Audience. In the item that follows, four different audiences are given for the same topic and purpose. Write answers for the numbered questions.

Topic: The driver's license test you failed
Purpose: To tell a story
Audiences: (a) Your friends,   (b) inspectors who test new drivers, (c) third-graders,   (d) people injured in automobile accidents caused by teen-age drivers

1. Which audiences would have more knowledge of the topic? Less knowledge?
2. For which audiences would terms need to be defined? Which terms?
3. Which audiences would need background information?
4. Which audiences might have strong feelings for or against the subject? How would those feelings affect your writing?
5. For which audience would you choose to write? Why?

EXERCISE 7. Rewriting Paragraphs for a Different Audience.
Rewrite any one of the three paragraphs in Exercise 5 for one of the following audiences.

   a. Aliens from a different planet
   b. A group of fifth-graders
   c. A group of tenth-graders in a world history class

CHOOSING AND LIMITING A SUBJECT

1c. Choose a subject that is appropriate for your audience.

The age, background, and interests of your audience should influence your choice of subjects to write about. You can probably write about any subject for any audience if you are able to explain enough terms and give enough background information. Nevertheless, avoid choosing a subject that is too difficult or complicated for your audience, because you would have to know it very well in order to simplify it enough—and even then the subject could still be too complicated. For example, third-graders could understand the subject "magnetism," but they would probably find Einstein's theory of relativity baffling, no matter how much you simplified it.

Your subject should also be appropriate to the audience's interests. For instance, people who live inland and have never sailed will have little interest in the latest designs for catrigged sailboats, but the topic will have great appeal to present catboat owners.

EXERCISE 8. Analyzing the Suitability of a Subject.   Answer *yes* or *no* to indicate whether each of the following subjects is appropriate for the audience given. Be prepared to explain your answers.

1. The training of Seeing Eye dogs—parents of blind children
2. Increasing highway tolls—readers of a local newspaper

3. Latest research in heart-transplant operations—college students studying to be doctors
4. A discussion of Shakespearean comedy—a class of third-graders
5. Cost-of-living increases for Social Security recipients—a junior-high English class

1d. Limit your subject so that it can be covered adequately in the form of writing you have chosen.

A *subject* is a broad, general area of knowledge, such as "music" or "car repairs." A *topic,* on the other hand, is a limited subject—one specific enough to serve as the basis for a paragraph or a composition. "The development of the first electric guitar" and "how to change a flat tire" are limited subjects, or topics. The briefer your form of writing, the more limited your topic must be. In a paragraph, you have only a few sentences in which to develop your ideas. In a composition, you may have several pages. You must match topic to form.

EXERCISE 9. Distinguishing Between Subjects and Topics. Identify each item below as (a) a broad subject, (b) a topic suitably limited for a single paragraph, or (c) a topic suitable for five or more paragraphs.

1. The sculptured faces on Mount Rushmore, South Dakota
2. Caring for a pet boa constrictor
3. Major themes of *My Ántonia* by Willa Cather
4. American women in politics
5. Three requirements for a good quarterback

CRITICAL THINKING:
Analyzing a Subject

You can find topics by dividing a broad subject into smaller parts. The basis for your analysis depends on the subject but may be time periods, examples, features, uses, or causes.

EXAMPLES   1. *Subject divided into time periods*
                    Subject: Government in Alaska
                    Topics: Russian territorial government—before 1867
                             U.S. territorial government—from 1867 to 1959
                             U.S. state government—from 1959 to present

2. *Subject divided into examples*
   Subject: American folk heroes
   Topics: John Henry
             Paul Bunyan
             Johnny Appleseed
3. *Subject divided into features*
   Subject: Photography
   Topics: History of earliest photography
             Equipment
             Advice to beginning photographers
             Famous photographers

Sometimes your first division will yield a topic suitably limited for the form in which you are writing. Usually, however, you will need to subdivide the topics further. The diagram below shows the subject "photography" divided into more limited topics. Those labeled 4 could be covered adequately in a short composition.

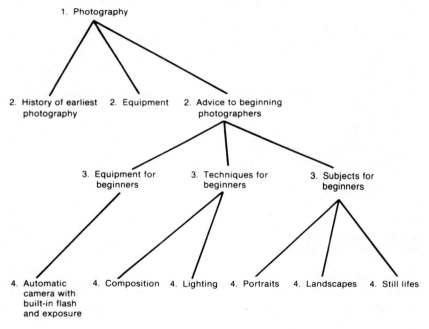

EXERCISE 10. Analyzing Subjects to Develop Topics. Choose five subjects and divide each one into at least three smaller parts. (*Note:* For each subject, different analyses are possible and correct, but be prepared to discuss the basis for your division.)

1. United Nations	6. Airplanes
2. Sports	7. Careers
3. Education	8. Popularity
4. Clothing	9. Eskimos
5. Songs	10. Health

EXERCISE 11. Limiting a Subject to Develop Topics Suitable for Paragraphs. Choose one of the subjects that you analyzed for Exercise 10. Could each topic be covered adequately in a paragraph of several sentences? If not, continue dividing to find at least three topics suitable for a paragraph. Show your analysis in a diagram like the one on page 12.

CREATING TONE

1e. Consider your attitude toward your topic and its expression through tone.

Your feelings about a topic—your attitude—influence the tone of your writing. Sometimes the topic or purpose determines your attitude, but sometimes you choose it: positive, negative, serious, humorous, angry, enthusiastic. Tone is the expression of that attitude, and it is created through both choice of details and language.

Consider the tone of the following paragraph. How does the author feel about her subject? How do you know? What particular words and observations convey her attitude and create the informal tone?

Though Faith Ringgold, artist and activist, has traveled everywhere, she's never really left Harlem. She was born at Harlem Hospital (in 1930), grew up in the areas known as the Valley and Sugar Hill, and lives today on West 145th, in Dinah Washington's old apartment. She studied art at City College, whose nearby Gothic buildings she views affectionately from her apartment window. She and her second husband first met as kids in the neighborhood; together they brought up in Harlem, too, her own two daughters by an earlier marriage. To Mrs. Ringgold, who smiles at "a sort of backwardness" in herself that keeps her there, Harlem is a small town that radiates warmth and a sense of shelter, and its life and people loom very large in her art. So it's only fitting that this summer a local institution, the Studio Museum in Harlem, is devoting its main exhibition galleries to a Faith Ringgold retrospective, celebrating 20 years of her art (through Sept. 4).

GRACE GLUECK

Your tone may be personal or impersonal, formal or informal, comical or serious, but be sure it is appropriate to your topic and purpose.

EXERCISE 12. **Identifying Tone.** Bring to class three paragraphs from different sources (articles, stories, advertisements). Identify the tone of each and the author's attitude toward the subject.

GATHERING INFORMATION

1f. Gather information appropriate to your purpose.

Your purpose for writing is a key to the kinds of information you must gather. To describe a famous pitcher in action, you need to collect keen visual details for your readers: appearance, expression, movements. To give information about careers in health care, you need to gather facts, examples, and statistics.

The following pages contain many techniques for gathering information for your writing. Used separately or in combination, they show you how to tap your own creativity and resources and how to approach a topic's analysis.

Direct and Indirect Observation

(1) Use your powers of observation to note specific details.

Observation, whether direct or indirect, is central to writing. *Direct observations* are firsthand experiences through your senses of sight, smell, sound, taste, and touch. In the following description of a jazz-rock concert in Tokyo, Japan, Kennedy Fraser brings the scene to life with many sensory details of sight and sound.

> Some ten thousand young people had arrived promptly at six-thirty for Hino's concert, settling into the giant arena as gently as snow. The jazz-rock star was a slight, almost fragile-looking young man with a small face, which puffed out as he played his trumpet. ("Like a blowfish" was how Miyake described Hino's cheeks at full toot.) Wearing black leather pants, a samurai dagger, and a particolored wingshoulder wetsuit-fabric jacket, Hino was holding his own against an elaborate backup band and a set with energetic lighting in which the words "Damon," "Pyramid," and "Hino" blinked, coursed, and pulsed in a ceaseless show of vivid color. "He was also a Suntory Personality," Miyake said to me, whispering, as though we were sitting at a string-quartet recital. Around us, indeed, were very few weaving

heads or tapping feet; the audience seemed almost eerily calm. The lit-up words clashed brightly on in a swirl of colored-smoke effects, like Hades. In shafts of purple air, the band turned blue, Hino red, and the teetering brass cymbals magenta.

KENNEDY FRASER—THE NEW YORKER

For *indirect observations,* you use the firsthand experiences of other people. You watch them, talk to them, or read their words. Kennedy Fraser's direct observations may give you indirect observations for an essay on Japanese popular music.

CRITICAL THINKING:
Observing Specific Details

Observing requires special attention to details of experience. You cannot see everything, of course, but you can learn to see more. Make a habit of paying attention. Focus on specifics.

EXERCISE 13. Testing Your Powers of Observation.   Answer each question from memory.

1. Whose face is on the United States quarter? The penny? The five-dollar bill?
2. How tall is your best friend? How much does he or she weigh?
3. What color stripe is at the top of the American flag? At the bottom?
4. On an FM radio dial, what is the number shown at the far left-hand side?
5. Draw a picture of a stop sign. What color is it?

A Writer's Journal

(2) Keep a writer's journal.

You may include anything you like in a writer's journal: random thoughts; opinions about music, books, and movies; overheard conversations; memorable quotations; reactions to people and events. By recording your ideas, experiences, and feelings, you create a source of topics and details for your writing. Remember, however, that your writer's journal should contain only ideas, experiences, and feelings you feel comfortable sharing with others. You may also want to keep a private journal for your personal use.

EXERCISE 14. Using a Journal Entry to Gather Ideas for Writing.
Read the following journal entry; then answer the questions that follow it.

> Sunday—October 5
>   Went on a three-hour canoe trip on the Fox River yesterday with Lynette and her dad. We drove in two cars. First, Lynette's dad put the canoe in (it's called "put in") at Lookout Park. He lifted the canoe all by himself from the car's top. Then he parked his car seven miles downstream, and we all drove back to the park in Lynette's car. Lynette's dad steered the canoe by paddling in back. Lynette in front—I was in the middle. We paddled slowly; sometimes we just drifted. Bright, sunny day. Smell of cool, fall leaf mold. Very quiet—no birds, no wildlife, no other river traffic. Part through densely overgrown river banks. When we got to where his car was parked, Lynette's dad hauled the canoe up and put it back on top of his car. He's been a Boy Scout leader for forty years and is one of a group that goes canoeing and birding before dawn every other week. He knows a lot about birds of north-central Illinois. Unfortunately, he didn't warn me about poison ivy on the river bank, and I have an awful case on my ankles and legs.

1. On the basis of this journal entry, the writer decided she could write a narrative essay about the trip. List as many other topics as you can think of, suggested by the entry, that she might write about.
2. Write at least three questions you could ask Lynette's dad about one of the topics you listed in question 1. Write as many questions as you can think of.

Brainstorming and Clustering

(3) Use brainstorming and clustering to stimulate ideas.

Both brainstorming and clustering are techniques that generate a free flow of ideas. Either technique is useful for finding topics or accumulating specific details.

To *brainstorm,* write your topic at the top of a piece of paper, relax, and list whatever ideas about the topic that come to mind. Work quickly, and do not stop to judge the ideas that you are listing. Stop only when you have run out of ideas.

Now you can evaluate what you have written. Decide which items are usable topics or details, and circle them. These circled words and phrases may stimulate new ideas.

Here is one student's list of brainstorming notes on the topic "the composition of outdoor portrait photographs." The parenthetical notes show the writer's evaluation of the ideas after the list was complete.

composition (arrangement of the elements within a photograph)
three main things to consider
brightest part of photograph (center of light; eyes drawn to center of light)
lines that draw the eye into a photograph (leading lines)
examples of good photos (Franny at beach; Lou in sleeping bag)
bad photos (faces shaded; too dark or too bright—but why?)
balance in photograph
rule of thirds (diagram photo as framed in viewfinder into thirds)
type of camera

Clustering, or *making connections,* is similar to brainstorming, but you create a diagram of related ideas rather than just a list. Write your topic in the center of the paper, and circle it. As ideas come to mind, write them down, circle them, and draw lines connecting them either to the central idea or to each other.

Here is a clustering diagram for the previous topic.

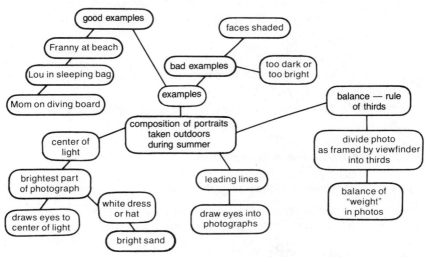

EXERCISE 15. Using Brainstorming or Clustering to Gather Information. Choose one of the topics you developed in Exercise 10,

or choose another limited topic. Use either brainstorming or clustering to gather information about the topic.

Asking the 5 *W-How?* Questions

(4) Ask the *5 W-How?* questions to gather information.

The basic *Who? When? Where? What? Why?* and *How?* questions can help provide specific details for your writing. Not every question will apply to every topic.

EXAMPLE   *Topic:* What the original Olympic Games were like
   Who? Who participated in the original Olympic Games?
   What? What events were included?
   Where? Where were the games held?
   When? When were they held?
   Why? Why were they held?
   How? How were the events different from events today?

EXERCISE 16. Gathering Information by Asking the *5 W-How?* Questions.   Use the *5 W-How?* questions to gather information about one of the following topics or a topic of your own. Write both your questions and the answers. Do research if necessary. Some of the *5 W-How?* questions may not apply to your topic.

1. History of basketball
2. An ideal holiday meal
3. Pros and cons of a national seventy-mile-per-hour speed limit
4. My earliest memory
5. Emergency procedures for home safety during severe storms

Asking Point-of-View Questions

(5) Use different points of view to gather information.

Another questioning technique is considering the topic from three different points of view: What is it? How does it change or vary? What are its relationships? These points of view generate many more questions. This technique is based on ideas in *Rhetoric: Discovery and Change* by Richard E. Young, Alton L. Becker, and Kenneth E. Pike (New York: Harcourt Brace Jovanovich, 1971).

1. *What is it?*

In this first point of view, you focus on the topic itself. If your topic is a place, person, or object, you may ask what the topic looks like, what it does, and how it differs from others of its kind. Because it defines, the *What is it?* question is useful even for an abstract idea.

EXAMPLE   *Topic*: How to prepare a résumé [What is a résumé? What is it used for? What does it look like? What information should it contain? How should the information be organized?]

2. *How does it change or vary?*

The second point of view focuses on how a topic changes over time. Its questions help bring out information about the topic's history and future.

EXAMPLE   *Topic*: Types of phonograph records [What were the first phonograph records like? When were they made? What are 78-rpm and 45-rpm records? What other ways are there of recording sound? What are compact disc (CD) recordings? What will records be like ten years from now? A hundred years from now?]

3. *What are its relationships?*

For the third point of view, you focus on how the topic's parts, or aspects, are related to each other, to the topic as a whole, and perhaps to other, similar topics. This is similar to the critical thinking skill of analysis.

EXAMPLE   *Topic*: A terrible adventure movie [What are the elements of the movie: story, writing, characters, acting, photography, directing, music, special effects? Which elements are terrible? Fair? Good? Are some more important than others? What makes this movie worse than other adventure movies?]

EXERCISE 17. Gathering Information by Asking Point-of-View Questions.   Using the three different point-of-view questions, gather information about two of the following topics. Write all the questions you think of, as well as your answers.

1. A specific place or neighborhood
2. A specific animal or species of animal
3. A character in a play
4. A type of job
5. A specific emotion

CLASSIFYING INFORMATION

1g. Classify your ideas and information by grouping related items.

The techniques for gathering information give you many ideas and details. The next step in the writing process is to classify the information, to sort it into groups. You must decide how the items are related.

CRITICAL THINKING:
Classifying Ideas

When you *classify,* you identify details that are somehow similar, and you group similar items under a heading that explains what they have in common. What is a possible heading for the following details?

EXAMPLE   Discounts at some movie theaters
           Discounts on airlines
           No fees at some banks for checking accounts
           In some communities, eligibility for free classes at colleges
           Reduced fares on public transportation
           Eligibility for Medicare

 The common element for this list can be expressed by the heading "Advantages for Senior Citizens."
   Classifying may yield more than one group. When this happens you must decide the relationship of the groups as well as of the items.
   Classifying also helps you spot information that is not useful for your purpose. Do not hesitate to discard items that do not fit into any of your groups or headings.

Techniques for Prewriting. Use the following questions to classify information.

● Which items have something in common? What is it? (Use the similarity to write a heading.)
● Are some items or groupings more important than others? Which are the most important (or main) ideas?
● Which items seem to be subdivisions (examples, parts, etc.) of the main ideas? If you have not listed any subdivisions for your main ideas, what do you think they might be?

EXERCISE 18. Classifying Information. Use the following four main headings to classify the listed items. (*Note:* One item will not fit under any of the headings.)

Expedition to the Ocean's Bottom
Discovery of Exotic Species of Life
Location of Discovery
Water Temperature

Redheaded worms discovered—up to five feet long
Water measured at 293° Centigrade
Deep-sea dive in submarine *Alvin*
Photosynthesis—process that lets plants use energy from sunlight
Water heated by vents miles below water's surface; vents lead to molten rock beneath ocean floor
Part of gigantic undersea mountain ridge
4,000-foot crater of axial volcano, underwater
Unusual species of clams discovered
Alvin holds three scientists: oceanographers (study the ocean) and geophysicist (studies physics of earth and ocean)
These animals feed on poisonous chemicals (sulfur compounds) in deep, ultrahot water

EXERCISE 19. Classifying Ideas and Information. Read the following ideas for a composition on how to study for a test. Decide which ideas can be grouped, and write a heading for each group. (*Note:* The headings are not in the list.) Then write the ideas below their proper headings. You may discard some items.

Memorize dates, formulas—whatever needs to be memorized
Last math test I got 79
Spend enough time
Find a quiet place with good lighting
Charts and diagrams
Notes from classes
Read captions under photographs and illustrations
Restate most important ideas in your own words
Chapters in textbook
Define important terms and symbols
Final exam in English next Tuesday
No TV or radio

ARRANGING INFORMATION

1h. Arrange your ideas in order.

A final step in prewriting is deciding how to order your information. You have created main headings; now consider how to put them in sequence for your audience. Once you have done this, you have an informal outline, or plan, for your writing.

Often your purpose suggests the order. For example, to explain how to stir-fry vegetables, you will probably follow chronological (time) order. To persuade readers to sign a petition, you will put the most important reasons first or last. If your purpose or the ideas themselves do not suggest an order, arrange your information in a way that is clear and interesting to your audience. (You will learn more about types of order in Chapter 2.)

REVIEW EXERCISE A. Following the Steps for Prewriting.   Prepare to write a paragraph on a topic of your choice. Decide on your purpose and your audience. Choose a subject, and limit it to a topic for a single paragraph. Using at least one of the techniques for gathering information, make a list of specific details. Classify the details under main headings. Decide on an order for the information, and write it down as an informal outline.

WRITING A FIRST DRAFT

All of the prewriting activities prepare you for the second stage in the writing process: writing a first draft, or *drafting*.

WRITING A FIRST DRAFT

1i. Write a first draft, keeping your audience and purpose in mind.

Before you begin a first draft, recall your purpose and audience. Then, with your notes or outline before you, express your ideas as clearly as possible, choosing specific details and language appropriate both for your audience and purpose. Remember that a draft is not your final, finished writing. You will evaluate and revise several times, changing both content and wording.

CRITICAL THINKING:
Synthesis

Synthesis means to put together separate parts, or elements, to create a new whole. All writing is a synthesis, for writers combine words and ideas in new ways to create letters, paragraphs, compositions, poems, stories, and plays.

As you synthesize ideas to write your draft, you will be rethinking all your writing plans. For example, you may decide to adjust your purpose, content, organization, or tone. You may think of a new detail or see a more logical arrangement of ideas. Use these discoveries in creating your first draft.

Techniques for Writing. As you write your first draft

- Use your prewriting plans as a guide
- Write freely, without correcting mechanical errors that would stop the flow
- Concentrate on clarity
- Consider including new ideas that occur as you write

EXERCISE 20. Writing a First Draft. Using the prewriting notes you developed for Review Exercise A (page 22), write a first draft of a paragraph.

EVALUATING

A first draft always has some weaknesses, or things that could be done differently to improve the draft. Even a professional writer must evaluate a draft in order to correct and improve it, and you too must be able to recognize the weaknesses, as well as the strengths, of your writing.

EVALUATING YOUR WRITING

1j. Evaluate your first draft.

Evaluation is the process of judging what works and what does not work. Any changes you make while creating a first draft, for example, are the result of evaluation. Finally, though, you must evaluate the finished draft as a whole, and this evaluation requires distance: you try to see the writing as if it were someone else's. You also try to judge the writing in its entirety: content, organization, and style. A thorough evaluation requires several rereadings of your first draft. You can use different techniques to make each reading profitable.

Techniques for Evaluating. Use the following techniques to gain different perspectives on your draft.

- Set your draft aside for a while so that you are seeing it fresh.
- Read aloud, to "hear" what you have said. Listen for confusing statements, missing details, unclear language, or a tone that is not appropriate.
- Have a classmate or someone else read your draft and comment on its strengths and weaknesses. (Professional writers almost always have a friend or an editor who evaluates their writing.)

CRITICAL THINKING:
Evaluating Content, Organization, and Style

When you *evaluate,* you judge your writing on the basis of carefully developed *criteria,* or standards. These criteria can be grouped in three categories:

Content	What have you said?
Organization	How have you arranged your ideas?
Style	How have you used words and sentences?

The following Guidelines for Evaluating apply to almost any form of writing. Use them as a checklist to identify problems in your draft. With the revising and proofreading symbols on page 36, you can then mark the problems for later revision. Note that the questions review the steps and ideas you should have followed in prewriting.

GUIDELINES FOR EVALUATING

Content

Purpose
1. Do the ideas and details in the paper support the primary purpose: to explain, to describe, to persuade, or to tell a story?

Audience
2. Will the intended audience find the paper interesting? Does the paper contain background information, and does it explain terms that the audience may need to know?

Topic Development
3. Is the information sufficiently detailed for the audience to understand the topic? Is information included that does not apply to the topic?

Organization

Order
4. Is similar information presented together, or must the reader jump back and forth among ideas? Does the order of the information make the main idea clear?

Transitions
5. Are sentences smoothly joined by connecting words and phrases? Does one idea lead clearly to another, or does information seem to be missing?

Style

Tone
6. Does the choice of words and details effectively convey the writer's attitude toward the topic? Does the paper sound serious enough, or light enough, for its purpose?

Sentence Variety
7. Do the sentences vary in length, begin in different ways, and follow different patterns to avoid monotony?

Word Choice
8. Does the writing contain precise, specific words? Do they make the meaning clear rather than vague and fuzzy? Are descriptive words vivid, creating concrete, sensory images?

EXERCISE 21. Evaluating a First Draft. Read the following draft, and evaluate it using the preceding guidelines. Number your paper 1–8, as the guidelines are numbered. As you judge the draft, write *yes* if the guideline is met and *no* if it is not. Give at least one specific example to support each answer.

One day more than thirty years ago, two cardiologists, Dr. Meyer Friedman and Dr. Ray Rosenbaum, in San Francisco noticed something strange about the chairs in their waiting room. Some of the chairs the patients sat in had fabric that was being worn out. The doctors wondered if perhaps this had something to do with the nervous, hurry-up, take-charge personality traits associated with Type A personalities. They decided to do a study to see if the behavior patterns of Type A patients could be changed and if such changes in behavior would decrease the chance of a second heart attack.

Dr. Friedman studied more than eight hundred men who had had heart attacks. Some of them went to group counseling meetings to learn how to stop being competitive, aggressive, and hurried. They actually learned to change their personalities and to calm down. They also watched themselves on videotape and saw how nervous they were. Dr. Friedman also had a control group, and he compared the results of the two groups. After three years, 79 percent of those who had gone for group counseling had changed their Type A behavior and had become more calm and relaxed. Only 9 percent of this group had a second heart attack. In the control group, after three years only 49 percent had changed their behavior, and 19 percent had suffered coronaries. Both groups were given advice on diet and the importance of exercise.

EXERCISE 22. Evaluating a First Draft. Use the Guidelines for Evaluating on page 25 to evaluate the first draft that you wrote for Exercise 20 or another piece of writing. Reread the draft several times. You may want to exchange with another student and evaluate that student's draft. Number a paper 1–8 for each guideline and indicate whether the guideline was met. If it was not, explain why.

REVISING

When you evaluate your paper, you uncover problems. When you revise, you make changes to improve your writing. You may make some revisions while writing the first draft, but you will make more following a thorough evaluation. You must find a specific way to improve each weakness in the paper.

REVISING YOUR FIRST DRAFT

1k. Revise your first draft.

After you have decided where your paper needs improvement, you must decide how to make the necessary changes. Four basic revision techniques can correct most problems in writing: adding, cutting, replacing, or reordering.

Techniques for Revising.   Use the following techniques to make changes after you have evaluated your draft.

TECHNIQUE	EXAMPLE
● *Add* add information, details, sentences, or words	*bloodless* A revolution toppled Prince Sihanouk in 1970.
● *Cut* take out information, details, sentences, or words	The most popular programming language for home computers ~~by far~~ is called BASIC.
● *Replace* take out information, details, sentences, or words and substitute something else	The calendar of the Assyrians was based on ~~lunation.~~ *the phases of the moon.*
● *Reorder* move information, details, sentences, or words to another place in the paper	In 1971, archaeological crews found the *Mary Rose*—sunk in 1545—forty feet below the surface. Finally, in 1982, a major portion of the hull saw the light of day. Some 24,000 dives recovered 14,000 well-preserved artifacts.

These techniques can be used for problems in content, organization, and style. Notice how the techniques are used to revise the following paragraph. (See page 36.)

Topic: Origin of standard time in the United States
Purpose: To explain
Audience: Classmates or teacher

¶ We owe the idea of standard time to the nation's railroad companies.
~~In the good old days~~ before ~~November 18,~~ 1883,   replace/cut

passengers traveling from Maine to California on a

railroad train had to set their watches back and

forth almost a hundred times, *because* Almost every city   add

and state ran on *a* different local times. ~~Not only~~ *e*   add/cut

~~that.~~ To make things *even* more confusing, every rail-   cut/add road clock was a little bit different. Clocks were not   add

~~yet~~
synchronized. ~~Railroads got together and some-~~   add/cut

~~body had a very bright idea.~~ Railroad company   cut

on November 18, 1833,

executives created the idea of "standard time" and   add

divided the United States into four time zones;   add

~~Today we have~~ Eastern Time, Central Time,   cut

Pacific

~~Rocky~~ Mountain Time, and ~~one other time zone I~~   cut/replace

also

~~forget which.~~ They synchronized the clocks in all of   cut/add

so that

the railroad stations. Within each time zone every   add

station's   *not only*

railroad clock showed the same time. This helped   add

run   *efficiently, but also*

~~them to run~~ the railroads more ~~better and to allow~~   cut/add replace

timetables.

passengers to follow exact railroad ~~schedules.~~ Con-   replace

which

gress passed the Standard Time Act of 1918. ~~This~~   replace

zones

made the railroad time ~~changes~~ official for the   replace

whole country.

   The following chart shows how the revision techniques can be combined with the evaluation guidelines (page 25) to solve the problems in any draft. The other composition chapters contain charts that apply the four revision techniques to specific forms of writing.

REVISING A DRAFT

PROBLEM	TECHNIQUE	REVISION
Content		
Unfamiliar terms are not explained.	Add/Replace	Add definitions or explanations. Replace unfamiliar terms with familiar ones.

PROBLEM	TECHNIQUE	REVISION
The ideas and details do not help explain, describe, persuade, or tell the story.	Add/Cut	Add explanations, arguments, descriptive details, or narrative details. Cut information that is not related to the purpose.
The audience will not find the paper interesting.	Add/Replace	Add interesting examples, anecdotes, dialogue, or additional details. Replace details unrelated to the audience's specific interests or background.
There are not enough details and information to help the audience understand what is being said.	Add	Add details, facts, examples, etc. to support the topic.
Some information does not support the topic and may confuse or distract the audience.	Cut	Cut out sentences or parts of sentences that do not relate directly to topic and purpose.
Organization The audience will find the arrangement of ideas unclear.	Reorder	Check the order of details in your informal plan. Move the draft's ideas or details to make the meaning clear.
The connections between the ideas in different sentences are not clear.	Add	Add words that will help link the sentences: *this, when, then, first, in addition, as a result,* etc. Add missing information.
Style The tone does not convey the writer's attitude.	Replace	Replace words or details that are not consistent with the intended attitude (angry, sad, enthusiastic, humorous, etc.).

PROBLEM	TECHNIQUE	REVISION
The tone is not suitable for the audience and purpose.	Replace	To create a lighter tone, replace formal words with less formal (slang, contractions, etc.). To create a more serious tone, replace slang and contractions with standard vocabulary.
The sentences are monotonous.	Replace/ Reorder	Combine sentences by joining them with *and, but, for,* or *or;* by making one subordinate to the other; or by making one a modifying phrase. Change the word order so that sentences do not all begin in the same way.
The words are dull and vague. They do not make the meaning clear.	Replace	Replace general terms with precise, exact words. Replace dull descriptions with vivid, sensory details.

EXERCISE 23. Revising a First Draft. Use the evaluation you completed for Exercise 21 to revise the paragraphs in that exercise. For each problem that you found, identify the strategy to correct it (add, cut, reorder, or replace). Then make the improvement.

EXAMPLE Evaluation: An unfamiliar term is not explained
Strategy: *Add* a definition for technical terms
Revision: Dr. Friedman also had a control group *of patients who received no counseling,* and he compared the results of the two groups.

REVIEW EXERCISE B. Revising a First Draft. Using the evaluation of your first draft from Exercise 22, revise the draft. Be sure to refer to the revising chart on pages 28–30.

PROOFREADING

In the next stage in the writing process, proofreading, you reread your revised paper to find and correct mistakes in grammar, usage, and mechanics (spelling, capitalization, and punctuation).

PROOFREADING YOUR WRITING

1I. Proofread your revised paper.

Proofreading, particularly of your own writing, requires keen attention. Some strategies will help you proofread your revised writing.

> *Techniques for Proofreading.* Use the following techniques to improve your proofreading accuracy.
>
> ● Put your paper aside for a while. When you return to it, you will see errors more quickly.
> ● Cover the lines below the one you are proofreading. You will concentrate better and not read ahead.

CRITICAL THINKING:
Applying the Standards of Written English

The purpose of proofreading is to apply the standards of written English to your writing. These standards, summarized in the Guidelines for Proofreading on pages 32–33, are the rules generally used in books, magazines, and newspapers. Writers follow these standards to prevent readers from being confused by mistakes or irritated by errors.

EXERCISE 24. Applying the Standards of Written English.   In each sentence, find and correct the error in grammar, usage, or mechanics. If you cannot correct an error, use the index of this book to find the rule in parentheses. Then make the correction.

1. Each of the topics have been limited adequately. (subject-verb agreement with indefinite pronouns)

2. The young woman, who is standing next to Maria, has just moved to Dallas from New York City. (punctuating adjective clauses)
3. Just between you and I, Charlene is a better racketball player than he. (using the objective case of pronouns for the object of a preposition)
4. When does the modern art exhibit at the school open. (punctuating questions)
5. If you are going to the concert on Saturday night next week. (sentence fragments)
6. First, think about the answers that seem possible, then choose the best one. (run-ons)
7. She had never before swam in an icy mountain lake. (past participles of irregular verbs)
8. I'm real glad that you called. (using adjectives and adverbs correctly)
9. Fred has laid in the sun all morning and is badly sunburned. (use of *lie* and *lay*)
10. Please meet me at 4:00 P.M. at the Commercial bank building on the corner of Main Avenue and Thirty-eighth Street. (capitalizing names of specific buildings)

EXERCISE 25. Proofreading a Revised Draft.   Proofread the draft you revised for Review Exercise B or another paper you have revised. Use the Guidelines for Proofreading that follow and the Revising and Proofreading Symbols on page 36.

GUIDELINES FOR PROOFREADING

1. Is every sentence a complete sentence? (pages 297–305)
2. Does every sentence end with a punctuation mark? Are other punctuation marks correct? (pages 564–623)
3. Does every sentence begin with a capital letter? Are all proper nouns and appropriate proper adjectives capitalized? (pages 548–63)
4. Does every verb agree in number with its subject? (pages 447–50)
5. Are verb forms and tenses used correctly? (pages 488–512)
6. Are subject and object forms of personal pronouns used correctly? (pages 468–87)
7. Does every pronoun agree with its antecedent in number and in gender? Are pronoun references clear? (pages 461–64)

8. Are frequently confused words (such as *lie* and *lay, fewer* and *less*) used correctly? (pages 530–47)
9. Are all words spelled correctly? (pages 624–43)
10. Is the paper neat and free from obvious corrections? (page 33)

WRITING THE FINAL VERSION

CORRECT MANUSCRIPT FORM

1m. Write the final version, following correct manuscript form.

The last step in the writing process is to prepare a final, clean copy of your revised and proofread paper. Although there is no single correct way to prepare a manuscript, the following standards are widely used.

1. Use lined composition paper or, if you type, $8\frac{1}{2}$ x 11-inch white paper.
2. Write on only one side of the paper.
3. Write in blue or black ink, or type, using double-spacing.
4. Leave a margin of one inch at the top, the sides, and the bottom of the page. The left-hand margin must be straight and the right-hand margin as straight as possible.
5. Indent the first line of each paragraph about one-half inch.
6. Follow your teacher's instructions for placing your name, the class, the date, and the title on the manuscript.
7. Number all pages. Place the number in the upper right-hand corner, about one-half inch from the top.
8. Write legibly and neatly. If you are typing, do not strike over letters or cross out words. If you have to erase, do it neatly.
9. Before handing in your final version, proofread it carefully to make certain your recopying is accurate.

The following rules will help you prepare a final version of any paper you write.

1n. Apply the rules for using abbreviations.

In most of your writing, you should spell out words rather than abbreviate them. A few abbreviations, however, are commonly used.

The abbreviations *Mr., Mrs., Ms., Dr., Jr.,* and *Sr.* are acceptable when they are used with a name. Spell them out in other uses.

EXAMPLES **Mr.** Rugelli, **Mrs.** Corning, **Dr.** Loesster, John S. Wilber, **Sr.**
She has an appointment with the **doctor**.
The **senior** law partner was consulted.

The abbreviations A.M. (*ante meridiem*—"before noon"), P.M. (*post meridiem*—"after noon"), A.D. (*anno Domini*—"in the year of the Lord"), and B.C. (*before Christ*) are acceptable when they are used with numbers.

EXAMPLES The *Queen Elizabeth 2* is scheduled to sail at 9:00 **A.M.**
Octavian (63 **B.C.–A.D.** 14) is now known as Augustus Caesar. [Notice that the abbreviation *A.D.* precedes the number, while *B.C.* follows it.]

Abbreviations for organizations are acceptable if they are generally known.

EXAMPLES My sister and I joined the **Y.W.C.A.** [or **YWCA**]
Thousands visit the **U.N.** headquarters. [or **UN**]
The **FBI** cooperates closely with state police agencies. [Abbreviations for government agencies are usually written without periods.]

1o. Apply the rules for writing numbers.

Numbers of more than two words should be written in numerals, not words. If, however, you are writing several numbers, some of them one word and some of them more than one word, write them all the same way.

EXAMPLES Edith traveled **675** kilometers on her trip to Texas.
Marlene weighs **ninety-seven** pounds.
To the north we have **750** acres, to the south **340**, to the west **182**, and to the east only **47**.

A number at the beginning of a sentence should be written out. Also write out numbers like *eleventh, forty-third,* and so on. If they are used with a month, however, it is customary to use numerals only.

EXAMPLE **Thirty-five hundred** pairs of terns were counted on the shore.
My brother placed **eleventh** [not *11th*] in the race.
School closes on **June 6.** [or **the sixth of June**; not *June 6th*]

1p. Apply the rules for dividing words at the end of a line.

Sometimes a long word will not fit at the end of a line. You may start the word on the next line; however, if that will leave a very uneven right-hand margin, divide the word, using a hyphen after the first part. Learn the rules for dividing words (see pages 616–17). You should try to avoid dividing words, however. A slightly irregular margin looks better than a hyphenated word.

EXERCISE 26. Writing the Final Version.   Write the final version of the paper you proofread for Exercise 25. Use the rules for correct manuscript form or rules your teacher provides. Proofread your final version carefully.

CHAPTER 1 WRITING REVIEW

Applying the Writing Process.   Write a paragraph on a topic of your choice. Follow these steps as you plan, write, evaluate, and revise your paragraph.

1. Identify your purpose and audience.
2. Choose a subject and limit it to a suitable topic.
3. Consider attitude and tone.
4. Gather information about the topic.
5. Classify and arrange your information.
6. Write a first draft.
7. Evaluate your draft's strengths and weaknesses.
8. Revise to eliminate the weaknesses.
9. Proofread the revised draft.
10. Prepare a final version.

REVISING AND PROOFREADING SYMBOLS

Symbol	Example	Meaning of Symbol
≡	Maple High school	Capitalize a lowercase letter.
/	the First person	Lowercase a capital letter.
∧	the first May	Insert a missing word, letter, or punctuation mark.
∧	seperate	Change a letter.
⌐	before the train arrived	Replace a word.
ℓ	Tell me the the plan.	Leave out a word, letter, or punctuation mark.
ℐ	an unussual idea	Leave out and close up.
⌒	a water fall	Close up space.
∽	recieve	Change the order of letters.
(tr.)	the last Saturday of September (in the month)	Transfer the circled words. (Write (tr.) in nearby margin.)
¶	¶"Help!" someone cried.	Begin a new paragraph.
⊙	Please don't go	Add a period.
⌄	Well what's new?	Add a comma.
#	birdcage	Add a space.
⊡	the following ideas	Add a colon.
;	Houston, Texas St. Louis, Missouri and Albany, New York	Add a semicolon.
=	two teen agers	Add a hyphen.
⌄	Sallys new job	Add an apostrophe.
(stet)	An extremely urgent message	Keep the crossed-out material. (Write (stet) in nearby margin.)

CHAPTER 2

Writing Paragraphs

STRUCTURE AND DEVELOPMENT

A paragraph is a group of closely related sentences that makes clear one idea about a topic. Whether it appears alone or as part of a longer composition, it is a complete unit of thought.

In this chapter you will study the structure and characteristics of effective paragraphs and learn how the stages of the writing process apply to the paragraph form.

THE STRUCTURE OF A PARAGRAPH

THE MAIN IDEA

2a. A paragraph is a series of sentences that presents and develops one main idea about a topic.

The sentences in a paragraph work together to communicate one main idea. Often, this idea is stated in a single sentence. In the following paragraph, for example, the topic is violence. The main idea, that violence as a way of achieving racial justice is impractical and immoral, is presented in the first sentence. The other sentences provide reasons that develop, or support, that idea.

> Violence as a way of achieving racial justice is both impractical and immoral. It is impractical because it is a descending spiral ending in

destruction for all. The old law of an eye for an eye leaves everybody blind. It is immoral because it seeks to humiliate the opponent rather than win his understanding; it seeks to annihilate rather than to convert. Violence is immoral because it thrives on hatred rather than love. It destroys community and makes brotherhood impossible. It leaves society in monologue rather than dialogue. Violence ends by defeating itself. It creates bitterness in the survivors and brutality in the destroyers. A voice echoes through time saying to every potential Peter, "Put up your sword." History is cluttered with the wreckage of nations that failed to follow this command.

DR. MARTIN LUTHER KING, JR.

THE TOPIC SENTENCE

2b. The *topic sentence* states the one main idea of a paragraph.

Many paragraphs, like the one above by Dr. King, have a general statement, or *topic sentence,* giving the main idea. This sentence controls the entire paragraph by restricting the ideas that can be included in the other sentences. (Some descriptive paragraphs and paragraphs in stories do not have topic sentences, but they are special cases.)

The topic sentence often comes at the beginning of the paragraph, where it tells the reader immediately what the paragraph is about. Putting the topic sentence first also helps the writer remember to keep to the point.

A topic sentence may instead appear in the middle of a paragraph or at the end. Coming at the end, as it does in the following paragraph, the topic sentence serves as a conclusion based on the information presented in the other sentences.

> The fourteenth century opened with a series of famines brought on when population growth outstripped the techniques of food production. The precarious balance was tipped by a series of heavy rains and floods and by a chilling of the climate in what has been called the Little Ice Age. Upon a people thus weakened fell the century's central disaster, the Black Death, an eruption of bubonic plague which swept the known world in the years 1347–1349 and carried off an estimated one-third of the population in two and a half years. **This makes it the most lethal episode known to history, which is of some interest to an age equipped with the tools of overkill.**
>
> BARBARA TUCHMAN

Topic and Restriction Sentences

Sometimes two sentences in a paragraph work together to present the main idea. The first sentence introduces a general idea; the second one restricts, or further limits, that idea by focusing on one particular aspect. These two sentences are called *topic* and *restriction* sentences.

In the following paragraph, notice that the first two sentences work together to state the paragraph's central idea.

> [Topic] **This farm, which was situated two miles west of the village, immediately won our love.** [Restriction] **It was a glorious place for boys.** Broad-armed white oaks stood about the yard, and to the east and north a deep forest invited exploration. The house was of logs and for that reason was much more attractive to us than to our mother. It was, I suspect, both dark and cold. I know the roof was poor, for one morning I awoke to find a miniature peak of snow at my bedside. It was only a rude little frontier cabin, but it was perfectly satisfactory to me.
>
> HAMLIN GARLAND

EXERCISE 1. Identifying Topic Sentences. Identify the topic sentence or the topic and restriction sentences in each of the following paragraphs.

1. People who say they do not want to pick flowers and have them indoors (the idea being, I suppose, that they are more "natural" in the garden than in the house) don't realize that indoors one can really look at a single flower, undistracted, and that this meditation brings great rewards. The flowers on my desk have been lit up one by one as by a spotlight as the sun slowly moves. And once more I am in a kind of ecstasy at the beauty of light through petals . . . how each vein is seen in relief, the structure suddenly visible. I just noticed that deep in the orange cup of one of these flat-cupped daffodils there is translucent bright green below the stamens.

   MAY SARTON

2. American Sign Language substitutes for speech a dizzying combination of animated hand gestures, facial expressions and body movements. In a signed performance of *Little Shop of Horrors,* for example, Carl Chopinsky and Marie Taccogna of Theater Access Project mouthed all of the words spoken or sung in perfect synchrony with the actor he or she was interpreting. Simultaneously, with their hands, each signer delivered the dialogue and, in time to the music, the lyrics. When a trio sang a song à la the Supremes, the interpreters, their hips rolling and swaying, created the harmonies by signing

in unison. Their hand movements were clipped and hiccuping, or rolling and sustained, mimicking the sound of the voices. At the climax of the show, when Audrey II, a huge man-eating plant, advanced toward the audience and the music swelled, the interpreters' signs grew broader, extending farther from their bodies, engulfing more space.

ELEANOR LUGER

3.   Fretting parents and educators can no longer accuse television writers of influencing the behavior of inner-city teenagers. The violence of day-to-day urban reality far exceeds any cruelties, atrocities or mayhem depicted in the current crop of television crime and adventure series, with the sole exception of the 6 o'clock news, which dramatically portrays the horrors of urban living. What is the most immediate consequence of a vicious murder committed by a young mugger, who is subsequently apprehended? The answer is instant stardom by way of the 6 o'clock news and the evening headlines. Regardless of the severity of the ensuing punishment, he had his moment of infamous glory.

CLAUDE BROWN

SUPPORTING SENTENCES

2c. **Other sentences in the paragraph give specific information that supports the main idea stated in the topic sentence.**

A paragraph with only one or two supporting details (specific information) is not effective. At least three details—examples, facts, statistics, or reasons—are needed to provide strong support for the main idea. Compare the following two versions of a paragraph.

WEAK   It was warm in the kitchen. Steam rose from the kettle, and every little noise seemed loud.

EFFECTIVE   It was warm in the kitchen. A blow-fly buzzed, a fan of whity steam came out of the kettle, and the lid kept up a rattling jig as the water bubbled. The clock ticked in the warm air, slow and deliberate, like the click of an old woman's knitting needle, and sometimes—for no reason at all, for there wasn't any breeze—the blind swung out and back, tapping the window.

KATHERINE MANSFIELD

EXERCISE 2. Revising a Weak Paragraph. The following paragraph is weak because it does not have enough supporting details. Study the paragraph and the questions that follow it. Using your answers to the questions, revise the paragraph so that it has enough information to support the main idea in the topic sentence. (You may revise the topic sentence also.) Write your revised paragraph on a separate piece of paper.

> Being outdoors just before sunrise is a special feeling. The streets are quiet and almost empty. Several cats are out.

1. Is the neighborhood in a city, a suburb, or the country? What kinds of houses are there? What do they look like in the early morning? Are any lights on in the houses?
2. Are there any signs of human life in the houses or on the streets? Are there joggers, walkers, bicyclists?
3. Are cars parked on the streets? What do they look like?
4. Where are the cats, and what are they doing? If they are moving, where and how? If they are still, where and how are they sitting or lying? Are they making any noise?
5. What other noises can you hear? Human voices? Traffic noises?

REVIEW EXERCISE A. Revising Weak Paragraphs. Revise each of the following weak paragraphs by adding sufficient supporting details to develop the paragraph's idea. You may also revise the topic sentence to make it more precise or more interesting. Write the revised paragraphs on a separate sheet of paper.

1

> Imagine what your life would be like if you had no "best" friend. Everyone needs someone with whom to share feelings and with whom to go places. (*Hint:* Add specific details and examples, and think of other functions that a best friend serves.)

2

> Last Saturday's football game was the most exciting game I have ever seen. Our team played badly during the first half. In the last ten minutes of the game, we scored 14 points. We won 14–12. (*Hint:* Add specific details about the action of the game, the players, how the fans reacted to the scores. You might even describe the weather.)

THE CLINCHER SENTENCE

2d. A paragraph may end with a clincher sentence.

Sometimes you may want to reemphasize the main idea of a paragraph by restating it in a concluding sentence. This kind of restatement is called a *clincher sentence.* A clincher sentence may instead summarize the information given or suggest a course of action.

Not all paragraphs need a clincher sentence. For example, such a sentence is unnecessary in a very short paragraph. Also, a clincher sentence should not just be tacked on to a paragraph that is effective without it.

The following paragraph shows the effective use of a clincher sentence. (Both the topic sentence and the clincher sentence are in boldfaced type.) The paragraph is from a review of the movie *Never Cry Wolf;* Tyler is a young biologist who spends a year in the Arctic studying the habits of wolves.

> **The cruel fact is that more wolves would have helped; wolves that were more accommodating would have helped, too.** The animals on the screen just don't seem eager to act out their roles, and they're not strong in the grandeur department—they look sort of scroungy. Children who went to see *The Black Stallion* could believe in that mythological horse because Ballard [the director] had fully created him; the wolves here are never characters. Despite the names that Tyler gives them, they have no discernible personalities, and nothing really happens between Tyler and the wolves. **These long-legged creatures with tiny, sharp eyes are playing out a script of their own devising.**
>
> PAULINE KAEL

EXERCISE 3. Writing Clincher Sentences.   For each of the following paragraphs, write a clincher sentence. Try writing several versions for each paragraph; then choose the one that you think is most effective.

1.   Like many other workers, lumberjacks, people who cut down trees for a living, have a colorful language all their own. For example, they never refer to themselves as lumberjacks. Instead, they call themselves *sawyers, fallers,* or *gypos* (short for *gypsies,* independent truckers). To lumberjacks, a *widowmaker* is a huge tree limb that crashes silently to the ground from high above. *Skidding* is dragging chain-wrapped felled trees with a tractorlike piece of equipment through the forest to the roadside.

2.   Since 1978 New York City's Ethnic Advisory Council has promoted understanding and peaceful accord among the city's 150 or so ethnic groups. Representatives for each of the twenty-five largest ethnic groups meet once a month to discuss problems in New York's diverse communities. Although the council advises the mayor and the groups that come before it, the council has no real power. The Korean representative, Mrs. Grace Lyu-Volckhausen, believes that the council would be

more effective if it had legal powers. The council has had some successes, however, according to Indian leader Swami G. Jagdishwaranand. For example, the Indian community, acting on the council's suggestion, contacted the public schools and local organizations to help end a four-year period of violence against Indians in a Queens neighborhood.

UNITY

2e. Every sentence in a paragraph should be directly related to the main idea.

A paragraph in which every sentence supports the main idea has *unity:* its sentences work together as a unit to develop one main idea. Any sentence that does not directly support the main idea should be removed.

As you read the following paragraph, look for the two sentences that break its unity. (The topic sentence is in boldfaced type.)

> [1]**American bald eagles, once an endangered species, are making a gradual comeback across the country.** [2]You can see the bald eagle on the United States coat of arms on the back of a dollar bill. [3]During the 1970's the bald eagle (or American eagle, as it is sometimes called) was put on the endangered species list because its numbers had steadily decreased and sightings of these eagles were extremely rare. [4]After the insecticide DDT was removed from use, their numbers slowly began to increase. [5]This year during the annual midwinter census taken by the National Wildlife Federation, almost 12,000 bald eagles—many of them immature birds—were counted in forty-two of the fifty states. [6]In 1979, during the first bald eagle census, only 20 percent of the eagles counted were young birds; now 30 to 35 percent are. [7]You can recognize an immature eagle by its brownish-black head; a mature eagle has a snow-white head. [8]The fact that the percentage of immature birds has been steadily increasing through the 1980's is a sign that the overall eagle population is growing and that the birds are producing healthier offspring.

Sentences 2 and 7 should be removed. Sentence 2 has nothing to do with the paragraph's main idea (that bald eagles were disappearing but now are making a comeback). Sentence 7 is somewhat related to sentences 5 and 6, but it is not directly related to the main idea in the topic sentence. Knowing how young eagles are recognized does not help the reader understand the paragraph's main idea.

To produce a unified paragraph, check each sentence against your main idea, asking "Does this sentence directly support my main idea?"

EXERCISE 4. Identifying Sentences That Destroy Unity. One or more sentences in each of the following paragraphs are not closely related to the main idea. Find these sentences, copy them onto your paper, and be ready to explain how they break the unity of the paragraph.

1.   Hikers backpacking in Glacier National Park in northwestern Montana are advised not to disturb the grizzly bears that live in the park. The park is larger than the state of Rhode Island. Because grizzlies have been known to react violently when surprised by visitors, hikers wear bells that warn any bears in the vicinity that intruders are coming. The black bears found in Yellowstone Park do not have the same frightening reputation as the grizzlies. Although there are only about two hundred grizzlies in Glacier National Park and although the chances of being attacked are about a million to one, visitors are uneasy because the grizzly has traditionally been considered America's fiercest and most dangerous animal. Even today a grizzly will occasionally attack a human being—with painful or fatal results.

2.   If you have ever paddled a canoe, you know that paddling is a skill that must be learned. Since a canoe can be pushed from its course by a slight breeze, the paddlers must sit in such a way that the bow will not be forced too high out of the water, where it will catch too much wind. In calm weather the canoeists should sit in the stern, but in windy weather they should kneel just aft of the middle, for in this position they can control their craft with less effort. They should paddle on the side opposite the direction of the wind because the wind then actually helps them to hold to a straight course. In a river with rapids and falls, canoeists should wear life jackets in case the canoe overturns. Try to float on your back with your feet pointed downstream so that your head does not smash against a rock. Steering a canoe is done by a twist of the paddle at the end of each stroke, the extent of the twist depending on the force of the stroke and the strength of the wind against the bow.

3.   Annie Peck's career as a mountaineer was astonishing for a nineteenth-century woman. This internationally acclaimed climber first became interested in mountaineering when she saw the majesty of the Matterhorn in the Alps. She climbed Mount Shasta in California and then, in 1895, ascended the Matterhorn. Climbing Mount Orizaba in southern Mexico won her recognition for achieving the highest point in the Americas reached by a woman up to that time. Peck was not satisfied with achieving something no woman had ever achieved before; she wanted to reach a height no person had ever reached before. Some people considered her climbing costume as

daring as her accomplishments. She continued searching for the right mountain, and she finally climbed the north peak of Huascarán in central Peru. This peak was named Huascarán Cumbre Ana Peck in her honor. Peck continued to be an active mountaineer until her death at the age of eighty-four.

COHERENCE

2f. The ideas in a paragraph should be arranged in a logical order and clearly connected.

A *coherent* paragraph is one in which the ideas flow smoothly from one sentence to the next and the relationships between the ideas are clear. Coherence is achieved in two ways: (1) by arranging the ideas in a logical order and (2) by providing clear transitions, or links, between the ideas.

Logical Order

The word *logical* means "reasonable" or "orderly." When ideas are arranged logically, the paragraph is easy to follow. Four ways of arranging ideas are in chronological order, in spatial order, in order of importance, and in an order that reveals comparison or contrast.

Chronological Order

(1) Ideas may be arranged in chronological order.

In a paragraph that relates an incident (a brief story), the logical way to organize information is to use *chronological order*—the order in which events happened in time. Chronological order is also used to explain a process, with the steps in the process arranged in the order in which they must be done. How many transitional expressions can you find in the following process paragraph?

> Salmon at its finest was traditionally baked over alder wood coals by Northwest Indians. The fish was split down the back and laid flat, then pressed between the parts of a split-cedar stake. It was held in place by thin cedar strips, like a sail on a mast; then the stake was pounded into the ground near the coals, leaning slightly over the smoke. The fish was baked until it was cooked through but still moist. Sometimes the salmon was brushed with seal oil to enhance its succulence. .

The following transitional expressions are often used to show chronological order:

after	earlier	moments later
afterward	finally	next
as soon as	first	since
at first	formerly	soon
at last	in the beginning (end)	then
at the same time	in the meantime	until
before	later	when
during	meanwhile	while

EXERCISE 5. Arranging Ideas in Chronological Order. Arrange sentences a–h in chronological order. Then write the paragraph, beginning with the topic sentence given.

Topic sentence: During last week's game with the Panthers, the Leesberg Eagles scored three runs in the ninth inning, winning the game 3–2.

a. Milewski advanced to third, and Goldstein slid safely into second.
b. Then the pitcher walked Milewski, the shortstop, putting an Eagles runner on base for the first time in the game.
c. The first Eagles batter struck out, and the second batter popped out to first.
d. Milewski and Goldstein trotted home, while Washington went around the bases to roaring applause.
e. The fourth batter, Goldstein, hit a long, hard drive that bounced off the center-field wall.
f. Tension mounted as the rookie Panthers pitcher finished warming up, with Washington, the Eagles center fielder, waiting near the batter's box.
g. On the first pitch, Washington hit a long drive to left field that landed in the upper deck.
h. With two players on base and only one out to go, the Panthers coach replaced the tired pitcher.

Spatial Order

(2) Ideas may be arranged in spatial order.

Arranging ideas in spatial order helps the reader visualize where the parts of a topic are in relation to one another. Notice how the writer of the following paragraph uses spatial order to describe Mark Twain's boyhood home, Hannibal, Missouri. The transitional expressions are italicized.

> One morning I stood *atop* 200-foot-high Cardiff Hill and surveyed the scene that stretched *before* me. Hannibal—an active town of 20,000 people that today is an agricultural, rail and light manufacturing center—nestles *in* a mile-and-a-half-wide fan-shaped valley. It rises gradually *from* the river *up to* residential areas *in* the low hills and knolls a mile or two *off to* the west. Above the riverfront's cobblestone levee *below to my left* towered the white silos of the Hannibal Grain Terminal, while directly *in front of* me Main Street passed *through the center* of the grid-like downtown area *on its way toward* Lover's Leap, the high bluff that overlooks the river *to the south.*
>
> TOM WEIL

The following paragraph shows how spatial order can be used to describe an object.

> The babe was done up as usual *in a movable cradle* made from an oak board two and a half feet long and one and a half feet wide. *On one side of it* was nailed with brass-headed tacks the richly embroidered sack which was open *in front* and laced *up and down* with buckskin strings. *Over the arms of the infant* was a wooden bow, the ends of which were firmly attached *to the board,* so that if the cradle would fall the child's head and face would be protected. *On this bow* were hung curious playthings—strings of artistically carved bones and hoofs of deer which rattled when the little hands moved them.
>
> CHARLES A. EASTMAN [OHIYESA]

The following transitional expressions are used to clarify spatial order:

above	below	in front of	throughout
across	beneath	in the middle	to the side of
against	beside	inside	toward
alongside	between	near	under
among	beyond	next to	underneath
around	down	on	up
at	facing	opposite	upon
before	in a corner	outside	within
behind	in back of	over	without

EXERCISE 6. Using Spatial Order. Choose three of the following topics, and decide in what order you would describe each one (from top

to bottom, left to right, near to far, etc.). Be prepared to explain your answers.

1. A baseball stadium
2. The inside of a car
3. The school cafeteria
4. The inside of a movie theater
5. The view from a goldfish bowl as seen by a goldfish

Order of Importance

(3) Ideas may be arranged in order of importance.

In an expository or persuasive paragraph, certain ideas may be more important than others. They may, for example, provide stronger support for the paragraph's main idea, or they may be more convincing to the audience. Using order of importance enables you to emphasize your more important ideas.

Ideas may be arranged from most important to least important or the other way around—from least important to most important. Persuasive paragraphs are often most effective when the most convincing reason is presented last, where it will linger in the reader's mind.

The ideas in the following paragraph are arranged from most important to least important. The topic sentence is in boldfaced type; the ideas are numbered in the order of their importance.

> **Specialists in children's television viewing suggest a number of ways parents can control their children's viewing.** [1]Most important, they say, is setting time limits, such as one hour a day, no viewing on school nights, or two or three hours on weekends. [2]Another suggestion is that parents discuss with the children which television programs to select, so that children learn to choose their programs instead of just watching whatever happens to be on. [3]It is generally agreed that parents should watch with their children occasionally, because shared viewing leads to discussion and evaluation of the programs. It may also bring the family closer together and increase understanding of different points of view.

The following transitional expressions are used to indicate order of importance:

above all	finally
another	first (second, third, etc.)
besides	for one reason

furthermore
in the first place
more (most) important
moreover

next
of greater (greatest) importance
of less (least) importance
to begin with

EXERCISE 7. Arranging Ideas in Order of Importance. Choose one of the following topic sentences (either *should* or *should not*). Then decide which of the reasons given support that topic sentence, and list them in order from least important to most important.

Topic sentence: Every young adult (should, should not) learn to drive a car.

Details: You never know when it will be necessary to drive in case of an emergency.

People who do not learn to drive as young adults may be too frightened to learn later.

Not everyone has a car or can afford to own one. Many people have no need to drive; they use public transportation.

Some jobs require being able to drive a car.

Driving is fun.

Some people are temperamentally unsuited for driving—they are too nervous or too aggressive.

If everyone learned how to drive, roads would be more crowded and the air more polluted.

Comparison and Contrast

(4) Ideas may be arranged in an order that reveals comparison or contrast.

A *comparison* shows how two things are alike; a *contrast,* how they are different. Facts, incidents, sensory or concrete details, or examples may be used to point out similarities or differences between two topics. Sometimes both comparison and contrast are included in the same paragraph, as in the following example.

Termites are not true ants, though many people call them "white ants." Like the ant, the termite has only two body sections, but the thorax of the termite is not so clearly separated from the abdomen. Most ants are shiny and dark in color; termites, however, are soft and pale. Termites also

topic sentence
comparison

contrast 1

contrast 2

differ from ants in matters of colony life. Worker   contrast 3
ants are all wingless females, but workers in a
termite colony may be either male or female.

In this paragraph, the ideas are arranged according to the
point-by-point, or *alternating, method.* For each feature that is compared or contrasted, both topics (termites and ants) are mentioned. For
example, the second sentence discusses the body sections and thorax of
both the ant and the termite.

A comparison or contrast may instead be arranged according to the
block method. With this method, all the ideas about one topic are
presented first, and then all the ideas about the second topic are given.
The following paragraph is an example of the use of the block method.

In one way, baby-sitting for a two-year-old child   topic and
is like dog-sitting for a two-month-old puppy. You   restriction
cannot trust either of them out of your sight.   sentences
Puppies must be watched constantly because their   topic 1
curiosity is endless and their teeth are sharp.
Nothing they can reach is safe. They can happily
destroy a shoe or a pillow or a book in a few
minutes. If you don't know where a puppy is, you
had better worry. Silence doesn't necessarily mean
sleep. Similarly, two-year-olds are never still. They   topic 2
run, climb, fall down, throw things, disappear
suddenly. They try to put everything into their
mouths. If you can't see or hear them, you had
better investigate. Silence often means mischief.

Following are some of the transitional expressions that may be used
in a paragraph of comparison or contrast.

COMPARISON		CONTRAST	
also	just as	although	on the other hand
and	like	but	though
besides	similar	by contrast	unlike
both	similarly	however	whereas
in the same way			

EXERCISE 8. Analyzing a Comparison. Read the following paragraphs about teaching drawing; then answer the questions that follow them.

> In many ways, teaching drawing is somewhat like teaching someone to ride a bicycle. It is very difficult to explain in words. In teaching someone to ride a bicycle, you might say, "Well, you just get on, push the pedals, balance yourself, and off you'll go." Of course, that doesn't explain it at all, and you are likely finally to say, "I'll get on and show you how. Watch and see how I do it." So it is with drawing. Most art teachers and drawing textbook authors exhort beginners to "change their ways of looking at things" and to "learn how to see." The problem is that this different way of seeing is as hard to explain as how to balance a bicycle, and the teacher often ends by saying, in effect, "Look at these examples and just keep trying. If you practice a lot, eventually you may get it." While nearly everyone learns to ride a bicycle, many individuals never solve the problems of drawing. To put it more precisely, most people never learn to *see* well enough to draw.

1. What is teaching drawing compared to in these paragraphs?
2. Name all of the ways mentioned in these paragraphs in which the two topics are alike.
3. According to the last paragraph, the two subjects are different in one important way. How are they different?
4. Which of the following features of learning to ride a bicycle might also be a point of comparison or contrast with learning to draw? For each feature you select, write a sentence making the comparison or contrast with learning to draw.
    a. Learning to ride a bicycle is fun.
    b. Learning to ride a bicycle can be dangerous.
    c. Learning to ride a bicycle provides good physical exercise.
    d. Some people learn to balance so well that they can ride a bicycle without using their hands.
    e. When you are learning to ride a bicycle, you must observe certain rules for your own safety.

EXERCISE 9. Writing a Paragraph of Comparison and Contrast. Use the following information to write a paragraph comparing *and* contrasting helium and hydrogen. You may use either the point-by-point method or the block method. You do not have to use all of the information provided.

FEATURES	HYDROGEN	HELIUM
Natural state	Colorless gas	Colorless gas
Weight	Lightest known substance	Second-lightest known substance
Ability to burn	Can burn	Cannot burn
Boiling point	−252.8° C	−268.9° C
Melting point	−259.14° C	−272.2° C
Uses	Combines with other elements to form water, carbohydrates, fats, oils acids, bases; used in nuclear materials	Used for inflating balloons, for low-temperature work, as part of air supply of deep-sea divers

REVIEW EXERCISE B. Choosing a Logical Order for Arranging Ideas. Number your paper 1–10. For each of the following topics, write the kind of order you would use: chronological, spatial, order of importance, or comparison and contrast. Be prepared to explain your choices.

1. Local political issues in 1986 and in 1987
2. Three factors that will affect the outcome of this year's election
3. Converting solar energy into electricity.
4. Sources of pollution in a local river
5. Nora's study area
6. The view from Point Jarvis in New Jersey
7. Italian and Spanish
8. Cross-country skiing and downhill skiing
9. An abandoned farm
10. Making muffins

Connections Between Ideas

To link the ideas within and between sentences, you can use direct references, transitional expressions, or both.

Direct References

Direct references are words and phrases that remind the reader of something presented earlier in the paragraph. They may be pronouns, repeated words and phrases, or synonyms.

As you read the following paragraphs, notice how the italicized words and phrases refer to ideas that come earlier in the passage.

A hundred years ago, the average workweek in the United States was about seventy hours. Today, *it* is about forty hours—and experts say that in the next decade or so *it* will be cut again, the predictions ranging from thirty-seven hours or thereabouts down to twenty or even less. *This reduction* might come as a shorter workday, fewer workdays per week, or longer—very much longer—vacations.

What shall we do with *all that free time?* Many people are profoundly troubled about *this question. They* feel that, far from being a blessing, the change may prove a catastrophe. Certainly, the growth of leisure time is an extremely serious matter. *It* deserves far more attention than *it* is getting.

BRUCE BLIVEN

EXERCISE 10. Identifying Direct References. In the following paragraphs, Eleanor Roosevelt's name is mentioned only twice, yet the ideas are clearly linked. List the words and phrases the writer uses to refer to Eleanor Roosevelt without repeating her name each time.

It was a childhood you wouldn't wish on anyone. The girl was born on October 11, 1884, into a confounding world of privilege and deprivation. She was rejected by a mother who called her "granny." She idolized a father who was at once loving and unstable. Orphaned by the age of 10, she went to live under the roof and rules of a grandmother so rigid that the girl rebelled by adding a bit of warm water to a cold bath.

The creature of this comfortlessness later described herself as "a solemn child, without beauty. I seemed like a little old woman entirely lacking in the spontaneous joy and mirth of youth." As a cousin put it, "It was the grimmest childhood I had ever known."

Yet, out of this, Eleanor Roosevelt became, quite simply, the greatest American woman of the century.

Those of us who pay homage at the centennial of this woman's birth, those of us who admire her, live now in a rampantly psychiatric age. We have the conceit that adult life is predictable to any nursery-school observer. Yet who could have predicted Eleanor, the First Lady of the World?

ELLEN GOODMAN

Transitional Expressions

Transitional expressions are words and phrases that indicate the relationships between ideas. Since different kinds of transitional expressions indicate different kinds of relationships, such expressions must be chosen with care.

EXAMPLES   Frieda had dreaded the recital, *yet* she danced quite well.
            Manny is the best math student in the sophomore class; *moreover,* he is a gifted artist.

Transitional Expressions

To link similar ideas or add an idea

again	equally important	likewise
also	further	moreover
and	furthermore	similarly
another	in addition	then
besides	in the same way	too

To limit or contradict an idea

although	however	on the contrary
and yet	in spite of	on the other hand
but	instead	otherwise
conversely	nevertheless	still
even if	nor	yet

To show time or place

above	beyond	nearby
across	eventually	next
after	finally	now
around	first (second, etc.)	opposite to
at once	here	thereafter
before	meanwhile	thereupon

To indicate an example, a summary, or a conclusion

as a result	in conclusion	to sum up
consequently	in fact	therefore
for example	in other words	thus
for instance	in short	
in brief	on the whole	

EXERCISE 11. Choosing Appropriate Transitional Expressions.

Number your paper 1–5. For each item, choose the transitional expression in the parentheses that most clearly indicates the relationship between the ideas. Write the expression on your paper after its number and be prepared to explain your choices.

1. Norrine enjoys playing the French horn. Unfortunately, (on the other hand, however, for instance), she has no place where she can practice without disturbing others.
2. (Because, Although, Even if) human beings have no gills, they cannot stay underwater for long periods of time without special breathing equipment.
3. Many adults discover talents that they never knew they had. Mother's cousin Ralph, (as a result, consequently, for example), became an accomplished metal sculptor in his fifties.
4. No one wearing street shoes is allowed to enter the Norikami Museum. If you wish to enter, (therefore, nevertheless, on the other hand), you must leave your shoes outside and wear paper slippers.
5. Kerri and Mitch were wearing their seat belts when a driver crashed into the rear of their car. (As a result, In addition, Finally), they were not injured badly, (although, similarly, and) their car was totaled.

REVIEW EXERCISE C. Analyzing and Revising a Paragraph. Read the following paragraph carefully. As you read, consider what is wrong with it and how it can be improved. Use the following questions to help you decide how the paragraph might be improved.

1. What is the topic sentence? Does it state the main idea clearly and precisely? How could it be improved?
2. What is the writer's purpose?
3. What details support the main idea? Are there enough details?
4. Does the paragraph contain any sentences that destroy the paragraph's unity?
5. In what order are ideas presented? Is this a logical order for the topic?
6. If you could add information or details, what would you add?
7. Does the paragraph have a clincher sentence? How effective is it? If you think a paragraph that does not have a clincher sentence would benefit from one, try to write several versions.

Revise the paragraph, and write your revised version on a separate sheet of paper. When you have improved the paragraph as much as possible, proofread it before making a final copy.

Graphology is the study of handwriting. Graphologists are experts in handwriting. They believe that they can analyze people's personalities by studying samples of their handwriting. To read a person's character traits, they look carefully at the slant of the writing and the spacing between words. They analyze the size of the letters, the shape of loops and crossbars, end strokes, and punctuation. My handwriting teacher, Mr. Smith, used to be furious at students who wrote small circles over their lowercase *i*'s and *j*'s instead of simply dotting them. The worst offense, according to Mr. Smith, was not crossing our *t*'s. According to graphologists, a straight capital *I* with no loops or curves suggests that a person is extremely confident. A person whose handwriting looks almost like printing is said to be creative, witty, and independent.

REVIEW EXERCISE D. Structuring a Paragraph. Choose one of the following topics or a topic of your own: packing a backpack, frying chicken, washing a car, kicking a field goal, two kinds of pasta, two varieties of roses, or the African elephant and the Indian elephant. Then plan a paragraph: Gather supporting information; select and arrange the information you will use; and write a topic sentence. Write a first draft of the paragraph.

THE DEVELOPMENT OF A PARAGRAPH

Now that you have reviewed the structure and characteristics of effective paragraphs, you will learn how the steps in the writing process apply to the paragraph form.

PREWRITING

CHOOSING AND LIMITING A SUBJECT

2g. Choose a subject and limit it to a topic that is suitable for a paragraph.

Although paragraphs vary in length, most are about 150 to 200 words long. Thus, you must limit a broad subject to a topic that you can develop clearly and precisely in only a few sentences. (See pages 10–13 for help with searching for subjects.)

A broad subject may be limited by focusing on a specific example, aspect, time, part, or use. The following diagram shows how one writer limited the subject "mystery stories" to find a topic suitable for a paragraph.

EXAMPLE

The writer first divided the subject into three parts and then subdivided each of those parts into two of its parts. Since the idea of fictional female detectives seemed most appealing, the writer thought of one specific example, Miss Jane Marple. This topic was still too broad for a paragraph, however, so the writer further limited it to "the characteristics of Miss Jane Marple." (See pages 10–13 for more information on limiting a subject.)

EXERCISE 12. Limiting Subjects to Find Topics.
Analyze each of the following items to find at least two topics limited enough for a paragraph.

EXAMPLE 1. Air conditioning
        1. a. *How a room air conditioner removes moisture from the air*
           b. *The first room air conditioner*

1. Holiday celebrations in our home
2. My hobbies
3. Women in American politics
4. Early exploration of America
5. American folk tales and legends

EXERCISE 13. Choosing and Limiting a Subject.
Select a subject from Exercise 12 or another subject that interests you. Then analyze the subject, dividing and subdividing it to find three topics that are suitable for paragraphs.

CONSIDERING PURPOSE AND AUDIENCE

2h. Determine your purpose for writing the paragraph.

You may want to *explain* an idea, *describe* a scene or a person, *tell* a story, or *persuade* your audience to do something. Occasionally you may write for a combination of purposes, as, for example, when you describe a dangerous intersection and then try to persuade the city council to install a traffic light there. Knowing *why* you are writing will help you keep firm control over your paragraph.

2i. Consider how your audience will affect your writing.

Your audience will affect your writing in three important ways. First, you will want to choose a *topic* that interests your audience. Suppose that you decide to write about denim jeans, for example. Tenth-graders would surely be more interested in reading about why the first denim jeans were called Levi's than about how to repair the machinery on which denim is woven.

Second, you will need to include *details and background information* that will help the audience understand your ideas. For instance, in writing for seventh-graders about the extinction of the passenger pigeon, you would point out that passenger pigeons were once abundant in America. For second-graders, you would need to define terms such as *species* and *extinct.*

Finally, your audience will affect the *language* you use. Although clarity is essential for all audiences, you would use shorter sentences and easier words for second-graders than adults. You should also choose words that will convey the intended tone to your audience.

> *Techniques for Prewriting.* . Consider how your audience will affect your writing. Ask yourself:
>
> - What topic will interest my audience?
> - What details and background information will they need in order to understand my ideas?
> - What words and sentence structures will they be able to understand?

EXERCISE 14. Analyzing How Purpose and Audience Affect Writing.
Read the following paragraph, and then answer the questions.

People who are adept at dealing with other people will find a wealth of jobs open to them by the turn of the century, predicts Christopher Dede, past president of the World Future Society and a visiting scientist at M.I.T. The need for their services, he said, will be largely a response to the problem of having so many jobs dependent upon computer interaction all day long. This, he said, will create a need for intensive human contact in every other sphere of life, helped along by professions. His list of such people includes therapists of all kinds, educators, people in dating services, and negotiators and conciliators to bring more disputes out of the courts and into mediation.

ANDREE BROOKS

1. What is the paragraph's main idea? State this idea in your own words.
2. What is the purpose of the paragraph—to explain, to persuade, to tell, or to describe?
3. Which of the following audiences do you think the paragraph was written for: (a) an audience of seventh-graders; (b) a general audience, that is, educated adults; (c) an audience of scientists? Support your answer with evidence from the paragraph.
4. Suppose you wanted to revise this paragraph for an audience of fifth-graders. Which words would you replace with easier words? How else would you change the language?

GATHERING INFORMATION

2j. Gather information about your limited topic.

For some topics you can gather all the information you need by drawing on your own knowledge and experience. For others, you will need to make some new observations or do research in outside sources by reading or talking to people.

Brainstorming and clustering are two techniques for getting onto paper ideas and details that you already know. Reading your journal can also help you remember ideas and details.

For topics that you do not know as well, use the *5 W-How?* questions (*Who? What? Where? When? Why?* and *How?*) or the *point-of-view* questions (*What is it? How does it change or vary?* and *What are its relationships?*). See pages 18–19 for more on these information-gathering techniques.

As you gather information, be sure to take notes. You will use them as you continue planning your paragraph and as you write your first draft.

EXERCISE 15. Developing Questions to Use in Gathering Information. Choose three of the following limited topics. Write all of the questions you can think of that will help you gather information about each topic.

1. The last birthday celebration you remember
2. Something you hope to accomplish this year
3. A career that interests you
4. A famous person no longer living
5. An incident that made you laugh very hard

EXERCISE 16. Gathering Information for a Paragraph. Gather information about one of the topics you chose for Exercise 15 or another limited topic.

DEVELOPING A WORKING PLAN

2k. Develop a working plan for your paragraph.

A *working plan* is made up of a topic sentence and a list of supporting details, arranged in a logical order.

EXAMPLE

Topic sentence: People vary a great deal in the conditions they prefer for studying.

Details: Some—silence and solitude
Others—noise and company
Some—with the radio on
Some—always same conditions
Some—conditions don't matter

Writing an Effective Topic Sentence

To be effective, a topic sentence must meet the following three requirements.

(1) A topic sentence should be neither too limited nor too broad.

A topic sentence is too limited if it merely states a fact; once you have stated a fact, there is nothing more to say.

TOO LIMITED Indira Gandhi served as Prime Minister of India.
TOO LIMITED Indira Gandhi was the daughter of Jawaharlal Nehru, India's first Prime Minister.
SUITABLE Indira Gandhi learned many of her leadership skills from her father, Jawaharlal Nehru, who served as India's first Prime Minister. [Paragraph goes on to talk about specific leadership skills Indira Gandhi learned from her father.]

A topic sentence is too broad if it presents an idea that cannot be made clear and precise within the space available in a paragraph.

TOO BROAD Women have proved themselves to be effective as national leaders.
TOO BROAD India has had many important leaders.
SUITABLE Indira Gandhi faced several complex economic problems during her years as Prime Minister of India. [Paragraph goes on to identify several of these economic problems.]

(2) A topic sentence should state the paragraph's main idea directly and precisely.

Word your main idea as directly and precisely as you can, eliminating wordiness and unnecessary phrases such as "In this paragraph I will explain." A topic sentence should not be vague; it should be clear and easy for a reader to understand.

WEAK I am going to tell you about my first deep-sea dive.
IMPROVED My first deep-sea dive convinced me that I had found a sport to last a lifetime.
WEAK Scuba diving is a fascinating sport.
IMPROVED Scuba diving opens up a whole new world of plants and animals vastly different from those on land.

(3) A topic sentence should arouse the reader's interest.

A topic sentence should make the reader want to read the whole paragraph. Try to attract the reader's attention—perhaps by including a vivid detail, perhaps by addressing the reader directly.

WEAK Our long-distance bicycle trip was fun.
IMPROVED If you've ever had aching muscles and a hard time sitting, you have some idea of the after effects of my recent bicycle trip.

WEAK   Making a list helps people remember what they have to do.
IMPROVED   If you have sixteen things to do and you can't remember even half of them, make a list.

Techniques for Prewriting. To evaluate your topic sentence, ask yourself:

- Is it neither too broad nor too limited?
- Does it state my main idea directly and precisely?
- Will it catch the interest of my audience?

EXERCISE 17. Improving Topic Sentences. Revise each of the following topic sentences so that it is an effective topic sentence for a paragraph. Add any information you need to make it more effective.

1. Many sports require special equipment.
2. Sojourner Truth led many slaves to freedom.
3. People are really funny.
4. Movies make you forget about your problems.
5. John Henry is an American folk hero.
6. The Eskimos are an interesting people.
7. People can suffer from poor nutrition even though they eat a lot.
8. In this paragraph you will find out about the order in which colors appear in a rainbow.
9. Life in the Pueblo villages of the Southwest was different.
10. Woodworking is a good hobby.

EXERCISE 18. Writing Topic Sentences. For each of the following lists of details, write an effective topic sentence that will be the first sentence in the paragraph. (You will not necessarily use all the details in a paragraph.)

1. *Details:* New service for joggers in Eugene, Oregon: rent a Doberman pinscher
    Dogs trained to protect female joggers
    Women joggers rent fierce-looking dogs
    Service started several years ago; 12 large black Doberman pinschers
    Women running in isolated areas vulnerable to attack and harassment

Not one assault reported by joggers with rented Doberman pinschers

Joggers hold dog on leash

Amazon Trail—$6\frac{1}{2}$-mile jogging trail along Willamette River in Oregon

2. *Details:* Kayaking an Olympic sport since 1936; women kayaking in Olympics since 1948

Kayaks first used by Eskimos for transportation

Olympic kayaks made of laminated wood or fiberglass; Eskimo kayaks made of sealskin stretched over wood frame

Paddler sits in middle of kayak, an enclosed shell

Olympic paddlers use double-bladed wood paddle; may average two strokes a second

White-water kayaking on rivers with rapids; Olympic kayaking races are flat-water (no rapids)

3. *Details:* In New York City since 1970's, "educational option" high schools providing training in broad career areas—each school specializing in one area

Existing programs in commercial art, business and banking, health professions

Open to high-school students in city

More than 28,000 applications to one high school, half of them for computer science program

Schools usually take only about 1,000 applicants

Local high schools losing best students to educational option schools; beginning to develop own specialized programs

Two thirds of city's high schools have or are developing such programs

CRITICAL THINKING:
Forming a Generalization

A *generalization* is a general conclusion about an entire group of people, events, objects or places, or ideas. A *valid* (sound) *generalization* is one that is based on a fairly large number of facts or unbiased observations. It suggests that additional facts or observations will also probably support the conclusion.

EXAMPLES   Seat belts save lives.
Flowering plants are pollinated by flying insects.
Long-term exposure to loud noise causes hearing loss.

The following statements are *not* generalizations because they cover only one specific instance, not a whole group.

EXAMPLES   Our pet parrot has wings.
This whale is a mammal.
Teresa makes her tortillas from either cornmeal or flour.

A *hasty generalization* is one that is based on insufficient or biased information; it is considered a fallacy in logical thinking. (See page 185.)

EXAMPLES   Redheads have bad tempers.
Potatoes are fattening.
Men are insensitive.

People make many generalizations that they use every day. For example, suppose that you have gone to see five or six films that the movie critic in the local newspaper has recommended highly. To your surprise, you found that you did not like these films at all. You will make the generalization "This movie critic's taste is very different from mine." You will probably not pay much attention to what the critic says about films in the future.

The topic sentence of a paragraph often states a generalization. The other sentences provide evidence (facts, examples, or reasons) that supports the generalization.

EXAMPLE   Violence as a way of achieving racial justice is both impractical and immoral. [Dr. King concludes that the use of violence to achieve racial justice has and will probably continue to have these two attributes.]

EXERCISE 19. Identifying Generalizations.   Some of the following topic sentences are generalizations, and some are not. Identify all the generalizations. Be prepared to explain your answers.

1. It is much better for elderly people to live as part of a family unit than in an institution.
2. The ability to play music "by ear" is a gift, not a skill that can be learned through practice.
3. The capital of Oklahoma is Oklahoma City.

4. Jane Austen wrote *Pride and Prejudice, Sense and Sensibility,* and *Emma.*
5. Water is essential to life.

EXERCISE 20. Identifying Generalizations. Look at all the topic sentences in the model paragraphs in this chapter, and identify the ones that are generalizations. Be prepared to explain your answers.

EXERCISE 21. Evaluating Generalizations. Number your paper 1–5. Study the following chart. Then, after the proper number, decide whether each generalization is true or false. If you cannot tell from the chart whether the generalization is true, write *can't tell*. Remember that each generalization must be drawn *only* from information in the chart.

NUMBER OF RESTAURANTS IN A MICHIGAN CITY
(BY ETHNIC SPECIALTY)

	THIS YEAR	LAST YEAR	THE YEAR BEFORE
Asian	14	8	4
French	3	4	8
Spanish	9	2	0
Italian	10	10	9
Jewish	3	4	4
Soul food	8	7	7
Russian	0	0	1
Hungarian	2	2	2
Scandinavian	1	1	0

1. Asian restaurants are becoming increasingly popular in this city.
2. There are more fast-food restaurants in this community than all the ethnic restaurants combined.
3. People in this community are not as interested in French restaurants as they were two years ago.
4. There are more Spanish-speaking people living in this city than there are people from the various Asian nations.
5. Interest in Italian, Jewish, and soul-food restaurants has increased considerably during the past three years.

EXERCISE 22. Forming Generalizations Based on Data. For each of the following charts, write two or more generalizations based on the data given.

1. **ESTIMATED ADVERTISING EXPENDITURES IN THE UNITED STATES**
(In millions of dollars; includes all types of local and national advertising)

1950	1955	1960	1965	1970	1975	1980	1982
5,700	9,150	11,960	15,250	19,550	27,900	53,550	66,580

2. **TOTAL DEATHS FROM ACCIDENTS IN THE UNITED STATES, 1960–1980**
(By type of accident; from 1970 on, figures include only U.S. residents)

TYPE OF ACCIDENT	YEARS				
	1960	1965	1970	1975	1980
Motor vehicle accidents	38,137	49,163	54,633	45,853	53,173
Water transport accidents	1,478	1,493	1,651	1,570	1,429
Air and space transport accidents	1,475	1,529	1,612	1,552	1,494
Railway accidents	1,023	962	852	508	632
Accidental falls	19,023	19,984	16,926	14,896	13,294
Accidental drowning	5,232	5,485	6,391	6,640	6,043
Accidents caused by:					
Fires and flames	7,645	7,347	6,718	6,071	5,822
Firearms	2,334	2,344	2,406	2,380	1,955
Electric current	989	1,071	1,140	1,224	1,095

Choosing and Arranging Details

Before you begin writing, analyze the material you have gathered to make sure that it will result in a unified paragraph. Look closely at each detail to see whether it is directly related to the main idea in your topic sentence. If any of the details do not support your main idea, remove them. Then arrange the remaining details in a logical order (see pages 118–22).

Techniques for Prewriting. To determine whether a detail is directly related to the main idea in your topic sentence, ask:

- Does this detail provide strong support for my main idea?
- Will the detail help the audience understand my main idea?
- How does the detail function within the paragraph—is it a fact? An example? A reason?

REVIEW EXERCISE E. **Developing a Working Plan.** Write a topic sentence for the limited topic you chose for Exercise 16. Then choose the details you will use, arrange them in a logical order, and prepare a working plan for your paragraph.

WRITING

WRITING A FIRST DRAFT

2l. Write the first draft of your paragraph.

In writing a first draft, you express your ideas clearly in sentences. Write freely, keeping your audience and purpose in mind, and remember that this draft is *not* your final version. You will have the opportunity to improve the content, organization, and style when you evaluate and revise your writing. Later, when you proofread your paragraph, you will correct any errors in grammar, usage, and mechanics.

Techniques for Writing. As you write the first draft of your paragraph:

- Use your working plan as a guide.
- Keep your purpose and audience in mind.
- Write freely, focusing on expressing your ideas clearly.
- Add related ideas as you think of them.
- Choose words that convey your tone accurately.

EXERCISE 23. Writing a First Draft. Use the working plan you prepared for Review Exercise E to write the first draft of your paragraph.

EVALUATING

EVALUATING YOUR PARAGRAPH

2m. Evaluate the content, organization, and style of your paragraph.

In order to improve a paragraph, you must be able to *evaluate,* or judge, it. Skill in evaluating is developed through practice and experience. It is also developed by exposure to good writing, which is why the model paragraphs in this book are by professional writers. If you had never read an example of a good paragraph, you could not be expected to recognize one.

Evaluating any piece of writing involves making judgments about whether the content, organization, and style (word choice and sentence structure) fulfill the purpose and meet the needs of the audience. You will find the following guidelines helpful for any paragraph you write. Specific guidelines for evaluating the four basic types of paragraphs (expository, persuasive, descriptive, and narrative) appear in Chapter 3.

GUIDELINES FOR EVALUATING PARAGRAPHS

Topic Sentence	1. Does the topic sentence identify the topic and clearly state one main idea? Does it indicate the purpose?
Topic Development	2. Are enough details given to develop the main idea fully?
Unity	3. Does each sentence directly support the main idea?
Conclusion	4. If a clincher sentence is used, does it provide a strong ending for the paragraph?
Sentence Order	5. Are the ideas arranged in a logical order? Is the order suitable for the purpose?
Relationships Between Ideas	6. Do the ideas flow smoothly from one sentence to the next? Are direct references and appropriate transitional expressions used to link ideas?
Word Choice	7. Is the language specific and vivid? Is it appropriate for the audience? Are technical terms and difficult words defined or explained?

EXERCISE 24. Evaluating Word Choices. From the choices in parentheses in the following paragraph, choose the ones that you think would be most effective. Be prepared to explain your choices.

Lunch-hour exercise classes at Johnson & Johnson and free physical exams at IBM are part of a growing nationwide (interest, trend, increase) in which employers offer "wellness programs" to their employees. Such programs are (hoped, planned, designed) to improve employees' physical health and, (in part, as a result, on the other hand), to decrease absenteeism and increase productivity. Company officials (say, think, report) that existing fitness programs have (hopefully, already, probably) saved them millions of dollars' worth of lost work time and employee (medical expenses, doctors' bills, hospital bills). Exercise classes and weight-loss programs are (unusually, sometimes, often) found in large companies, some of which also have programs to help (attack, eliminate, target) employees' smoking and alcoholism. Smaller companies that do not have their own exercise programs often pay all or part of employees' (money, bills, expenses) at private classes, such as those (offered, run, done) by the Y.M.C.A. Workers say that exercise classes and other wellness programs not only make them feel good about themselves but also make them feel (good, proud, friendly) about their employers.

EXERCISE 25. Evaluating a First Draft. Use the guidelines on page 68 to evaluate the following first draft of a paragraph. Answer each question on the guidelines in writing, numbering your answers to match the numbers of the guidelines.

On a cool September evening, Boston's Faneuil Hall and Quincy Market are very crowded. It must be the busiest place in Boston. Inside the marketplace, hundreds of young people stroll and visit the restaurants and food stalls, sampling foods from all nations. The smell of Greek souvlakia mingles with Belgian waffles, Israeli falafel, pizza, and Indian curry. Hundreds of restaurants and booths tempt the stroller with both ethnic foods and typical American foods. When they are not eating, strollers eye the passing crowds, looking for familiar faces or someone to meet and talk with. Outside the hall, in the cool, dark night, applause and laughter float on the air from the crowd that circles a mime and a juggler onstage in the courtyard between the two main buildings. Away from the entertainment, crowds browse through the dozens of pushcarts that line the sidewalks and streets. (It is possible to buy rugs from Peru, Boston T-shirts, mufflers from Scotland—anything from anywhere.) The trees and branches cast shadows on the brick sidewalks, the strollers, and the bench sitters. Above, brightly colored banners wave gently in the night air. The whole area seems ablaze with color and movement as the crowds of people move, stop, and move again. Serious shoppers enter the expensive and moderate-priced shops that line the sidewalks or browse the windows of closed stores.

EXERCISE 26. Evaluating Your Paragraph. Use the guidelines on page 68 to evaluate the first draft you wrote for Exercise 23. You may also want to use the appropriate guidelines for your specific type of paragraph (see Chapter 3).

REVISING

REVISING YOUR PARAGRAPH

2n. Revise your paragraph to improve the content, style, and organization.

Evaluating your paragraph enables you to identify areas that need improving. When you make those improvements, you are *revising* your writing.

Four basic strategies are useful for revising any piece of writing: *adding, cutting, reordering,* and *replacing.* The following chart shows how you can apply these four strategies to revising expository paragraphs.

REVISING PARAGRAPHS		
PROBLEM	**TECHNIQUE**	**REVISION**
The paragraph does not have a topic sentence.	Add	Add a sentence that identifies the topic and states the main idea.
The topic sentence is too broad.	Cut	Remove words, phrases, or clauses that do not keep to the one main idea of the paragraph.
The topic sentence is too narrow.	Add	Add words, a phrase, or a clause that will make the topic sentence cover all of the material in the paragraph.
The topic sentence is too dull.	Add/Replace	Add vivid, interesting details to the sentence. Replace general words with specific ones.

PROBLEM	TECHNIQUE	REVISION
One or more sentences do not directly relate to the main idea.	Cut	Remove the sentence(s).
The main idea is not clear.	Add	Add facts, statistics, details, examples, causes, effects, reasons, or an incident.
The paragraph trails off or ends abruptly.	Add	Add a clincher sentence: Restate the main idea, summarize the information, emphasize an important point, or suggest a course of action.
The ideas are not easy to follow.	Reorder	Rearrange the sentences in a logical order.
The ideas do not flow smoothly.	Add/Replace	Add direct references and transitional expressions. Substitute more appropriate transitional expressions. (See page 54.)
The language is dull.	Add/Replace	Add vivid nouns, verbs, and modifiers. Replace general words with specific ones.
The language is too difficult.	Add/Replace	Add definitions and explanations. Substitute easier words for difficult ones and shorter, simpler sentences.
The tone is inappropriate or inconsistent.	Replace	Substitute words that are more formal or informal, serious, enthusiastic, humorous, etc.

The following example shows the changes the writer made in revising the first draft of the paragraph on page 69.

On a cool September evening, Boston's Faneuil Hall
and Quincy Market ~~are very crowded.~~ *teem with activity.* ~~It must be the~~   replace
~~busiest place in Boston.~~ Inside the marketplace, *thousands* ~~hun-~~   cut/replace
~~dreds~~ *mostly* of young people ~~stroll and visit the restaurants and~~   add/cut
food stalls, *sample* ~~sampling~~ *savory aroma* foods from all nations. The ~~smell~~ of   replace
Greek souvlakia mingles with *the hot, sweet smell of* Belgian waffles, ~~Israeli~~   add/replace
and caramel apples and the spicy smell of
falafel, pizza, and ~~Indian~~ curry. Hundreds of restaurants   add/cut
and booths tempt the stroller with both ethnic foods and
apple-pie ~~typical~~ American foods. When they are not eating,   replace
those who walk or stand still or sit ~~strollers~~ eye the passing crowds, looking for familiar   replace
faces or perhaps someone to meet and talk with. Outside
the hall, in the cool, dark night, applause and laughter
float on the air ~~from the~~ *A laughing* crowd ~~that~~ circles a mime and a   add/cut
juggler ~~onstage~~ in the courtyard between the two main   cut
buildings. Away from the entertainment, *tourists and shoppers* ~~crowds~~ browse   replace
through the dozens of pushcarts that line the sidewalks
~~and streets.~~ *There one can* ~~(It is possible to~~ buy rugs from Peru, Boston   cut/replace
T-shirts, *scarves* ~~mufflers~~ from Scotland—anything from any-   replace
where.) The trees and branches cast shadows on the
brick sidewalks, the strollers, and the bench sitters.
Above, brightly colored banners wave gently in the night
air. The whole area seems ablaze with color and movement as the crowds of people move, stop, and move
on again. ~~Serious shoppers enter the expensive and moder-~~   add/cut
~~ate-priced shops that line the sidewalks or browse the~~
~~windows of closed stores.~~

EXERCISE 27. **Revising a First Draft.** Revise the following first draft of a paragraph. First copy the paragraph as it is printed here; then evaluate and revise it, using the guidelines on pages 28–30 and the chart on pages 70–71. Copy your revised version on a separate sheet of paper.

> A chain of grocery stores is cooperating with the police department in order that a missing children-identification program can be created in order to protect the children of this community. Every parent or guardian should have every child's fingerprints (all ten are suggested) on file and identification on the same form. Along with a current photograph and information about an accurate description. The grocery store supplies the form, and it also has a black square that can be used for fingerprinting. And there are also instructions on how to do the fingerprinting. Forms available from grocery stores ask for the child's full name and nickname, birthday, race, sex, eye color, height, and weight. They want to know about medications, allergies, scars, and additional identifying information. Parents should keep these forms on file so that they will be available to police just in case a child becomes missing. If a child becomes missing, parents are supposed to call the local police and the county sheriff's office, they should call a special toll-free number for the Missing Children's Information Center that has an office in the state capital.

REVIEW EXERCISE F. **Revising Your Paragraph.** Using your answers for Exercise 26, revise the first draft of the paragraph you wrote for Exercise 23. (See the chart on pages 70–71 for revision strategies.)

PROOFREADING AND PREPARING A FINAL COPY

PROOFREADING YOUR PARAGRAPH AND PREPARING A FINAL COPY

2o. Proofread your paragraph, prepare a final copy, and proofread again.

Proofread your paragraph to correct errors in grammar, usage, and mechanics. Before giving your paragraph to your audience, recopy it in correct manuscript form. Then proofread it again.

EXERCISE 28. **Proofreading Your Paragraph.** Use the Guidelines for Proofreading on pages 32–33 to proofread the paragraph you wrote for Review Exercise F. Then recopy the paragraph and proofread again.

CHAPTER 2 WRITING REVIEW

Writing an Effective Paragraph. Limit one of the following subjects to find a topic that is suitable for a paragraph (or choose and limit your own subject). Determine your purpose for writing, and identify your audience. Then gather information, and prepare a working plan by writing a topic sentence and listing in a logical order the details you choose. Write a first draft of your paragraph; then use the Guidelines for Evaluating Paragraphs on page 68 to judge your writing. Refer to the paragraph revision chart on pages 70–71 as you revise your writing; then proofread, using the guidelines on pages 32–33, prepare a final copy, and proofread again.

1. Computers
2. Teaching someone a skill
3. The South Pacific
4. Invertebrates
5. The Supreme Court

Writing Four Types of Paragraphs

PARAGRAPHS FOR DIFFERENT PURPOSES

Paragraphs usually can be classified into four types, depending on the writer's purpose:

TYPE OF PARAGRAPH	PURPOSE	EXAMPLE
Expository	To inform or explain	A paragraph explaining the origin of Mother's Day
Descriptive	To describe	A paragraph describing the gift you gave your mother for Mother's Day
Narrative	To tell a story	A paragraph relating an incident that took place on Mother's Day
Persuasive	To persuade	A paragraph persuading students to make greeting cards for Mother's Day

In this chapter you will learn methods of developing each of these types of paragraphs. The method or combination of methods you use for a paragraph will depend on your specific purpose and on your audience.

THE EXPOSITORY PARAGRAPH

The purpose of an expository paragraph is to give information or to explain. Expository paragraphs may be developed with facts and statistics, with examples, or by means of cause and effect.

The *tone* of an expository paragraph should be direct and unemotional. Expository paragraphs should also be objective; that is, the writer's personality should not intrude.

INAPPROPRIATE TONE   When I was mining for rubies in North Carolina, I spent two disgusting hours in the boiling-hot sun sifting through six buckets of mud, and I didn't find a single ruby.

APPROPRIATE TONE   Visitors to the ruby mines just north of Franklin, North Carolina, pay two dollars a bucket to sift through mud and clay in search of rubies.

Any of the four types of order (chronological, spatial, order of importance, and comparison and contrast) may be used in an expository paragraph. In general, your specific purpose will suggest a logical order. For example, if your purpose is to explain how something works or how to make or do something, using chronological order will make clear to the reader the order in which the steps must be performed. The following paragraph about supplying a space station illustrates the use of chronological order. (See pages 45–52 for more on logical order.)

[1] After blasting off, the booster rockets the entire double assembly up into the final reaches of the earth's atmosphere. [2] Having achieved proper altitude and velocity, the booster separates from the orbiter stage. [3] Then the booster extends its wings and, guided by its two-man crew, returns to earth in normal airplane fashion, using auxiliary jet engines as necessary. [4] The second stage, which carries the payload of personnel and supplies, takes up where the booster stage lets off. [5] It accelerates on into orbit and makes a rendezvous with the space station. [6] After transferring its crew and cargo, and picking up whatever personnel or equipment is scheduled for a return to earth, the orbiter casts off for the journey home. [7] Owing to its unique design, which includes small wings and efficient control surfaces, it is able to spiral downward and reenter the atmosphere at a safe, gentle angle, unthreatened by extreme friction heat.

(1) topic sentence

(2) first step

(3) second step

(4) third step

(5) fourth step

(6) fifth step

(7) concluding sentence

CHARLES COOMBS

Developing a Paragraph with Facts and Statistics

3a. Develop an expository paragraph with facts and statistics.

A *fact* is a statement that can be proved to be true. Historical events and dates are facts, as are scientific findings that can be checked or reproduced. It is a fact, for example, that the earth is the third planet from the sun. It is also a fact that the Bill of Rights was adopted on December 15, 1791.

Statistics are numerical facts that have been carefully collected and recorded. In the following paragraph, the writer uses both facts and statistics to develop the main idea in the topic sentence (the first sentence).

> In Hong Kong the shark fin is so important a luxury food that an industry worth more than $10 billion a year has grown up around its capture, sale and preparation. Many Hong Kong fishermen make their living catching sharks in the South China Sea and other waters near Hong Kong. And because the fins are so highly regarded, their importation from such places as India, Singapore, the Philippines, Taiwan, Japan, Norway, Mexico and South America is a big business. Fins are auctioned twice daily in Hong Kong, and more than 3,000 tons a year find their way to the city's restaurants through its 20 auction houses and more than 100 professional buyers.
>
> EILEEN YIN-FEL LO

In organizing a paragraph developed with facts and statistics, keep your audience clearly in mind. They may need to have certain points presented first to be able to understand the rest of the information.

CRITICAL THINKING:
Distinguishing Between Facts and Opinions

A *fact* is information that can be proved to be true; an *opinion* is a statement that cannot be proved. To write effective expository and persuasive paragraphs, you must be able to distinguish between facts and opinions. As a reader and as a listener, too, it is essential that you know whether the information you encounter is accurate and verifiable or merely someone's opinion.

FACT   The capital of Alaska is Juneau.
OPINION   Alaska is the most beautiful state in the United States.

FACT	Almost three fifths of the earth's surface is covered by water.
OPINION	Everyone should learn to swim.
FACT	Ella Fitzgerald was born in Newport News, Virginia, on April 25, 1918.
OPINION	Ella Fitzgerald is the greatest female jazz singer of the twentieth century.

Opinions often use "judgment" words, such as *most, should, should not, greatest,* and *best.* Although opinions are natural and useful responses to the world, they cannot prove anything; facts can.

EXERCISE 1. Distinguishing Between Facts and Opinions. Number your paper 1–10. Some of the following statements are facts, and some are opinions. After the proper number, write *F* for each fact and *O* for each opinion. (Assume that the statements that are written as facts are true.)

1. Booker T. Washington, an American educator, lived from 1856 to 1915.
2. The constellation Orion is named for a giant hunter in Greek mythology.
3. Greek myths are more interesting to read than Roman myths.
4. If anything can go wrong, it will.
5. A gargoyle is a grotesque human or animal figure that functions as a rain spout, carrying water away from the roof.
6. Greta Garbo was the most talented silent-film star.
7. Each of the signs of the zodiac is the name of a constellation.
8. Cigarette smoking is dangerous to human beings' health.
9. Everyone should be able to speak at least one foreign language.
10. Carry Nation led the American prohibition movement.

EXERCISE 2. Writing a Paragraph Using Facts and Statistics. Write an expository paragraph developed with facts and statistics. You may use one of the following topics or a topic of your own.

1. The world's fastest animals
2. The percentage of American women in the labor force
3. The destructive force of a volcanic eruption
4. The average age at which American women and men marry
5. Occupations expected to have the most job openings in ten years

PREWRITING   Use reliable reference books, such as those listed in Chapter 29, to gather accurate information on your topic. You will probably find more facts and statistics than you can use in a single paragraph. To decide which information to include, think about the needs and interests of your audience. Then arrange the material in an order that will be easy for your audience to follow, and write a topic sentence that states your main idea.

WRITING   Evaluate your choice of details again as you draft your paragraph; you do not want to overwhelm your audience with numbers. Remember to define or explain terms that your readers may find difficult or unfamiliar.

EVALUATING AND REVISING   Ask yourself: Does each fact and statistic help make my main idea clear? Have I included neither too many details nor too few? You may also ask someone else to read your paragraph and tell you whether it is easy to understand. Then use the Guidelines for Evaluating Expository Paragraphs on pages 86–87 to judge your paragraph, and refer to the paragraph revision chart on pages 70–71 as you improve your writing.

PROOFREADING AND MAKING A FINAL COPY   Proofread carefully, using the guidelines on pages 32–33. Then prepare a final copy and proofread it.

EXERCISE 3. Writing a Paragraph Using Facts and Statistics.   The following graph shows unemployment rates in the United States between 1965 and 1978. Write a paragraph explaining what trends the graph illustrates.

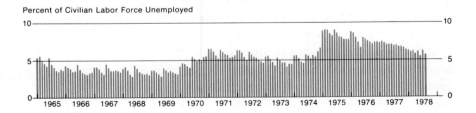

Percent of Civilian Labor Force Unemployed

EXERCISE 4. Writing a Paragraph Using Facts and Statistics. Research the unemployment rates for 1979 to 1987. Prepare a graph similar to the one in Exercise 3, and write a paragraph explaining what trends your graph illustrates.

Developing a Paragraph with Examples

3b. Develop an expository paragraph with examples.

An *example* is an item or instance that represents others of its kind. Using carefully chosen examples can help you make a general idea clear within the space available in a paragraph. In the following paragraph, how many examples are given to clarify the idea in the topic sentence?

> In *Lord of the Flies,* English novelist William Golding creates a feeling of nightmarish suspense. For example, there is always the question of whether the boys will find adult help before they destroy themselves. Then, too, there is the problem of the beast. Is the beast real or is it imaginary? If real, what kind of creature is it, and how should it be dealt with? The suspense becomes nearly unbearable during the chase near the end of the book, when Ralph is being hunted down by Jack and his fierce band.

The following paragraph uses a combination of facts and examples to develop the main idea in the topic sentence.

> Certain peculiarities make English difficult for speakers of another language to learn. In English, the position of a word is very important. By placing the word *only* before a different one of the seven words in the following sentence, you can change the meaning of the sentence seven times: "She told me that she loved me." English has a number of words that can be used with opposite meanings. *Seeded* rye has caraway seeds in it, but *seeded* raisins have had the seeds removed. A *fast* horse runs, but a *fast* color does not. When plants are *dusted,* chemical dust is sprayed on them, but when furniture is *dusted,* the dust is wiped off. Another source of confusion is the fact that in English the pronoun *I* has the plural form *we,* but the pronoun *you* is the same in the plural as in the singular.

topic sentence

fact 1

example

fact 2

examples

fact 3

EXERCISE 5. Analyzing a Paragraph Developed with Examples.
Read this paragraph, and answer the questions that follow it.

> Our lives are a series of births and deaths: we die to one period and must be born to another. We die to childhood and are born to adolescence; to our

high-school selves and (if we are fortunate) to our college selves and are born into the "real" world; to our unmarried selves and into our married. To become a parent is birth to a new self for the mother and father as well as for the baby. When Hugh and I moved from the city to live year round at Crosswicks, this was death to one way of life and birth to another. Then nine years later when we took our children, aged seven, ten, and twelve, out of a big house, a quiet village, a small country school, and moved back to New York and the world of the theatre, this was another experience of death and birth.

MADELEINE L'ENGLE

1. What is the topic sentence in the paragraph? How effective do you think it is?
2. Does the paragraph have a clincher sentence? If so, what is it? If not, try writing at least two possible clincher sentences for it.
3. List all the examples the writer gives of dying to one self and being born to another.
4. On the basis of your own observations and experiences, what other examples might the writer have included?
5. Part of the paragraph is a series of generalizations (general conclusions). At what point in the paragraph does the writer begin to give examples from her own life? How do these examples help make the paragraph effective?

EXERCISE 6. Writing a Paragraph Using Examples. Write an expository paragraph developed with examples. You may use one of the following topics or a topic of your own.

1. Professional athletes who continue to play well beyond an age when most athletes retire
2. Free or inexpensive places to take a date
3. The best mystery novels (or science fiction novels) of all time
4. The best jazz musicians playing today
5. Problems caused when people do not communicate well

PREWRITING Begin by jotting down examples and information that explains the examples. Arrange the material in an order that will be easy for your audience to follow, and write a topic sentence that states a general idea about your topic. Then review your list of details, and eliminate any that do not help clarify your main idea. Try to keep at least three examples that support the topic sentence. Decide in which order you want to arrange the examples.

WRITING Keep your audience and purpose in mind as you express your ideas in sentences. If any of your examples need to be explained, be sure to explain them before going on to the next example.

EVALUATING AND REVISING Ask yourself: Does each example help explain my main idea? Have I included enough examples? Use the Guidelines for Evaluating Expository Paragraphs on pages 86–87 to judge your paragraph. Refer to the paragraph revision chart on pages 70–71 for strategies for improving writing.

PROOFREADING AND MAKING A FINAL COPY Proofread your paragraph carefully, using the guidelines on pages 32–33. Proofread again after you prepare a final copy.

Developing a Paragraph by Means of Cause and Effect

3c. Develop an expository paragraph by analyzing cause and effect.

A *cause* is an event or situation that produces a result. An *effect* is anything brought about by a cause.

CAUSE Marcie slips on the wet floor in a supermarket and falls.
EFFECT Marcie breaks her wrist.

CAUSE There are twelve inches of rain over a twenty-four hour period.
EFFECT The river overflows and the downtown area is flooded.

Organizing a cause-and-effect paragraph helps your audience clearly distinguish between what is a cause and what is an effect. To explain why something has happened, for example, you begin by stating the effect in an introductory topic sentence, and then you discuss the cause or causes. (A complex event or situation nearly always has more than a single cause.) The following paragraph follows this pattern.

For the past two years, fewer students have been participating in after-school activities. One reason for this decline is that many students have jobs that begin immediately after school lets out. More than half of the 150 tenth-grade students surveyed recently work after school or must go home to take care of younger brothers and sisters. Other students who responded to the survey go directly home after school to watch favorite TV

effect

cause 1

cause 2

shows, such as "General Hospital." Still others do
not participate in after-school activities because   cause 3
they must depend for transportation on school
buses, which leave immediately after school. Finally, some students say that they are just "not   cause 4
interested" in the activities that are currently available, such as Drama Club, marching band, and the
school newspaper. Perhaps the time has come to
create some new after-school activities that will   clincher sentence
interest more of the students who have free time in
the afternoons.

Another way to organize a cause-and-effect paragraph is to state a
cause in the topic sentence and then detail its effects, or results. Such a
paragraph does not answer the question *Why?* but discusses the
consequences of a particular situation or action.

American society has become so mobile in the   cause
twentieth century that in any given year many
families move, usually because of a job change or a
search for work. Often the move is a considerable
one, involving a change of state or a change from
one region of the country to another. One result of
this mobility is that most children change school   result 1
systems frequently as they grow up. Few students
graduate from the same system in which they began
their schooling, which means that young adults do
not often maintain friendships from their early
years. Another result of frequent moves is the loss
of a sense of "roots" as fewer and fewer adults   result 2
remain in the same place where they were born and
their parents and grandparents lived. Perhaps the
most serious consequence of Americans' mobility,
however, is that families are widely separated as   result 3
children move to different parts of the country,
marry, and have families. Because travel is expensive, families do not regularly get together for

holidays and other family occasions, and children grow up never really knowing their cousins, aunts, uncles, and grandparents.

The following transitional expressions are among those that help clarify which statements are causes and which are results.

TO INDICATE CAUSE		TO INDICATE EFFECT	
because	since	as a result	if
cause	so that	consequently	therefore
reason	unless	effect	thus

EXERCISE 7. Planning a Cause-and-Effect Paragraph. Each of the following sentences states a cause. For each sentence, list all the possible effects (results) that you can think of.

EXAMPLE *Cause:* Enrollment in an already crowded high school increases by 10 percent in September.
Effects: a. *Class sizes are larger.*
b. *Halls are more crowded between classes.*
c. *The cafeteria is so crowded during lunch hour that some students have no place to sit.*

1. *Cause:* The high-school football team is having a spectacular season, winning all of its games so far this year.
2. *Cause:* Three new industries come to your community, employing a total of 1,350 new workers.
3. *Cause:* Legislation strictly controlling the disposal of toxic wastes is passed in your community.
4. *Cause:* A time machine suddenly propels you two thousand years into the future.
5. *Cause:* Your state's speed limit is raised to 75 miles per hour.

EXERCISE 8. Planning a Cause-and-Effect Paragraph. Each of the following sentences states an effect. For each effect, think of as many possible causes as you can. Each cause should be a complete sentence and help explain what brought about the effect.

EXAMPLE *Effect:* New car sales are less than half what they were a year ago.
Causes: a. *People have less money to spend on luxury items.*
b. *People are repairing their old cars instead of buying new ones.*
c. *New cars are too expensive.*
d. *Interest rates on car loans are at an all-time high.*

1. *Effect:* Only a small percentage of high-school students are taking two years of a foreign language.
2. *Effect:* Each year more high-school students are enrolling in work study programs, which allow them to spend half of each weekday working.
3. *Effect:* The percentage of men and women 65 years old and older in the American population is increasing each year.
4. *Effect:* Only slightly more than half of the citizens eligible to vote actually cast their votes in the last presidential election.
5. *Effect:* More women are working than ever before.

EXERCISE 9. Writing a Cause-and-Effect Paragraph. Write an expository paragraph developed by means of cause and effect. You may use one of the topics from Exercise 7 or Exercise 8, or a topic of your own.

PREWRITING Begin by identifying a cause (or an effect) that will interest your audience. Then list at least three related effects (or causes). Review your supporting statements and, if necessary, gather additional information such as facts, statistics, and examples. Then decide in what order you will present your supporting statements. To explain the causes of a situation, arranging the causes from most important to least important often works well; to give information about effects, the opposite order (from least important to most important) is often more effective. Finally, write a topic sentence that sets forth your main idea clearly. (For a topic from Exercise 7 or 8, simply reword the numbered item to make it clear and interesting.

WRITING Try to express your ideas clearly, incorporating the additional information you have gathered so that it directly supports the causes (or effects) that make up your main points. Use appropriate transitional expressions to help your audience distinguish between cause and effect and to link ideas within and between sentences.

EVALUATING AND REVISING Ask yourself: If my supporting statements are causes, do they clearly explain why the effect in the topic sentence came about? If they are effects, do they clearly explain the consequences of the cause in the topic sentence? Use the Guidelines for Evaluating Expository Paragraphs on pages 86–87 to judge your writing, and refer to the paragraph revision chart on pages 70–71 as you improve your paragraph.

PROOFREADING AND MAKING A FINAL COPY Use the Guidelines for Proofreading on pages 32–33 to correct your grammar, usage, and mechanics. Then make a final copy and proofread it.

Techniques for Writing. In preparing to write an expository paragraph, keep these points in mind:

- Determine the method of development you will use (facts and statistics, examples, or cause and effect).
- Arrange your information in a logical order that will be easy for your audience to follow.
- Write a topic sentence that identifies your topic and states your main idea clearly and concisely.
- Choose words that convey an unemotional tone.

Evaluating and Revising Expository Paragraphs

The following guidelines will help you evaluate, or judge, the expository paragraphs you write. Once you have determined where a paragraph needs to be improved, you can use the paragraph revision chart on pages 70–71 to revise your writing.

GUIDELINES FOR EVALUATING EXPOSITORY PARAGRAPHS

Topic Sentence
1. Does the topic sentence identify the topic and make clear that the purpose of the paragraph is to explain or give information?

Topic Development
2. Is the method of development (or combination of methods) appropriate for the main idea and the audience? Are enough details given to make the main idea clear? Is the information accurate?

Unity
3. Is each sentence directly related to the main idea in the topic sentence?

Conclusion
4. Does the clincher sentence, if there is one, provide a strong ending for the paragraph?

Order
5. Are the ideas arranged in an order that will be easy for the audience to follow?

Relationships Between Ideas
6. Do the ideas flow smoothly from one sentence to the next? Are they linked with direct references and appropri-

Word Choice

ate transitional expressions (*for example, because, as a result,* etc.)?

7. Is the language clear, specific, and appropriate for the audience? Are technical terms and difficult words defined or explained?

EXERCISE 10. Evaluating and Revising an Expository Paragraph.

Use the guidelines above to evaluate the following paragraph. Then revise the paragraph, using the paragraph revision chart on pages 70–71.

> Even before people speak, they give messages to others about the kind of person they are. Their clothes reveal a lot about their tastes and personalities. Their hair styles and jewelry send a message. Their facial expressions and the way they move their bodies say a lot even without words. All of these are part of nonverbal communication—communication without words.

REVIEW EXERCISE A. Writing an Expository Paragraph.

Write an expository paragraph on one of the following limited topics or a topic of your own. To plan your paragraph: Consider your purpose and audience; gather information; choose a method of development (facts and statistics, examples, or cause and effect) or a combination of methods; arrange the material in a logical order; and write a topic sentence. Then write a first draft, and use the guidelines on pages 86–87 and the chart on pages 70–71 to evaluate and revise it. Refer to the Guidelines for Proofreading on pages 32–33 as you proofread your revised draft and again as you check your final copy.

1. High-school dropouts in tenth grade this year
2. Attendance at school events (sports, dances, plays)
3. Newest fads in clothing
4. Anorexia among young adults
5. What teen-agers spend their money on

THE DESCRIPTIVE PARAGRAPH

Descriptive writing appeals chiefly to the senses. It shows a reader what something looks, tastes, smells, feels, or sounds like. A paragraph-length description usually concentrates on one person, place, object, or event.

Developing a Paragraph with Concrete and Sensory Details

3d. Develop a descriptive paragraph with concrete and sensory details.

In the following paragraph, the writer uses many concrete and sensory details that help the reader picture an event—a Pueblo Corn Dance. Which details show how the dancers are dressed? Notice how many times the writer mentions specific colors. Which details appeal to the reader's sense of hearing?

> The men dance together in double file, big-bellied men and skinny boys, toddlers and elders with gray hair flowing to the waist. Their torsos are painted with ocher clay, for these are the Squash People, who lead the dance. The Turquoise People, who follow, will be painted blue-gray. On their breasts are bandoleers of seashells and loops of turquoise and silver. High moccasins are on their feet, parrot feathers in their hair. Pine branches are tied to their upper arms. Their white wool kilts are tied by a long fringed sash, symbolic of rain, and by a belt of jingling sleigh bells. Fox furs hang down their backs like tails. In one hand each carries a rattling gourd; in the other a branch of evergreen. As they dance they will shake down the waters of the sky with their gourds and beat forth the waters of the earth with their feet.
>
> BETTY FUSSELL

Some paragraphs concentrate on only one sense. In the following paragraph, for example, notice how all of the sentences appeal to the sense of hearing.

> On a broiling afternoon when the men were away at work and all the women napped, I moved through majestic depths of silences, silences so immense I could hear the corn growing. Under these silences there was an orchestra of natural music playing notes no city child would ever hear. A certain cackle from the henhouse meant we had gained an egg. The creak of a porch swing told of a momentary breeze blowing across my grandmother's yard. Moving past Liz Virts's barn as quietly as an Indian, I could hear the swish of a horse's tail and knew the horseflies were out in strength. As I tiptoed along a mossy bank to surprise a frog, a faint splash told me the quarry had spotted me and slipped into the stream. Wandering among the sleeping houses, I learned that tin roofs crackle under the power of the sun, and when I tired and came back to my grandmother's house, I padded into her dark cool living room, lay flat on the floor, and listened to the hypnotic beat of her pendulum clock on the wall ticking the meaningless hours away.
>
> RUSSELL BAKER

In the following paragraph, the writer describes bus travel in rural India. As you read, note that the details appeal to the senses of sight and touch. The details in the last sentence appeal exclusively to the sense of touch.

> I have not yet traveled on a bus in India that has not been packed to the bursting-point, with people inside and luggage on top; and the buses are always so old that they shake up every bone in the human body and every screw in their own. If the buses are always the same, so is the landscape through which they travel. Once a town is left behind, there is nothing till the next one except flat land, broiling sky, distances and dust. Especially dust; the sides of the bus are open with only bars across them so that the hot winds blow in freely, bearing desert sands to choke up ears and nostrils and set one's teeth on edge with grit.
>
> RUTH PRAWER JHABVALA

Supporting details in a descriptive paragraph are often arranged in spatial order so as to direct the reader's attention from left to right, near to far, top to bottom, and so on (see pages 46–48). Russell Baker uses an unusual kind of spatial order in his paragraph: one that represents a journey around the neighborhood. He begins with the outdoor sounds on the farm, goes on to sounds heard on a walk through the neighborhood, and then focuses on sounds inside his grandmother's house. Ruth Prawer Jhabvala's paragraph uses the spatial order of inside to outside and back to inside again. She begins with a description of the inside of the bus, goes on to describe the landscape outside the bus, and ends by describing the dust inside the bus.

Often, the topic sentence of a descriptive paragraph creates a main impression of the topic. For example, Russell Baker creates the impression of "immense silences," and the sounds he describes in the supporting sentences are almost all quiet, "silent" sounds that help reinforce that impression. The first sentence in Jhabvala's paragraph gives an impression of the great discomfort of riding in such a bus, and the paragraph goes on to develop this idea of discomfort.

Techniques for Prewriting. To create a main impression in a descriptive paragraph:

- Gather precise concrete and sensory details about your topic.
- Select only those details that will help create a single impression, and arrange them in spatial order.
- Write a topic sentence that gives your main impression of the topic.

Evaluating and Revising Descriptive Paragraphs

You will find the following guidelines helpful for revising any descriptive paragraph you write. After you have identified the aspects of your paragraph that need to be improved, the revision chart on pages 70–71 will provide you with strategies for revising your writing.

GUIDELINES FOR EVALUATING DESCRIPTIVE PARAGRAPHS

Topic Sentence
1. Does the topic sentence identify a single person, place, object, or event? If it creates a single main impression of the topic, is the impression an effective one?

Topic Development
2. Are enough concrete and sensory details included to create a vivid picture of the topic?

Unity
3. Does each sentence directly support the main idea in the topic sentence?

Order
4. Are the details arranged in spatial order or in another appropriate and easy-to-follow order?

Relationships Between Ideas
5. Do the ideas flow smoothly from one sentence to the next? Are direct references and appropriate transitional expressions (*to the left, in the distance,* etc.) used to show where the parts of the topic are in relation to one another?

Word Choice
6. Is the language precise rather than general? Do the details help the reader picture the topic?

EXERCISE 11. Revising a Descriptive Paragraph. The following descriptive paragraph is weak because it does not contain enough concrete and sensory details. Use your imagination to add details that will make the paragraph vivid and interesting. Write your revised paragraph on a separate sheet of paper.

Jenny came out of the house. She was tall and thin. She wore a pair of jeans and a T-shirt. It was a hot summer day. Jenny sat on the front steps and waited. She heard a lot of sounds. She watched some people go by and said "Hello" to two of them. After a while she looked at her watch and frowned.

EXERCISE 12. Writing a Descriptive Paragraph. Use the following list of details to write a paragraph describing the United States one-dollar bill. You do not have to use all of the details, and you may use others you discover through observation. Before you draft your paragraph, arrange the details in an effective order, and write a topic sentence that creates a main impression. Use the guidelines on page 90 to evaluate your draft and the paragraph revision chart on pages 70–71 to revise it. Then carefully proofread the draft (see pages 32–33) and make a final copy.

> *Details:* George Washington, wise and serious-looking; labeled by his last name in case you don't recognize him
> Signature of the secretary of the treasury
> Front printed in black except for two green serial numbers and green seal of Department of the Treasury; seal has balanced scale above a key
> Back printed all in green
> Paper crisp and smooth when new; limp and creased when old
> Two seals on back
> One seal shows eagle holding 12 arrows in one claw and a branch in other; in its beak a banner reading *E Pluribus Unum,* which means "Out of many, one."
> Other seal mysterious-looking: cut-off pyramid, topmost part has one eye surrounded by glowing light. Wording on seal: *Annuit Coeptis,* which means, "He [God] has smiled on our undertakings"; *Novus Ordo Seclorum,* which means "A new order of the ages"
> Fine network of spiderwebs and curlicues, leaves, and border designs

REVIEW EXERCISE B. Writing a Descriptive Paragraph. Write a paragraph describing a place in your school, using concrete and sensory details to make the scene come alive for your readers.

PREWRITING Spend some time observing the place you have chosen. Decide in advance whether you will describe the place when there are people in it (during school hours) or when it is empty (before or after school). Take a pencil and paper with you, and ask yourself questions that will help you gather as many concrete and sensory details as possible. For example, if you are describing the empty gym, what do your footsteps sound like? What smells are there? Is the floor polished? Are the foul lines clearly painted, or are they dull? Then arrange the details in spatial order, and write a topic sentence that creates a single main impression of the place.

WRITING Concentrate on shaping your details into sentences that will reinforce your main impression. Use precise nouns, verbs, and modifiers to provide a vivid picture for the reader.

EVALUATING AND REVISING Ask yourself: Have I included enough concrete and sensory details? Does each detail help reinforce my main impression? Then use the Guidelines for Evaluating Descriptive Paragraphs (page 90) to judge your draft and the paragraph revision chart (pages 70–71) to improve it.

PROOFREADING AND MAKING A FINAL COPY Proofread your revised draft carefully, using the guidelines on pages 32–33. Prepare a final copy and proofread again.

THE NARRATIVE PARAGRAPH

If you want to develop a topic by relating a story or a series of events, you will write a narrative paragraph. Your purpose is to tell a story. The story may illustrate a point stated in the topic sentence, or it may simply entertain.

A paragraph-length narrative usually focuses on one action or one series of events.

Developing a Paragraph with an Incident

3e. Develop a narrative paragraph with an incident or an anecdote.

The topic sentence of a narrative paragraph may simply set the action in motion, or it may state a general idea, which is then illustrated by means of an incident or anecdote (brief story). Often, the story is drawn from the writer's own experiences. The writer is, in effect, telling the reader, "This is what I learned about life (topic sentence), and this is how I learned it (the incident or anecdote)."

In the following selection, Harry Crews tells about an experience with a car he once owned. What point is the writer making?

> The 1953 Mercury was responsible for my ultimate disenchantment with cars. I had already bored and stroked the engine and contrived to place a six-speaker sound system in it when I finally started to paint it. I spent the better half of a year painting that car. A friend of mine owned a body shop, and he let me use the shop on weekends. I sanded the Mercury down to raw metal, primed it, and painted it. Then I painted it again. And again. And then again. I went a little nuts, as I am prone to do, because I'm the kind of guy who if he can't have too much of a thing doesn't want any at all. So one day I came out of the house (I was in college then) and saw it, the '53

Mercury, the car upon which I had heaped more attention and time and love than I had ever given a human being. It sat at the curb, its black surface a shimmering of the air, like hundreds of mirrors turned to catch the sun. It had twenty-seven coats of paint, each coat laboriously hand rubbed. It seemed to glow, not with reflected light, but with some internal light of its own. I stood staring, and it turned into one of those great scary rare moments when you are privileged to see into your own predicament. Clearly, there were two ways I could go. I could sell the car, or I could keep on painting it for the rest of my life. If 27 coats of paint, why not 127? The moment was brief and I understand it better now than I did then, but I did realize, if imperfectly, that something was dreadfully wrong, that the car owned me much more than I would ever own the car, no matter how long I kept it. The next day I drove to Jacksonville and left the Mercury on a used-car lot. It was an easy thing to do.

HARRY CREWS

Notice that the writer does not tell everything about the car. He does not, for example, tell how many miles it had been driven before he bought it, how much it cost, or how much he sold it for. Instead, he focuses on his obsession with painting the car and how he dealt with that obsession.

The order of ideas in a narrative paragraph is usually chronological, the order in which the events occurred. If you have ever heard someone confuse the order of events in a story, you know how important chronological sequence is in a narrative paragraph.

Techniques for Prewriting.   To develop a narrative paragraph:

- Select an incident or anecdote that you think will interest your audience.
- Use the *5 W-How?* questions (*Who? What? When? Where? Why? and How?*) to gather details of the incident.
- Arrange the details in chronological order.
- If the paragraph illustrates a general idea, write a topic sentence that states that idea clearly.

Evaluating and Revising Narrative Paragraphs

The following guidelines will help you evaluate the narrative paragraphs you write. For strategies for improving your writing, see the paragraph revision chart on pages 70–71.

GUIDELINES FOR EVALUATING NARRATIVE PARAGRAPHS

Topic Sentence	1. Does the first sentence set the action in motion or state a general idea?
Topic Development	2. Are enough details included so that the audience can picture the incident and understand what happened or why it was important?
Unity	3. Have repetitive and unrelated details been left out?
Order	4. Are the actions arranged in the order in which they took place?
Relationships Between Ideas	5. Do the ideas flow smoothly from one sentence to the next? Are direct references and appropriate transitional expressions (before, later, in the meantime, etc.) used to link ideas?
Word Choice	6. Are precise nouns, verbs, and modifiers used to help the audience picture the action? Is the language suitable for the audience?

EXERCISE 13. Writing a Narrative Paragraph. Use the following details to write a paragraph developed with an incident. (The details are listed in chronological order.) First study the details and write a topic sentence that states a general idea. Then write the paragraph.

> *Details:* Took four-year-old cousin Annie to Sea World one day on a holiday weekend—very crowded
> Annie—curious, lively, self-confident
> Went to buy Annie a cold drink, waited in line
> Turned around, Annie gone; nowhere in sight
> Called her name; searched the dolphin area where we had just been
> Panicky—asked a guard to help me find Annie
> Annie's name and description broadcast on loudspeakers throughout park
> 10-minute wait seemed like hours; imagined Annie eaten by Shamu, famous killer whale
> Tear-stained Annie brought in by guard
> She had wandered into a training area for seals; guard found her asking baby seal how to get home

EXERCISE 14. Writing a Narrative Paragraph. Find a photograph in a newspaper or magazine, and write a paragraph relating an incident that might have happened just before or just after the photograph was taken. Make up a specific setting and characters as well as events and provide enough specific details to make the story interesting. If you prefer, you may instead relate an incident that happened just before or just after a family snapshot was taken. Attach the photograph to your paper.

PREWRITING Make a list of details that the reader will need to know in order to understand the incident. For example, where does the incident take place? If it is outdoors, what is the weather like? Who are the main characters? How can you describe them briefly yet interestingly? Where will you begin the story? Make a list of the actions that are necessary to understanding the incident, and arrange them in chronological order. Then consider what you (or the imaginary main character) learned from the incident, and write a topic sentence that comments on the meaning of the incident.

WRITING As you write, concentrate on telling the story clearly and concisely. Try to vary sentence beginnings and structure, avoiding sentences that begin, "And then I . . ."

EVALUATING AND REVISING Ask yourself: Have I included all of the details my audience will need to understand the incident? Does the incident clearly illustrate my general idea? Then use the Guidelines for Evaluating Narrative Paragraphs (page 94) and the paragraph revision chart (pages 70–71) to judge and improve your writing.

PROOFREADING AND MAKING A FINAL COPY Use the Guidelines for Proofreading on pages 32–33 to correct your grammar, usage, and mechanics. Prepare a final copy and proofread again.

REVIEW EXERCISE C. Writing a Narrative Paragraph. Write a narrative paragraph in which the main idea or topic is developed with a brief story. Be specific about time, place, and characters. Use one of the following general ideas or a general idea of your own.

1. The best things in life, it is said, are free.
2. Anger is a difficult emotion to learn to handle well.
3. When it comes to a test of willpower—especially regarding food and TV—more often than not I fail.
4. My mother always tells me that if something is worth doing, it is worth doing right.
5. In every family there are certain classic stories about something funny that a family member did or said.

THE PERSUASIVE PARAGRAPH

The purpose of persuasive writing is to convince an audience to agree with an opinion. Sometimes the writer also attempts to convince the reader to perform a specific action, such as contributing to a charity.

Developing a Paragraph with Reasons

3f. Develop a persuasive paragraph with reasons.

The topic for a persuasive paragraph should be a serious, debatable issue. The issue should be a meaningful one rather than merely a personal preference. Although personal preferences are debatable, they are not appropriate topics for persuasive writing.

NOT APPROPRIATE	Country music is better than rock music.
NOT APPROPRIATE	Maya Angelou is the best writer.
APPROPRIATE	Citizens should sign a petition to recall the mayor.
APPROPRIATE	TV commercials should be banned on children's programs.

The topic sentence, sometimes called the *position statement,* should state the writer's opinion as clearly and succinctly as possible. However, it should not be so brief that it is uninteresting.

TOO BRIEF	Leaded gasoline should be eliminated from the market.
TOO BRIEF	Leaded gasoline should be banned.
EFFECTIVE	For years, motorists have been offered a choice of leaded (regular) and unleaded gasoline, but it is time to eliminate leaded gasoline from the market.

An effective persuasive paragraph presents at least three *reasons,* statements that explain the opinion in the topic sentence. Reasons are most convincing when they are supported by evidence in the form of facts, statistics, or examples. Together, the reasons and the supporting evidence make up the writer's *argument.* Notice that each reason in the following paragraph is supported by a sentence or two providing additional information.

For years, motorists have been offered a choice of leaded (regular) and unleaded gasoline, but it is time to eliminate leaded gasoline from the market. Lead is highly poisonous. It can do considerable damage to the brain, especially in young children. Some learning experts have even speculated that a

topic sentence

reason 1

certain percentage of learning disabilities may be
caused by lead poisoning. Lead levels in the air are   reason 2
increasing, especially in urban areas. The lead
content in the atmosphere is caused by emissions
from automobiles using leaded gasoline. Voluntary
controls on the use of leaded gasoline are clearly
not effective. Although leaded gasoline is supposed   reason 3
to be used only in cars built before 1974, many car
owners buy converter attachments that allow
leaded gas to be pumped into newer cars designed
to use unleaded gas. Leaded paint was removed   clincher sentence
from the market when it was found to cause lead
poisoning; the time has come for leaded gasoline to
follow it into oblivion.

One type of reason that you may use to support an opinion is a
statement made by an *authority,* an expert in the field being discussed.
The following paragraph gives reasons and cites authorities to support
the idea that women are better suited than men for some sports.

Dr. Nicholas and several other doctors agreed   topic sentence
that physiological differences make women best
suited for sports that call upon endurance, like
marathons and English Channel swims, and those
that require balance, like certain gymnastics
events and skiing. They are least suited for events
that require upper body strength, such as the discus
or the pommel horse in gymnastics, or those that
require bursts of speed, like sprint races. Many
experts tentatively speculate that once women   reason 1
catch up in opportunity or training, they will sur-
pass men in endurance events. "Because of their
lighter bones," Dr. Marshall wrote, making the   reason 2
comparison between aluminum and steel, "women
have a chance to end up better marathoners."

JANE GROSS

Reasons in a persuasive paragraph are usually arranged in order of importance. In general, it is more effective to begin with the least important reason and build up to the most important one, thus achieving a forceful conclusion. In some situations, however, especially when you have one very important reason and several less important ones, it may be more effective to give the most important reason first. Whichever order you use, the reader should be able to distinguish important from less important reasons.

A persuasive paragraph may end with a *clincher sentence* that restates the main idea in the topic sentence, summarizes the writer's argument, or specifies a course of action. The clincher sentence in the model paragraph on page 97, for example, restates the main idea in the topic sentence. Although such a sentence is not required, it can provide an effective ending for a persuasive paragraph.

The tone of a persuasive paragraph should be serious and unemotional, thus creating the impression that the argument is fair and reasonable. Avoid name-calling and using words with negative connotations, such as *ignorant* and *unpatriotic*. The reasonable tone of a persuasive paragraph depends on the logical presentation of sufficient reasons and facts to back up your opinion. Be as specific as you can, and be accurate. Concentrate on expressing your ideas in clear, forceful, unemotional language.

Techniques for Prewriting. To plan a persuasive paragraph:

- Choose as a topic a serious, debatable issue.
- Write a topic sentence that states your opinion clearly and concisely.
- Gather at least three reasons that explain your opinion and evidence (facts, statistics, examples) that supports each reason.
- Arrange the reasons and their supporting details in order of importance.
- Plan to use a serious, unemotional tone.

Evaluating and Revising Persuasive Paragraphs

The following guidelines will help you revise the persuasive paragraphs you write. After you have identified areas that need to be improved, you can use the stategies suggested in the paragraph revison chart on pages 70–71 to revise your writing.

GUIDELINES FOR EVALUATING PERSUASIVE PARAGRAPHS

Topic Sentence	1. Does the topic sentence state an opinion about a serious, debatable issue? Is it clear, concise, and interesting?
Topic Development	2. Are at least three reasons given to explain the opinion in the topic sentence? Is each reason supported by accurate details?
Unity	3. Is each sentence directly related to the main idea in the topic sentence?
Conclusion	4. Does the clincher sentence, if there is one, provide a strong conclusion for the paragraph?
Order	5. Are the reasons arranged in order of importance?
Relationships Between Ideas	6. Is the line of reasoning easy to follow? Are transitional expressions used?
Word Choice	7. Have name-calling and words with negative connotations been avoided?
Tone	8. Is the tone consistently serious and unemotional?

EXERCISE 15. Analyzing a Persuasive Paragraph.   Read this paragraph, and answer the questions that follow it.

The many successful horror movies of recent years—both realistic movies about human and natural disasters and movies about fantastic supernatural events—are sheer moneymakers. They have little or no meaning or social value. Movies should convey some sort of meaningful message, yet we come away from a horror movie merely feeling glad that the scary events pictured on the screen did not happen to us. Nothing about such movies makes us better human beings. By boycotting mindless horror films, moviegoers can send a clear message to movie producers: that they want quality films that are meaningful as well as entertaining.

1. What is the topic sentence? How effective is it? Try writing at least two other topic sentences for this paragraph.
2. What is the writer's opinion about horror films? Do you agree or disagree with that opinion?
3. How many reasons does the writer give to support the opinion? Does the writer give separate reasons, or is the same reason repeated in different words?
4. Can you think of any additional reasons to support the opinion? Write a sentence for each additional reason.

5. What does the writer urge the reader to do?
6. Which of the following specific pieces of information would strengthen the paragraph?
   a. References to scary children's stories and fairy tales
   b. Statistics on (1) percentage of box-office successes that are horror movies, and (2) percentage of movies produced each year that are horror movies
   c. Detailed discussion of different types of horror movies
   d. Examples of specific titles, plots, and outcomes of recent horror movies
   e. Quotation from a movie critic on why horror movies are so successful
   f. Quotation from a psychologist on why horror movies are so successful
   g. Poll of movie viewers' reactions after seeing a particular horror movie
7. Does the paragraph have a clincher sentence? If so, what is it and how effective is it? Try writing one or more clincher sentences for this paragraph.

REVIEW EXERCISE D. Writing a Persuasive Paragraph. Write a persuasive paragraph developing one of the following topic sentences (*should* or *should not*). You may instead write a persuasive paragraph on a topic of your own choosing.

Topic sentence: Students (should, should not) be allowed to drive their own cars to high school.

Reasons:
Too many accidents involving students' cars in parking lot and on nearby streets
Students use parking lot as hangout—often cut classes
Parking lot area could be used for a new gym
School bus transportation available to all students who live more than a mile from school
Pressure on students to own cars
Many students have after-school jobs and need cars to get to work on time
Busing requires leaving home too early; cars more convenient
Many students have worked hard to pay for owning and driving cars; deserve to use them as they want to
Fewer students will need school buses, thus saving city money

PREWRITING Study the list of reasons carefully, and select the three or four that you think support your position most strongly. You may use any additional reasons that you think will be effective. (If you are writing on a topic of your own, you will need to develop and evaluate your own list of reasons.) Then think of evidence (facts, statistics, examples) to support each reason. Prepare an outline of your argument by arranging your reasons and evidence in order of importance, either from least important to most important or the other way around. Finally, consider rewording the topic sentence to make it more vivid and interesting.

WRITING Write your first draft, using the outline of your argument as a guide. Try to express your ideas clearly and unemotionally, and consider writing a clincher sentence that restates your opinion, summarizes your argument, or suggests a course of action.

EVALUATING AND REVISING Ask yourself: Have I built a strong argument for my position? Have I established and maintained a serious, unemotional tone? You may also want to have someone else read your draft and tell you how convincing it is. Then use the Guidelines for Evaluating Persuasive Paragraphs (page 99) to judge your writing and the paragraph revision chart (pages 70–71) to improve it.

PROOFREADING AND MAKING A FINAL COPY Use the Guidelines for Proofreading on pages 32–33 to proofread your revised draft. Then make a final copy and proofread again.

CHAPTER 3 WRITING REVIEW

Writing a Paragraph. Write a paragraph on one of the following limited topics or on a topic of your own. Begin by identifying the type of paragraph (expository, narrative, descriptive, or persuasive) that you plan to write. Then identify the audience for your paragraph. Gather information on your topic, arrange it in a logical order, and write a topic sentence that expresses your main idea. Then write a first draft and evaluate it by using the guidelines in this chapter for the particular type of paragraph. Refer to the paragraph revision chart on pages 70–71 as you revise your paragraph and to the Guidelines for Proofreading on pages 32–33 as you proofread it. Remember to proofread again after you make a final copy.

1. A high-school dress code
2. A close-up of a green pepper (or any other vegetable or fruit)
3. Time zones in the United States
4. Something funny you did when you were very young
5. The difference between ice hockey and field hockey

CHAPTER 4

Writing Expository Compositions

PLANNING AND WRITING THE LONGER COMPOSITION

In this chapter you will use the steps in the writing process to write expository compositions. A composition is made up of several closely related paragraphs that together develop a single topic. The paragraphs are arranged as an introduction, a body, and a conclusion.

Like the expository paragraph (pages 75–87), the expository composition has one of the following purposes: (1) to inform an audience about a topic, (2) to explain how to make or do something, or (3) to explain an opinion. Since the idea for a composition is broader than the main idea of a paragraph, an expository composition calls for more planning and more writing.

PREWRITING

SEARCHING FOR SUBJECTS

4a. Search for subjects for your expository composition.

Exposition, because it explains or informs, is the kind of writing you are most often assigned in school. Such assignments often provide specific limited topics for you to write about. Frequently, however, the responsibility for finding suitable subjects to write about falls to you. Searching for subjects—discovering something to write about—is your first step toward writing an expository composition. You can use your personal resources—your own interests, knowledge, and experiences—to begin the search for suitable subjects.

> **Techniques for Prewriting.** To find possible subjects, ask yourself:
>
> - What am I most interested in? Why?
> - What do I know a great deal about through reading, hobbies, participation in sports, TV viewing, out-of-school activities?
> - What firsthand experiences have I had? Which of these experiences are unusual?
> - What unusual experiences have I heard about, read about, or observed?

EXERCISE 1. Listing Your Personal Resources. Use the questions above to make a list of your interests, knowledge, and experiences. Your answers to each question will provide you with a personal resource inventory to which you may refer as you search for suitable subjects for expository compositions.

Tapping Your Personal Resources

Three techniques will help you tap your personal resources: keeping a writer's journal, brainstorming, and clustering.

A *writer's journal,* in which you record your ideas, thoughts, and experiences, can be a significant source of subjects to write about. As you review and react to your journal entries, you might find many possible subjects for expository compositions. For example, an entry about visiting the Grand Canyon might suggest the following subjects: natural wonders in the United States, formation of the Grand Canyon, disadvantages (or advantages) of organized sightseeing tours, and how to record a trip with a camera.

Another useful technique is *brainstorming,* in which you list as many ideas as possible without stopping to evaluate them. For example, one student developed the following list of possible subjects by brainstorming answers to the question "What am I most interested in?"

painting with watercolors
drawing still life of animals and insects
listening to rock music
exploring junk shops and flea markets
backpacking and hiking in wilderness areas
collecting family stories from relatives
playing computer games
reading about space travel
watching tennis matches on TV
collecting minerals

Whether you focus on your interests, knowledge, or experiences, brainstorming about yourself can be an excellent place to begin the search for subjects.

Clustering helps you generate ideas and make connections between them. You begin by writing and circling a word or phrase, then writing and circling each other word or phrase that occurs to you. You connect these circled ideas with lines; these connections allow you to follow your train of thought—to see how one idea suggests another, then another, and so on.

In the following example, one student starts by thinking about the seashore, and then uses clustering to continue a search for subjects suggested by this idea. Each of the circled phrases or words is a possible subject for an expository composition.

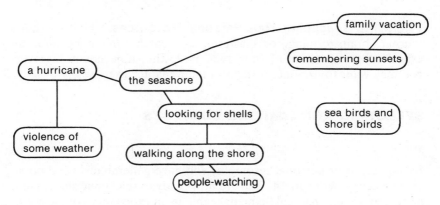

EXERCISE 2. Using a Writer's Journal to Search for Subjects. For three to five days, keep a writer's journal that you are willing to share with others. If you already keep such a journal, you may select several

entries to use in this exercise. By reviewing and reacting to your journal entries, list at least five possible subjects for expository compositions. You may choose to use any one of these subjects in later exercises in this chapter.

EXERCISE 3. Brainstorming to Search for Subjects. For each of the following questions, brainstorm at least five possible subjects for expository compositions. You may find it helpful to refer to the personal resource inventory you developed in Exercise 1 before you begin brainstorming. As noted in Exercise 2, you should save these subjects for use in later chapter exercises.

1. What interests me?
2. What do I know about?
3. What have I experienced?

EXERCISE 4. Using Clustering to Search for Subjects. Select any one of the subjects on the following list. Then use the clustering technique to search for subjects for an expository composition.

1. Holidays	5. Foods	8. Movies
2. Brothers and sisters	6. Hobbies	9. Books
3. Vacations	7. Sports	10. School
4. Seasons		

EXERCISE 5. Tapping Your Personal Resources. Use a writer's journal, brainstorming, or clustering to search for subjects for an expository composition of your own. Keep the subjects you discover; you may want to use one of them in later chapter exercises.

SELECTING AND LIMITING SUBJECTS

4b. Select and limit your subject.

By tapping your personal resources, you have generated several possible subjects to write about. You are now ready to select one subject and limit it to a topic that will be manageable in an expository composition.

Selecting a Subject

To select a subject, review the subjects you discovered through tapping your personal resources. Keep in mind, however, that the subject you choose should be one you are interested in, one you know well enough to explain to someone else, and one with which you have had some experience.

> **Techniques for Prewriting.** Use the following questions to select one subject to write about:
>
> ● Which subject am I interested in enough to want to explain it to someone else?
> ● Which subject do I know enough about to explain it to someone else?
> ● Which subject do I have enough experience with to explain it to someone else?

In answering these questions, you may discover that you do not have enough interest, knowledge, or experience to explain every subject you listed for Exercises 2–5. For example, consider the list of subjects brainstormed on page 105. Although you might be interested in collecting family stories, without ever having done so you probably lack the experience and knowledge to explain this subject to someone else. On the other hand, you might know a great deal about junk shops and flea markets because you visit them regularly with a relative in the business. Because your interest, knowledge, and experience come together on this subject, you might select junk shops and flea markets as a broad subject for an expository composition.

EXERCISE 6. Selecting Subjects. Study the following list of subjects. Review your interests, knowledge, and experiences; then select two subjects that you might enjoy writing about. For each subject you choose, think of several questions an expository composition on the subject should answer.

EXAMPLE   1. Science fiction writers
            1. *a. Who are the most popular science fiction writers?*
               b. Are these writers scientists?
               c. Are they hopeful about the future of humanity?
               d. What were the earliest science fiction stories about?
               e. Have science fiction themes changed?

1. Two authors with different attitudes toward youth

2. Financing your own college education

3. The tragic side of a comic
   character in a novel, movie,
   play, or TV program
4. Origins of place names in
   your area
5. Collecting records

6. Wildlife conservation
7. New steps in dancing
8. Training for the Olympics
9. New horizons in science
10. How advertisers attract
    customers

EXERCISE 7. Selecting a Subject. Using the lists of subjects you developed in earlier exercises, select one subject for an expository composition. Remember that the subject you select might be the one you will decide to write about in later exercises in this chapter. Use the questions on page 107 to help in your selection.

Limiting a Subject

After you have selected a subject, you should limit that subject so that you can explain it in an expository composition of five to eight paragraphs. If, for example, you choose a subject like "skin diving" (about which whole books have been written), you must limit your subject to some specific aspect of the sport to avoid writing too little about too much. Even one aspect—such as how Jacques Cousteau and Emil Gagnan invented scuba diving equipment for the French navy during World War II—offers more to write about than can be covered in a short composition.

To limit your subject to a manageable size, you should analyze it, or break it down into its smaller parts. The limited subject that results is called a *topic*. Notice how the following broad subject has been subdivided into more limited topics. Any of these topics might be covered fully in a short composition, whereas the broad subject would require several more pages of development. Think of the broad subject as the title of the book and each of the topics as the chapters. Then think of your expository composition as a very short chapter or even part of a chapter.

Broad Subject: Skin diving
Limited Topics:
    1. Nitrogen poisoning: what it is and how to avoid it
    2. Are sharks really dangerous?
    3. The advantages of the wet suit
    4. Scuba diving in nearby Marion Pond

Techniques for Prewriting. To limit a subject, ask yourself the following questions:

- What are some aspects, or smaller parts, of the broad subject?
- Which of these aspects are limited enough to cover fully in an expository composition of five to eight paragraphs?
- Which of these aspects lend themselves to the purpose of exposition: to inform or explain?

Then to select one topic to write about, ask yourself this question:

- Which topic best suits my interests, knowledge, and experiences?

EXERCISE 8. Limiting Subjects for Compositions. Select three of the following broad subjects. Then, using the questions above, list five limited topics for each broad subject you selected.

1. Cars
2. Sports
3. World leaders
4. Technology
5. Money

6. Television
7. Books
8. Hobbies
9. Politics
10. Travel

EXERCISE 9. Limiting Your Own Subject. Limit the subject you selected in Exercise 7, breaking it down into three topics that would be suitable for an expository composition.

CONSIDERING PURPOSE, AUDIENCE, AND TONE

4c. Evaluate your topic: consider purpose, audience, and tone.

Before you proceed with the writing process, take time to determine whether you have sufficiently limited your topic in terms of purpose, audience, and tone.

Considering Purpose

In writing an expository composition, your purpose is to inform or explain. You must therefore sufficiently limit your topic so that it can be explained clearly and adequately in several paragraphs. For example, in a short composition you would not have enough space to explain thoroughly all the parts of the topic "differences in quality and price of jogging equipment." A topic limited to one piece of jogging equipment —running shoes, for example—would be better suited to the purpose of a short expository composition.

Techniques for Prewriting. To evaluate your topic in terms of purpose, ask:

● Is my topic limited enough to explain clearly and adequately in several paragraphs?

EXERCISE 10. Evaluating Topics According to Purpose. Indicate which of the following topics are limited enough to be explained clearly and thoroughly in an expository composition. Write *L* for topics that are sufficiently limited and *NL* for those that are not.

1. Boring TV shows
2. Why I prefer first-run movies over made-for-TV movies
3. Making holiday decorations from bread dough
4. How rainbows form
5. Preparing picnics
6. Developing itineraries for visiting national parks
7. Phases in spontaneous combustion
8. Community activities
9. After-school jobs
10. How magicians make rabbits disappear

EXERCISE 11. Developing Limited Topics. Develop three limited topics for each topic you judged as too broad in Exercise 10. For example, the topic "weekend chores" can be further limited to the following topics: why doing weekend chores builds a teen-ager's character, how to start a weekend job service in your neighborhood, and the weekend chores I most dislike.

Considering Audience

The purpose of expository writing is to explain a topic *to someone.* This "someone"—your particular audience—also influences how your topic should be limited, that is, which aspects of the topic you ought to explain. Different audiences can differ greatly in what they bring to understanding your topic. You must therefore consider your audience's characteristics—their background, knowledge, viewpoints, and information needs—and limit the topic with this particular audience in mind.

Suppose, for example, that you are planning a composition about school fund raising. For your classmates, you might limit this topic to "organizing simple weekend fund-raisers." This topic reflects your audience's particular needs and backgrounds: Your classmates might want to know how to organize a fund-raiser; they might want to know what activities they can execute easily; and they might want to know what activities can be done in their free time. For parents who want to become involved in school activities, however, you might limit your topic to "three ways parents can help with school fund-raisers." Parents and classmates differ markedly, so the topic is limited differently for each audience.

Techniques for Prewriting. Use the following questions to evaluate your topic in terms of a particular audience:

- For whom am I writing?
- What aspect of this topic will be of special interest to my audience?
- What does my audience already know about this topic?
- What does my audience want to know or need to know about this topic?
- What will my audience be able to understand about this topic?

EXERCISE 12. Evaluating Topics According to Audience. Several topics for expository compositions are listed below. Following each topic are three different audiences. Indicate which audience the topic fits best. Be prepared to explain your choices.

1. Advanced resuscitation techniques
   a. Intermediate swimming students
   b. Lifesaving instructors
   c. Hospital emergency-room attendants
2. How to write a limerick
   a. Fifth-graders
   b. College poetry class
   c. Poetry society members

3. Economic difficulties of New England's fishing industry
   a. High-school social studies students
   b. National sports fishing association
   c. Advisers to state governors in the Northeast
4. Recreational opportunities through local colleges
   a. Foreign travelers
   b. Tourist bureau members
   c. Community newcomers
5. Job application procedures for June graduates
   a. High-school seniors
   b. Parents of high-school seniors
   c. Teachers of high-school seniors

EXERCISE 13. Limiting Topics for a Particular Audience. Limit each of the topics below for the audience given. Keep in mind that each topic should be limited for an expository purpose.

EXAMPLE *Topic:* Travel advice
Audience: a. Experienced travelers: *Traveling the back roads of France*
b. Inexperienced travelers: *How to make flight reservations to France*

1. *Topic:* Symbols of community pride
   Audience: a. Community newcomers
   b. High-school social studies teachers

2. *Topic:* American presidential elections
   Audience: a. Foreign tourists
   b. Readers of the local newspaper

,3. *Topic:* The pleasures of reading
   Audience: a. Your classmates
   b. Adults learning to read

Considering Tone

Tone is the writer's attitude, or point of view, toward a topic. The tone of an expository composition may be serious or humorous, formal or informal, personal or impersonal. Your attitude is often revealed through the way you have worded your topic. For example, the topic "decisions that have significantly changed my life" suggests a personal but serious tone. The same topic reworded to suggest a humorous tone might read "decision making through coin flipping."

As you evaluate your topic in terms of tone, make certain that your attitude is appropriate for the purpose of your exposition. If, for example, your purpose is to explain how to perform cardiopulmonary resuscitation (CPR), it would be inappropriate to adopt a humorous attitude toward this lifesaving procedure.

Similarly, you should consider whether your tone is appropriate for a particular audience. If, for example, you are writing to inform your classmates about student elections, it would be inappropriate to adopt the formal, impersonal attitude suggested by the topic "acceptable procedures for participating in student government." "Voting in student elections" suggests a more appropriate tone.

Techniques for Prewriting. Consider your attitude toward your topic:

- What attitude do I want to convey?
- Is that attitude appropriate for my purpose and my audience?
- Does the wording of my topic reflect my attitude?

EXERCISE 14. Identifying Tone. Identify the tone of each topic listed. Remember that tone can be serious, impersonal, formal, critical, humorous, enthusiastic, personal, informal, and so on. For example, the topic "jiffy hints for easy shopping" has an informal tone, whereas "building-evacuation procedures" has a formal tone.

1. How to perform the Heimlich maneuver
2. Three reasons for my amazing popularity
3. Camping without millions of "creepy-crawlies"
4. Similarities between *Romeo and Juliet* and *West Side Story*
5. Widespread causes of teen-agers' academic difficulties

EXERCISE 15. Limiting Topics According to Tone. Limit each of the following topics to convey the tone indicated. For example, for a formal tone, the topic "lifesaving techniques" can be limited to "vital resuscitation procedures." For an informal tone, the same topic can be limited to "ways to save a life."

1. *Topic:* Reasons for personal success
   Tone: a. Serious
      b. Humorous
2. *Topic:* Organizing a savings plan
   Tone: a. Personal
      b. Impersonal
3. *Topic:* How to read a play
   Tone: a. Formal
      b. Informal

REVIEW EXERCISE A. Evaluating Your Own Topic. Evaluate a topic of your own in terms of purpose, audience, and tone. (The topic may be one that you have selected and limited in earlier exercises.) Use the questions listed on pages 110, 111, and 113 to evaluate your topic.

CHOOSING A TITLE

4d. Choose a title that gives your purpose and topic.

A good title gives both topic and purpose in one phrase. It catches the audience's interest and suggests what the composition is about. For example, consider the topic "the popularity of jogging." If you are writing to amuse an audience, you might choose the title "Jogging: Flashy Outfits and Sore Feet." For a persuasive, more serious composition, you might choose the title "Run Today for a Healthful Tomorrow." For a straightforward expository composition you might choose the title "Dollars and Sense for Running Shoes." Notice that each title arouses the interest and clearly reflects the topic and purpose of each composition.

> **Techniques for Prewriting.** To choose a title for your expository composition, use these questions:
>
> - Does the title give in a single phrase both the topic and purpose of my composition?
> - Will the title catch the interest of my audience?

If you cannot immediately think of a suitable title, one may come to mind when you develop an outline for your composition.

EXERCISE 16. Writing Titles.   For each of the following topics, write a title that reflects both the topic and the expository, or explanatory, purpose. For example, a possible title for the topic "avoiding an exhausting vacation" might be "Coming Home Refreshed."

1. The benefits of summer travel
2. How the New York Stock Exchange works
3. Changes in fashions since 1900
4. Our school's grading system
5. How to start any collection

EXERCISE 17. Writing Your Own Title.   Write a title for a topic you have selected, limited, and evaluated in earlier exercises. Remember that this title may be revised at a later stage in the writing process.

GATHERING INFORMATION

4e. Gather information on your topic.

Several strategies that are already familiar to you will enable you to gather the information you will include in your expository composition.

   The *writer's journal* can be a valuable source of information on your topic. Suppose, for example, that one entry in your writer's journal details the time you assembled your ten-speed bicycle. If you were writing an expository composition, you might use this journal entry as a source of information—that is, specific details—on "how to assemble bicycles."

   Several questioning strategies can also be useful in gathering information on your topic. (1) The *5 W-How?* questions (*Who? What? When? Where? Why? How?*) enable you to assemble a wide range of information about any topic. (2) With *point-of-view* questions you can gather information about your topic by considering it from three different perspectives: What is it? How does it change or vary? What are its relationships? (3) You can also ask a series of questions about a particular topic: What is it? What are its parts? How is it put together? How is it made or done? What do I think about it? What is its value? What is it good for? Any one of these three questioning strategies will enable you to gather a great deal of information about any topic. (See pages 14–19 for more information on these strategies.)

Brainstorming is also a helpful strategy for gathering information. Suppose, for example, that you are gathering information on the topic "the appeal of cave exploring." To brainstorm about this topic, list every idea, impression, and recollection about exploring caves that might occur to you. The resulting list of ideas and details will not be solely the product of one session of brainstorming. It will be the outgrowth of your personal reading on the topic, conversations with other cave explorers, and, perhaps, other investigations (such as a trip to the library or a call or letter to an organization of cave explorers). The following list might result from brainstorming about cave exploring.

> the darkness of caves
> graffiti in caves and my anger at it
> formation of caves—geology
> appeal of darkness in caves
> sense of timelessness in caves
> the preservation of footsteps in a cave's protected atmosphere
> dangers—flash floods and unmarked passages
> age of caves in the United States
> descent in groups by experienced climbers
> cracks in ceilings—water seeping through
> breathtaking cave formations
> stalactites and stalagmites
> animal life in caves—insects and bats
> the growing popularity of cave exploring
> sense of discovery—as felt by astronauts and pioneers
> limestone mountains in the South
> appeal to senses—crisp sounds, pure air
> experience in rock climbing—a requirement?
> climate—cold and damp
> equipment needed for cave exploration
> physical requirements—strength for climbing and crawling

Regardless of which of the information-gathering strategies you use, the ideas and details you gather will later be classified and arranged when you develop a plan for your expository composition.

EXERCISE 18. Gathering Information on a Topic. Select any three topics from the following list; then use a different strategy to gather information for each topic. Be prepared to explain why, in your opinion, each strategy did or did not work well for that particular topic. Keep the information you gather for use in later exercises in this chapter.

1. Local facilities for water sports
2. Why personal talents need nurturing
3. Simplified foreign language study
4. Significant state historical figures
5. Preparing for careers in the arts
6. The excitement of rock music
7. How TV and movies differ
8. My most courageous moment
9. Why I cherish a family heirloom
10. Productive uses for leisure time

EXERCISE 19. Gathering Information on Your Own Topic. Gather information on a topic of your own, using any of the information-gathering strategies. You may use a topic you have developed in earlier exercises. Keep the information you gather for use in later exercises in this chapter.

CLASSIFYING AND ARRANGING IDEAS

4f. Classify and arrange your ideas.

To develop a plan for your expository composition, you must first organize the information you have gathered.

Classifying Ideas

The first step in organizing your information is to classify ideas and details. To do this, study the information you have gathered. Then group together the ideas and details that are related to the same aspect, or part, of your topic. By grouping ideas and details to discover main headings, you will be *classifying,* or organizing according to relationships.

For the sample brainstormed list on the topic "the appeal of cave exploring" (page 116), you might classify ideas and details according to what kind of appeal they explain. This might result in the following four groups.

GROUP 1: *Record of earth's history inside a cave*
formation of caves—geology
age of caves in the United States
limestone mountains in the South

GROUP 2:   *Dangers of caving*
dangers—flash floods and unmarked passages
descent in groups by experienced climbers
physical requirements—strength for climbing and crawling
experience in rock climbing—a requirement?

GROUP 3:   *Appeal to human need for adventure*
sense of timelessness in caves
appeal of darkness in caves
sense of discovery—as felt by astronauts, pioneers

GROUP 4:   *Beauty of caves and appeal to senses*
breathtaking cave formations
stalactites and stalagmites
climate—cold, damp
appeal to senses—crisp sounds, pure air

Several ideas from the list on page 116 have not been included. For example, "graffiti in caves and my anger at it" does not belong in any of the four groups because the idea is not closely related to the other ideas and details. Similarly, you may not be able to use all the information you have gathered on your topic.

Techniques for Prewriting. Use the following questions to classify the information you have gathered:

● Which ideas and details are related to the same aspect of the topic?
● What headings show how the ideas and details in each group are related?

EXERCISE 20. Classifying Ideas and Details.   Classify the ideas and details you gathered for any one topic in Exercise 18.

Arranging Ideas

Through classifying, you have developed several main headings for organizing the information gathered for your composition. Your next step is to arrange those main headings in the order in which you will discuss them in your composition.

Your specific purpose may suggest a logical order. A composition whose purpose is to explain an opinion, for example, proceeds logically in the order of importance—from least important reason to most important reason, or vice versa. A composition whose purpose is to explain how to make or do something logically follows the steps in the process in chronological, or sequential, order. For some compositions, the writer must determine what the most logical order is for that particular topic. For example, the information about the appeal of caves might proceed from what the writer sees as the simplest appeal to the most complex. Accordingly, the four main headings might be arranged in this order:

dangers of caving
beauty of caves and appeal to the senses
record of earth's history inside a cave
appeal to human need for adventure

Any composition is clearest when its elements are arranged in the right order; it is your task as the writer to determine the right order for your expository composition. To do so, experiment with the ideas and details on your own list. Rearrange them under your main groups until each has found its proper place and appears to belong nowhere else. As the example clearly indicates, some ideas and details will have to be rephrased, others combined, and still others—those that do not fit anywhere—will have to be eliminated entirely. This process of rephrasing, combining, and eliminating is natural, something that all writers experience. Items that are eliminated are not necessarily lost forever, however. They might be good points to include in the composition's introduction or conclusion.

Techniques for Prewriting. To arrange your ideas in logical order, use the following questions:

● What is the specific purpose of my composition?
● What order does that purpose suggest?

EXERCISE 21. Arranging Ideas and Details. Arrange the ideas and details you classified for Exercise 20.

EXERCISE 22. Classifying and Arranging Ideas and Details for Your Own Topic. Classify and arrange the ideas and details you gathered using the information-gathering strategies for Exercise 19. Keep your classification and arrangement of ideas for use in later exercises in this chapter.

Developing a Topic Outline

By classifying and arranging ideas and details, you have developed an informal plan, or outline, for your expository composition. This informal plan can be written more formally as a *topic outline,* one that has a specific format for entering main headings and details. The items in a topic outline (main topics and subtopics) are single words or phrases, not complete sentences. The main topics and subtopics are arranged so that the main ideas stand out. Observe the following rules when you prepare a topic outline for your own expository composition.

(1) Place the title and the statement of purpose above the outline. These items are not numbered parts of the outline.

(2) Use Roman numerals for the main topics. Subtopics are given capital letters, then Arabic numerals, then small letters, then Arabic numerals in parentheses, then small letters in parentheses.

Correct Outline Form

Title:
Purpose:
 I. Main topic
    A. Subtopics of I
    B.
        1. Subtopics of B
        2.
            a. Subtopics of 2
            b.
                (1) Subtopics of b
                (2)
                    (a) Subtopics of (2)
                    (b)
 II. Main topic
    A. etc.

(3) Indent subtopics. Indentations should be made so that all letters or numbers of the same kind will come directly under one another in a vertical line.

(4) When subtopics are included in an outline, there must always be more than one subtopic. Because subtopics are divisions of the topic above them, you must have at least two parts when you subdivide.

If you find yourself with a single subtopic, rewrite the topic above it to include the subtopic.

INCORRECT   D. The study of French culture
               1. The study of the French language
   CORRECT   D. The study of French culture and language

(5) Each number or letter in an outline must have a topic.

Never, for example, write *IA* or *A1* in an outline.

(6) A subtopic must be closely related to the topic under which it is placed.

(7) Begin each topic and subtopic with a capital letter. Since topics and subtopics are not sentences, they should not be followed by periods.

(8) The terms *introduction, body,* **and** *conclusion* **should not be included in a topic outline.**

Although you will have an introduction, a body, and a conclusion in your composition, these terms are not topics you intend to discuss.

Refer to the following sample topic outline as you develop an outline for your expository composition.

Topic Outline

CAVE EXPLORING: A TRIP INTO BEAUTY,
DARKNESS, AND DANGER

Purpose: To explain why people risk danger to explore the dark, mysterious world of caves

I. Dangers for cave explorers   main topic
    A. Unmarked passages
    B. Flash floods   subtopics
    C. Hazards of exploring alone
    D. Risks of being out of condition

II. Appeal of caves to the senses
    A. Cool, clean air
    B. Crispness of sounds
    C. Beautiful formations
       1. Stalactites   further divisions
       2. Stalagmites   of subtopics

III. Geology of caves
   A. Southern caves in limestone mountains
   B. Water tables over centuries
   C. Markings etched onto cave walls by water

IV. Caves as frontiers of exploration
   A. Similarity to astronauts' missions
   B. Similarity to pioneers' adventures

Note use of words and phrases, not sentences, throughout.

EXERCISE 23. Writing a Topic Outline.   Copy carefully the skeleton outline given below at the right. Then place each of the items in the list at the left in its proper position in the outline.

Title: Pleasures of travel
Purpose: To explain three enjoyable aspects of travel

Eiffel Tower in Paris	I.
Seeing natural wonders	A.
California's giant sequoias	B.
CN Tower in Toronto	C.
Seeing wonders created by human beings	II.
Victoria Falls in Africa	A.
Golden Gate Bridge in San Francisco	1.
Dog sleds in Alaska	2.
Aurora borealis	B.
Using unusual transportation	C.
Mexican pyramids	D.
Venetian gondolas	III.
Chesapeake Bay Bridge-Tunnel Complex	A.
Camelback in Egypt	B.
Towers	C.

EXERCISE 24. Developing a Topic Outline.   In Exercises 20 and 21 you classified and arranged information you previously gathered. Write a topic outline for this topic following correct outline form and using the classifications and arrangements you developed earlier. Keep your work for later use.

EXERCISE 25. Writing Your Own Topic Outline.   In Exercise 22 you classified and arranged ideas and details for a topic of your own. Write these same ideas and details as a formal topic outline. Save this topic outline for later use.

CRITICAL THINKING:
Synthesizing to Write a Thesis Statement

4g. Write a thesis statement.

Having gathered, classified, and arranged information on your topic, you are ready to write a thesis statement for your expository composition. A *thesis statement* indicates the purpose of the composition and makes clear what aspects of the topic you will discuss. The thesis statement focuses the attention of both the writer and the audience on the main idea of the composition.

To write a thesis statement, you use the critical thinking skill called synthesis. *Synthesis* comes from Greek words meaning "to place together." Placing together is exactly what you do in writing a thesis statement: you synthesize what you know or understand about your topic in a complete sentence.

In each step in the prewriting process, you have acquired a knowledge or understanding of your topic. As you limited your subject, evaluated your topic, and gathered information, you focused on specific aspects of the topic. Through classifying and arranging your ideas and details, you recognized relationships among these ideas and details. The thesis statement finally brings together what you now understand as a result of prewriting: what the specific aspects of your topic are and how they are related to one another. You have arrived at the understanding expressed in your thesis statement by synthesizing, or placing together, the relationships and information you have discovered through prewriting.

Through synthesizing, you might develop the following thesis statement for the topic "the appeals of cave exploring": *This paper will explain that cave explorers are searching for adventure and a strange beauty unknown in the upper world of light.* This statement, which should appear in the introductory paragraph, states the purpose of the composition (to explain) and suggests what aspects of the topic the composition will discuss (searching for adventure and for a strange beauty).

Techniques for Prewriting. In developing a thesis statement, keep these points in mind:

- Indicate the purpose of your composition.
- Make clear what aspects of your topic you will discuss.

EXERCISE 26. Writing Thesis Statements.   Using the topic outline you wrote in Exercise 24, write a thesis statement. You may want to exchange papers with your classmates to compare the thesis statements you have written on the same topic.

REVIEW EXERCISE B. Writing Your Own Thesis Statement.   Using the topic outline you wrote in Exercise 25, write a thesis statement for your expository composition.

WRITING

WRITING THE PARTS OF A COMPOSITION

4h. Write the parts of your composition: the introduction, the body, and the conclusion.

An expository composition has three main parts: (1) a beginning (the introduction), (2) a discussion of the topics in the outline (the body), and (3) an ending (the conclusion). Each part has a specific function.

Writing the Introduction

(1) The introduction arouses the audience's interest and presents the thesis statement.

Although the introduction does not appear as a heading in the topic outline, it is nevertheless a very important part of an expository composition. The introduction should catch the interest of your audience. It should clearly indicate the topic and your purpose in writing about it, and it should establish the tone of the composition. The thesis statement—either as originally written or in a revised form—is often the last sentence in the introduction.

Below are five ways to write the introduction for an expository composition. Notice how each arouses the interest of the audience and presents the thesis statement. (Each thesis statement is underlined in red.)

1. *Begin with an anecdote or an example.* The following introduction begins with a brief anecdote that leads naturally to the thesis statement.

> The newspapers in Carlsbad, New Mexico, recently carried a story about a cave explorer who missed a turn in one of the caves surrounding the main cavern in Carlsbad Caverns National Park. The explorer was lost for what must have been a frightening two hours before he was rescued and reunited with the rest of his party. When he was found, he greeted his friends with the words, "I feel as though I walked on the moon. Imagine—I was the first person to set foot in that cave." *In this paper, I will explain how the adventure of searching and the beauty of caves draws explorers to them.*

2. *Begin with a question.* A question that requires more than a yes or no response will encourage your audience to read your composition to find the answer.

> What is it about caves that makes certain people want to explore them? *My own reading and firsthand experience have convinced me that cave explorers are searching for adventure and a strange beauty unknown to the world above the ground.*

3. *Begin with a direct statement of your topic.* In a short composition —especially one on a topic of high interest—you may begin by stating your thesis.

> Cave explorers act out of two needs shared by most of humankind. *They are searching for adventure and a special kind of beauty.*

4. *Begin with a statement that contradicts your thesis and counter it with your thesis statement.* This technique arouses interest by surprising your audience.

> Many of us think of cave explorers as being foolhardy and irresponsible. *My own experience suggests, however, that they are simply in search of adventure and a strange kind of beauty unknown to those who never venture underground.*

5. *Begin with general background information.* This technique can be especially useful when the audience you are writing for is not familiar with your topic.

> Most of us are familiar with the natural wonders of the earth—the monuments in rock and water and sand that attract tourists to our national parks. For many, however, the most breathtaking of these wonders cannot be found on the earth's surface. *Every year, therefore, more and more cave explorers go underground in search of a special kind of beauty and what they think of as the most rewarding kind of adventure.*

> *Techniques for Writing.* When writing your introduction:
> - Arouse the interest of your audience.
> - Present your thesis statement.
> - Establish the tone of the composition.

EXERCISE 27. Writing Introductory Paragraphs. Select any one of the following five thesis statements. Then write two introductory paragraphs for this thesis statement, using a different technique for each. Refer to the examples just given and remember to include the thesis statement in each introduction.

1. Creativity demands both inspiration and discipline.
2. Rock musicians often combine musical talent with dramatic flair and a sense of poetry.
3. Establishing a school choral group involves finding a willing faculty sponsor and gathering interested and talented classmates.
4. Our community leaders are notable for their resourcefulness, far-sightedness, and sensitivity.
5. I enjoy fishing because it is a relaxing, rewarding, and challenging sport.

EXERCISE 28. Writing Your Own Introductory Paragraph. Write an introductory paragraph for your own expository composition, using the thesis statement and topic outline you have developed for your topic.

Writing the Body

(2) The body states and develops the main ideas in the outline.

The body of a composition consists of several paragraphs that develop the topic, as stated in your thesis statement. As you write your first draft, you should decide at which points new paragraphs should be started. The way you paragraph should show your reader the successive stages of your thinking. You may decide to devote one paragraph in your composition to each of the main headings in your topic outline or to each point in your thesis statement. This simple solution usually works out well in shorter compositions. In longer compositions, however, you will often find that you need to devote a paragraph to certain subheadings in your outline, or that a major point in your thesis statement might be developed best in two separate paragraphs.

In any case, each of your paragraphs should be built around a single aspect of your topic. Every time you consider a new aspect, begin a new paragraph that develops and supports your thesis statement. In this way your composition will be unified.

Each paragraph within the body should have a topic sentence supported by specific details, facts and statistics, examples, reasons, or incidents. (See Chapter 3.) Note that you might decide to relate an incident to explain an aspect of your topic. Here narration and exposition overlap as you try to achieve your informative or explanatory purpose. Refer to your topic outline for details to support each topic sentence.

Achieving Emphasis and Coherence

As you draft the body of your composition, you must also be concerned with achieving emphasis and coherence.

4i. Arrange your ideas to achieve emphasis.

All the parts of your composition are not necessarily of equal importance in explaining your topic to your audience. How you arrange and develop the paragraphs in the body of your composition should therefore clearly indicate to the reader which ideas and details you consider the most important. You can emphasize your most important ideas three ways:

1. *With a direct statement.* By using phrases like "the most important reason," "the major step in the process," and "the most significant result," you state directly which ideas you think are most important and should therefore receive the greatest emphasis.

2. *By position.* Ordinarily the strongest positions in the composition's body are the first and last parts. Ideas and details you want your audience to notice particularly should therefore be placed in these positions. Another type of arrangement for emphasis is the *order of climax,* which moves from the weakest to the strongest idea or reason.

3. *By proportion.* The amount of space you devote to an idea reflects its importance. Keep in mind, however, that the number of subtopics a topic has in an outline does not necessarily determine the amount of

emphasis the topic should receive. Sometimes a topic with several subtopics may concern the least important idea in your composition, while a topic with few subtopics may address the most important idea.

4j. Arrange your ideas to achieve coherence.

The paragraphs that form the body of your composition should be arranged in a logical order. The order you choose depends on the topic you are explaining. For example, in compositions that explain how to make or do something, paragraphs should be arranged in chronological or spatial order. Compositions that explain opinions often use order of importance, progressing from the least important idea to the most important idea, or just the opposite. For some topics, the order simply depends on which ideas are necessary for understanding later points and should therefore precede these points. By arranging the paragraphs in the body of your composition in a logical order, you will achieve coherence, or the smooth and logical flow of ideas. For a more extensive discussion of arranging ideas logically, see Chapter 2, pages 45–52.

4k. Connect your ideas to achieve coherence.

In an effective composition, the current of thought flows smoothly throughout the composition. It is not interrupted by the divisions between paragraphs; it is helped easily over these divisions by certain *transitions*. Examples of three kinds of transitions—transitional expressions, direct pronoun references, and repetition of key words—are given below. Use of these transitions connects ideas within and between paragraphs.

Transitional Expressions

To indicate another point: after that, also, another, at last, at the outset, further, besides, finally, first (second, etc.), furthermore, in addition, in conclusion, in other words, in the next place, lastly, moreover, then, then again, to begin with, too, to sum up

To indicate place or position: above, across from, adjacent to, around, before, below, beside, beyond, here, in the distance, nearby, next, on my left, on my right, opposite to, there, to the left, to the right

To indicate results: accordingly, as a result, as might be expected, consequently, hence, therefore, thus

To indicate time order or sequence: afterward, again, at last, at the present time, at the same time, at this point, eventually, finally, first (second, etc.), meanwhile, next, not long after, presently, soon, sooner or later, then, thereafter, thereupon

To introduce examples: an example of this, for example, for instance

To show comparison: again, also, and, besides, in addition, in a like manner, likewise, moreover, similarly, such, too

To show contrast: but, however, in spite of, instead, nevertheless, on the contrary, on the other hand, opposite to, otherwise, whereas, yet

To show order of importance: after that, also, equally important, furthermore, in addition, in conclusion, in the first (second, etc.) place, then, to begin with, to sum up

EXAMPLES   . . . Day after day the drought continued.

On the thirtieth day, **however,** the wind changed. It blew cool against the face and carried a faint breath of something new.

. . . scientists found that dolphins were intelligent.

An example of this intelligence is the way in which dolphins once avenged themselves on fishermen. A fishing boat in the Pacific had killed several dolphins. The next day about two hundred dolphins surrounded the fishing boat, stranding the fishermen aboard.

. . . it was the hottest day of the year.

The mayor, **accordingly,** declared a heat emergency.

Direct Pronoun References

EXAMPLE   . . . The lamb was uneasy too. **It** started violently at unexpected noises and cried piteously when left alone.

This was not the worst burden on *its* owner, however. . . .

Sometimes when you face a multiple-choice question on a test, you realize that you do not know the correct answer. You may, however, be able to determine **it** by a process of elimination. In this process, you consider all the choices one by one, questioning the reasonableness of **each. Some** will be obviously absurd and may be eliminated. The **one** that is left should be a safe guess.

Repetition of Key Words

EXAMPLES   . . . What is more, the car will accelerate from 0 to 60 miles per hour in only five seconds.

This blistering acceleration, however, is not its best feature. . . .

. . . A further advantage of using the play by Lorraine Hansberry is that it would require only a small cast of talented actors.

Having a small cast would allow us to increase our profits by at least 10 percent, a major goal since we are donating the proceeds to charity. Since our overhead costs. . . .

Techniques for Writing. In writing the body of your composition:

- Use your topic outline as your guide.
- Write a separate paragraph for each main point in your topic outline.
- Include in each paragraph a topic sentence developed by at least one of the methods of paragraph development.
- Emphasize your most important ideas.
- Use transitions to connect ideas within paragraphs and between paragraphs.

EXERCISE 29. Evaluating Coherence and Emphasis. In a magazine or newspaper that you may cut up, find three to five paragraphs written on one topic. Paste these paragraphs neatly on a sheet of paper. Indicate if the writer has achieved emphasis by position, proportion, or direct statement and if the writer has successfully indicated which ideas and details should receive the strongest emphasis. Underline the transitions, and summarize what kinds of transitions the writer uses. Be prepared to discuss why these are or are not appropriate for the paragraphs and how the writer has or has not arranged ideas in a logical order.

EXERCISE 30. Writing the Body of Your Composition. Using your own topic outline and thesis statement as guides, write the body of your composition.

Writing the Conclusion

(3) The conclusion clinches or extends the main points made in the body of the composition.

The conclusion, the last paragraph of your composition, leaves a final impression on your audience. That impression should give the composition a sense of completeness by reinforcing the main idea expressed in the thesis statement. Keep in mind, however, that the conclusion should not merely repeat what the audience has already read in the introduction of the composition. Rather, the conclusion should make a final statement that is an extension of the points discussed in the body.

In the following conclusion the writer brings a discussion of the rights of American Indians to a definite and strong close.

> The "vanishing Indian," the stereotype of the late nineteenth-century, is far from vanishing. Reservation home rule is more solidly established than ever, Indian self-esteem is on the rise, and the Indian world is in ferment. Where this will lead is anybody's guess, but at this writing the Indian's future, if not bright, certainly seems brightening. Alexander Pope's "poor Indian! whose untutor'd mind/Sees God in clouds, or hears him in the wind" has become a sophisticated and successful practitioner of the art of survival in the modern world.
>
> ROBERT A. HECHT

Techniques for Writing. When you write your conclusion, ask yourself:

- Does the conclusion reinforce the main idea presented in the thesis statement?
- Is the conclusion an outgrowth of the ideas discussed in the body of the composition?

EXERCISE 31. Evaluating a Conclusion. In a magazine or newspaper you may cut up, find a conclusion to an expository article or essay and bring it to class. Be prepared to explain why the conclusion does or does not provide an effective ending to the article.

EXERCISE 32. Writing the Conclusion for Your Own Composition. Write the conclusion for your expository composition.

STUDYING A SAMPLE COMPOSITION

A sample expository composition follows on the topic "the appeal of cave exploring." As you read the composition, notice how its parts work together to present and develop the main idea presented in the thesis statement. Also notice how the topics in the outline on pages 121–122 are developed.

CAVE EXPLORING: A TRIP INTO BEAUTY,   title
DARKNESS, AND DANGER

Caves are dark, cold tunnels inhabited by ants,   introduction
lizards, insects, and eyeless fish—weird, colorless

creatures that have never seen sunlight. Little from the world above can penetrate the black space of caves, except for water that seeps through cracks, occasional threads of light that sneak between rocks—and human beings who descend bravely into the dark. Every year, more and more people become interested in the unique hobby of cave exploring. What lures them into the murky depths? What pleasure do they get from crawling along narrow, jagged passages? <u>As we will see, they are searching for adventure and a strange beauty unknown in the "upper" world.</u>

specific details to arouse audience interest in topic

thesis statement

<u>For would-be adventurers, cave exploring offers unusual dangers.</u> Cave passages are seldom marked: therefore, it is quite easy to lose all sense of direction. Water often fills caves during flash floods, drowning anyone inside. Because of these dangers, explorers must never risk entering a cave alone. They also must be in good physical condition because maneuvering inside a cave requires strength for climbing and crawling.

body
topic sentence: states main topic I

specific details describe dangers of cave exploring

Once the explorer enters a cave's deep vaults, <u>however,</u> all the difficulties seem worthwhile. Cave air is cool and clean. Sounds echo crisply through the vast emptiness. Magnificent rock creations, shaped over centuries by drops of water seeping through the earth, dominate the interior. Like exotic sculptures in a secret museum, formations called stalactites droop ominously from a cave's ceiling, while stalagmites rise in massive pointed shapes from the floor. <u>For the cave explorer, the underground is a hidden realm of beauty.</u>

main topic II
transitional word

specific details illustrate appeal to the senses

topic sentence

<u>Many explorers know another secret hidden inside caves: a sense of intimacy with the earth's geologic past.</u> The caves of the Carolinas and

topic sentence: states main topic III; also includes transition

Georgia, for example, were originally formed out of limestone mountains. They were created by water tables—levels of water in the ground—that rose and fell over centuries, slowly dissolving the limestone bases of the mountains. The high, dry spaces left when the waters receded are the caves we know today. The explorer sees these water markings etched into the cave's floors and walls. They are vivid reminders of the earth's transformation and development.

Even more impressive than the beauty of a cave or its record of the past is its pull on the human imagination. A cave is a frontier of adventure, a last unexplored wilderness. Like an astronaut, a cave explorer is a wanderer into an alien world. Every "caver" has the pioneer dreams of being the first to find a new passageway and to take a fresh step into an undiscovered cavern. It is this call of the unknown that lures an explorer into the earth's depths—to enter a world where danger and beauty come together.

> transition; also indicates emphasis
>
> topic sentence: states main topic IV
>
> examples illustrate caves' pull on human imagination
>
> conclusion reinforces thesis statement

EXERCISE 33. Studying an Expository Composition. Answer each of the following questions about the sample composition. You may find it helpful to review the explanations on the introduction, body, and conclusion found on pages 124–31.

1. Which type of introduction (pages 124–26) is used in this composition? How effective, in your opinion, is this introduction in arousing the interest of the audience and in stating the main idea of the composition?
2. Review each paragraph in the body. What methods of paragraph development does the writer use? What other details, if any, do you think the writer could have included to support each topic sentence better?
3. How effective is the conclusion? What final impression does it leave on you? How does the conclusion reinforce the thesis statement?

4. What changes, if any, have been made from the writer's topic outline on pages 121–22? Why do you think the writer did or did not make changes?
5. How does the writer achieve emphasis in the composition? Coherence?

REVIEW EXERCISE C. Writing an Expository Composition. Select a topic of your own for an expository composition. Then, by referring to the Guidelines for Writing Expository Compositions on pages 140–41, write an expository composition on your topic.

EVALUATING

4l. Evaluate the content, organization, and style of your draft.

When you evaluate your draft, your goal is to identify its strong points and its weak points. You then need to decide what changes should be made to improve your draft. To do this, you must see your draft from a different perspective. That is, you must become a reader of your own writing, judging how well and how clearly you have explained your topic to your audience.

When you evaluate your draft, you should consider three aspects: (1) its content (what you say about your topic); (2) its organization (how your ideas are arranged); and (3) its style (how you use language to explain your topic). The following Guidelines for Evaluating Expository Compositions will help you discover what you should change to explain your topic clearly and thoroughly to your audience. Read each question and answer it honestly. When your answer is no, you have identified something that needs to be changed. (For further help in evaluating your draft, refer to the general evaluation guidelines in Chapter 1, page 25.)

GUIDELINES FOR EVALUATING EXPOSITORY COMPOSITIONS

Purpose | 1. Does the introduction tell the audience what the composition will be about? Does it attract the audience's attention?

Paragraph Unity	2. Does each paragraph in the body discuss only one main idea about the topic?
Thesis Development	3. Are enough points included to help the audience understand what the paper is about? (For a short paper, are there at least two supporting points?)
Conclusion	4. Is it obvious that the paper has ended? (The audience should not be left hanging.)
Emphasis	5. Can the audience easily identify the most important idea in the composition?
Coherence	6. Does the composition have a clear organizational pattern? Is that pattern logical? Does it suit the topic?
Coherence	7. Are ideas clearly connected, both within and between paragraphs? Do transitions like *this, those, another, first,* and *finally* link ideas?
Word Choice	8. Will the audience understand the language used in the composition? Are technical terms and unusual words defined or explained?

EXERCISE 34. Applying the Guidelines for Evaluating Expository Compositions. Below is a draft of the fourth paragraph in the sample composition on pages 132–33. As you read the draft, apply the Guidelines for Evaluating Expository Compositions. Then answer each question that follows the draft. Be prepared to explain your answers.

Many explorers get something from caves: a sense of intimacy with the earth's past. The caves of the Carolinas and Georgia were originally formed out of limestone mountains. They were made by water tables that rose and fell for years, slowly breaking up the limestone bases of the mountains. Limestone is a kind of rock composed of the organic remains of sea animals. The explorer sees these water markings, all kinds of crazy-looking squiggles, etched into the cave's floors and walls. The high, dry spaces left behind when the waters receded are the caves we know and love today. They are reminders of the earth's transformation and development.

1. What is the main idea of the paragraph? What details support it? Does the paragraph include any ideas that do not support the main idea? If so, what are they?
2. What organizational pattern does the paragraph follow? Which, if any, ideas seem to be out of order?
3. In which instances would the addition of transitions improve the logical flow of ideas in the paragraph?

4. In which instances would a change in wording improve the tone of the paragraph?
5. What specific changes do you think the writer should make in this paragraph? Be prepared to give at least one reason for each change you suggest.

EXERCISE 35. Evaluating Your Own Draft.   Evaluate your draft by applying each of the questions in the Guidelines for Evaluating Expository Compositions on pages 134–35. Mark places in your draft where you should make changes, and keep the marked draft for later use. You may also want to exchange papers with a classmate to evaluate one another's work.

REVISING

4m. Revise your draft, making changes to improve the content, organization, and style of your expository composition.

Four strategies are useful in revising any piece of writing: (1) you can cut, or omit, words, phrases and sentences; (2) you can add ideas and details; (3) you can reorder, or rearrange, words, sentences, and paragraphs; and (4) you can replace one thing with another. The chart that follows suggests how you can use these strategies to revise your expository compositions.

REVISING EXPOSITORY COMPOSITIONS

PROBLEM	TECHNIQUE	REVISION
The introduction has a weak thesis statement or none at all.	Add	Include a thesis statement that clearly states what the composition is about.
The introduction is dull.	Add	Begin with an anecdote or example, a direct statement, a contradictory statement, or some background information.

PROBLEM	TECHNIQUE	REVISION
A paragraph discusses more than one main idea.	Cut/Add	Remove details that do not discuss one main idea. Make a new paragraph with these details, or add them to an existing paragraph that discusses the same idea.
There is not enough support for the main idea of the composition.	Add	Add at least one more paragraph to support the main idea. (It should include a topic sentence backed up with facts, details, statistics, examples, incidents, or reasons.)
The composition does not end obviously.	Add	Add ideas and details that emphasize the main idea without repeating it word for word.
It is not clear which idea is the most important.	Add/Reorder	Show which point is the most important by (1) stating it in a sentence, (2) adding information about it, or (3) placing it at the beginning or at the end of the body of the composition.
The order of ideas doesn't make sense.	Reorder	Find the sentence or paragraph where the order of the composition becomes unclear; move it so the order of ideas is clear.

PROBLEM	TECHNIQUE	REVISION
It is not clear how ideas are related.	Add	Add words that help to link ideas, such as *these, other, first, then,* and *thus.*
Some of the words are not familiar to the audience.	Add/Replace	Add definitions and explanations. Replace technical terms or unusual vocabulary with familiar words.

   The revision below shows the changes made by the writer in the draft of the fourth paragraph (page 135) of the sample composition (pages 131–33). As you study the revisions, refer to the notes in the margin. They indicate the revision strategies used by the writer. The lines have been numbered for easy reference in Exercise 36.

1   Many explorers ~~get something from~~ *know another secret hidden inside* caves: a   replace

2   sense of intimacy with the earth's *geologic* past. The caves of   add

3   the Carolinas and Georgia *, for example,* were originally formed   add

4   out of limestone mountains. They were ~~made~~ *created* by   replace

5   water tables *— levels of water in the ground —* that rose and fell ~~for years,~~ *over centuries,* slowly   add/replace

6   ~~breaking up~~ *dissolving* the limestone bases of the mountains.   replace

7   ~~Limestone is a kind of rock composed of the~~   cut

8   ~~organic remains of sea animals.~~ The explorer sees   cut/reorder

9   these water markings, ~~all kinds of crazy-looking~~   cut

10   ~~squiggles,~~ etched into the cave's floors and walls.   cut

11   The high, dry spaces left ~~behind~~ when the waters   cut

12   receded are the caves we know ~~and love~~ today.   cut

13   They are *vivid* reminders of the earth's transformation   add

14   and development.

EXERCISE 36. Evaluating a Revised Paragraph. Answer each of the following questions by referring to the preceding revised paragraph.

1. The writer replaced words or phrases in lines 1, 5, and 6. Why do you think the writer made each change?
2. How does the addition of *for example* in line 3 help the reader? Why do you think the writer added *geologic* (line 2) and *vivid* (line 13)?
3. Why do you think the writer cut the sentence in lines 7–8, the phrase in lines 9–10, and the compound verb in line 12?
4. Why do you think the writer moved the sentence in lines 8–10?
5. Does the revision correct the problems you identified in Exercise 34? Do you think the revised version is better than the first draft? Why or why not?

EXERCISE 37. Revising Your Own Composition. Use the chart on pages 136–38 to decide what strategies you should use to revise your composition. Then make the necessary changes. For further help with revising, you may want to refer to Chapter 1. You may also want to exchange papers with a classmate.

PROOFREADING

4n. Proofread your composition for errors in spelling, grammar, usage, and mechanics.

Expository writing, if it is to fulfill its purpose, must be clear and precise. If a run-on sentence, misplaced comma, or misspelled word confuses your audience, they might miss the point of your exposition. You can make your expository composition more effective by correcting errors that may confuse or distract your audience.

Use the Guidelines for Proofreading on pages 32–33 to proofread your revised draft.

EXERCISE 38. Proofreading Your Expository Composition. Proofread the revised draft of your expository composition, using the Symbols for Revising and Proofreading on page 36. You may also want to double-check each other's proofreading by exchanging papers with a classmate.

WRITING THE FINAL VERSION

4o. Prepare the final copy of your composition.

After you have proofread your revised draft, you are ready to prepare the final version of your expository composition. As you do so, be sure to follow correct manuscript form (see Chapter 1) or your teacher's specific instructions. Proofread your final copy. Check for omitted words and other errors that may have been made in recopying.

EXERCISE 39. Preparing Your Final Copy. Prepare a final draft of any expository composition you have written in this chapter. Be sure to proofread again after you have recopied your composition.

CHAPTER 4 WRITING REVIEW 1

Writing an Expository Composition. Using the steps in the writing process, write an expository composition on a topic of your own choice. As you develop your composition, refer to the guidelines below.

CHAPTER 4 WRITING REVIEW 2

Using the Writing Process. Select any long expository paper you have written in a class other than English. Evaluate this composition, applying the Guidelines for Evaluating Expository Compositions on pages 134–35. Revise the composition, making the necessary changes. Exchange and compare papers with a classmate; then discuss how your knowledge of the writing process can improve the expository writing you do in your other classes.

GUIDELINES FOR WRITING EXPOSITORY COMPOSITIONS

PREWRITING

1. Select a topic you understand well enough to explain. Otherwise, you may find it difficult to explain the topic to someone else.

2. Be sure to limit your topic well so that you can discuss specific aspects in the available space.
3. Pay special attention to gathering information for your topic. Because your purpose is to give information, you need to have both the *right kind* of information and *enough* information to explain the topic well to your audience. Depending on your topic and audience, gather facts, statistics, specific details, examples, or incidents.
4. Determine if any technical terms or unusual vocabulary should be defined to help your audience.
5. Carefully organize the information you gather to explain your topic as well as possible. Group and arrange related ideas and details into an informal plan or topic outline, then use this plan or outline to draft a thesis statement.

WRITING

6. Select one of the methods for writing an introductory paragraph. Be sure to include a thesis statement.
7. Use your topic outline or informal plan to draft the body of your composition. Write one paragraph for each main topic in your outline, supporting the topic sentence in each with details from your outline. Achieve emphasis through position, statement, or proportion; arrange the paragraphs in the body logically; and use transitions to connect ideas and paragraphs.
8. As you write, be aware of language you use. Choose words that accurately convey your attitude toward the topic and that are appropriate for your audience.
9. Write a concluding paragraph that clinches the composition by restating your topic and by leaving your reader with a final impression about your topic.

EVALUATING, REVISING, AND PROOFREADING

10. Decide if you have included enough of the right kind of information to explain the topic to your audience. Also determine if the paragraphs in the body are arranged to explain your topic clearly. Consider how appropriate your language is for your audience and for the tone you wish to convey. Then revise, making the changes needed to improve your draft. Proofread for errors in spelling, grammar, usage, and mechanics. Proofread again after you prepare a final draft to catch any mistakes made in recopying.

CHAPTER 5

Writing Expository Compositions

SPECIFIC EXPOSITORY WRITING ASSIGNMENTS

The general principles of exposition discussed in Chapter 4 apply to most of the writing assignments you are likely to be given in school. There are, however, certain specific kinds of expository compositions that come up often enough to require special treatment: process explanations, critical reviews, and essays of literary analysis. Concentrate on one type at a time, and remember that the general ideas about using the writing process to write expository compositions apply to all expository writing.

PROCESS EXPLANATIONS

The explanation of a process gives a step-by-step account that explains either (1) how to make or do something or (2) how something works. Do-it-yourself instructions, recipes, or repair guides are examples of process explanations.

The hints, model, and guidelines that follow will help you plan and write an effective process explanation.

Prewriting Hints for Process Explanations

1. *Select and limit your subject.* Choose a process you can clearly

explain in a composition that contains an introduction, three or more paragraphs of explanation, and a concluding paragraph (or sentence). You could not fully explain the process of "how a car works" in a few paragraphs. You would need to limit this subject to a more manageable topic, such as "how a radiator cools an engine." In explaining your topic, you assume a position of authority, so be certain that you are fully informed about your subject.

2. *Gather sufficient information on your topic.* Assume that your audience is not familiar with your topic, and try to anticipate questions that someone might have. Ask yourself: What are my topic's parts? How is it put together? How does it work? How is it made or done? Be sure that you give every important step, but do not include unnecessary steps that will confuse your audience.

3. *Organize your information in a logical plan.* Arrange all the steps of the process in chronological order, using an informal plan or a topic outline (see pages 120–22). Read the outline over. Could someone follow this plan to make or to understand what you are explaining? If not, add or delete information, or clarify what you already have.

4. *Use the proper tone and language for your audience.* While you can assume that your audience is not familiar with your topic, do not "talk down" to them by oversimplifying or using childish language. Instead, treat your audience with respect by using specific words that show the relationships between the steps in the process.

5. *Define special terms.* Be sure that you explain any technical or special terms to your audience.

6. *Specify any materials, supplies, or tools that are needed.* Give exact amounts, measurements, or descriptions of any supplies or equipment needed in the process you are explaining.

7. *Include special notes and cautions.* Be sure to tell your audience about any special instructions or warnings. For example, if you were explaining how to service an automobile radiator, you would want to warn your audience about the danger of removing the radiator cap before the radiator is cool.

Writing Process Explanations

The following process explanation describes how to carve a wooden egg. After specifying what materials will be needed, the explanation gives a careful step-by-step presentation. Notice how the writer has used transitions to tie together parts of her explanation so that the audience can easily follow along.

In the following composition, notice how the writer announces her purpose, shows when it has been achieved, and tells the audience its value.

CARVING A WOODEN EGG FOR PRACTICE

Whether or not you have carved wood before, this practice project is a good way to begin. Use a block of wood of any kind (without knots) about $1\frac{1}{2}$ inches thick by $1\frac{1}{2}$ inches wide by $2\frac{1}{2}$ inches long, with the grain running the long way.

If you cannot find wood this thick, you can make such a block from two pieces of standard $\frac{1}{4}$-inch board, each $2\frac{1}{2}$ inches long. Measure and mark [the board] with the ruler and pencil the $2\frac{1}{2}$-inch lengths. Clamp the board in the vise of C-clamps, and with the crosscut saw cut off the measured pieces, <u>then</u> glue them with the flat sides together, using a thin coat of white glue. Press them in the vise or clamp them together, but not *too* tightly or all the glue will squeeze out. Let them dry for at least an hour, then use the piece exactly as if it were a single solid block. This method of gluing is called *laminating* wood, and although the joint may show a little, it will give you no trouble in carving if the two pieces are of the same kind of hardness of wood. All wood can be glued easily and permanently with the *flat sides* (long grain) together, but it is almost impossible to glue two *cut* ends (end grain) together to stay.

<u>Now</u> you need to make a simple pattern for the wooden egg. On a piece of the cardboard measure off and mark with ruler and pencil the $1\frac{1}{2}$-inch by $2\frac{1}{2}$-inch <u>rectangle</u> of one side of your block. In that <u>rectangle</u>, draw freehand the shape of an egg that almost touches each of the four sides. <u>Now</u>, using the scissors, cut out the cardboard-egg pattern and draw around it with the pencil on each of the four

Margin annotations:

introduction

gives specific measurements

gives special instructions

body

topic sentence

(1) first step gives special equipment

signals transition

gives special instructions

defines special term that is emphasized

gives special instruction emphasis: draws attention to definition of special terms

signals transition

(2) second step gives specific measurements; repetition for coherence

signals transition

sides of your wooden block. To start work on the egg, *first* shave away with the knife the four corners of the block outside the drawn lines and *then* slowly shape the piece into an egg just like those in the refrigerator. We are not going to give you a single further hint or bit of instruction. You are on your own to experiment and to learn some of the things about using your knife and about carving wood that you must find out for yourself. Try using first one blade and then the other to discover how your knife works. This practice is more important than it is to make a perfectly oval-shaped egg, so don't worry too much if the wood splits, or if you finally wind up with nothing but a scrap of wood. This is an important way to learn—to do a project by yourself in your own way.

(3) third step; signals first operation

signals next operation

conclusion; final advice

FLORENCE H. PETTIT

GUIDELINES FOR EVALUATING PROCESS EXPLANATIONS

Topic	1. Is the topic limited to a process that can be explained adequately in a few paragraphs?
Purpose	2. Does the introduction tell the audience exactly what the composition will show them how to do or help them understand?
Development	3. Are all materials, along with specific amounts and descriptions, included, as well as all steps the audience will need to understand the process?
Coherence	4. Are the steps in the process, including any special notes or cautions, presented in chronological order? Should any sentences or details be moved to make the explanation clearer?
Transitions	5. Is the order of the steps in the process clear to the audience? Do transitional words and phrases make this order clear?
Word Choice	6. Are any terms that might be unfamiliar to the audience explained in appropriate language?

EXERCISE 1. Writing a Process Explanation. Use the following steps to write a process explanation five to seven paragraphs long.

1. Select, limit, and develop a subject of your own that clearly involves explaining how to make or do something or how something works. Refer to the prewriting hints on pages 142–43; then write a first draft of your process explanation.
2. Using the Guidelines for Evaluating Process Explanations and the Guidelines for Evaluating Expository Compositions on pages 86–87, identify changes that are needed in your first draft.
3. Using the revising chart on pages 136–38, revise your first draft.
4. Referring to the Guidelines for Proofreading (pages 32–33), proofread your revised draft for any errors.
5. As you write the final draft, follow correct manuscript form (see pages 33–35) or your teacher's instructions. Proofread your paper once again to check for any errors made in recopying.

CRITICAL REVIEWS

The critical review evaluates a particular work so your audience can decide whether they would enjoy the work. Works to review include books, films, recordings, television programs, or any other creative forms. A critical review does not necessarily find fault with a work, although it may. Your critical review should include (1) a concise summary of the work's subject, thesis, or story line; (2) an objective examination of the work's elements; and (3) an evaluation, or a subjective impression, of the work's effectiveness.

Prewriting Hints for Critical Reviews

1. *Identify and limit your subject.* Begin by classifying the work into a category, such as subject matter (fiction or nonfiction), type (comedy, tragedy, documentary), genre (western, science fiction, biography), or audience (adults, teen-agers, historians). Next, take notes on the main sections or scenes of the work. Your summary must be short, only one or two paragraphs, so limit your notes to the central topic or story by asking yourself: What information is vital to understand this work?

2. *Gather information on your topic.* Become familiar with the work you are reviewing by rereading parts or all of a book or by seeing a film more than once. Write down specific quotations that express or support your views. Determine the purpose of the work by asking yourself:

What elements of the work are repeated? What elements are given the most space or time? What elements are emphasized (for example, with italics or boldfaced type in a book; with slow motion or music in a film)?

3. *Organize your information in a logical plan.* Present the information in your summary in the same order in which it appears in the work. Then organize your list of major points and elements either in the order in which they appear, in order of importance, or in chronological order. Conclude your review with an evaluation of the work. Ask yourself: Has this work made me aware of something new? Has it presented an argument or dramatization that changed or confirmed my views? Why would I recommend (or not recommend) this work to someone else? List specific information from the work to support your evaluation.

4. *Give your audience an accurate representation of the work.* Your review should provide an accurate representation of the content and effectiveness of the work you are reviewing. So, be sure to include all important points and not to distort the work's content, style, or theme.

5. *Describe any special features of the work.* Mention and evaluate any special features that would make the work more—or less—useful to your audience. For books these include illustrations, indexes, bibliographies, footnotes, and other aids. Special features in films include the soundtrack, color, subtitles, distinctive techniques (time-lapse photography, 3-D, fade-outs), and other special effects.

6. *Give your individual response to the work.* Do not simply state, "This is a good book" or "I think this was a bad movie." Instead, look over your summary and your list of major points, and decide exactly what makes the work effective or ineffective, enjoyable or unenjoyable. Then use specific details about the work to support your judgments of how successfully the work achieves its purpose.

Writing Critical Reviews

Two critical reviews follow: the first of a nonfiction book and the second of a film. Notice that each review is preceded by the work's title. In a book review, the author's and publisher's names and the date of publication are usually given. In a film review, the film's title is often accompanied by the director's name, along with the names of the production company, the starring performers, and sometimes the screenwriter or author, especially if either is well known.

The review of *Shinohata* begins with background information and includes a statement of purpose and specific support from the book. Notice that the review ends with reasons for the reviewer's favorable conclusion about *Shinohata*.

Shinohata
by Ronald P. Dore
Pantheon © 1978

title, author, and publisher

The Western vision of Japanese society rarely goes much further than picturing the entire nation uniformly dressed in dark suits and shiny slim ties, walking submissively behind a tour leader with a pennant in his hand. The other more congenial, but equally superficial, impression of the Japanese comes from the foreign traveler who has returned home laden with gifts, praising Japanese hospitality, the Tokyo taxi drivers who refuse tips, the friendly natives who ever so politely offer directions at Ginza street corners. Excluded, coddled, taunted, charmed, confused Westerners shift between enchantment at the warm mysteries of the Japanese sensibility and anger at what frequently seems a spitefully unapproachable, thoroughly hermetic society.

introduction

audience

In his chatty, friendly description of life in the village of Shinohata, Ronald P. Dore has done much to give us the brains and blood and humor of the puzzling Japanese. When Dore, an eminent Japanologist, visited Shinohata in 1955, the villagers were finally recovering from the ravages of the war, and upon his return in 1975, he found the people prospering from the Japanese industrial boom. Tracing the effects of the development upon his old friends, Dore makes a fascinating exploration of the changes in farming techniques, transportation, land ownership, and family life. Economic well-being has brought farm machinery, color televisions, indoor toilets, and automobiles to many Shinohata families, but some old-timers complain that wealth has destroyed reverence for small,

purpose

indicates author's authority on topic

summary of contents

specific examples used to present one element of conflict explored in the book

lovingly tended details: There is a particularly Japanese regret for the loss of "the preciousness of things."

Shinohata lives most vividly in the talk of the villagers, which Dore has transcribed verbatim. We hear the lament of the mother-in-law, once the all-powerful tyrant over her daughter-in-law's existence, who complains about the disobedience of the new, independent brides. Or the modern farmer, his nose too sensitized to bear the smell of cow manure ("The stink gets into your clothes and into your hair. . . ."), now completely dependent upon manufactured chemical fertilizer. Comfortable with the Japanese and their language, Dore has combined the precision of a scholar, the anecdotal talents of a novelist, and the heart of a humanist. He could have given his hosts in Shinohata no greater gift than this affectionate and informative portrait of their lives.

PHYLLIS BIRNBAUM

discussion of distinctive elements of the book accompanied by specific examples

specific quote from the book

general evaluation

personal response

In the review of *The Last Starfighter*, the introduction presents the movie's premise and identifies the opposing forces and the primary conflict. The review goes on to include information about the plot and details about the main scenes. Notice how effectively the reviewer states his criticisms.

THE LAST STARFIGHTER

Nice idea: a video game that is designed not merely as an amusement for idle teen-age reflexes but as aptitude test and recruiting device for Starfighters. These warriors are needed to defend a space frontier, maintained by the Star League, an interplanetary alliance threatened by the dread, yucky Ko-Dan.

Nice performance: Robert Preston as a sort of intergalactic Music Man who markets the games

introduction

film's main premise

main plot conflict

character discussion

here below and lures earthlings skyward to battle for righteousness. After almost a half-century, Preston's energy and infectious pleasure in performance remain delightful.

Curious lapse: once young Alex Rogan (Lance Guest) reluctantly leaves his dismal trailer park and his pert girlfriend (Catherine Mary Stewart) and arrives on Rylos, staging area for the paltry battle to come, he is either too polite or too dense to mention its uncanny resemblance to the mechanical landscapes scattered about the *Star Wars* galaxy. Of course, he can't hear the score (marked down John Williams) and is perhaps too caught up in the action to notice how much everyone and everything he meets resembles software, hardware and ideas people have all had just about enough of. Inexpressively written by Jonathan Betuel and languidly directed by Nick Castle, Jr., *The Last Starfighter* offers the audience little more than the pleasure of naming its previous movie bases as it touches them. Let's see: *TRON . . . E.T. . . . Close Encounters* . . . and so to sleep.

RICHARD SCHICKEL

Side annotations:
- more about plot
- evaluation of actor
- character identification
- plot development
- evaluation of character and sets
- opinion of music
- response to costumes, props, and sets
- evaluation of scriptwriter
- director
- response to movie in general

GUIDELINES FOR EVALUATING CRITICAL REVIEWS

Purpose	1. Does the review give an accurate, complete summary of the work's subject, thesis, or story line?
Topic Development	2. Is the audience given enough information about the major elements of the work?
Topic Development	3. Does the review mention distinctive features of the work, such as illustrations and reference aids in a book and elaborate sets or unique camera angles in a film?
Topic Development	4. Are specific elements of the work used to support critical evaluations and opinions?
Purpose	5. Does the review help the audience decide whether the work is worthwhile?

Purpose	6. Does the review offer the reviewer's personal response? Is this response logically related to other information in the review?
Coherence	7. Are points presented in a logical order that the audience can follow easily? Are ideas clearly linked?

EXERCISE 2. Writing a Critical Review.   Use the following steps to write a critical review three to five paragraphs long.

1. Select, limit, and develop a subject for a critical review. You may review a nonfiction or fiction book, a film, a record, or any other suitable creative work. Refer to the prewriting hints on pages 146–47; then write a first draft of your review.
2. Use the Guidelines for Evaluating Critical Reviews and the Guidelines for Evaluating Expository Compositions on pages 134–35 to identify changes that would improve your first draft.
3. Referring to the revising chart on pages 136–38, revise your first draft.
4. Use the proofreading guidelines on pages 32–33 to locate errors in mechanics, grammar, and usage. Pay special attention to the rules governing quotation marks and other marks of punctuation with quotation marks.
5. Follow correct manuscript form (see pages 33–35) or your teacher's instructions to prepare a final copy. Proofread your paper one last time to catch any errors made in recopying.

ESSAYS OF LITERARY ANALYSIS

A literary analysis develops and supports a specific thesis about a literary work that will help the audience better understand and appreciate the work. The literary analysis does this by revealing meanings, allusions, and other insights that give the work added dimensions.

Before you begin your literary analysis, become familiar with the work's major literary elements. In analyzing a short story, for example, you would examine plot, setting, character, dialogue, and so on. For a poem or a song, you would consider rhyme scheme, meter, and figurative language. Some elements—such as, imagery, symbolism, irony, theme, and point of view—apply to nearly all literary works.

A literary analysis is similar to all expository compositions. The introduction identifies the work to be analyzed and states your thesis, the body develops and supports the thesis, and the conclusion summarizes or completes the analysis.

Prewriting Hints for Essays of Literary Analysis

1. *Identify and limit your subject.* Begin to limit your subject by choosing some aspect of the work that interests you. Considering different categories can suggest topics. You might focus on a literary category (such as plot, imagery, or rhyme scheme), a sociological category (social class, family relations, criminal codes), a psychological category (emotion, motivation, intelligence), or any other category of human activity. Generally, you should limit your subject by applying more than one category, for example, how a particular character (literary category) is motivated (psychological category) to be a criminal (sociological category). Another way to generate ideas for topics is to pose questions about the work that do not have obvious answers. By precisely stating one of these questions, you are likely to develop a suitably limited topic. Before you use this topic as your thesis, examine the literary work to make certain you can gather enough information to support that thesis.

2. *Gather sufficient information on your topic.* To gather information, reread the work at least once and analyze it carefully. Reexamine its plot, theme, figurative language, and other elements. Note all ideas, images, quotations, and relevant information that apply to your topic.

3. *Organize your information in a logical plan.* To organize your information, group together related details and quotations. Do not try to force stray passages and details that do not fit in anywhere into a group; instead, just let them drop and turn your attention to your ordered information. As you organize the information, look for relationships between specific details and between groups of details. Comparison, which establishes likenesses between separate items, and contrast, which points out differences between like items, are two common relationships. (For further discussion of comparison and contrast see Chapter 2, pages 49–52.) Analyzing and grouping your information might suggest ways that a specific aspect, such as character or theme, could be expanded or clarified. You might also interpret the work, which means to give the meaning or to offer a particular reading of it. When analyzing a poem, you might give an explanation, in which a short passage or an entire poem is examined line by line to illuminate its content and technique. Make sure that your analysis expands knowledge about the work and does not simply summarize the work's plot. Your analysis should investigate some aspect of the work so that you and your audience gain insight into the work's meaning, significance, or composition. This insight then becomes your thesis statement, and the groupings of details become the main points of your analysis.

4. *Consider your audience's familiarity with the work.* Determine whether your audience is familiar with the work you are analyzing. If so, you need not summarize the work at all and can simply refer to it in your essay. If not, give your audience a brief summary of the work's main elements, such as its plot, characters, and other significant components. Present a large part of this summary in a paragraph at the beginning of your essay and then give additional specific summary information at appropriate points in your analysis.

5. *Support your analysis with specific information from the work.* Each point that you develop in your analysis should be supported by quotations, details, or incidents from the work. When you use direct quotations, make sure that they fit smoothly and correctly into your sentences.

Writing Essays of Literary Analysis

Read the following poem:

GOD'S WORLD

O world, I cannot hold thee close enough!
    Thy winds, thy wide grey skies!
    Thy mists, that roll and rise!
Thy woods, this autumn day, that ache and sag
And all but cry with colour! That gaunt crag
To crush! To lift the lean of that black bluff!
World, World, I cannot get thee close enough!

Long have I known a glory in it all,
    But never knew I this:
    Here such a passion is
As stretcheth me apart—Lord, I do fear
Thou'st made the world too beautiful this year;
My soul is all but out of me—let fall
No burning leaf; prithee, let no bird call.
              EDNA ST. VINCENT MILLAY

A literary analysis of "God's World" could focus on any number of aspects: the poet's use of language, a theme in the poem, or the poem's symbolism. The following essay is an explication that explores the relationship between the emotions the poet expresses and her controlled use of poetic elements. The first step in explicating a poem is to reread it several times, both silently and aloud, to familiarize yourself with its content and sound. During each reading, make notes of passages and details that you think are significant. For example, to investigate the relationship between emotion and poetic control in "God's World," you would want to note specific statements of emotion in the poem, such as the poet's response to the beauty of an autumn day. In any explication, attention is always given to how language is used in the poem. In this case, you might note the use of exclamation, the direct expression of intense feelings, and the use of repetition for emphasis.

Another element that is usually examined in an explication is the poem's structure. "God's World" contains fourteen lines divided into two stanzas with a pair of short lines appearing in the same place in both stanzas. The rhyme scheme is *abbccaa*. Ask yourself what purpose the structure serves in the relationship between emotion and poetic control. After looking at and noting examples of the poem's statements of emotion, language, and structure, you could develop a thesis and organize these notes into an outline of specific supporting information. Read the following essay, and notice what conclusions the writer draws from analyzing the poem and what examples the writer uses as support.

POETIC CONTROL OF EMOTION IN "GOD'S WORLD"   *title*

The apparent subject of the lyric "God's   *introduction*
World," by Edna St. Vincent Millay, is the beauty
of nature. However, the center of the poem is not
the autumn landscape but the intense personal
emotion that it arouses in the poet. <u>Millay's artistry</u>   *thesis*
<u>lies in giving the effect of a spontaneous out-pour-</u>
<u>ing of feeling while she exercises strict control over</u>
<u>her materials.</u>

The poet's response to the autumnal scene is so   *topic sentence*
ecstatic that the experience is painful. In the first
ten lines, the poet addresses the world and expresses her wonder and delight in the unspoiled natural
landscape. The scene she describes is romantic,   *body*
with its gray skies, rolling mists, and spectacular
crags and cliffs. The poet desires to embrace this   *supporting details*
beauty, to draw near to it. At the same time, the   *from work*
experience is so intense that it causes her pain:

"Here such a passion is/As stretcheth me apart."
In the last four lines, the poet addresses God and
asks that He withhold any more beauty from the
scene. The ecstasy she feels is already so intense
that a single leaf or bird call will be unbearable.
The poem ends with an expression of the poet's
reverence for God and nature.

specific supporting
quotation from work

The language of the poem conveys the emotional intensity of the poet's feelings. The apostrophe
to the world (in lines 1 and 7), as if it were alive,
adds immediacy to the poem. Every statement in
the first stanza is an exclamation, an outcry of
emotion. The poet relies on the direct expression of
her feelings and on overstatement. Her use of
exaggeration is a means of achieving emotional
intensity: she cannot get close enough; the world is
too beautiful; the woods *all but cry*; her soul is *all
but out* of her. The poet chooses words that have
connotations of pain or effort: *ache, sag, cry,
crush, stretcheth, apart, burning.* She also uses
repetition for emphasis in the opening and closing
lines of the first stanza.

topic sentence

specific supporting
details from work

The powerful emotions of the poem do not
seem excessive or unrestrained because the poet
imposes control through regular patterns of rhyme
and rhythm. The rhyme scheme, *a b b c c a a,* is
strictly adhered to in both stanzas. The basic
iambic pentameter pattern is varied in both stanzas
by the trimeter couplet (lines 2–3; 9–10). This
contraction and expansion of the lines not only
adds metrical variety to the poem, but suggests the
way the poet's emotions are pulled.

topic sentence

In "God's World," Millay successfully balances
content and form. The result is a poem that com-
municates a fresh and genuine experience.

conclusion

GUIDELINES FOR EVALUATING ESSAYS OF LITERARY ANALYSIS

Purpose
1. Does the introduction give the author's name and the title of the work? Does it include a specific thesis that states how the work will be analyzed and what the analysis will attempt to show?

Topic Development
2. Does the body of the essay present a complete and convincing analysis that develops the thesis statement?

Topic Development
3. Do details, incidents, and quotations from the work support each point in the analysis?

Audience
4. Is enough summary given so an unfamiliar audience will understand the essay? Is too much summary avoided for an audience familiar with the work?

Audience
5. Have definitions been given for all words, images, characters, and other elements that the audience might not know?

Conclusion
6. Does the conclusion summarize how the analysis has developed the idea(s) stated in the thesis?

EXERCISE 3. Writing an Essay of Literary Analysis. Follow the steps listed below to write an essay of literary analysis.

1. Select, limit, and develop a subject for an essay of literary analysis. Begin by choosing a short story, poem, novel, or play. Then select an element to analyze: the main character, setting, plot, theme, figurative language, imagery, or symbolism. Refer to the prewriting hints on pages 152–53, and write a first draft of your essay.
2. Use the Guidelines for Evaluating Essays of Literary Analysis and the Guidelines for Evaluating Expository Compositions on pages 134–35 to identify changes that would improve your essay.
3. Use the revising chart on pages 136–38 to make the revisions of your first draft.
4. As you proofread your revised draft for errors in mechanics, grammar, and usage, refer to the Guidelines for Proofreading on pages 32–33. Be especially careful that all quotations are exactly copied and are enclosed in quotation marks.
5. Follow correct manuscript form (pages 33–35) or your teacher's instructions to prepare your final copy. Proofread once more to be certain that you have not made any errors in recopying.

CHAPTER 6

Writing Persuasive Compositions

BUILDING AN ARGUMENT

Persuasive writing requires that you think clearly about what you believe is true. You must decide what you think about an issue and back up your opinion with sound reasons and evidence. In doing so, you build an argument—a logical and convincing presentation of opinion.

As you improve your ability to write persuasively, you will improve other skills as well. You will be able to speak more convincingly about your opinions. When you listen or read, you will be better able to judge the argument of an advertiser, a political candidate, or anyone else trying to convince you to do or think something.

PREWRITING

CONSIDERING FORM, TONE, AND AUDIENCE

One form of written persuasion is the *letter to the editor,* a brief essay that appears on the editorial page of a newspaper or magazine. A *persuasive composition* is a longer essay of opinion. It often has at least five paragraphs: an introduction, three or more paragraphs in the body, and a conclusion. The longer form allows more space to build an argument. By contrast, a letter to the editor must be brief and to the point.

In either form, the *tone* of your essay usually should be formal and unemotional. A serious, reasonable tone will help convince your reader that you are being fair and logical.

The *audience* for a letter to the editor depends on the publication. For letters to the school newspaper, the audience is people your own age (your peers), plus teachers, administrators, and some parents. When you write to a local newspaper, your audience is the general public, a cross section of your community's population. Readers of a magazine usually share particular interests, such as music or woodworking.

For a persuasive composition, your audience is often your teacher and classmates. Your readers may also be a specific audience outside of school, such as a civic club or political group.

It is especially important to recognize any special *audience attitude* about your topic. For example, you may present an argument for increasing city real-estate taxes. As you might guess, certain audiences will have a particular *bias*—already held opinions for or against the idea. Property owners, who must pay the tax, are likely to oppose it. City council members, knowing the need for additional funds, may be biased in favor of the tax increase. Other audiences may have no particular bias. For each audience, you must be able to tailor your argument to appeal to the readers' interests.

Techniques for Prewriting. To consider your audience, ask yourself:

● Will the readers be interested in the topic?
● How much background information do they need?
● Are they likely to hold a particular bias on the issue?

EXERCISE 1. Identifying Audience Bias. For each stated opinion, decide which of the listed audiences is likely to oppose the opinion. (*Hint:* Some items may have more than one answer.)

1. *Opinion:* Students in this high school should have at least a B+ average in all of their classes to be eligible to participate in a sport.
   a. Members of the football team
   b. Coaches for all the athletic teams
   c. Members of the general student body
   d. Members of the committee for excellence in academic subjects in the high school

2. *Opinion:* All adults who work in the United States should be required to donate one day's pay a month to local charities.
    a. Workers in a local factory
    b. Retired workers
    c. A sixth-grade class
    d. Workers in an organization devoted to helping poor families in the community
3. *Opinion:* The state should provide a free four-year college education to any high-school graduate who qualifies for college by means of an entrance exam.
    a. Parents of students who plan to attend college
    b. Students who plan to attend college
    c. State legislators who know what such a program would cost
    d. Students who do not plan to attend college

EXERCISE 2. Analyzing a Letter to the Editor. Read the following letter to the editor and answer the questions that follow.

To the Editor:
    I live near the high school on Twelfth Avenue and N.E. 171st Street. Before and after school each day, student drivers speed up and down Twelfth Avenue. Even though this is a residential area, and 30-mph speed-limit signs are clearly posted, many drivers (and not just students) use Twelfth Avenue as a highway, averaging 50–55 mph.
    Yesterday my dog was hit by a speeding car. An eyewitness reported that the car slowed briefly, and then sped away. My dog was killed, but not instantly. She was in terrible pain before she died.
    Something must be done immediately to stop the speeding cars. Next time it could be a child or an elderly person that is killed.
    The city should put up two four-way stop signs along Twelfth Avenue in the ten blocks between N.E. 175th Street and the high school. This will slow the traffic, provided, of course, that drivers stop at the stop signs. I urge that police officers patrol the area (especially before and after school) in order to ticket drivers who do not stop at the new stop signs.
    If you are concerned about life-threatening traffic in residential neighborhoods, write to your city council representative to ask for stop signs and police patrols. Come to next Tuesday's council meeting to demand safety for our neighborhood streets.

                                                                    YOLANDA DOWNS

1. What is the topic of the letter?
2. In your own words, what is the writer's main opinion?
3. Where in the letter does the writer state her opinion? (*Hint:* There may be more than one sentence.)

4. Who would you say is the intended audience for the letter, aside from the editor?
5. What is the tone of the letter and how appropriate is it?

CHOOSING A TOPIC AND WRITING A POSITION STATEMENT

6a. Choose a debatable, serious topic.

A persuasive essay must be about an *issue;* that is, an idea or problem on which opinions can differ. Facts are not debatable, because they are statements that can be proved true or false. Opinions cannot be proved and therefore may be debatable.

NOT SUITABLE   Surgeons can transplant corneas to restore a person's vision. [fact]

SUITABLE   You should carry a donor card giving permission for your cornea to be used in a transplant operation in the event of your sudden death. [opinion]

NOT SUITABLE   Puerto Rico is an island. [fact]

SUITABLE   Puerto Rico should become the fifty-first state. [opinion]

Not all opinions are debatable. You cannot debate, for example, the opinion that blue is the nicest color for cars. That opinion is simply a *personal preference.* The opinion you choose as a topic for persuasion must be about an issue that is serious and important, one which people can reasonably argue for or against.

NOT SUITABLE   Parrots are better pets than parakeets. [personal preference]

SUITABLE   People who live in apartment houses should not be allowed to have dogs or cats.

6b. Express your opinion clearly in a position statement.

The opinion you choose to support in your essay should be expressed concisely in a single sentence, called a *position statement* (or a *proposition*). A position statement should let your readers know exactly where you stand on the issue.

EXAMPLES   Employers should make special efforts to hire handicapped persons who are able to work effectively.

During presidential elections, polls should be open for 24 hours.

If you are interested in a particular debatable topic but do not as yet have an opinion, research the issue before you decide.

Techniques for Prewriting. To decide what your position is, ask yourself:

- What different conclusions can people draw on the issue?
- Which conclusion do I favor?
- What action do I think should be taken?

CRITICAL THINKING:
Evaluating Position Statements

The position statement should be as specific as you can make it. For example, which of the following three statements is the most general? Which is the most specific?

1. Maybe changing the day on which school dances are held would increase attendance.

2. Something needs to be done about school dances to increase attendance.

3. For the next two months, school dances should be held on Saturday night instead of Friday night to see if this increases attendance.

Statement 2 is the most general and far too vague to be a position statement. Statement 1 focuses on the idea of changing the day but is not at all specific about the proposed change. Also, statement 1 begins with the word *maybe,* which weakens the opinion. Statement 3 is the most specific, mentioning a detailed proposal for change. This statement, then, is an acceptable position statement.

EXERCISE 3. Evaluating Position Statements. Number your paper 1–5. Decide whether each statement is suitable as the position statement for a persuasive essay. After the proper number, write *S* for suitable or *NS* for not suitable.

1. Every school should have a psychologist available for students who feel they have problems they want to talk about.
2. Penalties for drunken driving should be increased.

3. Sales of personal and home computers have been decreasing in recent years.
4. Susan B. Anthony was the greatest American leader of the women's rights movement.
5. Avocados taste better than tomatoes.

EXERCISE 4. Making Position Statements Specific. Each of the following opinions is too vague or general to be a position statement. Rewrite each one as a suitable position statement. Make up any information you need to make the statement specific enough.

1. The high-school curriculum needs to be improved.
2. Something should be done about litter in the hallways.
3. We need to stop vandalism in schools.
4. It would be nice to have outdoor concerts during the summer.
5. It is really a shame that some of the city's parks are so run-down.

EXERCISE 5. Choosing Your Topic and Writing a Position Statement. Choose three of the following broad subjects. Limit each of the three to a debatable topic (see pages 10–13 to review limiting a subject). Then express your opinion by writing a suitable position statement.

EXAMPLE   *Broad subject:* City income taxes
         Position statement: All major cities should impose city income taxes to fund their services.

1. Sports
2. Nuclear arms race
3. Election campaigns
4. Traffic problems
5. Jobs for teen-agers
6. Movies
7. Pollution
8. Education
9. Government
10. Military service

BUILDING AN ARGUMENT

6c. Support your opinion with reasons and evidence.

To be convincing when you write and when you speak, you need to back up your opinion with logical reasons and evidence. Nobody is going to agree with your opinion just because you say it.

Choosing Reasons

As you saw with the persuasive paragraph (pages 96–101), the position statement must be directly supported by reasons. A reason is a statement that explains to the reader why you hold the stated opinion. For a persuasive essay, you should have at least three sound reasons.

CRITICAL THINKING:
Evaluating Reasons

An argument is convincing if the reasons are relevant and distinct. Each reason should be a statement that directly explains or justifies the main opinion. Such reasons are said to be *relevant*. A reason that is irrelevant does not relate directly to the position statement. A reason is *distinct* if it does not simply rephrase the position statement or a reason already given. In other words, each reason must be a separate reason. Consider the following example.

Position statement: Every elementary-school child should have his or her fingerprints on file with the local police department.

STRONG REASONS Fingerprints are the most accurate way to identify a human being. Fingerprints would help identify a missing child. An increasing number of children disappear each year.

These two reasons give strong support for the position statement because each reason is distinct and relevant to the main opinion.

All of the following reasons are weak. They would make the argument less convincing.

WEAK REASONS Police departments should have access to fingerprints of your children. [restates position]
Fingerprints are fun to take. [irrelevant]
All criminals have fingerprints on file. [irrelevant]
Every human being has unique fingerprints. [restates first strong reason]

EXERCISE 6. **Evaluating Reasons.** For each position statement, decide which reasons strongly support the opinion. On a separate sheet, write the letter of the reasons you would choose. Be prepared to explain your choices. (*Hint:* Some reasons are irrelevant or repeat the position.)

1. *Position statement:* Workers should not be forced to retire when they are sixty-five years old.
   a. Many workers are productive and capable at sixty-five and well past that age.
   b. Workers at sixty-five sometimes have health problems.
   c. Workers at sixty-five are usually highly paid.
   d. In countries with no mandatory retirement age, older workers make significant contributions to the society.
   e. Given a choice, many workers would want to continue working after age sixty-five.
2. *Position statement:* The break between class periods should be extended from four minutes to six minutes.
   a. Four minutes is not enough time for students who have to go from one end of the school to the other end.
   b. More students are needed to patrol the halls between periods.
   c. Rushing students can injure other students.
   d. Students are not allowed to use the elevator without a special pass.
   e. Instead of four minutes, students should be given at least six minutes to reach their next class.

EXERCISE 7. Choosing Your Reasons.   Choose one of the following position statements, or one of the position statements you wrote for Exercise 5. Write at least three relevant and distinct reasons to support the position statement.

1. All high-school students should be required to take a one-year course in speech.
2. People should not marry before the age of twenty-one.
3. Every adult male and female should be required to serve two years in the armed forces or in the Peace Corps.

Selecting and Gathering Evidence

Evidence is the specific factual information that you use to back up a reason. Evidence usually consists of facts such as statistics. It may also be examples, incidents, and quotations from experts. Remember that opinions, unlike facts, cannot be *proved*. You can, however, make your opinion *seem believable* if it is supported with strong reasons and if the reasons, in turn, are backed up by evidence. Evidence should either come from a reliable source or be the result of many personal observations—not just one or two. Usually, a mixture of kinds of evidence is more effective than only one kind. Consider what kinds of evidence would best suit each reason. Then look for that evidence.

Techniques for Prewriting. To gather evidence:

- Use techniques such as observation and interviews for familiar topics.
- Use library sources such as magazines for topics less familiar to you.

CRITICAL THINKING:
Evaluating Evidence

Just as reasons must be relevant to the position statement, evidence must be relevant to the reasons. A fact, example, or quotation should directly relate to the reason it is supposed to support. Irrelevant evidence should be eliminated from the argument. The following list is part of an argument for keeping grocery stores open until 10:00 P.M. on weekdays. One reason is given, and several pieces of evidence are suggested. Which pieces of evidence are relevant to the reason?

> *Reason:* Many people who work cannot get to the grocery store before its present closing time (6:00 P.M.).
>
> *Evidence:*
> a. Seventy-two percent of shoppers in a poll taken in the grocery store on Saturday said they cannot get to the store before 6:00 P.M.
> b. Gas stations in the neighborhood are open till 10:00 P.M.
> c. Many shoppers say that they try to shop only once a week.
> d. Mrs. Janet Lopez, who works downtown, does not leave her office till 6:00 P.M.
> e. Todd Lewis, president of Lakeland Supermarket, says, "We have had hundreds of complaints each month from working people who cannot get to our stores before they close at six."

Only three pieces of evidence (a, d, and e) are relevant to the reason. Items b and c are irrelevant and should be discarded.

EXERCISE 8. Selecting Relevant Evidence. For each numbered item, decide whether the evidence is relevant to the particular reason given. On a separate sheet, write the letter of each piece of relevant evidence.

1. *Position statement:* Employers should allow workers to work flexible hours, not just from 9:00 to 5:00 or 8:30 to 4:30.

   Reason: Flexible work hours would help working mothers of young children.

   Evidence:
   a. Statements by working mothers explaining why they want flexible working hours
   b. Statistics on the profits of a particular company during the past five years
   c. Statistics on the number of employees in a particular company during the past ten years
   d. Statement by an industrial psychologist about the benefits to employers of allowing working mothers to work flexible hours
   e. Statement by a labor union leader requesting a shorter workweek
   f. Example of how flexible hours benefit a specific working mother

2. *Position statement:* The faculty adviser should have the power to censor the student newspaper and to take out any material that is not appropriate.

   Reason: Student editors do not have the maturity to decide what is appropriate material for a student newspaper.

   Evidence:
   a. Specific example: the editorial in last week's student newspaper that caused a riot
   b. A statement by the student editor about why that editorial was published
   c. Statistics on the number of students who read the school newspaper
   d. Statement by the principal about the expected maturity of student editors
   e. Statistics on the number of high-school newspapers that have faculty advisers who censor all material
   f. Statement by a local professor of journalism about the number of journalism students

EXERCISE 9. Selecting and Gathering Your Evidence. Using the position statement and reasons that you listed for Exercise 7, think of the kinds of evidence you would look for to support each reason. Write as many kinds of relevant evidence as you can think of. (*Note:* If you cannot think of any evidence to support a reason, change the reason to one you can support.) Once you have decided on the kinds of evidence that would work for your argument, gather the details you need.

EXAMPLE OF KINDS OF EVIDENCE

> *Reason:* Many students have difficulty in distinguishing facts from opinions.
> *Evidence:*
>> 1. Statistics on facts and opinions from a nationally standardized test
>> 2. Statement from a reading teacher on students' difficulties in distinguishing facts from opinions
>> 3. Examples based on personal observations of students who have difficulty distinguishing facts from opinions

OUTLINING THE ARGUMENT

6d. Outline your argument as an effective writing plan.

The outline for an argument consists of the position statement followed by each reason and its supporting evidence. If you intend to ask readers to do something, such as write a letter or attend a meeting, add that statement at the end as a "call to action." Your outline should take this form:

> *Position statement:*
> *Reason 1:*
> *Evidence:* a.
>   b.
>   c.
> *Reason 2:* etc.
> *Call to action:*

Think about the order in which you list your reasons. For persuasion, writers most often use order of importance, from least important to most important. Decide which reason is your strongest. Save it for last, so that your argument builds up to it.

Make sure that your reasons are supported by specific, relevant evidence to help strengthen your argument.

EXERCISE 10. Outlining Your Argument. Outline the argument for a persuasive composition. Use the topic you worked with in Exercise 9, or develop another debatable topic. Make sure that your outline includes the position statement, reasons, detailed evidence, and a call to action, if you plan to have one.

CRITICAL THINKING:
Evaluating an Argument

You can apply the skill of evaluating an argument not only to your own writing but also to persuasive writing and to speeches. To judge how convincing an argument is, you must identify the various parts of the argument: the position statement, the reasons, and the evidence. Then you must consider the logic of each part. Use the following guidelines.

GUIDELINES FOR EVALUATING AN ARGUMENT

1. Is a specific position clearly stated?
2. Are there at least three reasons to support the position?
3. Is each reason relevant to the position statement?
4. Is each reason distinct from the other reasons and the position statement?
5. Is each reason backed up by evidence?
6. Is the evidence for each reason relevant and reliable?

The following interviews present arguments for ("pro") and against ("con") a state law requiring all motorists to wear seat belts. The interview in favor, with Representative David Hollister, supports the position that a law should be passed requiring all motorists to wear seat belts. In the interview against, Assemblyman Michael Nozzolio gives reasons against such a law. Read the arguments carefully so that you can answer the items in Exercise 11.

Should Motorists Be Forced to Wear Seat Belts?

Interview with David Hollister, Michigan state representative

PRO

QUESTION: Representative Hollister, why do you favor state laws that require motorists to wear seat belts?

ANSWER: Because studies of 36 countries and municipalities which have laws to that effect show conclusively that there is a dramatic reduction in highway deaths and injuries and large savings of money. In this country, we would save over 12,000 lives each year. In the U.S. each year, there are over 400,000 moderate-to-serious injuries and 2.8 million minor injuries caused by auto accidents. These would be reduced substantially.

QUESTION: The Reagan Administration will start requiring passive restraints, such as air bags or automatic seat belts, in new cars unless states with two thirds of the population pass mandatory-seat-belt laws. Won't that make ordinary belts obsolete?

ANSWER: By no means. Under the administration's plan, it will take some 10 years before all cars on the road have such passive restraints. Meanwhile, only the rich—the ones who can afford to buy new cars—will be protected. On the other hand, we already have seat belts in virtually all cars, if people would only use them. Besides, while air bags are effective in head-on collisions, they don't give you protection in rollovers, rear-end and side collisions, where seat belts do. The ideal protection may be both a seat belt and an air bag, but in a choice between the two I'd pick the belt. The economics and effectiveness are with the belt.

QUESTION: Do mandatory seat-belt laws infringe on people's constitutional rights?

ANSWER: Such as the right to go through the windshield? I'm a civil libertarian myself, but the lives and dollars saved far outweigh the individual-rights issue in this case.

QUESTION: Shouldn't people be able to decide for themselves?

ANSWER: No, they should not. Accidents always involve other people. Injuries and death disrupt families. They create major social costs: Lost work time, lost wages, high medical bills and welfare outlays. It is estimated that each traffic fatality costs the state and family about $330,000. Injuries and lost wages caused by the non-use of belts cost society $2,500 per accident.

QUESTION: Could such laws be enforced without harassing motorists?

ANSWER: Yes. Our traffic laws are largely self-enforcing. I stop at a stop sign at 3 in the morning not because I think there's a police officer on the corner but because it's the law. With a seat-belt law, a police officer who pulled up alongside of you and saw you weren't buckled up could ticket you—a $10 or $50 fine or whatever amount is set—or just give a warning. Police stopping a driver for any reason would also check for belt use. Not much more would be required.

QUESTION: Why wouldn't education bring about compliance?

ANSWER: Because it has never worked. In this country, voluntary compliance is only about 12 percent. In those countries that have passed mandatory laws, compliance has gone from 11 percent to 70 percent. It would happen here as well.

Interview with Michael Nozzolio, New York state assemblyman

CON

QUESTION: Assemblyman Nozzolio, why do you oppose mandatory-seat-belt laws?

ANSWER: Because the government has neither the right nor the responsibility to prescribe conduct to its citizens simply because it deems such conduct to be in their best interest.

QUESTION: Doesn't using seat belts greatly reduce injuries and deaths?

ANSWER: I concede that. I wear a seat belt myself. But the government shouldn't prescribe it. What if tomorrow the government ordered everyone to get 8 hours of sleep each night, take a daily dose of vitamins and a daily jog and get an annual medical checkup—on the ground that this could enhance and maybe even save lives?

QUESTION: Don't individuals have to accept reasonable restrictions on their freedom for the common good?

ANSWER: Certainly, up to a point. But there's a difference between restrictions and prescriptions. It's one thing to make motorists stop at a red light or stop sign or impose speed limits; it's quite another to prescribe what individuals must do inside their own automobiles. Furthermore, such laws will be extremely difficult to enforce.

QUESTION: Why?

ANSWER: Because it is easy enough to fool a policeman by quickly buckling up when you see a patrol car approaching. It's harder to cheat with a shoulder harness, so those who have both a harness and a seat belt will face tougher enforcement than those who have a seat belt only.

You're going to see a lot of court litigation on whether or not a driver can be held guilty of negligence if the passengers in his car failed to buckle up and an accident occurred.

New York is the first state to pass a mandatory seat belt law. There will certainly be a lot of confusion for tens of millions of people traveling from other states who drive through New York annually.

Also, I disapprove of diverting the scarce resources of our police away from fighting real crime in order to enforce the seat-belt law.

QUESTION: If motorists generally obey laws regarding stop signs even without policemen around, why wouldn't the same hold true for seat-belt laws?

ANSWER: Because seat-belt laws represent a far greater interference with personal freedom of choice. As such, they're likely to be widely resented, disrespected and disobeyed. Persuasion and education are the right road to follow.

QUESTION: Haven't efforts to encourage voluntary seat-belt use been a failure?

ANSWER: Voluntary measures such as public-service announcements and driver-education courses will gradually create a pro-seat-belt generation. We're already seeing more seat-belt use by young motorists.

EXERCISE 11. Evaluating an Argument. Referring to the interviews above, answer the following items.

1. Are you for or against mandatory seat-belt laws? Explain how these arguments did or did not help to convince you.
2. Summarize the argument that you agree with: Write a position statement and three reasons given to support that position.
3. What evidence is given to support the reasons in the argument that you favor?
4. What other reasons and evidence can you think of to support your position?
5. Do you think the argument you favor could have been stronger? If so, in what way? If the argument seems very strong already, explain why.

EXERCISE 12. Evaluating Your Argument. Using the guidelines on page 168, evaluate the argument you outlined for Exercise 10. Revise your outline as needed to strengthen your argument. Do more research on the issue, if necessary, to make sure you have relevant reasons and evidence.

WRITING THE FIRST DRAFT

WRITING THE ARGUMENT

6e. Write a first draft based on your outline.

Your outline of the argument serves as the work plan for your persuasive essay. The essay has three parts: an *introductory paragraph*, a *body*, and a *concluding paragraph*.

The *introductory paragraph* should arouse the reader's interest in the topic and should end with your position statement. This paragraph may also provide any background information that the reader needs to understand the topic.

The middle part of the essay is called the *body*. In a letter to the editor, the body may be only one or two paragraphs. In a persuasive composition, the body has at least three paragraphs: Each reason, together with its supporting evidence, takes up one paragraph. You may also respond in the body to the opposing viewpoint. By *refuting* this argument (showing why it is weak), you can show that you are knowledgeable and have researched your topic thoroughly. You can put "refuting the opposing argument" wherever it fits into your list of reasons.

The *concluding paragraph* may ask the reader to perform some specific action. Such a call to action makes an effective and forceful ending for a composition or a letter to the editor. Whether or not the paragraph contains a call to action, it should summarize your opinion and the main supporting reasons.

Techniques for Writing. Remember to
- Consider any audience bias.
- Keep your tone serious and formal.

A Sample Composition

DRIVER TRAINING FOR ALL

On a single weekend last month, there were three serious highway accidents caused by teen-age drivers in this country. One of the results of this tragic weekend was a renewed public demand that high-school students be required to take a course in driver training. True, most of the high schools in this area have offered driver-training courses for many years, but these courses have always been elective rather than required, and sometimes only a small fraction of the student body has actually been enrolled in the course. I believe that a course in driver training should be required for all tenth-grade students.

specific example to arouse reader's interest

background information

position statement

Opponents of this idea have argued that providing driver training for every student would be very expensive and that the results would not be worth the price. It is true that the courses would be costly. Our town school board has estimated that to provide driver training for every high-school student, the school would need at least two more

opposing viewpoint

full-time instructors and two additional training cars, as well as extra lab space and equipment.

However, the cost of this program must be weighed against the much greater cost—in both money and human suffering—of continuing to allow inexperienced and poorly trained people to join the ranks of licensed drivers. An effective driver-training program would certainly be worth the expense.

There is little question that driver training courses are effective. According to Ms. Shue, the instructor in charge of the course at our school, only two of the forty-three students who took and passed the course last year failed to pass the state driver's license examination on the first try; both of them passed on the second try. This compares very favorably with the statewide average of nearly 20 percent failures on the examination. Furthermore, Ms. Shue reports that only one of the students who has completed the course during the past five years has been involved in a serious accident since getting a license and that in this case the other driver was judged at fault. Although Ms. Shue does not have figures for accidents involving students who have *not* taken the course, she says that each year at least three or four such students from our school have been arrested for speeding, while no student who has completed the course has been arrested for any traffic violation.

Some people grant that driver training courses are effective but still do not feel that driving instruction should be a required subject in a public high school. I think that if we are to turn out a generation of well-trained drivers, the public school is the logical place to provide the training,

refutation of opposing viewpoint

reason 1

reason 2

statistics

statistics

reason 3

because all young people are in school until they are at least sixteen. Sixty years ago driving an automobile may have been a hobby of the rich, but today it is an essential part of nearly every adult's workaday life. It would be in the public interest to train all citizens to drive well and wisely. The only present alternative to teaching driving in the schools is to continue the haphazard practice of leaving the instruction to parents or older friends, a system that in too many cases has proved ineffective.

fact 1

fact 2

The schools have shown that they can train good drivers. Since they have access to all of our young people, let's give them the job of teaching all students to drive well. Beginning next semester, driver training should be a required course for all tenth-grade students in this city's public high schools.

summary of position statement and reasons

EXERCISE 13. Writing Your Persuasive Essay. Using the argument you evaluated in Exercise 12, draft a persuasive essay. Include your position statement in the introduction. If you plan to have a call to action, be sure to make that part of your concluding paragraph.

EVALUATING

EVALUATING A FIRST DRAFT

6f. Evaluate the content, organization, and style of your draft.

Read your draft carefully three times, so that you can concentrate on one aspect at a time. Use the following guidelines to decide where your draft needs improvement.

GUIDELINES FOR EVALUATING PERSUASIVE COMPOSITIONS

Position Statement 1. Does a position statement clearly express a specific opinion about a debatable, serious topic?

Introduction 2. Is the position statement in the introductory paragraph? Does the introduction catch the reader's interest?

Argument Development 3. Is the opinion supported by at least three relevant and distinct reasons? Is each reason the main idea of a separate paragraph?

Evidence 4. Is each reason supported by relevant, reliable evidence?

Coherence 5. Are the reasons arranged in an effective order?

Background Information 6. Is all necessary background information included?

Conclusion 7. Does the concluding paragraph summarize the argument? Does it include a "call to action," if appropriate?

Tone 8. Is a serious, formal tone used throughout the draft?

EXERCISE 14. Evaluating a First Draft. Read the following first draft of a letter to the editor. Use the Guidelines for Evaluating Persuasive Compositions to make a list of problems you see in the draft. Keep in mind that a letter to the editor needs to be brief.

Dear Editor:

I'd like to write something about the new Metrorail system. It's all very nice, but it doesn't run after 8:00 P.M. or on the weekends at all. That's when lots of people like us high-school students would like to ride it. We'd go downtown to movies, museums, and restaurants on dates and stuff. The downtown area, which is totally and really dead at night, would get busy and attract more people if the Metrorail system were open later hours and on weekends.

The guys who head up the transportation department say they're waiting for "public demand" to extend the hours at night and on weekends.

Most people are too lazy to give them a call or write a letter, so there never will be enough "public demand." Really, my friends and I would use the Metrorail system if it were open. Just last Saturday we wanted to go downtown to a movie but couldn't. Why don't they try running it on weekends for a couple of months and see if it takes off?

Also, I think the dollar fare is too high and that the Metrorail should service more parts of the city.

DAVID B. SMITH

EXERCISE 15. Evaluating Your First Draft. Use the guidelines on this page to evaluate the first draft you wrote for Exercise 13.

REVISING

REVISING A FIRST DRAFT

6g. Revise your draft to improve its content, organization, and style.

As with any other type of composition, you need to reread the first draft of a persuasive essay several times. With each reading, focus your attention entirely on just one aspect of the composition as you try to improve it.

Remember the four revising techniques you can use: *cut,* or leave out, words, phrases, or sentences; *add* words or ideas; *reorder,* or rearrange, words, sentences, or paragraphs; and *replace* words or ideas. The following chart suggests how you can use these techniques based on your evaluation of a first draft.

REVISING PERSUASIVE COMPOSITIONS		
PROBLEM	**TECHNIQUE**	**REVISION**
The position statement is not clear.	Replace/Add	Make sure you say whether you are "pro" or "con" on a debatable topic. Add a suggested action to your opinion.
The introduction is dull.	Add	Begin with an incident or example that makes the issue more personal for the reader.
A reason repeats another reason, or repeats the main opinion.	Replace/ Reorder	Replace the weak reason with a distinct reason. Consider using the weak reason as evidence or discarding it.
The argument does not respond to a known audience bias or opposing argument.	Add	Add ideas that clearly refute opposing views. Make sure you have considered audience attitude.

PROBLEM	TECHNIQUE	REVISION
A reason or some evidence does not back up the argument.	Cut/Replace	Remove irrelevant ideas and information. Make sure you still have sufficient reasons and evidence supporting the argument. Do more research, if needed.
There is no background information.	Add	Include ideas and details that will clarify the issue and help the audience understand the topic better.
The argument does not build up.	Reorder/Add	Rearrange the reasons, moving the strongest reasons and evidence toward the end, before the conclusion. Add or reorder ideas in the last paragraph to emphasize the logic of the argument forcefully.
The conclusion is flat.	Add	Add a specific call to action that offers the readers something to do about the issue.
The tone is informal or too emotional.	Replace/Cut	Replace slang, contractions, and other informal words with serious, formal wording. Remove emotional wording, or replace it with objective, reasonable language.

EXERCISE 16. **Revising a First Draft.** Using the revising chart on pages 176–77, revise the letter to the editor that you evaluated for Exercise 14. Make up any additional information you need to strengthen the argument. Make sure that there is a clear position statement and a concluding sentence.

EXERCISE 17. Revising Your First Draft. Revise your own composition that you evaluated for Exercise 15. Be sure to refer to the revising chart on pages 176–77.

PROOFREADING AND WRITING THE FINAL VERSION

6h. Proofread your revised essay and make a final copy.

Read your revised version several times, focusing on one aspect each time. Use the Guidelines for Proofreading on pages 32–33 to check your spelling, punctuation, capitalization, grammar, and word use. Refer to the index of this book to find a point of grammar or usage that you want to review.

When you have finished proofreading, write the final version on a separate sheet of paper, following the manuscript form required by your teacher. Be sure to proofread this version once more to check for copying errors.

EXERCISE 18. Completing an Essay. Proofread and write the final version of the letter to the editor that you revised for Exercise 16. Use the Guidelines for Proofreading on pages 32–33.

EXERCISE 19. Completing Your Composition. Proofread and write the final version of the persuasive composition you revised for Exercise 17.

REVIEW EXERCISE A. Writing a Persuasive Essay. Read carefully the following four brief persuasive essays about saving the Olympics. Then write your own brief essay telling what you think should be done to save the Olympics.

PREWRITING Decide which of the four ideas seems the best. Or you might think of an entirely different idea that makes more sense to you. Decide what your opinion is and write a position statement. Then build and outline your argument for a persuasive essay. Before you begin writing, evaluate your argument, using the guidelines on page 175.

WRITING THE FIRST DRAFT Plan to have at least four paragraphs in your essay: an introductory paragraph containing the position statement; two reasons, each developed in a separate paragraph; and a concluding paragraph. As you write, concentrate on expressing your ideas clearly and concisely.

EVALUATING AND REVISING   Review your draft to make sure that the position statement, reasons, and evidence are all relevant and distinct. Eliminate any unnecessary words or phrases. Add, replace, or reorder words and ideas to express yourself clearly and briefly and to strongly support your position. Use the chart on revising persuasive compositions on pages 176–77 to improve your essay.

PROOFREADING AND WRITING THE FINAL VERSION   Proofread your revised draft, using the Guidelines for Proofreading on pages 32–33. Make a final copy and make sure you have not made any mistakes in the final copying.

FOUR IDEAS TO SAVE THE OLYMPICS

1. *Return the Games to Greece*   Senator Bill Bradley (Democrat, New Jersey), member of the gold-medal Olympic basketball team in 1964

    Since 1976, I have proposed that the Olympics be moved to a permanent site, preferably Greece, the birthplace of the games. In 1980, when the U.S. boycotted the Moscow Olympics, the Greeks proposed a 1,250-acre site near ancient Olympia, but the idea was opposed by the International Olympic Committee. In the wake of the Soviet boycott, President Constantine Caramanlis of Greece has again called for returning the games to that nation.

    Construction costs for facilities in Greece would be paid by the participating nations. It would be a matter of spending 10 billion dollars once — rather than spending that amount or more every four years.

    Such a step is necessary to spare the Olympics the inevitable political repercussions that come from moving them from site to site. If there had been a permanent site, the boycotts of 1980 and 1984 would not have occurred.

2. *Protect the Athletes*   David Scheffer, attorney and associate, Harvard University Center for International Affairs

    A basic principle of the modern Olympics is that the games are designed for individual achievement, not the achievement of nations. The Olympics have moved away from that principle, but they need to return to it through an international treaty.

    Under the treaty, which could perhaps be negotiated through the United

Nations, countries would agree to uphold the rights of their athletes. Thus, if a nation determined that it would not officially participate in the Olympic Games, individual athletes would still be allowed to compete on their own, provided that they meet Olympic qualifications and pass the review of an arbitration panel set up to hear complaints of athletes.

This method would keep countries from pulling the rug out from under qualified athletes at the 11th hour.

3. *Split Up the Games* Buck Dawson, executive director, the International Swimming Hall of Fame

I favor decentralizing the Olympics into five separate sets of games —aquatics, winter sports, land individual sports, land team sports, and cultural competition—held in five different places. This would be consistent with the Olympic symbol, which is composed of five rings.

Since the whole world would not be congregated in one place, this would reduce the temptation to use the Olympics for political purposes. If a host country tried to politicize the games, you could shift the event somewhere else—something you can't do now with so much preparation and detail involved in one huge Olympics.

Decentralization would also make it possible to expand the number of Olympic events. For instance, at present they don't have the full quota of swimming events because Olympic officials feel that the games are already too big. They're reluctant to take on new sports for the same reason.

In addition, this system would reduce the incredible cost of hosting the games and make it possible for smaller countries to serve as hosts.

4. *Pick a Neutral Site* John Lucas, professor of physical education, Pennsylvania State University

The solution to the political problems that beset the Olympic Games is establishment of a permanent site in a politically neutral country. Central Switzerland would be ideal since it has both snow-capped mountains and an idyllic summer environment. The money for establishing the facilities would come primarily from the huge cache that the IOC [International Olympic Committee] has accumulated over the past 25 years from TV revenue. This location is preferable to Greece, where during July and August the temperature reaches 110 degrees in the Peloponnesus, home of the original games. Moreover, Greece is very unstable politically.

So far, the International Olympic Committee has rejected this plan because members feel the games should change sites every four years. But the IOC can't have the chaos that now exists and expect the games to last much longer.

If the IOC won't approve a permanent location, it should at least limit the games to a few already established sites. The summer games could rotate among Tokyo, Montreal, and Munich. The winter games could be shifted among some of the European spas, such as Grenoble, France, that have already hosted the Olympics. The important thing is to keep the games away from the territory of the two superpowers.

RECOGNIZING ILLOGICAL PERSUASION

6i. Avoid emotional appeals and fallacies in your writing.

Persuasive writing often includes emotional appeals and fallacies, or errors in logic. Neither enables the writer to build a sound, logical argument for a position. You should avoid these kinds of errors in your writing.

Identifying Emotional Appeals

An argument can be most convincing when it is based on sound reasoning—on logic. Nonetheless, you will find that many of the arguments you read, hear, or see are based almost entirely on emotional appeals. These appeals are used often because they can be quite effective with readers and listeners who do not recognize them. Always be alert to emotional appeals, which are intended to make you think or act in a certain way. When you write persuasion yourself, you may on occasion find an emotional appeal helpful—for example, in making a forceful conclusion to your argument. Generally, however, you should avoid emotional appeals.

Loaded Words

Loaded words tend to make a reader or listener feel either positive or negative toward the subject being discussed. *Flag, decency, patriotism, mother, freedom, democracy*, and *the public good* are loaded words and phrases, because they are associated with positive feelings. (See pages 283–84 for more information about the positive and negative connotations of words.) *Grotesque, diseased, arrogant,* and *untrustworthy* are examples of loaded words with negative connotations.

In the following paragraph the writer describes the contents of a vacant lot in the middle of a city block and tells what should be done about it. See if you can identify the loaded words.

The time has come to do something about the filth that exists in the middle of our city. Wherever there is a vacant lot, people have dumped their refuse. The lot in the middle of the 5400 block of Sherman Street contains six torn, stained mattresses; four broken chairs; a rusty refrigerator; two discarded stoves; one abandoned and rusting bicycle; sixty-seven empty soda cans; and hundreds of pounds of decaying food. People live and work next to these illegal garbage dumps. Pedestrians walk by, cars drive by, businesses carry on nearby, and hundreds of citizens live in neighboring lots, while the garbage rots in their midst. The sanitation department should clean up these vacant lots and bill the owners for their services. Once the lots are clean, law-abiding citizens should organize a "Lot Watch," reporting to the police anyone who dumps any kind of refuse in a vacant lot. Violaters must be promptly punished to the full extent of the law.

Filth, garbage, abandoned, decaying, illegal, and *rots* are loaded words with negative connotations. *Law-abiding citizens* and *full extent of the law* are loaded phrases with positive connotations. Notice the amount of loaded words with negative connotations compared to the amount of words with positive connotations.

Bandwagon Appeal

When a writer uses the *bandwagon appeal,* the reader is urged to *jump on the bandwagon* before it is too late. In other words, "everyone else" is doing or has already done whatever it is the writer wants the reader to do. In order not to feel left out, the reader is supposed to take a specific action.

EXAMPLES Student response to the school play has been overwhelming. Buy your tickets now before they are all gone.

According to our latest figures, 99 percent of all registered voters have already cast their ballots. Polls close in exactly one hour. Don't miss your chance to make your vote count.

Name Calling

In political campaigns, opponents sometimes label each other as *radical, liberal,* or *conservative.* Such labels are emotional appeals because they arouse positive or negative connotations. Without knowing anything specific about the candidate, the reader is already prejudiced by the emotional connotations of the label.

EXAMPLE Candidate X, my opponent, is a bleeding-heart liberal and a big spender. If elected, Candidate X will lead this nation into debt.

Glittering Generalities

Some loaded words with extra-positive connotations are *glittering generalities*. They make the reader feel good without understanding why. Words like *honor, integrity, justice,* and *freedom* are examples of glittering generalities.

EXAMPLE   You know that you are a person of integrity, a person with a sense of social justice. You cannot stand idly by while your neighbors go hungry or have no shelter. It is your duty, therefore, to make your annual contribution to the United Charities drive.

Testimonial

One type of evidence often used in persuasive writing is a quotation by an expert or authority on the subject being discussed. Such a quotation is an acceptable logical appeal because it is reasonable to expect that an expert in the field has information and opinions that are believable. However, when a famous person who is *not* an expert in the field endorses a product or a candidate, such a *testimonial* is an emotional appeal. The glamor or glory surrounding the famous person should not be a basis for believing everything the person says. Testimonials are often used in advertising and in politics.

EXAMPLES   Frankie T., the famous rock-jazz guitarist, says, "I always eat this brand of cereal because it is absolutely the most nutritious brand on the market. Look how much energy it gives me!"
Ruth W., the gorgeous movie star, is voting for Candidate Morrison for state senate, so you should, too.

Plain-Folks Appeal

Advertisers use the *plain-folks appeal* when they show average-looking, middle- and working-class people using their product and having a wonderful time. Although it is rarely stated directly, the message is that you, too, should buy the product or vote for the candidate because "plain folks" just like you are doing it already.

EXAMPLES   Candidate X is the choice of the people who struggled to build America by working long, hard hours in the factories and on the farms.

Folks in this town know it's important to eat right, so we buy Hometown applesauce—it's just like the kind your grandma used to make.

Snob Appeal

Snob appeal is the opposite of the plain-folks appeal. When advertisers show glamorous, well-dressed people using their products, they imply that your life will be more glamorous and exciting if you buy the products that these "beautiful people" are using. Snob appeal also implies that you are one of the special, privileged few.

EXAMPLE   Readers of this magazine are among the most successful people in their fields. Doctors, lawyers, and business executives subscribe to our magazine to learn how to make the most of every second of their lives. Subscribe today and find out what these successful people know.

EXERCISE 20. Identifying Emotional Appeals.   Read each of the following paragraphs carefully. Be prepared to discuss the loaded words and other emotional appeals that you find.

1

Everything in the world can be yours with your World Extravaganza credit card. You can have everything you've always wanted—cars, clothes, houses, travel. Enjoy the finest things in life today and pay for them tomorrow. Be one of the special few who are invited to enjoy the privilege of having a World Extravaganza credit card. Just fill out the enclosed application, and you can start making all your dreams come true.

2

Commissioner Neil Frank should be removed from office by means of the special recall process outlined in our city charter. Commissioner Frank has not served the public well in his year of office. He has been absent from more commission meetings than he has attended, and he has been a consistent troublemaker. Joe O'Rourke, the restaurant owner, and Lisa Craig, the violinist, both believe that Commissioner Frank should be recalled from office. We ordinary citizens of this county, who wholeheartedly believe in good government, must join together to protect our community from this troublemaker. If you are a registered voter, please sign a petition for the recall of Commissioner Frank.

Identifying Fallacies

Persuasive writing, as you have seen, needs to be based on logical thinking. Errors in logic are called *fallacies*. Recognizing fallacies will help you avoid them altogether in building your own arguments and will help you become a better, more critical thinker when you read and when you listen to speakers.

Hasty Generalization

A generalization that is made without sufficient evidence to back it up is called a *hasty generalization*. Often a hasty generalization is made on the basis of only one or two experiences.

EXAMPLES I have a French pen pal who loves to tell jokes. I guess French people have a terrific sense of humor.

Jeff says, "It's impossible to learn to play a musical instrument once you get past the age of 10. I know this is true because I tried piano lessons for a month last year and just couldn't do it."

A sound generalization is based on a whole series of observations and experiences. The more evidence you gather before making a generalization, the likelier you are to form a sound generalization.

Stereotype

A *stereotype* is a hasty generalization. According to a stereotype, all members of a particular group share certain qualities or characteristics —usually negative ones. Instead of judging people as individuals, stereotypes "prejudge" individuals by their group membership.

EXAMPLES Skinny people are too tense and serious.

All college graduates are snobs.

Cause–Effect

The *cause–effect* fallacy occurs when one event is said to be the cause of another just because the two events happened in sequence. You cannot assume that an event caused whatever happened afterward.

EXAMPLES My brother visited the Modern History Museum on Saturday. On Saturday night he came down with a bad cold that lasted a week. Museums are certainly unhealthy places.

I bought a new houseplant yesterday, and my bird died last night. That new plant must be giving off poisonous fumes.

Attacking the Person

If you are discussing your opponent's views, your focus should be on the opponent's argument—the reasons and evidence given to support the opposing point of view. If, instead, you attack the opponent's character or situation, you are guilty of the fallacy of *ad hominem,* or *attacking the person.*

EXAMPLES   George's ideas about the presidential candidates shouldn't be taken too seriously. You know that cars and baseball are all that George cares about.

Of course Tara will defend the hospital's position on containing health costs. Her mother's a doctor, isn't she? What else could Tara possibly say?

Circular Reasoning

In *circular reasoning,* you might appear to be giving a reason to support your opinion, but all you are actually doing is restating the opinion in different words. You are saying, in effect, that a statement is true because you say it is true.

EXAMPLES   Louis is the best candidate for Student Council treasurer because of all the candidates he is clearly the superior one.

People should not be allowed to smoke cigarettes in public places such as supermarkets and movie theaters because smoking should be banned from such places.

Either–Or

The *either–or* fallacy occurs when a person says that there are only two possible causes or courses of action and ignores all other possibilities. To the *either–or* thinker, the world is either good or bad, right or wrong, black or white; there are no in-between shades of gray.

EXAMPLES   If you loved me, you'd do my chores for me. But since you won't, you obviously don't love me.
If I don't get accepted at State University this fall, I will never be able to attend college.

EXERCISE 21. Identifying Fallacies.   Identify the fallacy in each numbered item.

1. It's silly to try to talk to JoAnn about sports. You know that women just aren't interested in sports.
2. Either you take this vitamin pill right now, or you will be sick tomorrow.
3. The only time I've been camping, a bear came into the camp-

grounds and stole someone's food. I'll never go camping again—it's far too dangerous!

4. Whenever I travel by plane (and it's happened to me twice), the airport is closed because of a blizzard. Flying is really an undependable form of transportation.

5. Jason thinks that the United States should retaliate against terrorists, and he has a lot of statistics and examples to prove his point. But everyone knows that Jason has some really weird ideas and a terrible temper, so I wouldn't waste time listening to what he has to say.

6. If I don't learn to ski, I'll never be popular with my classmates.

7. Physical education classes should be required for all four years of high school because I firmly believe that physical education should be mandatory for all students.

8. Chess players are cold and have no sense of humor.

9. Mrs. Applegate should win the Teacher-of-the-Month award because she is the teacher most deserving of the award.

10. The day Jenny broke up with Bob, we had an earthquake; and the night she broke up with Larry, there was a blizzard. There's bound to be some kind of natural disaster the next time Jenny ends a romance.

REVIEW EXERCISE B. Identifying Emotional Appeals and Fallacies. Read the editorials and letters to the editor in several issues of a daily newspaper, a news magazine, or a school newspaper. Bring to class the examples that you find of emotional appeals or fallacies. You might display the examples on a bulletin board.

CHAPTER 6 WRITING REVIEW

Writing to Persuade. Compile a list of debatable topics by consulting magazines and newspapers, interviewing adults, and talking with classmates and friends. Choose one of these issues and write a persuasive composition. Follow the steps detailed in this chapter: Consider your form, tone, and audience; write a position statement; build and outline an argument; write a first draft; evaluate and revise the draft; proofread and write a final version.

CHAPTER 7

Writing Narration and Description

STORIES; CHARACTER AND BIOGRAPHICAL SKETCHES

Literary writing—novels, short stories, poetry, biographies, personal narratives—is a combination of narration and description. Sometimes narration dominates the work and description adds detail and interest. Sometimes description dominates and narration illustrates an idea. Combining the two helps writers create a range of emotional responses in their audience.

WRITING CREATIVELY

All writing is creative: any piece of writing is a creation, something that never existed before. However, the term *creative writing* most often refers to stories, personal essays, and poems. Creative writing is literary and imaginative rather than practical and factual. It attempts to stir an audience's feelings, to amuse and entertain them, rather than merely to inform or to explain. By enabling the writer to add interest, color, and life, creative writing skills may be used to good advantage in any kind of writing.

Developing the Habit of Close Observation

7a. Develop the habit of close observation.

Creative writers are deeply interested in the people, places, and events of their world. They become close observers in order to vividly describe what they perceive.

In the following paragraph, Annie Dillard describes a "wonder" she experienced on the Atlantic coast of Florida. Because she has observed closely and remembered accurately, she conveys to us the full excitement of her experience.

EXERCISE 1. Analyzing Descriptive Writing.   Read the passage and visualize the scene. Then answer the questions following the passage.

> Another time I saw another wonder: sharks off the Atlantic coast of Florida. There is a way a wave rises above the ocean horizon, a triangular wedge against the sky. If you stand where the ocean breaks on a shallow beach, you see the raised water in a wave is translucent, shot with lights. One late afternoon at low tide a hundred big sharks passed the beach near the mouth of a tidal river, in a feeding frenzy. As each green wave rose from the churning water, it illuminated within itself the six- or eight-foot long bodies of twisting sharks. The sharks disappeared as each wave rolled toward me; then a new wave would swell above the horizon, containing in it, like scorpions in amber, sharks that roiled and heaved. The sight held awesome wonders: power and beauty, grace tangled in a rapture with violence.
>
> ANNIE DILLARD

1. What details indicate time and place?
2. What accurate details specify size and shape?
3. Point out a particularly well-chosen verb and an adjective.
4. What comparison makes the experience vivid?

EXERCISE 2. Writing Vivid Description.   Write a paragraph like Annie Dillard's describing an impressive sight. Make clear what you saw and how you felt.

Sharpen your powers of observation by recording in your journal, every day for a week, brief but detailed descriptions of things you see, preferably ordinary, unimportant things you may not have observed or noticed before. The following examples, describing things observed on the way to school, illustrate this kind of recording.

1. water standing in the gutter, a film of oil reflecting in rainbow swirls

2. a worker—stomach like a basketball above his belt—drinking coffee from a white cup held with enormous hands
3. a discarded aluminum can on the school lawn, its silver end reflecting in the sun like a bright flashlight

---

CRITICAL THINKING:
Analysis

In examining material and determining its parts and their relationships, you use the critical thinking skill of *analysis*. You analyze when you study a piece of writing to see how effectively the writer has used detailed observation.

EXERCISE 3. Analyzing Effective Use of Observation. Detailed observation is used in the following description of an old-fashioned oil lamp, the kind of lamp found in most houses before the advent of gas and electric lighting. Read slowly and try to see the lamp exactly as it is. Note each detail and answer the questions that follow.

1. It is of glass, light metal-colored gold, and cloth of heavy thread.
2. The glass was poured into a mold, I guess, that made the base and bowl, which are in one piece; the glass is thick and clean, with icy lights in it. The base is a simply fluted, hollow skirt; stands on the table; is solidified in a narrowing, a round inch of pure thick glass, then hollows again, a globe about half flattened, the globe-glass thick, too; and this holds oil, whose silver line I see, a little less than half down the globe, its level a very little—for the base is not quite true—tilted against the axis of the base.
3. This "oil" is not at all oleaginous,[1] but thin, brittle, rusty feeling, and sharp; taken and rubbed between forefinger and thumb, it so cleanses their grain that it sharpens their mutual touch to a new coin edge, and the odor is clean, cheerful, and humble, less alive by far than that of gasoline, even a shade watery; and a subtle sweating of this oil is on the upward surface of the globe, as if it stood through the glass, and as if the glass were a pitcher of cool water in a hot room. I do not understand nor try to deduce this, but I like it; I run my thumb upon it and smell of my thumb, and smooth away its streaked print on the glass; and I wipe my thumb and forefinger dry against my pants, and keep on looking. . . .

---

[1] *oleaginous:* oily

4. In this globe, like a thought, a dream, the future, slumbers the stout-weft[1] strap of wick, and up this wick is drawn the oil, toward heat; through a tight, flat tube of tin, and through a little slotted smile of golden tin, and there ends fledged with flame, in the flue; the flame, a clean, fanged fan.

JAMES AGEE and WALKER EVANS

1. Reread the second paragraph and draw a rough picture of the lamp. Compare your picture with those of your classmates. What information was omitted that would be helpful?
2. From paragraph 2, select three or four descriptive details that were most helpful as you drew the lamp.
3. Is the authors' description limited to the lamp and oil, or does it include their feelings about what they observe? Explain.
4. Explain the meaning of the following descriptions:
   paragraph 2 *solidified in a narrowing*
   paragraph 3 *it sharpens their mutual touch to a new coin edge*
                                   as if the glass were a pitcher of cool water in a hot room
   paragraph 4 *In this globe, like a thought, a dream, the future, slumbers the stout-weft strap of wick*
5. Find evidence that supports this statement: In their description of the lamp, the authors show that they are close observers.

REVIEW EXERCISE A. Writing a Detailed Description. Take any object that interests you, observe it closely, and write a detailed description of it.

PREWRITING A small object like the lamp will be easier to describe than a large object like a car. You might describe a beat-up book bag or a classmate's shoe. After you have chosen the object, observe it closely, questioning yourself about it. Is it unusual in any way? What color is it? What are its size and shape? Then ask yourself how you feel about it. Is it something special to you? Are you emotionally attached to it, or do you think of it as purely practical? Consider organizing the details according to their location on the object.

WRITING, EVALUATING, AND REVISING Try to describe the object so precisely that a reader could draw a picture of it. Let the reader know

---

[1] *weft:* woven

your feelings about the object, as Agee and Evans did. After you have
finished writing, evaluate, revise, and proofread your description. Use
the Guidelines for Evaluating on page 25 and the Guidelines for
Proofreading on pages 32–33.

Selecting Words That Appeal to the Senses

7b. In descriptive writing, select words that appeal to the senses.

Experience comes through our senses. In descriptive writing you should
appeal to the senses by using words that describe or identify the various
sights, sounds, smells, tastes, and feelings or physical sensations you
want to convey to your audience.

EXERCISE 4. Identifying Sensory Words. Number your paper
1–20. Copy the following list of words and write the sense or senses to
which each refers.

1. hot	6. salty	11. whisper	16. glassy
2. spicy	7. icy	12. bitter	17. glittering
3. sour	8. bright	13. tart	18. thump
4. loud	9. roar	14. coarse	19. empty
5. green	10. moist	15. smoky	20. burnt

Describing the Sense of Sound

Many words that describe sounds suggest the sounds themselves. *Clang*
suggests metal striking metal; *bong* suggests a large bell; *jingle* suggests
a small bell. The use of these words is called *onomatopoeia,* and the
words are said to be *onomatopoeic.*

EXERCISE 5. Using Onomatopoeia. Number your paper 1–10. For
each number, write the entire item on your paper, supplying an
onomatopoeic, or sound-imitating, word for the blank. You may also
add adjectives; for example, "the crash of thunder" might become "the
ear-splitting crash of thunder."

1. the —— of turning pages
2. the —— of footsteps
3. the —— of the wind
4. the —— of wheels on gravel
5. the —— of water dripping
6. the —— of a fire
7. the —— of a piano
8. the —— of distant gunfire
9. the —— of a door opening
10. the —— of a jet plane

Describing the Senses of Smell and Taste

Because smell and taste are closely related, the same words may often describe both. For example, the words *pungent, bitter, musty,* and *stale* refer to both senses.

In the following paragraph, Thomas Wolfe describes the sounds and smells he associated with the arrival of the circus when he was a young boy. Discuss with your classmates the effectiveness of Wolfe's descriptions.

> And to all these familiar sounds, filled with their exultant prophecies of flight, the voyage, morning, and the shining cities—to all the sharp and thrilling odors of the trains—the smell of cinders, acrid smoke, of musty, rusty freight cars, the clean pineboard of crated produce, and the smells of fresh stored food—oranges, coffee, tangerines and bacon, ham and flour and beef—there would be added now, with an unforgettable magic and familiarity, all the strange sounds and smells of the coming circus. The gay yellow sumptuous-looking cars in which the star performers lived and slept, still dark and silent, heavily and powerfully still, would be drawn up in long strings upon the tracks. And all around them the sounds of the unloading circus would go furiously in the darkness. The receding gulf of lilac and departing night would be filled with the savage roar of the lions, the murderously sudden snarling of great jungle cats, the trumpeting of the elephants, the stamp of the horses, and with the musty, pungent, unfamiliar odor of the jungle animals: the tawny camel smells, and the smells of panthers, zebras, tigers, elephants, and bears.
>
> THOMAS WOLFE

EXERCISE 6. Choosing Words to Describe Smell and Taste. Number your paper 1–5. Supply a specific descriptive adjective for each blank.

1. the —— taste of coffee
2. the —— odor of strong cheese
3. the —— taste of pickles
4. the —— aroma of fresh bread
5. the —— smell of pizza

Describing the Sense of Touch

Smooth, rough, icy, and *slimy* describe the feeling of a surface when we touch it or are touched by it. We can also describe our own physical sensations in an experience. In the following passage, Lois Hudson recalls the sensations she experienced as a young girl on a North Dakota farm when the temperature dropped to 50 degrees below zero.

I was well acquainted with the shock of stepping from the warm kitchen into a winter night. But none of the freezing memories of the past could prepare me for the burning air that night. It was like strong hot smoke in my nostrils, so that for one confused instant I thought I was going to suffocate with the cold that was so cold it was hot. I gasped for breathable air, and my father said, "Don't do that! Breathe through your nose—your breath is warmer that way when it gets to your lungs."

We walked carefully down the hill to the barn; then I slithered down the steps, chopped in a snowdrift in front of the door, and slid it open. The barn was very old, but, always before, it had been warm with the heat of the animals kept in it all day long. But that night being inside didn't seem to make any difference. I still had the kind of ache in my temples and cheekbones that I always got when I took too big a mouthful of ice cream.

LOIS HUDSON

EXERCISE 7. Choosing Words to Describe the Sensation of Touch. Write an adjective or a phrase that describes the sensation of touching each of the following items:

1. velvet	3. silk	5. denim	7. fish
2. marble	4. corduroy	6. earthworm	8. tire

Using Vivid Details

7c. Fill your writing with vivid details.

Most writing moves from the general to the particular. General statements are backed up with the supporting details needed to convey a picture clearly. In the following paragraph, Edmund G. Love recalls the barber from his childhood. Find two general statements about Joe Gage, and point out the supporting details.

I do not think that Joe Gage overcharged for his haircuts. A boy certainly got his money's worth. He was the first barber I ever knew who gave away lollipops to his customers. He also gave balloons, tops, kites, and baseballs. He entertained his customers as he cut their hair. He would stop in the middle of whatever he was doing and put on the boxing gloves and go a quick round with a boy. He would Indian-wrestle, play mumblety-peg, or teach a boy how to whittle. He would repair a coaster wagon or paint a name on a sled. He was a talented man in many ways. He was the best whistler who ever came to Flushing. He could imitate birds or whistle a song. He could sing. He could tell stories. Sometimes in the middle of a haircut he would get so engrossed in one of his own stories that he would draw up a stool and sit down. When my brother Walter stalked into his shop and asked for a shave, a shave was forthcoming. Joe lathered Walter's face, used the back of a comb to shave off the lather, applied a hot towel, and finished off with a generous application of witch hazel and lilac water.

EDMUND G. LOVE

EXERCISE 8. Writing a Description with Vivid Details.   Select one of the following places or a place not listed here. Write a one-paragraph description (approximately 150 words) conveying its atmosphere. Support your general statements with specific details, appealing to as many of the senses as possible. Let your reader know your feelings through your choice of details.

pizza parlor	indoor swimming pool
car repair shop	library
city playground	schoolroom
city street	zoo
restaurant	

Using Figurative Language: Similes and Metaphors

7d. Use similes and metaphors to make your writing clear and interesting.

Skillful writers often think in terms of comparison. Annie Dillard writes of *scorpions in amber* when referring to the sharks inside the waves, and she refers to a wave as a *triangular wedge against the sky.* James Agee and Walker Evans describe the lamp's base as a *fluted, hollow skirt,* comparing the lamp base and an article of clothing. Their lamp wick *slumbers* in oil, as if it is a live thing, and the flame at the top of the wick is a *clean, fanged fan.* Comparisons like these are called *figures of speech,* and the language in which they are expressed is called *figurative language.*

An expression is figurative when it compares things that are not alike in fact but are alike in the writer's imagination. For example, a writer literally describing a passenger on the bow of a ship on a winter night might say, "The wind in her face was strong and cold." A figurative description might say, "The wind cut her face like a knife."

You often use comparisons without thinking: "busy as a bee," "hard as a rock," "straight as an arrow." A person may be "a good egg" or "at death's door." These everyday comparisons are to be avoided in writing because they have been overused. Fresh, original comparisons can surprise and delight your audience.

The two most common figures of speech are simile and metaphor. A *simile* compares things essentially unlike, expressed *directly* with a comparing word such as *like* or *as:*

> They slept *like* the dead all day.
> The flame rose *like* a pointed flower.

A *metaphor* also compares things essentially unlike, but it is expressed *indirectly,* without a comparing word such as *like* or *as.* The comparison is suggested rather than stated:

> Between steep walls flowed the *swollen stream* of rush-hour traffic.
> The sun *hammered* at our uncovered heads.

EXERCISE 9. Identifying Similes and Metaphors. Identify each quotation below as a simile or metaphor by writing *S* or *M*. Be prepared to state what is being compared and to evaluate the effectiveness of each figure of speech.

1. The modern racehorse, inbred for speed, carrying the maximum amount of muscle on the minimum amount of bone structure, is as frail as a pastry shell.—ERNEST HAVEMAN
2. A tree of pain takes root in his jaw.—JOHN UPDIKE
3. I could not bear to see her dimmed.—MARY RENAULT
4. An island [Manhattan] uttered incandescent towers like frozen simultaneous hymns to trade.—MALCOLM COWLEY
5. The Possible's slow fuse is lit / By the Imagination!— EMILY DICKINSON

EXERCISE 10. Writing Similes. Using your imagination, complete the following similes in a fresh and original way.

1. Bright beach umbrellas like . . .
2. To press his hand was like . . .
3. The heavy fog was like . . .
4. High above us a jet plane moved across the sky like . . .
5. The room was as quiet as . . .

REVIEW EXERCISE B. Writing a Description of an Experience.
Write a three-paragraph composition (approximately 300 words) describing the experience of waking up in the morning or falling asleep at night.

PREWRITING   Keep a notebook beside you for a few nights as you go to bed or wake up. Observe everything around you: What sounds do you hear? What can you see? Can you smell anything—breakfast cooking, perhaps? How does the air in the room feel? Jot down your ideas.

Select a method of organization. In *chronological order,* start with the moment you turn out the light or when you first wake up. In *spatial order,* organize details by their physical location in the room. You might begin by describing the ceiling, moving from there to the walls and the floor. In *order of importance,* organize the details from the least to the most important or just the opposite.

WRITING   Using spatial order, chronological order, or order of importance, organize your specific details. Be sure to describe your sensations and remember your notes about senses other than sight.

EVALUATING, REVISING, AND PROOFREADING   Evaluate and revise your draft carefully. Use the Guidelines for Evaluating on page 25. Then proofread your paper using the Guidelines for Proofreading on pages 32–33.

Techniques for Prewriting.   Remember that effective creative writing includes

- Details drawn from close observation
- Words that appeal to all the senses
- Vivid details that support general statements
- Figurative language that creates fresh, unexpected pictures

---

WRITING SHORT STORIES

A short story is an imaginative narrative. Good storytellers use the techniques which are important to descriptive writing: accurate details, words that appeal to the senses, and comparisons. They add elements of plot (what happens), characters (who is involved), setting (the time and place of the action), and point of view (who is telling the story).

PREWRITING

Choosing a Struggle or Conflict

7e. Choose a struggle or a conflict that is appropriate for a short story.

A short story contains a situation or problem leading to a struggle or conflict. Without this conflict, there is no story. A character can be in conflict with society, with another character, with a natural force, or with competing desires or needs. These conflicts are not necessarily violent or physical; they may be strong disagreements or tests of will.

Ideas for conflicts that can be imaginatively treated in short stories are all around you. A newspaper story about a family attacked by a bear in Yellowstone Park can be developed into a conflict between the people and the park service. Other sources of ideas include reading your journal and recalling your own experiences, observing the actions of other people, reading and watching television, and interviewing family members and neighbors.

As you use these sources, remember that a short story is fictional. You may draw on *what happened* for ideas; but you must shape events into a plot and add imaginary details to your account.

EXERCISE 11. Choosing a Conflict. Using television, the newspaper, your journal, and observation of people around you, list five real conflicts or struggles. For each real conflict, develop two *imaginary* related conflicts.

EXAMPLE *Actual Conflict:* A conflict between a hotel owner and a fire marshal over fire hazards in a building
Imaginary Conflict 1: A conflict between a landlord and a tenant over fire hazards in a building
Imaginary Conflict 2: A conflict between a firefighter and a life-threatening hotel fire

Identifying Audience and Tone

7f. Analyze how the audience will affect your writing.

Although you may not have a specific audience for your short story, you still must be aware that an audience exists. A short story is written to be read and enjoyed. The readers, whoever they are, must be able to understand the story and must find it interesting.

If you do have a specific audience—the students who read your school magazine, for example—consider how the interests and background of that audience will affect what you should include in your story. If your school is in the city and most of the students lack actual experience in forests, how will you describe a forest fire so they can understand the power and devastation of that natural event? If most of the students in your school have lived in the same neighborhood all their lives, how can you make them understand the fear of a teenager whose family is moving to a foreign country? Even when you are writing for a general audience, remember to think about your readers as real people who may need background information, who may have certain biases, and who will need to find your story interesting.

Techniques for Prewriting. To analyze how your audience might affect your writing, ask yourself:

● Will this audience be naturally interested in this conflict?
● What details or actions can be included to make the story more interesting to this audience?
● Will any special information have to be provided for this audience to understand and appreciate this struggle? If so, what information should be included?
● What natural bias in favor of or against this struggle or the main character might this audience have?

EXERCISE 12. **Analyzing the Effect of Audience.**   Analyze how the audience would affect a story on the following conflict: During a blizzard, a woman nearly freezes to death right outside her own front door. Answer the preceding questions to analyze the effect of *each* audience. Be prepared to discuss your answers in class.

Audiences: 1. A group of elementary school students who live in southern Florida
2. A general audience in Nome, Alaska

7g. Choose a tone that is appropriate for your audience and your purpose.

Your general purpose in writing a short story is to entertain or interest your audience; more specifically, you may want to make your readers laugh, fill them with suspense and horror, or help them understand some basic, everyday conflict. That specific purpose reflects your attitude toward the conflict: For example, you want to make your readers laugh because you feel the conflict is humorous.

Consider your purpose and how you will share that purpose with your audience. Then choose a tone that will accurately reflect your purpose and your attitude toward the conflict.

To make your audience laugh, choose details and language that will convey a humorous tone. To make your audience tremble with fear, choose details and language that will convey the conflict's mystery and horror.

In the following excerpt from a short story by Kurt Vonnegut, Jr., the tone is light and humorous. The author enjoys the characters and the conflict, and he wants the audience to enjoy them also. Notice how Vonnegut uses words and details to reveal his attitude.

> The North Crawford Mask and Wig Club, an amateur theatrical society I belong to, voted to do Tennessee Williams's *A Streetcar Named Desire* for the spring play. Doris Sawyer, who always directs, said she couldn't direct this time because her mother was so sick. And she said the club ought to develop some other directors anyway, because she couldn't live forever, even though she'd made it safely to seventy-four.
>
> So I got stuck with the directing job, even though the only thing I'd ever directed before was the installation of combination aluminum storm windows and screens I'd sold. That's what I am, a salesman of storm windows and doors, and here and there a bathtub enclosure. As far as acting goes, the highest rank I ever held on stage was either butler or policeman, whichever's higher.
>
> KURT VONNEGUT, JR.

1. How does the title of the drama club reflect the story's tone?

2. If the story's tone were very serious, how might the last sentence in the first paragraph be rewritten?

3. What word in the first sentence of the second paragraph helps reveal the story's light tone?

4. How does the phrase *whichever's higher* contribute to the tone?

5. What details about the narrator's occupation contribute to the story's tone?

EXERCISE 13. Analyzing Audience, Purpose, and Tone. Choose one conflict from Exercise 11 and answer the following questions.

1. What is my specific purpose in telling this story?
2. What is my attitude toward the conflict?
3. Am I writing this story for a general or specific audience? If it is intended for a specific audience, what are that audience's unique needs?
4. What can I have my characters say or do that will convey my tone and purpose? What details can I include to reflect the story's tone?
5. Might the audience be surprised by or concerned about the tone I intend to use? If so, should I consider changing the tone?

Selecting a Point of View

7h. Select a point of view that is appropriate for your story.

When you plan your short story, decide what kind of narrator you will use to tell the story. You may use the *first-person* point of view; here the narrator is either someone directly involved in the conflict or a witness to the conflict. This point of view makes the audience feel close to the action, but the first-person narrator cannot know what any other character is thinking or feeling.

You may also write a story from the *third-person* point of view; here the narrator is someone outside the story. The *third-person, omniscient* (all-knowing) narrator knows what is going on in any character's mind and can show what all the characters are saying and doing. The following examples illustrate these points of view.

First-person, directly involved in the conflict. The blisters on my feet were raw, and I felt that every step would be my last.

First-person, a witness to the conflict. I saw Jane's pained expression as she sprinted around the corner into the final stretch of the race.

Third-person, omniscient. As Jane rounded the corner into the final stretch of the race, she struggled with the pain to keep running. From the sidelines, Martin also suffered.

When you choose a point of view for your story, decide whether you want to show what more than one character is thinking and feeling. Third-person, omniscient point of view gives writers the most freedom.

EXERCISE 14. Writing from Different Points of View. Using the following situation and characters, write a sentence or two illustrating each of the following points of view: (1) first-person, directly involved in

202 < Writing Narration and Description

the conflict; (2) first-person, a witness to the conflict; (3) third-person, omniscient. Use the examples above as a model.

Situation and Characters: Two teen-agers spot what appears to be a spaceship in a forest clearing. One goes up to investigate while the other watches from a distance.

Organizing a Plot for a Short Story

7i. Organize a plot for your short story.

The plot of a short story is the plan of action. It consists of the situation or *conflict,* the *series of actions* resulting from the conflict, the *climax* (the moment of greatest interest or excitement) of those actions, and the final *resolution* or outcome of the conflict. After choosing the basic conflict, a writer must decide how to begin, what events to include and in what order, and how to resolve the conflict.

> *Techniques for Prewriting.* To organize the plot of your short story, remember that
>
> - The opening of the story establishes the nature of the conflict and stimulates the interest of the audience.
> - The actions, told in chronological order, should keep the reader interested and in suspense about how the conflict will be resolved.
> - The climax, the highest point of interest for the audience, should come near the end of the story.
> - The resolution, or outcome, should occur immediately after the climax. Whether it's happy or unhappy, the outcome should be the likely result of the story's actions and events.

In the following very brief short story, observe the beginning, the middle, and the end.

The boy lay huddled on his side, his hands thrust deeply into the pockets of his jacket. Down the mountain, he could see the patches of snow that had lured him away from the camp. He remembered telling himself at the time that his

beginning: nature of conflict established; interest aroused

tracks would guide him back to camp. He hadn't expected most of the snow to melt long before he had reached the ledge on which he had lain all night. He felt once again the onset of tears as he recalled the emptiness of knowing he was lost and alone. The numbing cold and the ever-present pangs of hunger added to his desolation.

As the sun began to warm the ledge, the boy forced himself to stand upright, his arms and legs protesting after a full night in one cramped position. Suddenly, despite his miseries, he felt alive. Maybe someone had missed him. Maybe even now they were searching for him.

the middle: actions and events leading to climax

"Hey!" he shouted. Then, testing to hear how much voice he had left after all the cries for help the day before, he shouted as long and as loud as he could, "HEY!"

From down the slopes an echo seemed to come back, "Hey!" Then from not too far away came the words, "Is that you Jim? Show us where you are."

the end: outcome of the situation

The boy shook his head in disbelief. Then —cramps gone, cold vanished, hunger forgotten —he crashed downhill toward the sound of his name, yelling jubilantly as he ran.

EXERCISE 15. Organizing the Plot for Your Short Story. Using one of the conflicts from Exercise 11 or another conflict of your choice, develop a plot outline or plan. Follow this format as you develop your plan:

1. Describe the event or situation you will use to establish the nature of the conflict and to interest the audience.
2. List in chronological order the actions that lead to the climax. Describe how you will build suspense into the actions.
3. Describe the climax of the action.
4. Describe how the conflict will be resolved—either happily or unhappily.

WRITING

Developing Characters

7j. Develop characters through description, dialogue, and action.

Some stories focus on developing characters; others focus more on plot. In any story, however, it is important that the characters be well defined. The main character, or *protagonist,* faces the problem or conflict. The *antagonist* opposes the plans or wishes of the protagonist. A narrative may also include other characters, of course, depending on the writer's plan.

> *Techniques for Writing.* Follow Laurence Perrine's suggestions, noted in *Literature: Structure, Sound, and Sense,*[1] to make your characters convincing:
>
> - Make the characters behave consistently. For example, a basically greedy character should not spend money with abandon unless you give some reason for that change.
> - Help the reader understand why the characters behave as they do. If the avid mountain climber turns back before reaching the peak, the reader should know what motivates that decision.
> - Make the characters believable people who could actually exist in real life. Few people are perfect or entirely evil.

To create characters that are convincing and interesting, you will need to use description, dialogue, action, or a combination of these. In the following excerpt from "The Story of Muhammad Din," the writer combines all three techniques to develop character.

Next day, coming back from [the] office half an hour earlier than usual, I was aware of a small figure in the dining room—*a tiny, plump figure in a*   physical description
ridiculously inadequate shirt which came, perhaps, halfway down the tubby stomach. It wandered round the room, thumb in mouth, *crooning to itself*

---

[1] Laurence Perrine, *Literature: Structure, Sound, and Sense,* copyright © 1983 by Harcourt Brace Jovanovich, p. 69.

as it took stock of the pictures. Undoubtedly this was the "little son."   action

He had no business in my room, of course, but was so deeply absorbed in his discoveries that *he never noticed* me in the doorway. I stepped into the room and startled him nearly into a fit. *He sat down on the ground with a gasp. His eyes opened, and his mouth followed suit.* I knew what was coming, and fled, followed by *a long, dry howl which reached the servants' quarters* far more quickly than any command of mine had ever done. In ten seconds Imam Din was in the dining room. Then despairing sobs arose, and I returned to find Imam Din admonishing the small sinner who was using most of his shirt as a handkerchief.   action   action   action

"This boy," said Imam Din, judicially, *"is a budmash¹—a big budmash. He will, without doubt, go to the jailkhana² for his behavior."* Renewed yells from the penitent, and an elaborate apology to myself from Imam Din.   another character describing the character

"Tell the baby," said I, "that the *Sahib³* is not angry, and take him away." Imam Din conveyed my forgiveness to the offender, who had now gathered all his shirt round his neck, stringwise, and the yell subsided into a sob. The two set off for the door. "His name," said Imam Din, as though the name were part of the crime, "is Muhammad Din, and he is a budmash." Freed from present danger, Muhammad Din turned round in his father's arms, and said gravely, *"It is true that my name is Muhammad Din, Tahib,⁴ but I am not a budmash, I am a man!"*   character revealed through own words

RUDYARD KIPLING

¹ *budmash:* a bad character; a worthless fellow
² *jailkhana:* prison, jailhouse
³ *Sahib:* Master: a title used by natives in addressing European gentlemen
⁴ *Tahib:* Muhammad Din's childish mispronunciation of *Sahib*

Kipling begins developing Muhammad Din with a physical description: *a small figure in the dining room—a tiny, plump figure in a ridiculously inadequate shirt which came, perhaps, halfway down the tubby stomach.* Examples of the child's actions and a discussion between the boy's father and the narrator continue the development by showing that the father thinks his son is a problem. The boy's own words—"It is true that my name is Muhammad Din, Tahib, but I am not a budmash, I am a man!"—reveal Muhammad Din's strength of character, his willingness to assert himself, even to an English gentleman. Through the description, the action, and the dialogue, we see the complexity of the character.

Techniques for Writing. Consider the following points in developing characters for your own stories:

- *Description.* Your readers do not need an exact, complete physical description; use only the physical characteristics that are important to *who* the character is. Kipling does not describe Muhammad Din's height, weight, or hair color; he reveals only that Muhammad Din is little more than a baby.
- *Action.* One or two important actions can reveal some important trait or characteristic. Kipling shows Muhammad Din curiously exploring a room and crying with fear and surprise, two actions that reveal his character.
- *Dialogue.* Effective dialogue is brief. Sentences are short, and characters usually do not give long speeches. It is also appropriate to each speaker's age, occupation, and educational background. For example, Muhammad Din's mispronunciation of the word *Sahib* is appropriate for a young child.

EXERCISE 16. Developing a Character. Select one of the conflicts from Exercise 11, and assume that you are writing a short story about it. Think about the main character. Write two or three sentences that include a physical description of the character, a brief description of an action revealing personality traits, and a brief dialogue or quotation in which the character's own speech reveals personality traits.

Developing Setting

7k. Develop setting with descriptive details.

Short-story writers use descriptive details to reveal when and where a story takes place. Occasionally a writer includes a complete paragraph or two containing only a description of the setting. More often, the details of setting are sprinkled in with the development of the story. In the following excerpt, Kipling mixes details of setting with the action.

Heaven knows that I had no intention of touching the child's work then or later; but, *that evening, a stroll through the garden* brought me unawares full on it; so that I *trampled,* before I knew, *marigold heads, dust bank, and fragments of broken soap dish* into confusion past all hope of mending. Next morning I came upon Muhammad Din *crying softly* to himself over the ruin I had wrought. Someone had cruelly told him that the Sahib was very angry with him for spoiling the garden, and had scattered his rubbish, using bad language [all] the while. *Muhammad Din labored for an hour at effacing every trace of the dust bank and pottery fragments,* and it was with a tearful and apologetic face that he said "Talaam, Tahib," *when I came home* from [the] office. A hasty *inquiry resulted* in Imam Din informing Muhammad Din that, by my singular favor, he was permitted to disport himself[1] as he pleased. *Whereat the child took heart and fell to tracing the ground plan of an edifice* which was to eclipse the marigold-polo ball creation.

For some months, the chubby little eccentricity[2] *revolved in his humble orbit among the castor-oil bushes and in the dust*; always fashioning magnificent palaces from *stale flowers thrown away by the bearer, smooth water-worn pebbles, bits of broken glass, and feathers* pulled, I fancy, from my fowls —always alone, and *always crooning* to himself.

RUDYARD KIPLING

Marginal notes: time and place · action · details of setting · action · action related to setting · time and action · action related to setting · action related to setting · details of setting · action

[1] *disport himself*: play.
[2] *eccentricity*: odd person.

Techniques for Writing. Answer the following questions to develop the setting of your short story:

- Where does the story take place? In what country? In a small town, in a city, or in the country?
- What is the climate like? What is the weather like on the day or days when the story takes place?
- What is the relationship, if any, between the conflict and the location of the setting? Between the conflict and the weather at the time?
- Does the time of day affect the conflict? If so, what time of day is it when the conflict begins and ends?
- What senses—sight, smell, touch, taste, sound—would help to describe this setting? (See pages 192–94 for a discussion of sensory details.)

EXERCISE 17. Using Descriptive Details for Setting. Using the conflict from Exercise 13 or 15, or another conflict of your choice, assume that you are writing a short story. Answer each of the preceding questions to develop an appropriate setting for the story.

Writing a First Draft of Your Short Story

7l. Write a first draft of your short story.

Writing the first draft of a story is like writing any other first draft. After you have thought about your topic (in this case, the conflict) and developed an outline (a plot outline), you are ready to write. Think of this first draft as an opportunity to get your ideas on paper and to begin to think through some of the problems in your writing task. Remember that you will be able to improve the story later when you evaluate and revise.

EXERCISE 18. Writing a First Draft. Write a first draft of your story. Create an interesting beginning and build suspense into the actions leading to the climax of the story. You may use the plot outline, characters, and setting you developed in earlier exercises, or you may select a new conflict and develop a new plan.

EVALUATING

Evaluating a First Draft

7m. Evaluate the first draft of your short story.

The first draft of a short story, like any other piece of writing, should be evaluated to pinpoint its strengths and weaknesses. Use the following Guidelines for Evaluating Short Stories to evaluate your draft. Mark your draft to note where improvements should be made. You might also ask a friend or classmate to use the guidelines to evaluate your draft.

GUIDELINES FOR EVALUATING SHORT STORIES

Plot Development
1. Does the beginning of the story establish the conflict and arouse the interest of the reader?
2. Do the actions lead to a climax and develop suspense? Is the conflict resolved logically? Has the reader been prepared for the resolution?

Coherence
3. Are the actions in the story in clear chronological order?

Point of View
4. Is one point of view used consistently in the story? Is the point of view appropriate for the story?

Character Development
5. Are the characters convincing? Do they behave consistently? Is it clear why they behave as they do?
6. Has the main character been fully developed through description, dialogue, action, or a combination of these?

Dialogue
7. Is the dialogue natural and appropriate for the characters?

Setting
8. Do the details of setting help the reader understand the characters and the conflict? Does the setting convey the right mood?

EXERCISE 19. Evaluating a First Draft. Use the Guidelines for Evaluating Short Stories to evaluate the first draft you wrote for Exercise 18. Note on your draft where improvements should be made, and save your draft for later use.

REVISING AND PROOFREADING

Revising and Proofreading Your Story

7n. Revise and proofread your story.

Professional writers often write many drafts of their stories. They may write these drafts over a long period of time—sometimes months or even years. By evaluating your short story, you discover problems or areas for improvement. The following chart suggests how to use the four revising techniques (cutting, adding, replacing, and reordering) to solve these problems.

REVISING SHORT STORIES		
PROBLEM	**TECHNIQUE**	**REVISION**
The beginning fails to catch the audience's interest.	Replace	Write new opening dialogue, an anecdote, or a description to arouse the reader's interest and curiosity.
The beginning does not establish the conflict.	Cut/Replace	Cut opening material that clutters the beginning. Replace with action or description that involves the reader with the conflict immediately.
The resolution is not logical.	Replace	Substitute a resolution consistent with the characters, conflict, actions, and climax in the story.
The actions are not clearly organized.	Reorder	Rearrange the incidents in the plot so that the actions logically lead to the climax and resolution.

PROBLEM	TECHNIQUE	REVISION
The point of view changes.	Cut/Replace	Cut information the narrator could not logically know. Reword other information, if necessary, to include the material you cut.
The characters are not convincing.	Cut/Add	Cut actions or words that are not consistent with the characters' personalities. Add background information that explains the characters' behavior and makes them more believable.
The main character is not fully developed.	Add	Add physical details and details of character to present the dominant character trait. Add actions or dialogue that reveal character.
The dialogue is not convincing.	Cut/Replace	Cut long speeches and sentences. Replace unreal dialogue with contractions and informal expressions as appropriate for each character. (Improvise orally with a classmate to listen for the natural sound of dialogue.)
The setting does not create a mood.	Cut/Add	Cut details of setting that do not support the desired mood. Add precise words and sensory details that will make the setting come alive.

The following paragraphs are from the beginning of a short story. Notice the techniques the writer used to revise the first draft after evaluating it.

Hang on to

‸"Please ~~grip~~ the rope ~~better~~," Marcia/~~said~~ *yelled* as she   replace/cut

moved up the side of the cliff.

"Okay! Okay!" I yelled back. "Give me ‸~~the~~ *a*   replace

break!

‸~~benefit of the doubt~~. My hands are‸ *half frozen!"* ~~just too cold to~~   replace

~~hold on to the rope.~~"‸   cut

~~George's brother was a mountain climber. The~~   cut

Marcia I   just spent the last

‸~~man~~ and‸~~woman~~ had‸~~been on the mountain for~~ six   replace

trying to move ten feet up the face of that cliff

hours‸ and neither‸ had much strength or patience left.   add

although I was in good physical condition

‸~~George was six feet tall and weighed a hundred and~~   replace

and Marcia had more endurance than

‸~~ninety pounds, and Marcia had dark hair and dark~~

anybody I knew, we both had reached our

‸~~eyes. Marcia was strong for her size.~~   *limits ⊙*

1. Why did the writer change Marcia's words?
2. Why were the words of the second speaker changed?
3. Why was the first sentence of the last paragraph eliminated?
4. Why were the words *The man and woman* changed to *Marcia and I*?
5. Why did the writer change the last two sentences?

Allow as much time as possible for revising. After completing the final version, proofread it carefully and prepare a clean copy.

EXERCISE 20. Revising and Proofreading Your Short Story.
Revise your story, and proofread your final copy. Carefully examine your use of quotation marks, other punctuation, and paragraphing in your story's dialogue. Review the rules for punctuating dialogue on page 603. Also refer to the proofreading guidelines on pages 32–33.

WRITING CHARACTER SKETCHES AND BIOGRAPHICAL SKETCHES

A *character sketch* tells what someone is or was like. A *biographical sketch* tells about what someone has done by relating the major events and accomplishments in that person's life. Both combine narrative and descriptive techniques.

PREWRITING

Choosing a Character and Gathering Information

7o. Choose an interesting character, and gather information for a character sketch or a biographical sketch.

Choosing Characters

Whether a character sketch or biographical sketch stands alone or is part of a larger work (such as a short story or an essay), the character you write about should be interesting. In fiction you can *create* an interesting personality. For true stories, choose a character who, because of appearance, peculiarities, characteristics, occupation, or achievements, is naturally interesting. A character sketch can be written about imaginary or real characters; the subject of a biographical sketch is usually a real person.

Gathering Information About People

Your own mind will be the source of information about imaginary characters for a character sketch. Refer to journal notes, literature or history books, or television for ideas, but create the details in your own mind and imagination.

Sources of information about real people will vary, depending on the subject. For someone you know, find information by reading your journal, by interviewing friends or family members, or by observing. For someone you do not know, look in books or magazines and interview people associated with the person. For biographical sketches, you should probably consult one or more books to compile the major accomplishments and events in the person's life. For character sketches, identify one or two incidents that reveal the character's dominant personality trait.

Use the following questions to gather information about people.

A Character Sketch

1. What are the person's outstanding physical characteristics? What are the person's most striking, most unusual features?

2. What is this person's dominant personality trait? Is the person friendly, generous, proud, courageous, domineering, timid?

3. How does this person act, talk, dress, move, treat other people? How do other people feel about this person?

4. What events or actions reveal what this person is really like?

5. Is there a particular setting that helps reveal the person's dominant personality trait? What are the features of that setting?

A Biographical Sketch

1. When was this person born? In what major period of time did the person live—Civil War, Great Depression, Middle Ages?

2. In what city or country did this person live?

3. What were the important periods in this person's life?

4. What were the major events in this person's life?

5. What were this person's major achievements? What did this person do that affected the lives of other people?

6. What did this person look like? How did appearance affect this person's accomplishments?

7. What were the outstanding personality traits of this person? How were those personality traits and this person's accomplishments related?

EXERCISE 21. Gathering Information for a Character Sketch. Use prewriting techniques to identify a real or an imaginary person as a subject for a character sketch. Use the questions on pages 213–14 to gather information. Write down the answers to the questions, and be prepared to discuss the personality of this character.

EXERCISE 22. Gathering Information for a Biographical Sketch. Use prewriting techniques to identify a subject for a biographical sketch. Use the questions on pages 213–14 to gather information. Write down the answers to the questions, and be prepared to discuss the highlights of the person's life.

Considering Purpose and Audience

7p. Consider the purpose and the audience of your character sketch or biographical sketch.

The purpose of a character sketch is to reveal the personality of a character. The purpose of a biographical sketch is to recount the major accomplishments and events of a person's life. For either sketch, the writer may also want to communicate a specific attitude toward the character or person being described. If the writer's attitude is that the person is a scoundrel, a clown, or a saint, the tone of the sketch should reflect that attitude. Consider your attitude toward the person and how you will choose events, details, and language to reflect that attitude or tone.

You should also consider your intended audience. Your teacher may suggest a general audience or some specific audience. For any audience, specific or general, think about the background information you need to provide, the biases your audience might have, and the kinds of details you will need to provide.

Techniques for Prewriting. To consider the purpose and audience of your sketch, ask yourself the following questions:

- What is my purpose—to reveal this person's character or to highlight the achievements in this person's life?
- What is my attitude toward this person? What do I want my audience to think of this person?
- What actions and details will convey my attitude to my audience?
- What does my audience already know about this person?
- What background information will my audience need?
- How can I interest my audience in this person?

EXERCISE 23. Considering Purpose and Audience. Using the material you developed for Exercise 21 or 22, write the answers to the preceding questions about purpose and audience. Be prepared to discuss them.

Organizing a Character Sketch or a Biographical Sketch

7q. Organize a character sketch around a dominant personality trait.

You will normally not develop a character as fully in a brief character sketch as a novelist would in a book. To avoid painting a jumbled picture, emphasize one main impression. Your character sketch thus studies in depth one of the character's outstanding qualities.

To decide on this main impression, think about your attitude toward the character. Using the information you have gathered, what kind of picture do you want to create? What is this person's dominant characteristic: pettiness, gentleness, wisdom, strength of will? Once you have decided on a main impression, eliminate unrelated details.

Arrange the remaining details logically. For example, a revealing incident could lead into the details of physical characteristics and personal habits. Another arrangement might group physical details at the beginning and follow them with personality and behavioral details. Analyze the organization of the following character sketch.

The family was at the very core and ripeness of its life together. Gant lavished upon it his abuse, his affection, and his prodigal provisioning. They came to look forward eagerly to his entrance, for he brought with him the great gusto of living, of ritual. They would watch him in the evening as he turned the corner below with eager strides, follow carefully the processional of his movements from the time he flung his provisions upon the kitchen table to the rekindling of his fire, with which he was always at odds when he entered, and onto which he poured wood, coal, and kerosene lavishly. This done, he would remove his coat and wash himself at the basin vigorously, rubbing his hands across his shaven, tough-bearded face with the cleansing and male sound of sandpaper. Then he would thrust his body against the door jamb and scratch his back energetically by moving violently to and fro. This done, he would empty another half can of kerosene on the howling flame, lunging savagely at it and muttering to himself.

Then, biting off a good hunk of powerful apple tobacco, which lay ready to his use on the mantel, he would pace back and forth across the room fiercely, oblivious to his grinning family who followed these ceremonies with exultant excitement, as he composed his tirade. Finally, he would burst in on Eliza in the kitchen, plunging to the heart of denunciation with a mad howl.

His turbulent and undisciplined rhetoric had acquired, by the regular convention of his usage, something of the movement and directness of classical epithet[1]: his similes were preposterous, created really in a spirit of vulgar mirth, and the great comic intelligence that was in the family—down to the youngest—was shaken daily by it. The children grew to await his return in the evening with a kind of exhilaration.

As he stormed through the house, unleashing his gathered bolts, the children followed him joyously, shrieking exultantly as he told Eliza he had first seen her "wriggling around the corner like a snake on her belly," or, as coming in from freezing weather, he had charged her and all the Pentlands with malevolent domination of the elements.

[1] *epithet*: a word or phrase used to characterize something or someone.

"We will freeze," he yelled, "we will freeze in this . . . cruel and God-forsaken climate. . . . Merciful God! I have fallen into the hands of fiends incarnate, more savage, more cruel, more abominable than the beasts of the field. . . . They will sit by and gloat at my agony until I am done to death!"

As his denunciation reached some high extravagance, the boys would squeal with laughter, and Gant, inwardly tickled, would glance around slyly with a faint grin bending the corners of his thin mouth.

THOMAS WOLFE

1. Why does Wolfe begin by mentioning the family?
2. Wolfe announces early the person's dominant characteristic. What is it?
3. Wolfe uses a series of typical behaviors to support his impression. What are those behaviors?
4. What is the effect of the quotation Wolfe uses in the next-to-last paragraph? Why is the quotation placed near the end?
5. What detail at the very end of the selection sums up the dominant characteristic? Why does Wolfe place it at the end?

EXERCISE 24. Organizing a Character Sketch. Using your work from Exercise 21, develop an informal plan for a character sketch. First, identify the dominant characteristic you want to reveal. Then list events, physical traits, personal habits, and other details in a logical order.

7r. Organize a biographical sketch in chronological order, according to the major periods in the person's life.

Since a biographical sketch highlights the important events in a person's life, the most logical organization is chronological. Divide the person's life into major periods (youth, early adulthood, middle age, and so forth). Next, organize the main events and achievements within each period. Details about the person's personality and physical characteristics may go in an introductory paragraph or alongside the major events and achievements in that person's life.

The following two paragraphs are from the beginning of Louis Untermeyer's biographical sketch of Susan B. Anthony. Notice how the sketch begins with background information on the status of women's rights before Anthony's efforts.

What is perhaps the most radical alteration of social relationships in the last century is already so taken for granted that its newness is generally overlooked. Yet less than one hundred years ago women had no rights.

The first organized demand occurred as late as 1848 and asked for such essentials as the right "to have personal freedom, to acquire an education, to earn a living, to claim her wages, to own property, to make contracts, to bring suit, to testify in court, to obtain a divorce for just cause, to possess her children, to claim a fair share of the accumulations during marriage." Only one college in the United States admitted women; there were no women doctors or lawyers in the country. Married women literally "belonged" to their husbands as slaves or chattels. If they earned money or inherited it, legally it was not theirs but their husbands'. Single women had to be represented by male guardians. Obviously, no woman was entitled to vote. Except in ancient Egypt and under Roman law, this approximately had been the status of women from the beginnings of time.

In the second paragraph, Untermeyer introduces Susan B. Anthony. Chronological details about her family and childhood lead up to a significant detail about her personality: her *inquiring mind* that *was bound to rebel.*

The dogged seventy-five-year campaign of prodding, petitioning, and pleading that emancipated modern woman owed its strength and its strategy to Susan Brownell Anthony, sometimes called "the Napoleon of Feminism." She was born February 15, 1820, in Adams, Massachusetts, the second child in a family of eight. Her father, Daniel Anthony, was a man of strong intellect and liberal inclinations. Though a Quaker, he was not a conformist. For his wife, he picked Lucy Read, who was not only a Baptist but a young woman of lively disposition. However, when she became Mrs. Anthony she observed all the Quaker customs. Susan was brought up in a household that, in her childhood, wore Quaker clothes, spoke in Quaker terms, and proscribed frivolity. Though Daniel was a prosperous mill owner, it was incumbent on his wife to do all her own work, including farm chores, as well as board and serve the mill hands who lived with them from time to time. The children, particularly the older girls, were trained early in household accomplishments. But their education was far from neglected. Before she was five, precocious Susan could read and write. As her schooling progressed, whenever she came to a subject in which she was interested (such as more and more advanced arithmetic) she insisted on being taught it—even though it was nothing that girls were supposed to know. The early learning was obtained at home from a governess. In her teens, Susan was sent to an inexpensive finishing school near Philadelphia, Miss Deborah Moulson's Select Seminary for Females. Miss Moulson's task, as she saw it, was to mold her pupils in the prevailing forms, rather than direct an inquisitive spirit, and Susan's inquiring mind was bound to rebel.

Untermeyer then presents Anthony's early years in teaching and in the movement for women's rights. The following paragraphs, taken from the middle of the sketch, relate Anthony's activities and experiences during the Civil War. Notice how concisely Untermeyer treats the important events over a period of several years.

Meanwhile, the Civil War was embroiling the nation. Immediately upon Lincoln's election the extreme Abolitionists, with whom Susan had always identified herself, had campaigned—at first against Lincoln who was trying to prevent the war—for immediate emancipation. During the war the women's rights fight was suspended. The New York State legislature took advantage of the situation by repealing that part of the law they had passed two years earlier covering women's rights over children. Susan was immobilized on her father's farm. In her journal she noted: "Tried to interest myself in a sewing society; but little intelligence among them." Besides the farm work, she passed the time reading Elizabeth Barrett Browning and George Eliot, storing up energy towards the next battle. The call for it sounded in the clanging notes of the Emancipation Proclamation. Free the women as well as the slaves, Susan demanded. Let this be a government of the people, by the people, including women, she insisted—assuming that women are people.

Arguing that women's rights could be tied in with Negro rights, Elizabeth Stanton and Susan organized large numbers of women to campaign for a constitutional amendment abolishing slavery; the signatures they succeeded in getting to a petition helped effect the passage of the Thirteenth Amendment. It was with dismay, then, that they read the proposed Fourteenth Amendment and learned that civil rights were reserved for previously disenfranchised *male* citizens only. If they could have that one word struck out of the amendment, then all women, white as well as Negro, would win the vote at one stroke. The amendment, however, was passed as written. Susan retired to home ground, concentrating on the votes-for-women issue in Albany. It was at this time that the famous exchange of discourtesies took place between her and Horace Greeley.

"Miss Anthony," said Greeley with deadly suavity, "you are aware that the ballot and the bullet go together. If you vote, you are also prepared to fight?"

"Certainly, Mr. Greeley," Susan retorted. "Just as you fought in the last war—at the point of a goose-quill."

The writer includes the information about the Civil War and the Thirteenth and Fourteenth Amendments because these political events directly affected the efforts and motivations of Susan B. Anthony. The exchange between Greeley and Anthony serves two purposes: (1) It shows the kind of opposition Anthony was facing, and (2) it reveals her courage and wit.

Notice how the following last paragraphs in the sketch continue the chronological development of Anthony's life but also comment on her achievements and contributions.

> In 1904, when the International Woman Suffrage Alliance was formed, she was automatically acknowledged by the women of the world as their undisputed leader. Early in 1906, she attended what she suspected would be her last convention and told the delegates: "The fight must not stop. You must see it does not stop!" On her eighty-sixth birthday, she insisted on going to Washington to attend a dinner in her honor and ended her remarks by insisting, "Failure is impossible."
>
> It was success, however, that seemed impossible. When, as the result of a cold caught on the trip to Washington, she died on March 13, 1906, though the country flew its flags at half-mast in grief at her passing, she was eulogized as "The Champion of a Lost Cause."
>
> Thirteen years later, on May 21, 1919, the lost cause was won; an amendment giving women the full rights of citizenship was added to the United States Constitution. It was called the Susan B. Anthony Amendment.

Untermeyer includes information about Anthony's death in the next-to-last paragraph. In the last paragraph he tells of an event after her death which culminated the efforts of her life.

1. What is the purpose of the first paragraph in the sketch? Would the sketch be as effective if Untermeyer had left it out? Why or why not?

2. The second paragraph provides information on Anthony's developing personality. Why does the writer include this?

3. Why doesn't Untermeyer include information about the great battles of the Civil War?

4. Where does Untermeyer show the impact of the Civil War and the Thirteenth and Fourteenth Amendments on Anthony?

5. Would the sketch be as effective without the final paragraph? Why or why not?

CRITICAL THINKING:
Evaluating Information

To judge the relative value of information, you use the critical thinking skill of *evaluation*. As you gather information for a biographical sketch, you develop a list of events and achievements, some of which are more important than others. You must evaluate the information on that list, judging whether each individual event or achievement is important enough to include in your sketch.

EXERCISE 25. Evaluating the Importance of Information. The following list of events and achievements is taken from the life of an imaginary person, a scientist. Evaluate the importance of the information, and divide it into two lists: minor events and achievements and major events and achievements. In evaluating the importance of the information, consider the writer's purpose. Be prepared to discuss your lists in class.

Writer's Purpose: To show the significance of the scientist's contributions to the scientific world and to society.

Events and Achievements:

4.0 grade average in high school
sixteenth-birthday party
4.0 grade average in college
named to *Who's Who*
became a gourmet cook
invited to make presentation before Congressional committee
a barbecue at the home of a friend
graduation from college, *summa cum laude*
Nobel Prize award ceremony
birth of first child
knee surgery
discovered a cure for cancer
married childhood sweetheart

received National Science Foundation Grant
elected president of college Science Club
death at age 37
appeared on television talk show
received Nobel Prize for Science
received second Nobel Prize
founded a scientific think tank
discovered an unknown bacterium
served in the Air Force
taught science at a university
applied for National Science Foundation grant
received fellowship for graduate study

EXERCISE 26. Organizing a Biographical Sketch. Using your work from Exercise 22, evaluate the relative importance of events and achievements, and eliminate the minor ones. Arrange the remaining events and achievements in chronological order under major periods in the person's life. Under each event or achievement, list any important related details (physical characteristics, personality traits, setting) that should be included in the sketch.

WRITING

Writing Character Sketches and Biographical Sketches

7s. Write a first draft of your character sketch or biographical sketch.

Writing a First Draft of a Character Sketch

Write the first draft of your character sketch with the following suggestions in mind:

1. As you begin, place the character in a setting that either reflects or contrasts with the personality. Do not describe the setting in too much detail; a few brief strokes will do. Recall the brief, natural way Wolfe wove details of setting into the sketch on pages 216–17.

2. Show your character in action: how the person walks, sits, gestures, and expresses anger, amusement, love, confusion, and so on. In Wolfe's sketch, the reader discovers how the character *flung his provisions upon the kitchen table,* and how *he would remove his coat and wash himself at the basin vigorously.*

3. Let dialogue contribute to the sketch. Use idioms and expressions that would be characteristic of the person. The sketch on pages 216–17 includes only one paragraph of dialogue, but those few sentences demonstrate the character's dominant characteristic, "gusto."

4. Select vivid physical details that contribute to the dominant impression. To describe features, use striking, original comparisons whenever possible; avoid clichés. (For help with figurative language, see pages 195–97.)

5. To describe the setting and the character's appearance, choose sensory details that will help the reader see, feel, hear, and smell. (See pages 192–94.)

6. Be precise: Use specific and concrete nouns (not "he wore a sweater," but "he wore a red wool cardigan"). Use active and sharp verbs and adverbs; use vivid adjectives.

EXERCISE 27. Writing a First Draft of a Character Sketch. Using your plan from Exercise 24 and the suggestions above, write a first draft of a character sketch. Allow your thoughts to flow freely. You will have an opportunity to evaluate and revise later.

Writing a First Draft of a Biographical Sketch

Write the first draft of your biographical sketch with the following suggestions in mind:

1. In your opening paragraph, arouse the audience's interest. Begin with an incident, a summary of the person's accomplishments, background information related to the person's accomplishments, or the person's birth. Notice how Untermeyer begins with background information in his sketch (page 217).

2. Include significant events and accomplishments only. They should be organized chronologically according to the major periods in the person's life.

3. You will have many events to relate, so be as concise as possible. Untermeyer dealt with Anthony's early childhood in one sentence: *Before she was five, precocious Susan could read and write.*

4. If there is any connection among events—cause and effect, for example—show that connection. As Untermeyer discusses the Civil War years, he shows how the Emancipation Proclamation affected Anthony's campaign for women's rights (page 219).

5. If the person is dead, you may end the sketch with the person's death or with a paragraph that ties together the person's major accomplishments. After Anthony's death, Untermeyer concludes with the passage of the Susan B. Anthony Amendment (page 220). If the person is still alive, you may want to end with a recent significant event, a summary, or a prediction of what the person might accomplish in the future.

EXERCISE 28. Writing a First Draft of a Biographical Sketch. Using your plan from Exercise 26, write the first draft of your biographical sketch. Follow the suggestions for biographical sketches above and remember that you will evaluate and revise later.

EVALUATING

Evaluating a First Draft

7t. Evaluate the first draft of your character sketch or biographical sketch.

As with any other writing, you should take time to evaluate your character sketches and biographical sketches. It may help to set your draft aside for awhile before you begin. If possible, share your draft with friends or classmates and listen carefully to their suggestions. You can use the following questions to evaluate your character sketches and biographical sketches. As you work, mark your draft to note places that need improvement.

GUIDELINES FOR EVALUATING CHARACTER SKETCHES AND BIOGRAPHICAL SKETCHES

Character Sketches

Character Development	1. Is the character shown in action? Are gestures, movements, and responses pictured vividly? Is speech used effectively to reveal character and feeling?
Setting	2. Does the setting help the reader see the character? Can the setting be visualized easily?
Descriptive Details	3. Do descriptive details make the character's dominant trait clear? Does the description effectively appeal to the senses? Do sensory images contribute to the total effect?
Word Choice	4. Are precise, specific, and vivid words used effectively? Does figurative language (similes and metaphors) make the description clearer and more colorful?
Tone	5. Does the tone of the character sketch suit the subject, the audience, and the purpose?

Biographical Sketches

Introduction	6. Does the introduction arouse the audience's interest?
Topic Development	7. Does the sketch include only the *major* accomplishments and events in the person's life?
Coherence	8. Have events and accomplishments been arranged chronologically into periods in the person's life?
Tone	9. Does the tone of the writing suit the purpose and the audience of the sketch?
Conclusion	10. Does the end satisfy the audience's need to know what happened to the person or where the person's life may be heading?

EXERCISE 29. **Evaluating Your Character Sketch.** Using the Guidelines for Evaluating Character Sketches on page 224, evaluate the character sketch you wrote for Exercise 27.

EXERCISE 30. **Evaluating Your Biographical Sketch.** Using the preceding guidelines, evaluate the biographical sketch you wrote for Exercise 28.

REVISING AND PROOFREADING

Revising and Proofreading Character Sketches and Biographical Sketches

7u. Revise and proofread your character sketch and your biographical sketch.

You can revise your character sketch and biographical sketch by applying the four revising techniques: adding, cutting, replacing, and reordering. The following chart suggests how you can use the techniques to improve your draft. After revising your draft, you should proofread it (see the guidelines on pages 32–33) and prepare a final copy.

REVISING CHARACTER AND BIOGRAPHICAL SKETCHES

PROBLEM	TECHNIQUE	REVISION
Character Sketches The character is not shown in action.	Cut/Add	Cut details that merely describe the character. Add scenes or details showing the character actually saying or doing something.
The character's speech does not show what he or she is like.	Replace	Think about the character's dominant trait and reword the dialogue so that it reflects this trait.

PROBLEM	TECHNIQUE	REVISION
The setting is hard to visualize.	Add	Add descriptive words to paint a vivid picture of the setting. (Ask a reader to describe the setting you created and compare this with what you intended to convey.)
There is so much descriptive detail that the dominant trait is not clear.	Cut/Add	Cut descriptive details that are unimportant. Review the character's main trait; then add details that specifically reveal it.
Descriptive details are dull and do not appeal to the senses.	Replace/Add	Replace details that are dull by consulting a dictionary or thesaurus for fresh descriptive words. Add similes or metaphors which create sharp images.
Biographical Sketches The beginning is dull.	Add	Add an incident, dialogue, or background material that will catch the audience's interest.
Too many minor accomplishments and events are included.	Cut	Cut accomplishments and events that are unimportant and that do not contribute to your purpose.
Events and accomplishments are in a confusing order.	Reorder	Rearrange events chronologically under each major heading or time period in the person's life so that the order is made clear.
The tone is inconsistent or is not right for the story.	Replace	Replace unsuitable details or words with ones that will fit your subject, purpose, and audience.

PROBLEM	TECHNIQUE	REVISION
The ending is unsatisfying or seems incomplete.	Replace	Replace the ending by adding an important recent accomplishment or a prediction. If the person is dead, make the ending meaningful by noting the person's overall accomplishments.

As you read the following paragraph from a character sketch, note the changes the writer made in the first draft.

My grandfather was attractive, but he was not handsome. He was too thin, even scrawny, was stooped from years of working over a machine in a factory. and he stooped when he walked. My grandmother was crazy about him! I think He was attractive, though, and his attractiveness came almost entirely from his personality. What made my special ability to see the humor in life. grandfather great was his sense of humor. He was soft-spoken and gentle, but he a twinkle in his eye and always had a big smile on his face. bright

1. Why did the writer shorten the first sentence?
2. Why do you think the writer added the information about working in a factory?
3. Why did the writer cut the third sentence?
4. Why did the writer reorder the last two sentences?
5. Why did the writer change the word *great* to *special* and add the phrase "had a twinkle in his eye"?

The following paragraphs are from the middle of a biographical sketch about an imaginary photographer. As you read them, study the changes the writer made.

When he was twenty-four, Harold Tinker sailed off to Europe, where he planned to establish his career in photography. After two years of adventure, the money he had inherited from his aunt had disappeared. He had visited cathedrals and museums and castles; dinner parties, tennis parties, and all kinds of he went to parties. He stayed in touch with his friends

back in the United States, even flying home for a good friend's birthday party.
While in Europe he kept pace with the European jet set and had no time for
~~he had such wonderful adventures that he~~
photography.

and He was forced to take photography seriously. He went back to the sights
cathedrals and the castles
with a new eye and determination. ~~His father had taken him to Washington~~
new
~~Cathedral when he was a child, and he had never forgotten it.~~ Tinker turned his
Still in need of money,
attention to the photography of people. The resulting collection was published
of photography
under the title *The Eye and the Spirit: Cathedrals and Castles of Western Europe.*

1. Why did the writer add the phrase to the first sentence?
2. Why did the writer move the second sentence?
3. Why did the writer cut two sentences?
4. Why did the writer add details to explain the types of parties and sights?
5. Why did the writer move the last sentence in the second paragraph?

EXERCISE 31. Revising and Proofreading Your Character Sketch.
Using the revising chart on pages 225–27 and the Guidelines for
Proofreading on pages 32–33, revise and proofread your character
sketch. Follow correct manuscript form or your teacher's directions to
prepare your final copy.

**EXERCISE 32. Revising and Proofreading Your Biographical
Sketch.** Using the revising chart on pages 225–27 and the Guidelines
for Proofreading on pages 32–33, revise and proofread your biographical sketch. Follow correct manuscript form or your teacher's directions
to make your final copy.

CHAPTER 7 WRITING REVIEW 1

Writing a Short Story. Write a short story about a nonphysical
struggle or conflict. The struggle may be a difficult decision or a
problem between two characters. Use the third-person omniscient point
of view.

PREWRITING   To select a conflict, use your journal, the newspaper or television, brainstorming, or interviews with other people. Then ask yourself questions about the conflict. What could happen? How could it happen? To whom could it happen? When could it happen? Why could it happen? Think about how you will reveal your characters' personalities. Will you use action, description, dialogue, or all three? What details will you include? Organize your information into the beginning, the middle, and the end of the story.

WRITING   Follow your plan, but feel free to make changes as you write. After an interesting beginning, build suspense toward the climax, or high point of the action. Include any details of setting that are important to the plot. Make dialogue brief, natural-sounding, and appropriate for your characters. Maintain a consistent third-person omniscient point of view and follow chronological order.

EVALUATING, REVISING, AND PROOFREADING   Set the story aside before you begin evaluating. Think about organization, character development, interest and suspense, and the beginning and ending as you use the evaluation guidelines on page 25. Then revise your draft by referring to the chart on pages 210–11, and proofread carefully, using the guidelines on pages 32–33. Be sure to prepare a neat final copy.

CHAPTER 7 WRITING REVIEW 2

Writing Character Sketches and Biographical Sketches.   Choose a real person who has made some significant contribution to society. The person may or may not be alive. Write both a character sketch and a biographical sketch of that person.

PREWRITING   Choose a person you have discussed in a class, seen on TV, or read about in a newspaper, magazine, or book. A subject might be someone from entertainment or athletics, from the sciences or professions, from business, or from the military. Use the questions on pages 213–14 to gather information for each sketch. Select an audience that would have a natural interest in the person you are writing about. Organize the information for a character sketch around a dominant characteristic. Organize the information for your biographical sketch chronologically, according to the major periods in the person's life.

WRITING   As you write your character sketch, keep the dominant characteristic in mind. Show your character in action, using description and speech to reveal character. Use sensory detail and vivid language to add interest.

As you write your biographical sketch, concentrate on major periods and significant achievements. Arouse the audience's interest in the beginning, and make sure the ending satisfies the audience's need to know what happened or what may happen to the person.

EVALUATING, REVISING, AND PROOFREADING   After you have written the sketches, ask a friend or classmate to make suggestions for changes. Use the evaluation guidelines on page 224 to locate areas that need improvement. Revise, referring to the chart on pages 225–27; proofread carefully, consulting the Guidelines for Proofreading on pages 32–33; and follow correct manuscript form (see pages 33–35) or your teacher's directions to make a clean copy.

CHAPTER 8

Writing a Research Paper

RESEARCH, WRITING, DOCUMENTATION

The research, or library, paper is a relatively long factual paper based on outside sources rather than personal knowledge.

A research paper is generally written in language suitable for an educated audience. It tends to be formal in tone and usually does not include personal comments by the writer. In other ways, however, a research paper is much like any other composition. It should be interesting, well written, and appropriate for its intended audience.

Preparing a research paper involves many steps. The steps are presented separately in this chapter, with examples and practice exercises at each stage.

PREWRITING

SELECTING A SUBJECT

8a. Begin with an interesting subject that is appropriate to your audience and purpose.

Your audience will be interested in your report if you give new and specific information about your subject. Therefore, you should avoid subjects your audience already knows well unless you have a new way of presenting them. On the other hand, you should also avoid highly technical or complex subjects that will be too difficult for your audience to understand.

Techniques for Prewriting. To find an appropriate subject for a research paper

● Thumb through the subject cards in your library's card catalog and list all the subjects that interest you.
● Skim articles in current magazines and newspapers for interesting subjects.
● Spend some time looking at the articles and pamphlets in your library's vertical file.
● When you have several possible subjects in mind, check the card catalog and *Readers' Guide to Periodical Literature* to find out what resources are available. Make sure your library has adequate and up-to-date information on the subject you select. If there does not seem to be enough available material, select another subject.

EXERCISE 1. **Evaluating Subjects for Research.** Each of the following subjects is a preliminary choice for a research report. Based on the preceding points, which of the subjects do you find appropriate? (Assume that you are writing for a general audience and that your only source of information is your school library.) Be prepared to explain your answers.

1. Discrimination against obese people in the United States
2. Operations in the mechanical drive of the Jarvik-7 artificial heart
3. Quality of life for artificial-heart transplant patients
4. Safe disposal of methyl isocyanate toxic waste
5. Simplified federal income tax proposals
6. Effectiveness of hijacking-prevention procedures at major U.S. airports
7. Combating street-gang violence in large U.S. cities
8. Lengthening life through macrobiotic dieting
9. Job discrimination against attractive women
10. The new poor in America—the unemployed factory worker

EXERCISE 2. Selecting Subjects for Research. Write down five preliminary subjects for a research paper. When choosing subjects, follow the techniques listed on page 232.

GETTING AN OVERVIEW OF YOUR SUBJECT

8b. Use library resources to get an overview of your subject.

Reading general articles and scanning books to get an overview, or broad understanding, of your subject will help you decide how to limit the subject. An overview will also help you determine what questions about your subject you want to answer through your research. You may know, for example, that you want to write about the brain's communication system—how signals that control or affect human thoughts, emotions, and perceptions are sent and received. By getting an overview of the subject, you can determine that you need answers to questions such as the following ones: (1) What roles do both electricity and chemicals play in the brain's communication system? (2) How is the structure of the nerve cell designed for efficient communication? (3) What happens when this vital communication system breaks down?

Techniques for Prewriting. To get an overview of your subject

- Start by reading two or three general articles in reference books such as encyclopedias, atlases, and almanacs. Note how the subject is divided. The headings and subheadings in the article may suggest ways to limit the subject or important subdivisions to cover in your report.
- Find your subject in the *Readers' Guide* and read the descriptions of all articles listed there. Jot down any general questions or topic ideas that come to mind.
- Using the subject cards in your library's card catalog, locate two or three books on your subject. Read the jacket flaps (if any) and look carefully at the chapter headings in the table of contents. Use this information to think about limited topics and general questions to guide your research.
- Look up your subject in the vertical file, quickly read through any pamphlets and articles available, and write down questions or ideas that come to mind after your reading.

EXERCISE 3. Forming an Overview.   Select a subject for a research paper from the preliminary subjects you developed for Exercise 2. Then carry out all the suggestions listed in the Techniques for Prewriting on page 233.

LIMITING THE SUBJECT TO A SUITABLE TOPIC

8c. Limit the subject to a topic that can be treated in sufficient detail.

In this textbook the word *subject* refers to a broad area. The word *topic* refers to a much more limited area that can be treated in detail given the length and scope of a piece of writing. When limiting a subject, you must remember not only your audience and the resources of your library but also the limitations of time and space. The general subject of the brain, for example, would probably appeal to a wide audience, and it is likely that your library would have a great many sources with information about it. That subject, however, is obviously too large (a vast number of books have been written on it) and must be limited to a suitable topic.

As you think about limiting your subject, remember that most subjects are too general for these reasons:

1. The subject covers too many years.

EXAMPLES   Seventy-five years of space research [Seventy-five years is a long time. A suitable topic, which limits the time covered, is the space shuttle, a project developed only within the last twenty years.]

Women's fashions through the years [*Years* may include every year since the beginning of time. One suitably limited topic is the "dress for success" movement among women during the 1980's.]

2. The subject covers too great a geographical area.

EXAMPLES   Public-housing problems in the United States [Every major city in the United States has housing supported by city, state, or federal funding. A suitably limited topic could focus on specific problems in one major city, perhaps your own.]

Fads among the world's teen-agers [Fads differ among teen-agers throughout the world. Limit the subject to a topic you can treat in enough detail to be interesting, such as the strange fads of American college students during the 1950's who swallowed goldfish and stuffed themselves into telephone booths.]

3. The subject has too many parts, or features.

EXAMPLES The brain [This subject includes many parts, such as brain structure and chemistry, mental retardation, sensory perception, movement, mental illness, creativity, learning and memory, and sleep. A topic limited to one part of the brain is the use of recent brain research to improve memory.]

Long life [This broad subject includes such parts as people who have lived extraordinarily long lives, reasons for longevity, the practice of cell rejuvenation, and special diets for prolonging life. A suitably limited topic might be a report on new research about how diet and exercise can prolong life.]

EXERCISE 4. Analyzing Broad Subjects. Analyze each of the following subjects to decide why it is too broad for a high-school research report. Does the subject cover too many years or too great a distance? Does it have too many parts? Is it too broad for a combination of these reasons?

1. Personal computers
2. Bandits through history
3. High-school grading systems
4. The history of money
5. Americans and their pets

EXERCISE 5. Developing Limited Topics. Develop five limited topics for the subject you used in Exercise 3. Before deciding on the topics, think about your audience, the resources of your library, and the length of your paper. Refer to pages 234–35 for more help in limiting subjects.

DEVELOPING A PURPOSE STATEMENT

8d. Once you know more about the specific information needed to develop your topic, write a purpose statement.

A *purpose statement* is simply one or more sentences that state what you plan to accomplish in your paper.

EXAMPLES I plan to explain the causes of the 1984 drought in Ethiopia and to discuss steps to prevent future droughts.

> I will explain the basic structure of the brain's nerve cells and discuss how the structure works to send signals back and forth through the brain.

The purpose statement will not appear in your final paper. As you will recall, sentences beginning with phrases such as "I plan to describe . . ." are not effective beginnings for any type of writing. Also, during your research you will probably find or delete information that will change your purpose statement. You might, for example, add a description of the *effects* of the Ethiopian drought on the inhabitants of that country and so revise the purpose statement as follows:

> I plan to explain the causes of the 1984 drought in Ethiopia, to describe its effects on the inhabitants, and to discuss steps to prevent future droughts.

EXERCISE 6. Forming a Purpose Statement. Choose one of the five limited topics you developed for Exercise 5 and write a purpose statement.

DEVELOPING A PRELIMINARY OUTLINE

8e. Develop a preliminary outline to guide your research.

A preliminary outline is simply an informal list of ideas to cover in your paper in the order that you plan to cover them. The headings in this first outline come from the general information gathered during the overview stage and from your purpose statement. The outline does not have to be detailed; its purpose is to guide and organize your research.

The order of headings in your outline reflects your purpose. If you plan to discuss research on communication within the brain, you might first discuss early research and then proceed to the present (chronological order). If you plan to describe the structure of a nerve cell, you might describe how it appears under an electron microscope as your eye scans the cell (spatial order).

As you begin your research, you will probably find some subheadings that do not belong in this preliminary outline and discover new subheadings that should be added. Throughout your research, you will add, delete, and rearrange material in the preliminary outline.

Following is a preliminary outline for a research paper about how brain cells send and receive information.

REACHING ACROSS THE GAP:
COMMUNICATION IN THE HUMAN BRAIN

Early knowledge of brain function
    Heart as center of body
    Brain as center of body
Electricity as basis for brain communication
Chemicals as basis for brain communication
Basic nature of nerve cell
    Axon
    Dendrite
    Synapse
Breakdown of brain communication system
    Physical illness
    Mental illness
New research on brain communication system

Notice that this informal outline, unlike the formal outline, does not use a numbering system and that it is a topic, rather than sentence, outline. If your teacher directs you to use a formal sentence outline, review pages 120–22.

EXERCISE 7. Developing a Preliminary Outline. Develop a preliminary outline for your research paper topic, using information from the overview and purpose statement. Use the outline form your teacher prefers.

LOCATING SOURCES AND GATHERING INFORMATION

8f. Locate sources with specific information about your topic.

You can find specific information necessary for detailed, interesting writing in sources such as books, magazines, newspapers, journals, governmental and other types of pamphlets, films, radio and television programs, and so on. You can often begin locating these sources through encyclopedias, where articles on various topics often refer readers to more specific sources. Books usually have bibliographies on their topics, and the subject cards in the library's card catalog can again be a valuable aid. (See pages 647–61 for more help using the library to locate information.) Once you have located a source, always evaluate its usefulness.

Techniques for Prewriting. To evaluate a source's usefulness, ask yourself the following questions:

- How current is this information? What is the copyright date? (If your topic is the last presidential election, a book published in 1982 will be of little use.)
- Is the author an expert on this topic? Can this author be relied on to give accurate information and to discuss the topic fairly? (For a report on the drawbacks of contact lenses, an article written by a noted eye surgeon is a better source than a pamphlet published by a company that makes contact lenses.)
- Do encyclopedias or other books list this source in their bibliographies? (A source that appears more than once in your research is usually reliable.)
- If the source is an article, does it appear in a reputable, special-interest magazine written to inform readers (*Science, Smithsonian, American Heritage*) or in a magazine designed primarily to amuse and entertain? Does the magazine have a reputation for treating topics accurately and knowledgeably?
- If the source is an article, how long is it? (A fifteen-page special report will provide more information than a four-paragraph article.)
- If the source is a book, have you examined the table of contents or index to determine how many pages are devoted to your topic? (A book with three chapters on your topic will be more useful than one that treats the topic in two pages.)

COMPILING A WORKING BIBLIOGRAPHY

8g. Prepare a working bibliography.

A working bibliography is a list of sources you consult during your research. For convenience, keep entries in a working bibliography on separate note cards, one card for each source. Each card should have all of the information illustrated below. This information will be extremely important as you prepare your final bibliography, so check the information carefully against the source. For a book, most of the necessary information appears on the title and copyright pages. General publishing information about a magazine (date, volume, issue) is usually found on the first two or three pages of the issue.

EXAMPLES *Working bibliography card for a book*

Source number circled

call number

Author

Title

Publs. infor.

②

616.89

Andreasen, Nancy C. The Broken
Brain: The Biological
Revolution in Psychiatry.
New York: Harper & Row, 1984.

(*book from city library*)

Special infor. locate book

Working bibliography card for an article

①

Alper, Joseph. "Biology
and Mental Illness."
Atlantic Monthly
Dec. 1984: 70-76.

(*On microfilm; see Mr. Griffin*)

Techniques for Prewriting.   To prepare bibliography cards

- Record all necessary information about the source.
- Use punctuation correctly.
- Number bibliography cards consecutively in the upper right corner. (Later, when you take notes, you can identify the source of each note simply by repeating this source number.)
- Write each book's call number under the source number.
- Write any special information at the bottom of the card.

EXERCISE 8. Evaluating Sources. Using your limited topic, locate at least three books and two magazine articles that give specific information about it. Evaluate each source by answering the questions listed in the prewriting techniques on page 238.

EXERCISE 9. Preparing Bibliography Cards. Prepare a working bibliography card for each source that you used in Exercise 8. For each card, provide the information shown in the examples on page 239.

TAKING NOTES FROM YOUR SOURCES

8h. Take notes on material that relates directly to a heading or subheading in your preliminary outline.

At this point, discard sources that do not relate to headings or subheadings in your outline or that cannot help you achieve your paper's purpose. Once you have decided on sources, use note cards as a convenience in recording information. For each note on a different heading or subheading, use a new card. Change cards also when you move to a different source. Even though each source may treat the same heading or subheading, make sure you keep the sources on separate cards.

Before taking notes, read quickly over the relevant material in each of your sources. This reading will help you absorb general information.

There are three ways to take notes:

1. *Summarize.* Summarize when you need to capture only the main ideas of a passage. When summarizing, use your own words to record information.

2. *Paraphrase.* Paraphrase, or restate in your own words, when you want to record the specific facts or ideas in a passage. (For more information on summarizing and paraphrasing, see pages 703–705.)

3. *Quote.* Quote when the author's language, as well as ideas, is important. Copy the author's material word for word. When quoting, always check your notes against the original material to be certain that you have copied exactly. Also, include the exact page or pages from which you have quoted; place quotation marks around the author's exact words.

EXAMPLE

Mental illness ②

Schizophrenia may be caused by "overheated" circuits — too many messages sent and received

page 222

Techniques for Prewriting. To take notes from a source

- Put the number you assigned to that source in the upper right corner of the note card.
- Include a "slug" (a heading or subheading from your preliminary outline that the note develops) in the upper left corner of the note card.
- Do not put notes about two different headings or subheadings on the same card.
- Do not put notes from different sources on the same card.
- Write the page number on which the information appears in the bottom right corner of the note card.
- Think carefully about the kind of notes you want to take from a source: *summarize* to record main ideas; *paraphrase* to record specific facts or information; and *quote exactly* to record an author's language and ideas.

EXERCISE 10. Taking Notes. Take notes on the sources for your topic. For each note card, be prepared to indicate whether you have summarized, paraphrased, or quoted the material. Prepare your note cards as directed above.

Indicating Sources on Note Cards

Giving authors credit for their words and ideas is called documentation. Failing to document constitutes plagiarism. (The word *plagiarism* comes from a Latin word meaning "kidnapper.") Whether you summarize, paraphrase, or quote, you must acknowledge words and ideas that are not your own. It is not necessary, however, to acknowledge the following information:

1. *Information that is general knowledge.* This is information that can easily be found in general reference sources such as dictionaries and encyclopedias. (The capital of Mexico is Mexico City.)

2. *Information that most educated people know.* (The brain is made up of nerve cells. Snow is formed when particles of water vapor freeze in the upper air and fall to the ground.)

3. *Information you routinely acquire from public sources such as radio, television, magazines, and newspapers.* (The winter of 1978 was one of the coldest in Chicago's history. Future plans for space shuttles include retrieving communications satellites.)

When preparing your note cards, scrupulously record source information and page references. Also, in the beginning stages of research paper writing, remember that a good policy to follow is, "When in doubt, document."

PREPARING THE FINAL OUTLINE

8i. Prepare a final outline from which you will write your paper.

A final outline, from which the first draft of your paper is written, is usually a formal outline. (See pages 120–22.) Your teacher will indicate whether you should prepare a topic or a sentence outline.

Following is a final outline for the research paper on brain communication. How does this outline differ from the preliminary outline on page 237?

REACHING ACROSS THE GAP:
COMMUNICATION IN THE HUMAN BRAIN

  I. Early knowledge of human brain
    A. Early belief in heart as center of life
    B. Later discovery of brain as center
 II. Knowledge of brain communication process
    A. Galvani's discovery of electricity's role
    B. Woewi's discovery of chemical role

III. Nerve cells as center of brain communication
   A. Structure of cell
      1. Nucleus
      2. Axon
      3. Dendrites
   B. Importance of synapse
      1. Role of electricity
      2. Role of chemicals
IV. Breakdown in brain communication system
   A. Results
      1. Physical illness
      2. Mental illness
   B. Causes
 V. New research in brain communication
   A. Research into development of synapses
   B. Applications of knowledge for improving quality of human life

Techniques for Prewriting. To prepare a final outline, ask yourself these questions:

- What general categories do the notes fall into? What headings best describe each category? (For example, a stack of note cards on the early history of research in brain communication might have the heading "Early history.")
- How will the first and last headings identify the content of the paper's introduction and conclusion? (The words *introduction* and *conclusion* do not appear in the outline.)
- What new headings or subheadings should be added to the outline? What items in the preliminary outline should be omitted or changed?
- Are Roman numerals, capital letters, and Arabic numerals used correctly to indicate smaller and smaller divisions of the topic? (See pages 120–22 in Chapter 5.)
- Are all subtopics under a heading closely related to that particular heading? (For help in organizing ideas, see pages 120–22.)
- Are items arranged in a logical order that will be easy for readers to follow?

EXERCISE 11. Preparing a Final Outline. Sort through your note cards, making at least three stacks, and give each stack a general heading describing its contents. Then decide on the content of your introduction and conclusion, and give each a heading. Prepare a final outline, writing the headings in a logical order. Refer to the example on pages 242–43.

REVIEW EXERCISE. Analyzing the Steps in Planning a Research Paper. In this chapter, the steps in planning a research paper are taught in a particular order. Discuss problems you might encounter by omitting, reordering, or changing any of the steps listed below.

1. Selecting a subject
2. Getting an overview of the subject
3. Developing a suitable topic
4. Developing a purpose statement
5. Developing a preliminary outline
6. Locating and gathering information
7. Compiling a working bibliography
8. Taking notes from the sources
9. Preparing the final outline

WRITING

WRITING THE FIRST DRAFT

8j. Know the correct form for the research paper.

The format of a research paper includes such aspects as how sources are documented, how pages are numbered, how the bibliography is presented, and so on. The format described in this chapter is that of the Modern Language Association (MLA), a highly respected organization of English language and literature scholars. There are, however, other acceptable formats for preparing research papers; your teacher may prefer that you use one of these other styles.

8k. Begin with a rough draft.

A rough draft is your first attempt to write in a logical order the material that supports your purpose statement. Before you begin this draft, organize your note cards according to your final outline, using the logical order appropriate for your topic. (See also pages 242–43.) Once again, discard any material that does not relate to the headings in your final outline.

As you write, you may find that each item in your outline develops easily into one or two paragraphs. However, you may also find that you lack sufficient details on a particular topic and must do more research. If so, stop immediately and gather the additional information before you continue your first draft.

When writing your rough draft, you should pay particular attention to two matters of format: documenting sources and incorporating quotations.

Documenting Sources

In your research paper, you should document the material used. This documentation may take the form of notes within the paper, called *internal* or *parenthetical* notes; notes at the bottom of each page, called *footnotes;* or notes at the end of the paper, called *endnotes.* Your teacher will indicate which form you should use.

The latest *MLA Handbook for Writers of Research Papers* (1984) recommends that parenthetical notes follow summarized, paraphrased, or quoted material. This parenthetical information is usually very brief; its main purpose is to refer the reader to the complete source information in the bibliography at the paper's end. Use the following MLA guidelines to document sources within your paper:

1. When you use an author's words or ideas, follow them with a pair of parentheses in which you place the author's last name and the page number or numbers from which the information was taken. (Complete information about the source will be in the bibliography.) There is no punctuation between the author's last name and the page reference. The words *page* and *pages* and their abbreviations do not appear in the parentheses. Place your final punctuation mark after the parentheses. Follow quoted material with closing quotation marks. Then insert the necessary parenthetical information, followed by the closing punctuation mark.

EXAMPLE The Spanish neurologist Santiago Ramon y Cajal once referred to each of the individual cells that make up this network as "the aristocrat among the structures of the body, with its giant arm stretched out like the tentacles of an octopus" (Restak 26).

2. If your bibliography has two or more entries by authors with the same last name, use both the first and last names of each author.

EXAMPLE (Richard Restak 26) (John Restak 93)

3. If the work has more than one author, use all the last names or the last name of the first author followed by *et al.* (and others). Do not use a comma between *et al.* and the page reference.

EXAMPLE (Ornstein and Thompson 134–138) (Roby et al. 22)

4. If the author's name is used within the text of your paper, add parenthetical page numbers only to identify the location of the material you used.

EXAMPLE Ornstein and Thompson point out that the connections that seem actually to determine the quality of life are not simple: "The mind cannot exist in a single identified nerve cell, or even in many thousands of them; it is the product of the interaction among the myriad neurons in the vertebrate brain" (81).

5. Parenthetical information about your source is best placed at the end of the sentence that contains the information, as close as possible to the material to which it refers. End punctuation for the phrase, clause, or sentence containing the parentheses follows the parentheses.

EXAMPLE This electrical force, Galvani believed, was produced by the brain and stored in the nerves for later use (Restak 31). It seemed that this electrical current, which the French writer Montaigne described as a "miraculous force," was used to send signals by the brain throughout the body (Restak 30).

Study the sample research paper on pages 255–59 for more examples of documentation.

EXERCISE 12. Preparing Documentation. First, summarize the following information on the history of medicine in the United States. In your summary, use at least one quotation. Then paraphrase the same information, using at least one different quotation. In both your summary and paraphrase, use parenthetical notes to document the source.

Most ailments were, in the terminology of the day, "self-limited." In the great majority of cases a patient could expect to recover—with or without the physician's ministrations. This was understood and acted upon; even the wealthy did not ordinarily call a physician immediately except in the case of severe injury or an illness with an abrupt and alarming onset. The decision to seek medical help would be made gradually; first a family member might be consulted, then a neighbor, finally perhaps a storekeeper who stocked drugs and patent medicines—all before turning to a doctor. Many housewives kept "recipe books" that included everything from recipes for apple pie and soap to remedies for rheumatism and croup. Guides to "domestic practice" were a staple for publishers and peddlers. It is no wonder that doctors a century ago were so critical of the care provided by what they dismissed as uneducated and irresponsible laymen.

(This selection is from page 24 of an article by Charles E. Rosenberg, appearing in the October/November 1984 issue of *American Heritage* magazine.)

Incorporating Quotations

Quotations should be worked into the general text of your paper. Use the following MLA guidelines to include quotations in your paper:

1. Use quotations sparingly, only when the author's words, as well as ideas, are important.

2. Copy the quotation exactly as it appears in the source, including capitalization and punctuation. Place quotation marks around the author's exact words.

3. If the quotation is a short piece of prose (four lines or less), run it into your text. Remember that you do not always have to quote whole sentences. You may quote only a word or phrase that you place within your own sentence.

EXAMPLE Joseph Jacobs Thorndike describes his ancestor of eight generations back, George Jacobs. In Salem, Massachusetts, in 1692, Jacobs was accused of witchcraft and brought to court before examining magistrates. As he confronted his accusers, Jacobs said, "You tax me for a wizard. You may as well tax me for a buzzard" (Thorndike 82).

4. Long prose quotations (more than four lines) are set off from the text. Indent the quotation ten spaces from your paper's left margin, without using quotation marks. Introduce the quotation in your own words, followed by a colon. Even if the quotation is a complete paragraph, do not indent the first line.

EXAMPLE In her book *An Unfinished Woman,* Lillian Hellman describes how, as a child, she learned the pleasures of reading while sitting in a fig tree:

It was in that tree that I learned to read, filled with the passions that can only come to the bookish, grasping, very young, bewildered by almost all of what I read, sweating in the attempt to understand a world of adults I fled from in real life but desperately wanted to join in books. (I did not connect the grown men and women in literature with the grown men and women I saw around me. They were, to me, another species) (84).

5. Occasionally, you may need to shorten a quotation by leaving out words. Use an ellipsis, three periods with a space between each period (. . .), to show where words have been omitted.

EXAMPLE   According to Ornstein and Thompson, "the mind . . . is the product of the interaction among the myriad neurons in the vertebrate brain" (81).

8l. Remember to use paragraph- and essay-writing skills.

Writing a research paper involves many technical points, so it is sometimes difficult to remember to apply the paragraph- and essay-writing skills you use with other types of writing. Your research paper should have an effective introduction and conclusion; ideas should be arranged logically; and transitions should smoothly link paragraphs. In addition, enough specific details should be included to make the writing interesting. (See pages 124–34 for help on writing effective compositions.)

EXERCISE 13. Writing a First Draft. Following the final outline, write the first draft of your research paper. First organize your note cards in the order listed in your final outline. Follow the MLA format for documenting sources and for incorporating quotations into your text. As you write, apply the paragraph- and essay-writing skills you have already learned. Also, review the Guidelines for Writing Research Papers on page 260.

EVALUATING AND REVISING

EVALUATING A FIRST DRAFT

8m. Evaluate the content, organization, style, and format of your research paper.

Considering the length of a research paper, it is wise to concentrate on evaluating one aspect at a time. You should also pay particular attention to the paper's format, especially to documenting sources and to incorporating quotations from your research. Use the following guidelines to evaluate your research paper.

GUIDELINES FOR EVALUATING RESEARCH PAPERS

Introduction	1. Does the introduction clearly state the purpose of the paper? Does it catch the audience's attention?
Topic Development	2. Does each paragraph in the body develop one idea about the topic? Does each paragraph include specific details and examples?
Topic Development	3. Is there enough information for readers to follow the line of reasoning? Is there any unrelated or unnecessary information? Are quotations and ideas from sources incorporated into the text?
Conclusion	4. Does the end of the paper obviously conclude the presentation and reinforce the main ideas?
Coherence	5. Are ideas about the topic presented in a logical order? Are there clear and logical transitions, or connections, between paragraphs and between major sections in the paper?
Word Choice	6. Are technical terms and unusual vocabulary defined or explained? Does the language reveal the serious tone appropriate for a research paper? Does the title clearly indicate the paper's topic?
Format	7. Have sources been documented in the text, using the MLA format (parenthetical notes) or some other acceptable format? Have short quotations been incorporated into the text? Have longer quotations been set off from the text?

CRITICAL THINKING:
Evaluating a First Draft

When you make judgments by applying criteria to your writing, you use the critical thinking skill of *evaluation*. In doing so, you must bring together and apply not only specific information about writing a research paper, but also general information about writing paragraphs and essays. The following two paragraphs are from the first draft of the sample research paper on brain communication (see pages 254–59). As you read the paragraphs, be prepared to discuss the following questions:

1. What inaccuracies are there in the documentation of sources, using MLA format?
2. How accurately, according to MLA format, are quotations placed within the text?
3. Do these paragraphs display effective paragraph- and essay-writing skills? Is the introduction effective? Are ideas arranged logically? Are the transitions between sentences and paragraphs smooth? Is the topic of each paragraph developed with sufficient specific detail? Be prepared to give reasons for your answers.
4. What details should be omitted because they do not relate to topics in the final outline on pages 242–43?
5. What suggestions do you have for revising these paragraphs?

REACHING ACROSS THE GAP:
COMMUNICATION IN THE HUMAN BRAIN

Little was known about the function of the brain until after the 14th century. It was only then that scientists finally understood the basic function of the brain. Before then, scientists believed that the heart, in the center of the body, was the organ that controlled thoughts and feelings. It was an early observation that when the heart stopped beating, the body became cold. The heart had provided heat to all parts of the body. Then scientists learned that blood vessels from the heart went to all parts of the body. Today, scientists know so much about the heart that heart transplants can be performed. (Restak, *The Brain*, pp. 21–24.)

Scientists learned that the brain controlled thoughts and emotions, but how did the brain send this information? Scientists also knew that the brain and the body were made up of individual cells. How did communication take place between the cells? In the 18th century Galvani used the muscles of frogs to show that living creatures contained electricity. (Even then animals were used for scientific experimentation.) It seemed that this electrical current, which the French writer Montaigne described as a "miraculous force" (Restak, 30), could be used to send signals throughout the body. Galvani was not the first to know about electrical forces in living creatures. Pictures on ancient Egyptian tombs proved that Egyptians knew about electric catfish.

EXERCISE 14. Evaluating Your First Draft. Using the guidelines on page 249, evaluate the first draft of your research paper. You may also refer to the Guidelines for Evaluating Expository Compositions on pages 134–35. Keep notes, either on your draft or on a separate sheet of paper, about items you need to improve. It may also be helpful to exchange papers with a classmate and to evaluate each other's papers. If you do so, take and exchange notes about problems in the draft.

REVISING A FIRST DRAFT

8n. Make revisions to improve your first draft.

By evaluating your draft, you identify strengths and weaknesses in your research paper. To make the changes necessary to improve your paper, you should analyze each problem you have discovered and determine what can be done to correct the problem. You can apply any or all of four techniques to revise your draft: adding, cutting, reordering, and replacing. To revise the draft of your research paper, use the chart on pages 136–38, Revising Expository Compositions.

EXERCISE 15. Revising the First Draft. Revise the first draft of your research paper. Before you begin, you may want to review the revising chart on pages 136–38.

PREPARING A FINAL VERSION

PREPARING THE FINAL COPY

8o. Proofread the final draft and prepare a clean copy using correct manuscript form.

Preparing the final copy of your paper consists of proofreading and preparing a clean copy. To proofread you should check for and correct errors in usage, grammar, and mechanics. Then you should rewrite your final draft, incorporating the corrections you made in proofreading. To prepare this clean copy, use the following MLA guidelines or your teacher's specific instructions.

1. Type or write your paper neatly and legibly on one side of acceptable paper.

2. Leave one-inch margins at the top, bottom, and sides of your pages.

3. Double-space throughout, including title, quotations, and bibliography.

4. Place your name, information about your class, and the date on separate lines starting one inch from the top of the first page, even with the left margin. Double-space between these lines. Center the title, with double-spacing between the information at the top of the page and the title. Double-space twice between the title and the first line of your paper. Do not put quotation marks around the title.

5. Number pages consecutively throughout your paper, including bibliography pages. Place page numbers in the upper right corner of each page, one-half inch below the top of the page and fairly close to the right margin. Use a number without the word *page* or *pages* or their abbreviations.

EXERCISE 16. Proofreading the Final Draft. Using the proofreading guidelines on pages 32–33, proofread your final draft.

EXERCISE 17. Preparing a Clean Copy. Prepare a clean copy of your final draft, following the preceding MLA guidelines or your teacher's instructions. Then proofread once again. Your teacher may allow you to make brief (and very neat) corrections on the clean copy, but if you have many corrections, you may need to recopy the paper a second time.

PREPARING THE BIBLIOGRAPHY

8p. Prepare a list of the works you have cited in your research paper.

The bibliography, or "Works Cited," gives the reader complete information about sources used in the paper. Do not include general reference sources, such as encyclopedias, that you used in your overview unless they are referred to specifically in your report. The MLA guidelines for preparing a bibliography follow:

1. Begin the bibliography on a separate page from the text of the paper itself. Continue numbering pages from the text. For example, if your research paper ends on page 13, the first page of your bibliography will be page 14.

2. Center the words *Works Cited* one inch from the top of the page.

3. Double-space between the title and the first entry. Begin the first entry even with the left margin. If the entry runs more than one line, indent all other lines five spaces from the left margin. Double-space all lines in entries and double-space between entries.

EXAMPLE   Alper, Joseph. "Biology and Mental Illness." The Atlantic Dec.
          1984:70–76.

4. For books, give information in the following order: author's name, book title, place of publication, name of publisher, and date of publication. Alphabetize entries by the author's last name, followed by a comma and then his or her first name. Place a period after the author's name and skip two spaces before the book's title. Underline the title, placing a period after it. Then skip two spaces and write the city of publication (if more than one city appears on the copyright page, use the first city listed), followed by a colon, a space, and the name of the publishing company. Follow this name with a comma and the year of publication. End every entry with a period.

EXAMPLE   Andreasen, Nancy C. The Broken Brain: The Biological Revolution
          in Psychiatry. New York: Harper & Row, 1984.

For a book by two or more authors, list the names as they are shown on the title page (not necessarily alphabetized). Reverse only the name of the first author, and add a comma.

EXAMPLE   Wender, Paul H., and Donald F. Klein. Mind, Mood, and Medicine:
          A Guide to the New Biopsychiatry. New York: Farrar, Straus &
          Giroux, 1981.

5. For articles from magazines published every week or every two weeks, you need the following information: the author's name (last name first); the title of the article (in quotation marks); the title of the periodical (underlined); the day, month (abbreviated), and year of the issue; a colon, a space, and the page number or numbers of the article. Place periods after the author's name, after the title of the article, and at the end of the entry. (Note: May, June, and July are not abbreviated.)

EXAMPLE   Shreve, Anita. "The Working Mother as a Role Model." New York
Times Magazine 9 Sept. 1984: 39–54.

6. For magazines published monthly, give the month or months of publication and the year, but not the day.

EXAMPLE   Alper, Joseph. "Biology and Mental Illness." The Atlantic Dec.
1984: 70–76.

7. For newspapers (daily), follow the format for magazines published every week or two weeks. If the newspaper appears in sections and each section begins numbering anew, add the section number followed by a colon and the page number or numbers. (See the final entry of the sample research paper bibliography on page 259.)

EXERCISE 18. Preparing a Bibliography. On a sheet of paper, center the heading "Bibliography" or "Works Cited" (without quotation marks) as your teacher directs. Then prepare a final bibliography that lists each of the following sources. Alphabetize the entries and use the MLA format for entry content, format, and punctuation.

1. A book by Isaac Asimov published by Houghton Mifflin (Boston) in 1984 titled *Opus 300*
2. An article by Victoria Horstmann titled "Career Metamorphosis," published in the magazine *Working Woman* in the May 1984 issue on pages 114–117
3. A book published in 1980 by Harcourt Brace Jovanovich (Orlando) titled *A Double Discovery: A Journey,* written by Jessamyn West
4. An article by Herbert R. Lottman published in the weekly periodical *Publishers Weekly* titled "What's New in France's Publishing Capital," appearing on pages 22–40 of the November 9, 1984, issue

EXERCISE 19. Preparing a Final Bibliography. Using your working bibliography cards, prepare the final list of works cited for your research paper. Refer to the sample bibliography on page 259 and use the MLA format described in this chapter.

A Sample Research Paper

REACHING ACROSS THE GAP:
COMMUNICATION IN THE HUMAN BRAIN

For thousands of years, the brain has been a source of wonder. Protected as it is by the thick bones of the skull, the brain has never been easily studied. In fact, so little was known about the brain

Leave one-inch margins at top, sides, and bottom.
Center and double-space title.
Double-space paper throughout.

that it was not until after the fourteenth century that its basic function was finally understood. Before that time, most scholars believed that the heart, in the center of the body, controlled thoughts and feelings. This belief was reinforced by the early observation that when the heart stopped beating, life stopped, and the body became cold. Such an event seemed to show that the heart, during life, had provided heat to all parts of the body and was thus central to its being. By the fifteenth century, scientists had learned that blood vessels coming from the heart spread out into the body. Again, this design seemed to confirm the central role of the heart in human life (Restak 21–24).

Parenthetical information includes author's last name and page reference.

Only by the eighteenth century did scientists learn that the brain, not the heart, determined thoughts, emotions, movements, and so on. By then they also knew that, in some way, the brain received and processed information from all over the body and then sent back "directions" for action. In addition, scientists, who had known for some time that the brain, like the rest of the body, was made up of individual cells, reasoned that communication was somehow taking place between the cells. The knowledge that remained missing for many more years was exactly how this communication was accomplished. How did the brain, in less than a split second, receive a message from a finger touching a red-hot iron and then return the message to the finger, telling it to move? Even more baffling, how did the brain send and receive information that caused one person to behave "normally" and another to hear voices and see images that were not there? The beginning of an answer to these questions lay in a frog's leg.

In the late eighteenth century an Italian scientist named Luigi Galvani, using the leg muscles of frogs, showed that the bodies of living creatures contain electricity. He demonstrated this fact by exposing the muscles on either leg of a frog. When one exposed muscle was placed against another, the second muscle twitched, obviously in response to a force coming from the first muscle. This electrical force, Galvani believed, was produced by the brain and stored in the nerves for later use (Restak 31). It seemed that this electrical current, which the French writer Montaigne described as a "miraculous force" (Restak 30), was used to send signals from the brain throughout the body.

Thanks to Galvani, scientists were getting closer to understanding the mystery of communication within the brain. By the end of the nineteenth century, they knew that electricity flowed within the brain and between the brain and other parts of the body, but they still were not certain how information was actually carried by the current. In 1921, Austrian scientist Otto Woewi performed an experiment showing that certain chemicals played an important role in carrying signals to and from the brain (Gilling and Brightwell 128).

Today, scientists know that brain communication involves both electricity and chemicals. This electrochemical process begins in each of the ten billion or more nerve cells that make up the brain. Each nerve cell, or *neuron*, consists of a *nucleus*, or center, and a number of fibers. Each cell body has one long, thick fiber called an *axon*. At the other end of the cell, however, small hair-like fibers called *dendrites* (from the Greek word for "tree") branch out in all directions toward other cells.

This and the next paragraph develop the second major topic of the final outline.

source

source

Note the two authors for this source.

The words "brain communication" are used as a transition between the previous paragraph and this one.

Under a powerful microscope, this network of fibers, both axons and dendrites, is clearly visible. The Spanish neurologist Santiago Ramon y Cajal once referred to each of the individual cells that make up this network as "the aristocrat among the structures of the body, with its giant arms stretched out like the tentacles of an octopus" (Restak 267). Nerve cells within this network do not actually touch each other, however. Instead, each cell is separated from other cells by a gap called the *synapse*. It is across this synapse that communication within the brain actually takes place (Ornstein and Thompson 68).

> Incorporate quotations into your text, unless more than five lines.

> Final punctuation for this sentence is placed after the parentheses.

Communication from cell to cell begins when an electrical impulse travels down the axon of one cell to the synapse. At the synapse, small sacks of chemicals, called *neurotransmitters*, are stored. Under the right conditions, the sacks of chemicals are released. Once they burst from their sacks, they flow across the synapse to the dendrites of the second cell. In this way the electrical impulse that travels down the axon is translated to a chemical impulse when it reaches the synapse. Upon reaching the second cell, however, the chemical signal is translated back into an electrical impulse (Ornstein and Thompson 77–79).

> source

The second cell, the receiver of the electro-chemical signal, may or may not respond to the signal sent by the first cell. If it does respond, the cell sends an electrical impulse down its own axon, where the signal is ferried across the synapse in the form of a chemical impulse, and so on. The response of the receiver cell is crucial because without it no communication, and thus no movement, thought, emotion, and so on, takes place.

[*The next two pages of the paper, omitted here, describe what happens when the electrochemical system breaks down in some way. Both physical diseases, such as epilepsy, and mental diseases, such as schizophrenia, may result from malfunctions in chemical messengers.*]

Unfortunately, most researchers today believe that the breakdowns that may lead to physical and mental illnesses are more complex than a simple deficiency or excess of a particular chemical messenger. Certain cells might be stimulated too easily by the chemicals, thus firing too often. Or, once it crosses the synapse, the chemical might not be properly reabsorbed or broken down and continue causing cells to fire. Other scientists believe that even a slight change in the production of one chemical can throw an entire part of the system into chaos (Alper 427). Researchers are now learning that the system is simply more complex than has yet been imagined. As a result, a cure for diseases caused by breakdowns in the electrochemical system is much further away than had been hoped.

source

As research in brain communication continues, scientists are looking closely at the brain cells themselves—how they develop and how they mature. Although the brain is unable to replace damaged or dead brain cells, scientists have learned that the brain can establish new synapses, thus creating new pathways for new and more complex information to travel through the brain. These new pathways, scientists believe, are formed only when there is sensory stimulation from the environment. Thus, an environment rich in sights, sounds, smells, tastes, and textures, one that stimulates thinking and feeling, can actually lead to a more complex brain, capable of a much richer quality of life (Ornstein and Thompson 81).

Further research on the brain is almost certain to be on the brain's electrochemical communication system. A better knowledge of how this system works will help scientists to understand better how the brain develops and how it functions to control and affect thoughts, feelings, and sensory information from the outside world. Perhaps understanding the brain and its communication system can help us to provide the quality of environment that seems the right of every human being.

source

The last paragraph, the conclusion, develops the final subtopic of the outline.

A Sample Bibliography

WORKS CITED

Allen, Oliver E. "The State of Medical Care, 1984: An Interview with Dr. David E. Rogers." American Heritage Oct.–Nov. 1984:32–40.

Alper, Joseph. "Biology and Mental Illness." The Atlantic Dec. 1984:70–76.

Andreasen, Nancy C. The Broken Brain: The Biological Revolution in Psychiatry. New York: Harper & Row, 1984.

Gilling, Dick, and Robin Brightwell. The Human Brain. New York: Facts on File Publications, 1982.

Ornstein, Robert, and Richard F. Thompson. The Amazing Brain. Boston: Houghton Mifflin, 1984.

Restak, Richard. The Brain. Toronto: Bantam, 1984.

Wender, Paul H., and Donald F. Klein. Mind, Mood, and Medicine: A Guide to the New Biopsychiatry. New York: Farrar, Straus & Giroux, 1981.

Wolfson, Jill. "Increased Funding Adds Troops to Battle Against Alzheimer's." Chicago Tribune 22 July 1984, sec. 6: 1+.

(*Note:* When you study the sample bibliography, refer to pages 252–54. The "1+" in the last entry indicates that the article begins on page one of section six and continues on following pages.)

CHAPTER 8 WRITING REVIEW

Develop a limited topic and write another research paper, following the procedures you have learned in this chapter. As you prepare your paper, refer to the following guidelines.

GUIDELINES FOR WRITING RESEARCH PAPERS

1. Before you begin work on your paper, make a chart outlining the steps involved. Note any deadlines your teacher gives you for completing each step. Then check off each step as you complete it.
2. Select a subject that is interesting, appropriate to your audience, and for which there is sufficient current information. After getting an overview of the subject, limit it to a topic suitable for the audience, the available resources, and the paper's length.
3. Develop a purpose statement and a preliminary outline to guide your research. Then locate sources and gather information about your topic. Evaluate the usefulness of each source. Try not to return any of your sources until your final draft is complete, for as you write, you may find information on your note cards that is incomplete or that needs further checking.
4. Prepare a working bibliography card for each source. Include the author's name, the title, publication data, and a source number, and double-check all spellings. Accuracy now will save time later when you prepare your final bibliography.
5. Take notes from your sources, summarizing, paraphrasing, or quoting material as needed. Use a new card for each heading, subheading, or source, and use special symbols, such as a star (*), to indicate notes you especially want to use.
6. Develop a final outline that details the ideas the paper will cover.
7. Write a first draft, applying the skills you have learned about writing paragraphs and compositions.
8. Evaluate and revise your draft, referring to the guidelines on pages 249 and 136–38 and to the revising chart on pages 28–30.
9. Prepare a final copy of your paper, including a final bibliography. If possible, make a copy of your paper for yourself before handing it in. In this way you not only protect yourself against loss of your paper but also have a model to keep for future reference.

CHAPTER 9

Writing Business Letters and Completing Forms

BUSINESS WRITING SKILLS

The business letters you write and the forms you complete are permanent records that represent you to people you may never meet. To do their job of representing you well, your business letters must be appropriate in tone, attractive in appearance, and clear. The forms and applications you complete must also be neat and free of errors.

WRITING BUSINESS LETTERS

Your message in a business letter should be unmistakably clear and direct; you need to be brief—without seeming curt. You should choose your words carefully to be sure that your tone is polite and businesslike. How your letter looks is just as important as what it says.

PREWRITING

APPEARANCE AND FORM OF A BUSINESS LETTER

As you prepare to write business letters, recognize the conventions—or standard practices—of letter-writing form.

9a. Observe standard practices in writing business letters.

You should type your letter, if possible, on $8\frac{1}{2}$ x 11-inch plain white stationery. A typewritten letter is more legible and therefore more quickly read than a handwritten one. If you write the letter by hand, use dark ink on plain white stationery. Also, remember to type or write carefully; never send a letter that has typeovers or messy corrections.

Before beginning your letter, estimate the amount of space it will occupy on the stationery you are using. Center the letter as nearly as possible by making sure you will have approximately the same margin at the top and bottom of your page and the same margin on both the left and right sides. If you need a second page, be sure that you will have at least three lines on it. Never write on the back of a page.

Letter Form

The six parts of a business letter are the *heading, inside address, salutation, body, closing,* and *signature.* These parts are labeled in the illustrations below.

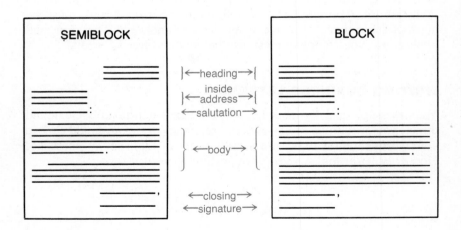

Model Business-Letter Forms

The parts of a business letter are arranged in standard patterns. The two most frequently used patterns are the block form and the semiblock form. The block form (see page 267) may be used only if the letter is typed. In this style, you begin each line at the left-hand margin. Allow one line of space between each paragraph, but do not indent paragraphs. The block form is easy for a typist to use since there is no need to set paragraph tabs or computer codes. Some businesses prefer not to use block form, however, because letters typed this way tend to look unbalanced at the left.

With the semiblock form, you place the heading, closing, and signature just to the right of the center of your page. You may indent paragraphs consistently throughout the letter (see page 270) or begin all of them at the left margin (see page 269).

1. Heading

Before you begin your business letter, decide whether you want to use block or semiblock form. Then write your *complete* address and the full date, beginning at least one inch from the top of the page. Many businesses use the two-letter code recommended by the postal service for states.

EXAMPLE   49 Surrey Lane   49 Surrey Lane
          Clinton, Iowa 57232   (or)   Clinton, IA 57232
          June 4, 1988   June 4, 1988

2. Inside Address

Start the inside address at the left-hand margin about four spaces below the heading. It should include the full name of the company to which you are writing, as well as its complete address. If you are writing to an individual, use the full name and title, with a comma between the two if they are on the same line; if the name and title are long, put the title on the next line.

EXAMPLES   The Helen Mills Company
           RFD 4
           Cross Corners, Oklahoma 73028

           Ms. Marjorie Berg, Vice-President
           Newland and Company
           40 Fifth Avenue
           Lewiston, Maine 04240

           Mr. Reginald B. Macpherson
           Secretary to the President
           Wilbur Field and Sons
           218 South Street
           Fort Hamilton, Virginia 24437

3. Salutation

The salutation is placed two spaces below the inside address and flush with the left-hand margin. For addressing an individual within the firm, the correct salutation is *Dear Mr. . . .* (*Mrs., Ms.,* or *Miss*) followed by a colon. If you are writing to a professional man or woman, use the title instead:

EXAMPLES   Dear Dr. Grayce:
                 Dear President Tyson:

When you write to a company or to a person whose name you do not know, you may have just *Personnel Department, President,* or *Editor* on the first line of the inside address. You may then use an impersonal salutation (*Editor, Personnel Department*) or the traditional salutation (*Dear Sir, Gentlemen*) followed by a colon.

    In using traditional salutations, it is understood that the group to which you are writing may be composed of both men and women.

4. Body

Keep your paragraphs fairly short and use a double space between paragraphs if you are typing. Remember that paragraph indentations are acceptable only if you use the semiblock form, and that if you indent one paragraph, you must indent the others. If your typewritten letter is seven lines or less, you may either put it on a smaller sheet of stationery ($5\frac{1}{2}$ x $8\frac{1}{2}$ inches) or double-space the entire body of the letter on $8\frac{1}{2}$ x 11-inch stationery.

5. Closing

In business letters, appropriate closings are *Very truly yours, Yours truly, Yours very truly, Sincerely yours,* and *Yours sincerely.* The closing is placed two spaces below the last line of the body of your letter. It is followed by a comma.

    Avoid ending your letter with an outmoded phrase such as "Hoping to hear from you soon, I am, . . ." or "Thanking you in advance, I am . . ." End the body of your letter with a *period.* Begin the first word of your closing with a capital letter.

EXAMPLES   Very truly yours,
                 Yours truly,
                 Sincerely yours,

6. Signature

Sign your full name to your letter. A signature should always be handwritten. If your letter is typewritten, type your name below your signature, flush with the first letter of the closing.

EXAMPLES   Very truly yours,   Sincerely yours,

Elena Montera   *Minh Luu*
Elena Montera   Minh Luu

The Envelope

Two envelope sizes are acceptable for business letters: $6\frac{1}{2}$ x $3\frac{1}{2}$ inches and $9\frac{1}{2}$ x $4\frac{1}{2}$ inches. If your letter is on $5\frac{1}{2}$ x $8\frac{1}{2}$-inch stationery, use the smaller size envelope and fold the letter in this way: up from the bottom about a third of the way and then down from the top. When the letter is unfolded, it will be right side up for the reader.

Either a small or a large envelope may be used for a letter on $8\frac{1}{2}$ x 11-inch stationery. If you have a large envelope, fold your letter the same way you folded a small sheet for a small envelope. If the envelope is small, fold your letter up from the bottom to within a quarter of an inch of the top; then fold the right side over a third of the way; finally, fold the left side over.

On the lower half of your envelope, use the same address as the inside address of the letter. Put the return address in the upper left corner of the envelope on the same side as the receiver's address. Use block form for both addresses.

Folding the Letter

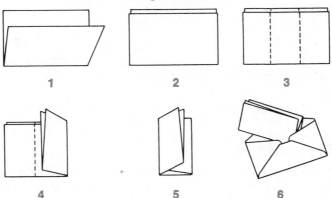

1   2   3

4   5   6

```
Theodora Jonas
303 Clayton Street
Huntington, WV 25703




              Executive Secretary
              Chamber of Commerce
              Mystic, CT 06355
```

Model Envelope

The post office also requests that you use a ZIP code number in both your return address and the receiver's address. The ZIP code should appear on the last line of the address, with a double space between the last letter of the state and first digit of the code. Do not use a comma between the state name and the ZIP code.

CONTENT OF THE BUSINESS LETTER

Even though the tone of a business letter will be formal, you should still strive for naturalness and simplicity of expression. Come right to the point in your letter; avoid wordy beginnings. Make sure you have supplied all the necessary information.

WRITING

TYPES OF BUSINESS LETTERS

9b. Learn how to write different types of business letters.

The Request Letter

A letter of request asks for something: information, a free brochure, or a speaker, for example. It is important to be very clear, specific, and reasonable about what you want. When you ask for information, you are more likely to get a reply if you enclose a stamped, self-addressed envelope. When you write to ask someone to send a speaker to your school, be sure to write early and give all the information that the person will need about time, place, and audience.

Be sure to be courteous in the phrasing of your request. You may want to conclude the request letter with a polite acknowledgment like: "I shall certainly appreciate any help you can give me with this request." Finally, make your request simple. Companies handling a large volume of mail cannot afford to spend time reading lengthy letters.

> 76 Brixton Place
> Phoenix, Arizona   85008
> July 8, 1988
>
>
> Model Airways, Inc.
> 410–12 Second Avenue
> Flagstaff, Arizona   86001
>
> Mail Order Department:
>
>   Will you please send me a copy of your
> latest catalog on model planes?   I have three
> of your models and would like to add some of the
> later ones to my collection.
>
> Very truly yours,
>
> *Frank Tyndall*
> Frank Tyndall

MODEL REQUEST LETTER—Semi-block Form

EXERCISE 1. Writing a Request Letter. Decide with your classmates which colleges and trade schools most interest the class. Make a list of these; then choose one school from the list and write to it, asking for its catalog. If you think the catalog may not include all the information you need, ask specifically for whatever you wish to know.

Another type of request letter is the kind you write when you ask a firm to send a representative to your school for a specific purpose. With your classmates, select a local business firm. Then, write a request letter, asking for one of the firm's representatives to address your class. Include all necessary details.

EXERCISE 2. Writing a Request Letter. Copy in proper form the business letter given below.

420 Jackson Avenue, Iola, Texas 77861, January 8, 1986. Miss R. F. Hawkins, Business Manager, Perry and Company, 480–96 Fuller Street, Fort Worth, Texas 76104. Dear Miss Hawkins: Our junior class of 170 students will decide this month on our class rings and pins. We expect to have representatives from several companies here on Monday, January 21, to show us samples of the rings and pins their firms make, together with price lists. We would very much like to have someone from your company here on that date, if possible. Your representative should come to Room 31, between 2:45 and 3:30 P.M. Very truly yours, Sarah Porter, Secretary of the Junior Class, Iola High School.

EXERCISE 3. Writing a Request Letter. As head of the student assembly program at your school, you wish to have a neighboring high school send its glee club to perform during one of your assembly periods. Give the time, date, place, length of program, type of song (if you wish), and any other information you think is necessary.

EXERCISE 4. Writing a Request Letter. Using the following information, set up this material in the form of a business letter. You must compose the letter.

Ms. Elsie Dowing of 22 Twin Oaks Road, Carlsburg, Ohio 43316, writes on April 6, 1988, to the George C. Buckeye Company, 240 Lexington Avenue, Cleveland, Ohio 44102, stating that while shopping there the week before, she lost a valuable gold ring. It contained a diamond and two pearls in an old-fashioned setting. She would like to know if it has been found and if so, where she may call for it.

The Order Letter

If you are writing an order letter, you should list the items you wish to purchase, one below the other, with complete information (catalog number, style, size, price, etc.) about each item. The price should be put at the right-hand side (flush with the right-hand margin), and each amount should be placed directly under the one above, to make it easier to add the prices. List the cost of shipping, if you know it, and include it in the total, unless you know the firm pays for shipping. Be sure to specify how the articles are to be paid for—check, C.O.D., etc.

```
                              58 Crane Street
                              Canton, Iowa 52542
                              December 1, 1988


Webb and Sons
140-156 Seventh Avenue
Des Moines, Iowa 50311

Gentlemen:

I should like to order the following articles, as ad-
vertised in the Des Moines Register of November 29.

2 white silk scarves, fringed, one with black
    initials A.J., the other with red initials M.W.,
    @ $7.98                                        $15.96
1 size 15-34 Supercron white shirt                  16.50
                                    Postage          1.20
                                    Total           $33.66

I am enclosing a check for $33.66 to cover the total
amount.

                              Very truly yours,

                              Amy Ladd
                              Amy Ladd
```

**MODEL ORDER LETTER—Semiblock Form
without Paragraph Indentation**

EXERCISE 5. Writing an Order Letter. Write to Ritz Camera Center, 1147A Sixth Avenue, New York, New York 10036, a letter ordering the following items: 1 Star D Model D–18 tripod, price $19.75; 3 rolls 35mm Kodachrome film at $3.50 a roll. Include $1.50 postage. You are enclosing a money order for the amount.

The Letter of Application

When you apply for a position, your letter of application comes before your interview with your prospective employer. It is the first contact the

98 Oxford Street
St. Cloud, Minnesota 56303
April 2, 1988

Mrs. O. A. Lester, Director
Camp Carlson
Oneidaga Lake
Big Pines, Minnesota 56680

Dear Mrs. Lester:

Ben Nichols, one of your regular campers, told me this week that you have a vacancy for a swimming counselor on your camp staff this summer, and I would like to apply for the position.

I am a senior at St. Cloud High School and am eighteen years old. For the last two years I have been the junior swimming counselor at Camp Winnebega, Cauhoga Falls, Wisconsin. I have just received my Examiner's badge in lifesaving and am now certified for the position of senior swimming counselor.

The following people have given me permission to use their names as references:

Mrs. J. B. Morse, Director, Camp Winnebega, Box 150, Cauhoga Falls, Wisconsin 54612 (414)936-1212

Mr. Chester Roberts, Principal, St. Cloud High School, 525 Ancona Avenue, St. Cloud, Minnesota 56303 (612)452-2323

I will be glad to come for a personal interview at your convenience.

**MODEL LETTER OF APPLICATION—Semiblock Form
with Paragraph Indentations**

two of you have. Therefore, you must "put yourself across" in a way that will suggest confidence that you can do the job called for. You will have an advantage if you can put some original, personal touch into your letter (but only if it comes naturally to you) to distinguish you favorably from the rest of the applicants this employer may be considering.

Remember to include the following information:

1. Include a statement of what position you are applying for and how you learned about it.

2. Show that you know what qualifications are needed and that you believe you can fill them. State your age, experience, and education.

3. List names, addresses, and telephone numbers of two or three people who can be contacted for references as to your character and ability. Always make sure first that these people are willing to be listed.

4. Request an interview at the employer's convenience.

EXERCISE 6. Writing a Letter of Application. You have learned from a friend that a couple she knows in another city are looking for a high-school student to spend the summer with their family at their summer home. They want the student to take care of three children, ages two, four, and six. Write to the couple (make up a name and address) and apply for this job. State your qualifications. Try to make your letter interesting as well as informative.

EXERCISE 7. Writing a Letter of Application. A drugstore in a neighboring town needs someone to deliver orders from 4:00 to 6:00 P.M. schooldays and all day Saturdays. Write your letter of application.

COMPLETING FORMS AND APPLICATIONS

9c. Learn how to complete common forms and applications.

All forms are alike in that they ask you to provide specific, often detailed information before you sign your name at the end. It is extremely important to fill out forms carefully, keeping these points in mind:

1. Always read through the entire form and any accompanying directions before you begin to fill in the blanks.

2. Most forms ask you to print or type information. Use black or blue ink if you print, unless the form specifically asks you to use pencil. Be sure that anything you print is legible and that you have supplied each item of information on the correct line.

3. After you have finished filling out the form, read through it again before you sign. Proofread to make sure that you have made no spelling, punctuation, or factual errors.

The Personal Check

Keeping most of your money in the bank is safer than carrying it around or having it at home. Many people keep money in checking accounts. A personal check is a form that tells the bank to take money from your account to pay the person or company whose name you have written on the check.

```
Anita Grayson                                    ① 589
5676 Mountain Road
Berkeley, CA 94705          ③ December 12 19 88

                                    ⑨  80-21
                                        580A
Pay to the ④ Allen's Bookstore      ⑤ $ 18.95
order of

⑥ Eighteen and 95/100 ~~~~~~~~ DOLLARS

    Bell National Bank
  ⑧ 89 West Street
    Berkeley, CA 94705
                                ⑦ Anita Grayson

  ② ' " 321160589:0211  089:::5862"
```

Model Check

All personal checks are organized in the same way even though various ways of personalizing checks make them look quite different from one another. Checks are numbered in sequence. The bank identifies each of your checks by (1) this number, but more importantly, by (2) the code number in computer language. When you write a check, you fill in (3) the date; then you write (4) the name of the company or person that you are paying. Notice that you write the amount of the check twice. First you write it in (5) numbers to the right of the dollar sign. On the next line, use (6) words to indicate how many dollars and a fraction to show how many cents. Draw a wavy line to fill in the rest of the space on this line. Write (7) your signature on the check the way you signed the signature card that the bank has on file. Notice that (8) the name of the bank is always printed on the check and (9) a code number for the bank appears near the date.

The Deposit Slip

Your checkbook may have forms at the back of the checks. You should use these forms, called deposit slips, when you make a deposit to your account. These deposit slips usually have your name, address, and account number already printed on them.

Notice that (1) the bank's name is printed on the slip. When you want to make a deposit, you write (2) your account number and the date in the appropriate spaces at the left. Then you print (3) your name and address below the account number. You write (4) the amounts that you are depositing in the columns at the right and indicate (5) the subtotal. If you want cash back from your account, you write (6) the amount to be taken out on the line beside "less cash," and subtract from the subtotal to get the total, which is (7) your net deposit. Then you write (8) the amount of cash received, and (9) your signature on the slip. If you are not getting cash back, you need not sign the deposit slip.

Notice also that a similar kind of deposit slip can be used for other bank accounts, such as a savings account.

Model Deposit Slip

The Social Security Card Application

The Social Security System records the amount of money that U.S. workers earn and the amounts that the workers and their employers are required to contribute to the Social Security fund. When workers retire, become disabled, or die, they or their survivors receive benefits from the fund. For this reason, it is important that all workers have a Social Security card.

Before you receive your first paycheck, apply for a Social Security card. The application form, which you can obtain from any Social Security office, appears on the following page. Study this completed form very carefully so that you will know exactly how to complete your own form when you get one.

With your application form, you will receive three pages of instructions and an explanation of why the government requires the information. Wherever the form (1) refers to "page 1" or "page 2," it refers to these instructions. Notice that the form includes (2) several references to "required evidence." Examples of such evidence include a birth certificate, driver's license, U.S. passport, alien registration card, or other original documents that prove your age, identity, and U.S. citizenship or legal alien status. Notice also (3) the use of NA (not applicable). If an item does not apply to you, write *NA* or a dash (—) in that space.

Everyone must complete items 1–4, 6–10a, and 11–14. You are not, however, required to complete item 5, but the government would like you to do so. If you have never before requested a Social Security card, you skip over items 10b–10e. These items are primarily for people who want to change the name on their Social Security records (as in the case of marriage) or correct their date of birth. You should ignore (4) the capital letters at each item number as well as the numbers in parentheses at 10a and 10b. These letters and numbers are used by the clerks in the Social Security office who carefully examine and process all card applications.

EXERCISE 8. Completing a Form. If your teacher provides the forms, write a check and a deposit slip or an application for a Social Security card. Proofread the form carefully. Then exchange your work with a classmate. If you receive a check and a deposit slip, examine them as a bank teller would. If you receive an application for a Social Security card, examine it as a clerk in the Social Security office would. Write your comments on a separate sheet of paper, and share them with your classmates.

DEPARTMENT OF HEALTH AND HUMAN SERVICES
SOCIAL SECURITY ADMINISTRATION

Form Approved
OMB No. 0960-0066

FORM SS-5—APPLICATION FOR A SOCIAL SECURITY NUMBER CARD (Original, Replacement or Correction)

Unless the requested information is provided, we may not be able to issue a Social Security Number (20 CFR 422-103(b))

INSTRUCTIONS TO APPLICANT — Before completing this form, please read the instructions on the opposite page. Type or print, using pen with dark blue or black ink. Do not use pencil. SEE PAGE 1 FOR REQUIRED EVIDENCE.

NAA 1
NAME TO BE SHOWN ON CARD — First: Janine Middle: Marie Last: Big Elk
FULL NAME AT BIRTH (IF OTHER THAN ABOVE) — First: NA Middle: NA Last: NA
OTHER NAME(S) USED: NA

STT 2 MAILING ADDRESS: 59 Poplar Road
CITY: Helena STATE: Montana ZIP CODE: 59601

CSP 3 CITIZENSHIP: ☒ a. U.S. citizen ☐ b. Legal alien allowed to work ☐ c. Legal alien not allowed to work ☐ d. Other
SEX 4 ☐ MALE ☒ FEMALE
ETB 5 RACE/ETHNIC: ☒ d. Northern American Indian or Alaskan Native

DOB 6 DATE OF BIRTH — MONTH 9 DAY 15 YEAR 72 AGE 7 PRESENT AGE 16 PLACE OF BIRTH — CITY: Helena STATE: Montana

MNA 9 MOTHER'S NAME AT HER BIRTH — First: Mary Middle: NA Last: Old Horn
FNA FATHER'S NAME — First: Tyrone Middle: NA Last: Big Elk

PNO 10 a. Has a Social Security card ever been requested? ☒ NO(1) b. Was a card received? —

DON 11 TODAY'S DATE — MONTH 10 DAY 18 YEAR 88
12 Telephone: (406) 732-6170 HOME

13 YOUR SIGNATURE: Janine M. Big Elk
14 ☒ Self

DO NOT WRITE BELOW THIS LINE (FOR SSA USE ONLY)

Form SS-5 (8-85) 5/84 and 1/85 editions may be used until supply is exhausted 3

Application for a Social Security Card

EVALUATING AND REVISING

EVALUATING AND REVISING LETTERS AND FORMS

9d. Evaluate and revise your business letters and forms.

Like any other writing, business letters and forms require very careful evaluation and revision to insure their accuracy and clarity. Use the following guidelines to evaluate the business letters and forms you write.

GUIDELINES FOR EVALUATING BUSINESS LETTERS AND FORMS

Purpose	1. Will the reader know right away why the letter was written?
Clarity	2. Is all the necessary information given? Is the letter brief and to the point? Are all applicable parts of the form completed correctly?
Tone	3. Is the tone of the letter courteous and businesslike?
Form	4. Does the letter consistently follow either block or semi-block form? Is each part of the letter correctly placed and accurately punctuated? Are the salutation and closing appropriate?
Appearance	5. Does the letter look attractive? Is it centered on the page? Is the typing or handwriting as neat as possible? Has plain white stationery in a standard size been used? Is the form neatly completed?
Envelope	6. On the envelope, are the address to the receiver and the return address accurate, complete, and correctly positioned? Has the letter been folded appropriately to fit the envelope?

After you evaluate your business letters and forms for their accuracy and clarity, you should revise them. Use the revising chart on the following page to make the changes necessary to improve your letters or forms.

REVISING BUSINESS LETTERS AND FORMS

PROBLEM	TECHNIQUE	REVISION
The purpose is unclear.	Add	Add an introductory sentence that states the purpose. Add details that explain what kind of information or service is needed.
Not enough details are included.	Add	Add pertinent details, such as the order number, or add information to complete each item on the form.
The letter is not polite or sounds too informal.	Cut/Replace	Omit discourteous remarks. Replace informal words with businesslike ones.
The form is not consistent.	Replace	Use either block or semiblock form throughout.
The salutation or the closing does not sound right.	Replace	Use the impersonal or traditional forms, such as *Dear Madam* or *Sincerely yours.*
The addresses inside the letter and on the envelope do not match.	Replace	Substitute the correct information.

After you revise your letters or forms, you should proofread carefully. Refer to the Guidelines for Proofreading on pages 32–33; then prepare a neat, legible final copy. Proofread once again before you send your letter or form.

EXERCISE 9. **Evaluating and Revising a Letter.**   Choose any business letter you wrote in this chapter (except Exercise 2). Evaluate your letter, using the guidelines on page 276. Then make the revisions that will improve your letter, referring to the chart on page 277. Address an envelope for your letter, fold the letter, and insert it in the envelope.

You may also want to exchange letters with a classmate to offer each other suggestions for improvement.

EXERCISE 10. Preparing Your Final Copy.   Prepare a final copy of the business letter and accompanying envelope that you evaluated and revised. Proofread again after you have copied your letter and the envelope.

☞ NOTE: The United States Postal Service recommends the use of two-letter codes for states, the District of Columbia, and Puerto Rico. The service also recommends the use of nine-digit ZIP codes. When you use these codes, the address should look like this:

EXAMPLE   Ms. Laura Braverman
72 White Plains Blvd.
Dallas, TX 75231-2424

The two-letter code is in capital letters and is never followed by a period. Refer to the following list of two-letter codes:

Alabama AL	Maryland MD
Alaska AK	Massachusetts MA
Arizona AZ	Michigan MI
Arkansas AR	Minnesota MN
California CA	Mississippi MS
Colorado CO	Missouri MO
Connecticut CT	Montana MT
Delaware DE	Nebraska NE
District of Columbia DC	Nevada NV
Florida FL	New Hampshire NH
Georgia GA	New Jersey NJ
Hawaii HI	New Mexico NM
Idaho ID	New York NY
Illinois IL	North Carolina NC
Indiana IN	North Dakota ND
Iowa IA	Ohio OH
Kansas KS	Oklahoma OK
Kentucky KY	Oregon OR
Louisiana LA	Pennsylvania PA
Maine ME	Puerto Rico PR

Rhode Island RI
South Carolina SC
South Dakota SD
Tennessee TN
Texas TX
Utah UT

Vermont VT
Virginia VA
Washington WA
West Virginia WV
Wisconsin WI
Wyoming WY

CHAPTER 10

Effective Diction

THE MEANINGS AND USES OF WORDS

In composition, the quality of the words you select to express your ideas is just as important as the quality of your sentence structure. The words you choose constitute your *diction*. One way to improve your diction is to expand your vocabulary. But keep in mind that a better vocabulary is not one with a lot of long or rare words. It is one that allows you to call on a broader range of words that most of the people you know understand. A good vocabulary allows you to convey the exact meanings you intend. This chapter will help you explore the levels of word meanings and select your words wisely.

SEMANTICS: THE MEANINGS OF WORDS

Linguistics is the science of language. One of its most interesting branches is *semantics*—the study of what words mean and how their meanings change.

A word is a symbol. The thing or idea that it symbolizes, or refers to, is its *referent*. If a word is to be useful in communication, its referent must be the same for the person who uses it as for the person who reads or hears it.

If your teacher says, "Please give me the chalk," you immediately comprehend the references to *give, me,* and *chalk*. Had your teacher said, "Please give me the *glub*," you would have been confused. *Glub* is not customarily used to refer to anything. It has no referent.

Concrete Words

Think of words as being either *concrete* or *abstract*. A concrete word is one whose referent can be seen or touched: *book, cloud, car, chalk.* An abstract word is one whose referent is beyond our vision or touch. Its referent is an idea: *peace, need, love, freedom.*

Some concrete words are more precise in their meaning than others. For example, the word *vehicle* describes something that can be seen and touched, but the word is not very specific. *Vehicle* does not call up a well-defined image. The word *car* is more specific; *station wagon* is still more specific. "John was driving a dilapidated vehicle" will not convey as clear a picture as "John was driving a dilapidated station wagon." When you consider several different words to describe something or express an idea, look for the one that is most precise.

EXERCISE 1. Classifying Words According to Their Precision. Arrange the words in each of the following groups so that the word with the least specific referent comes first, and the word with the most specific referent comes last.

1. seat, desk chair, chair, furniture, swivel chair
2. quadruped, creature, mammal, spaniel, dog
3. fruit juice, drink, lemonade, juice, liquid
4. storm at sea, typhoon, occurrence, storm
5. laborer, carpenter, employee, human being, woman

EXERCISE 2. Classifying General and Specific Words. For each of the following general words, list three words that have a more specific referent:

1. food   3. elevation   5. educational institution
2. boat   4. reward   6. restaurant

Abstract Words

Abstract words usually refer to general ideas. You must use abstract words with care, because each one may have many referents.

The word *freedom,* for example, has only a vague referent until you define it. To a prisoner, *freedom* means getting out of jail. To Mr. Barnes, who resents the neighbors' criticism of his noisy family, *freedom* means the right of his family to make as much noise as they wish.

Franklin D. Roosevelt defined the freedoms in which Americans believe as freedom of speech, freedom of worship, freedom from want, and freedom from fear. Each of these definitions provides a more specific referent for the word *freedom,* and each could be even more narrowly defined.

Sometimes an example will help clarify the meaning of an abstract word. In the following passage, the meaning of *quality,* in the context "a man of quality," is made clear by an example.

> Mansfield was a man of quality. Although he never pushed himself forward or tried to assert his superiority, you could tell by his bearing, his quiet sense of humor, and his manner of speaking that he was a superior person.

EXERCISE 3. Defining Abstract Words.   Without using a dictionary, write a one- or two-sentence definition of each of the following words. In discussion, compare your definitions with those of your classmates.

1. fairness   3. success   5. skill
2. beauty   4. failure   6. happiness

Synonyms

Synonyms are words that are similar, but rarely identical, in meaning. For example, the words *disciple, partisan,* and *satellite* are synonyms in that each refers to a person who is a *follower* of a leader. Yet their meanings are different. *Follower,* the most general in meaning, may be used in place of any of the other three, but it is inexact. A writer who has in mind the followers of a professor or religious leader, for instance, probably will choose the word *disciples.* If the writer is referring to devoted followers of a political or military leader, the word *partisans* might be preferable. Servile followers who circulate about a powerful leader in hope of favors might be described as *satellites.* Since the first synonym that occurs to you may not be the best one, use a thesaurus or dictionary to search for the synonym with the exact meaning for your purpose.

EXERCISE 4. Identifying Meanings and Referents of Synonyms. Without using the dictionary, explain the differences in meaning of the words in each of the following groups. Describe a situation in which each word would be appropriate.

1. road, boulevard, expressway, trail
2. compel, coerce, force, constrain
3. reveal, divulge, tell, betray
4. repulsive, obnoxious, abhorrent, distasteful
5. laughing, giggling, snickering, guffawing

Denotation and Connotation

Compare the meaning of the following sentences:

Nan's persistence surprised everyone.
Nan's stubbornness surprised everyone.

Of course, the two sentences may mean the same thing. *Persistence* is another word for *stubbornness,* the quality of not giving up easily. This is the *denotative* meaning of the words. But the *effect* of the words on the reader or listener can be quite different. *Stubbornness* suggests that Nan is unreasonable, narrow-minded, and unwilling to listen to others. This suggestive meaning of a word is its *connotation,* or *connotative* meaning. Most words have connotations. There is nothing wrong in choosing a word for its connotations, but you must be aware of what they are to avoid saying or writing something you do not intend.

EXERCISE 5. Evaluating Word Connotations. Number your paper 1–5. As you read the following list, write *F* if the word or phrase has favorable, pleasing connotations for you. Write *U* if it has unfavorable connotations. Write *N* if the connotations are neutral—that is, if the word or phrase does not stir any feeling in you. Compare your answers with those of your classmates.

1. liberal
2. propaganda
3. mother
4. bureaucrat
5. grand opera

Loaded Words

A word whose connotations carry strong feelings is said to be *loaded.* The propagandist, the newspaper columnist, and the political speaker are likely to use loaded words. They are trying to appeal to people's emotions. Clear thinkers disapprove of the deliberate use of loaded words.

EXERCISE 6. Analyzing Word Connotations. Discuss with your classmates and teacher the connotations of the following words:

1. plump, fat, potbellied, stout
2. visionary, crackpot, idealist
3. crowd, gang, mob, assemblage
4. youth, teen-ager, minor, young adult
5. determined, persevering, dogged, resolute

THE WRITER'S CHOICE OF WORDS

When you speak, you can supplement your words with additional explanatory words or with body language. When you write, your meaning depends upon which words you choose and how you use them. Only by selecting your written words carefully will you deliver your message clearly, fulfilling your purpose by reaching and possibly influencing your audience.

Figurative Language

Figures of speech will help you create interesting and vivid writing. You encounter many of them in literature, especially in poetry. The most common figures of speech are *metaphor, simile,* and *personification.* In each of these, the writer compares two things that are not really alike but are similar in at least one respect. The writer thus is able to express meaning more clearly, vividly, and convincingly than he or she could by writing a literal description or explanation.

   D. H. Lawrence describes a row of distant houses on a ridge at night: "The homes stood . . . black against the sky, *like wild beasts glaring curiously with yellow eyes down into the darkness.*" Lawrence knows, of course, that houses and beasts are quite different, but the houses with lighted windows suggest to his imagination beasts with yellow eyes. His figurative description is more arresting than some literal statement, such as "The lighted houses were black against the sky," would have been.

   Note the striking effect of the four figures of speech used by Pearl Buck in describing a handful of precious jewels: "There were such a mass of jewels as we had never dreamed could be together, jewels *red as the inner flesh of watermelons, golden as wheat, green as young leaves in spring, clear as water trickling out of the earth.*"

Simile

A *simile* is a comparison between things essentially unlike, expressed directly through the use of a comparing word such as *like* or *as*.

EXAMPLES   Her hair was **like** silk.
He was thin **as** a stick.

If the things compared are really alike, the comparison is neither a simile nor a figure of speech.

NOT A SIMILE   He wore a hat like mine.
SIMILE   He wore a hat **like an overturned pail.**

NOT A SIMILE   Her sister was like her mother.
SIMILE   Her sister was **like an angel.**

Metaphor

A *metaphor* is a comparison between things essentially unlike, expressed without a comparing word such as *like* or *as*. The comparison is implied rather than directly stated.

EXAMPLES   The silver lace of the branches above the river . . . .
The road was a ribbon of moonlight.

ALFRED NOYES

Personification

Personification is a figure of speech in which the characteristics of a human being are attributed to an animal, a thing, or an idea.

EXAMPLES   But, look, **the morn in russet mantle clad**
Walks o'er the dew of yon high eastern hill.

SHAKESPEARE

Only through the rusty hinges and swollen sea-moistened wood-work certain airs, detached from the **body of the wind** (the house was ramshackle after all) **crept** round corners and **ventured** indoors.

VIRGINIA WOOLF

EXERCISE 7. Explaining and Evaluating Figures of Speech.   Copy the figures of speech from the following passages. After each, tell whether it is simile, metaphor, or personification. Be prepared to explain the figure of speech and to evaluate its effectiveness.

1. When Alma went down into the audience room, in the midst of the chattering singers, who seemed to have descended like birds, from song flights to chirps, the minister approached her.—MARY E. WILKINS FREEMAN
2. The silence is cloven by alarm as by an arrow.—JAMES JOYCE
3. Spring was a very flame of green.—D. H. LAWRENCE
4. The edge of the colossal jungle, so dark green as to be almost black, fringed with white surf, ran straight, like a ruled line, far, far away along a blue sea whose glitter was blurred by a creeping mist. —JOSEPH CONRAD
5. Are there no water-lilies, smooth as cream
   With long stems dripping crystal?—ELINOR WYLIE

EXERCISE 8. Using Figures of Speech in Sentences. Make each of the descriptions below more vivid by writing a sentence using simile, metaphor, or personification.

1. hot August scene on a city street
2. sensations while walking in a hurricane or a blizzard
3. a person's reaction to sudden fear
4. a fruit tree in bloom
5. cars in bumper-to-bumper traffic
6. sensations while shoveling snow
7. a sleeping kitten
8. a drink of cool water after hours of thirst
9. autumn leaves floating on a lake
10. a plane taking off

Hazards of Figurative Language

The habit of thinking metaphorically, of seeing life in terms of comparisons, can help a writer—in prose as well as in poetry—to enliven style and clarify meaning.

Yet, three pitfalls await the glib or careless user of figurative language. The first is the selection of similes and metaphors that weaken style because they have been used too often. Examples of such clichés are *clear as crystal, ran like the wind, silence reigned,* and *clear as day.* The second pitfall is the use of comparisons that sound too strained or far-fetched: "Like a boiling lobster, the dawn turned from black to red." This fault is more common in verse than in prose. The third pitfall is the error of mixing figures of speech.

Mixed Figures of Speech

The *mixed figure of speech* is sometimes referred to as a "mixed metaphor." It is one in which the writer starts with one comparison and then shifts to another that is not consistent with the first. The following examples illustrate this danger.

MIXED Flailing both wings, Mr. McCall flew to the platform and barked for silence. [The first metaphors compare Mr. McCall to a bird, and the last to a dog.]

BETTER Flailing his arms like wings, Mr. McCall **flew** to the platform and **screeched** for silence.

MIXED Her face reddened as great waves of embarrassment broke over her, all but drying up the little confidence she had. ["Great waves" suggest water, which would hardly "dry up" anything.]

BETTER Her face reddened as great **waves** of embarrassment broke over her, all but **washing away** the little confidence she had.

EXERCISE 9. Selecting an Appropriate Figure of Speech. Each item in the following exercise contains a figure of speech and a space where a portion of the sentence has been omitted. Beneath the sentence, four wordings are suggested for the space. One of them is preferable if the figure of speech is to be maintained consistently. After the proper number, write the letter of the wording that best fits the blank space.

1. Mr. Gross, who was up to his neck in debt, . . . when his company went on strike.
   a. collapsed
   b. nearly went under
   c. was caught off base
   d. suffered a setback
2. Her path was strewn with serious problems that threatened . . .
   a. to drop on her with crippling effect.
   b. to engulf her completely.
   c. to trip her up at every step.
   d. to wreck her career.
3. The book is a treasure chest of wisdom in which you will find . . .
   a. a rich supply of bonbons to sweeten your speech.
   b. a greenhouse of rare flowers to decorate your speech.
   c. new clothes to dress up your speech.
   d. a hoard of verbal gems to adorn your speech.

4. Heavy income taxes, which exert a stranglehold on the economy, have . . . sources of new investment capital.
   a. crippled
   b. choked off
   c. tied up
   d. destroyed
5. Like a person tenderly raking leaves from a new lawn, we must always be careful that in removing the old and unwanted, we do not . . . the new.
   a. uproot
   b. bury
   c. undermine
   d. drown out

EXERCISE 10. Revising Sentences By Using Consistent Figures of Speech. Seven of the sentences below contain mixed figures of speech. Revise the sentences to remove the conflict. If a figure is consistently maintained, write + following its number on your paper.

1. After enduring an hour of Carl's insane driving, we ordered him into the asylum of the back seat.
2. The senator said he would lay his cards on the table, since his life was an open book, with no skeletons in the closet.
3. Bionics researchers are on a small island of knowledge in the midst of a sea of ignorance, but, like corals, they are building reefs, extending their knowledge in all directions.
4. Unfortunately the speaker did not know he was flying too high over the head of his audience until their general restlessness made him realize he had better get out of the depths and into the shallow water, where they were.
5. In college she changed course abruptly, and instead of foundering on the submerged rocks of low grades and expulsion from school, she got on the beam, which eventually led her to a safe landing.
6. Elisa dived into her studies, afraid she would never reach the top of the heap, but determined not to give up before the final whistle blew.
7. The productive field of psychiatry, once considered a pseudo-science, has now achieved respectability and may become a most important branch of medical research.
8. Every morning a chorus of starlings in the trees outside her window awakened her, their harsh, dissonant voices jangling her nerves unbearably.

9. She spent the morning of her career groping through the dark halls of obscurity, until the publication of her third novel thrust her above the surface of the black waters into the brilliant noonday sun.
10. Unless the mayor sets a new course, our city is likely to be buried beneath a mound of debt.

Trite Expressions

Trite expressions, sometimes called *clichés,* are expressions that have grown stale through too frequent use. They have lost all originality. No doubt "butterflies in my stomach" was strikingly apt the first time it was used to describe stage fright, but we have heard it all too often. Similarly, such comparisons as *blanket of snow, busy as a bee,* and *on the fence* are so familiar that they make our writing dull. Clichés suggest laziness and a lack of originality in the writer who fails to guard against them. The simple, straightforward statement of an idea is preferable to the use of a worn-out expression.

TRITE	SIMPLE, STRAIGHTFORWARD
bury the hatchet	stop fighting, make peace
at loose ends	disorganized
on speaking terms	friendly
fair and square	completely honest
at death's door	near death

You have probably noticed that some clichés are comparisons (*busy as a bee*), while others are ways of stating an idea (*fair and square*). Studying the following list of clichés will make you sensitive to trite expressions. The list is far from complete. See what you and your classmates can add to it.

TRITE EXPRESSIONS

a good time was had by all	brown as a berry
accidents will happen	budding genius
add insult to injury	bury the hatchet
after all is said and done	busy as a bee
at death's door	by the sweat of one's brow
at loose ends	calm before the storm
beat a hasty retreat	clear as crystal
beauty is only skin-deep	depths of despair
beyond the shadow of a doubt	diamond in the rough
bite off more than you can chew	discreet silence
blushing bride	doomed to disappointment
break the ice	each and every

easier said than done
eternal triangle
fair sex
Father Time
few and far between
fond parents
gala occasion
green with envy
hale and hearty
in no uncertain terms
in this day and age
irony of fate
last but not least
long arm of the law
make a long story short
none the worse for wear

on speaking terms
on the fence
out of the frying pan into the fire
point with pride
quick as a flash
ripe old age
sadder but wiser
silence reigned
straight and narrow path
supreme sacrifice
to the bitter end
trials and tribulations
view with alarm
viselike grip
white as a sheet
word to the wise

EXERCISE 11. Revising Sentences by Replacing Trite Expressions. Rewrite each of the following sentences, substituting simple, straightforward language for the trite expressions.

1. After our sumptuous repast, we agreed that a good time had been had by all.
2. In this day and age, political figures who remain on the fence when burning questions are argued will be doomed to disappointment on Election Day.
3. Although warned not to bite off more than I could chew, I signed up for six courses with the result that after all was said and done I was a sadder but wiser woman.
4. To make a long story short, I failed two courses, and to add insult to injury, my parents sent me to summer school.
5. Among the novel's characters are two members of the fair sex who wander from the straight and narrow path and are eventually embraced by the long arm of the law.
6. In the depths of despair, each and every one of us maintained a discreet silence.
7. Sensing that Mr. Stern's pleasant greeting was only the calm before the storm, I tried to beat a hasty retreat, which was nipped in the bud as, with a viselike grip, he led me into his office.
8. Busy as a bee in her ripe old age, Grandmother always pointed with pride to the beautiful garden she had made by the sweat of her brow.

9. Having known the agony of defeat as well as the dizzying heights of success, Jim was determined to fight to the finish in this tennis match, which seesawed back and forth, continually swaying the balance.
10. Green with envy, Ira watched from the sidelines as Fred kicked up his heels and danced up a storm.

Jargon

There are two kinds of *jargon*. One is technical language used by specialists in the same profession. An engineer may use engineering jargon in a report to other engineers. An educator may use educational jargon in an article for a teacher's magazine. The practice in such cases is expected and usually acceptable. There is always the danger, however, that a writer may carry jargon to such an extreme that it will obscure rather than clarify meaning, even for members of the same profession. When this happens, jargon becomes a stylistic fault. The specialist should, whenever possible, use simple, everyday language rather than terms known only to his fellow professionals. As a high-school student you may encounter the specialist's jargon in your reading, but you will not be likely to use it in your writing.

The second type of jargon consists of vague, puffed-up, pretentious or unnecessary language that tends to confuse the reader. Some jargon words are so unspecific as to be almost meaningless. Examples might be *case, factor, field, aspect, matter,* and *concept.* Vague and unnecessary phrases usually characterize jargon: *as for the fact that, under the circumstances pertaining, along the line of, in the case of, relative to the matter, as to whether,* and *with reference to.* Perhaps these examples show why jargon has been called "fuzzy language."

Users of jargon often overwrite. They prefer the big word to the simple word, the unusual word to the ordinary one. To them, knives are cutlery; table napkins are napery; dogs are canines; a trailer truck is a behemoth of the highways. They rarely start or begin—they initiate or commence. In short, the "jargonist," in using vague, wordy, overwritten language, not only obscures meaning but also confuses and irritates the reader.

EXAMPLE OF COMMON JARGON

In spite of the fact that government aviation agencies were not in agreement with respect to the question of the cause of the accident at Kennedy Airport, the court decided that one of the contributing factors was a propeller that had been structurally weakened.

REWRITTEN WITHOUT JARGON

Although government aviation agencies disagreed on the causes of the accident at Kennedy Airport, the court decided that one cause was a structurally weakened propeller.

EXERCISE 12. Revising a Passage Obscured by Jargon. In the following passage, jargon somewhat obscures the meaning. Read the passage several times until you are sure what the writer was trying to say. Then write a jargon-free version.

Owing to the fact that a number of social factors along the line of unemployment and dislocation follow consequentially from the automation of industry, government, as well as labor and management, must concern itself with the implementation of the processes of adjustment of affected persons.

Degrees of Informal English

As explained in Chapter 17, there are two kinds of standard English —formal and informal. We use informal English in much of our conversation and in most of our writing, but there are degrees of informality. The most extreme degree is never "bad" English, but it is sometimes inappropriate. Because it is light in tone and sometimes very close to slang, extremely informal English should be carefully limited in serious composition.

Slang

Slang is highly informal language that does not conform to conventional usage. For that reason, slang is found only in standard *informal* English. Slang often consists of new words and phrases, or established words and phrases with new meanings. Many linguists believe slang actually began as a secret means of expression—called an *argot*—among thieves and beggars who wanted to avoid being understood by police.

Slang today is most often used by close-knit groups, such as students, military recruits, musicians, and sailors, as a mark of membership in these groups. The slang may be confined to the group for a while, but then, thanks to radio and television, it spreads to a larger population. The following slang expressions, for example, were first used by jazz musicians in everyday conversations among themselves. Notice that many of the expressions are now familiar to general audiences.

EXAMPLES   the Big Apple—New York City
            bad—good
            bread—money
            bug—to bother
            clinker—a missed note
            cut—to leave
            dig—to understand or agree with
            gas—as a noun, something that especially pleases
            hep—in the know, as in "hip"
            put down—to belittle another's playing

Even though many of these words and phrases may be familiar to you, most slang is short-lived. That is why slang from your parents' generation probably seems outdated to you. Slang is generally considered acceptable only when used in the most informal situations. Writers often use it to depict informal speech.

EXERCISE 13. Understanding the Use of Slang. Which of the following slang expressions are still current? If necessary, use your dictionary to find their meanings.

1. apple polisher
2. crackerjack
3. fuzz
4. bag (noun)
5. bughouse

Colloquialisms and Idioms

Colloquialisms are words and phrases that are characteristic of spoken informal English. In informal occasions, such as a letter to a close friend, they are used in writing as well. Unlike slang, colloquialisms are not confined to particular groups. Instead, they tend to be widespread. Also unlike most slang expressions, colloquialisms tend to remain in the language, becoming after some time a part of standard English.

Colloquialisms often have an idiomatic meaning. An *idiom* is a word or phrase that cannot be accepted literally. For example, to say you are "down in the mouth" does not mean your jaw is sagging. It means you are "depressed" or "unhappy."

EXERCISE 14. Understanding the Use of Colloquialisms. Each of the following expressions is colloquial. If you do not know the meaning

294 < Effective Diction

of a phrase, look it up. Write two sentences for each phrase. In one, use the phrase as you might in a letter to a friend. In the other, substitute a slightly more formal meaning for the phrase, using it as you might in a school report.

1. hang back
2. from the horse's mouth
3. clue me in
4. run out on (someone)
5. slip one over on (someone)

CHAPTER 10 WRITING REVIEW

Evaluating a Writer's Choice of Language.   Select two articles from your local newspaper. Take one from the national news section, the other from a section such as sports, style, or entertainment. Identify in each article the characteristics of the language the writer chose. Is the language appropriate to the subject matter, the purpose, and the audience for which it was written? Be prepared to discuss your evaluation in class.

PICTURE T H E POSSIBILITIES:

IDEAS FOR WRITING

Pictures have the power to prompt the memory, stir the emotions, and spark the imagination. In this section you will learn how to use pictures as a powerful source of ideas for writing.

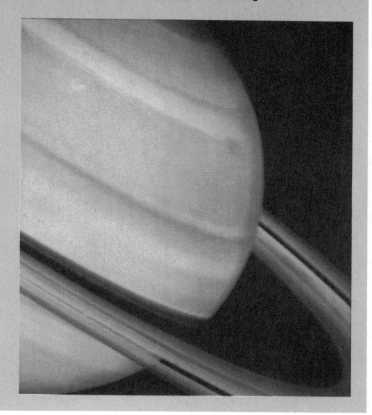

Probing the Picture

This picture lends itself well to **descriptive** writing. To create a main impression, you could focus on the picture's strongest elements: the nearly vertical horse and man and the intensity of their struggle. Or, you could imagine yourself in the place of the would-be rider and gather concrete and sensory details by asking questions such as *What sounds do I hear? What odors do I smell? How does the horse's mane feel against my face? How do the muscles in my shoulders, arms, and back feel?* For a different perspective altogether, you could (without attributing human thoughts and emotions to the horse) ask similar questions to gather details that an onlooker concentrating on the horse might observe.

Another way to use the picture would be as a source of ideas for **persuasive** writing. To find debatable issues, you could consider the relationship between the picture's principal elements: horse and man. Using brainstorming, you could develop a list of debatable issues such as *Should wild horses be allowed to roam free on private land? Should they be slaughtered? Should they be relocated to other parts of the country? Should people contribute to a fund set up to pay for the relocation of the horses?*

Writing Activities

Using the steps of the writing process, complete one of the following activities.

- Write a description of the picture from the perspective of the man.
- Write a persuasive composition on one of the issues mentioned above or on another issue the picture suggests.

Probing the Picture

Your first response to this picture might be to wonder why the theater closed—what happened? This question naturally suggests a **narrative.** For a short story, you could use the closing of the theater as the event that sets other events in motion, as the climax of the story, or as the outcome of the conflict. In any case, asking the 5 W-How? questions would help you develop the other elements of a narrative. For example, *Who* are the characters? *When* and *where* does the action take place? With *whom* or *what* is the main character in conflict? Your answers to these and other questions would help you develop a plot outline.

Another approach would be to use the picture for an **expository** paragraph analyzing cause and effect. Once you had decided whether to treat the theater's closing as a cause or as an effect, you could use the *point-of-view questions* to gather information on related effects (or causes). For example, if you think of the closing as a cause, you might ask questions such as *How did the closing affect business in the community? The way in which the townspeople spent their leisure time?* Thinking of the closing as an effect, you might ask, *Did the theater close because a shopping mall with a multi-screen theater came to town? Because the townspeople preferred to rent videocassettes? Because the town's major industry collapsed?*

Writing Activities

Using the steps of the writing process, complete one of the following activities.

- Write a short story about the picture.
- Use the picture to write an expository paragraph analyzing cause and effect.

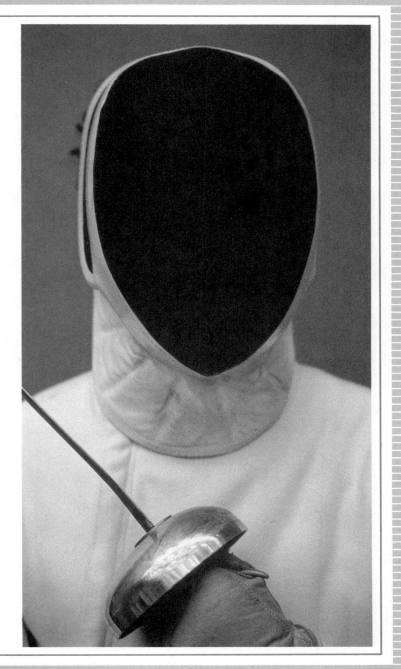

Probing the Picture

Although this picture strongly suggests description, it can prompt you in other directions as well. For example, you could use "cactuses" as the subject for an **expository** composition. Once you had limited the scope of the subject to find a manageable topic, you could develop a list of *questions about the topic* to guide your research. To gather information on the topic "features that enable cactuses to survive in hot, dry climates," for example, you might consider such questions as *How does a cactus store water? What function does the stem serve? The root system? The spines? How does a cactus reproduce itself?*

You might instead use the picture to generate ideas for a **narrative.** For example, you could begin by brainstorming to find possible settings in which the cactus might be found: *Is it in a desert? In a botanical garden? In the greenhouse of a country estate? In a one-room city apartment?* You might then consider what specific function the cactus serves in the story: *Is it the characters' only source of shade? An unwelcome gift from a close friend? A symbol of the main character's personality or of his or her endurance in a harsh environment?* Using the *5 W-How?* questions would help you develop the other elements of a narrative.

Writing Activities

Using the steps of the writing process, complete one of the following activities.

- Write an expository composition on the subject "cactuses."
- Use the picture to develop a plot outline, and write a short story.

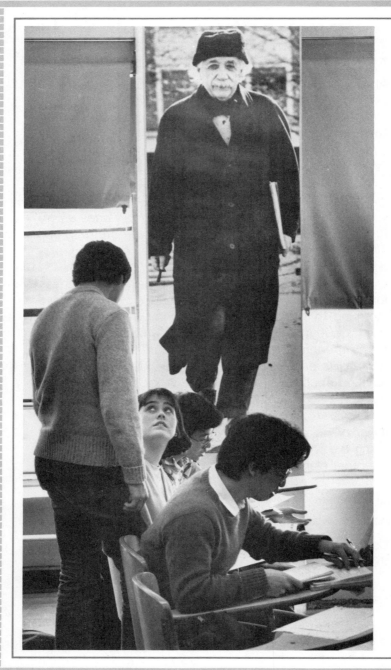

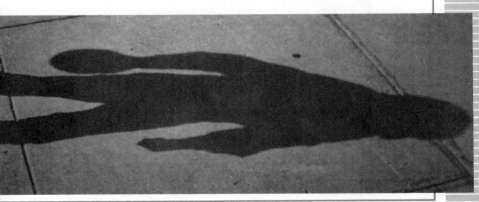

Probing Pictures to Discover Writing Ideas

The following questions will help you use any picture to discover ideas for writing.

1. What is it about this picture that interests me most? What specific idea does it suggest?
2. For what purpose could I use this idea?
3. What are the strongest elements of the picture? How could I combine those elements to achieve my purpose?
4. Would using the *5 W-How?* questions help me gather information to use?
5. What might have happened just before or just after the picture was taken? What might the person(s) have said?
6. What main impression do I get from this picture?
7. What concrete and sensory details do I observe as I examine the picture? What details do I imagine when I think of myself as being in the scene?
8. Could I explain how to make or do what the picture shows?
9. Could I give information about what the picture shows by telling what the subject is, what its history is, or how it is related to others of its kind?
10. What debatable issues does the combination of elements in the picture suggest to me?

On Your Own

Using any of the pictures you have not written about, write a paper for your classmates. You may choose the form (paragraph, composition, letter to the editor, short story, etc.) and the purpose (to narrate, to describe, to explain or to give information, or to persuade). Follow the steps of the writing process as you prepare your paper.

PART TWO

COMPOSITION:
Writing and Revising
Sentences

CHAPTER 11

Writing Complete Sentences

SENTENCE FRAGMENTS AND RUN-ON SENTENCES

Two of the most common errors in student writing result from carelessness in marking the end of one sentence and the beginning of the next. The first kind of error, the *sentence fragment,* occurs when a part of a sentence—a phrase or subordinate clause, for example—is written as a complete sentence. The second, *the run-on sentence,* occurs when two or more sentences are run together with only a comma, or no punctuation at all, between them.

SENTENCE FRAGMENTS

11a. A *sentence fragment* is a group of words that does not express a complete thought. Since it is only a part of a sentence, it should not be allowed to stand by itself but should be kept in the sentence of which it is a part.

A group of words is not a sentence unless it has both a subject and a verb and expresses a complete thought. The following examples are fragments because they fail to meet one or both of these conditions.

FRAGMENT   The referee calling the foul. [The *-ing* form of a verb cannot be the verb in a sentence unless it has a helping verb with it.]

FRAGMENT   Because the referee was calling the foul. [The subordinating conjunction *Because* signals that what follows is part of a larger sentence; it does not express a complete thought.]

Both of these fragments are really parts of a longer sentence.

EXAMPLES   The referee calling the foul was waving her arms in the air.
Because the referee was calling a foul, she was waving her arms in the air.

Good writers sometimes punctuate fragments as sentences for stylistic reasons. For example, notice the use of the following fragment.

FRAGMENT   Paul rides to school every day. *On his younger brother's tricycle.*

The writer used a capital letter at the beginning and a period at the end of the prepositional phrase for humorous effect, thinking that the point would be otherwise lost to the reader.

Paul rides to school every day on his younger brother's tricycle.

Another solution might have been to use a dash, thus gaining the desired emphasis while retaining conventional punctuation.

Paul rides to school every day—on his younger brother's tricycle.

Although the use of fragments can be justified, the practice requires experience and judgment; the beginning writer should avoid it.

The Phrase Fragment

A phrase is a group of words acting as a single part of speech and not containing a verb and its subject.

Verbals (See pages 394–406 for more information on verbals.) that present participles and gerunds are words ending in *-ing*. Words ending in *-ing* cannot be used as verbs unless they follow a helping verb. With a helping verb like *am, are, has been, will be,* they become complete verbs. It is the same with infinitive phrases. Like participial and gerund phrases, infinitive phrases can never stand alone. In order to make sense, they must be attached to a preceding or following sentence or be completed by being developed into a proper sentence. A participial phrase must not be written as a sentence.

FRAGMENT   The woman giving us directions. [a phrase; no verb]
CORRECTED   The woman **was giving** us directions. [The present participle has been made into a complete verb by adding the helping verb *was*.]

FRAGMENT   We admired the seascape. Painted and signed by Winslow Homer. [The participial phrase modifies the word *seascape*. It must be included in the sentence with the word it modifies.]

CORRECTED   We admired the seascape **painted and signed by Winslow Homer.** [The fragment is corrected by including the participial phrase in the sentence with the word it modifies.]

A gerund phrase must not be written as a sentence.

FRAGMENT   Many of us dislike working in the kitchen. Cleaning and scrubbing objects that in a few hours will be dirty again. [Here a gerund phrase functioning as an appositive of *working* is cut off from it by the period. It must be reconnected.]

CORRECTED   Many of us dislike working in the kitchen, **cleaning and scrubbing objects that in a few hours will be dirty again.** [The gerund phrase fragment is corrected by including it in the sentence.]

An infinitive phrase must not be written as a sentence.

FRAGMENT   You must first learn to float. To swim properly and with confidence. [The phrase cannot stand alone. It should be attached to the preceding sentence.]

CORRECTED   **To swim properly and with confidence,** you must first learn to float.

A prepositional phrase or a succession of prepositional phrases must not be written as a sentence.

FRAGMENT   The post office is two blocks from here. Near the corner on the north side of the street. [Here three successive prepositional phrases are isolated. They make sense only when included in the sentence.]

CORRECTED   The post office is two blocks from here **near the corner on the north side of the street**.

EXERCISE 1. Correcting Phrase Fragments.   Convert each of the following phrase fragments into a complete sentence by using one of two methods: (1) attach the fragment to an independent clause, or (2) develop the phrase into a complete sentence.

EXAMPLE   1. putting on her jacket
         1. *Putting on her jacket, Cindy left the theater.* [attached]
              or
         1. *Cindy was putting on her jacket.* [developed]

1. standing on the deck beside the captain
2. to make set shots consistently from outside the pivot position
3. on lower Main Street under the Lexington Bridge
4. puzzled by the question
5. to stay alert
6. finishing her assignment
7. murmuring something about a meeting
8. burned and blistered by the sun
9. playing tennis in the hot sun
10. performing the chemistry experiments

The Appositive Fragment

An appositive is a noun or pronoun that follows another noun or pronoun to identify or explain it. An appositive phrase (an appositive and its modifiers), should not be written as a separate sentence.

EXAMPLES   Mike, **the best mechanic in the garage,** worked on my car. [*The best mechanic in the garage* is an appositive. It is in apposition with *Mike*.]

In two years I will graduate from Madison High School, **a red brick building with a golden dome**. [*A red brick building with a golden dome* is in apposition with *Madison High School*.]

Sometimes a hasty writer will treat an appositive phrase as a complete sentence and leave it standing alone, even though it lacks a verb and subject and does not express a complete thought.

FRAGMENT   The amateur boat-builder was constructing a simple model. A small outboard cruiser of conventional design.

CORRECTED   The amateur boat-builder was constructing a simple model, **a small outboard cruiser of conventional design.** [The appositive phrase has been attached to the sentence in which it belongs.]

EXERCISE 2. Correcting Appositive Phrase Fragments. Number your paper 1–5. If an item consists of a sentence followed by an appositive fragment, write the last word in the sentence, a comma, and the first word of the appositive. If an item consists of two sentences, write *C*.

1. Before railroads, much inland transportation of freight was done by means of canals. Hand-dug, water-filled ditches that connected natural waterways.

2. An essential feature of the canals was their locks. Devices by which boats were raised or lowered from one level to another to accommodate changes in the terrain.
3. Canal boats were towed by horses walking on towpaths alongside the canals. This was a slow method of transportation.
4. The horses were driven on the paths by youths between the ages of twelve and seventeen. They were called loggees.
5. On the Erie Canal in 1850, a thousand people were employed as loggees. They were exposed to rough weather and if they let their towlines become tangled with those of a passing boat, to the wrath of boat captains.

The Subordinate Clause Fragment

Although a subordinate clause does have a subject and verb, it depends upon an independent clause to complete its meaning. Standing alone, a subordinate clause suggests a question which it does not answer.

EXAMPLES   Because the machine is so dangerous. [What will happen?]
           If you do not know how to operate it. [What will happen?]

A subordinate clause must be attached to an independent clause in order to complete its meaning. It should not be written as a sentence.

FRAGMENT   Television make-up differs from stage make-up. Because it must withstand the intense heat from the studio lamps.

CORRECTED   Television make-up differs from stage make-up **because it must withstand the intense heat from the studio lamps**.

FRAGMENT   Lamps that burned fat or olive oil served as the only source of artificial light until 1600. When petroleum was discovered.

CORRECTED   Lamps that burned fat or olive oil served as the only source of artificial light until 1600, **when petroleum was discovered**.

☞ NOTE   In combining an adverb clause with an independent clause, the adverb clause may either precede or follow the independent clause.

EXAMPLES   **If you bring your guitar to the picnic,** we can have some music. [adverb clause first]
           We can have some music **if you bring your guitar to the picnic.** [adverb clause last]

EXERCISE 3. Revising by Correcting Subordinate Clause Fragments. Copy the paragraphs, changing the punctuation and capitalization to eliminate the subordinate clause fragments which they contain.

Have you ever taken a course in film history? Some film historians believe that Alice Guy Blache was the first person. Who used the medium of motion pictures to tell a story. After she had worked as a director for Gaumont in Paris. She came to the United States. Where she formed her own production company in 1919. When she closed it down and began making films for Metro and Pathé. She returned to France in 1922. Since she was unable to find work in France. She retired from the cinema industry. Still in existence are some of this enterprising woman's American films. Which were made under the Solax company name. Alice Guy Blache died in an American nursing home in 1968 at the age of ninety-five. Her death received little public notice.

In the opinion of many critics, Sarah Maldoror is one of the most important of the film makers. Who are emerging from the Third World. Among her best films is *Sambizanga*. Which is set in Angola during the period before the uprising against Portuguese rule in 1961. *Sambizanga* deals with the conflicts between the Angolans and the Portuguese.

Do you know what a documentary film is? Have you ever seen one? While some people use the camera to present a fictional story. Others use the camera to try to capture life exactly as it is. In this latter category is Chick Strand, another important film maker. Whose films are part documentary and part personal interpretation of people and events. Her deep concern with anthropology and ethnography is reflected in each of her films. Which attempt to present all of the elements that will enable the viewer to see the people she is filming exactly as they are.

Check your local papers and see if you can find a showing of films by any of these three women.

EXERCISE 4. Using Subordinate Clauses in Sentences. Add an independent clause either at the beginning or at the end of each of the following subordinate clauses to make five complete sentences. When an adverb clause comes at the beginning of a sentence, it should be followed by a comma.

1. if we do well on the test
2. when they send the message
3. who can play several musical instruments
4. which I have never read
5. as we shut off the motor

EXERCISE 5. Identifying and Correcting Fragments. On your paper, mark each complete sentence with an *S*, and correct each fragment by making it part of a complete sentence.

1. Furnished with beautifully finished cottages, the resort was one of the finest in the area.
2. Running and dodging are features of lacrosse. Whose original object among its creators seems to have been the development of endurance and agility.
3. If you decide to go.
4. The friends shopped all day at the new shopping mall.
5. Elected by an overwhelming number of the students.
6. As she opened the door and peered out.
7. Because it was foggy and the visibility was poor.
8. Located in the middle of a swamp. The cabin was four miles from the highway.
9. Driving at night can be dangerous. Blinded by the lights of an approaching car. We almost hit a tree.
10. Because they wanted to escape the heat. They left for the mountains. Setting out in the early part of August.

THE RUN-ON SENTENCE

11b. Avoid the run-on sentence. Do not use a comma between sentences. Do not omit punctuation at the end of a sentence.

Independent clauses can be combined in a single sentence (1) by means of a comma plus a word like *and* or *but* or (2) by means of a semicolon. The following examples illustrate these two methods.

> Peanuts were more than just food to George Washington Carver, and in his laboratory he used them to make such things as ink and shampoo. [A comma plus *and* is used to join the two independent clauses.]

> Peanuts were more than just food to George Washington Carver; in his laboratory he used them to make such things as ink and shampoo. [A semicolon is used to join the clauses.]

The colon or the dash is sometimes used, but a comma alone is never enough between independent clauses. Using a comma or no punctuation at all in this situation results in the run-on sentence:

Peanuts were more than just food to George Washington Carver, in his laboratory he used them to make such things as ink and shampoo.

The run-on sentence is used effectively by experienced writers, especially when its parts are very short. A famous example is the translation of Julius Caesar's boast "I came, I saw, I conquered."

An easy test for spotting run-on sentences consists of simply reading your compositions aloud. The rise or fall of your voice and the pause you make at the end of a sentence sound quite different from the intonation and pause that a comma usually signals.

EXERCISE 6. Revising by Correcting Run-ons. The following passages contain a number of run-on sentences. Determine where each sentence properly begins and ends, and write the last word in the sentence with the proper mark after it. Then write the first word of the following sentence with a capital letter.

1

Having been excused early, we hurried to the locker room and changed to our uniforms, when the coach called us, we were ready to go the big bus drew up in the drive, and just as we had done a dozen other times, we piled in and took our usual seats this trip was different, however, everybody knew how different it was we would return either as champions of the state or as just another second-rate team.

2

Working on a lake steamer all summer was monotonous, it was also better than any other job I could have obtained, I loved the water and the ships and the rough and ready crew with whom I worked, the food was good the work was not too strenuous, if it hadn't been for the sameness of the routine day after day, I would probably never have left.

REVIEW EXERCISE. Revising Paragraphs by Eliminating Fragments and Run-ons. The following paragraphs contain sentence fragments and run-on sentences. Rewrite the passage correctly, changing the punctuation and capital letters whenever necessary.

Our national bird is the great bald eagle. As most Americans know. Similar to the bald eagle is the golden eagle. Which has a wingspread up to seven-and-a-half feet. The national bird is protected by law, but the golden eagle is not, the result is that hunters are rapidly diminishing the number of these great birds. If the golden eagles are not also given the protection of the law, they may become extinct. In a few years.

The National Audubon Society says that the annual slaughter of golden eagles is a national disgrace. Some hunters bagging hundreds of eagles a year. Texas and Oklahoma are the principal hunting territories, the birds are often shot from airplanes by gunners. Who are paid both by sheep ranchers and by manufacturers. Who want the feathers. Sheep ranchers claim the eagles menace sheep, tourists buy the feathers. Protecting the golden eagle will also provide further protection for the bald eagle. Because hunters often mistakenly kill bald eagles. Which, at a certain stage in growth, resemble golden eagles.

The golden eagle migrates to Texas and Oklahoma from northern regions. Such as Canada, Alaska, and our other Northwestern states. Golden eagles will be protected. If Congress amends the Bald Eagle Act. To include golden eagles.

CHAPTER 12

Writing Effective Sentences

SENTENCE COMBINING AND REVISING

Although a knowledge of grammar and punctuation is of obvious help in learning to write correct sentences, there is much more to effective writing than avoiding errors in sentence structure. The main difference between good writing and bad writing is not a matter of correctness, but a matter of *style*.

Style can be thought of as "a way of doing something." In writing, as in most things, there is a difference between doing things well and doing them any old way. In the pages that follow, you will find principles that will help you to write sentences that are more varied and therefore more interesting for your readers.

SENTENCE COMBINING

Short sentences are often effective in a composition, but a long series of short sentences tends to irritate readers. Notice how the short, choppy sentences in the following paragraph sound immature and make the paragraph less interesting to read.

> The first person to go over Niagara Falls in a barrel and live was Annie Edson Taylor. She was a schoolteacher. She was from Michigan. On September 24, 1901, she entered the upper Niagara River. She entered the river above the Horseshoe Falls. The Horseshoe Falls drops 51 meters to the

lower Niagara River. Seventeen minutes passed. Then Canadian rescuers pulled Annie from the river. She was badly bruised and shaken. She had escaped serious harm. Annie did not gain fame for her dangerous act. She did not gain fortune. Years later she died in a poorhouse.

Notice how the short, choppy sentences in the previous passage can be combined into longer, smoother sentences.

> The first person to go over Niagara Falls in a barrel and live was Annie Edson Taylor, a schoolteacher from Michigan. On September 24, 1901, she entered the upper Niagara River above the Horseshoe Falls, which drops 51 meters to the lower Niagara River. After seventeen minutes had passed, Canadian rescuers pulled Annie from the river. Badly bruised and shaken, she nevertheless escaped serious harm. Annie did not gain fame or fortune for her dangerous act, and years later she died in a poorhouse.

A number of sentence-combining devices have been used to rewrite the original passage. For example, the first three sentences have been combined by the use of an appositive phrase. Other sentences have been combined through the use of coordination and subordination.

12a. Combine short, related sentences by inserting adjectives, adverbs, or prepositional phrases.

TWO SENTENCES	The coach praised the players. The coach was delighted.
ONE SENTENCE	The **delighted** coach praised the players. [adjective]
TWO SENTENCES	The tired fans left the stadium. The fans left quietly.
ONE SENTENCE	**Quietly,** the tired fans left the stadium. [adverb]
THREE SENTENCES	The deer were feeding. The deer were on the hill. The hill was behind our house.
ONE SENTENCE	The deer were feeding **on the hill behind our house.** [prepositional phrases]

When you join short sentences by inserting adjectives, adverbs, or prepositional phrases, you may invent different ways of combining the same sentences. In such instances, the choice of word order is up to you, the writer. The combined sentences, however, should not change the meaning of the original sentences, nor should adjectives, adverbs, or prepositional phrases be misplaced within the combined sentence.

EXERCISE 1. Combining Sentences by Inserting Adjectives, Adverbs, or Prepositional Phrases.

Combine each group of short, related sentences into one sentence by inserting adjectives, adverbs, or prepositional phrases. Several combinations may be possible.

EXAMPLE   1. The basketball game will be televised.
            The game is tonight.
            The game is in the school gym.
         1. *The basketball game tonight in the school gym will be televised.*

1. Basketball has a history.
   The history is interesting.
2. The inventor was James Naismith.
   He was the inventor of basketball.
   He was from Springfield, Massachusetts.
3. In the first games, players shot a soccer ball at a peach basket.
   There were nine players on each team.
   The peach basket was suspended.
4. Basketball rules have changed.
   The rules have changed since 1891.
   The rules have changed greatly.
5. Basketball is popular.
   It is popular today.
   It is popular among men and women.
   It is popular all over the country.
6. Women basketball players compete.
   They are professional players.
   They compete before large crowds.
   They compete regularly.
7. The speed of modern basketball is surprising.
   It is often surprising.
   It is surprising to the spectator.
8. Dribbling, leaping, and shooting are the skills players practice.
   Dribbling, leaping, and shooting are skills in basketball.
   Most players practice these skills.
   They practice them for many hours.
9. Players concentrate on passing, shotblocking, and playmaking.
   They concentrate during team practice.
   They concentrate under a coach's direction.
   They usually concentrate.

10. Players may organize a play and then execute the play.
They may organize a play for hours.
They execute the play during a game.
They execute the play in seconds.

12b. Combine short, related sentences by using participial phrases.

A participial phrase (see pages 397–99) is a group of related words that contains a participle and that acts as an adjective. In the following examples, the participial phrases are boldfaced.

EXAMPLES   **Galloping across the meadow,** the horse neared the forest.
Elated by the news, we prepared a celebration.

Two closely related sentences can be combined by making one sentence a participial phrase.

TWO SENTENCES   The dogs yelped loudly.
The dogs ran down the trail.

ONE SENTENCE   **Yelping loudly,** the dogs ran down the trail.

A participial phrase must be placed close to the noun or pronoun it modifies. Otherwise the phrase might confuse the reader.

MISPLACED   **Flying overhead,** we saw an eagle.

CORRECTED   We saw an eagle **flying overhead.**

EXERCISE 2. Combining Sentences by Using Participial Phrases.

Combine each of the following pairs of sentences into one sentence by using a participial phrase. There may be more than one correct way to combine the sentences. Add commas where necessary. (See pages 576–77 for the use of commas to set off introductory phrases.)

EXAMPLE   1. His radio blared.
It woke up the house.
1. *His blaring radio woke up the house.*

1. Juanita Platero writes about Navajo culture.
The writing describes the conflict between old and new ideas.
2. Richard Wright was born a sharecropper's son.
He fought valiantly for an education.
3. *Meridian* was written by Alice Walker.
It is a novel about hope and courage.

4. Eudora Welty's stories are full of eccentric characters.
   The stories are set in rural places.
5. James Baldwin's essays depict his youth in Harlem.
   These essays are very popular.

12c. Combine short, related sentences by using appositive phrases.

Appositive phrases (see pages 406–07) explain or identify nouns or pronouns. In the following sentence, the appositive phrase is boldfaced.

EXAMPLE   The poodle, **a very intelligent dog,** is a most popular breed.

Two related sentences can be combined by using an appositive phrase.

TWO SENTENCES   The Shetland stands about one meter tall at the shoulders.
                 The Shetland is the smallest of ponies.
ONE SENTENCE   The Shetland, **the smallest of ponies,** stands about one meter tall at the shoulders.

EXERCISE 3. Combining Sentences by Using Appositive Phrases.
Combine each pair of sentences by turning one sentence into an appositive phrase. Be sure to put the phrase next to the noun or pronoun it identifies. Punctuate the sentence correctly. (See page 579 for the use of commas to set off appositive phrases.)

EXAMPLE   1. The kiwi has a strong sense of smell.
              The kiwi is a flightless bird of New Zealand.
           1. *The kiwi, a flightless bird of New Zealand, has a strong sense of smell.*

1. The railroad worm looks like a train with a red headlight.
   The railroad worm is actually a light-producing beetle.
2. The weaver may build nests measuring five meters across.
   The weaver is a sparrowlike African bird.
3. The flounder is a flat fish that swims on its side.
   The flounder has both eyes on one side of its head.
4. The walking catfish can survive on land for a long time.
   This catfish is a recent import to North America.
5. The zoo has a colony of animals that never need to drink water.
   The animals are kangaroo rats.

12d. Combine short, related sentences by using compound subjects and compound verbs.

Compound subjects and verbs (see pages 365–67) are joined by conjunctions such as *and, but,* or *or* and by correlative conjunctions such as *either—or, neither—nor,* or *both—and.*

EXAMPLES   Mom **and** Dad took us to see Williamsburg.
The committee could **neither** agree on the amendment **nor** vote on the motion.
Both students **and** teachers arrive early **and** leave late.

Short, related sentences may often be combined by using a compound verb, compound subject, or both.

TWO SENTENCES   We went to the movie theater.
We saw the new horror film.

ONE SENTENCE   We went to the movie theater **and** saw the new horror film.

FOUR SENTENCES   The players rushed to home plate.
The coach rushed to home plate.
The players protested the umpire's call.
The coach protested the umpire's call.

ONE SENTENCE   **Both** the players **and** the coach rushed to home plate **and** protested the umpire's call.

EXERCISE 4. Combining Sentences by Using Compound Subjects and Compound Verbs. Combine the following groups of sentences into one sentence by using compound subjects and compound verbs. Be sure the subjects and verbs agree in number.

1. Refined sugar is not necessary in a healthful diet.
   Too much salt is also not necessary in a healthful diet.
2. We should include a food from the bread group in every meal.
   We should avoid overeating carbohydrates.
3. A healthy person eats a varied diet.
   A healthy person exercises regularly.
   A healthy person gets enough sleep.
4. Meat provides essential protein.
   Beans provide essential protein.
   Rice provides essential protein.
5. Long-distance runners control their diet.
   Football players control their diet.
   The runners drink plenty of fluids.
   Football players drink plenty of fluids.

312 < Writing Effective Sentences

REVIEW EXERCISE A. **Revising a Paragraph by Combining Sentences.**   Revise the following paragraph so that it is appropriate for an English report to be read to your class. Combine short and choppy sentences.

Romeo and Juliet are two young people from rival families. They fall in love. They marry secretly. Romeo is exiled for killing Juliet's cousin in a duel. Romeo returns at night. He finds Juliet lying in a deep coma. Romeo thinks she is dead. Romeo kills himself with poison. Juliet awakens. She discovers Romeo's corpse. She kills herself with his dagger. Their senseless deaths stun the rival families. The deaths bring reconciliation.

12e. Combine short, related sentences by writing a compound sentence.

A compound sentence (see page 425) is really two or more simple sentences joined together by the conjunctions *and, but, or, nor, for, so,* or *yet.*

EXAMPLE   We started for home, **but** the rain made travel difficult.

When writing a compound sentence, be sure the ideas you connect are related and equal in importance.

UNRELATED IDEAS   The actors rehearsed their lines, and snow fell in record amounts.

RELATED IDEAS   The actors rehearsed their lines, and the musicians tuned their instruments.

EXERCISE 5. **Combining Sentences into a Compound Sentence.**
Combine each pair of sentences which contains closely related ideas into a compound sentence, adding commas as necessary. (For use of commas in compound sentences, see pages 572–73.) If a sentence pair contains unrelated ideas, write *U.*

1. The *Voyager* space probes have discovered much about Jupiter.
   We still have much to learn.
2. Earlier pictures had suggested that Jupiter's atmosphere was calm.
   The *Voyager* craft uncovered high-speed winds.
3. *Voyager* photographs showed lightning flashes.
   Scientists detected a new moon orbiting the planet.
4. Jupiter has several moons.
   Scientists are especially interested in the moon named Io.

5. *Voyager* passed close to Io.
   Scientists wanted a clear look at this small moon.

12f. Combine short, related sentences into a complex sentence by putting one idea into a subordinate clause.

A complex sentence (see page 426) has an independent clause and at least one subordinate clause.

(1) Use an adjective clause to combine sentences.

An adjective clause (see pages 416–19) is a subordinate clause that modifies a noun or a pronoun and begins with one of the relative pronouns: *who, whom, whose, which,* or *that.* In the following example, the adjective clause is boldfaced.

EXAMPLE We found a book **that had been printed more than two hundred years ago.**

To combine two sentences with an adjective clause, supply the necessary relative pronoun.

TWO SENTENCES The driver reported the accident.
The accident had blocked traffic in both directions.

ONE SENTENCE The driver reported the accident, **which** had blocked traffic in both directions.

EXERCISE 6. Combining Sentences by Using an Adjective Clause.
Combine each of the following groups of sentences into one sentence by using an adjective clause. Add commas where necessary. (For information about the use of commas with nonessential clauses, see pages 574–76).

1. Sacajawea guided Lewis and Clark.
   Lewis and Clark explored the Louisiana territory.
2. Matthew Henson was among the first explorers to reach the North Pole.
   Robert Peary chose Henson as his chief assistant.
3. Margaret Mead studied families in Samoa, Bali, and New Guinea.
   Her books are very popular today.
4. E. A. Martel pioneered in cave exploration.
   He charted deep vertical caves in Europe.

5. Amelia Earhart tried to fly around the world at the equator.
   She crashed into the Pacific Ocean.
6. Silvia Earle tests diving suits.
   The suits enable her to descend 380 meters.
7. Heinrich Schliemann unearthed an ancient city.
   This city, he believed, was the Troy of Homer's *Iliad*.
8. Inez Mexia was a famous botanical explorer.
   She spent months in the jungles of South America.
9. Antarctica has a harsh climate.
   It has never been fully explored.
10. Tenzing Norgay finally scaled Mount Everest.
    He had been climbing mountains for many years.

(2) Use an adverb clause to combine sentences.

An adverb clause (pages 419–21) is a subordinate clause that, like an adverb, modifies a verb, an adjective, or an adverb.

EXAMPLE **If the team scores this goal,** it will win the divisional championship.

Adverb clauses, like adverbs, may tell *when, how, where, to what extent,* or *under what condition* an action is done. An adverb clause begins with a subordinating conjunction. Study the following list:

Common Subordinating Conjunctions

after	before	than	whenever
although	if	unless	where
as	since	until	wherever
because	so that	when	while

When you combine two sentences by turning one into an adverb clause, be careful to choose a subordinating conjunction which shows the true relationship between clauses.[1] A poorly chosen conjunction will show a false or meaningless relationship. For example, a number of subordinating conjunctions could be used to join these two sentences, but not all of them would show a relationship that makes sense.

TWO SENTENCES At camp we get up. The sun rises.

UNCLEAR At camp we get up until the sun rises.

CLEAR At camp we get up **when** the sun rises.

---

[1] Choosing a subordinate conjunction is further discussed on pages 419–20.

EXERCISE 7. Combining Sentences by Using an Adverb Clause.
Combine each of the following groups of ideas into one sentence by putting one idea into an adverb clause. Refer to the list of subordinating conjunctions on page 419. Vary the conjunctions you choose. Add commas where necessary. (For the use of commas with introductory clauses, see page 577.)

1. A bill begins its passage into law.
   A representative sends a bill to the clerk of the House.
2. The Speaker of the House routes all bills to House committees.
   Relatively few bills pass beyond the committee stage.
3. A committee sends the approved bill to the full House.
   All representatives can have a vote.
4. The House passes the bill.
   It must also win the approval of the Senate.
5. A Senate committee approves or amends a similar bill.
   It moves to the full Senate.
6. The Senate bill is approved.
   The bill must agree with the House version.
7. The two bills go to a House-Senate conference committee.
   A compromise bill is agreed to.
8. A bill passes both the Senate and the House.
   It goes to the President to be signed into law.
9. The bill becomes law.
   The President vetoes it.
10. A vetoed bill can become law.
    A two-thirds majority in both House and Senate can override the President's veto.

(3) Use a noun clause to combine sentences.

Noun clauses (see pages 422–24) are usually introduced by *that, what, whatever, who, whoever, whom,* or *whomever.*

EXAMPLE   The jury decided **that the defendant was innocent of the charges.**

Two ideas can be combined by using a noun clause.

TWO SENTENCES   The doctor said something about nutrition.
                It was important.

ONE SENTENCE   **What the doctor said about nutrition** was important.

EXERCISE 8. Combining Sentences by Using a Noun Clause.
Combine each of the following groups of ideas into one sentence by
turning one of the ideas into a noun clause. There may be more than one
correct way to combine them.

1. We are going to the fair tonight.
   Nancy told me.
2. The wheel was invented long ago.
   Exactly when is still unknown.
3. The ticket seller refused to admit us.
   My father wanted to know why.
4. Bernie told us something.
   We wanted to hear it.
5. Fifteen players were injured.
   This fact did not affect the coach's game plan.

REVIEW EXERCISE B. Combining Sentences. Combine each of
the following groups of sentences into one sentence. There may be more
than one correct way to combine them. Add commas where necessary.
In some of the items, you may have to change some elements to create
parallel elements.

1. Marisol Escobar prefers to use only her first name.
   She has displayed her work at the Museum of Modern Art.
   She has displayed her work in a special room at the museum.
2. Gwendolyn Brooks has been recognized as a major American poet.
   She has been recognized for a long time.
   She has been elected to the National Institute of Letters.
3. Hiroko Yajima is originally from Tokyo.
   She is a young violinist.
   She came to New York.
   There she made her professional debut.
4. Fernando Bujones has lived in New York City.
   He is Cuban-born.
   He has been a dancer with the American Ballet Theater.
5. Cicely Tyson is a native-born American.
   She has appeared on television.
   She appeared as a young African woman.
   This woman refused to adopt Western culture.

NOT VARIED

The trial had been scheduled for two o'clock. The audience was noisily settling itself in the courtroom for the coming show. The lawyers were quietly talking and shuffling piles of papers at the polished tables in the front of the room. The bell in the courthouse tower struck two in resounding tones. Judge Perez, dignified in her long black gown, walked slowly to her bench. The clerk rasped out, "Everyone rise." The room seemed suddenly to lift for a moment; then it settled back into an ominous silence. The judge opened the case of *The People v. John Strong* in a manner which seemed to imply that such trials happened every day of her life.

VARIED

The trial had been scheduled for two o'clock. In the courtroom the audience was noisily settling itself for the coming show. At the polished tables in the front of the room, the lawyers were quietly talking and shuffling piles of papers. When the bell in the courthouse tower struck two in resounding tones, Judge Perez, dignified in her long black gown, walked slowly to her bench. "Everybody rise," rasped the clerk. Suddenly the room seemed to lift for a moment; then it settled back into an ominous silence. In a manner which seemed to imply that these trials happened every day of her life, the judged opened the case of *The People v. John Strong.*

You need not avoid the normal order of sentences merely for the sake of variety, but often you can increase the force and clarity of a statement by beginning it with an important modifier. The use of different kinds of sentence openers, in moderation, will improve your writing.

(1) You may begin a sentence with a single-word modifier—an adverb, an adjective, or a participle.

EXAMPLES **Instantly** I felt better. [adverb]
Thick and slimy, the mud oozed from under the truck's wheels. [adjectives]
Grinning, Myra tuned in her favorite radio program. [present participle]
Dejected, the coach sat on the bench and brooded over his team. [past participle]

For additional information about adverbs, adjectives, and participles, see Chapters 13 and 15.

EXERCISE 10. Revising Sentences by Beginning with Single-Word Modifiers. The following sentences contain single-word modifiers that can be placed at the beginning of the sentences. Rewrite each sentence, placing the modifier first. (For the use of commas with introductory single-word modifiers, see page 576.)

EXAMPLE 1. Our system of measurements will eventually be changed.
        1. *Eventually our system of measurements will be changed.*

1. The United States is planning cautiously to introduce the metric system.
2. Our vocabulary of measurement will gradually be replaced by a new one.
3. The metric system, tested and refined, has been in use in Europe and most of the rest of the world since the early nineteenth century.
4. The metric system, comprehensive and orderly, includes measurements of length, weight, volume, and temperature.
5. An inch converts metrically to 2.54 centimeters; an ounce to 28.3 grams; a quart to .946 liters; and 32° Fahrenheit to 0° Celsius (or Centigrade).

(2) You may begin a sentence with a phrase: a prepositional phrase, a participial phrase, an appositive phrase, or an infinitive phrase.

EXAMPLES **At the sound of the bell,** the teacher collected the papers. [prepositional phrase]
Having examined the records, the lawyer prepared a new deed. [participial phrase]
An excellent example of modern architecture, the new city hall is a favorite tourist attraction. [appositive phrase]
To learn to swim better, we took lessons. [infinitive phrase]

For additional information about phrases, see Chapter 15.

EXERCISE 11. Revising Sentences by Beginning with Phrase Modifiers. The following sentences contain phrase modifiers that can be placed at the beginning of the sentences. Revise each sentence by placing the modifying phrase at the beginning. Place a comma after each introductory phrase.

1. Pompeii was a well-to-do commercial city at the foot of Mt. Vesuvius.
2. Its population at the time of its destruction was about 30,000.
3. Archaeologists have discovered many facts about the life and times of ancient Pompeii to add to our knowledge of bygone days.

4. Wealthy Romans, attracted by the beauty of the location and healthfulness of the climate, built many villas there.
5. The streets, paved with blocks of lava, were usually wide and straight.
6. The Forum was a square, completely surrounded by temples and public buildings, near the western edge of the city.
7. Mt. Vesuvius had never given any indication of its volcanic character up to the year A.D. 63.
8. The inhabitants, still rebuilding their city from the ravages of earthquakes, were overwhelmed by the sudden eruption of August 24, A.D. 79.
9. The people fled the city to save their lives.
10. The existence of Pompeii was forgotten during the Middle Ages, and it was not until 1763 that excavations of the city began.

(3) You may begin a sentence with a subordinate clause.

EXAMPLES   I was unable to attend the Junior Prom because I had the flu.
Because I had the flu, I was unable to attend the Junior Prom.

Katsura was interested in joining the Masquers Club and the Film Group, but she did not have time to attend the meetings.

Although Katsura was interested in joining the Masquers Club and the Film Group, she did not have time to attend the meetings.

Subordinate clauses at the beginning of sentences usually begin with a subordinating conjunction. For a list of subordinating conjunctions, see page 419.

EXERCISE 12. Revising Sentences by Beginning with Subordinate Clauses.   Revise each sentence so that it begins with a subordinate clause instead of the subject. Place a comma after an adverb clause coming first in the sentence.

1. The praying mantis is a welcome guest in any garden because it destroys many harmful pests. [Because . . .]
2. The insects are not large in this country, but their South American relatives are big enough to devour small birds. [Although . . .]
3. The mantis was once highly regarded, and its landing on any person was considered a token of saintliness and an omen of good fortune. [Since . . .]

4. They watch patiently for their prey, and these creatures hold their claws in a kind of praying position. [When . . .]
5. Superstitious people believed these insects to be engaged in prayer, and so mantises were often called soothsayers or prophets. [Because . . .]
6. This insect can fly, but it prefers to wait on shrubs for its unsuspecting dinner to come by.
7. The mantis moves quietly and carefully, and seldom does its prey get away.
8. The forelegs shoot out like lightning, and the victim is caught in the mantis' trap.
9. The female mantis harbors no love for her mate, and a male mantis may find himself his wife's dinner if he is not fast on his feet.
10. These voracious eaters of destructive pests are protected by law in many areas, and a person may be fined for harming them.

EXERCISE 13. Revising Sentences by Beginning with Single-Word, Phrase, and Clause Modifiers. Change each of the following sentences in the manner suggested.

1. The steak was thick and juicy, and it just seemed to melt in my mouth. [Begin with single-word modifiers.]
2. The batter swung wildly at the ball. [Begin with a single-word modifier.]
3. The Student Council at Springfield High elected a parliamentarian to settle all disputes about conducting a meeting. [Begin with an infinitive phrase.]
4. Myron forgot his lines in the middle of the second act. [Begin with prepositional phrases.]
5. The house was appraised at $40,000 last year and sold for $45,000 this week. [Begin with a past participial phrase.]
6. The bookstore in our town gives special discounts at Christmas time. [Begin with a prepositional phrase.]
7. The coach was annoyed at Christine's failure to show up for practice and benched her for two games. [Begin with a past participial phrase.]
8. Ms. Wentworth came into the room and told us to report to the auditorium for our seventh-period class. [Begin with a subordinate clause.]

The band members rehearse every day after school **so that they can give a good performance at their concert.** [The idea in the subordinate clause states the reason for the idea in the independent clause.]

The following words, when used at the beginning of a subordinate clause, help to make clear the relationship between the sentence ideas:

CAUSE   because, since, as
RESULT OR REASON   so that, in order that
TIME   when, while, as, since, until, after, before, whenever

Whenever you are combining ideas, make sure that your connectives are appropriate.

EXERCISE 14. Changing Compound Sentences into Complex Sentences.   Change each of the following compound sentences into a complex sentence by expressing one of the ideas in a subordinate clause. Begin each subordinate clause with a word which will show how the ideas in the sentence are related: cause, result or reason, time.

1. Last week I visited New York City with my parents, and we saw the Dance Theater of Harlem at the Uris Theater.
2. Melva Murray-White danced in *Don Quixote,* and I was fascinated by her performance.
3. She danced with a powerful grace, and her movements radiated energy and exhilaration.
4. My favorite dance was *Agon,* and I enjoyed its theme of life and combat.
5. Its movements were like flashes of electricity, and the dancers darted back and forth across the stage with computerlike precision and timing.

EXERCISE 15. Revising a Composition by Changing or Combining Sentences into Complex Sentences.   The following paragraphs consist chiefly of simple and compound sentences. Revise them, varying the style by changing or combining some of the sentences into complex sentences. Do not try to make all your sentences complex, for your purpose is to achieve sentence variety.

1. My first day in high school was one of the most hectic days of my life. It all seems ridiculous now, but it was no joke then. With my

heart in my mouth, I boarded the school bus that morning. Many of my old friends from junior high days were seated there, but for some strange reason they did not want to talk very much. Everybody was abnormally quiet, and the air was electric with the tension. Gus, the bus driver, must have enjoyed the ride. Usually he has to tell us about twenty times to pipe down.

2. The silent bus soon arrived at the high school, and we filed quickly into the courtyard. For the tenth time in five minutes, I looked at my instructions for the first day. These instructions had come in the mail the week before, and by now I had practically memorized them. Still, I did not want to lose them. "Proceed to the student lobby and check your name on the lists posted there," stated the valuable paper. To make a long story short, I did just that and soon located my name on the bulletin board. The next step was to find Room 134, my official homeroom according to the list on the wall.

3. I wandered all over the school looking for Room 134. I should have asked for directions and saved myself a lot of trouble, but I was too stupid. At least, that's my excuse today. I bumped into Ray and Mike, my best friends last year. They were looking for Room 147. They didn't know the location of 134, but Ray did have a map of the school. I looked at it closely and found that Room 134 was right next to the student lobby.

4. I entered Room 134 slowly and glanced around. There wasn't a familiar face in sight. Where could all these strange people have come from? A short, red-haired man strode toward me and told me to take a seat. Sitting in the front makes me feel very conspicuous, so I selected a choice spot in the back of the room. I just can't stand a million eyes bouncing off the back of my head. The red-haired man was our homeroom teacher, and he explained about fire drills, cafeteria procedure, absentee notes, and countless other school rules. He was wasting his time. It sounded like mumbo jumbo to me, and it went in one ear and right out the other. Soon he distributed the program cards and a map of the school and told us to report to the first class at the ringing of the bell. The bell cut the silence of the room, and off I went on my big adventure.

5. The rest of the day was a real nightmare. I got lost many times, I got pushed around in the halls, and I felt like a rat prowling around in a gigantic maze. Some upperclassmen, chuckling to themselves, tried to sell me a ticket to the swimming pool on the third floor. I didn't fall for that, however. There isn't any swimming pool, and there isn't any third floor. I met all my new teachers, and each one kindly presented me with

a book weighing about three pounds. I could hardly walk around. The books kept slipping out of my arms. And so I came to the end of that first day and boarded the bus with my head swimming with *do's* and *don't's*. The ride home was just like old times. It wasn't quiet, and sure enough, Gus had to exercise his lungs and tell us to pipe down.

REVIEW EXERCISE C. Writing a Composition Using a Variety of Sentence Structures. Write a narrative composition about one of your own experiences. The purpose of your writing is to show that you can avoid a monotonous style by varying the form of your sentences. Before writing, review the three ways of beginning a sentence. Include some complex sentences in your composition. Check your writing for parallel structure.

PART THREE

TOOLS FOR
WRITING AND REVISING

Grammar ▪ Usage ▪ Mechanics

CHAPTER 13

The Parts of Speech

THEIR IDENTIFICATION AND FUNCTION

Words are classified according to the jobs they perform in sentences. There are eight main ways in which words are used in sentences; the eight kinds of words that perform these jobs are called *parts of speech.* They are *noun, pronoun, adjective, verb, adverb, preposition, conjunction,* and *interjection.*

DIAGNOSTIC TEST ✓

Identifying the Parts of Speech.   Number your paper 1–20. After the proper number, write each italicized word in the following sentences and indicate what part of speech it is. Use the abbreviations *n.* (noun), *pron.* (pronoun), *adj.* (adjective), *v.* (verb), *adv.* (adverb), *prep.* (preposition), *conj.* (conjunction), and *interj.* (interjection).

1. In the *thirty* years following the Civil War, millions of longhorn cattle were driven *over* long trails from ranches in Texas to railroads in Kansas.
2. When the drive was *over,* the cattle *were shipped* to northern cities to meet the need for hides, meat, and tallow. [*were shipped* = single part of speech]

3. During this *period,* the cowboy *became* an American hero.
4. Novels *and magazine* articles glorified life on the range.
5. Cowboys *who* rode the range, however, endured *many* hardships.
6. Even on *unusually* long drives, the cowboy spent *most* of his time in the saddle.
7. There *were few* comforts on the trail.
8. In fact, on early drives *each* cowboy cooked for *himself.*
9. Some *improvement* came after *Charles Goodnight* put together the first chuck wagon.
10. A hinged lid swung *down* to form a simple *but* complete kitchen.
11. The *first* chuck wagons were pulled *by* oxen.
12. *These* were later replaced by mules *or* horses.
13. The cook *not only* prepared meals *but also* served as a barber, a doctor, and a dentist.
14. Details of life on the trail are shown in the paintings of Charles M. Russell, which became *quite popular.*
15. His paintings show that cowboys worked *unbelievably* hard but that *they* also enjoyed many light moments.
16. *Most* of the cowhands who took part in the historic cattle drives remain *nameless.*
17. *In spite of* their anonymity, cowboys have added color to *our* history.
18. Moreover, they were *instrumental* in opening trails used by the men and women who *settled* the frontiers.
19. *Railroads soon* began to crisscross the country; the cowboy was no longer needed to drive cattle.
20. *Oh,* how the bravery and independence of the cowboy continue to stir the *imagination!*

THE NOUN

13a. A *noun* is a word used to name a person, place, thing, or idea.

A noun names something. Your own name is a noun. The name of your state is a noun. *Tree* is a noun. The names of things that you cannot see or touch are nouns: for example, *sympathy, fairness, width, generos-*

ity, magic, truth. These words do not name tangible things, but they do name qualities or ideas.

EXERCISE 1. Identifying Nouns in Sentences.✓ Number your paper 1–10. After the proper number, write the nouns that appear in each of the following sentences. Treat as single nouns all capitalized names of more than one word. Do not include years (for example, 1820).

1. Elizabeth Cady Stanton, an outspoken leader in the suffragist movement, was born in Johnstown, New York, in 1815. 2. She received a superior education in the classics and in mathematics both at home and at the Troy Female Seminary, from which she graduated in 1832. 3. From an early age she watched as her father practiced law; she was struck by the injustices suffered by women, especially in education and politics. 4. She became interested in the antislavery cause and in 1840 married Henry Stanton, a prominent abolitionist. 5. At an antislavery convention in London, Mrs. Stanton was outraged at the denial of recognition to the female delegates, among them Lucretia Mott. 6. She and Mrs. Mott later organized the first meeting addressed to the rights of women. 7. At this convention, held in Seneca Falls, New York, Mrs. Stanton read her "Declaration of Sentiments," outlining the inferior status of women and calling for reforms. 8. Later she joined forces with Susan B. Anthony, and for fifty years both women planned campaigns and spoke in statehouses and before congressional committees. 9. Mrs. Stanton, an accomplished writer and orator, was complemented by Miss Anthony, a superb organizer and tactician. 10. Both women also worked tirelessly for the abolition of slavery.

The Proper Noun and the Common Noun

Nouns may be divided into two classes: *proper nouns* and *common nouns.* A proper noun names a *particular* person, place, or thing; a common noun names a *class* of things.

PROPER NOUNS	COMMON NOUNS
Atlanta, Nantucket, Mount McKinley	city, island, mountain
Louisa May Alcott, General Patton	novelist, general
Museum of Fine Arts, the World Trade Center	museum, building
Queen Elizabeth 2	ship

GRAMMAR

☞ NOTE Compound nouns are made up of two or more words put together to form a single noun. Some compound nouns are written as one word (*basketball*), some as two or more words (*car pool, Arts and Crafts Club*), and some with hyphens (*passer-by, sister-in-law*). Notice that in the following example, the compound nouns are in boldfaced type.

EXAMPLE   His **mother-in-law** is a member of the **Tennis Club,** which holds its tournaments at the **Greenvale Courts.**

EXERCISE 2. Writing Proper Nouns. ✓For each of the following common nouns, write a proper noun after the corresponding number.

EXAMPLE   1. river
             1. *Mississippi River*

1. play   4. song   7. president   9. poem
2. state   5. ocean   8. writer   10. car
3. street   6. newspaper

WRITING APPLICATION A:
Using Nouns to Make Your Writing Specific

Nouns that name a quality or an idea are called *abstract nouns*. For example, *freedom* is an abstract noun. A good way to make abstract nouns clear is to give examples using nouns that a person can clearly picture in his mind.

EXAMPLE   kindness: 1. my *mother* washing my PE clothes 2. my *friend* listening to my problems 3. a *person* helping someone with heavy packages 4. a *driver* who helps someone with a dead battery 5. a *friend* who loans you some money when you forget yours

Writing Assignment

Select one of the following abstract nouns. Beside it, jot down six specific nouns that come to your mind as you think about your subject. Underline these nouns.

CHOICES   fear   compassion   liberty
           happiness   success   beauty

GRAMMAR

THE PRONOUN

13b. A *pronoun* is a word used in place of a noun or of more than one noun.

EXAMPLE   Susan watched the monkey make faces at her little sister and brother. **She** laughed at **it** more than **they** did. [*She* is used in place of *Susan, it* in place of *monkey, they* in place of *sister and brother.*]

Personal Pronouns

The boldfaced words in the preceding example are *personal* pronouns. Here, *personal* refers to one of the three possible ways of making statements: A person speaking about himself or herself (first person) or about the person being spoken to (second person) or about anyone or anything else (third person). The few pronouns in English that have different forms to show person are called *personal pronouns.*

	Singular	*Plural*
FIRST PERSON	I, my, mine, me	we, our, ours, us
SECOND PERSON	you, your, yours	you, your, yours
THIRD PERSON	he, his, him	they, their, theirs, them
	she, her, hers	
	it, its	

Here are some other kinds of pronouns that you will encounter as you study this textbook.

RELATIVE PRONOUNS   (used to introduce adjective and noun clauses; see pages 416–17, 422–23)

who   whom   whose   which   that

INTERROGATIVE PRONOUNS   (used in questions)

Who . . . ?   Whose . . . ?   What . . . ?
    Whom . . . ?   Which . . . ?

DEMONSTRATIVE PRONOUNS   (used to point out a specific person or thing)

this   that   these   those

INDEFINITE PRONOUNS   (not referring to a definite person or thing)

all	anybody	both	everybody
another	anyone	each	everyone
any	anything	either	everything

few	much	no one	some
many	neither	one	somebody
more	nobody	other	someone
most	none	several	such

REFLEXIVE PRONOUNS (the *-self, -selves* forms of the personal pronouns)

myself	ourselves
yourself	yourselves
himself, herself, itself	themselves

☞ NOTE   Never write or say *hisself* or *theirselves*.

EXERCISE 3. Identifying Pronouns in Sentences. ✓ Number your paper 1–7. Write after the proper number the pronouns in each of the following sentences. You should find at least twenty-five pronouns.[1] If a pronoun is used more than once, write it each time it appears.

1. Everybody in my family likes to go camping, but few of us enjoy the experience more than I do.   2. Last summer several of my cousins and I stayed at a rustic camp in the mountains, which are not far from our hometown.   3. At camp we all learned how to build a campfire and how to keep it going.   4. A group of us even went beyond that—we learned to cook meals over the open fire.   5. One of our counselors showed those who were interested how to cook simple meals.   6. Each of his recipes was easy to follow, and everyone ate everything in sight.   7. Anything cooked over an open fire tastes good, don't you agree?

THE ADJECTIVE

13c. An *adjective* is a word used to modify a noun or a pronoun.

Adjectives are words used to make the meaning of a noun or a pronoun more definite. Words used in this way are called *modifiers*.

---

[1] When words in the list on page 335 immediately precede a noun (*my* friend, *your* brother, etc.), they are considered possessive *pronouns* in this book, rather than *adjectives*.

An adjective may modify a noun or a pronoun by telling *what kind* it is.

blue ink   **old** friends   **strong** winds

An adjective may indicate **which one.**

this park   **these** papers   **that** house

An adjective may tell **how many**.

twenty-five kilometers   **two** men   **several** apples

An adjective is not always placed next to the word it modifies. It may be separated from the word it modifies by other words.

The sky was **cloudy.** [cloudy sky]

That joke is **clever.** [clever joke]

☞ NOTE   An adjective modifying a pronoun is almost always separated from the pronoun.

They look **happy.**   She is **strong.**

Articles

The most frequently used adjectives are *a, an,* and *the.* These little words are usually called *articles.*

A and *an* are *indefinite* articles; they refer to one of a general group.

EXAMPLES   **A** ranger helped us.
We kept watch for **an** hour.
They planted **an** acre with corn.

A is used before words beginning with a consonant sound; *an* is used before words beginning with a vowel sound. Notice in the second example above that *an* is used before a noun beginning with the consonant *h* because the *h* in *hour* is not pronounced. The *sound* of the noun, not the spelling, determines which indefinite article will be used.

The is the *definite* article. It indicates that a noun refers to someone or something in particular.

EXAMPLES **The** ranger helped us.
The hour dragged by.
They planted **the** acre with corn.

EXERCISE 4. √Identifying the Words that Adjectives Modify.
Number your paper 1–10. Write the adjective after the appropriate
number, and after each adjective, write the word it modifies.

1. By the 1890's, an *extraordinary* craze for bicycling had swept the
United States. 2. Though bicycles had been *available* for years, the
early versions made for an *awkward* ride. 3. These *ungainly* cycles
featured a very *tall* wheel in the front and a *small* wheel in the
back. 4. In 1885, however, a more *sensible* bicycle was introduced,
one that resembled the *modern* vehicle. 5. *Energetic* people everywhere suddenly took to *this* bicycle. 6. Bicycling soon became a
national sport. 7. Cyclists joined *special* clubs that planned *vigorous*
tours through the countryside. 8. A *typical* ride might cover *twenty*
miles, with a *welcome* stop for refreshments. 9. Races were also
popular with *enthusiastic* spectators, who often outnumbered those at
ball games. 10. The fans enjoyed watching *these* tests of endurance,
which sometimes lasted *six* days.

**EXERCISE 5. Supplying Interesting Adjectives to Complete
Sentences.** Write the following sentences, supplying adjectives in the
blank spaces. Use meaningful, interesting adjectives. Read the paragraph through before you start to write.

1. Hillcrest Gardens offers the visitor a —— oasis within
the —— , —— jungle of city life. 2. It is especially —— in the
springtime. 3. Everywhere you will discover the —— sights
and —— scents of plants blooming after a —— winter. 4. You can
take a —— walk along the —— paths or simply relax on one of
the —— benches in this —— garden. 5. As you meander, feast your
eyes on the —— beds of —— and —— tulips and on the —— clusters
of daffodils. 6. Your visit will not be complete until you stroll under
the —— canopy of —— flowering fruit trees. 7. Nearby are
—— , —— bushes of —— lilacs. 8. They fill the air with
a —— fragrance. 9. However, the most —— spot for —— visitors is
the goldfish pond. 10. Here rays of —— sunlight cause the —— fish
to gleam like —— jewels.

GRAMMAR

WRITING APPLICATION B:
Using Adjectives to Describe an Imagined Self

Have you ever imagined what it would be like to be an object or an animal? Some outstanding writers have done just that. In one of his stories, Franz Kafka writes about a man who awakens to discover that he is changed into a cockroach! One characteristic of a creative writer is a fruitful imagination.

EXAMPLE   The speaker in a poem by Sylvia Plath is a mirror:

I am silver and exact . . .
I am not cruel, only truthful —

Writing Assignment

Imagine that you are changed into an animal or an object. Using at least ten carefully chosen adjectives, describe yourself. Underline these adjectives. Do not count articles as adjectives.

Pronoun or Adjective?

Some words may be used either as adjectives or as pronouns (*this, which, each,* etc.). To tell them apart, keep in mind what they do.[1]

Adjectives *modify* nouns, while pronouns *take the place of* nouns. In the first sentence in each of the following pairs, the boldfaced word is used as a pronoun. In the second sentence of each pair, the word is used as an adjective.

PRONOUN   **Those** are excited fans.
ADJECTIVE   **Those** fans are excited.
PRONOUN   **Many** cheered the famous athlete.
ADJECTIVE   **Many** fans cheered the famous athlete.

Notice that a noun must follow immediately if the word is used as an adjective.

EXERCISE 6. Identifying Words as Adjectives or Pronouns.   Write the numbered, italicized words in a column on your paper. After each

---

[1] Pronouns used before nouns (*my* friend, *your* brother) are sometimes called adjectives because they modify a noun. In this book such pronouns are called *possessive pronouns.* Follow your teacher's wishes in referring to such words.

word, tell whether it is used as a pronoun or an adjective (*pron.*, *adj.*). For each adjective, write the word it modifies.

a. Ants, (1) *which* are related to wasps, are significantly unlike (2) *those* insects.
b. (3) *All* ants are social; (4) *most* wasps are solitary.
c. (5) *Most* of the solitary wasps are hunting wasps.
d. (6) *These* make nests in soil or in decaying wood.
e. (7) *These* wasps congregate to form a permanent colony of adults and young.
f. There are 35,000 species of ants; (8) *each* contains three castes: males, queen, and workers.
g. (9) *Some* colonies include half a million ants; (10) *others* may be much smaller.

Nouns Used as Adjectives

Sometimes nouns are used as adjectives.

salad bowl	**grocery** store
chicken dinner	**gold** chain

When you are identifying parts of speech and find a noun used as an adjective, call it an adjective.

REVIEW EXERCISE A: Identifying Nouns, Pronouns, and Adjectives. Number your paper 1–10. Next to the proper number write and label the nouns (*n.*), pronouns (*pron.*), and adjectives (*adj.*) used in the following sentences. After each adjective, write the word that it modifies. (Do not include the articles *a, an,* and *the.*)

1. Our teacher, Mr. Lopez, identified the various trees along the nature trail.
2. The bird feeder in the elm tree in my yard attracts cardinals and chickadees.
3. The flag over the hotel was a welcome sight to the two travelers.
4. The antique doll was dressed in a sailor hat and a blue suit.
5. Autumn leaves colored the highway along the Hudson River with bright splashes of red and orange.
6. A large cake sat in the center of the kitchen table.

7. Someone has filled the fruit bowl with dates and walnuts.
8. As a child Susan B. Anthony was taught the religious tenets of the Quakers, which include the belief in the equality of women.
9. Because some streams are impure, fish cannot survive in them.
10. The book cover on that anthology has seen better days.

THE VERB

13d. A *verb* is a word that expresses action or otherwise helps to make a statement.

All verbs help to make statements. Some do it by expressing action, others by telling something about the subject.

Action Verbs

Words such as *bring, say, shout,* and *jump* are action verbs. Some action verbs express an action that cannot be seen—for example, *ponder, trust, evaluate,* and *review.*

There are two general classes of action verbs—*transitive* and *intransitive.* A verb is *transitive* when the action it expresses is directed toward a person or thing named in the sentence.

EXAMPLES   She **flew** the airplane. [The action of the verb *flew* is directed toward *airplane.* The verb is transitive.]
Zora Neale Hurston **wrote** novels.

In these examples the action passes from the doer—the subject—to the receiver of the action. Words that receive the action of a transitive verb are called *objects.*

A verb is *intransitive* when it expresses action (or helps to make a statement) without reference to an object. The following sentences contain intransitive verbs.

EXAMPLES   The birches **swayed.**
The train **stops.**

The same verb may be transitive in one sentence and intransitive in another. A verb that can take an object is often used intransitively when the emphasis is on the action rather than on the person or thing affected by it.

EXAMPLES   Miss Castillo **weeds** the garden every day. [transitive]
Miss Castillo **weeds** every day. [intransitive]

Elsa **swam** the channel. [transitive]
Elsa **swam** for many hours. [intransitive]

EXERCISE 7. Identifying Verbs as Transitive or Intransitive.   Some of the verbs in the following sentences are transitive and some are intransitive. Write the verb of each sentence after the proper number, and label it as a dictionary would—*v.t.* for transitive, *v.i.* for intransitive.

1. The strong winds died down.
2. We quickly packed lunch for a trip to the seashore.
3. The whitecaps on the ocean had disappeared.
4. The sun sparkled on the gently splashing surf.
5. At low tide, Rosita suddenly spotted a starfish.
6. She noticed its five purplish arms.
7. She touched a soft, brown sponge floating nearby.
8. She added it to her collection of shells and dried seaweed.
9. Her collection includes several conch shells.
10. Three horseshoe crabs swam in the tidal pool.

WRITING APPLICATION C:
Using Verbs to Enliven Your Writing

Have you noticed the many ways sports writers avoid the monotony of saying that one team *defeated* another?

EXAMPLES   Johnson High *Rocks* Jefferson
Wakulla *Smashes* Blountstown
Hamilton *Blasts* Eastern

Writing Assignment

Revise each of the following sentences by thinking of new, lively verbs to substitute for the underlined words.

1. Cham opened the door and told Tom to hurry up.
2. Mother suddenly stepped on the brakes and the car stopped.
3. He frowned as I sang loudly the words to our alma mater.
4. She lay down on her bed and began to cry.

GRAMMAR

Linking Verbs

Linking verbs help to make a statement not by expressing an action but by serving as a link between two words.   Such verbs are intransitive.

The most commonly used linking verbs are forms of the verb *be*. You should become thoroughly familiar with these.

be	were	shall have been	should have been
being	shall be	will have been	would have been
am	will be	should be	could have been
is	has been	would be	
are	have been	can be	
was	had been	could be	

Any verb ending in *be* or *been* is a form of the verb *be*. In addition to *be*, the following verbs are often used as linking verbs.

Other Common Linking Verbs

appear	grow	seem	stay
become	look	smell	taste
feel	remain	sound	

In the following sentences each verb is a link between the words on either side of it. The word that follows the linking verb fills out or completes the meaning of the verb and refers to the subject of the verb.

Kelp **is** the scientific name for seaweed. [*Kelp* = name]
Kelp **tastes** good in a salad. [good kelp]
Most seaweed **becomes** brown as it ages. [brown seaweed]
Kelp **can be** a basic source of iodine. [Kelp = source]

> ☞ NOTE   Many of the linking verbs listed above can be used as action (nonlinking) verbs as well.

Emilia **felt** calm at the seashore. [linking verb: calm Emilia]
Emilia **felt** the rubbery strands of the ribbon kelp. [action verb]
Some kelps **grow** long. [linking verb: long kelps]
Some kelps **grow** large bulbs. [action verb]

Even *be* is not always a linking verb. It may be followed by only an adverb: *They are here.* To be a linking verb, the verb must be followed by a word that refers to (names or describes) the subject.

EXERCISE 8. Writing Sentences Using Verbs as Both Linking and Action Verbs. For each of the following verbs, write two sentences. In the first sentence, use the verb as a linking verb; in the second sentence, use it as an action verb.

1. appear   2. sound   3. smell   4. grow   5. look

The Verb Phrase

A verb frequently has one or more *helping verbs*. The verb and the helping verbs make up a unit that is called the *verb phrase*.

Commonly used helping verbs are *will, shall, have, has, had, can, may, might, do, does, did, must, ought, should, would*, and the forms of the verb *be* (see page 343).

EXAMPLES   This year's budget **has been approved.**
Sally **will launch** the canoe.
Did she **paint** the house?
You **might have helped** with the trim.

EXERCISE 9. Identifying Verbs as Action Verbs or Linking Verbs. Study each italicized verb in the following sentences. Tell whether it is an action verb or a linking verb.

1. Situated on the banks of the Nile in Egypt, the ruins at Karnak *are* some of the most impressive sights in the world.
2. The largest ruin *is* the Great Temple of Amon.
3. Its immense size is astonishing to people who *know* little about the scale of Egyptian architecture.
4. If you *should follow* the avenue of sphinxes which leads to the entrance, you *would be amazed* at the 42-meter-high gateway.
5. The ceiling of the temple *is* extremely high—more than 23 meters above the floor.
6. The central columns that *support* the stone roof *are* enormous.
7. The columns' surfaces *are decorated* with low relief carvings.
8. Even an amateur engineer *can appreciate* the tremendous efforts which *must have gone* into the completion of this temple.
9. We now *know* that inclined planes, combined with levers and blocking, *enabled* the ancient Egyptians to raise the large stones.
10. Nevertheless, the temple *seems* an incredible undertaking.

GRAMMAR

EXERCISE 10. Identifying Verbs and Verb Phrases. Number your paper 1–10. Write the verbs in each of the following sentences. Be sure to include all the helping verbs.

> ☞ NOTE The word *not* in a phrase such as *could not go* is not a verb. *Not* is an adverb.

1. The first performance of the marching band would occur tonight on the football field.   2. Marcia and the other flute players were clapping their hands vigorously, because their fingers had already become numb in the raw, chilly air.   3. It would not be funny if their fingers froze to the keys of their flutes.   4. Music would stream out in a shrill blast, and the spectators would be startled.   5. The other band members would no doubt skip a beat, and chaos might spread across the field.   6. With all the musicians out of step, the flute players might stumble into the clarinet players, who would certainly collide with the trombone players, who just might trip over the drummers.   7. As the time for their performance drew near, Marcia and her friends rolled their eyes and laughed about the dreadful scene they had just imagined. 8. Surely such a disaster could not possibly happen.   9. "Oh, no!" Marcia exclaimed as the band marched onto the field. "It is snowing!" 10. People were already leaving the stands when the principal announced over the loudspeaker: "Ladies and gentlemen, please remain in your seats; the band will now play 'Jingle Bells.'"

THE ADVERB

13e. An *adverb* is a word used to modify a verb, an adjective, or another adverb.

Adverbs qualify the meaning of the words they modify by telling *how, when, where,* or *to what extent.*

Adverbs Modifying Verbs

Just as there are words (adjectives) that modify nouns and pronouns, there are words that modify verbs. For example, the verb *sing* may be modified by such words as *loudly, softly, haltingly,* or *cheerfully.* A word that modifies a verb is an *adverb.* An adverb qualifies the meaning of the verb.

EXAMPLES   The bird was chirping **downstairs.** [*where*]
The bird chirped **today.** [*when*]
The bird chirped **loudly.** [*how*]
Our bird chirped **constantly.** [to *what* extent]

EXERCISE 11. Identifying Adverbs and the Verbs They Modify. There are ten adverbs in the following sentences. Write them after the proper number. After each adverb, write the verb that it modifies.

1. The first balloonists floated gently above Paris in a hot-air balloon that had been cleverly designed by the Montgolfier brothers. 2. Although their earlier attempts had failed, the Montgolfiers never stopped trying and finally settled on a balloon made of paper and linen. 3. These early balloons differed significantly from modern balloons, which are sturdily constructed of coated nylon. 4. Despite their ingenuity, the Montgolfiers first thought that smoke would effectively push a balloon skyward. 5. In their first experiments, they bravely prepared fuel from rotten meat and old shoes.

Adverbs Modifying Adjectives

Sometimes an adverb modifies an adjective.

EXAMPLES   It was a **fiercely** competitive game. [The adverb *fiercely* tells *how* and modifies the adjective *competitive.*]
The police officer was **exceptionally** brave. [The adverb *exceptionally* modifies the adjective *brave.*]

☞ NOTE   Probably the most frequently used adverb is *very.* It is so overworked that you should avoid it whenever you can and try to find a more exact word to take its place.

EXERCISE 12. Identifying Adverbs and the Adjectives They Modify. Number your paper 1–10. In each of the following sentences, there is an adverb modifying an adjective. After the proper number, write these adverbs. After each adverb, write the adjective it modifies.

1. An immensely long wagon train started out from Denver.
2. Both oxen and mules were used to pull unusually large wagons.
3. The trail through the mountains was fairly hazardous.
4. A moderately hard rain could turn the trail into a swamp.
5. When the trail was too muddy, the heavier wagons became mired.
6. Wagons that were extremely heavy then had to be unloaded before they could be moved.
7. Stopping for the night along the trail was a consistently welcome experience.
8. It offered relief to thoroughly tired bones and muscles.
9. Nights in the mountains could be quite cold.
10. On terribly cold nights, the travelers would roll themselves in blankets and sleep close to their campfires.

Adverbs Modifying Other Adverbs

You have learned that an adverb may modify a verb or an adjective. An adverb may also modify another adverb.

EXAMPLE   The guide spoke **too** slowly.

You can recognize *slowly* as an adverb modifying the verb *spoke*. It tells *how* the guide spoke. You can also see that *too* modifies the adverb *slowly*. It tells *how* slowly.

> ☞ NOTE   Many adverbs end in *-ly*. Do not make the mistake, however, of thinking that all words ending in *-ly* are adverbs. For instance, the following words are adjectives: *homely, kindly, lovely, deadly.* Moreover, some common adverbs do not end in *-ly*: for example, *always, never, very, soon, not, too.*

EXAMPLE   The U.S. hockey team did **not** win an Olympic gold medal between 1960 and 1980. [The adverb *not* comes between the parts of the verb phrase *did win.*]

EXERCISE 13. Identifying Adverbs and the Words They Modify.
There are twenty-five adverbs in the following paragraph. Write them after the proper numbers on your paper: After each, write the

word that the adverb modifies and tell whether this word is a verb, an adjective, or another adverb.

1. Yesterday my sister June and I shopped for houseplants. 2. The large ones were too expensive for us. 3. We also knew that large plants are almost always raised in hothouses. 4. They do not adjust easily to homes in extremely cold climates. 5. Suddenly June had a brainstorm. 6. "Let's buy some seeds and grow them indoors. 7. That way we can choose a rare species, and the seedlings will automatically adapt themselves to the climate in our house." 8. At the seed store the owner, Mrs. Miller, greeted us cheerfully. 9. We told her we wanted seeds for a plant seldom sold in local shops. 10. We mentioned that our room hardly ever gets bright sunlight and that during the winter it is especially dark. 11. "I know what you need," Mrs. Miller promptly replied. 12. "These are seeds of the bo tree, an unusually hardy member of the fig family native to India. 13. There it is sacred to Buddhists, for it is said that the Buddha received enlightenment under a bo tree." 14. At home we carefully planted the seeds in a container filled with moist dirt and a layer of damp peat moss. 15. We then covered the container with a sheet of transparent plastic film. 16. Eventually the seeds sprouted and our trees grew. 17. To our surprise, we discovered that each leaf of the bo tree ends in a delicately tapered tip. 18. The leaves were the most unusual ones we had ever seen!

EXERCISE 14. Using Words as Adjectives or Adverbs. The following words may be used as either adjectives or adverbs. Write a pair of sentences for each word. In the first sentence, use the word as an adjective; in the second, use it as an adverb.

EXAMPLE   1. kindly
1. *She had a kindly manner.* [adjective]
1. *She spoke kindly.* [adverb]

1. daily   2. fast   3. late   4. more   5. far

REVIEW EXERCISE B. Identifying the Parts of Speech of Words. Number your paper 1–25. After the proper number, write the italicized words in the following paragraphs. After each word, tell its part of speech. For each adjective and adverb, write the word modified.

With a (1) *thunderous* roar an avalanche (2) *slides* (3) *swiftly* down a mountainside. (4) *It* sometimes travels at speeds of more than 200 miles an hour and poses a (5) *deadly* threat to skiers, mountain climbers, and the people (6) *who* live and work in the mountains.

The (7) *best* way to survive an avalanche is to make swimming motions in order to remain on top of the snow. People who are caught in an avalanche, however, (8) *rarely* survive. They are (9) *usually* completely (10) *immobilized,* and the slide (11) *itself* forces snow into the victim's nose and mouth.

Avalanche workers both in the (12) *United States* and abroad have (13) *long* realized the (14) *potential* (15) *destructiveness* of selected slide paths. They (16) *have concluded* that an avalanche can be (17) *substantially* reduced if (18) *explosives* (19) *are used* to trigger a (20) *series* of (21) *smaller* slides before (22) *one* large mass of snow can build up. (23) *Today* the detonation of explosives has become a standard (24) *practice* for controlling avalanches in (25) *this* country.

WRITING APPLICATION D:
Using Adverbs to Express Intense Feeling

Perhaps you have strong opinions and feelings about such issues as environmental pollution, inadequate facilities for the handicapped, and so forth. The careful use of adverbs helps you express intense feelings and opinions.

EXAMPLE   I am *ardently* concerned about world hunger.

Writing Assignment

Select an issue that affects many people. Write a paragraph in which you express your opinions and feelings about this topic. Use at least three adverbs. Underline them. Try to avoid *very, extremely,* or *quite.*

THE PREPOSITION

13f. A *preposition* **is a word that shows the relationship of a noun or a pronoun to some other word in the sentence.**

Prepositions are important because they point out different relationships. Notice in the following examples how the prepositions in bold-faced type show three different relationships between *village* and *rode* and between *river* and *park*.

I rode **past** the village.	The park **near** the river is quiet.
I rode **through** the village.	The park **beside** the river is quiet.
I rode **beyond** the village.	The park **across** the river is quiet.

A preposition always introduces a phrase (see page 389). The noun or pronoun that ends a prepositional phrase is the *object* of the preposition which introduces the phrase. In the previous examples the objects of the prepositions are *village* and *river*.

Commonly Used Prepositions

aboard	below	for	past
about	beneath	from	since
above	beside	in	through
across	besides	inside	to
after	between	into	toward
against	beyond	like	under
along	but (meaning	near	underneath
amid	"except")	of	until
among	by	off	up
around	concerning	on	upon
at	down	onto	with
before	during	outside	within
behind	except	over	without

Compound prepositions consist of more than one word.

according to	in addition to	instead of
because of	in front of	on account of
by means of	in spite of	prior to

☞ NOTE   The same word may be either an adverb or a preposition, depending on its use in a sentence.

EXAMPLES   Marge climbed **down.** [adverb]
Marge climbed **down** the ladder. [preposition]

EXERCISE 15. Writing Sentences Using Words as Prepositions.

Use the following words as prepositions in sentences. Underline the phrase that each preposition introduces. Be able to tell between which words the preposition shows a relationship.

1. during   2. with   3. beyond   4. into   5. aboard

EXERCISE 16. Writing Sentences Using Words as Adverbs. Use the following words as adverbs in sentences.

1. up   2. on   3. past   4. along   5. by

THE CONJUNCTION

13g. A *conjunction* **joins words or groups of words.**

Conjunctions are used to join parts of a sentence that function in the same way or in a closely related way. The parts joined may be words, phrases, or clauses. In the following examples the conjunctions are in boldfaced type, and the words they join are underscored.

EXAMPLES   The orchestra played one *waltz* **and** two *polkas*.
We can *walk to the shopping mall* **or** *take a bus*.
I looked for Hal, **but** *he had already left*.

There are three kinds of conjunctions: *coordinating, correlative,* and *subordinating.*

Coordinating conjunctions. Conjunctions that join equal parts of a sentence are called *coordinating conjunctions*. They are *and, but, or, nor, for, so,* and *yet.*[1]

Correlative conjunctions. Some conjunctions are used in pairs. Examples of these are *either...or, neither...nor, both...and, not only...but also.* Study the pairs of conjunctions in the following sentences. Conjunctions of this kind, used in pairs, are *correlative conjunctions.*

Either the head coach **or** the assistant coach will time your sprint.
Neither the baseball team **nor** the football team has practice today.
Both the track team **and** the volleyball team enjoyed a winning season.

Their victories sparked the enthusiasm **not only** of students **but also** of teachers and townspeople.

[1] The conjunctions *and, but, or,* and *nor* can join words, phrases, and clauses. *For, so,* and *yet* usually join clauses. For this reason some grammarians consider these last three words subordinating conjunctions, not true coordinating conjunctions. Follow your teacher's wishes in classifying these last three conjunctions.

Subordinating conjunctions will be discussed later in connection with subordinate clauses (pages 419–20).

EXERCISE 17. Identifying Coordinating and Correlative Conjunctions. Write the coordinating and correlative conjunctions in the following sentences.

1. Once Nantucket and New Bedford were home ports of great whaling fleets. 2. Whaling channeled tremendous profits into these ports, but the golden days of whaling ended about the time of the War Between the States. 3. A whaling trip was no pleasure cruise for either the captain or the crew, for they worked long hours during a day on the sea. 4. Maintaining order was no easy task on a long voyage, because the food and living conditions gave rise to discontent. 5. Inevitably the sailors had time on their hands, for they didn't encounter a whale every day. 6. To relieve the dullness and boredom on long voyages, whaling ships often would exchange visits. 7. Not only the captain but also the whole crew looked forward to such visits. 8. All enjoyed the chance to chat and exchange news. 9. The decline of whaling and of the whaling industry began about 1860. 10. Our country no longer needed large quantities of whale oil; for kerosene, a cheaper and better fuel, had replaced it.

THE INTERJECTION

13h. An *interjection* **is a word that expresses emotion and has no grammatical relation to other words in the sentence.**

There are a few words that can be used to show sudden or strong feeling, such as fright, anger, excitement, or joy.

EXAMPLES **Ouch!   Ugh!   Wow!   Oops!   Oh!**

These words are usually followed by an exclamation mark. An interjection that shows only mild emotion is followed by a comma.

Well, I'm just not sure.

EXERCISE 18. Writing a List of Interjections. Make a list of ten interjections other than those given above. Be sure to include an exclamation point after each interjection.

DETERMINING PARTS OF SPEECH

13i. What part of speech a word is depends on how the word is used.

In the following sentences you will see that one word is used as three different parts of speech. What part of speech is *light* in each sentence?

> Rich heard the **light** patter of raindrops.
> The room was filled with **light.**
> Let's **light** some candles this evening.

EXERCISE 19. Determining the Parts of Speech of Words. Number your paper 1–20. Study the use of the italicized words in the following sentences. Write the part of speech of each italicized word after the proper number. Be prepared to explain why the word is that part of speech.

1. They decided that the hedge needed a *trim.*
2. Their hedges always look *trim* and neat.
3. We usually *trim* the tree with homemade ornaments.
4. Mother always *shears* a couple of inches off the top of the tree.
5. Later she uses garden *shears* to cut straggling branches.
6. My brother *spices* fruit pies with nutmeg and allspice.
7. These *spices* are available in most stores.
8. Sage adds a tangy *flavor* to stew.
9. Many chefs also *flavor* stew with basil.
10. In their family, a *cross* word is rarely spoken.
11. You will find their house where Pine Avenue and Hazelnut Street *cross.*
12. We looked for a constellation of stars shaped like a *cross.*
13. After sundown, the two counselors *spin* tales for their eager audience.
14. In the evening, we sometimes go for a *spin* in the car.
15. One night we spotted wild horses near a *turn* in the road.
16. "*Turn* off the headlights!" we cried.
17. We were all *safe* and sound after our adventure.
18. Her mother keeps her important papers in a *safe.*
19. To get back home, we must make the next *right* turn.
20. Turn *right* when you see the old barn.

REVIEW EXERCISE C. Writing Sentences Using Words as Different Parts of Speech. Write three sentences for each of the following words, using the word as a different part of speech in each sentence. At the end of the sentence, write the part of speech.

1. long   2. cut   3. back   4. fast   5. iron

REVIEW EXERCISE D. Determining the Parts of Speech of Words. Number your paper 1–25. After the proper number, write the part of speech of each italicized word or expression.

(1) *Early* farmers on the (2) *Great Plains* eked out a rough existence, (3) *for* there were few towns, stores, (4) *or* other hallmarks of civilization. Their first homes were constructed with sod bricks, (5) *which* were cut out of the prairie. Trees were in short supply on these vacant lands, (6) *but* the resourceful settler might find a few (7) *cottonwoods* growing (8) *along* a stream. (9) *These* (10) *could be used* to build a frame for the roof, which was then covered (11) *lightly* with grassy earth. Grass (12) *both* on the roof (13) *and* in the sod cemented the structure together. The door to (14) *this* primitive house might be constructed from timber, (15) *but* usually a cowhide (16) *was draped* across the entrance. Inside was a dirt floor that was covered with (17) *either* a bearskin (18) *or* a buffalo robe.

Furnishings were (19) *always* (20) *homemade*. Pioneers usually slept in (21) *rustic* beds made with rawhide strips that were pulled (22) *tautly* (23) *across* a wooden frame. (24) *Their* mattresses were often straw-filled ticks, somewhat lumpy but sweet-smelling. With a few crude benches, a wooden table, and cooking utensils, the house of the early settler was (25) *complete*.

CHAPTER 13 REVIEW: POSTTEST 1

Determining the Parts of Speech of Words. After the proper number, write each italicized word and indicate what part of speech it is. Use the abbreviations *n.* (noun), *pron.* (pronoun), *adj.* (adjective), *v.* (verb), *adv.* (adverb), *prep.* (preposition), *conj.* (conjunction), and *interj.* (interjection).

Since the (1) *condition* of the roads prevented (2) *extensive* use of wheeled vehicles, the most reliable means of transportation in colonial times was the (3) *saddle horse*. Some (4) *exceptionally* wealthy people kept carriages, but (5) *these* were usually heavy vehicles (6) *that* were pulled by two or more horses. The carriages were (7) *satisfactory* for short trips, (8) *but* they were not practical for long journeys.

Stagecoaches were introduced in (9) *America* about 1750. By this time roads ran (10) *between* such major cities as New York and Boston. Although these roads (11) *were* little more than muddy tracks, (12) *most* were wide enough for a four-wheeled coach. Three (13) *or* four pairs of horses (14) *were harnessed* to a coach. The vehicles were so heavy, however, that (15) *coach* horses tired (16) *quite* (17) *rapidly* and (18) *either* had to be rested frequently (19) *or* changed at post houses along the route.

On the (20) *frontier* there were no roads at all. The (21) *Conestoga wagon* was developed for long trips. It had huge wheels that were sometimes (22) *six* feet in diameter, and (23) *its* body was built like a barge. When a Conestoga wagon (24) *approached* a river that was too deep to be forded, the wagon was floated (25) *across*.

CHAPTER 13 REVIEW: POSTTEST 2 √

Writing Sentences with Words Used as Different Parts of Speech.
Number your paper 1–20. Use each of the following words in a sentence. Then write the part of speech of the word in the sentence.

EXAMPLES 1. gold
          1. *Maria bought a gold bracelet. adjective*
          2. that
          2. *That is a very funny story! pronoun*

1. novel	8. but	15. often
2. Park Avenue	9. both...and	16. inside
3. this	10. silver	17. underneath
4. are laughing	11. hiked	18. oh
5. yesterday	12. appeared	19. whew
6. tomorrow	13. tasted	20. in
7. or	14. quietly	

GRAMMAR

SUMMARY OF PARTS OF SPEECH

Rule	Part of Speech	Use	Examples
13a	noun	names	**Larry** picks **grapefruit.**
13b	pronoun	takes the place of a noun	**You** and **he** sing well. Do not let **anyone** guess.
13c	adjective	modifies a noun or a pronoun	That was a **happy** sight. They were very **noisy.**
13d	verb	shows action or helps to make a statement	He **jumps** and **spins.** She **might take** the prize.
13e	adverb	modifies a verb, an adjective, or another adverb	He learns **quickly.** She is **always** right. It flies **quite** high.
13f	preposition	relates a noun or a pronoun to another word	The cats are **in** the shade **under** the oak tree **near** the garage.
13g	conjunction	joins words	Nancy **and** Sheila passed the test.
13h	interjection	expresses strong emotion	**My goodness!** **Hey,** stop that!

CHAPTER 14

The Sentence

SUBJECTS, PREDICATES, COMPLEMENTS

DIAGNOSTIC TEST

A. Identifying Subjects, Verbs, and Complements. Number your paper 1–10. After the proper number, write the italicized word or word group in the following sentences. Correctly identify each, using these abbreviations: *s.* (subject), *v.* (verb), *p.a.* (predicate adjective), *p.n.* (predicate nominative), *d.o.* (direct object), *i.o.* (indirect object).

1. Native *cactuses* in the Southwest are in trouble.
2. Some species are already *vulnerable* to eventual extinction.
3. Cactuses *are being threatened* by landscapers, collectors, and tourists.
4. Many people illegally harvest these wild *plants*.
5. There are many unique and unusual *species* in Arizona.
6. Arizona is therefore an active *battlefield* in the war against the removal of endangered cactuses.
7. "Cactus cops" *patrol* the streets of Phoenix on the lookout for places with illegally acquired cactuses.
8. Authorized dealers must give *purchasers* permit tags as proof of legal sale.
9. First violations are *punishable* by a minimum fine of five hundred dollars.
10. Illegally owned cactuses *are impounded*.

B. Classifying Sentences as Declarative, Interrogative, Imperative, or Exclamatory. Number your paper 11–20. After the proper number, classify each of the following sentences as declarative, interrogative, imperative, or exclamatory. After each classification write the proper end punctuation in parentheses.

11. What a thorny problem cactus rustling has become
12. Why are illegal harvesters so hard to keep track of
13. Many work at night and sometimes use permit tags over and over
14. Go to the library and read about imperiled cactuses in the December 1980 issue of *Smithsonian*
15. The author describes a trip into the desert with a legal hauler
16. Can you imagine a saguaro worth three hundred dollars
17. A crested saguaro is even rarer and can sell for thousands of dollars
18. No wonder illegal harvesting is booming
19. Always examine a large cactus for bruises
20. Legally harvested plants should not show any damage

In speech, we often leave out parts of our sentences. For example, we often answer a certain kind of question in a few words, not bothering to speak in sentences.

> "What happened to Laura?"
> "Sprained wrist."
> "Too bad."
> "Sure is."

When we write, however, our words have to convey the whole message. Our readers cannot hear us, and if they do not understand, they cannot ask for a repetition. Therefore, when we put our thoughts on paper, we are expected to express them in complete sentences.

14a. A *sentence* is a group of words containing a subject and a verb and expressing a complete thought.

The two parts of this definition are closely related. To express a complete thought, a sentence must refer to someone or something (the subject), and it must tell us something about that person or thing. This job of telling about something is done by the predicate, which always contains a verb.

GRAMMAR

SUBJECT AND PREDICATE

14b. A sentence consists of two parts: the *subject* and the *predicate*.

The *subject* of the sentence is the part about which something is being said. The *predicate* is the part that says something about the subject.

subject	*predicate*
Some residents of the desert	have ingenious ways of evading the life-threatening effects of a drought.

predicate	*subject*
Bizarre and unbelievable is	the method of the Australian frog.

subject	*predicate*
These water-holding frogs	can lie in a trance for as long as three years between rainfalls.

EXERCISE 1. Identifying Subjects and Predicates. Write each sentence on your paper; draw *one* line under the complete subject and *two* lines under the complete predicate. Keep in mind that the subject may come after the predicate.

1. The discovery of platinum has been credited to a variety of countries.
2. Spanish explorers in search of gold supposedly found the metal in the rivers of South America.
3. They considered it a worthless, inferior form of silver.
4. Their name for platinum was *platina,* or "little silver."
5. Back into the river went the little balls of platinum!
6. The platinum might then become gold, according to one theory.
7. Europeans later mixed platinum with gold.
8. This mixture encouraged the production of counterfeit gold bars and coins.
9. Platinum commands a high price today because of its resistance to corrosion.
10. Such diverse products as jet planes and jewelry require platinum in some form.

GRAMMAR

The Simple Predicate and the Complete Predicate

The *complete predicate* of a sentence is the part that says something about the subject. Within the complete predicate, there is always a word or word group that is essential because it is the key word in completing the statement about the subject. This word or word group is called the *simple predicate,* or *verb.*

14c. The principal word or group of words in the complete predicate is called the *simple predicate,* or the *verb.*

EXAMPLES   Spiders **snare** their prey in an intricate web. [complete predicate: *snare their prey in an intricate web;* verb: *snare*]

The Verb Phrase

The simple predicate, or verb may consist of more than one word. It may be a verb phrase: *are walking, will walk, might have walked.* When this is so, look for all parts of a verb phrase when you are asked to pick out the simple predicate of any sentence.

EXAMPLES   **Has** Sally **helped** you? [simple predicate: *has helped*] The new theater **will** not **have** permanent seats. [simple predicate: *will have*]

In the following sentences, the verb is underscored; the complete predicate is in boldfaced type. Study the sentences carefully.

The fishermen **steered** **their boat toward the middle of the lake.**
They **had heard** **about this popular spot.**
They **switched** **off the motor.**
Paul **is using** **his best lures.**
Everyone **is** **optimistically** **looking** **forward to a winning season.**

Throughout the rest of this book, the simple predicate is referred to as the verb.

EXERCISE 2. Identifying Verbs or Verb Phrases in Sentences. Number your paper 1–10. Write the verb in each of the following sentences. Be sure to include all parts of a verb phrase.

1. Scientists throughout the world have expressed concern about the fate of the giant panda of China.
2. The animal's natural habitat has slowly become smaller.
3. Many forests of bamboo have died.

4. A panda may devour as much as forty pounds of bamboo daily.
5. Each tender, green shoot of bamboo contains only a small amount of nutrients.
6. The large but sluggish panda is not known as a successful hunter of small animals.
7. In their concern for the panda's survival, scientists are now studying the daytime and nighttime habits of this animal.
8. They hold a captured panda in a log trap for several hours.
9. During this time, the scientists attach a radio to the panda's neck.
10. The radio sends the scientists valuable information about the released animal's behavior.

The Simple Subject and the Complete Subject

The *complete subject* of a sentence is the part about which something is being said. The principal word (or group of words) within the complete subject is called the *simple subject*.

14d. The *simple subject* is the main word or group of words in the complete subject.

EXAMPLE   A **dog** with this pedigree is usually nervous. [complete subject: *A dog with this pedigree;* simple subject: *dog*]

In naming the simple subject, consider compound nouns as one word.

EXAMPLE   The **Taj Mahal** in India is one of the most beautiful buildings in the world. [complete subject: *The Taj Mahal in India;* simple subject: *Taj Mahal*]

Throughout the rest of this book, unless otherwise indicated, the word *subject* will refer to the simple subject.

Caution: Remember that *noun* and *subject* do not mean the same thing. A *noun* is the name of a person, place, thing, or idea. A *subject* is the name of a part of a sentence; it is usually a noun or pronoun.

How to Find the Subject of a Sentence

You will find it easier to locate the subject if you pick out the verb first. For example:

The shutters on that house are painted green.

The verb is *are painted.* Now ask yourself: Who or what are painted? The answer is *shutters,* so *shutters* is the subject. In the sentence *Beyond the brook stands a cabin,* the verb is *stands.* Ask yourself: Who or what stands? The answer is *cabin,* so *cabin* is the subject.

EXERCISE 3. Identifying Subjects and Verbs. Number your paper 1–10. Write the subject and verb of each sentence, subject first. Underline the subject once and the verb twice.

1. Despite their fragile appearance, butterflies often fly over a thousand miles during migration.
2. The painted lady, for example, has been seen in the middle of the Atlantic Ocean.
3. In northern Europe, this species was once spotted over the Arctic Circle.
4. During the spring, millions of painted ladies flutter across North America.
5. This huge flock of colorful butterflies leaves its warm winter home in New Mexico.
6. These butterflies' impressive journey sometimes takes them as far north as Newfoundland, Canada.
7. In September, the brilliant orange-and-black monarch flies south from Canada toward Florida, Texas, and California.
8. The migratory flight of the monarch may cover a distance of close to two thousand miles.
9. Every winter for the past sixty years, monarchs have gathered in a small forest not far from San Francisco.
10. The thick clusters of their blazing orange wings make this forest very popular with tourists.

14e. The subject is never in a prepositional phrase.

A prepositional phrase is a group of words that begins with a preposition and ends with a noun or pronoun: *through the yard, of mine.* Finding the subject when it is followed by a phrase may be difficult.

EXAMPLE   One of my relatives has taken a trip to Europe.

You see at once that the verb is *has taken.* When you ask "Who has taken?" you may be tempted to answer *relatives.* However, that is not what the sentence says. The sentence says, "*One* of my relatives has

GRAMMAR

taken a trip to Europe." The subject is *One*. Notice that *relatives* is part of the phrase *of my relatives*. In many sentences you can easily isolate the subject and verb simply by crossing out all prepositional phrases.

EXAMPLE The team ~~with the best record~~ will play ~~in the state tournament~~.
[verb: *will play;* subject: *team*]

EXERCISE 4. Identifying Subjects and Verbs. Write the following sentences on your paper. Cross out each of the prepositional phrases. Underline each verb twice and its subject once.

1. A book about the Chinese experience in America has been written by Victor G. Nee and Brett de Bary Nee.
2. The title of the book is *Longtime Californ': A Documentary Study of an American Chinatown.*
3. The book traces the history of Chinese immigration and the development of the Chinese American community.
4. The first immigrants came for the jobs in the gold mines and on the railroads in the 1850's.
5. In the beginning only men could immigrate.
6. In time the early immigrants sent to China for their wives.
7. During the 1920's the cohesive family society of Chinatown developed.
8. Interviews of old and young residents of Chinatown give the book its authentic character.
9. A good example of this technique is the interview with Lisa Mah about her return to Chinatown after her family's departure.
10. The spirit of the Chinatown community is subtly captured.

EXERCISE 5. Completing Sentences by Supplying Predicates; Identifying Subjects and Verbs. Complete each of the following sentences by adding predicates to the complete subject. After you have done so, underline the subject once and the verb twice.

1. Last month —— .
2. A white fence —— .
3. The surf —— .
4. The road by my house —— .
5. The students in our school —— .

REVIEW EXERCISE A. Identifying Complete Subjects and Predicates and Identifying Subjects and Verbs. Write the following sentences on your paper. Insert a vertical line (|) between the last word

GRAMMAR

in the complete subject and the first word in the complete predicate. Then underline the subject once and the verb twice.

1. Benjamin Banneker was born in Maryland of a free mother and a slave father.
2. Banneker himself was considered free.
3. As a result, he attended an integrated private school.
4. With the equivalent of an eighth-grade education, this young man became a noteworthy American astronomer and mathematician.
5. His knowledge of astronomy led to his acclaimed prediction of the solar eclipse of 1789.
6. The first of his almanacs was published a few years later.
7. These almanacs contained tide tables and data on future eclipses.
8. A number of useful medicinal products were also listed.
9. Banneker's almanac appeared annually for more than a decade.
10. Banneker is best known, however, for his contribution as a surveyor during the planning of Washington, D.C.

The Subject in an Unusual Position

Two kinds of sentences may confuse you when you wish to find the verb and its subject. These are (1) sentences that begin with the words *there* or *here* and (2) sentences that ask a question.

Sentences Beginning with *There* or *Here*

When the word *there* or *here* comes at the beginning of a sentence, it may appear to be the subject, but it is not. Use the "*who* or *what*" formula to find the subject.

EXAMPLE There are two apples in the refrigerator. [What are? *Apples.*]

Sentences That Ask Questions

Questions usually begin with a verb or a verb helper. Also, they frequently begin with words like *what, when, where, how,* and *why.* Either way, the subject usually follows the verb or verb helper.

EXAMPLES Why is **he** running?
How do **you** feel?

In questions that begin with a helping verb, the subject always comes between the helping verb and the main verb. Another way to find the subject is to turn the question into a statement, find the verb, and ask "Who?" or "What?" in front of it.

EXAMPLES   *Question:* Were your friends early?
Statement: Your friends were early.
[Who were early? *Friends. Subject:* **Friends**]

Question: Has Mrs. Williams read our compositions?
Statement: Mrs. Williams has read our compositions.
[Who has read the compositions? *Mrs. Williams.*
Subject: **Mrs. Williams**]

EXERCISE 6. Identifying Subjects and Verbs. Number your paper 1–10. Write the verb and the subject in each of the following sentences. Select the verb first.

1. There were three questions on the final exam.
2. Here is my topic for the term paper.
3. What did you choose for a topic?
4. Will everyone be ready on time?
5. There will be no excuse for lateness.
6. When should we go to the library?
7. There were very few books on the subject.
8. Are there any magazine articles about the bald eagle?
9. Where will our conference be held?
10. Have you begun the next chapter?

Sentences in Which the Subject is Understood

In requests and commands, the subject is usually left out of the sentence. The unexpressed subject of a command or request is *you.*

EXAMPLES   Rake the yard.
Pick up the fallen branches.

In these sentences the verbs are *rake* and *pick.* In both sentences the subject is the same. Who must *rake* and *pick?* The subject is *you,* even though the word does not appear in either of the sentences. A subject of this kind is said to be *understood.*

Compound Subjects and Verbs

14f. Two or more subjects connected by *and* or *or* and having the same verb are called a *compound subject.*

EXAMPLE **Mr. Oliver** and his **daughter** planted a vegetable garden. [verb: *planted;* compound subject: *Mr. Oliver* (and) *daughter*]

14g. Two or more verbs joined by a connecting word and having the same subject are called a *compound verb.*

EXAMPLES At the street festival, we **danced** the rumba and **sampled** the meat pies. [compound verb: *danced* and *sampled;* subject: *we*]
I **have written** these letters and **addressed** the envelopes. [The subject is *I;* the compound verb is *have written* and (*have*) *addressed.* Notice that the helping verb *have* is understood with *addressed.*]

EXERCISE 7. Identifying Subjects and Verbs. Number your paper 1–10. Write the subject and the verb of each sentence. If the subject of a sentence is understood, write (*you*).

EXAMPLES 1. My grandmother and my aunt will drive to New Mexico and visit Santa Fe.
1. *grandmother, aunt will drive,* (*will*) *visit*
2. Show me the map.
2. (*you*) *Show*

1. Jackets and ties are required in the dining room.
2. Are there bears living in these woods?
3. There are five new students in our class this semester.
4. Bring both a pencil and a pen to the exam on Thursday.
5. Frank neither sings nor plays an instrument.
6. Where do you and Liz buy your cassettes?
7. Both of the math problems were difficult.
8. Play ball!
9. There is much wisdom in folk sayings and proverbs.
10. Is one of the kittens sick?

REVIEW EXERCISE B. Identifying Subjects and Verbs. Number your paper 1–10. Write the subject and verb of each sentence. If the subject is understood, write (*you*). Underline the subject once and the verb twice.

1. Only birds, bats, and insects can fly.
2. Other animals can move through the air without flying.
3. The flying fish swims fast and then leaps out of the water.
4. How does the flying squirrel glide from tree to tree?

5. There are flaps of skin between its legs.
6. Why can birds fly?
7. Their wings lift and push them through the air.
8. Look carefully at an insect's wings.
9. Most have two sets of wings.
10. The pair in front covers the pair in back.

WRITING APPLICATION A:
Adding New Interest to Your Writing
by Placing Subjects in Different Positions

One of the ways people sometimes approach a routine task is to do it in a different way. Taking a different route can make a daily walk to school or drive to work more pleasant. Similarly, you can make your writing more interesting by selecting different positions for the subjects of your sentences.

EXAMPLES 1. Awakened by a strange noise, *I* was instantly alert.
2. Waking up in the night, *I* heard an unfamiliar noise.
3. From far down the hall came a strange, unfamiliar *noise*.
4. Suddenly *I* heard a strange noise.
5. Although soft and low, the strange *noise* was frightening.

Writing Assignment

Think back to an incident in your life that taught you something important. It may have been a time when you learned the value of friendship, when you realized the importance of honesty, when you recognized that you are responsible for the consequences of your actions, or when you suddenly understood how much a relative meant to you. Write a paragraph describing that incident in detail. Read what you have written; see if you can make it more interesting. In at least three sentences, try to place the subject somewhere other than first. Underline the subject each time you do this.

FRAGMENTS

A sentence contains a verb and its subject. However, not all groups of words containing a subject and a verb are sentences. For example,

Because she concentrates contains a verb and its subject—the verb is *concentrates,* and the subject is *she.* Yet the group of words is not a sentence because it does not express a complete thought. It suggests that more is to be said. It is a fragment, a part of a longer sentence.

> She does well in tennis because she concentrates.

Now you have a sentence. The thought has been completed.

EXERCISE 8. Identifying Sentences and Fragments.   Number your paper 1–20. If a word group is a sentence, write *S* beside its number on your paper. If it is not a sentence, write *F* for fragment.

1. Willa Cather was born in Back Creek Valley, in northern Virginia.
2. In 1883, when she was ten years old.
3. Her family moved to the treeless prairie of Nebraska.
4. Fascinated by the wild and rolling plains.
5. She tracked buffalo and collected prairie flowers.
6. Listened to the stories of neighboring settlers.
7. They told memorable tales about the harsh struggles of the home-steaders.
8. In her first novel, *O Pioneers!*
9. She describes how farmers turned the unruly plains into neat fields of wheat and corn.
10. After high school in the village of Red Cloud, Nebraska.
11. She attended the recently established University of Nebraska in Lincoln.
12. Although she was first interested in science.
13. She discovered her talent for writing.
14. Stories and reviews by Willa Cather soon appeared in the local newspapers of Lincoln.
15. At first, her writing was relatively unnoticed.
16. She worked for several years as a schoolteacher and then as a magazine editor in New York City.
17. Although she relished the glamour of New York.
18. She never lost touch with the sights and sounds of her childhood in the Midwest.
19. *My Ántonia* describes Nebraska's open spaces as well as its grueling challenges.
20. In this novel a boy grows up and leaves the Midwest yet holds a deep reverence for his past.

THE SENTENCE BASE

Every sentence has a base, the part upon which all other parts rest. The sentence base is usually composed of two parts—the subject and the verb.

EXAMPLES   A gaggle of geese flew overhead. [base: *gaggle flew*]
The animals in the barnyard have been fed. [base: *animals have been fed*]

In these examples, the sentence base consists of only a subject and a verb. In many sentences, however, something else is required in the predicate to complete the meaning of the subject and verb. This third element is a *complement* (a "completer").

COMPLEMENTS

14h. A *complement* is a word or group of words that completes the meaning begun by the subject and verb.

The following example will show you how the complement completes the meaning.

```
        S     V            C
    Snow covered the hillside.
```

"Snow covered" would not be a complete statement by itself, even though it contains a subject and a verb. "Snow covered *what*?" a reader would ask. The word *hillside* completes the meaning of the sentence by telling *what* the snow covered. Study the following sentences, in which subjects, verbs, and complements are labeled. Name the part of speech of each complement.

```
          S   V        C
    That book is an autobiography.

          S        V      C
    Mark Twain wrote novels about his boyhood.

          S        S    V        C
    Both Eric and Bob felt rather gloomy.
```

EXERCISE 9. Writing Sentences with Subjects, Verbs, and Complements. Construct sentences from the following sentence bases. Do not be satisfied with adding only one or two words.

SUBJECT	VERB	COMPLEMENT
1. cyclists	planned	trip
2. musicians	performed	duet
3. speaker	looked	enthusiastic
4. problem	was	identified
5. novel	is	suspenseful

> ☞ NOTE   Like the subject of a sentence, a complement is never part of a prepositional phrase.

I intercepted **one** of the passes. [The complement is *one*, not *passes; passes* is part of a prepositional phrase.]

An adverb modifying a verb is not a complement. Complements may be nouns, pronouns, or adjectives.

Lucy plays **hard**. [*Hard*, an adverb, is not a complement.]
These pears are **hard**. [*Hard*, an adjective, is a complement.]

EXERCISE 10. Identifying Subjects, Verbs, and Complements.
Number your paper 1–10. Label three columns: *Subject, Verb, Complement.* For each sentence, write the subject, the verb, and the complement, if any.

1. A hurricane is actually a tropical cyclone.
2. These large, revolving storms are accompanied by destructive winds.
3. The rains of a hurricane are almost always heavy.
4. A hurricane has no fronts but has a strange central area.
5. This area is the eye of the hurricane.
6. Here there is neither wind nor rain.
7. Around the eye, however, the winds whirl violently.
8. All hurricanes originate on the western side of the ocean, in the doldrums.
9. A hurricane moves slowly through the tropics and speeds up only in the middle latitudes.
10. The tracks of most hurricanes are shaped like parabolas.

GRAMMAR

GRAMMAR

The Subject Complement

14i. A *subject complement* is a noun, pronoun, or adjective that follows a linking verb. It identifies, describes, or explains the subject.

EXAMPLES   Jerry is a soccer **player.**
                Susan seems **confident.**

In the first example, *player* identifies the subject, *Jerry*. In the second, *confident* describes the subject, *Susan*.

    There are two kinds of subject complements. If the subject complement is a noun or a pronoun, it is a *predicate nominative*. If it is an adjective, it is a *predicate adjective*.

    Predicate nominatives (nouns and pronouns) explain the subject or give another name for the subject. Predicate adjectives describe the subject. Both predicate nominatives and predicate adjectives are linked to the subject by linking verbs. The common linking verbs are *be, become, feel, smell, taste, look, grow, seem, appear, remain, sound, stay.*[1]

EXAMPLES   The caterpillar becomes a **butterfly.** [predicate nominative]
                The rug looks **green**, but it is actually *blue.* [predicate adjectives]

EXERCISE 11. Identifying Subject Complements as Predicate Nominatives or Predicate Adjectives.

Number your paper 1–10. Write the subject complement from each of the following sentences. After each complement, write what kind it is: predicate nominative or predicate adjective.

1. The last scene of the play is very tense.
2. The two small birds are finches.
3. The music sounded lively.
4. This costume looks elegant.
5. My goldfish is growing larger every day.
6. Andrea's report on digital recording is a detailed one.
7. The setting of the story is an old castle.
8. Your solution to this algebra problem is clever.
9. We felt full after our huge dinner.
10. His entire story seems almost unbelievable.

---

[1] The forms of *be* are *am, is, are, was, were,* and verb phrases ending in *be* or *been,* such as *can be* and *has been.*

Distinguishing Between Subject and Complement

When the subject is not in the normal position before the verb, it is sometimes hard to tell the subject from the complement. When the word order is normal, there is no problem—the subject comes before the verb and the subject complement comes after:

$$\overset{S}{\text{Martin Luther King, Jr.,}} \overset{V}{\text{is}} \overset{C}{\text{a national hero.}}$$

When the word order is reversed, as in questions, the subject still comes before the subject complement in most cases:

$$\overset{V}{\text{Was}} \overset{S}{\text{he}} \overset{C}{\text{a recipient of the Nobel Peace Prize?}}$$

Sometimes, however, a writer or speaker may put the subject complement first for emphasis.

$$\overset{C}{\text{How elusive}} \overset{V}{\text{is}} \overset{S}{\text{victory!}}$$
$$\overset{C}{\text{What a fine speaker}} \overset{S}{\text{the Reverend King}} \overset{V}{\text{was!}}$$

When this happens, you must consider which word is more likely to be the subject of the sentence. Usually the subject will be the word that specifically identifies the person or thing that the sentence is about. The first example above presents little difficulty because *elusive* is an adjective and cannot be the subject. In the second example, however, both the subject complement (*speaker*) and the subject (*Reverend King*) are nouns. In this case you must ask yourself which noun more specifically identifies the subject. *Reverend King* has a more specific meaning than *speaker;* consequently, it is a more likely subject for the sentence.

EXERCISE 12. Identifying Subjects, Verbs, and Subject Complements. Write the following sentences. Label the subject of the sentence *S*, the verb *V,* and the subject complement *C*.

1. Are those girls your cousins?
2. How friendly everyone seems!
3. Ginger is a superb athlete.
4. "A Rose for Emily" is a haunting story.
5. How bright the stars seem tonight.
6. What a fine cook your father is!

7. When does a house become a home?
8. Our dog is usually friendly.
9. Clara Maass was a nurse of extraordinary dedication.
10. Life is a precious gift.

Direct Objects and Indirect Objects

Another kind of complement, the *direct object,* does not refer to the subject. Instead, it receives the action of the verb or shows the result of the action.

EXAMPLE The receptionist answered the **phone.** [base: *receptionist answered phone*]

14j. The *direct object* is a word or group of words that directly receives the action expressed by the verb or shows the result of the action. It answers the question *What?* or *Whom?* after an action verb.

```
                  S     V      DO
EXAMPLES   The mechanic fixed our car.

           S    V              DO
           She replaced the broken muffler.
```

In the first example, *car* is the direct object. It directly receives the action expressed by the verb. It answers the question *What?* after the verb. Fixed what? Fixed *car.* In the second sentence, *muffler* is the direct object. Replaced what? Replaced *muffler.*

Objects are used after action verbs only. Verbs like *study, dream, understand,* which express mental action, are just as much action verbs as are verbs that express physical action: *push, leap, stumble.*

EXERCISE 13. Identifying Verbs and Their Direct Objects.
Number your paper 1–10. Write the direct objects in the following sentences. Be able to name the verb whose action the object receives. *Caution:* The direct object is never part of a prepositional phrase.

1. I borrowed my parents' new camera recently.
2. First I loaded the film into the camera.
3. Then I set the opening of the shutter.
4. I focused the camera on a distant object.
5. I could read the shutter speed in the viewfinder.
6. A flashing red light means an incorrect setting.
7. Slowly and carefully I pressed the button.

8. I then moved the film forward for the next shot.
9. By the end of the day, I had snapped thirty-six pictures.
10. Unfortunately, the film processor lost my roll of film.

14k. An *indirect object* is a noun or pronoun in the predicate that precedes the direct object. It tells *to whom* or *for whom* the action of the verb is done.

EXAMPLES   The teacher read the assignment.
            The teacher read **us** the assignment.

In both examples *assignment* is the direct object. In the second example, however, another word also receives the action of the verb *read.* The word *us,* which comes before the direct object, tells *to whom* the assignment was read. It is an indirect object.

What is the indirect object in this sentence?

    The chef showed the diners the new kitchen.

Kitchen is the direct object. *Diners* is the indirect object. It is the diners *to whom* the kitchen was shown.

If the words *to* or *for* are used in the sentence itself, the word following them is part of a prepositional phrase and not an indirect object. Compare the following pairs.

Jeff served me fresh vegetables. [indirect object: *me*]
Jeff served fresh vegetables to me. [no indirect object]
We bought my family several souvenirs. [indirect object: *family*]
We bought several souvenirs for my family. [no indirect object]

Caution: When identifying complements, do not be confused by adverbs in the predicate.

They turned **right.** [*Right* is an adverb telling *where.*]
You have the **right** to remain silent. [*Right* is a noun used as a direct object.]

Compound Complements

Complements may be compound.

EXAMPLES   The names of our cats are **Jezebel** and **Koomba.** [compound predicate nominative]
            The alley is **long** and **narrow.** [compound predicate adjective]

We used paper **plates** and **napkins.** [compound direct object]
The trip had given my **sister** and **me** the best vacation ever.
[compound indirect object]

EXERCISE 14. Identifying Direct and Indirect Objects. Number
your paper 1–10. After the proper number, write the objects in each
sentence. Write *i.o.* after an indirect object and *d.o.* after a direct
object. Not all sentences contain both kinds of objects.

1. Last spring Steve told us his plans for the Olympics.
2. He wants a place on the swim team.
3. This goal demands hours of hard practice.
4. We all gave Steve encouragement and support.
5. Steve showed us the practice pool in the college gym.
6. Every day Steve swims a hundred laps in the pool.
7. His coach teaches him the fine points of swimming.
8. Such intense training has cost Steve a social life.
9. A rigorous schedule leaves an athlete little time to spend with
   friends.
10. Nevertheless, Steve wants that gold medal.

**REVIEW EXERCISE C. Identifying Sentences and Fragments;
Identifying Complements.** If one of the following word groups is not
a complete sentence, write *F* (for *fragment*) after the proper number. If
a word group is a complete sentence, write it, adding end punctuation.
Underline the subject once and the verb twice. If a sentence has a
complement, label it, using these abbreviations: *p.a.* (predicate adjective), *p.n.* (predicate nominative), *d.o.* (direct object), *i.o.* (indirect
object).

1. Has the committee announced the date of the school carnival
2. Perhaps next week
3. Linda gave us a summary of her science project
4. It was long and interesting
5. Although it was well written
6. Books and papers covered the desk and spilled onto the floor
7. One of those dogs is obedience-trained
8. Helen gave the children a box of oatmeal cookies
9. Kim, Juan, and Tracey were winners at the track meet
10. How happy they were

SENTENCES CLASSIFIED BY PURPOSE

14l. Sentences may be classified according to their purpose.

There are four kinds of sentences: (1) declarative, (2) imperative, (3) interrogative, and (4) exclamatory.

(1) A sentence that makes a statement is a *declarative* sentence.

Its purpose is to declare something. Most of the sentences you use are declarative.

EXAMPLES   As a matter of fact, this yard needs more shade trees.
            An oak would thrive in the west corner.

(2) A sentence that gives a command or makes a request is an *imperative* sentence.

EXAMPLES   Pass the salt, please.   Speak softly.

(3) A sentence that asks a question is an *interrogative* sentence.

An interrogative sentence is followed by a question mark.

EXAMPLES   Can you speak Spanish?   What did you say?

(4) A sentence that expresses strong feeling is an *exclamatory* sentence.

An exclamatory sentence is followed by an exclamation point.

EXAMPLES   What a beautiful day this is!
            How we love cool, sunny weather!

Caution: A declarative, an imperative, or an interrogative sentence may be spoken in such a way that it is exclamatory. In this case it should be followed by an exclamation point.

EXAMPLES   This is inexcusable! [Declarative becomes exclamatory.]
            Stop the car! [Imperative becomes exclamatory.]
            How could you say that! [Interrogative becomes exclamatory.]

EXERCISE 15. Classifying Sentences as Declarative, Imperative, Interrogative, or Exclamatory.

Classify each sentence as declarative, imperative, interrogative, or exclamatory. Write the proper classification after the number of each sentence.

1. The loudspeakers in our living room are small yet powerful.
2. Turn down the sound!
3. Is that music or noise, Shirley?
4. Listening to loud music every day can damage one's hearing.
5. How many watts does your amplifier produce?
6. Sound levels are measured in units called decibels.
7. Do you know that an increase of ten decibels represents a doubling in the sound level?
8. Do not blast your sound system.
9. Keep it quiet!
10. Music played softly is relaxing.

WRITING APPLICATION B:
Catching a Reader's Interest with
Appropriately Varied Sentences

When a fisherman sees another boat full of fish, one of the first questions he wants to ask is, "What are you using for bait?" In order to catch your reader's interest, you should also use the right bait. Your opening sentence contains this bait. Select the most appropriate opening sentence.

EXAMPLES
1. I don't need eight hours' sleep every night (declarative)
2. Be sure to get eight hours' sleep every night. (imperative)
3. Do all people need eight hours' sleep every night? (interrogative)
4. How silly to think that all people need the same amount of sleep! (exclamatory)

Writing Assignment

Sometimes it is fun to disagree with something that other people have always seemed to accept without question. Select one of the following topics, or think of one of your own. Write different opening sentences for your topic, one for each classification (declarative, imperative, interrogative, and exclamatory). Select the one that is the best "bait" for your ideas. Write the paragraph.

Ideas: 1. Don't walk in the rain.
2. Don't talk back.
3. Keep your elbows off the table.

DIAGRAMING SENTENCES

The first thing to do in making a diagram is to draw a horizontal line on your paper. On this horizontal line you will write the sentence base. In approximately the center of the line you will draw a short vertical line cutting the horizontal one. This vertical line is the dividing point between the complete subject and the complete predicate. The subject and all words relating to it go to the *left* of this vertical line; the verb and all words relating to it go to the *right*.

Diagraming the Subject and Verb

The subject of the sentence is written on the horizontal line to the left of the vertical line. The verb is written to the right of the vertical line.

For an understood subject, write the word *you* in parentheses as the subject in your diagram.

EXAMPLE   Answer the phone.

Diagraming Modifiers

Modifiers of the subject and verb (adjectives and adverbs) are written on slanting lines beneath the subject or the verb.

EXAMPLE   **The blue** car **quickly** swerved **left.**

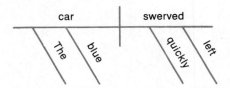

Diagraming Compound Subjects and Compound Verbs

If the subject is compound, diagram it as in the following example. Notice the position of the coordinating conjunction on the broken line.

EXAMPLE **Maria** and **Patsy** are hiking.

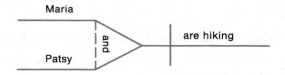

If the verb is compound, diagram it this way:

EXAMPLE Roger **swims** and **dives**.

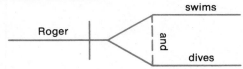

If the sentence has both a compound subject and a compound predicate, diagram it this way:

EXAMPLE **She** and **I dance** and **sing**.

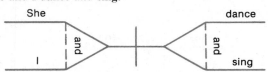

Notice how a compound verb is diagramed when the helping verb is not repeated:

EXAMPLE Sally **was reading** and **studying**.

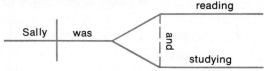

Since *was* is the helping verb for both *reading* and *studying,* it is placed on the horizontal line, and the conjunction *and* joins the main verbs *reading* and *studying.*

When the parts of a compound subject or a compound predicate are joined by correlative conjunctions, diagram the sentence this way:

EXAMPLE   **Both** Nancy **and** Beth will **not only** perform **but also** teach.

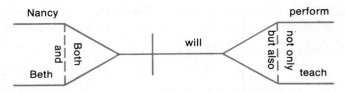

Diagraming *Here, There,* and *Where* as Modifiers

When the words *here, there,* and *where* are modifiers of the verb, diagram them in the following way:

EXAMPLE   **Here** come the astronauts!

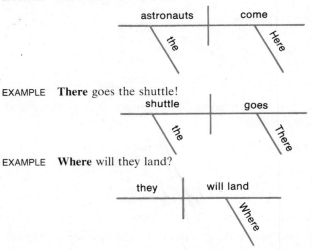

EXAMPLE   **There** goes the shuttle!

EXAMPLE   **Where** will they land?

Diagraming *There* When It Is Not a Modifier

When *there* begins a sentence but does not modify either the verb or the subject, it is diagramed on a line by itself, as in the following example. When used in this way, *there* is called an *expletive.*

EXAMPLE   **There** are seven astronauts.

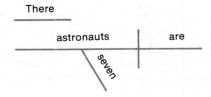

Diagraming a Modifier of a Modifier

A word that modifies another modifier is diagramed like this:

EXAMPLE   They performed **exceptionally** well.

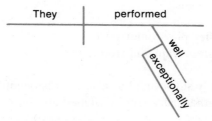

EXERCISE 16. Diagraming Sentences.   Diagram the following sentences. Diagrams of the first five are provided for you to copy and fill in.

1. Clouds move very swiftly.

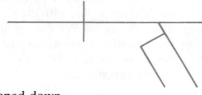

2. A hawk swooped down.

3. The rabbit moved suddenly and hopped quickly away.

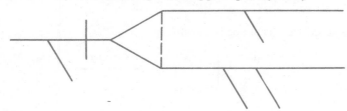

4. There was a sudden noise.

GRAMMAR

5. Never drive too fast.

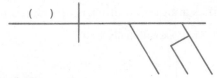

6. Where will they play tomorrow?
7. Does the express train still stop here?
8. Run ahead!
9. Karen not only sings well but also dances beautifully.
10. This car and that truck were designed and built here.

Diagraming the Predicate Nominative and the Predicate Adjective

A subject complement (predicate nominative or predicate adjective) should be placed on the same horizontal line with the simple subject and the verb. It comes after the verb, and a line drawn upward from the horizontal line and slanting toward the subject separates it from the verb. The line slants toward the subject to show that the subject complement is closely related to the subject.

PREDICATE NOMINATIVE   Some dogs are good **companions**.

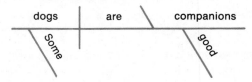

PREDICATE ADJECTIVE   That dog is **friendly**.

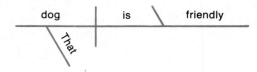

EXERCISE 17. Diagraming Sentences with Predicate Nominatives and Predicate Adjectives.   Diagram the following sentences:

1. Some old books are very valuable.
2. Does the recording sound scratchy?

3. That might have been her fastest race.
4. Hockey is my favorite sport.
5. Most cats are seldom affectionate.

Diagraming the Direct Object and the Indirect Object

The direct object is diagramed in almost the same way as the predicate nominative. The only difference is that the line separating the object from the verb is vertical (not slanting).

EXAMPLE   Cathy led the **band.**

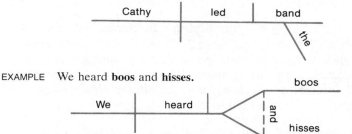

EXAMPLE   We heard **boos** and **hisses.**

The indirect object is diagramed on a horizontal line beneath the verb. A slanting line connects the horizontal line and the verb. Notice how the slanting line extends slightly below the horizontal line in the following example.

EXAMPLE   They gave **her** a present.

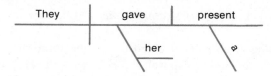

EXERCISE 18. Diagraming Sentences with Complements. Diagram the following sentences. Be sure to distinguish between subject complements and object complements.

1. The sky was blue and cloudless.
2. The sunlight seemed unusually harsh.
3. The intense heat wilted the roses.
4. My neighbors and I always plant a vegetable garden.
5. My coach patiently taught me a new stunt.

REVIEW EXERCISE D. Understanding the Parts of a Sentence. Number your paper 1–10. In your own words, give a definition of each of the following parts of a sentence, and make up an example to illustrate it.

1. A sentence
2. A complete subject
3. A verb (simple predicate)
4. A verb phrase
5. A complete predicate
6. A subject (simple)
7. A subject complement
8. A direct object
9. An understood subject
10. An indirect object

REVIEW EXERCISE E. Identifying Subjects, Verbs, and Complements. Number your paper 1–20. After the proper number, write the italicized word or word group in the following paragraphs. Correctly identify each, using these abbreviations: *s.* (subject), *v.* (verb); *p.a.* (predicate adjective), *p.n.* (predicate nominative), *d.o.* (direct object), *i.o.* (indirect object).

The (1) *pyramids* of Egypt certainly are a wonder. How could an ancient (2) *race,* even with 100,000 workers, build such enormous (3) *monuments?* Almost every visitor (4) *makes* a trip out into the desert to see the massive tombs. They appear (5) *majestic* from a distance. The Great Pyramid of Khufu is (6) *one* of the wonders of the ancient world. (7) *It* was once encased with blocks of polished limestone. However, weather and thievery (8) *have combined* to destroy its original casing. The pyramids (9) *look* (10) *weather-beaten.* Still, they are impressive (11) *sights.*

One invading Arab ruler decided to rob the tomb of Khufu. With hundreds of workers at his disposal, the ruler gave the (12) *men* his (13) *instructions.* The workers hacked through the solid blocks of granite. The stone was (14) *hard.* By accident, they suddenly broke into a tunnel. Imagine the (15) *excitement!* All too soon they (16) *discovered* an enormous (17) *plug* of granite blocking their way. They cut around the passage plug and soon reached the inner (18) *chamber.*

Strangely enough, there was no (19) *gold.* No vast treasures (20) *sparkled* under the light of the torches. The tomb had probably been robbed many centuries earlier by Egyptians familiar with its secret entrances.

CHAPTER 14 REVIEW: POSTTEST 1

A. Identifying Subjects, Verbs, and Complements. Number your paper 1–15. After the proper number, write the italicized word or word group in the following sentences. Correctly identify each, using these abbreviations: *s.* (subject), *v.* (verb), *p.a.* (predicate adjective), *p.n.* (predicate nominative), *d.o.* (direct object), *i.o.* (indirect object).

1. Have *you* ever met a robot?
2. In the field of robotics, scientists have built vastly improved *robots*.
3. Today these machines *have been put* to work in factories, laboratories, and outer space.
4. How were these complex *machines* first used?
5. There are a *number* of interesting early examples of robots at work.
6. One of the first robots was a mechanical *figure* in a clock tower.
7. It raised a hammer and struck a *bell* every hour.
8. At the 1939 New York World's Fair, Sparko and Elektro were popular *attractions*.
9. Elektro was *tall,* more than seven feet high.
10. Electric motors gave *Elektro* power for a variety of amazing tricks.
11. Sparko was Elektro's *dog*.
12. Sparko *could bark* and even *wag* his tail.
13. Today *some* of the simplest robots are drones in laboratories.
14. Basically, they are *extensions* of the human arm.
15. They can be *useful* in many different ways.

B. Classifying Sentences as Declarative, Interrogative, Imperative, or Exclamatory. Number your paper 16–20. Study the following sentences. After the proper number, classify each of the sentences as declarative, interrogative, imperative, or exclamatory. After each classification, write the proper end punctuation in parentheses.

16. Can you picture a robot twenty-five feet tall
17. Step up and say hello to Beetle
18. Perhaps you have already heard of CAM, an even more advanced robot
19. It can travel on long legs across rough terrain as rapidly as thirty-five miles an hour
20. How like a science-fiction creature it looks

GRAMMAR

CHAPTER 14 REVIEW: POSTTEST 2

Writing Sentences. Write sentences according to the following guidelines. Underline the subject once and verb twice in each sentence. If the subject is understood write (*You*).

1. a declarative sentence with a verb phrase
2. a sentence beginning with *There*
3. an interrogative sentence
4. an exclamatory sentence
5. an imperative sentence
6. a sentence with a compound subject
7. a sentence with a predicate nominative
8. a sentence with a compound direct object and an indirect object
9. a sentence with a predicate adjective
10. a sentence with a compound verb

CHAPTER 15

The Phrase

PREPOSITIONAL, VERBAL, APPOSITIVE PHRASES

DIAGNOSTIC TEST

Classifying Phrases. Number your paper 1–20. After the proper number, write each italicized phrase in the following sentences and indicate what kind of phrase it is. Use the abbreviations *prep.* (prepositional phrase), *part.* (participial phrase), *ger.* (gerund phrase), *inf.* (infinitive phrase), and *app.* (appositive phrase). Do not identify a prepositional phrase that is part of a larger phrase.

EXAMPLE   1. The sundial was one of the first instruments for *telling time.*
             1. *telling time, ger.*

1. *Regarded chiefly as garden ornaments,* sundials are still used in many areas *to tell time.*
2. The shadow-casting object *on a sundial* is called a gnomon.
3. Forerunners of the sundial include poles or upright stones *used as gnomons by early humans.*
4. *Setting the gnomon directly parallel to the earth's axis* greatly improved the accuracy of the sundial.
5. The development of trigonometry permitted more precise calculations for *constructing sundials.*
6. A sundial is not difficult *to make with simple materials.*
7. First find a stick *to use as a gnomon.*

8. *At high noon,* put the stick *in the ground.*
9. It is important *to tilt the stick slightly northward.*
10. *To mark the first hour,* place a pebble at the tip of the shadow made by the stick.
11. An hour later put another pebble at the tip *of the shadow.*
12. Continue this process *throughout the afternoon.*
13. *Starting the next morning,* repeat the hourly process.
14. Be sure *to place the last pebble at high noon.*
15. *Observing the completed sundial,* you will note that the pebbles are not equidistant.
16. The unevenly spaced markers, *a characteristic of the sundial,* demonstrate that shadows move faster in the morning and the evening than at noon.
17. For everyday use, *owning a watch* has obvious advantages over *using a sundial.*
18. However, sundials were long employed for *setting and checking watches.*
19. The heliochronometer, *a sundial of great accuracy,* was used until 1900 *to set the watches of French railway workers.*
20. The difference *between solar time and clock time* is correlated by the use of tables *showing daily variations in sun time.*

You already know that a group of words used as a verb is a verb phrase. In a verb phrase, one or more helping verbs and a verb are used together as one verb: *have been writing, is writing.* Similarly, other groups of related words are sometimes used as a single part of speech. Such phrases may be used as adjectives, adverbs, or nouns.

15a. A *phrase* is a group of related words that is used as a single part of speech and does not contain a verb and its subject.

In the first of each of the following pairs of examples, a single word is boldfaced. In the second part of each pair, a *phrase* that performs the same function in the sentence is boldfaced.

Carbon monoxide is an **odorless,** very toxic gas. [adjective]
Carbon monoxide is a very toxic gas **without an odor.** [adjective phrase]

Why not plant the rosebushes **here**? [adverb]
Why not plant the rosebushes **near the fence**? [adverb phrase]

The phrases in the preceding examples are *prepositional phrases*. You have already learned something about this kind of phrase. In this chapter you will study prepositional phrases in greater detail, and you will also explore verbal phrases and appositive phrases.

PREPOSITIONAL PHRASES

15b. A *prepositional phrase* is a group of words beginning with a preposition and usually ending with a noun or pronoun.

The prepositional phrases are boldfaced in the following examples:

> The woman **with the helmet** is a motorcyclist.
> The cashier gave the change **to me.**

The preposition in the last example is *to*. Do not confuse this common preposition with the *to* that is the sign of the infinitive form of a verb: *to watch, to learn, to drive.*

15c. The noun or pronoun that ends the prepositional phrase is the *object* of the preposition that begins the phrase.

PHRASE	PREPOSITION	OBJECT
before the second stoplight	before	stoplight
along the highway	along	highway
from him	from	him

A preposition may, of course, have a compound object:

> near **forests** and **rivers**
> despite the **rain, snow,** and **ice**

Prepositional phrases usually do the work of adjectives and adverbs in sentences.

Adjective Phrases

Prepositional phrases may be used to modify nouns or pronouns in much the same way as single-word adjectives.

EXAMPLES   a **hopeful** sign   a sign **of hope**
                Israeli cousins   cousins **from Israel**

15d. A prepositional phrase that modifies a noun or pronoun is an adjective phrase.

The cottages **by the lake** are quite picturesque.

The families **on my block** are very friendly.

Two or more adjective phrases often modify the same noun:

The picture **of the candidate in today's paper** is not flattering.

An adjective phrase may also modify the object of another prepositional phrase:

The coconut palms in the park **near the bay** were planted a long time ago. [*Near the bay* modifies *park,* the object of the preposition *in.*]

EXERCISE 1. Identifying Adjective Phrases and the Words They Modify. Each of the following sentences contains two adjective phrases. Write them in order on your paper. After each phrase, write the noun or pronoun it modifies.

EXAMPLE   1. Julius Caesar was one of the most popular generals in ancient Rome.
1. *of the most popular generals—one; in ancient Rome—generals*

1. The roads of ancient Rome linked the far corners of the empire.
2. Large blocks of the hardest stone paved the surface of the major routes.
3. Close communication between provinces strengthened the position of the Roman rulers.
4. Caesar's interest in military roads showed his concern with communication.
5. Roman roads were one reason for the success of Caesar's military operations.

Adverb Phrases

15e. A prepositional phrase that modifies a verb, an adjective, or another adverb is an *adverb phrase*.

EXAMPLES   The mole burrowed **under the lawn.** [The phrase modifies the verb *burrowed.*]

Althea Gibson was graceful **on the tennis court.**
[The phrase modifies the adjective **graceful.**]

The party lasted long **into the evening.** [The phrase modifies the
adverb *long.*]

Adverb phrases tell *when, where, why, how,* or *to what extent.*

EXAMPLES   The town grew quiet **after the storm.** [*when*]
They peered **through the window.** [*where*]
Most street musicians play **for tips.** [*why*]
This summer we're going **by car.** [*how*]
She won the game **by two points.** [*to what extent*]

Unlike adjective phrases, which always follow the words they
modify, adverb phrases can appear at various places in the sentence.
More than one adverb phrase can modify the same word.

EXAMPLE   **In the first inning** she pitched **with great control.** [The adverb phrases
In the first inning and *with great control* both modify the verb *pitched.*
The first adverb phrase tells *when* and the second adverb phrase tells
how.]

EXERCISE 2. Identifying Adverb Phrases and the Words They Modify.

Number your paper 1–10, and write the adverb phrases in the
following sentences. After each phrase, write the word it modifies and
the part of speech of that word.

1. Eerie sounds came from the abandoned house.
2. Are some old houses haunted by ghosts?
3. My parents and I weren't afraid of any ghosts.
4. On a moonlit night, we searched throughout the unused house.
5. In the cellar we found two alley cats.
6. The strange noises were made by these animals.
7. We carefully placed the cats in a box.
8. They both seemed happy with their temporary home.
9. We walked up the steps, out the door, and across the lawn.
10. At a leisurely pace, we returned to our own house.

Diagraming Prepositional Phrases

The preposition that begins the prepositional phrase is placed on a
slanting line leading down from the word the phrase modifies. The

object of the preposition is placed on a horizontal line drawn from the slanting line. As with the indirect object, the slanting line extends slightly below the horizontal line.

EXAMPLE: The steep slopes **of the mountains** are covered **with forests.**

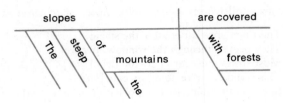

EXAMPLE   They sailed late **in the fall.** [adverb phrase modifying the adverb *late*]

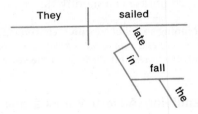

EXAMPLE   They were imprisoned **without food and water.**

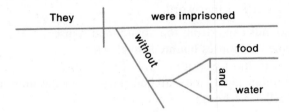

EXAMPLE   **Down the valley** and **over the plain** wanders the river.

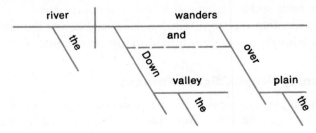

EXAMPLE   The princess lived **in a castle on the mountain.**

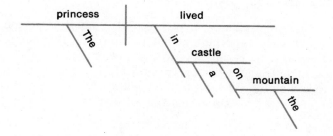

EXERCISE 3. **Diagraming Sentences with Adjective and Adverb Phrases.**   Diagram the following sentences:

1. She paints portraits of young children.
2. The sailor steered through the perilous channel and toward the open sea.
3. They waved to each passer-by on the road.
4. In Illinois during the fall, maple trees turn brilliant red.
5. The dunes on the coast of Australia are unbelievably high.

REVIEW EXERCISE A. **Completing Sentences by Inserting Prepositional Phrases.**   Complete each sentence by inserting an appropriate prepositional phrase in each blank. Be able to tell whether it is an adjective or an adverb phrase.

EXAMPLE   1.   —— Mrs. Bowen reads the newspaper.
          1. *In the evening Mrs. Bowen reads the newspaper.*

1. —— the children played hopscotch.
2. I saw a spider —— .
3. We planned a drive —— .
4. Her team played —— .
5. The sky divers jumped fearlessly —— .
6. Hundreds —— stared.
7. —— the cyclists unpacked their lunch.
8. There —— winds a narrow road.
9. This movie runs —— .
10. —— the dancers swayed with the music.

WRITING APPLICATION A:
Using Prepositional Phrases to Clarify Your Directions

Being able to explain something so that another person can understand is an important communication skill. Explaining how something is done is called a process explanation. In this kind of writing, details and accuracy are critical. The reader should be able to accomplish the same task by following your steps. Prepositional phrases are useful in this kind of writing.

EXAMPLES   **Before beginning,** read the recipe carefully.
Place **within easy reach** everything you will need.
Coat the pan **with vegetable oil or shortening.**

Writing Assignment

Think of something you know how to do—how to change a tire, how to overcome stage fright, how to serve a tennis ball, how to decorate your house for a party—that might be a help to someone else. Write a paragraph explaining exactly how to accomplish this task. Be sure to include all the necessary steps in the process and to put them in the order in which they should occur. Use at least five prepositional phrases; underline these phrases.

VERBALS AND VERBAL PHRASES[1]

Verbals are forms of a verb that are used not as verbs but as other parts of speech. Verbals act very much like verbs. They may be modified by adverbs and may have complements. Their chief function, however, is to act as other parts of speech: adjectives, nouns, adverbs.

There are three kinds of verbals: *participles, gerunds,* and *infinitives.*

The Participle

15f. A *participle* is a verb form that can be used as an adjective. Since the participle can function as a verb or an adjective, it might be called a "verbal adjective."

---

[1] For work on verbal phrases as sentence fragments, see pages 298–99. For verbals as dangling modifiers, see pages 524–25.

EXAMPLES   The **simmering** soup smelled delicious.
A **chipped** fingernail can be annoying.

In the first example, *simmering* is part verb because it carries the action of the verb *simmer*. It is part adjective because it modifies the noun *soup*: *simmering soup*. In the second example, *chipped* is part verb because it carries the action of the verb *chip*. It is part adjective because it modifies the noun *fingernail*: *chipped fingernail*. Because *simmering* and *chipped* are formed from verbs and used as adjectives, they are both participles.

There are two kinds of participles: *present* and *past*.

(1) *Present participles* consist of the plain form of the verb plus -*ing*.

EXAMPLES   The **smiling** graduates posed for the photographer.
Checking the weather forecast, the captain changed course.

In the first example, *smiling* (formed by adding -*ing* to the plain form of the verb *smile*) is a present participle modifying the noun *graduates*. In the second example, *checking* (formed by adding -*ing* to the plain form of the verb *check*) is a present participle modifying the noun *captain: checking captain*. In both examples, the present participles are verbals.

In addition to its use as a verbal, the present participle can be part of a verb phrase.

EXAMPLES   The graduates **were smiling**. The captain **is checking** the weather forecast.

A present participle alone cannot be a verb. It can, however, be part of a verb phrase if it is preceded by a helping verb: *were smiling*.

(2) *Past participles* consist of the plain form of the verb plus -*d* or -*ed*. A few are formed irregularly.[1]

EXAMPLES   **Discovered** by the guard, the **startled** burglar was led away. [The past participles *discovered* and *startled* modify the noun *burglar*.]
Pleased by the capture, the guard continued her rounds. [The past participle *pleased* modifies the noun *guard*.]

Like a present participle, a past participle can also be part of a verb phrase.

EXAMPLES   The burglar **was startled** when he **was discovered** by the guard.
The guard **was pleased** by the capture.

---

[1] See the discussion of irregular verbs on pages 491–92.

EXERCISE 4. Identifying Participles and the Words They Modify.
Write all the present and past participles in the following sentences.
After each one, write the word that the participle modifies. Be careful
not to confuse participles with the main verbs of the sentences.

1. Killer whales, long known as "wolves of the sea," have suffered
   from an undeserved notoriety.
2. Seeking to test the supposedly ferocious nature of the killer whale,
   scientists have studied their behavior.
3. After extensive study, scientists discovered that there is no documented case of an attack on a human by a killer whale.
4. Trainers, teaching killer whales to perform at amusement parks,
   learned that their charges were intelligent and gentle.
5. Congregating in Johnstone Strait, a narrow channel between Van-
   couver Island and British Columbia in Canada, killer whales swim
   and mate all year round.
6. Choosing this spot to observe the mammals, researchers were able
   to identify over one hundred individual whales.
7. Noting the unique shape of each whale's dorsal fin, this team of
   scientists named each whale to keep more accurate records.
8. Impressed by the long life span of killer whales, scientists have
   estimated that males may live fifty years and females may survive a
   century.
9. Cruising in groups called pods, killer whales are highly social
   animals.
10. During the summer and fall in Johnstone Strait, many pods gather,
    splashing and playing in "superpods."

EXERCISE 5. Revising Sentences by Using Participles. Each of
the following sentences is followed by a participle inside parentheses.
Rewrite each sentence by inserting the participle next to the noun it
modifies.

EXAMPLES 1. The candidate thanked each of her supporters. (*winning*)
          1. *The winning candidate thanked each of her supporters.*

          2. We collected funds for the restoration of the building. (*damaged*)
          2. *We collected funds for the restoration of the damaged building.*

1. The train was greeted loudly this afternoon. (*arriving*)
2. The committee selected three television shows for their educational
   value. (*nominating*)

3. My sister in the living room did not hear the doorbell. (*ringing*)
4. The carpenter was supposed to teach us how to fix this chair. (*broken*)
5. The Tasmanian wolf is a species seen only rarely since 1930. (*endangered*)
6. The stream crosses the farmer's land at three places. (*winding*)
7. A message on the back of an envelope was handed to me. (*crumpled*)
8. The book included three interesting facts about dinosaurs. (*illustrated*)
9. A Douglas fir had become the haven for several small creatures. (*fallen*)
10. The plane narrowly missed a tall radio antenna. (*circling*)

The Participial Phrase

A participle may be modified by an adverb or by a prepositional phrase used as an adverb, and it may have a complement. These related words combine with the participle to make a participial phrase.

15g. A *participial phrase* consists of a participle and its related words, such as modifiers and complements, all of which act together as an adjective.

The participial phrase in each of the following sentences is in boldfaced type. An arrow points to the noun or pronoun that the phrase modifies.

> ☞ NOTE Some participial phrases contain one or more prepositional phrases.

EXAMPLES **Climbing the tree,** the monkey disappeared into the branches.

I heard him **whispering to his friend.**

We watched the storm **blowing eastward.**

Nominated unanimously by the delegates, the candidate thanked her supporters.

The concert **scheduled for tomorrow** has been postponed until the week after next.

Cheered on by the spectators, the little bay horse swept past the finish line in record time.

EXERCISE 6. Identifying Participial Phrases and the Words They Modify.

Each of the following sentences contains one or more participial phrases. Write each participial phrase, and after it, write the noun or pronoun it modifies.

EXAMPLE   1. Hindered by bad weather, the British expedition lost the race to the South Pole, arriving a month after the Norwegians.
1. *Hindered by bad weather—expedition*
   arriving a month after the Norwegians—expedition

1. Hoping to be the first to reach the South Pole, the British explorer Robert Scott, taking four men with him, began his final dash to the pole on January 4, 1912.
2. Leading Scott by sixty miles, however, a Norwegian expedition, commanded by Roald Amundsen, was moving swiftly.
3. Having learned about Amundsen, Scott realized a race to the pole was on.
4. Plagued by bad weather and bad luck, Scott fell farther behind Amundsen.
5. Reaching the pole on January 17, the British found the Norwegians had already been there.
6. Weakened by scurvy, frostbite, and exhaustion, the five explorers, knowing they had little hope of survival, set out on the eight-hundred-mile journey back to their base ship.
7. One member of the party, overcome by exhaustion and injuries, died before half the journey had been completed.
8. On March 15, another member, leaving the camp at night, walked deliberately to his death in a violent blizzard.
9. Eight months later, a rescue mission, sent to find out what had happened, found the bodies of Scott and his companions.
10. Today the ill-fated Scott expedition, acclaimed for its heroism, is better known than the successful Amundsen expedition.

WRITING APPLICATION B:
Using Participial Phrases for Clear, Vivid Writing

Participial phrases can make your writing more vivid. However, be sure to place the participial phrase close to the noun or pronoun it modifies. Otherwise the phrase might create confusion or, as in the following example, some unexpected amusement.

CONFUSING   Waddling by the lake, we saw two ducks.
CLEAR   We saw two ducks waddling by the lake.

Writing Assignment

Write two sentences for each of the following participial phrases. In the first sentence, place the participial phrase in a position that creates an amusing meaning. In the second sentence, place each participial phrase near the noun or pronoun it modifies.

1. sheltered from the tornado
2. filmed in Mexico
3. screaming in terror
4. clustered in groups
5. written last week
6. scrawled illegibly
7. breaking all the rules
8. keeping a tight grip

The Gerund

Gerunds and present participles are formed exactly alike. Both are formed by adding -ing to the plain form of the verb. The difference between them is in their use. Present participles are used as *adjectives;* gerunds are used as *nouns.*

15h. A *gerund* is a verb form ending in -ing that is used as a noun.

Study the boldfaced gerunds in the following sentences. Note that each word is part verb and part noun. For instance, *reading* in the first sentence is formed from the verb *read;* it names an action. Yet it also names something and is the subject of its sentence; therefore, it is used as a noun.

EXAMPLES   **Reading** will increase your vocabulary.
Tobogganing is a winter sport.
I enjoyed **seeing** you again.
Peppering the soup improved its flavor.
She cleared a path by **shoveling** the snow.

In some sentences the gerund is used as the subject; in one it is used as the object of the verb; in the last sentence it is used as the object of a preposition. Note that gerunds always end in *-ing*.

EXERCISE 7. Identifying Gerunds and Participles. Number your paper 1–10. In each of the following sentences, you will find verbals ending in *-ing*. Write each verbal and label it either *ger.* for gerund or *part.* for participle. If the verbal is a gerund, tell how it is used (subject, object, predicate nominative, object of a preposition). If the verbal is a participle, tell what word it modifies.

EXAMPLES 1. Sleeping on the job is foolish.
　　　　　　 1. *Sleeping—ger.—subject*
　　　　　　 2. Let sleeping dogs lie.
　　　　　　 2. *sleeping—part.—dogs*

1. Their giggling annoyed the other viewers.
2. Virginia looks forward to fishing.
3. After studying, how do you relax?
4. A fascinating mystery is my favorite kind of book.
5. Making new friends in a large school can be difficult.
6. The highlight of the season was watching our team win the regional tournament.
7. Spinning around three times, she performed a pirouette.
8. Cindy makes money by walking dogs.
9. My grandmother and I enjoy digging for clams.
10. Sensing the danger nearby, he began to shout for help.

The Gerund Phrase

15i. A *gerund phrase* consists of a gerund together with its complements and modifiers, all of which act together as a noun.

EXAMPLES **Jaywalking in heavy traffic** is especially risky. [The gerund phrase is the subject of the sentence. The gerund *Jaywalking* is modified by the prepositional phrase *in heavy traffic*.]
　　　　　 She enjoys **hiking in the mountains.** [The gerund phrase is the direct object of the verb *enjoys*. The gerund *hiking* is modified by the prepositional phrase *in the mountains*.]
　　　　　 He improved his appearance by **losing weight.** [The gerund phrase is the object of the preposition *by*. The gerund *losing* has a direct object, *weight*.]

EXERCISE 8. Writing Sentences with Gerund Phrases. Write five sentences, each containing one or more gerund phrases. Underline each phrase, and label it using the following abbreviations: *subj.* (subject), *obj.* (object), *p.n.* (predicate nominative), *o.p.* (object of a preposition). Include an example of each use.

The Infinitive

15j. An *infinitive* is a verb form, usually preceded by *to*, that is used as a noun, adjective, or adverb.

An infinitive consists of the plain form of the verb, usually preceded by *to*. It can be used as a noun, an adjective, or an adverb. Study the following examples carefully.

Infinitives used as nouns

> **To err** is human. [The infinitive *to err* is the subject.]
> Betty wants **to act.** [The infinitive *to act* is the direct object of the verb *wants.*]

Infinitives used as adjectives

> The candidate **to believe** is Villegas. [The infinitive *to believe* modifies the noun *candidate.*]
> They are the easiest dogs **to train.** [The infinitive *to train* modifies the noun *dogs.*]

Infinitives used as adverbs

> The favored team was slow **to score.** [The infinitive *to score* modifies the adjective *slow.*]
> Grandmother has come **to stay.** [The infinitive *to stay* modifies the verb *has come.*]

> ☞ NOTE *To* plus a noun or a pronoun (*to bed, to the movies, to her*) is a prepositional phrase. *To* is the sign of the infinitive only when it is followed by a verb (*to go, to see, to have finished*).

EXERCISE 9. Identifying Infinitives and Their Uses in Sentences. Write the infinitives in the following sentences. After each infinitive, tell how it is used—as subject, object, predicate nominative, adjective, or adverb. You may use abbreviations.

1. Do you want to meet at the corner?
2. We are eager to go.
3. One way to relax is to listen to classical music.
4. I am easy to please.
5. We are waiting to talk with the principal.
6. The soup is still too hot to eat.
7. To excel, one must practice.
8. This summer she hopes to travel in the West.
9. To hike through the woods is fun.
10. To forgive is sometimes difficult.

The Infinitive Phrase

15k. An *infinitive phrase* consists of an infinitive together with its complements and modifiers.[1]

Like infinitives alone, infinitive phrases can be used as adjectives, adverbs, and nouns.

EXAMPLES   **To hit a curve ball solidly** is very difficult. [The infinitive phrase is used as a noun and is the subject of the sentence. The infinitive has an object, *ball,* and is modified by the adverb *solidly.*]

It is sometimes difficult **to listen attentively.** [The infinitive phrase is used as an adverb and modifies the adjective *difficult.* The adverb *attentively* modifies the infinitive.]

She wants **to be a lawyer.** [The infinitive phrase is the direct object of the verb *wants.* The infinitive is followed by the predicate nominative *lawyer.*]

The Infinitive Without *to*

Occasionally, the *to* that is usually the sign of the infinitive is omitted in a sentence. This happens frequently after such verbs as *see, hear, feel, watch, help, know, dare, need, make, let,* and *please.*

EXAMPLES   Did you watch her [to] play volleyball?
He will help us [to] paddle the canoe.
We don't dare [to] go outside during the storm.

---

[1] Unlike the other verbals, an infinitive may have a subject: *I asked him to come to my party.* (*Him* is the subject of the infinitive *to come.*) An infinitive phrase that includes a subject may sometimes be called an *infinitive clause.*

EXERCISE 10. Identifying and Classifying Infinitive Phrases.
Write the infinitive phrases from the following sentences. After each
phrase, tell how it is used—as subject, object, predicate nominative,
adjective, or adverb.

1. Our assignment was to read *I Know Why the Caged Bird Sings.*
2. We were asked to examine Maya Angelou's descriptions of her
   childhood.
3. To grow up in Stamps, Alabama, in the 1930's was to know great
   hardship.
4. Maya Angelou tried to show the everyday lives of black families
   during the Great Depression.
5. To accomplish this purpose meant including many descriptions; one
   such passage told about the process for curing pork sausage.
6. Angelou has an extraordinary ability to capture vivid details in her
   writing.
7. She helps us see her grandmother's store through the eyes of a
   fascinated child.
8. However, Angelou was eager to experience life beyond Stamps,
   Alabama.
9. Her ambitions enabled her to gain success as a writer, a dancer, and
   an actress.
10. To dramatize her Afro-American heritage was a dream she realized
    by writing a television series.

Diagraming Verbals and Verbal Phrases

Participles and participial phrases are diagramed as follows:

EXAMPLE **Walking to school,** Ted saw the first spring robin.

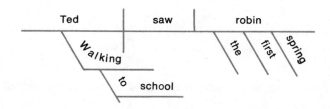

EXAMPLE **Waving her hat,** Sara flagged the train **speeding down the track.**

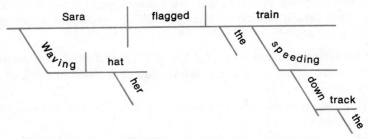

Gerunds and gerund phrases are diagramed differently.

EXAMPLE **Waiting patiently for hours** is usually a sure means of **observing wild animals.** [The gerund phrase *Waiting patiently for hours* is the subject of the verb *is;* the gerund phrase *observing wild animals* is the object of the preposition *of.* The first gerund phrase is modified by the adverb *patiently* and the prepositional phrase *for hours.* In the second gerund phrase, the gerund has a direct object, *animals.*]

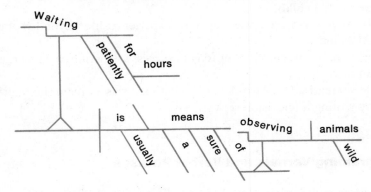

Infinitives and infinitive phrases used as modifiers are diagramed like prepositional phrases.

EXAMPLE He plays **to win.**

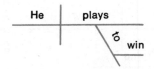

Infinitives and infinitive phrases used as nouns are diagramed as follows.

EXAMPLE   **To always be on time** is often difficult.

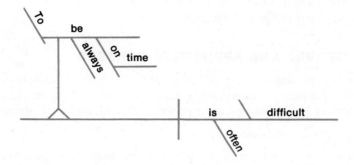

EXAMPLE   She is hoping **to see him again.**

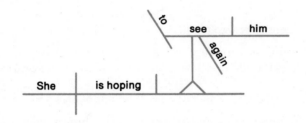

In the following sentence, notice how the subject of an infinitive is diagramed and how the infinitive itself is diagramed when *to* is omitted.

EXAMPLE   My brother watched **me climb the tree.**

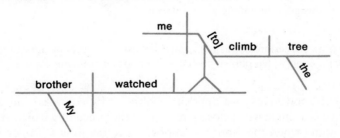

EXERCISE 11. Diagraming Sentences with Verbal Phrases. Diagram the following sentences.

1. Slowing down, the driver changed gears.
2. We always enjoy picnicking in the park.

3. Jean dreams of traveling to Africa.
4. To join clubs is often a good way to make friends.
5. Joe watched me groom the horses.

APPOSITIVES AND APPOSITIVE PHRASES

Nouns and pronouns, as you know, are modified by adjectives and adjective phrases. Occasionally a noun or pronoun will be followed immediately by another noun or pronoun that identifies or explains it.

EXAMPLE   My cousin **Bryan** is a philatelist.

In this sentence the noun *Bryan* tells which cousin. The noun *Bryan* is said to be in apposition with the noun *cousin*. In this sentence *Bryan* is called an *appositive*.

15l. An *appositive* **is a noun or pronoun that follows another noun or pronoun to identify or explain it.**

Like any noun or pronoun, an appositive may have adjective or adjective phrase modifiers. If it does, it is called an *appositive phrase*.

15m. An *appositive phrase* **is made up of an appositive and its modifiers.**

Examine the appositives and the appositive phrases in the following examples. They are in boldfaced type.

EXAMPLES   His grandparents, **the Vescuzos,** live on Miller Road, **a wide street lined with beech trees.**
A diligent and quick-witted student, Mark is studying hard to reach his goal, **becoming a veterinarian.**

> ☞ NOTE   Occasionally (as in the first appositive in the second example above) an appositive phrase precedes the noun or pronoun explained.

Set off appositives and appositive phrases by commas, unless the appositive is a single word closely related to the preceding word. Always use a comma when the word the appositive refers to is a proper noun.

EXAMPLES   Dr. Rosen, **our family dentist,** is a cheerful woman.
Her daughter **Karen** is a tennis player.
Jeff, **her younger son,** is a tennis coach.

In diagraming, place the appositive in parentheses after the word with which it is in apposition.

EXAMPLE   Ed Robbins, **our newest classmate,** comes from Goshen, **a town near Middletown.**

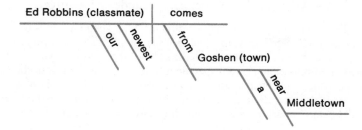

EXERCISE 12. Identifying Appositive Phrases and the Words They Modify.   Write the appositive phrases in each of the following sentences and underline them. Then write the word each modifies.

1. Soccer, my favorite sport, is very popular in South America.
2. Pelé, the internationally famous soccer star, is from Brazil.
3. Hausa, a Sudanese language, is widely used in western Africa.
4. Mr. Zolo, an old friend of the family's, will stay with us.
5. Susan, my youngest sister, speaks fluent Spanish.

WRITING APPLICATION C:
Writing Sentences with Appositive Phrases

Use appositive phrases to make your writing more specific for your readers. In the following pair of sentences, for example, notice how much more specific the second sentence is than the first.

EXAMPLE   Mr. Jones will be taking our class to see *Macbeth.*
            Mr. Jones, *our teacher,* will be taking our class to see *Macbeth.*

Writing Assignment

Think of ten people you admire. Write a sentence about each person, with an appositive phrase describing him or her.

EXAMPLES   Will Simon Le Bon, the lead singer of Duran Duran, appear on *Saturday Night Live?*
             Bernard King, the forward for the New York Knicks, scored two points off a jump shot.

GRAMMAR

REVIEW EXERCISE B. Identifying Verbal Phrases. There are twenty verbal phrases in the following sentences. Write them in order and tell what kind each is: participial, gerund, or infinitive.

Finding a summer job can be a difficult task. The first step is to scan the classified ads listed in your local newspaper. After discovering available opportunities, you can embark on the second step, matching your skills with the varied requirements of a specific job. In most cases you can then get in touch with a prospective employer by phoning the office or by writing a letter. If you are asked to interview for a job, preparing for the interview will be an important step in landing a summer job. To make a good impression, be sure to arrive on time, to dress neatly, and to speak courteously. Remember to avoid such nervous habits as constantly checking your watch or shuffling your feet. Within a day or two after an interview, it is permissible to call the interviewer. By presenting yourself as calm, confident, and courteous, you may hear the magic words, "We'd like you to work for us."

REVIEW EXERCISE C. Identifying Verbal and Appositive Phrases. The following sentences contain verbal and appositive phrases. Write the ten phrases and tell what kind each is: participial (*part.*), gerund (*ger.*), infinitive (*inf.*), or appositive (*app.*). Modifiers and complements of a verbal are considered part of the phrase.

EXAMPLE 1. To win a marathon, an athlete trained for this race must concentrate on developing stamina.
  1. *to win a marathon—inf.*
  trained for this race—part.
  developing stamina—ger.

1. The Brooklyn Bridge, a remarkable feat of design, spans the East River in New York City.
2. Linking the boroughs of Brooklyn and Manhattan, it was once the longest suspension bridge in the world.
3. Hart Crane, an American poet, immortalized the bridge.
4. Pedestrians walking across the bridge are struck by the grandeur of its graceful cables.
5. Despite its beauty, the bridge is remembered for having cost the lives of many of its builders.
6. To support the twin towers on the bridge, the brilliant John A. Roebling, its engineer, designed airtight caissons filled with concrete.

7. Working underwater on the caissons was painstakingly slow and extremely dangerous.
8. Another perilous job was spinning the cables from one side of the river to the other.

CHAPTER 15 REVIEW: POSTTEST 1

Identifying Prepositional, Verbal, and Appositive Phrases. Number your paper 1–20. After the proper number, write each italicized phrase and indicate what kind of phrase it is. Use the abbreviations *prep.* (prepositional phrase), *part.* (participial phrase), *ger.* (gerund phrase), *inf.* (infinitive phrase), or *app.* (appositive phrase).

EXAMPLE   An interesting career (1) *to consider* is (2) *practicing law.*
1. *to consider—inf.*
2. *practicing law—ger.*

(1) *To become a lawyer,* one must first earn a degree (2) *from a four-year college.* Then the undergraduate must take the Law School Admissions Test (3) *to gain acceptance at an approved law school.* After (4) *completing three full years of law school,* the graduate is awarded an L.L.B. degree or a J.D. degree. Before (5) *practicing law,* however, the graduate must take an exam (6) *given by the state board of bar examiners.* Only after (7) *passing this exam* is a lawyer ready (8) *to be admitted to the bar* and (9) *to practice law.*

The duty of a lawyer, (10) *also called an attorney or a counselor at law,* is (11) *to provide service and advice* (12) *relating to legal rights.* (13) *Representing a client in court* is only part (14) *of a lawyer's job.* Lawyers must spend hours (15) *gathering enough evidence* (16) *to defend a client.* Lawyers also devote time (17) *to research* and are required (18) *to write numerous reports.*

Some lawyers spend most of their time (19) *trying cases in court.* Others work hard (20) *to keep cases* out of court.

CHAPTER 15 REVIEW: POSTTEST 2

Writing Sentences with Prepositional, Verbal, and Appositive Phrases. Write ten sentences using the following phrases. Follow the directions in the parentheses.

1. in the cottage (use as an adjective phrase)
2. for our English class (use as an adverb phrase)
3. for *Nineteen Eighty-Four* (use as an adverb phrase)
4. by the train (use as an adverb phrase)
5. walking by the lake (use as a participial phrase)
6. playing the piano (use as a gerund phrase that is the subject of the sentence)
7. to get a home run (use as an infinitive phrase that is the direct object of the sentence)
8. the new student in our class (use as an appositive phrase)
9. the President of France (use as an appositive phrase)
10. my favorite actress (or actor) (use as an appositive phrase)

GRAMMAR

CHAPTER 16

The Clause

INDEPENDENT AND SUBORDINATE CLAUSES

A clause, like a phrase, is a group of related words used together as part of a sentence. Clauses, however, contain a subject and verb, whereas phrases do not.

PHRASE   We had our midterms **before spring.** [The prepositional phrase *before spring* contains neither a subject nor a verb.]

CLAUSE   We had our midterms **before spring began.** [*Spring* is the subject of the clause and *began* is the verb.]

DIAGNOSTIC TEST

A. Identifying Independent and Subordinate Clauses; Classifying Subordinate Clauses.   Number your paper 1–10. Identify each of the italicized clauses in the following sentences as an independent clause or a subordinate clause. Tell how each subordinate clause functions in the sentence, using the following abbreviations: *adj. cl.* (adjective clause), *adv. cl.* (adverb clause), *n. cl.* (noun clause).

EXAMPLES 1. A soccer field measures 115 yards by 75 yards, and *the netted goals are 8 yards wide by 8 feet high.*
         1. *independent clause*
        2. Soccer, *which is the national sport of many European and Latin American countries,* has enjoyed only limited success in the United States.
         2. *subordinate clause, adj. cl.*

1. During a career *that spanned twenty years,* Pelé was probably the most popular athlete in the world.
2. He was named Edson Arantes do Nascimento, but *hardly anyone recognizes that name.*
3. Soccer fans the world over, however, knew Pelé, *who was considered the world's best soccer player.*
4. *While he was still a teen-ager,* he led his Brazilian teammates to the first of their three World Cup titles.
5. *Whenever he played,* his skill and agility awed fans.
6. Once, he juggled the ball on his foot for fifty yards, eluding four opponents *who were trying to take the ball away from him.*
7. *That he soon became a superstar* is not surprising.
8. *Even though soccer never became a major sport in the United States,* Pelé managed to spark considerable interest in the game.
9. After he signed with the New York Cosmos, *people flocked to the stands to watch him play.*
10. They soon saw *that Pelé was a great entertainer as well as a great athlete.*

B. Classifying Sentences as Simple, Compound, Complex, or Compound-Complex.   Number your paper 11–20. After the proper number, identify each of the following sentences as simple, compound, complex, or compound-complex.

EXAMPLE   1. Tennis originated in France in the fifteenth century as indoor court tennis, but it did not take its present form as lawn tennis until 1870.
   1. *compound*

11. As the youngest member of a tennis-playing family, Tracy Austin appeared on the cover of *Tennis World* when she was only four.
12. At fourteen she had run out of opponents her own age; therefore, she began to look for older competitors.
13. In 1977 she became the youngest player to compete at Wimbledon, but she did not win any major tournaments that year.
14. At age sixteen, she decided to turn professional.
15. She proved equal to the challenge when she defeated a number of more experienced players.
16. By 1979 she had defeated the top women players and eventually won her first major tournament.

17. She defeated Billie Jean King and then went on to break Martina Navratilova's winning streak.
18. When she defeated Chris Evert Lloyd, she became the youngest player to win the U.S. Women's Open.
19. She traveled extensively on the tournament circuit, but she attended school, where she regularly earned good grades.
20. The determination that enabled her to win at tennis also made her an A student.

16a. A *clause* is a group of words that contains a verb and its subject and is used as part of a sentence.

KINDS OF CLAUSES

All clauses have a subject and verb, but not all of them express a complete thought. Those that do express a complete thought are called *independent clauses*. Such clauses could be written as separate sentences. We think of them as clauses when they are joined with one or more additional clauses in a single larger sentence. Clauses that do not make complete sense by themselves are called *subordinate clauses*. Subordinate clauses may function as nouns, adjectives, or adverbs, just as phrases do.

Independent Clauses

16b. An *independent* (or *main*) *clause* expresses a complete thought and can stand by itself.

Each of the following two sentences is the same as an independent clause:

> The outfielders were missing easy fly balls.
> The infielders were throwing wildly.

To show the relationship between these two ideas, we can combine them as independent clauses in a single sentence:

> The outfielders were missing easy fly balls, **and** the infielders were throwing wildly.

Independent clauses may also be joined by the conjunctions *but, or, nor, for,* and *yet.*

Should we go for a walk, **or** is it too hot outside?
Gladys was not tired, **but** her tennis partner was.

Subordinate Clauses

16c. A *subordinate* (or *dependent*) *clause* **does not express a complete thought and cannot stand by itself.**

Subordinate means "lesser in rank or importance." Subordinate clauses are so called because they need an independent clause to complete their meaning.

SUBORDINATE CLAUSES   who spoke to our class yesterday
that many students are eligible for scholarships
because no students have applied for them

Notice that each of these subordinate clauses has an incomplete sound when read by itself. Each one leaves you expecting more to be said. Words like *if, when, although, since,* and *because* always make the clause they introduce sound unfinished. These words signal that what follows is only part of a sentence: **although** *the store was closed;* **since** *you are leaving.* The subordinate clauses given as examples above fit into sentences as follows:

The woman **who spoke to our class yesterday** informed us of financial aid for college applicants.
She said **that many students are eligible for scholarships.**
Some scholarships are still available **because no students have applied for them.**

EXERCISE 1. Identifying Independent and Subordinate Clauses.
Number your paper 1–10. After the proper number, identify each italicized clause as *independent* or *subordinate*.

1. Anne, *who enjoys watching baseball,* is a loyal fan of the Chicago Cubs.
2. *The burglar easily picked the lock;* next, he carefully cut the wires to the alarm system.
3. Mr. Wilson always waves to us *whenever we drive past his house.*
4. *As soon as the movie begins,* you should stop talking.
5. *We played croquet in the back yard* until the mosquitoes began to attack us.
6. The cat *that jumped through my bedroom window* is a stray.

7. Since the tropical storm is gathering force, *it may become a hurricane.*
8. *Donna sang ten beautiful songs,* but the audience wanted to hear many more.
9. He assumed *that we had already met.*
10. People *who belong to tenants' organizations* usually get better service from their landlords.

Complements and Modifiers in Subordinate Clauses

A subordinate clause, like an independent clause or a simple sentence, may contain complements and modifiers.

EXAMPLES   Here is the portrait **that** he painted. [*That* is the direct object of *painted.*]
   We couldn't tell **who** they were. [*Who* is a predicate nominative: They were *who.*]
   Since she told **us** the *truth* . . . [*Us* is the indirect object of *told; truth* is the direct object of *told.*]
   When I am **busy** . . . [*Busy* is a predicate adjective.]
   After he had cooked **for us** . . . [*For us* is an adverb phrase modifying *had cooked.*]

EXERCISE 2. Identifying Subjects, Verbs, and Complements in Subordinate Clauses.   Write the italicized subordinate clauses in the following sentences. In each clause, underline the subject once and the verb or verb phrase twice, and identify any complements, using the abbreviations *d.o.* (direct object), *p.n.* (predicate nominative), *i.o.* (indirect object).

EXAMPLE   1. *After he shows us his new boat,* we will go swimming.
                     i.o.   d.o.
      1. *After he shows us his new boat*

1. We couldn't see *who had won the race.*
2. They could see *who the winner was,* but they couldn't tell *which country she was from.*
3. She is the celebrity *whom we saw at the restaurant.*
4. Look for the mouse *that you heard last night.*
5. He spotted a horse *that galloped away.*
6. *After we passed the test,* we celebrated.
7. I wake up *whenever I hear a strange noise.*

8. *Because you had not given us the right address,* we missed the party.
9. The package will arrive on time *if you ship it today.*
10. *Until Mike loaned me this book,* I had never heard of John Steinbeck.

THE USES OF SUBORDINATE CLAUSES

Subordinate clauses fulfill the same function in sentences as adjectives, adverbs, and nouns. Subordinate clauses are named according to the job they do in sentences.

The Adjective Clause

16d. An *adjective clause* is a subordinate clause used as an adjective to modify a noun or pronoun.

EXAMPLES   The novel **that I borrowed from the library** is about the Irish revolt of 1798.
Our town's civic center, **which was renovated last year,** has just been declared a landmark.

An adjective clause always follows the noun or pronoun it modifies. It is sometimes set off by commas and sometimes not. If the clause is *needed* to identify the word modified, no commas are used. Thus in the first example, the adjective clause is not set off because it is needed to identify *which* novel the sentence is about. If the clause merely adds information that is *not essential,* as in the second example, commas are used. (See pages 574–75.)

Relative Pronouns

Adjective clauses are usually introduced by the pronouns *who, whom, whose, which,* and *that.* These pronouns are called *relative pronouns* because they relate the adjective clause to the word the clause modifies (the antecedent of the relative pronoun). In addition to referring to the word the clause modifies, the relative pronoun has a job to do within the adjective clause.

EXAMPLES   Isabella Baumfree was an abolitionist **who was popularly known as Sojourner Truth.** [The relative pronoun *who* relates the adjective clause to *abolitionist. Who* also functions as the subject of the adjective clause.]

GRAMMAR

She is the person **whom I trust most.** [*Whom* relates the adjective clause to *person. Whom* also functions in the adjective clause as the direct object: *I trust whom.*]

The topic about **which he is writing** is controversial. [*Which* relates the clause to *topic. Which* also functions in the adjective clause as the object of the preposition *about.*]

Do you know the name of the group **whose recording is number one on the charts?** [*Whose* relates the clause to *group. Whose* also functions in the clause as a modifier of *recording.*]

In some cases the relative pronoun is omitted. The pronoun is understood and still is thought of as having a function in the clause.

EXAMPLES Ms. Chung is the legislator **[that] we met.** [The relative pronoun —*that* or *whom*—is understood. The pronoun relates the adjective clause to *legislator* and functions in the adjective clause as the direct object.]

Are these the books **[that] you read?** [The relative pronoun—*that* or *which*—is understood.]

In addition to relative pronouns, adverbs are sometimes used to introduce adjective clauses.

EXAMPLES This is the season **when it rains almost every day.**
Here is the spot **where we will have lunch.**

EXERCISE 3. Identifying Adjective Clauses and the Words They Modify.
Write the adjective clauses in the following sentences. Underline the subject of each clause once and the verb twice, and circle the relative pronoun that introduces the clause. After the clause, write the word it modifies.

EXAMPLE 1. The topic that Melissa chose for her paper was a difficult one.
1. (that) *Melissa chose for her paper—topic*

1. A speech community is a group of people who speak the same language.
2. There are speech communities that consist of millions of people and some that contain only a few hundred.
3. The language that we use during our childhood is called our native language.
4. A person who has mastered a second language is bilingual.
5. People who conduct business internationally should know more than one language.

6. English, French, and Spanish, which many diplomats can speak, are among the six official languages of the United Nations.
7. Russian, Chinese, and Arabic are the other three languages that are used officially at the UN.
8. People for whom language study is important include telephone operators, hotel managers, and police officers.
9. Tourists who travel to other countries need to know a language that is understood in different parts of the world.
10. French, for example, is a language which is spoken in Europe, Africa, and Southeast Asia.

Diagraming Adjective Clauses

An adjective clause beginning with a relative pronoun is joined to the noun it modifies by a broken line. This line runs from the modified word to the relative pronoun.

EXAMPLE   The coat **that I wanted** was too expensive.

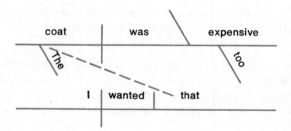

EXAMPLE   The box **that contained the treasure** was missing.

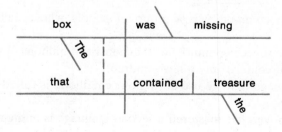

EXAMPLE   She is the woman **from whom we bought the used car.**

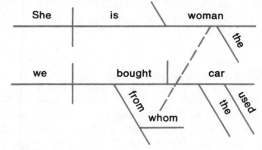

The Adverb Clause

16e. An *adverb clause* is a subordinate clause that modifies a verb, an adjective, or an adverb.

Like adverbs, adverbial clauses modify words by telling *how, when, where,* or *under what condition.*

EXAMPLES   Donna sounds **as if she has caught a cold.** [*As if she has caught a cold* tells *how* Donna sounds.]
Before we left, we turned off the lights. [*Before we left* tells *when* we turned off the lights.]
You will see our house **where the road turns right.** [*Where the road turns right* tells *where* you will see our house.]
As long as he starts early, he will arrive on time. [*As long as he starts early* tells *under what condition* he will arrive on time.]

The Subordinating Conjunction

Adverb clauses are introduced by subordinating conjunctions. As its name suggests, a subordinating conjunction makes its clause a subordinate part of the sentence—a part that cannot stand alone. Unlike relative pronouns, which introduce adjective clauses, subordinating conjunctions do not serve a function within the clause they introduce.

Common Subordinating Conjunctions

after	before	unless
although	if	until
as	in order that	when
as if	since	whenever
as long as	so that	where
as soon as	than	wherever
because	though	while

GRAMMAR

☞ **NOTE** Many of the words in this list can be used as other parts of speech. For instance *after, as, before, since,* and *until* can also be used as prepositions.

Diagraming Adverb Clauses

An adverb clause is written on a horizontal line below the independent clause and is joined to it by a broken line connecting the verb of the adverb clause to the word in the independent clause (usually the verb) that the clause modifies. On the broken line, write the subordinating conjunction that introduces the subordinate clause.

EXAMPLE **Before a hurricane strikes,** ample warning is given.

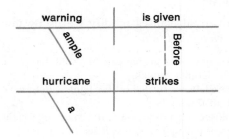

EXERCISE 4. Identifying Adverb Clauses and Subordinating Conjunctions. Write the adverb clause in each of the following sentences. Circle the subordinating conjunction in each clause.

1. Ruth mowed the lawn while we weeded the flower beds.
2. The grass looked as if it had not been cut in months.
3. Because the house had been empty for so long, the lawn and gardens were choked with weeds.
4. We borrowed tools so that we could weed more efficiently.
5. Until we had pulled out the weeds, we could not see the roses.
6. When we cut through the heavy undergrowth, we used a scythe.
7. In one corner we stacked a mound of debris so that it could be hauled away.
8. After Ruth had mowed about half the lawn, she was exhausted.
9. When we stopped for a rest, we stretched out in the shade.
10. Long hours in the hot sun had made us feel as though the day would never end.

EXERCISE 5. Writing Sentences with Adverb Clauses. Write ten sentences, using in each sentence a different one of the subordinating conjunctions in the list given on page 419. After each of the sentences, state whether the clause tells *how, when, where, why,* or *under what condition.*

WRITING APPLICATION A:
Using Subordination to Create a Mature Style

Mature writers generally avoid a long series of short, choppy sentences. One way to express your thoughts in a mature way is to use subordination. Some of the thoughts in the example with short, choppy sentences were combined by using a subordinate clause. The clause is in boldface.

EXAMPLE I like impressionism. Mary Cassatt is an American artist. I enjoy her painting. She is an impressionist.
I enjoy the works of Mary Cassatt, **who is an American impressionist painter.**

Writing Assignment

Is there a certain artist, musician, or author who particularly appeals to you? In a paragraph of 100 to 150 words, discuss this person. Use specific details and include at least five subordinate clauses. Underline these clauses.

REVIEW EXERCISE A. Distinguishing Between Adjective and Adverb Clauses. Write on your paper the subordinate clauses in the following sentences. After each clause, state whether it is an adjective clause or an adverb clause.

1. In 1978, aeronauts Ben Abruzzo, Max Anderson, and Larry Newman, whose home was Albuquerque, New Mexico, became the first people to pilot a balloon across the Atlantic Ocean.
2. Although Abruzzo and Anderson had been forced to land in the ocean in an earlier attempt in *Double Eagle,* they were not discouraged by this failure.
3. They acquired a new balloon, which they named *Double Eagle II.*
4. Since experience had shown the need for another crew member, they took Newman with them.

5. A balloon rises because it is filled with helium, which is a light-weight gas.
6. If a balloon loses altitude, the crew moves it upward by discarding ballast.
7. When it gains too much altitude, the crew lowers it by releasing some of the gas.
8. Aeronauts must know meteorology so that they can take advantage of favorable winds.
9. As the aeronauts were eager to point out, *Double Eagle II* was flown across the Atlantic; it did not just drift across.
10. On its journey from Maine to France, *Double Eagle II* was airborne for 137 hours, which is a little less than six days.

The Noun Clause

16f. A *noun clause* is a subordinate clause used as a noun.

Compare the two sentences in each of the following pairs. Notice that in the second sentence in each pair, *a subordinate clause takes the place of a noun in the first sentence.* Tell whether the clause in each sentence is used as a subject, a direct object, an indirect object, a predicate nominative, or an object of a preposition.

> She believes that **saying.**
> She believes **that lost time is never found again.**
>
> The municipal **garage** is the main item on tonight's agenda.
> **Where the municipal garage will be built** is the main item on tonight's agenda.
>
> She has written an article about her **election.**
> She has written an article about **how she was elected to the Senate.**
>
> The store owner will give the **winner** a substantial prize.
> The store owner will give **whoever wins the contest** a substantial prize.
>
> The happiest time in my life was our **summer** in Colombia.
> The happiest time in my life was **when we went to Colombia for the summer.**

Noun clauses are usually introduced by such connectives as *that, whether, what, who, whoever, whose, where,* and *why.* Sometimes the introductory word does not have any function in the clause.

EXAMPLE I know **that she is worried.** [The connective *that* has no function in the clause.]

(above "she is": S   V)

At other times, the introductory word does have a function in the clause.

EXAMPLE Do you know **what the problem is?** [The connective *what* functions in the clause as the predicate nominative.]

(above: PN   S   V)

Like adjective clauses, noun clauses are sometimes used without the usual introductory word. Compare the noun clauses in the following paired sentences.

He told us **that attendance is improving.**
He told us **attendance is improving.** [The connective *that* is understood.]

EXERCISE 6. Identifying and Classifying Noun Clauses.   Write the noun clauses in the following sentences. Label the subject and the verb of each. Then identify each clause using these abbreviations: *s.* (subject of the sentence), *d.o.* (direct object), *i.o.* (indirect object), *p.n.* (predicate nominative), or *o. prep.* (object of a preposition).

1. Mr. Perkins told us what we would play at half time.
2. We can never predict what he will choose.
3. We never know whether he will choose a march or a show tune.
4. The drummer told Mr. Perkins she did not like Sousa marches.
5. How she could say that was a mystery to me.
6. Mr. Perkins told us we would play a medley of marches.
7. Whoever did not like this choice could leave the band.
8. His reason is that the band director must have the final say.
9. Whoever shows the most talent will play the solos.
10. The crowd always applauds enthusiastically for whoever plays a solo.

Diagraming Noun Clauses

A clause used as subject, object, predicate nominative, or object of a preposition is supported by an upright line resting on the line of the subject, object, predicate nominative, or object of a preposition.

NOUN CLAUSE AS SUBJECT **What she said** convinced me. [*What* functions in the clause as the direct object.]

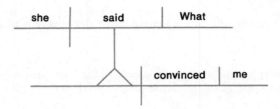

NOUN CLAUSE AS OBJECT We know **that you won the prize.** [*That* has no function in the clause.]

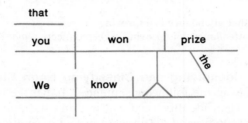

REVIEW EXERCISE B. Identifying Adjective, Adverb, and Noun Clauses. The following sentences contain adjective, adverb, and noun clauses. Write each clause, label its verb and subject, and name the kind of clause.

1. When the circus is in town, be sure to go.
2. Jack and Joan, who were in town last week, visited me.
3. After we went to the museum, we strolled through the park.
4. This is what I would call an excellent meal.
5. Camping out was difficult for those who had never done it before.
6. While we ate breakfast, the kitten played with the ball of yarn.
7. One of Marge's complaints was that the weather had been bad.
8. This is the hat that I want for my birthday.
9. We visited Jerusalem before we left Israel.
10. Here is the clothing store that sells leather jackets.

SENTENCES CLASSIFIED BY STRUCTURE

16g. When classified according to structure, there are four kinds of sentences: *simple, compound, complex,* and *compound-complex.*

GRAMMAR

(1) A *simple sentence* **is a sentence with one independent clause and no subordinate clause.**

EXAMPLE   The Hudson is a historic waterway.

Although we often think of simple sentences as short, this is not necessarily so.

EXAMPLE   In the stands at half time, we bragged to friends from another school about our team's prospects for the season. [Notice that there are several phrases but only one subject and one verb.]

(2) A *compound sentence* **is a sentence composed of two or more independent clauses but no subordinate clauses.**

EXAMPLES   A strange dog chased us, but the owner came to our rescue. [two independent clauses]

The film is long, but it is suspenseful, and the time passes quickly. [three independent clauses]

A coordinating conjunction or a semicolon is generally used to connect the independent clauses in a compound sentence. Other words, called *conjunctive adverbs,* used to join the clauses of a compound sentence are *consequently, therefore, nevertheless, however, moreover,* and *otherwise.* When a word of this kind is used between two independent clauses, it is preceded by a semicolon and followed by a comma.

Each independent clause in a compound sentence is diagramed like a separate sentence. A broken line is drawn between the verbs of the two clauses, and the conjunction is written on a solid horizontal line connecting the two parts of the broken line.

EXAMPLE   I bought the blouse, but the brooch was given to me.

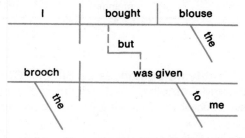

Caution: Do not confuse the compound predicate of a simple sentence with the two subjects and two predicates of a compound sentence.

EXAMPLES

     S   V   V

She played basketball and won a sports scholarship. [simple sentence with compound predicate]

     S   V   S   V

She played basketball, and she won a sports scholarship. [compound sentence with two independent clauses]

(3) A *complex sentence* is a sentence containing one independent clause and at least one subordinate clause.

EXAMPLE   As night fell, the storm reached its climax.

Since you have already learned how to diagram a sentence containing a subordinate clause (adjective, adverb, and noun clause), you know how to diagram a complex sentence.

(4) A *compound-complex sentence* contains two or more independent clauses and at least one subordinate clause.

EXAMPLE   The room that Carrie painted had been white, but she changed the color. [two independent clauses and one subordinate clause]

In diagraming a compound-complex sentence, first diagram the independent clauses. Then attach the subordinate clauses to the words they modify. Give yourself plenty of room.

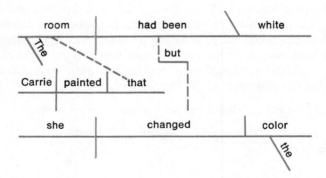

EXERCISE 7. Identifying Sentences as Simple, Compound, Complex, or Compound-Complex.   After the proper number, write what kind of sentence each of the following is: simple, compound, complex, or compound-complex.

1. The Key Club sponsored a rummage sale and accepted donations from everyone.

2. The principal donated a bird cage, and the coach made lemonade for the volunteers.
3. We used whatever had been donated, but we welcomed housewares most.
4. One customer bought a set of encyclopedias, which she'd long wanted, and her husband purchased an antique wood bookcase with a brass trim.
5. The Key Club gave all the profits that it made from the sale to a local charity.

EXERCISE 8. Diagraming the Four Kinds of Sentences. Diagram the sentences in Exercise 7.

WRITING APPLICATION B:
Using Variety in Sentence Structure to Enliven Your Writing

Would you enjoy eating exactly the same kinds of food for supper every night? Probably not. Looking forward to something different increases interest as well as appetite. This is somewhat the way your reader feels. You should serve different kinds of sentences to maintain interest. Keep in mind that you have four kinds of sentences to choose from: simple, compound, complex, and compound-complex.

EXAMPLE   This morning I looked at the kitchen. (simple) The dirty dishes were piled high on the cabinet, and the trash was overflowing the container. (compound) When I looked in a skillet on the stove, I saw leftover grease. (complex) I knew that I had to clean it all up, but I hated to get started. (compound-complex) Never will I leave the kitchen dirty again! (simple)

Writing Assignment

Write a description of one of the following areas. Include at least one of each kind of sentence. Write the kind of sentence in parentheses after the sentence, as the writer did in the example above.

AREAS   1. your room   3. a game room
        2. skating rink   4. school cafeteria

GRAMMAR

CHAPTER 16 REVIEW: POSTTEST 1

A. Identifying Independent and Subordinate Clauses; Classifying Subordinate Clauses. Number your paper 1–10. After the proper number, identify each of the italicized clauses in the following sentences as an independent clause or a subordinate clause. Tell how each italicized subordinate clause functions in the sentence, using the abbreviations *adj. cl.* (adjective clause), *adv. cl.* (adverb clause), and *n. cl.* (noun clause).

EXAMPLE 1. The Brooklyn Bridge, *which was built in the latter half of the nineteenth century,* is still considered one of the world's foremost suspension bridges.
1. *subordinate clause—adj. cl.*

1. The Brooklyn Bridge, *which spans the strong tides of the East River between Brooklyn and Manhattan,* is one of the engineering wonders of the world.
2. Massive granite towers *that are supported by pneumatic caissons* are its most remarkable feature.
3. *The bridge was designed and built by John and Washington Roebling, a father-and-son engineering team* who were pioneers in the use of steel-wire cables.
4. Because of the steel-wire cables used in its construction, the bridge is a graceful structure *that resembles a spider's web.*
5. *That the bridge combines strength with beauty* remains a tribute to the Roebling family.
6. The Roeblings discovered *that construction work could be both slow and dangerous.*
7. *Although she was not an engineer,* Nora Roebling assisted in the efforts to complete the bridge.
8. *Because at times they were required to work underwater in airtight chambers,* many workers, including Washington Roebling, suffered from caisson disease.
9. Sailors, *who were used to working at great heights,* were hired to string the miles of cable.
10. *John Roebling's foot was injured in an accident,* and he died before the bridge's completion.

B. Classifying Sentences as Simple, Compound, Complex, or Compound-Complex. Number your paper 11–20. After the proper number, identify each of the following sentences as simple, compound, complex, or compound-complex.

EXAMPLE 1. John Augustus Roebling was the German-born engineer who designed and built the Brooklyn Bridge.
1. *complex*

11. As an aftermath of caisson disease, Washington Roebling, who succeeded his father, was confined to bed.
12. The Roeblings lived in a house that was in the vicinity of the construction site, and Washington supervised by observing progress through a telescope.
13. He dictated instructions to Nora, who was his energetic go-between.
14. No one can say whether the work on the bridge could have continued without her assistance.
15. When the bridge was finally completed, President Chester A. Arthur attended the dedication ceremonies.
16. Because of his illness, Washington was unable to attend.
17. The President, however, came to the Roebling home to honor the man who had struggled so valiantly to complete the bridge.
18. The bridge had taken fourteen years to build; it was hailed by some as the eighth wonder of the world.
19. The bridge stands as a monument to the artistry, sacrifice, and determination of the people who had planned and built it.
20. The Roeblings had envisioned cable cars to carry people across the bridge, but today only motorized vehicles pass along the six-lane thoroughfare.

CHAPTER 16 REVIEW: POSTTEST 2

Writing a Variety of Sentence Structures. Write your own sentences according to the following guidelines:

1. A simple sentence with a compound verb
2. A compound sentence with two independent clauses joined by the conjunction *but*

3. A compound sentence with two independent clauses joined with the conjunction *and*
4. A complex sentence with an adjective clause
5. A complex sentence with the adverb clause placed at the beginning of the sentence
6. A complex sentence with an adverb clause placed at the end of the sentence
7. A complex sentence with a noun clause used as the direct object of the verb
8. A complex sentence with a noun clause used as the subject of the sentence
9. A complex sentence with a noun clause used as the object of a preposition
10. A compound-complex sentence

CHAPTER 17

The English Language

HISTORY AND USAGE

THE HISTORY OF ENGLISH

The Early Beginnings

The history of a language resembles a family tree in many ways. You may someday become so interested in your own ancestry that you will trace it back as far as available records can take you, possibly to a little village in England, continental Europe, Asia, or Africa. You would realize that members of your present family are like the smallest branches at the ends of limbs. You and the hundreds of other branches sprang from the same source—the original parents, or trunk of the family tree.

Language experts might say that the tree in this analogy is like a *language stock,* or group of languages that grew from a single original tongue. There are several such stocks in the world. They have given us more than 2,500 languages in all.

How could such an incredible number develop? For thousands of years much of the world's population was on the move. Tribes and armies wandered over the entire face of the globe, splitting up to form additional tribes, fighting, intermingling, sometimes settling down, sometimes moving on again. Throughout this process, languages, like the people who spoke them, evolved. They influenced or combined with or departed from one another. The process will in fact never end.

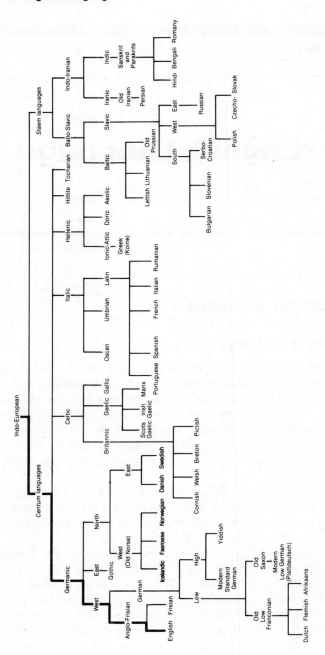

Indo-European languages

The family tree of which English is a branch can be traced back 6,000 years, or to about 4000 B.C. Our "trunk" was Proto- (first or earliest) Indo-European; we drop the "Proto" in identifying the large family of languages that descended from it.

The areas from which the tribes who spoke Proto-Indo-European started their wanderings were eastern Europe and western Asia. We need not trace the tribes' movements in detail. Suffice it to say that one movement was responsible for the modern-day languages of India and the Iranian peninsula. Another led to several languages of Greece and the coastal areas of Asia Minor. Another resulted in Latin and the succeeding Romance (Roman-origin) languages, such as French, Spanish, Italian, Portuguese and Romanian. Still another led to the Germanic tongues, of which English is one. (Study the diagram on page 432.)

Proto-Indo-European was spoken so long ago that language scholars must content themselves with a few words they believe can be traced back that far. The linguists are fairly certain that such basic words as *heart, lung, head, mother, father, sun, moon, star,* and the numerals from one to ten all were used—in different form, of course—by the Proto-Indo-Europeans. The full collection of these words is called the Indo-European *base.* Many dictionaries include these words in their etymologies. Such words are indicated with asterisks: **bher-* (bear).

In contrast, linguists know almost everything about the later evolution of languages. We will examine some of it in our study of the history of English. Let us begin by noting that languages derived from a common stock, no matter how different they may seem, share certain words to a recognizable extent. An example is *mother.* Here are its forms in eight languages derived from Indo-European:

English	mother	Greek	meter
Sanskrit	mata	Italian	madre
French	mère	Latin	mater
German	Mutter	Russian	mat'

EXERCISE 1. Investigating the Indo-European Language. Use your school library to study the history of the Indo-European language. Look for answers to the following questions:

1. What evidence led scholars to establish the location of the Indo-European homelands?
2. What have we discovered about the life of the Indo-Europeans?
3. What language stocks are there besides Indo-European? What are some languages that have developed from them?

EXERCISE 2. Applying Knowledge of Word Origins. Each of the following words has its origins in Indo-European. Using a dictionary that gives Indo-European origins, look up each word and write down its Indo-European base form.

1. mother   6. heart
2. sun   7. head
3. cup   8. weave
4. sky   9. moon
5. two   10. wolf

Old English

About thirteen centuries have passed since the first English of which we have any record, but the stage was set for the language two or three centuries earlier, or between A.D. 400 and 500. The islands of Great Britain and Ireland, as we now call them, were governed by the Romans, who kept peace between the Celts in the south and the Picts and Scots to the north. All these peoples had crossed over from Europe much earlier.

By this time—around A.D. 450—the Roman Empire was disintegrating. The Romans in the British Isles were called home. They were no sooner gone than the Picts and Scots began attacking the peaceful Celts, who started looking for help. They thought they had found it in the Angles, Saxons, and Jutes, Germanic tribes who heeded the call and came from their lands just across the North Sea. But having been invited as guests, the newcomers stayed as conquerors. By the year 600 they had driven the Celts into a small part of the main island. By 700 the principal language of the islands was not Celtic but a mixture of the languages that had been spoken by the Angles, Saxons, and Jutes. It was given the name "Englisc." The islands had come to be known as "Angle Land," after the largest group of new inhabitants. That name is the obvious source of "England."

Our own name for the language that evolved under these circumstances is Old English. We usually date it from around A.D. 450. You would hardly recognize Old English as being anything like the language we use. Consider this line from the greatest Old English poem, *Beowulf:* "*Thone sithfaet him snotere ceorlas lythwon logon.*" The rough translation is "The wise men criticized that journey to him not at all." To know that, however, you would have to be familiar not only with the roots of the words but also with the word endings. The endings changed according to the role of the words in the sentence.

Some of the endings were determined by the gender of the nouns, each of which was masculine, feminine, or neuter. This still holds true in such modern languages as German, in which, for example, the article "a" or "an" can be *ein, eine, einer, eines, einem,* or *einen,* depending on the gender and case of the noun it modifies.

A significant side influence in the formation of Old English was the arrival of missionaries, led by St. Augustine, around the year 600. They came to Christianize the people of the islands, and they succeeded. The Latin they brought with them helped shape both the grammar and the vocabulary of the language they had to learn upon their arrival.

EXERCISE 3. Applying Knowledge of Word Origins. Each of the following English words came from Latin. Look each up in dictionaries (checking more than one). Write down what you learn about the source of each word and the changes in its meaning over time.

1. angel
2. candle
3. disciple
4. hymn
5. cleric
6. martyr
7. mass
8. minister
9. devil
10. priest

Middle English

Around the beginning of the eleventh century, Old English began a change into the second great phase of our language, Middle English. We usually date it from the year 1066, and for an extremely good reason. In October of that year, William, Duke of Normandy, a province in France, crossed the English Channel with a powerful army, defeated his chief rival for the British throne in a historic battle near the town of Hastings, and became England's king. His successful invasion is known as the Norman Conquest, and it had a profound influence on the development of the English language.

For a time English may have seemed actually imperiled. William confiscated the English estates and gave them, along with all the top positions in government, to his followers, who spoke only French. For generations, French was to be the language of the new aristocracy, the government, the law, and the arts.

Yet no one need have worried that French would become the only language in England. The common people, who greatly outnumbered the aristocracy, went right on speaking their native tongue. English kept right on evolving—as Middle English. In the end it was merely enriched by French, to the extent of some 10,000 words. English gradually reasserted itself even in the upper classes during the period beginning about 1200. By the early fourteenth century, it had reclaimed its dominance in law, education, business, and literature.

Another significant influence on Middle English vocabulary—from about 1300—was the Renaissance, a revival of interest in classical Latin and Greek. The literature, art, music, and philosophy of those languages were much explored and discussed in England, and many of their words found their way into English.

The language was changing in more important ways, however, and as a student you may have some cause to be thankful for them. The speakers of English gradually began to simplify it. In the end they abandoned most of the multiple, or inflected, endings for nouns, verbs, and adjectives. They stopped giving gender to nouns. The word order in sentences became more regular. Middle English is far more recognizable to us than Old English. We can see that in the following lines from *The Canterbury Tales,* the story of a group of pilgrims on their way from London to a saint's shrine in Canterbury. In this excerpt, the narrator describes how he happened to meet the other pilgrims at an inn, the Tabard. Try to translate the lines into modern English as you read them.

> Bifel that, in that sesoun on a day,
> In Southwerk at the Tabard as I lay
> Redy to wenden on my pilgrymage
> To Caunterbury with ful devout corage,
> At nyght was come into that hostelrye
> Wel Nyne and twenty in a compaignye,
> Of sondry folk, by aventure yfalle
> In felaweshipe, and pilgrymes were they alle,
> That toward Caunterbury wolden ryde.
> The chambres and the stables weren wyde,
> And wel we weren esed atte beste.
> And shortly, whan the sonne was to reste,
> So hadde I spoken with hem everichon,
> That I was of hir felaweshipe anon,
> And made forward erly for to ryse,
> To take oure wey ther as I yow devyse.

EXERCISE 4. Applying Knowledge of Word Origins. The following French words were absorbed into English after the Norman Conquest. Look them up in a dictionary that shows word origins. Write down each word and tell the meaning it had in French or Latin. Be prepared to explain how each word's meaning changed over time.

1. court
2. council
3. power
4. realm
5. fete

6. countenance
7. jury
8. plaintiff
9. prison
10. robber

EXERCISE 5. Applying Knowledge of Word Origins. The Renaissance was responsible for the following English words. Look each of them up and write it down as it appeared in Greek or Latin. Be prepared to explain changes in each word's history.

1. arithmetic
2. logic
3. geometry
4. comedy
5. tragedy

6. nucleus
7. ignoramus
8. radius
9. virus
10. formula

Modern English and American English

We have noted that many new English words during the Middle English period were the result of Renaissance influences. The Renaissance, in fact, extended well beyond what we consider the transition period between Middle and Modern English. We date Modern English from around 1450, by which time the grammatical simplifications we noted were essentially complete. Yet, the English of 1550 or even of the 1600's (Shakespeare's time) would not seem exactly modern to you. Some of the spellings and word usages are too different from ours. The original Shakespeare manuscripts, however, would be much more recognizable to you than our excerpt from *The Canterbury Tales*.

You would have no trouble carrying on an intelligent conversation if a time machine took you back to 1607 and put you among the first English settlers to arrive in the New World. And had you been one of those immigrants, you would have begun to pick up new words almost immediately from the Indians and to invent words to name unfamiliar objects in your new world of experience. It was inevitable that the English of the people in America would begin to change from the language they left behind. Later generations would pick up words from the people arriving from other nations in Europe and elsewhere.

USAGE

Our country has been called a melting pot of nationalities. To a lesser extent it has been a melting pot of words, for all the differences of our scattered dialects. The point is that the language we now speak deserves its distinctive title of American English.

EXERCISE 6. Investigating Word Origins. Using a map of your state, see how many cities, lakes, rivers, and mountains have names you can identify as having come from Indian words. Use a dictionary to see how they have changed from their original form.

REVIEW EXERCISE A. Reviewing the History of English. Answer the following questions.

1. What is a language stock?
2. What was the *Indo-European* language?
3. How do we know that such different languages as Sanskrit and English are related?
4. Who were the Celts? What happened to their language?
5. Describe briefly how Old English developed.
6. What influence did St. Augustine and his missionaries have on the English language?
7. Why did so many French words become a part of English?
8. In what ways did English become less complex during the Middle English period?
9. How did the Renaissance influence the English language?
10. What were the influences on the formation of American English?

USAGE

Regional Dialects

A *dialect* is a form of language that varies in its vocabulary, grammar, and pronunciation from other forms. A *regional* dialect is a variation of language shared by a group of people in a geographical area. There are three major American dialect areas—Northern, Midland, and Southern—although there are some smaller ones as well. The dialects are determined largely by the origins of the first settlers. Much of New England, for example, was settled by residents of London (southern England). Later, people from northern parts of England, who spoke a different dialect, settled many areas of the southern United States.

A few examples will illustrate differences in regional dialects. In the Northern area, many speakers tend to drop the *r* and lengthen the /a/ sound, so that *barn* sounds like "bahn." In the Midland and Southern areas, an *r* sound often is inserted into such words as *wash* so that the word sounds like "warsh."

Differences in grammar include the Southern "sick at my stomach," and the Northern "sick to my stomach." Differences in vocabulary are probably the most noticeable. For example, a certain insect may be called a "darning needle" in the Northern area, a "snake doctor" in the Midland area, and a "mosquito hawk" or "dragonfly" in other areas. The object that is commonly referred to in the Southern area as a "skillet" may in the Midland area be a "frying pan" and in the Northern area a "spider."

Differences in regional dialects actually are not as clear-cut as they often seem and may be slowly disappearing. Not everyone in the Southern dialect area, for example, refers to a "skillet," nor may everyone in the Midland area say "warsh" for *wash*. Today, because we all travel much more extensively, people are exposed to many different dialects. Radio and television also have promoted a kind of "national" language, one that lacks distinctive features of grammar, vocabulary, and pronunciation. It is usually difficult to identify any distinctive Northern, Midland, or Southern dialect features in the speech of radio and television announcers and newscasters.

USAGE

EXERCISE 7. Evaluating Features of Regional Dialects. The following dialogue is from the play *The Homecoming,* which was an episode of the television show *The Waltons.* The time is Christmas Eve, 1933. The mother, Olivia, and the children discuss a cardinal they see outside and worry about their father's late arrival. The family lives in the Virginia mountains, and their speech contains Appalachian dialect features. See if you can identify them. Which features differ from those of your own regional dialect? What vocabulary, grammar, and pronunciation would you use to express the same thought?

> **Luke:** That red bird is goen to freeze tonight.
> **Olivia:** He won't freeze. Not that bird.
> **Clay-Boy:** Looking back, I don't know if Nana was talking about the cardinal, or if she was trying to say something to her red-headed children.
> **Olivia:** A red bird has got the knack of surviving winter. He knows it, too. Otherwise, he'd of headed South with the wrens and gold finches and the bluebirds back when the leaves started to turn.
> **Luke:** But the red birds don't have to?

Olivia (Touching his hair): Because they've got the knack of surviving.

Shirley: I wish my daddy could fly. Then he wouldn't have to wait for the bus.

Mark: If Daddy goes flyen around, somebody's liable to think he's a turkey buzzard and shoot him down.

Olivia (Emphatically): Don't you worry about our daddy. He's goen to be home for Christmas. You stop fretten about it.

Notice: This play may not be copied. It is illegal to make copies of this play which is fully protected by copyright. If you wish to produce this play you must obtain permission from the owner and pay the appropriate royalty fee. Inquiries concerning production will be answered promptly and should be addressed to: The Dramatic Publishing Company, 4150 N. Milwaukee Ave., Chicago, Ill. 60641

EXERCISE 8. Evaluating Features of Regional Dialects. Find some works with regional dialects in your school library. Copy down examples of regional words and phrases and bring them to class for discussion.

Standard and Nonstandard English

In the fifteenth century an Englishman named William Caxton invented the printing press. This historic development opened the world of books to the average person. The question arose as to which of England's many dialects would be used for the mass printings. The logical answer was the dialect of the nation's business and cultural center, London. The London dialect became *standard* English. So it has remained, although with some five centuries of evolution and some different preferences among the various English-speaking nations.

We think of standard English as the form most often used in books and magazines, on radio and television, and in the business and academic communities. It is the form high-school teachers and college professors teach their students. Its features are detailed in the Usage chapters of this textbook.

It is important to know that the characterizations "right" and "wrong" do not properly apply to standard and nonstandard English. It is also important to know that standard and nonstandard English are not rigidly separated categories into which language neatly fits. Almost everyone, at one time or another, departs from standard English. This happens more often when you speak than when you write—and more often still when you talk with close friends. Some features that are considered nonstandard may gradually become a part of standard English. Many linguists believe, for example, that the distinction between *who* and *whom* is becoming less important. The usage *"Who are you calling?"* has been considered nonstandard, but the linguists believe it will soon be accepted as a part of standard English because it is so commonly used.

EXERCISE 9. Analyzing the Use of Standard/Nonstandard English. The following paragraph includes both standard and nonstandard English. Revise it to eliminate the nonstandard features. For help, refer to the Usage chapters of this textbook.

This club ain't going to get nowheres except us members cooperate. For one thing, we have to start getting more enthused about coming to the meetings. Also, there's been too many absences, with too many excuses like "I could of come, but I had to feed my dog." We meet only once a month, and everyone knows about the meeting ahead of time, so it's kind of dumb to say that you don't. Another thing is that the members they should sort of take part of the responsibility for the club. The same people hadn't ought to be always taking care of refreshments, planning the program, and making arrangements with the school for the meeting room. I don't mean to infer that you're all deadbeats, but we've got a ways to go to get this club straightened out.

Formal and Informal English

Even standard English can vary from the very formal to the very informal, depending on the occasion or the speaker's or writer's purpose. Differences in formal and informal English include those listed here:

Formal:	*Informal:*
Used more in writing than in speech	Used more in speech than in writing
Most often used for highly ceremonial occasions	Most often used on casual occasions, with friends and small audiences
Sentences are often long and complex	Sentences are usually shorter, less complex, and may even be incomplete
Sentences are most often complete	
Vocabulary is most often precise and complex	Vocabulary is often general and imprecise
Little if any use of slang or colloquialisms	Likely to include slang and colloquialisms

Formal English

Formal English is most often used for such occasions as weddings, formal speeches, and inaugurations. It lends dignity and solemnity to an event. Formal English also is used for most legal and government documents. The following excerpt, for example, is from the 25th Amendment to the Constitution of the United States. The amendment establishes the procedure to be followed if a President dies or becomes disabled in office.

Whenever the Vice-President and a majority of either the principal officers of the executive departments or of such other body as Congress may by law provide, transmit to the President pro tempore of the Senate and the Speaker of the House of Representatives their written declaration that the President is unable to discharge the powers and duties of his office, the Vice-President shall immediately assume the powers and duties of the office as Acting President.

Notice how specifically this section is written: "either the principal officers of the executive departments *or* of such other body"; "the powers *and* duties." Notice also the formal terminology: "transmit" rather than "send," "written declaration" rather than "letter," "discharge" rather than "perform."

Informal English

Informal English is used for most everyday matters. Because it is spoken more often than written, it is sometimes called *conversational English*.

Informal English often is sprinkled with colloquialisms and slang. A *colloquialism* is a word or expression used in informal conversation but not accepted in formal written English. It is often an expression not to be taken literally. If you say someone is "down in the mouth," you are using a colloquialism. *Slang* more often consists of the colorful use of words to describe items or offer comments. For example, money is called *bread,* and something admired is *far out.* (See pages 292–94 for further treatment of colloquialism and slang.)

Like standard and nonstandard English, formal and informal English are not completely separate categories. Think of formal and informal English as being at opposite ends on a line. Our use of English tends to slide back and forth along the line, depending on our needs and inclinations at a given time. The possible points on this language line are referred to as *levels of usage.* The effective speaker or writer is one who knows the choices along the line—the various levels—and the appropriate time to use each of them.

EXERCISE 10. Evaluating Language Use. The purpose of and audience for each of the following selections is indicated. Note the features of formal or informal usage that each contains. How appropriate is the language in each selection for the audience? Be prepared to give the reasons for your answers.

1

From the keynote address to the 1976 Democratic Convention, delivered by Congresswoman Barbara Jordan:

In this election year we must define the common good and begin again to shape a common future. Let each person do his or her part. If one citizen is unwilling to participate, all of us are going to suffer. For the American idea, though it is shared by all of us, is realized in each one of us.

And now, what are those of us who are elected public officials supposed to do? We call ourselves public servants, but I'll tell you this: We as public servants must set an example for the rest of the nation. It is hypocritical for the public official to admonish and exhort the people to uphold the common good if we are derelict in upholding the common good. More is required of public officials than slogans and handshakes and press releases. More is required. We must hold ourselves strictly accountable. We must provide the people with a vision of the future.

If we promise as public officials, we must deliver. If we as public officials propose, we must produce. If we say to the American people it is time for you to sacrifice, if the public official says that, we [public officials] must be the first to give. We must be. And again, if we make mistakes, we must be willing to admit them. We have to do that. What we have to do is strike a balance between the idea that government should do everything and the idea, the belief, that government ought to do nothing. Strike a balance.

2

From an article written by a teen-ager for other teens explaining why the colonists did not adopt the American Indian word for turkey but chose instead to name the bird after that faraway country.

In any event, the sixteenth- and early-seventeenth-century English bred these birds that they thought came from Turkey and so were well acquainted with them by the year 1620. Thus, on that first Thanksgiving Day at Plymouth, Massachusetts, in 1621—featuring Gov. William Bradford, Miles Standish, Priscilla Mullins, John Alden, and all that crowd—when the Wampanoag chief Massasoit came forward and offered a wild bird for the feast, saying, "This bird is mighty good eating, folks—it's called a *neyhom*," the Pilgrims no doubt made a reply something like this: "Gee, thanks, Chief. We'll pluck this bird and roast it right away. These birds are well known to us in England; we call them *turkeys*."

USAGE

EXERCISE 11. Rewriting Formal and Informal English. Select the passage from Exercise 10 that is informal and rewrite it in more formal language. Then rewrite the formal passage in informal language. Why are the rewritten passages less suitable for the intended purpose and audience?

REVIEW EXERCISE B. Evaluating the Use of Language. The article in Exercise 15 of Chapter 12 of this book was written to tell about a student's first day in high school. Read it. Discuss the following questions.

1. Is the article in standard or nonstandard English? Give examples of features that support your answer.
2. Is the article in formal or informal English, or does it fall somewhere in between? Give examples of features that support your answer.
3. What—if any—examples of slang do you find in the article? What —if any—colloquialisms in the article affect its formal/ informal usage level? (See pages 292–94 for additional help with this.)
4. This article was written for a general audience. How appropriate is the language for such an audience? Give reasons to support your answer.
5. Select one paragraph from the article, and rewrite it to reverse its formal or informal features. For example, if the paragraph is moderately informal, rewrite it so that it is moderately formal. How appropriate is the new level of usage to the intended audience and purpose? Give reasons to support your answer.

Agreement

SUBJECT AND VERB, PRONOUN AND ANTECEDENT

Subjects are closely related to their verbs, and a careful speaker makes them agree with each other by matching verb forms to subject forms. In the same way, pronouns and their antecedents are closely related and must be made to agree with each other by matching forms. When such words are correctly matched, we say that they *agree*. When they fail to match, we say there is an error in *agreement*.

DIAGNOSTIC TEST

A. Selecting Verbs That Agree with Their Subjects.   Number your paper 1–10. For each sentence choose the verb in parentheses that agrees with the subject. Write the verb after the proper number.

EXAMPLES   1. Neither of the coats on display (is, are) the color I want.
     1. *is*
   2. Both coats (is, are) on sale this week.
     2. *are*

1. The jury (has, have) been paying close attention to the evidence in this case.
2. There (is, are) four herbs that any gardener can grow: basil, thyme, marjoram, and oregano.

3. All of these old letters (was, <u>were</u>) tied with ribbon and stored in a trunk in the attic.
4. Each of them (<u>is,</u> are) penned in bold, flowing handwriting, embellished with many flourishes.
5. Alicia and Isabel (thinks, <u>think</u>) that the former owner of the house put the letters in the attic.
6. Neither of them (<u>knows</u>, know) for sure who wrote them.
7. It (<u>doesn't</u>, don't) seem right to read letters addressed to someone else.
8. *Archy & Mehitabel* (<u>is,</u> <u>are</u>) a series of poems about a cockroach that lives in a newspaper office and his friend, a cat.
9. Here (is, <u>are</u>) the latest scores of today's baseball games.
10. Neither potatoes nor corn (is, are) grown on this farm.

B. Writing Verbs That Agree with Their Subjects and Pronouns That Agree with Their Antecedents. In many of the following sentences, either a verb does not agree with its subject, or a pronoun does not agree with its antecedent. Number your paper 11–20. After the proper number on your paper, write the correct forms of the incorrect verb or pronoun. If a sentence is correct, write *C*.

EXAMPLES 1. The flock of birds, almost blackening the sky, were an awe-inspiring sight.
    1. *was*
    2. Only a decade ago their number was declining.
    2. *C*

11. The meeting got out of hand when the discussion period began, since everyone tried to express their opinion at the same time.
12. There on the corner of your desk is the books that I returned and that you claimed you never received.
13. Two students from each class is going to the state capital to attend a special conference on education.
14. Each of them are expected to bring back a report on the objectives of the conference so that classmates can get firsthand information.
15. Since they will be on vacation next month, neither Miguel nor his sister are going to enter the mixed-doubles tennis tournament.
16. The audience expressed their admiration for the dancer's grace and skill by applauding wildly.

17. After the senator had read the proposed amendment, anyone who disagreed with the ruling was allowed to state their reason.
18. When she saw the locker room, Ellen became angry because not one of the children had picked up after themselves.
19. She is one of those competitive people who perform best under pressure.
20. Although she owns several pieces of fine china, her most prized possession are the little cups inherited from a great-aunt.

SINGULAR AND PLURAL NUMBER

18a. When a word refers to one person or thing, it is *singular* in number. When a word refers to more than one, it is *plural* in number.

The boldfaced words below agree in number.

EXAMPLES   **One** of the players **was** not wearing **his** glove. [singular]
Several of the players **were** not wearing **their** gloves. [plural]

Nouns and pronouns have number. The following nouns and pronouns are singular because they name only one person or thing: *airplane, child, I, idea.* The following are plural because they name more than one person or thing: *airplanes, children, we, ideas.*[1]

EXERCISE 1. Identifying Words as Singular or Plural in Number.
List the following words on your paper. After each plural word, write *P* for plural; after each singular word, write *S* for singular.

1. books
2. one
3. several
4. lights
5. people
6. mouse
7. many
8. civics
9. ability
10. area
11. mathematics
12. love
13. both
14. data
15. woman

AGREEMENT OF SUBJECT AND VERB

Verbs, too, have number; certain forms are used when a verb's subject is singular and others when the subject is plural. In standard English, verbs agree with their subjects.

---

[1] For rules regarding the formulation of plurals of nouns, see pages 629–32.

18b. A verb agrees with its subject in number.

(1) Singular subjects take singular verbs.

EXAMPLE Marcia **attends** college, but Laura **goes** to computer school. [The singular verb *attends* agrees with the singular subject *Marcia;* the singular verb *goes* agrees with the singular subject *Laura.*]

(2) Plural subjects take plural verbs.

EXAMPLE Marcia and Laura **attend** college, but the other girls **do** not. [The plural verb *attend* agrees with the plural subject *Marcia and Laura,* and the plural verb *do* agrees with the plural subject *girls.*]

In general, nouns ending in *s* are plural (*aunts, uncles, towns, crimes*), but verbs ending in *s* are singular (*gives, takes, does, has, is*). Singular *I* and *you,* however, generally take verbs that do not end in *s* (*I think, you think, I am, you are*).

☞ NOTE The form *were* is normally plural except when used with the singular *you* and in sentences like the following:

If I were in charge, I would make some changes.
Were Albert home, he could fix this.

EXERCISE 2. Selecting Verbs That Agree with Their Subjects. Decide which one of the verbs in parentheses should be used to agree with the subject given.

1. people (walks, walk)
2. one (is, are)
3. several (runs, run)
4. we (talks, talk)
5. Joan (was, were)
6. house (stands, stand)
7. the result (is, are)
8. both (believes, believe)
9. crews (sails, sail)
10. women (seems, seem)

18c. The number of the subject is not changed by a phrase following the subject.

Since the subject is never a part of a phrase, a word in a phrase cannot influence the verb.

EXAMPLE **One** of the women **is singing.** [The phrase *of the women* does not affect the number of the subject *one: one is,* not *women are.*]

One	is singing

EXAMPLE Both **women** from the senate **were** at the meeting. [The phrase *from the senate* does not affect the number of the subject *women: women were,* not *senate was.*]

women	were

Even prepositional phrases beginning with expressions like *with, together with, in addition to, as well as,* and *along with* do not affect the number of the verb.

EXAMPLES Tammy, along with her mother and aunt, **is** going to the concert. [Tammy . . . is]
The wind, together with the rain and fog, **was** making navigation difficult. [The wind . . . was]
Jack's imagination, as well as his sense of humor, **was** delightful. [Jack's imagination . . . was]

The logic of this will be clearer to you if you rearrange the first sentence about Tammy.

EXAMPLE Tammy **is** going to the concert along with her mother and aunt.

Another source of trouble is the negative construction. When such a construction comes between the subject and its verb, it is often mistakenly allowed to affect the number of the verb and throw it out of agreement with its proper subject. Treat negative constructions exactly like phrases following the subject.

EXAMPLE Carl, not Juan and I, is doing the artwork.

EXERCISE 3. Selecting Verbs That Agree with Their Subjects.
Write the subject of each of the following sentences. Then write the verb in parentheses that agrees in number with the subject.

1. Two of these cassettes (is, are) mine.
2. A heaping basket of beets (was, were) on the counter.

3. Disregard for the rights and comforts of others (is, are) rude.
4. The community college course on collecting stamps and coins (attracts, attract) many people.
5. The members of the family (meets, meet) for a reunion every year.
6. The roar of the waves (was, were) deafening.
7. Lois, as well as Tricia and Raphael, (has, have) volunteered to count votes.
8. That big tree with the oddly shaped leaves (seems, seem) to be dying.
9. The carpeting in the upstairs and downstairs rooms (is, are) worn.
10. The price of haircuts (is, are) going up again.
11. The package of radio parts (was, were) smashed in the mail.
12. These jars of mustard (is, are) broken.
13. The cost of two new snow tires (was, were) more than I expected.
14. Burt, not Anne and Laura, (has, have) the bicycle pump.
15. The three boxes of dried mint (fits, fit) easily on the bottom shelf.
16. The members of the winning band (feels, feel) jubilant.
17. The escape of three snakes from the laboratory (has, have) created quite a stir.
18. The chief, along with two of the firefighters, (gives, give) lectures on home safety.
19. In the movie, a ring of dancers (performs, perform) a folk dance.
20. Participation in class discussions, not just high test scores, (counts, count) toward one's final grade.

18d. The following pronouns are singular: *each, either, neither, one, everyone, everybody, no one, nobody, anyone, anybody, someone, somebody.*

These words are called *indefinite pronouns* because they refer only generally, indefinitely, to some thing or person. Very often they are followed by a prepositional phrase containing a plural word. When this situation occurs, be sure to make the verb agree with the indefinite pronoun, not with a word in the prepositional phrase.

NONSTANDARD   One of the guitar strings were broken. [The verb *were* does not agree with the singular subject, *one.*]

STANDARD   **One** of the guitar strings **was** broken. [The verb agrees with the subject.]

Read the following pairs of sentences aloud, stressing the subjects and verbs in boldfaced type.

EXAMPLES **Neither was** sure of the answer.
Neither of the scientists **was** sure of the answer.

No one leaves early.
No one except the band members **leaves** early.

Someone raids the refrigerator at night.
Someone among the guests **raids** the refrigerator at night.

18e. The following pronouns are plural: *several, few, both, many.*

EXAMPLES **Several** of the women **were** joggers.
A **few** in the crowd **are** troublesome.
Both have tried harder.
Many of the tourists **stop** here and **rest.**

18f. The pronouns *some, all, any, most,* and *none* may be either singular or plural, depending on the meaning of the sentence.

A writer may use either a singular or a plural verb to agree with the words *some, all, any, most,* and *none,* depending on the meaning of the sentence. These words are plural if they refer to a plural word; they are singular if they refer to a singular word.

SINGULAR **Most** of the day **was** already gone. [*Most* refers to *day,* which is singular.]

PLURAL **Most** of the steers **were** grazing. [*Most* refers to *steers,* which is plural.]

SINGULAR **Has any** of the shipment arrived? [*Any* refers to *shipment,* which is singular.]

PLURAL **Have any** of the coins been spent? [*Any* refers to *coins,* which is plural.]

SINGULAR **None** of the damage **was** serious. [*None* refers to *damage,* which is singular.]

PLURAL **None** of the students **have** finished. [*None* refers to *students,* which is plural.]

In each of the last six examples, the prepositional phrase following the subject provides a clue to the number of the subject. You may think of this as an exception to rule 18c. These pronouns can also be used without a prepositional phrase after them.

USAGE

EXAMPLES   Most were grazing. [a number of horses, steers, cows, etc.]
            Most was interesting. [a portion of a book, movie, conversation, etc.]

EXERCISE 4. *Oral Drill*. Stressing Subjects and Verbs in Sentences.   Repeat each of the following sentences aloud three times, stressing the italicized words.

1. *One* of those cups *is* broken.
2. Either *one* of the bikes *is* ready to go.
3. A *few* of the girls *are* experienced riders.
4. *Each* of them *has* a complete set of maps.
5. *Some* of the mice *were* caught.
6. *Most* of the milk *is* gone.
7. *Neither* of the cars *has* a radio.
8. Every *one* of the packages *is* heavy.

EXERCISE 5. Writing Sentences with Verbs That Agree with Their Subjects.   Rewrite each of the following sentences according to the directions in parentheses. If necessary, change the number of the verb to agree with the new subject or to accord with the altered sense of the sentence.

1. Everyone quickly understands the rules of this game. (Change *everyone* to *most people*.)
2. Neither of the actresses was nominated. (Change *neither* to *both*.)
3. There is fried chicken for everybody. (Change *chicken* to *potatoes*.)
4. Some of the trees were destroyed. (Change *trees* to *crop*.)
5. Have any of the apples been harvested? (Change *apples* to *wheat*.)
6. Nobody visits that haunted house. (Change *nobody* to *many of our neighbors*.)
7. Each is well trained. (Change *each* to *both*.)
8. Each of the tires needs air. (Change *each* to *several*.)
9. All of the fruit was eaten. (Change *fruit* to *pears*.)
10. Has each of your cousins had a turn in the game? (Change *each* to *both*.)

EXERCISE 6. Identifying Subject-Verb Agreement in Sentences.
Number your paper 1–20. If the verb and subject of a sentence agree, write a + after the proper number. If the verb and subject do not agree, write a 0.

1. Many of the knives is dull. ○
2. Not one of the keys fits. ✦
3. Several of the crew was commended by the captain. ○
4. One of the cartoonist's favorite characters was Delbert Duck. ✕
5. Most of the questions on the test was hard. ○
6. Neither of the coaches were happy with the decision.
7. Each of us are going to make a large poster for the upcoming election.
8. Some of the ice cream has started to melt.
9. Every one of the entrants have to pass a special exam.
10. Either of those albums are good background music.
11. All of the seats were too near the movie screen.
12. Each one of the machines are thoroughly tested at the automobile factory.
13. Does both of those games require special equipment?
14. Either of the assistants goes for the mail.
15. Each of the ingredients is carefully measured.
16. None of the buildings were damaged by the hail.
17. None of the food has been frozen.
18. Neither of the book reports were finished on time.
19. Every one of the players gets a trophy.
20. Most of the birds were quiet.

The Compound Subject

18g. Most compound subjects joined by *and* take a plural verb.

EXAMPLES   Ramon and she **like** hiking.
Her brother and her cousin **are** teachers.
The mother dog and her puppy **sleep** here.

A few compound subjects joined by *and* name a single person or thing and therefore take a singular verb.

EXAMPLES   Pork and beans **goes** well with hot dogs. [one dish]
Rock and roll **is** here to stay. [one kind of music]

18h. Singular subjects joined by *or* or *nor* take a singular verb.

EXAMPLES   Neither Mark nor Donna **knows** the address.
Does either Father or Mother have the key?
Neither our phone nor our doorbell **was** working.

USAGE

Note that the word *either* may be omitted, but the number of the subject is not changed so long as the parts are joined by *or*.

EXAMPLE   Jim or Peggy **is** taking the letters to the post office.

Note also that this use of *either . . . or, neither . . . nor* should not be confused with that of the correlative conjunction *both . . . and,* which takes a plural verb.

EXAMPLES   Both the scout and the counselor **were** helpful guides.
Neither the scout nor the counselor **was** helpful as a guide.

18i. When a singular and a plural subject are joined by *or* or *nor,* the verb agrees with the nearer subject.

EXAMPLES   Either Horace or his aunts **were** up to something strange. [aunts were]
Neither the potatoes nor the roast **seems** done. [roast seems]

In the first sentence *aunts* is nearer to the verb *were* than *Horace,* the other part of the compound subject. The verb must be plural to agree with the nearer subject, *aunts.* Likewise, in the second sentence the verb *seems* must agree with *roast,* since this singular part of the compound subject is nearer to it. This kind of construction is often awkward, however, and it is usually best to avoid it.

EXAMPLES   Either Horace **was** up to something strange, or his aunts **were.**
The potatoes **do** not seem done, and neither **does** the roast.

EXERCISE 7. *Oral Drill.* **Stressing Subjects and Verbs in Sentences.**   Repeat each of the following sentences aloud three times, stressing the italicized words.

1. Every *one* of the kittens *has* been given away.
2. A *few* of us *are* going to Chicago.
3. *Each* of the photographs *was* in black and white.
4. *Neither* Sam *nor* Miguel *likes* sports.
5. *Either* Judy or Claudia *does* the dishes tonight.
6. Not *one* of the stations *is* coming in clearly.
7. *Several* of the plates *were* cracked.
8. *Both* Marilyn *and* Marge *have* summer jobs.

EXERCISE 8. Selecting Verbs That Agree with Their Subjects.
Number your paper 1–10. For each sentence write the verb in parentheses that agrees with the subject of the sentence.

1. Neither my brother nor I (has, have) a car.
2. Marlon and she (is, are) the dance champions.
3. Our relatives and theirs (is, are) having a picnic together.
4. Both John and his mother (plays, play) a good game of tennis.
5. Either the director or the actors (is, are) going to have to compromise.
6. Neither the grapes nor the cantaloupe (was, were) ripe.
7. Both the Los Angeles Lakers and the Boston Celtics (is, are) popular with fans.
8. Our class or theirs (is, are) going to sponsor the dance.
9. Either the faucet or the shower head (leaks, leak).
10. Either a transistor or a capacitor (has, have) burned out in this receiver.

Other Problems in Agreement

18j. Collective nouns may be either singular or plural.

You may be in doubt at times about the number of a word that names a group of persons or objects. This kind of word is known as a *collective noun.*

A collective noun is singular and takes a singular verb when the group is thought of *as a unit or whole.*

A collective noun is plural and takes a plural verb when members of the group are thought of *as individuals acting separately.* Study the following pairs of sentences.

The class **has** a substitute teacher. [*Class* is thought of as a unit.]
The class **were** disagreeing with one another about **their** answers. [*Class* is thought of as a number of individuals.]

Kathy's club **is** visiting the museum. [*Club* is a unit.]
Kathy's club **are** all wearing **their** new uniforms. [The *club* is thought of as individuals.]

The following is a list of some collective nouns:

army	crowd	jury
audience	faculty	swarm
choir	family	team
class	flock	troop
club	group	
committee	herd	

EXERCISE 9. Writing Sentences with Collective Nouns. Select five collective nouns, and write five pairs of sentences like those on page 455, showing clearly how the words you choose may be either singular or plural.

EXERCISE 10. Writing Sentences with Verbs That Agree with Their Subjects. Rewrite the following ten sentences according to the instructions in parentheses, changing the number of the verb if necessary.

1. Both of the records are in the top forty. (Change *both* to *neither*.)
2. The choir has been arguing with the conductor. (Change *with the conductor* to *among themselves*.)
3. Either my cousins or Julie is bringing the pizza. (Reverse the order of the subjects.)
4. Neither Carrie nor Jana is in the Pep Club. (Change *neither . . . nor* to *both . . . and*.)
5. Jerry and Manuel are going to win. (Change *and* to *or*.)
6. All of your papers were graded. (Change *all* to *each*.)
7. Some of the time was needlessly wasted. (Change *time* to *supplies*.)
8. The delighted team was waving and grinning widely. (Change *waving and grinning widely* to *assembling to accept their medals*.)
9. Everybody in the chorus is trying out for the play. (Change *everybody* to *no one*.)
10. Baked chicken and white corn always taste good. (Change *and* to *or*.)

18k. A verb agrees with its subject, not with its predicate nominative.

In the following examples the subject is marked s and the predicate nominative PN.

EXAMPLES
$\quad$ The greatest **threat** to campers **is bears.**
$\qquad\qquad$ s $\qquad\qquad$ PN

$\quad$ **Bears are** the greatest **threat** to campers.
$\qquad\quad$ s $\qquad\qquad$ PN

$\quad$ The main **ingredient** of my hot sauce **is** jalapeño **peppers.**
$\qquad\qquad$ s $\qquad\qquad\qquad$ PN

$\quad$ Jalapeño **peppers are** the main **ingredient** of my hot sauce.
$\qquad\quad$ s $\qquad\qquad$ PN

Often this kind of agreement problem can be avoided by changing the sentence so as to avoid using a predicate nominative:

EXAMPLE **I use** jalapeño **peppers** as the main ingredient of my hot sauce.

18l. When the subject follows the verb, as in sentences beginning with *there* and *here,* be careful to anticipate the subject, and make sure that the verb agrees with it.

NONSTANDARD   Here is the brushes you need. [not *brushes . . . is*]
STANDARD   Here **are** the brushes you need. [*brushes . . . are*]

EXERCISE 11. Identifying Sentences with Subject-Verb Agreement. Number your paper 1–10. Read each sentence aloud. If the verb agrees with the subject, write a + after the proper number. If the subject and verb do not agree, write a 0 after the proper number. Be ready to explain the reasons for your choice.

1. Soap and water is the best cleanser for my face.
2. There's the boats I told you about.
3. Both my father and sister wants to see the Cubs game.
4. Either the twins or Jamie are playing a practical joke.
5. How was the swimming and sailing at the beach?
6. Ham and eggs are a great combination for breakfast.
7. Neither the windows nor the door is locked.
8. Each of the newspapers have clippings cut out.
9. There's always dozens of football games on television on New Year's Day.
10. Where's my socks?

18m. Words stating amount are usually singular.

EXAMPLES   Two years **is** a long time.
Fifty cents **was** the price.
Ninety percent of the student body **is** present.

When the sense of the sentence indicates that the subject designates a collection of individual parts rather than a single unit or quantity, the verb must be plural in number.

EXAMPLES   Sixty short minutes **fly** by.
Three quarters **were** in my pocket.
Ninety percent of the students **are** present today.

USAGE

Two such amount-stating expressions deserve special mention: *the number of* and *a number of*. They should not be confused. *The number of* takes a singular verb, and *a number of* takes a plural verb.

EXAMPLES   **The number of** female athletes **is** growing.
            A number of girls **like** strenuous sports.

18n. *Every* or *many a* before a word or a series of words is followed by a singular verb.

EXAMPLES   **Every** mother, father, and grandparent **is looking** on proudly.
            Many a hopeful performer **has** gone to Broadway in search of fame and fortune.

18o. The title of a work of art, literature, or music, even when plural in form, takes a singular verb.

EXAMPLES   Paul Laurence Dunbar's *Majors and Minors* **is** a collection of his poetry.
            Millet's *The Gleaners* **is** a famous nineteenth-century French painting.
            Gertrude Stein's *Three Lives* **has** influenced many writers.

18p. *Don't* and *doesn't* must agree with their subject.

With the subjects *I* and *you,* use *don't* (*do not*); with other singular subjects use *doesn't* (*does not*); with plural subjects use *don't* (*do not*).

EXAMPLES   **I don't** have any paper.
            You don't need special permission.
            It (he, she) doesn't show up in this picture.
            They don't feel nervous.

Do not use *don't* after *he, she,* or *it.*

NONSTANDARD   It don't look right.   He don't like spinach.
STANDARD   It **doesn't** look right.   He **doesn't** like spinach.

EXERCISE 12. Using *Don't* and *Doesn't* Correctly in Sentences.
Number your paper 1–10. After the proper number, write the correct form (*don't* or *doesn't*) for each of the following sentences.

1. The calf —— look very strong.
2. It —— matter if the weather is bad.
3. She —— play racquetball.

4. He —— write many letters.
5. I —— mind helping out.
6. You —— have to watch the program.
7. Loretta —— enjoy cleaning house.
8. A few of the contests —— award cash prizes.
9. —— it arrive soon?
10. —— he tinker with cars?

EXERCISE 13. Selecting Verbs That Agree with Their Subjects.

Number your paper 1–20. Write the correct one of the two verbs given in parentheses in each of the following sentences.

1. The coach, along with two assistants, (was, were) yelling at the players.
2. Georgia O'Keeffe, of all painters, (captures, capture) the mystery of the West.
3. They (wasn't, weren't) interested in learning how to play the accordion.
4. Carlos, not Martha or Jan, (was, were) answering all the letters.
5. Many of them (has, have) already read the novel.
6. *The Birds* (was, were) one of Hitchcock's great movies.
7. Samantha, a Persian cat with expensive tastes, (is, are) partial to lobster.
8. That collection of short stories (is, are) fun to read.
9. Mrs. Williams, as well as two of her neighbors, (is, are) on the budget committee.
10. A few of the men, including Mr. Gomez, (isn't, aren't) convinced the mayor is right.
11. Could it be that nobody among all the world's animal lovers (wants, want) to take these puppies off my hands?
12. (Doesn't, Don't) Chuck want to join the Air Force when he graduates?
13. Caroline, like most of her classmates, (wishes, wish) vacation could last forever.
14. A package of nuts and bolts (was, were) delivered to the hardware store.
15. There (is, are) some good programs on the educational television station.
16. Neither of his teammates (was, were) open for the pass.

17. The collection of Jill Krementz' photographs (is, are) drawing large crowds at the gallery.
18. It (doesn't, don't) look good for our school's baseball league this season.
19. (Doesn't, Don't) all of you remember your very first swimming lesson?
20. Both of the skaters (is, are) hoping to become members of the Olympic team.

WRITING APPLICATION A:
Using Subject-Verb Agreement to Make Your Writing Clear

Who are your two favorite teachers? Are these two teachers alike in some ways? Are they unlike in other ways? Being able to write about how people, things, or ideas are alike and unlike is an important skill. It requires careful checking of subject-verb agreement.

Writing Assignment

Pointing out likenesses is generally called comparing. Pointing out differences is generally called contrasting. Write a paragraph comparing and contrasting two people, things, or ideas. In the paragraph, use at least three of the following expressions, making sure subject and verb agree. When you use the expressions, underline them.

1. each of   4. one of
2. both of   5. either of
3. neither of   6. several of

EXAMPLE   One of my favorite teachers is a fifth-grade teacher.

REVIEW EXERCISE A. Making Verbs Agree with Their Subjects.
Number your paper 1–20. If the verb and subject agree in a sentence, write *C* after the proper number. If the verb and the subject do not agree, supply the correct form of the verb.

1. Each of you are invited.
2. Barbara Parsons, along with her cousin, wants to visit Washington, D.C.

3. Not one of those pictures or plaques is hung straight.
4. Neither the class nor Ms. Johnson have heard the news.
5. There are a strain of measles that lasts only three days.
6. Where's the best bargains in clothing in town?
7. Few objections, besides the one about chartering the bus, was raised.
8. *Six Characters in Search of an Author* is a modern play that raises many interesting questions about art and reality.
9. Some of this land is far too hilly to farm.
10. Either he or she are doing the advertising layouts for the school paper.
11. Fifteen dollars is a lot to pay for an album.
12. Every one of these handy mango peelers come with a one-year guarantee.
13. In Maine there's many miles of rocky coastline.
14. The committee is prepared to hold its elections.
15. Four minutes were his record time in that race.
16. It don't really make any difference.
17. Two thirds of a cup of flour is needed for this recipe.
18. The band was tuning their instruments nervously.
19. There are, in my opinion, a number of good reasons for the proposed change.
20. Every student, teacher, and administrator are contributing to the fund-raising drive.

AGREEMENT OF PRONOUN AND ANTECEDENT

Personal pronouns (*I, you, he,* etc.) have matching forms that must agree with their antecedents. The antecedent is the word to which a pronoun refers.

18q. A pronoun agrees with its antecedent in gender and number.

A small number of nouns in English name persons or things that are clearly masculine: *father, ram, stallion.* About the same number name persons or things that are clearly feminine: *mother, ewe, mare.* Most nouns name persons or things that may be either masculine or feminine (*adult, reader*) or to which the idea of gender does not apply (*town, report*). Nouns that apply to both masculine and feminine, or that do not carry any idea of either masculine or feminine, are said to be *neuter* or to have *common gender*.

Personal pronouns usually match the gender of their antecedents.

EXAMPLES   Does **Margaret** like **her** dance class? [The pronoun *her* is feminine to agree with *Margaret*.]

Because the **car** would not start, **it** had to be towed. [The pronoun *it* agrees in gender with *car*.]

Personal pronouns also have forms that reflect the number of their antecedents.

EXAMPLES   The **riders** readied **their** horses. [The pronoun is plural to agree with *riders*.]

The **rider** adjusted **his** stirrups. [Because the antecedent is singular now, the pronoun is singular.]

(1) The words *each, either, neither, one, everyone, everybody, no one, nobody, anyone, anybody, someone, somebody* **are referred to by a singular pronoun:** *he, him, his, she, her, hers, it, its.*

The use of a phrase after the antecedent does not change the number of the antecedent.

EXAMPLES   **Each** of the teams had **its** mascot at the game.

Either Sharon or Juanita lost **her** glove.

Someone in the class left **his** notes behind.

Everybody on the bus is supposed to stay in **his** seat.

When the antecedent can be either masculine or feminine, as in the last two examples, it has been standard formal usage to use only the masculine pronoun. However, more writers are beginning to use both the masculine and feminine forms of pronouns in such cases.

EXAMPLE   **Everybody** has **his or her** card.

You can avoid the awkward *his or her* construction by rephrasing the sentence using the plural form of the pronouns.

EXAMPLE   **All** students have **their** cards.

In conversation, you might find it more convenient to use a plural personal pronoun when referring to singular antecedents that can be either masculine or feminine.

EXAMPLES   **Nobody** rode **their** bikes.

Everybody brought **their** fishing rods.

No one brought **their** umbrellas.

USAGE

> ☞ USAGE NOTE   On certain occasions when the *idea* of the sentence (the meaning of the antecedent) is clearly plural, one must use the plural pronoun even though the singular form of the pronoun is called for grammatically. For example, to use a singular pronoun in the following sentence would be absurd.
>
> EXAMPLE   When **everybody** has arrived, explain the situation to **them** [not *him*].
>
> It is usually possible to avoid such constructions.
>
> BETTER   When **all** the people have arrived, explain the situation to **them.**

(2) Two or more singular antecedents joined by *or* or *nor* should be referred to by a singular pronoun.

EXAMPLE   Neither Heidi nor Beth took **her** umbrella with **her.**

(3) Two or more antecedents joined by *and* should be referred to by a plural pronoun.

EXAMPLE   The guide and the ranger wrapped **their** rain ponchos in **their** saddle rolls.

(4) The number of a relative pronoun (*who, which, that*) is determined by the number of the word to which it refers—its antecedent.

EXAMPLES   Miriam is one of those **students who are** always striving to do **their** best. [*Who* is plural because it refers to *students*. Therefore, the plural forms *are* and *their* are used to agree with *who*.]
Anyone who wants to volunteer should raise **his** hand. [*Who* is singular because *anyone* is singular. Therefore, the singular forms *wants* and *his* are used to agree with *who*.]

EXERCISE 14. Selecting Pronouns That Agree with Their Antecedents.
Number your paper 1–20. For each blank in the following sentences, select a pronoun that will agree with its antecedent, and write it after the proper number on your paper.

1. After the long hike through the woods, all of the scouts complained that —— feet hurt.
2. Either Camille or Rose will bring —— cassette player.
3. Everyone at the campground will need to bring —— own tent and bedroll.

4. Some of the women wrote to —— local newspapers about the pollution problem.
5. Every driver checked —— car before the race.
6. Each of the actors had —— own odd superstition.
7. Both of the girls practiced —— dives off the high tower.
8. Marcia and her younger brother are saving money to have —— car repaired.
9. Someone has parked —— car in my space.
10. All of the girls knew —— parts perfectly by opening night.
11. Neither of the sweaters had —— price tag removed.
12. Everybody should exercise —— right to vote.
13. Many of the crew got —— first case of seasickness in the violent storm.
14. Gina and her grandfather proudly showed us —— string of rainbow trout.
15. One of the houses had —— windows broken by the hail.
16. Everyone bought —— own copy of the textbook.
17. The President and the Vice-President expressed —— separate opinions about the issue.
18. Anyone who needs a pencil should raise —— hand.
19. Either Stu or Mike will lend me —— fishing gear.
20. Each of the cars has —— own parking place.

WRITING APPLICATION B:
Using Pronoun-Antecedent Agreement to Make Your Writing Clear

Good writers have different and individual ways of thinking. This is a characteristic of creativity. One way to develop your creative thinking ability is to ask questions that start with "What if . . .?"

Writing Assignment

Write ten questions that begin with "What if . . . ?" In at least five of the questions, include a pronoun that must agree with its antecedent, as illustrated below. Underline the pronoun and its antecedent when they occur.

EXAMPLE   What if a <u>girl</u> discovered that <u>her</u> exact twin was sitting across the table in the cafeteria?

REVIEW EXERCISE B. Identifying Subject-Verb Agreement and Pronoun-Antecedent Agreement in Sentences. In some of the following sentences, either a verb does not agree with its subject or a pronoun does not agree with its antecedent. Number your paper 1–20. If a sentence is correct, write a +; if it is incorrect, write a 0.

1. Both Sid and Nikki like their new neighborhood.
2. Neither of the transmitters were affected by the storm.
3. Antonio, in addition to the other singers, were ready for the competition to start.
4. One of the local police officers was the top scorer on the rifle range today.
5. Neither John nor Bruce has recovered from their disastrous camping trip.
6. *The Three Little Pigs* are my young nephews' all-time favorite animated feature.
7. There was a set of salt-and-pepper shakers on the counter.
8. Where is the Athletics Department?
9. Each of the waitresses were hurrying as fast as possible.
10. A few of the crowd was murmuring impatiently.
11. Is there any of those peanuts left?
12. Either Lois or Maria is in charge of the equipment.
13. Every one of those cattle are going to have to be rounded up.
14. An additional feature of these models is the built-in stereo speakers.
15. Somebody has gone off and left their car running.
16. If anybody calls, tell them I'll be back by this evening.
17. Each team has its own colors and symbol.
18. One of the goats were nibbling on a discarded popcorn box.
19. Here's the pair of gloves that you forgot.
20. Are there no end to these questions?

REVIEW EXERCISE C. Selecting Verbs That Agree with Their Subjects and Pronouns That Agree with Their Antecedents. Number your paper 1–20. In each sentence, write the correct one of the two forms given in parentheses.

1. Neither the manager nor the two salespeople (was, were) prepared for the number of customers.
2. Everybody got to listen to a recording of (his, their) own voice.

USAGE

3. Each of the cyclists (was, were) beginning to feel the effects of the long trip.
4. If anyone comes in now, (he, they) will see what a mess we've made.
5. Neither of the sets of barbells (was, were) easy to lift.
6. Both Karen and the two firefighters (is, are) having difficulty getting the cat out of the tree.
7. Ms. Lo, along with her students, (visits, visit) the museum once a semester.
8. Where (is, are) the box of nails that came with the kit?
9. A few of our classmates (was, were) invited.
10. "Birches" (is, are) a poem by Robert Frost.
11. There (is, are) leftover macaroni and cheese on the top shelf in the refrigerator.
12. If anybody likes a spectacle, (he, they) will love seeing a drum corps competition.
13. Several of the audience (was, were) frightened.
14. Nobody knows what (his, their) future may hold.
15. The great auk, as well as the dodo and the passenger pigeon, (is, are) extinct.
16. Where (has, have) the sports section of my paper gone?
17. Neither of the planes had (its, their) cargo loaded.
18. Anyone who wants (his, their) plate refilled had better hurry.
19. Every one of these mosquitoes (seems, seem) to want to bite me.
20. A philosopher once said that if someone built a better mousetrap, the world would beat a path to (his, their) door.

CHAPTER 18 REVIEW: POSTTEST

Selecting Verbs That Agree with Their Subjects and Pronouns That Agree with Their Antecedents. Number your paper 1–20. After the proper number on your paper, write the correct form of each incorrect verb or pronoun. If a sentence is correct, write *C*.

EXAMPLES
1. Each leaf, flower, and seedpod were glimmering with frost.
1. *was*

2. Were any tickets left at the box office for me?
2. *C*

1. There was women, as well as men, who set out on the perilous journey into new territory.
2. Everyone who works at the machines wears goggles to protect their eyes.
3. The test results showed that about 80 percent of the class was in the average group.
4. A hostile crowd gathered outside the courtroom to show their disapproval of the verdict.
5. Many of Gwendolyn Brooks' early poems was printed in the *Chicago Defender*.
6. *Bronzeville Boys and Girls* are a collection of her poems.
7. None of the travelers went to their seats immediately, making passage through the aisle impossible.
8. Jesse, who don't like classical music, was not pleased to learn that the evening's concert was all Haydn.
9. Neither of the candidates has prepared his speech.
10. Their biggest problems are apathy and indecision.
11. Mr. Ortega, in association with other members of his firm, have established a scholarship fund for art students.
12. To apply for the scholarship, a student must submit at least four samples of their work.
13. Every teacher in the audience hopes that their pupil will win.
14. Chester or Nina, I think, have the best chance of winning.
15. About half the dog owners at the dog show was complaining about the judges' incompetence and threatening to remove their dogs.
16. For Ellen, one of those exasperating people who is always late, eight o'clock means half past nine.
17. Mr. Johnson and Mr. Golding is repairing the roof now.
18. My committee is preparing their speeches for Tuesday's meeting.
19. Neither the lawyer nor the defendants were satisfied with the judge's decision.
20. All of the bread are on the table.

USAGE

Using Pronouns Correctly

NOMINATIVE AND OBJECTIVE CASE

A small number of pronouns have three forms, or *cases*: a *nominative* form that is used when the pronoun is a subject or predicate nominative; an *objective* form that is used when it is a direct or indirect object or the object of a preposition; and a *possessive* form that is used to show ownership or relationship. For example:

NOMINATIVE CASE **We** heard from Sheila.
She is staying in Ohio.

OBJECTIVE CASE I wrote to **her**.
Sheila phoned **me**.

POSSESSIVE CASE **Her** vacation is almost over.
She is at **their** farm.

DIAGNOSTIC TEST

Using Pronouns Correctly in Sentences. Number your paper 1–20. After the proper number, write the correct one of the two pronouns in parentheses.

EXAMPLE 1. Was it (he, him) driving the car when the accident occurred?
1. *he*

1. Francis said that in a few years he would give his stamp collection to his brother and (I, me).
2. I need to know today if you and (she, her) plan to go with us on the trip.
3. Everyone was waiting impatiently to find out (who, whom) the new cheerleader would be.
4. I am going to vote for (whoever, whomever) can present the best solution to environmental problems.
5. After he had spoken at the assembly, the senator agreed to meet with our class president and (we, us).
6. My little sister is a much better chess player than (I, me).
7. She is one of those people (who, whom) can analyze opponents' moves quickly.
8. After the bake sale, give the remaining cookies and cakes to everyone (who, whom) worked.
9. We found that it was (she, her) who called twice while we were out of town.
10. Before the debate started, I noticed that my opponent was as nervous as (I, me).
11. She is the teacher (who, whom) will coach the varsity golf team this year.
12. The teacher said that (whoever, whomever) was ready could give a speech first.
13. As the runners approached the finish line, we saw Lisle and (he, him) break ahead of the others.
14. An argument broke out between Mr. Morales and (they, them) over the location of the property lines.
15. Although her grandfather was the person for (who, whom) the town was named, she moved away immediately after graduation.
16. Seeing a car with an out-of-state license plate in my driveway, I ran inside, and (who, whom) do you think was there?
17. My coach, Mr. Lopez, said that he would choose between Leslie and (I, me) for the starting position.
18. Please give my message to (whoever, whomever) answers the phone.
19. Mrs. Martin and (she, her) have been the best of friends since childhood.
20. For (who, whom) is this criticism intended?

USAGE

CASE FORMS OF PERSONAL PRONOUNS

Personal pronouns change form in the different persons.

> First person is the person speaking: *I (We)* do.
> Second person is the person spoken to: *You* were doing.
> Third person is a person or thing other than the speaker or the person spoken to: *He (She, It, They)* will do.

Study the following list of personal pronouns, noticing the changes in person and case form.

Personal Pronouns

Singular

	NOMINATIVE CASE	OBJECTIVE CASE	POSSESSIVE CASE
FIRST PERSON	I	me	my, mine
SECOND PERSON	you	you	your, yours
THIRD PERSON	he, she, it	him, her, it	his, her, hers, its

Plural

	NOMINATIVE CASE	OBJECTIVE CASE	POSSESSIVE CASE
FIRST PERSON	we	us	our, ours
SECOND PERSON	you	you	your, yours
THIRD PERSON	they	them	their, theirs

Two of these pronouns (*you* and *it*) have the same form in the nominative and objective case; therefore, they present no special problems. Ignore these two pronouns and concentrate on the following forms:

NOMINATIVE CASE	OBJECTIVE CASE
I	me
he	him
she	her
we	us
they	them

You should review the nominative and objective forms until you know them thoroughly.

EXERCISE 1. Personal Pronouns. Write from memory the following personal pronouns.

1. First person plural, objective case
2. Third person singular, nominative case, feminine
3. Third person plural, nominative case
4. First person plural, nominative case
5. Third person singular, possessive case, masculine
6. First person singular, objective case
7. Third person singular, objective case, feminine
8. Third person plural, objective case
9. First person singular, nominative case
10. Third person singular, possessive case, neuter

THE NOMINATIVE CASE

19a. The subject of a verb is in the nominative case.

EXAMPLES   Both **he** and **I** solved the problem. [*He* and *I* are subjects of the verb *solved*.]

Her brothers and **she** cleaned the house. [*She* is the subject of *cleaned*.]

They knew **we** were going. [*They* is the subject of *knew*, and *we* is the subject of *were going*.]

Most errors involving pronouns as subjects arise when the subject is compound. People who would never say "Me went to the movies" often do make the mistake of saying "George and me went to the movies." The best way of avoiding this error is to try each subject separately with the verb, adapting the verb form as necessary. Your ear will tell you which form is correct.

NONSTANDARD   Her and me study English. [*Her* studies English? *Me* studies English?]

STANDARD   **She** and **I** study English. [*She* studies English. *I* study English.]

The pronouns *we* and *they* frequently sound awkward as part of a compound subject. In such cases, it is usually easy enough to revise the sentence.

AWKWARD   We and they will go to the movie.

BETTER   We will go to the movie with them.

Pronouns are sometimes used with a noun appositive:

We road racers run every day.

To determine the right case form to use in such a situation, try reading the sentence without the appositive.

We run every day.

EXERCISE 2. *Oral Drill.* **Stressing Pronouns in the Nominative Case.** Read each of the following sentences aloud several times, stressing the italicized words.

1. *She* and *I* gave the dog a bath.
2. Irving and *he* plan to try out for the soccer team.
3. *We* sophomores organized the drive.
4. Wendy and *she* can help you in the lab.
5. Are *you* and *he* doing the report?
6. Either *we* or *they* may go to the championship finals.
7. The drill team and *we* band members took the bus.
8. The twins and *they* go everywhere together.

EXERCISE 3. Inserting Pronouns in the Nominative Case to Complete Sentences. Number your paper 1–10. Choose correct pronouns for the blanks in the following sentences. Vary your pronouns. Do not use *you* or *it*.

1. The judge and —— studied the evidence.
2. Ted and —— took the wrong train.
3. Linda and —— are planning a party.
4. —— students are having a science fair.
5. Either Julius or —— will give you a ride.
6. —— and —— have been rivals for years.
7. I'm sure —— knew about the meeting.
8. Soon —— and —— will be graduating.
9. Miss Arami said that —— and —— would be nominated for class president.
10. —— and —— have overdue library books.

EXERCISE 4. Writing Sentences with Pronouns in the Nominative Case. Use the following subjects in sentences of your own.

1. We teen-agers
2. My family and I
3. He and his friends

4. Liz, Michelle, and she
5. They and their classmates

EXERCISE 5. Using Pronouns in the Nominative Case Correctly in Sentences. Number your paper 1–10. Read each of the following sentences *aloud*. If all the italicized pronouns in a sentence are correct, write a + after the proper number; if any one of them is not, write a 0 followed by the correct form of the incorrect pronoun.

EXAMPLES 1. Stuart and *she* have studied as hard as you and *I* have.
 1. +
 2. Mrs. Jackson said that you and *me* wrote vivid descriptions.
 2. O, I

1. I heard from my mother that Kate and *she* were home from school again.
2. Lenny and *he* arrived before Kevin and *I* did.
3. *Him* and *me* went downtown last Saturday.
4. *Us* music students give a recital every spring.
5. You and *I* have to cut up a frog in biology soon.
6. Sharon and *her* missed their bus this morning.
7. *He* and the professor were intently discussing the new scientific discovery.
8. We thought you and *her* were related to each other.
9. *She* and *they* wrote the words and music.
10. You and *he* can help us carry these costumes for the play to the drama room.

19b. A predicate nominative is in the nominative case.

A predicate nominative is a noun or pronoun in the predicate that explains or renames the subject of the sentence. It follows a linking verb. The exercises and examples in this chapter concentrate on pronouns as predicate nominatives.

COMMON FORMS OF *be*		PREDICATE NOMINATIVE
am		I
is, are		he
was, were	*are*	she
may be, can be, will be, etc.	*followed*	we
may have been, etc.	*by*	you
want to be, like to be, etc.		they

USAGE

EXAMPLES It was **I** who chopped down the cherry tree.
The winner might be **he**.
Could the caller have been **she**?

☞ USAGE NOTE It is now perfectly acceptable to use *me* as a predicate nominative in informal usage: *It's me.* (The construction rarely comes up in formal situations.) The plural form (*It's us*) is also generally accepted. However, using the objective case for the third person form of the pronoun (*It's him, It's them*) is still often regarded as unacceptable. When you encounter any of these expressions in the exercises in this book or in the various tests you take, you will be wise to take a conservative attitude and use the nominative forms in all instances.

EXERCISE 6. Using Predicate Nominatives in Sentences. Remembering that a predicate nominative is in the nominative case, supply the pronouns specified for the following:

1. Do you think it was ——— ? (third person singular, masculine)
2. It must have been ——— . (third person singular, feminine)
3. Good friends are ——— . (third person plural)
4. The pranksters were ——— . (first person plural)
5. It was ——— at the door. (third person plural)

REVIEW EXERCISE A. Using Pronouns in the Nominative Case Correctly in Sentences. Number your paper 1–20. Complete each of the following sentences by writing an appropriate pronoun for each space. Use as many different pronouns as you can. Do not use *you* or *it*. Be ready to explain the reasons for your choice.

1. I couldn't believe it was ——— .
2. My brother and ——— won the road rally.
3. ——— art students are making posters for the play.
4. It was Pilar and ——— who won the award.
5. Everyone applauded when Patty and ——— took a bow after our piano recital.
6. Have you asked if ——— and ——— can come with us?
7. Where did Barry and ——— go after school?
8. Jimmy and ——— caught the runaway piglets.
9. The tuba players are ——— and ——— .

USAGE

10. Nellie and —— made waffles for breakfast.
11. It is —— that you need to see.
12. Skip argued that it was Lana and —— who made the error in the calculation.
13. Was it Teresa or —— who hit the home run?
14. Either David or —— might be able to do it.
15. It was decided that —— girls could play in the county softball tournament.
16. —— and —— both forgot their lunches today.
17. My sister and —— are going to visit Provo, Utah.
18. —— linemen have to practice our plays.
19. I believe that the Masked Marvel has to be —— .
20. Do you think that —— and —— can work well together on the science project?

THE OBJECTIVE CASE

The pronouns *me, him, her, us,* and *them* are in the objective case. These pronouns are used as direct and indirect objects and as objects of prepositions.

19c. The object of a verb is in the objective case.

EXAMPLES   Our coach has been training **us**. [direct object]
          I paid **him** a compliment. [indirect object]

As with the nominative forms, the objective forms are troublesome mainly in compound constructions. It is unnatural to say, "The explosion frightened *I*," but you might carelessly say, "The explosion frightened Jim and I." Once again, the solution is to try the parts of the compound object separately.

Pronouns in the objective case may also have noun appositives. Whenever a pronoun is used with a noun in this way, you can always determine the case by omitting the noun.

Everyone knows **us** pranksters. [They know *us*, not *we*.]

EXERCISE 7. Using Pronouns in the Objective Case in Sentences.
Number your paper 1–10. Supply appropriate pronouns for the blanks in the following sentences. Use a variety of pronouns. Do not use either *you* or *it*.

USAGE

1. The old sailor warned —— about the danger.
2. The city awarded —— its highest honor.
3. You could ask Deborah or —— .
4. The crowd cheered —— heartily.
5. Be sure to ask —— for her social security number.
6. The shark in that movie didn't scare —— at all.
7. How can I recognize —— ?
8. We saw Norman and —— in their horse costume.
9. Did you give Paula and —— their assignments?
10. I bought my father and —— birthday presents.

EXERCISE 8. Writing Sentences Using Pronouns in the Nominative and Objective Cases. Write ten sentences using personal pronouns (except *you* and *it*). Include three using pronouns in compound subjects of verbs, three using pronouns in compound predicate nominatives, and four using pronouns in compound objects of verbs.

REVIEW EXERCISE B. Selecting Pronouns in the Nominative or Objective Case to Complete Sentences. Number your paper 1–10. Write the correct one of the two pronouns in parentheses after the proper number. Be ready to explain your answers.

1. Last fall, Tina talked Susan and (I, me) into going on a canoe trip with her.
2. My father told Susan and (I, me) to wrap our food and equipment well.
3. He warned both Tina and (we, us) that we would probably get a good dunking before we were through.
4. When we first started, Susan and (I, me) could barely steer our canoe.
5. We watched another canoeist and saw how (she, her) and her partner maneuvered their craft.
6. They and (we, us) both did well until we hit the rapids, or rather, the rapids hit (we, us).
7. Susan grabbed for our sleeping bags, and (she, her) and (I, me) both scrambled for our food cooler.
8. All of (we, us) would-be campers were drenched, but no quitters were (we, us).

USAGE

9. My father's warning haunted all of (we, us) as (we, us) starved adventurers stared at waterlogged hot dogs, soaked rolls, and biscuits with tadpoles in them.
10. Later, Susan and (I, me) discovered that our bedrolls had become portable water beds; after a squishy, cold night I decided wise are (they, them) who heed the voice of experience.

REVIEW EXERCISE C. Using Pronouns in the Nominative and Objective Cases in Sentences. Number your paper 1–10. Write the personal pronoun that can be substituted for each italicized expression. In those sentences calling for a first person pronoun, use one of the following pronouns: *I, we, me, us.*

EXAMPLES   1. Did you see Judy or *Faye*?
            1. *her*
            2. Both Ray and [first person pronoun] are related.
            2. *I*

1. Last weekend, Coach Welber showed Rita and *the other girl* the new play.
2. Uncle Walt gave her and [first person pronoun] some sound advice yesterday.
3. The cooks will be Charlie and *Al*.
4. The pilot and *navigator* were puzzled by the readings.
5. Give Bob or [first person pronoun] your dirty dishes.
6. Did my brother tell you and *Jennifer* about the dance?
7. Could it have been *Larry* that called?
8. How soon do you want to see Claire and [first person pronoun]?
9. In charge of entertainment will be Tom and *Wally*.
10. You can bet that if anybody can accomplish the task, it is *Wes and Craig*.

19d. The object of a preposition is in the objective case.

A prepositional phrase begins with a preposition and ends with a noun or pronoun that is the *object of the preposition*. When the object of a preposition is a pronoun, it must be in the *objective* case.

EXAMPLES   to them, for you and us, with him

Errors in usage occur most often when the object of a preposition is compound. You can usually tell the correct pronoun by trying the parts of the compound object separately.

EXAMPLES   We spoke with Gwen and (she, her).
            We spoke with she. [nonstandard]
            We spoke with her. [standard]
            We spoke with Gwen and her.

Try this test on the following correct examples:

EXAMPLES   I sent cards to my *uncle* and *him*.
            The hostess brought menus for *Franny* and *me*.
            We can ride with *Joan* and *her*.

EXERCISE 9. Selecting Pronouns in the Objective Case to Complete Sentences Correctly.   Select the correct one of the two pronouns in parentheses, and write it on your paper.

1. The referee called fouls on (he, him) and (I, me).
2. Maggie is off fishing with grandfather and (he, him).
3. We didn't want to leave without you and (she, her).
4. They assigned the same locker to (they, them) and (we, us).
5. The duke directed a haughty sneer at the jester and (he, him).
6. A package arrived for Pat and (he, him).
7. Nobody understood the problem but Kevin and (he, him).
8. The player tried to dodge between Sherrie and (I, me).
9. The wary skunk circled around (she, her) and (I, me).
10. Uncle Vic will get the details from you and (she, her).

EXERCISE 10. Writing Sentences Using Pronouns in the Objective Case.   Write sentences of your own, using each of the following prepositions with a compound object, at least one part of which is a pronoun.

1. against   2. for   3. except   4. without   5. by

EXERCISE 11. *Oral Drill.* Stressing Prepositions and Their Pronoun Objects.   Read *aloud* five times each of the following sentences, putting the stress on the italicized words.

1. There were calls *for* Walker and *us*.
2. This message is *from* Delores and *her*.
3. We sat *with* Arnie and *them*.
4. Margo looked *toward* Sue and *me*.
5. They gave copies *to* him and *me*.
6. This drawing is *by* either Max or *him*.

USAGE

7. Don't hold this *against* Barb and *her*.
8. I walked *between* Vince and *him*.

WRITING APPLICATION A:
Considering Your Audience by Using Pronouns Correctly

Some games have an unwelcome "tilt" light that appears when you do something wrong. When this happens, everything just shuts down and you have to start over. Unfortunately, similar situations occur in writing. If your readers stumble across a glaring error, their concentration goes "tilt." Careful and considerate writers try to avoid causing their readers' thinking to be distracted by such errors.

TILT Mrs. Smith promised my sister and *I* a baby-sitting job every weekday morning this summer.

Writing Assignment

A narrative relates a series of events. When you write a narrative, you usually explain what happened, when it happened, and to whom it happened. The narrative can be either a true story or an imaginary one. Write a narrative, either truth or fiction, about something that happened to you and another person. In your narrative, illustrate the following use of pronouns:

1. pronoun in compound subjects of verbs
2. pronoun in compound objects of verbs
3. pronoun in compound objects of prepositions

SPECIAL PROBLEMS IN PRONOUN USAGE

Who and Whom

The use of *who* and *whom* in questions can no longer be reduced to a strict law. In modern spoken English the distinction between *who* and *whom* is gradually disappearing altogether, and *whom* is going out of use. *Who do you mean?* and *Who do you know?* are standard, even though, according to the rule you have learned about the case of the object of a verb, the speaker should say *whom* in these sentences. For the exercises in this book, follow the rules of standard formal usage. However, the rules are applied strictly only in formal writing.

Using *who* and *whom* in subordinate clauses, however, is a different matter. In subordinate clauses the distinction between *who* and *whom* is generally observed in both formal and informal writing.

19e. The use of *who* and *whom* in a subordinate clause is determined by the pronoun's function in the clause.

EXAMPLE   Dani is the actress **who played the lead.**

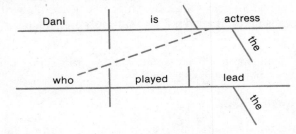

EXAMPLE   Dani is the actress **whom the audience applauded most loudly.**

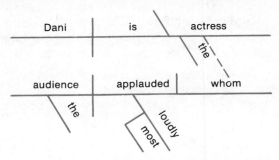

EXAMPLE   She was the student **about whom the story was written.**

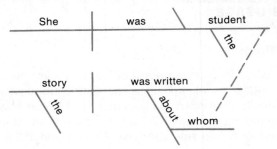

Follow these steps in deciding whether to use *who* or *whom* in a subordinate clause:

1. Pick out the subordinate clause.
2. Decide how the relative pronoun is used in that clause.
3. Determine the case of the pronoun according to the usual rules.
4. Select the correct form of the pronoun.

PROBLEM   Alex is the student (who, whom) got a perfect score.
Step 1   The subordinate clause is (*who, whom*) *got a perfect score.*
Step 2   The relative pronoun is the subject of the clause.
Step 3   Since it functions as a subject, the pronoun must be in the nominative case.
Step 4   The nominative form is *who.*
SOLUTION   Alex is the student **who** got a perfect score.

PROBLEM   I saw Ellen, (who, whom) I knew from school.
Step 1   The subordinate clause is (*who, whom*) *I knew from school.*
Step 2   The relative pronoun is the object of the verb *knew: I knew* (*who, whom*).
Step 3   The object of a verb is in the objective case.
Step 4   The objective form of *who* is *whom.*
SOLUTION   I saw Ellen, **whom** I knew from school.

PROBLEM   Do you know (who, whom) she is?
Step 1   The subordinate clause is (*who, whom*) *she is.*
Step 2   The relative pronoun is the predicate nominative: *she is* (*who, whom*).
Step 3   A predicate nominative is in the nominative case.
Step 4   The nominative form is *who.*
SOLUTION   Do you know **who** she is?

It is important to remember that no words outside the clause affect the case of the pronoun. In the third problem, the whole clause *who she is* is the object of the verb *know* in the independent clause. Within the subordinate clause, however, *who* is used as a predicate nominative and takes the nominative case.

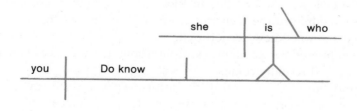

USAGE

> ☞ USAGE NOTE   *Whom* is often omitted (understood) in subordinate clauses.

EXAMPLES   The actor [whom] I wrote to sent these photos. [*Whom* is understood as object of preposition.]
The man [whom] we saw on the elevator looked familiar. [*Whom* is understood as direct object of *saw.*]

EXERCISE 12. Determining the Use of Who and Whom in Subordinate Clauses.

Number your paper 1–10. After the proper number, write the subordinate clause containing *who* or *whom* in each of the following sentences. Then tell how the relative pronoun (*who* or *whom*) is used in its own clause—as subject, predicate nominative, object of a verb, or object of a preposition.

EXAMPLE   1. She is someone whom we all admire.
1. *whom we all admire, object of verb*

1. The people who are born in Puerto Rico live in a commonwealth, with its own senate, supreme court, and governor's cabinet.
2. In 1969 the governor needed a secretary of labor on whom he could depend.
3. The person whom he appointed would occupy the most difficult and sensitive position in the cabinet.
4. Do you know who the choice was?
5. The choice fell to Mrs. Julia Rivera De Vincenti, who became the first woman to occupy a cabinet post in her country.
6. Mrs. De Vincenti, on whom Cornell University had bestowed a Ph.D. in management and collective bargaining, was a good choice for the appointment.
7. Mrs. De Vincenti, who was later appointed to the U.S. Mission to the UN, was the first Puerto Rican to serve in that capacity.
8. She addressed the General Assembly and showed that she was a woman who knew her job well.
9. She praised her compatriots, from whom new advances in agriculture had recently come.
10. And Mrs. De Vincenti made history again, for she was the first woman who ever wore a pantsuit to address the General Assembly!

USAGE

WRITING APPLICATION B:
Using *Who, Whoever, Whom,* and *Whomever* Correctly

Though you may use *who* and *whoever* for *whom* and *whomever* in spoken English, you should always follow the rules for standard English usage for *who* and *whoever* in your school writing.

NONSTANDARD *Who* did you call?
STANDARD *Whom* did you call?

In addition, always observe standard English usage for *who* and *whoever* when you use them in subordinate clauses.

INCORRECT I asked her *who* she had spoken with.
CORRECT I asked her *whom* she had spoken with.

Writing Assignment

Write ten sentences according to the following guidelines:

1. Use *who* as the subject of the subordinate clause.
2. Use *who* to begin a question.
3. Use *whom* as the object of the preposition in a sentence.
4. Use *whom* as the direct object in a sentence.
5. Use *whomever* as the direct object in a sentence.
6. Use *whomever* as the object of the preposition in a subordinate clause.
7. Use *whom* to begin a question.
8. Use *whom* as the direct object in the subordinate clause.
9. Use *whoever* to begin a question.
10. Use *whomever* as the object of the preposition in the subordinate clause.

REVIEW EXERCISE D. Selecting Pronouns to Complete Sentences Correctly. Number your paper 1–20. After the proper number, write how the pronoun in parentheses is used. Use the abbreviations *s.* (subject), *p.n.* (predicate nominative), *d.o.* (direct object), *i.o.* (indirect object), *o.p.* (object of preposition). Following the abbreviation, write the correct pronoun.

1. Did you get the post card from Margaret and (I, me)?
2. We all knew (who, whom) the winner would be.

3. Will Meg and (she, her) run the concession stand?
4. The coach asked you and (I, me) for help with the team's new equipment.
5. Becky and (she, her) rode their bikes to the meeting.
6. Grandfather joked with my sister and (I, me).
7. The lighting crew for the play was Manuel and (I, me).
8. (He, him) and (I, me) were watching the soccer game.
9. They treat (whoever, whomever) they hire very well.
10. We didn't see (whoever, whomever) had knocked.
11. Could it be you or (she, her) that called me?
12. Everyone except Louis and (he, him) was watching.
13. Who is that writer (who, whom) you were with?
14. They met Jennie and (she, her) at the airport.
15. The hostess and (he, him) greeted everyone.
16. The cheerleaders teased Matt and (I, me) about the fumble.
17. I didn't know (who, whom) to give the letter to.
18. I think that the people who were costumed as pirates are (they, them).
19. I looked for someone (who, whom) could give me directions to the theater.
20. My aunt and (we, us) went swimming last weekend.

REVIEW EXERCISE E. Determining Proper Case of Pronouns in Sentences. Number your paper 1–20. For each sentence in which the pronouns are all in the proper case, write a +; for each incorrect sentence, write a 0.

1. Be careful who you tell.
2. Will Marie and I be in the outfield?
3. My brother and me like water-skiing.
4. My family goes to the dentist who Ms. Calhoun recommended.
5. They will be going in place of Charlie and me.
6. Coretta said there would be other flag bearers in addition to Hugh and I.
7. The disc jockey gave Eileen and I each a free record.
8. Have you shown your new card to Linda and he?
9. At the head of the parade were us Girl Scouts.
10. The mayor awarded Marcus and him citizenship medals.
11. Maybe you should ask Rene or he.
12. Nobody except Josh and him finished the marathon.

13. Sonia and I want to work at Graceland next summer.
14. We wish we had neighbors like Sylvia and him.
15. Should you and me sign up for that course?
16. Did your father and them reach an agreement about the boundary dispute?
17. Joanne and us found a great beach.
18. Marilyn told Emily and me about her test.
19. There were us girls with a flat tire and no spare.
20. The incident happened after he and I had left.

The Pronoun in Incomplete Constructions

19f. After *than* and *as* in an incomplete construction, use the form of the pronoun you would use if the construction were completed.

The following are examples of incomplete constructions. In each one, part of the sentence is omitted and is included in the brackets.

> She is taller than **I**. [than *I* am tall]
> The news surprised Andrea more than **me**. [than the news surprised *me*]

In an incomplete construction, you should use the form of the pronoun you would use if you completed the sentence. Thus in the first sentence *I* is correct because it is the subject of the clause *I am tall*. In the second sentence *me* is correct because it is the object of the verb *surprised* in the clause *the news surprised me*.

Now examine this pair of sentences:

> I understand Mac better than **he**. [than *he* understands Mac]
> I understand Mac better than **him**. [than I understand *him*]

As you can see, the case of the pronoun depends on how the sentence is completed. Both these sentences are correct, but they are quite different in meaning; they are completed in different ways.

EXERCISE 13. Selecting Pronouns to Complete Incomplete Constructions in Sentences.   Write out each of the following sentences, supplying the omitted part and using the correct form of the pronoun. After the sentence, write the use of the pronoun in its clause. Some of the sentences may be completed in two different ways.

1. We played defense better than (they, them).
2. Margo works as slowly as (I, me).

USAGE

3. Nobody tried harder than (she, her).
4. You are a month younger than (he, him).
5. I know Millie better than (she, her).
6. Did you get as far in that book as (I, me)?
7. Richard wanted more tickets than (we, us).
8. Bianca lives farther away than (we, us).
9. She visited Lisa more than (I, me).
10. I hope you aren't as sick as (she, her).

REVIEW EXERCISE F. Selecting Pronouns to Complete Sentences. Number your paper 1–20. Write the correct one of the two pronouns given in parentheses. Be prepared to give reasons for your answer.

1. Heather and (he, him) live on a blueberry farm.
2. The teacher gave the assignment to (whoever, whomever) was absent yesterday.
3. The supporting players were Dina, Janelle, and (she, her).
4. Do you intercept passes as well as (she, her)?
5. We took Megan and (he, him) for a boat ride.
6. We wondered (who, whom) started the rumor.
7. I was standing in line right behind Dave and (he, him).
8. You and (I, me) could do a cartoon strip for the school paper.
9. You did as well on the test as (she, her).
10. We knew you'd arrive sooner than (he, him).
11. The skit was written by Cy and (he, him).
12. Aunt Stephanie brought Jack and (I, me) some mangoes from Florida.
13. Kathleen struck out Karen and (I, me).
14. The electrician warned (he, him) and (I, me) about the frayed wires.
15. These apricots are for (he, him) and (we, us) to share.
16. You sing much better than (I, me).
17. Did the bus leave without Zack and (he, him)?
18. Can you run the two hundred meters as fast as (them, they)?
19. The author, (who, whom) the critics had praised, autographed a copy of his novel for me.
20. The sleet whirled about George and (he, him) until they could barely see.

CHAPTER 19 REVIEW: POSTTEST

Determining the Proper Case of Pronouns in Sentences. Number your paper 1–20. If a sentence contains an incorrect pronoun, write the correct form after the proper number on your paper. For each correct sentence, write *C* after the proper number.

1. Del can't do math any better than her.
2. If anyone calls, ask whom it is.
3. You and him will guard their center.
4. There was some misunderstanding between him and his brother.
5. We saw Mike and he at the clambake.
6. The lab assistant gave Nora and I our equipment.
7. To who was the letter addressed?
8. Inez is better at physics than me.
9. Give a program to whoever asks for one.
10. I showed the negatives to Debbie and she.
11. It can't be they; that's not their car.
12. Ben and you can come with me and them.
13. Here's a list of people whom we can invite.
14. Did everyone finish the experiment except Donna and I?
15. Juanita and him showed us how to start the motor.
16. We band members have to be at school early to practice marching.
17. We saw Carla and her at the auto show.
18. He's the sportscaster who irritates me with his pretentious talk.
19. Martin and me performed as professionally as them.
20. She can ask Harry and I what the assignment is.

USAGE

Using Verbs Correctly

PRINCIPAL PARTS, TENSE, VOICE

People frequently use verbs in a nonstandard way when they speak. You may hear someone say, "He has brang," "She had drank," or "I was laying down." Fiction writers sometimes use nonstandard speech to add lifelike detail to dialogue. However, nonstandard verb usage is not appropriate on occasions, such as job interviews, when formal standard English is expected. This chapter will help you learn the standard usage of verbs in speaking and writing.

DIAGNOSTIC TEST

A. Writing the Past or Past Participle Form of Verbs. Number your paper 1–10. After the appropriate number write the past or past participle of the verb given at the beginning of the sentence.

EXAMPLE   1. *do*   Because he —— his work so well, he got a raise.
              1. *did*

1. *write*   Although Emily Dickinson —— poetry most her life, very little of her work was published until after her death.
2. *drink*   When he saw that the animals had —— all the water from the pails, he refilled them at the faucet.
3. *throw*   Regarding those weeds as unwanted intruders, she pulled them from the ground and —— them over the fence in the yard.

4. *swim*   The water was cold and daylight was fading, so he —— only a short distance before turning back to shore.

5. *freeze*   The dew —— during the night, covering each twig and blade of grass with a silvery coating.

6. *give*   After my brother had —— his new puppy a bath, he seemed to be wetter than the dog.

7. *speak*   She —— in such a low voice that the audience strained to hear her remarks.

8. *shrink*   Frightened by the strangers who crowded around, the deer —— back in its cage.

9. *ride*   Leading the parade was an officer who —— a prancing black horse.

10. *ring*   When the church bell ——, the villagers became alarmed.

B. Revising Verb Tense or Voice. Revise the following sentences, correcting verbs that are in the wrong tense or use an awkward passive voice. If a sentence is correct, write *C* after the proper number.

11. Geraldine A. Ferraro was born on August 26, 1935, in Newburgh, New York.

12. She attends Fordham University Law School and received a J.D. degree from the Law School in 1960.

13. In 1974 she becomes an assistant district attorney of Queens, New York.

14. She ran against Republican Alfred A. DelliBovi in the Congressional race in 1978; she defeats him and became the Democratic congresswoman for Queens, New York.

15. Reelection to this office was won by Geraldine Ferraro in 1980 and 1982.

C. Determining Correct or Incorrect Use of *Lie—Lay, Sit—Set,* and *Rise—Raise* in Sentences. Number your paper 16–20. If a sentence is correct, write a + after its number; if it is incorrect, write a 0.

16. The landlord asked us not to leave our lawn furniture setting in the hallway.

17. The construction workers lain the bricks in a pile next to where the mortar was set.

USAGE

18. When the dough has risen for fifteen minutes, turn it out onto the floured board.
19. When we are rising from our beds, the Chinese are laying down to sleep.
20. I was laying in the hammock on the porch watching the leaves fall in the wind.

KINDS OF VERBS

All verbs help to make a statement about their subjects. *Action* verbs do so by expressing an action performed by the subject.

Linking verbs help to make a statement by linking with the subject a word in the predicate that explains, describes, or in some other way makes the subject more definite. (See Chapter 13 for more information about action verbs and linking verbs.)

PRINCIPAL PARTS

Verbs have four basic forms from which all other forms are made. These are called the *principal parts* of the verb.

20a. The principal parts of a verb are the *infinitive*, the *present participle*, the *past*, and the *past participle*.

INFINITIVE	PRESENT PARTICIPLE	PAST	PAST PARTICIPLE
walk	(is) walking	walked	(have) walked
see	(is) seeing	saw	(have) seen

The words *is* and *have* are included to remind you that the present participle is used with some form of the helping verb *be* and the past participle mainly with a form of the helping verb *have*.

Regular Verbs

20b. A *regular verb* is one that forms its past and past participle by adding *-ed* or *-d* to the infinitive form.[1]

---

[1] A few regular verbs have an alternative past form ending in *-t;* for example, it *burns* (present), it *burned* or *burnt* (past), and it has *burned* or *burnt* (past participle).

INFINITIVE	PAST	PAST PARTICIPLE
work	worked	(have) worked
receive	received	(have) received
saddle	saddled	(have) saddled

Irregular Verbs

20c. An *irregular verb* **is one that forms its past and past participle in some way other than a regular verb does.**

Some irregular verbs form the past and past participle forms by changing the vowels, some by changing the consonants, and others by making no change at all.

INFINITIVE	PAST	PAST PARTICIPLE
bring	brought	(have) brought
begin	began	(have) begun
fly	flew	(have) flown
burst	burst	(have) burst
sit	sat	(have) sat
tear	tore	(have) torn

Since irregular verbs form their past and past participles in unpredictable ways, there is nothing to do but memorize the forms of at least the most common ones. You doubtless already know most of the irregular verbs on the list that follows. Nevertheless, you should study all of them carefully, concentrating on the ones that might give you some trouble.

Common Irregular Verbs

INFINITIVE	PRESENT PARTICIPLE	PAST	PAST PARTICIPLE
begin	(is) beginning	began	(have) begun
blow	(is) blowing	blew	(have) blown
break	(is) breaking	broke	(have) broken
bring	(is) bringing	brought	(have) brought
burst	(is) bursting	burst	(have) burst
choose	(is) choosing	chose	(have) chosen
come	(is) coming	came	(have) come
do	(is) doing	did	(have) done
drink	(is) drinking	drank	(have) drunk
drive	(is) driving	drove	(have) driven
fall	(is) falling	fell	(have) fallen

USAGE

INFINITIVE	PRESENT PARTICIPLE	PAST	PAST PARTICIPLE
freeze	(is) freezing	froze	(have) frozen
give	(is) giving	gave	(have) given
go	(is) going	went	(have) gone
ride	(is) riding	rode	(have) ridden
ring	(is) ringing	rang	(have) rung
run	(is) running	ran	(have) run
see	(is) seeing	saw	(have) seen
shrink	(is) shrinking	shrank	(have) shrunk
speak	(is) speaking	spoke	(have) spoken
steal	(is) stealing	stole	(have) stolen
swim	(is) swimming	swam	(have) swum
take	(is) taking	took	(have) taken
throw	(is) throwing	threw	(have) thrown
write	(is) writing	wrote	(have) written

USAGE

EXERCISE 1. Writing the Past and Past Participle Forms of Irregular Verbs. Your teacher will dictate to you the first principal part of the twenty-five irregular verbs listed above. Write from memory the past and the past participle. Place *have* before the past participle.

EXERCISE 2. Writing the Past or Past Participle Form of Irregular Verbs to Complete Sentences. Number your paper 1–25. Write the correct form (past or past participle) of the verb given at the beginning of the sentence. If necessary, refer to the list above.

1. *blow* All last night the wind —— wildly.
2. *shrink* Mrs. Ming feared that the jeans she washed had —— .
3. *begin* I had already —— my homework.
4. *steal* Did you see how Lou —— second base yesterday?
5. *freeze* Last winter the rosebushes —— .
6. *tear* Oops, I think my jacket has —— .
7. *do* Look what that nuisance of a cat has —— now.
8. *fly* Last summer we —— in a lighter-than-air balloon.
9. *sit* During my last class, someone —— on my lunch.
10. *come* Yesterday afternoon the mail —— late.
11. *write* She has —— a letter to the newspaper.
12. *see* When Clark was on vacation, he —— Mount Rushmore and the Grand Tetons.
13. *ride* Nobody except Walt has ever —— that horse.
14. *take* My sister has —— that course.

15. *burst* When she stuck the pin into the bubble, it ——— .
16. *choose* Which college has Mickey ——— ?
17. *bring* Hadn't she ——— her sleeping bag?
18. *drink* Bill ——— three glasses of orange juice at breakfast.
19. *swim* Every day on vacation my mother ——— a mile.
20. *ring* No one has ——— the bell yet.
21. *fall* He had ——— on the icy walk.
22. *throw* The horse had ——— its shoe.
23. *go* The teachers had ——— to a meeting.
24. *break* We hoped we hadn't ——— the machine.
25. *speak* Last semester our teacher ——— about England and Wales.

EXERCISE 3. Selecting the Past or Past Participle Form of Verbs.
Number your paper 1–25. Write the correct one of the two verbs in parentheses. When your paper has been corrected, read each sentence to yourself several times, using the correct word.

1. The robot glided into the control room and (began, begun) blinking its lights.
2. She had (wrote, written) her ideas on scraps of paper.
3. Someone actually (threw, throwed) a chocolate cream pie at the actor.
4. We (did, done) everything we could to help him.
5. Who has (drank, drunk) the rest of the orange juice?
6. My sister (came, come) into my room to remind me to clean up the mess in the kitchen.
7. Last night I (saw, seen) a TV show about whales.
8. Someone has already (tore, torn) out the coupon.
9. Who's (took, taken) the phone off the hook?
10. Once again the cat has (broke, broken) the lamp.
11. Who (give, gave) you the right to mark up my book?
12. She (ran, run) the copying machine last week.
13. I wish you had (spoke, spoken) to me about it sooner.
14. I dived off the high board and (swam, swum) the length of the pool.
15. You must have (rang, rung) the doorbell when I was out.
16. They just (came, come) back from the rink.
17. They could have (went, gone) to the movies.
18. Nancy had never (ate, eaten) a tamale before.
19. Lois (blowed, blew) up the balloon.

20. Suddenly the balloon (burst, bursted).
21. Ice cream that has (froze, frozen) is like a rock.
22. Joyce was (chóse, chosen) to represent our school.
23. Marc's new puppy was (brought, brung) back to him by a thought-ful neighbor.
24. We were (drove, driven) to the train station in a taxi.
25. My suitcase had (fell, fallen) off the luggage rack.

TENSE

Verbs change form to show the time of the action or the idea they express. The time indicated by the form of a verb is called its *tense*. There are six tenses, each of which is formed in one way or another from the principal parts of the verb. A systematic listing of the verb forms used in the six tenses is called a *conjugation*.

The conjugations that follow for the verbs *talk* and *throw* illustrate the tense forms of two common verbs, one regular and the other irregular.

20d. Learn the names of the six tenses and how the tenses are formed.

Conjugation of the Verb Talk

Present infinitive: *to talk*   Perfect infinitive: *to have talked*

Principal Parts

INFINITIVE	PRESENT PARTICIPLE	PAST	PAST PARTICIPLE
talk	talking	talked	talked

Present Tense

Singular	*Plural*
I talk	we talk
you talk	you talk
he, she, it talks	they talk

Present progressive: *I am talking,* etc.[1]

---

[1] The present progressive is not a separate tense but a form of the present tense since it shows present time. There is a progressive form for each of the six tenses.

Past Tense

Singular	Plural
I talked	we talked
you talked	you talked
he, she, it talked	they talked

Past progressive: *I was talking,* etc.

Future Tense

(*will* or *shall* + the infinitive[1])

Singular	Plural
I will (shall) talk	we will (shall) talk
you will talk	you will talk
he, she, it will talk	they will talk

Future progressive: *I will (shall) be talking,* etc.

Present Perfect Tense

(*have* or *has* + the past participle)

Singular	Plural
I have talked	we have talked
you have talked	you have talked
he, she, it has talked	they have talked

Present perfect progressive: *I have been talking,* etc.

Past Perfect Tense

(*had* + the past participle)

Singular	Plural
I had talked	we had talked
you had talked	you had talked
he, she, it had talked	they had talked

Past perfect progressive: *I had been talking,* etc.

Future Perfect Tense

(*will have* or *shall have* + the past participle)

Singular	Plural
I will (shall) have talked	we will (shall) have talked
you will have talked	you will have talked
he, she, it will have talked	they will have talked

Future perfect progressive: *I will (shall) have been talking,* etc.

[1] For a discussion of the use of *shall* and *will*, see pages 539–40.

Conjugation of the Verb **Throw**

Present infinitive: *to throw*   Perfect infinitive: *to have thrown*

Principal Parts

INFINITIVE	PRESENT PARTICIPLE	PAST	PAST PARTICIPLE
throw	throwing	threw	thrown

Present Tense

Singular	*Plural*
I throw	we throw
you throw	you throw
he, she, it throws	they throw

Present progressive: *I am throwing,* etc.

Past Tense

Singular	*Plural*
I threw	we threw
you threw	you threw
he, she, it threw	they threw

Past progressive: *I was throwing,* etc.

Future Tense

(*will* or *shall* + the infinitive)

Singular	*Plural*
I will (shall) throw	we will (shall) throw
you will throw	you will throw
he, she, it will throw	they will throw

Future progressive: *I will (shall) be throwing,* etc.

Present Perfect Tense

(*has* or *have* + the past participle)

Singular	*Plural*
I have thrown	we have thrown
you have thrown	you have thrown
he, she, it has thrown	they have thrown

Present perfect progressive: *I have been throwing,* etc.

Past Perfect Tense

(*had* + the past participle)

Singular	*Plural*
I had thrown	we have thrown
you had thrown	you had thrown
he, she, it had thrown	they had thrown

Past perfect progressive: *I had been throwing,* etc.

Future Perfect Tense

(*will have* or *shall have* + the past participle)

Singular	*Plural*
I will (shall) have thrown	we will (shall) have thrown
you will have thrown	you will have thrown
he, she, it will have thrown	they will have thrown

Future perfect progressive: *I will (shall) have been throwing,* etc.

20e. Learn the uses of the six tenses.

Each of the six tenses has its own uses. Sometimes the tense of a verb expresses time only; at other times tense may tell whether or not the action is still going on. Study the following explanations and examples carefully; then refer to these pages frequently as you work to complete the exercises.

(1) The *present tense* is used to express action (or to help make a statement about something) occurring now, at the present time.

EXAMPLES   Sonja **owns** a calculator.
Larry **is** in the Chess Club.
We **are rehearsing** the play.

> ☞ NOTE   The third example illustrates the present progressive tense. Each tense has a progressive form which is used to indicate that the action expressed by the verb is continuing.

In addition to indicating present time, the present tense has some special uses. It is used to indicate habitual action:

He **runs** two miles a day.

The present tense is also used to express a general truth—something that is true at all times.

Gary believed that the pen **is** [not *was*] mightier than the sword.

(2) The *past tense* **is used to express action (or to help make a statement about something) that occurred in the past but did not continue into the present. The past is regularly formed by adding** *-d* **or** *-ed.*

EXAMPLES   I **lunged** toward the door.
I **was lunging** toward the door.

(3) The *future tense* **is used to express action (or to help make a statement about something) that will occur at some time in the future. The future tense is formed with** *will* **or** *shall.*

EXAMPLES   I **will read** a lot.
I **will be reading** a lot.

There are several other ways of indicating future time.

EXAMPLES   I **am going to read** a lot this week.
I **leave next month.** [present tense with another word or phrase clearly indicating future time]

(4) The *present perfect tense* **is used to express action (or to help make a statement about something) that occurred at no definite time in the past. It is formed with** *have* **or** *has.*

EXAMPLE   She **has visited** Chicago.

The present perfect tense is also used to express action (or to help make a statement about something) that occurred in the past and continues into the present.

EXAMPLES   She **has worked** there several years. [She is still working there.]
I **have been playing** guitar for six months. [I am still playing it.]

(5) The *past perfect tense* **is used to express action (or to help make a statement about something) completed in the past before some other past action or event. It is formed with** *had.*

EXAMPLES   After she **had revised** her essay, she handed it in. [The action of revising preceded the action of handing it in.]
When he **had washed** the dishes, he sat down to rest. [He washed the dishes before he rested.]

(6) The *future perfect tense* **is used to express action (or to help make a statement about something) that will be completed in the future before some other future action or event. It is formed with** *shall have* **or** *will have.*

EXAMPLES   By the time I leave, **I will have packed** all my clothes. [The packing will precede the leaving.]

At the end of next year, I **shall have been going** to school for eleven years.

EXERCISE 4. Explaining the Uses of the Tenses of Verbs in Sentences. Explain the difference in meaning between the sentences in the following pairs. Both sentences in each pair are correct. Name the tense used in each sentence.

1. When you get here, I will start work.
   When you get here, I will have started work.
2. How long have you been a pilot?
   How long were you a pilot?
3. What happened at the game?
   What has been happening at the game?
4. She lived in Cleveland for four years.
   She has lived in Cleveland for four years.
5. When I am seventeen, I will get a driver's license.
   When I am seventeen, I will have gotten a driver's license.
6. Lynette was a cheerleader for one semester.
   Lynette has been a cheerleader for one semester.

EXERCISE 5. Using the Different Tenses of Verbs in Sentences. Number your paper 1–10. After the proper number, write the following sentences on your paper, changing the tenses of the verbs as indicated.

1. Otto lived here a month. (Change to past perfect.)
2. When the alarm goes off, I will get up. (Change *will get* to future perfect.)
3. Is she sleeping? (Change to present perfect progressive.)
4. When I get back, will you go? (Change *will go* to future perfect.)
5. Were they at the party? (Change to past perfect.)
6. Were you invited? (Change to present perfect.)
7. The soloist sings well. (Change to present perfect.)
8. The bus arrives on time. (Change to future.)

9. By the time you get here, Cammi will find out. (Change *will find* to future perfect.)
10. Ken was in town all summer. (Change to past perfect.)

Consistency of Tense

Young writers, especially when writing essays or narratives, sometimes begin their compositions in one tense and then lapse into another tense. Such lapses are due largely to carelessness, for students usually understand the error when it is pointed out to them.

20f. Do not change needlessly from one tense to another.

CARELESS	Roy *raised* (past) his telescope and *sees* (present) a large bear as it *raced* (past) back to the woods. [mixture of past and present tenses]
CORRECT	Roy *raised* (past) his telescope and *saw* (past) a large bear as it *raced* (past) back to the woods. [past tense throughout]
CORRECT	Roy *raises* (present) his telescope and *sees* (present) a large bear as it *races* (present) back to the woods. [present tense throughout]

EXERCISE 6. Identifying Verbs in the Wrong Tense. Number your paper 1–20. After the proper number, list the verbs that are in the wrong tense. After each, write the appropriate tense form. If there are no incorrectly used verbs in a particular sentence, write *C*.

1. One of the most important battles of the Revolutionary War occurred in September and October 1777 at Saratoga, New York. 2. The leader of the British troops, General John Burgoyne, had set up camp near Saratoga and is planning to march south to the city of Albany. 3. Burgoyne's army has been recently weakened by an attack from an American militia, which had ambushed some of his troops at Bennington, Vermont. 4. Although the march to Albany is dangerous, Burgoyne decided to take the risk because he feels bound by orders from London.

5. Meanwhile, also near Saratoga, the American troops under General Horatio Gates and General Philip Schuyler gather reinforcements and supplies. 6. The American forces outnumbered their British enemies by a margin of two to one. 7. The Americans are much better equipped than the British, whose provisions are badly depleted.

8. In spite of these disadvantages, the British open an attack on the Americans on September 19, 1777.   9. After four hours of fierce fighting, the Americans, led by Benedict Arnold (who later became an infamous traitor to the American cause), withdraw.   10. The British, however, have suffered serious losses, including many officers. 11. Burgoyne quickly sends a message to the British command in New York and asked for new orders.   12. He never received a response from his superiors, possibly because the message is intercepted. 13. Burgoyne's tactics became desperate.   14. He boldly leads a fresh attack against the Americans on October 7.   15. This time, however, his troops endure even worse casualties, and the next day Burgoyne prepares to retreat.

16. The Americans surround Burgoyne's army before it leaves Saratoga.   17. Trapped and helpless, Burgoyne begins negotiating his surrender.   18. The Convention of Saratoga, by which Burgoyne gave up his entire force of six thousand troops, is signed on October 17.   19. Saratoga becomes a turning point in the Revolutionary War. 20. Six years later, in 1783, the British signed a peace treaty with the Americans, and the Revolutionary War ended.

USAGE

WRITING APPLICATION A:
Avoiding Unnecessary Shifts in Tense

To communicate effectively, your writing must be clear. One way to achieve clarity in your writing is to select a tense and to avoid shifting tense unnecessarily.

Writing Assignment

Write an essay explaining why you think a particular historical event occurred. Be sure to limit your topic for the length of your essay. Use the past tense, and avoid shifting tense unnecessarily.

ACTIVE AND PASSIVE VOICE

In most English sentences the subject performs the action of the verb. If there is a receiver of the action, it is expressed by the object of the verb, as in this example:

```
                    S        V                  O
```
EXAMPLE   The blazing fire **blistered** the outside walls. [The subject, *fire,* performs the action; the object, *walls,* tells what was blistered.]

A verb that expresses action performed by the subject is said to be in the *active voice.*

For reasons of emphasis, however, such sentences are often switched around so that the object becomes the subject:

```
                    S        V
```
EXAMPLE   The outside walls **were blistered** by the blazing fire.

Notice that the object has been moved forward to the subject position and that the original subject is now expressed in a prepositional phrase. In addition, the verb has been changed from *blistered* to *were blistered.* Verbs that express action performed *upon* their subjects are said to be in the *passive voice.* A passive verb is always a verb phrase consisting of some form of *be* (*is, was,* etc.) plus the past participle.

ACTIVE   She **grows** tomatoes and corn on her farm.

PASSIVE   Tomatoes and corn **are grown** on her farm.

ACTIVE   She **will plant** the corn in two weeks.

PASSIVE   The corn **will be planted** in two weeks.

These passive sentences do not identify the performer of the action. When it is important to know who or what performed the action in a passive sentence, the performer of the action is identified in a prepositional phrase.

Although the passive construction is useful in situations in which the performer of the action is unknown or unimportant, it can easily be overused. A succession of passive sentences has a weak and awkward sound and should be avoided.

WEAK PASSIVE   The party was enjoyed by all the guests.

BETTER   All the guests enjoyed the party.

EXERCISE 7. Identifying Sentences in the Active or Passive Voice.   Indicate whether the verb in each sentence is active or passive. Then rewrite each passive-voice sentence in the active voice.

1. The art of Lucia Wilcox was admired by artists around the world.
2. Her blindness during her last years made her final works particularly interesting.

3. Dufy, Leger, Motherwell, and Pollock were among her teachers and friends.
4. Exhibits of her paintings were shown all over the art world.
5. Her blindness was sudden, though not wholly surprising.
6. It was caused by a tumor near the optic nerve.
7. After she became blind, she claimed she had better sight than anyone else.
8. Her vision and her mind were "free of static and distractions."
9. Her style was altered from energetic silhouettes to larger canvases in lush spreading colors.
10. These visions during her period of blindness were imitated by many well-known artists.

WRITING APPLICATION B:
Using the Passive Voice to Create Suspense

In many of the art forms, it is fairly easy to establish mood. If a film director wants the mood to be frightening, for example, he may select eerie music. He may show a dark, rainy night with the wind blowing long, stringy moss that is hanging from old trees. If a dancer wants the same mood, her dance movements become sharp and fragmented. The canvas artist can use deep, dark tones. All of these artists can create sights or sounds or both to reinforce mood. In writing, however, you have to use words alone. One technique in creating suspense in a written work is to keep the performer of the action unknown by using the passive voice, as in the following example.

EXAMPLE What disturbed me about the room? Suddenly I noticed that the window *had been opened*. As I walked over to close it, I felt I *was being watched* from the darkness outside.

Writing Assignment

Think of a situation in which suspense is created because the audience does not know who is performing the action. Write a narrative paragraph telling what happened. Use the passive voice to keep the performer of the action unknown. Your aim is to create suspense.

SIX TROUBLESOME VERBS

Three pairs of verbs in English account for many usage errors: *lie—lay, sit—set,* and *rise—raise.* Because the meanings of each pair are related and their forms are similar, it is easy to get them mixed up. The exercises in this section will help you to keep these common verbs straight.

Lie and Lay

The verb *lie* means "to recline" and does not take an object. Its principal parts are *lie, (is) lying, lay, (have) lain.*

The verb *lay* means "to put or place" and takes an object. The principal parts of lay are *lay, (is) laying, laid, (have) laid.*

INFINITIVE	PRESENT PARTICIPLE	PAST	PAST PARTICIPLE
lie (to recline)	(is) lying	lay	(have) lain
lay (to put or place)	(is) laying	laid	(have) laid

EXAMPLES The cat **lies** on the porch, sunning itself.
A thick fog **lay** over the city.
The old papers **had lain** on the desk for months.

Lay your packages down here.
The masons **laid** the bricks.
He **had laid** his keys on the ledge.

When faced with a *lie—lay* problem, ask yourself two questions:

1. What is the meaning I intend? (Is it "to be in a lying position" or is it "to put something down"?)
2. What is the time expressed by the verb? (Only one of the principal parts will express this time accurately.)

PROBLEM Feeling drowsy yesterday, I (lay, laid) on the couch.
Question 1: The meaning is "to remain in a lying position."
Therefore the proper verb is *lie.*
Question 2: The time is past. Therefore, the proper principal part is *lay* (lie, *lay*, lain).
SOLUTION Feeling drowsy yesterday, I **lay** on the couch.

PROBLEM The teacher (lay, laid) the cards on the desk.
Question 1: The meaning is "to put." Therefore, the proper verb is *lay.*
Question 2: The time is past. Therefore, the proper principal part is *laid* (lay, *laid*, laid).
SOLUTION The teacher **laid** the cards on the desk.

EXERCISE 8. *Oral Drill*. Stressing the Correct Forms of *Lie—Lay* in Sentences. Read each of the following sentences aloud three times, stressing the italicized verbs. Be able to explain, in the light of the information given, why each verb is correct.

1. The ketchup bottle should *lie* on its side.
2. A light haze *lay* over the hills.
3. The cat *laid* its toy on the doorsill.
4. Someone's books are *lying* in the hall.
5. She had *lain* down for a nap.
6. We *laid* new tiles in our kitchen.
7. *Lay* the material on the counter.
8. You could *lie* down and relax.

EXERCISE 9. Selecting the Correct Form of *Lie—Lay* to Complete Sentences. Number your paper 1–10. Write the correct one of the two words in parentheses after the proper number.

1. He (lay, laid) out the silverware.
2. Don't (lie, lay) your books in that puddle.
3. The pasture (lies, lays) in the valley.
4. A sheet (lay, laid) over the rug to catch the paint.
5. The clothing had (lain, laid) strewn about the room all week.
6. Kitty (lay, laid) the book down.
7. Marty had (lain, laid) in the sun too long.
8. The theories developed by Albert Einstein (lay, laid) the ground-work for many later scientific discoveries.
9. The cat has been (lying, laying) on my coat.
10. (Lying, Laying) the tip by my plate, I rose to leave the restaurant.

EXERCISE 10. Determining the Correct Use of *Lie—Lay* in Sentences. Number your paper 1–20. If the verb in each of the following sentences is correctly used, write a + after the proper number; if it is incorrect, write a 0. Think of the *meaning* of the verb.

1. She had just lain down with a good book when the phone rang.
2. The towels laying in the corner all need to be washed.
3. The patient laid on the operating table.
4. Did you ever lay down on a water bed?
5. After I had tripped, I sat there feeling embarrassed, my groceries lying all around me.

USAGE

6. After lunch he will lay down and take a nap.
7. Exhausted, she crossed the finish line and laid down in the grass.
8. The peddler lay out his wares.
9. The fox was lying hidden in the thicket.
10. She found the dog laying under the porch.
11. Saturday all we did was lie around and play records.
12. He was lying under the car tinkering with the muffler.
13. The factory has lain off several workers.
14. The sun worshipers were lying on the beach.
15. My gym bag was laying right where I had left it.
16. Last week he lay great emphasis on footnote form.
17. I laid the pie crust in the pan carefully.
18. The cougar was laying in wait for its prey.
19. She sighed and lay down the phone receiver.
20. As I remember it, he laid the letters in one of the drawers of the desk in the den.

Sit and Set

The verb *sit* means "to be in a seated position." The principal parts of *sit* are *sit, (is) sitting, sat, (have) sat.*

The verb *set* means "to put," "to place (something)." The principal parts of *set* are *set, (is) setting, set, (have) set.*

INFINITIVE	PRESENT PARTICIPLE	PAST	PAST PARTICIPLE
sit (to rest)	(is) sitting	sat	(have) sat
set (to put)	(is) setting	set	(have) set

Study the following examples:

You may **sit**.   The cars **sit** in the lot.
You may **set** your books here.   We **set** the stand on the street.

You will have little difficulty using these verbs correctly if you will remember two facts about them: (1) Like *lie*, the verb *sit* means "to be in a certain position." It almost never has an object. (2) Like *lay*, the verb *set* means "to put (something)." It may take an object. *Set* does not change form in the past or the past participle. Whenever you mean "to place" or "to put," use *set*.[1]

---

[1] Several uses of the verb *set* do not mean "to put" or "to place"; for example: *the sun sets, setting hens, set your watch, set a record, set out to accomplish something.*

USAGE

EXERCISE 11. *Oral Drill.* **Stressing the Correct Forms of** *Sit—Set* **in Sentences.** Read each of the following sentences aloud three times, stressing the italicized verb.

1. *Set* the groceries on the counter.
2. *Sit* down anywhere you like.
3. Would you *set* the table?
4. The bird *sat* on the wire.
5. Rosita *set* her watch.
6. We had *sat* in the lobby an hour.
7. They have been *sitting* on the porch.
8. We *sat* by the sea.

EXERCISE 12. **Selecting the Correct Form of** *Sit—Set* **to Complete Sentences.** Select from each sentence the correct one of the two words in parentheses, and write it after the proper number.

1. A few of us were (sitting, setting) at our desks.
2. He (sat, set) in the rocker, reading.
3. He (sat, set) the package on the doorstep.
4. Thomas was (sitting, setting) out the appetizers for the party guests.
5. We had been (sitting, setting) on a freshly painted bench.
6. They (set, sat) the seedlings in the window boxes.
7. She (sits, sets) in front of me.
8. He (set, sat) the mousetrap, baiting it with peanut butter.
9. I could (sit, set) and watch the sunset every evening.
10. Mick and Sheila (sat, set) the dials on the machine.

REVIEW EXERCISE A. **Selecting the Correct Form of** *Lie—Lay* **and** *Sit—Set* **to Complete Sentences.** Number your paper 1–20. Write the correct verb in parentheses after the proper number.

1. (Sitting, Setting) on the table was a pair of scissors.
2. Please (sit, set) the carton down carefully.
3. She (lay, laid) in the hammock, watching the clouds.
4. (Sit, Set) all the way back in your seat.
5. The dirty dishes had (lain, laid) in the sink for hours.
6. Yesterday Tom (lay, laid) the blame for his lateness on his alarm clock.
7. The cat always (sits, sets) on the couch.

USAGE

8. If only we could have (lain, laid) our hands on that buried treasure!
9. My eyeglasses were (sitting, setting) right where I left them.
10. King Tut's tomb (lay, laid) undisturbed for centuries.
11. Have you ever (sat, set) around with nothing to do?
12. She (sat, set) down at her desk with her checkbook and calculator in front of her.
13. The two children were (sitting, setting) in the playpen.
14. The beached rowboat (lay, laid) on its side.
15. She (sat, set) looking toward the horizon.
16. Laura had just (sat, set) down when the phone rang.
17. Julie (lay, laid) her handbag on the counter.
18. Pieces of the jigsaw puzzle were (laying, lying) on the floor in the living room.
19. Jack was (sitting, setting) outside on the top step.
20. Were you (laying, lying) down for a while before dinner?

Rise and Raise

The verb *rise* means "to go in an upward direction." It is an *irregular* verb. Its principal parts are *rise, (is) rising, rose, (have) risen.*

The verb *raise* means "to move something in an upward direction." It is a *regular* verb. Its principal parts are *raise, raising, raised, (have) raised.*

Study the following:

INFINITIVE	PRESENT PARTICIPLE	PAST	PAST PARTICIPLE
rise (go up)	(is) rising	rose	(have) risen
raise (force upward)	(is) raising	raised	(have) raised

Just like *lie, rise* never has an object. Like *lay* and *set, raise* may have an object.

EXERCISE 13. Selecting the Correct Form of *Rise—Raise* to Complete Sentences. Number your paper 1–10. Write the correct one of the two words in parentheses in each sentence.

1. Has the moon (risen, raised) yet?
2. The tower (rose, raised) high into the darkening air.
3. The temperature (rose, raised) as the sun climbed higher.
4. When speed limits go up, the number of accidents (rises, raises).

5. A serious problem has (risen, raised).
6. Trails of mist were (rising, raising) from the lake.
7. How much did the river (rise, raise) during the flood?
8. Has anyone (rose, raised) that question before?
9. The butterfly (rose, raised) from the leaf and flitted away.
10. The dough for the biscuits was (rising, raising) in the bowl on the sill.

EXERCISE 14. Writing the Correct Form of *Rise—Raise* to Complete Sentences. Number your paper 1–10. For each sentence, write the correct form of *rise* or *raise* required by the meaning.

1. If you know the answer, —— your hand.
2. —— the flags higher, please.
3. The tide —— and falls because of the moon.
4. Last year Marietta —— money for the charity by baking cookies.
5. Up toward the clouds —— the jet.
6. The crops we —— were sugar beets and corn.
7. Prices have —— in the last few years.
8. The traffic officer —— his hand to signal us.
9. Sonia —— before the sun came up this morning.
10. A question was —— by a member of the council.

REVIEW EXERCISE B. Determining Correct or Incorrect Use of *Lie—Lay, Sit—Set,* and *Rise—Raise* in Sentences. Number your paper 1–10. If a sentence is correct, write a + after the proper number; if it is incorrect, write a 0.

1. Set down the eggs carefully.
2. The frog was setting on the lily pad, croaking loudly.
3. The judge carefully studied the papers, then lay them beside her gavel.
4. The cattle were lying in the shade by the stream.
5. Is the thermometer raising, or do I just think it's hotter?
6. Wanda sat out the equipment for the experiment.
7. Why don't you lie those things down?
8. Instead of laying down, you should be getting some type of strenuous exercise.
9. A strange noise raised from the motor.
10. Set down for a while and relax.

USAGE

REVIEW EXERCISE C. Writing the Correct Forms of Verbs to Complete Sentences. Number your paper 1–20. After the proper number, write the correct one of the two words in parentheses.

1. Have you (wrote, written) the address down?
2. Little Billy was (lying, laying) in wait for us.
3. Why don't you (lie, lay) the beach towels over the railing to dry in the sun?
4. He had accidentally (thrown, throwed) his homework away.
5. The spilled laundry (lay, laid) in a wet heap.
6. We ate until we almost (burst, bursted).
7. The kitten (shrank, shrunk) back from the barking dog.
8. The pack rat had (stole, stolen) my watch during the night.
9. Haven't you ever (swam, swum) in a lake before?
10. They certainly have (ran, run) a successful campaign.
11. When the winners appeared, a cheer (rang, rung) out.
12. When we arrived, the movie had already (began, begun).
13. I had put the pineapple juice in the freezer to cool, and it had (froze, frozen).
14. We should have (gone, went) with the first bus.
15. Have you ever (rode, ridden) a roller coaster?
16. I knew I should have (brought, brung) my camera.
17. In New York, we (saw, seen) a Broadway play.
18. Uh-oh, I think this phone is (broke, broken).
19. A strange figure (rose, raised) up out of the mist.
20. I accidentally (sat, set) the dripping cup on the clean tablecloth.

CHAPTER 20 REVIEW: POSTTEST

A. Writing the Past or Past Participle Form of Verbs. Number your paper 1–10. Write the past or past participle of the verb given at the beginning of each sentence.

1. ride   Jeffrey and Lee have —— their bikes fifty miles today.
2. write   I read the love letters Grandpa —— to Grandma in 1930.
3. take   After you have —— algebra, you may try calculus.
4. fall   All that winter day the snow ——, blanketing everything.
5. see   Rebecca soon —— why the old house had sold so cheaply.

6. drink   The gerbil has —— all its water and is still thirsty.
7. begin   As dark fell and the children still did not return, I —— to worry.
8. bring   Margot has —— popcorn for the postgame party.
9. speak   Sargeant Liakos —— about responsible driving at the assembly yesterday.
10. give   The teacher told me that she had already —— directions for the test.

B. Revising Verb Tense or Voice.   Rewrite the following sentences, correcting verbs that are in the wrong tense or use an awkward voice. If a sentence is correct, write *C* after the proper number.

EXAMPLES   1. The Congressional Medal of Honor was received by Mary Walker, one of the first women doctors, who served as a surgeon during the Civil War.
   1. *Mary Walker, one of the first women doctors, who served as a surgeon during the Civil War, received the Congressional Medal of Honor.*
   2. The mason poured the cement and then smoothes it.
   2. *The mason poured the cement and then smoothed it.*

11. Captain Cook, one of the greatest explorers of all time, sailed large areas of the Pacific Ocean and makes accurate maps of the region.
12. Cook joins the navy as a seaman in 1755 and many promotions were received by him before becoming a master of his own ship in 1759.
13. Because of his knowledge of mathematics, astronomy, and geography, he is selected to lead a scientific expedition to the Pacific.
14. The purpose of the expedition is to observe the passage of Venus between the earth and sun, a very rare occurrence.
15. On the voyage, Cook wins a battle against scurvy, a serious disease caused by lack of vitamin C.
16. Raw cabbage, which was rich in vitamin C, was eaten by the sailors to prevent scurvy.
17. By the time the voyage is over, the ship traveled around Cape Horn to Tahiti in the Pacific Ocean.
18. After he observes the passage of Venus, Cook sails off to explore the east coast of New Zealand, which was claimed by him for England.

19. On a second voyage, the Hawaiian Islands were identified by Cook, which were named the Sandwich Islands by him.
20. In a dispute over a canoe, Cook was killed by island inhabitants and in naval tradition was buried at sea in 1779.

C. Determining Correct or Incorrect Use of *Lie—Lay, Sit—Set,* and *Rise—Raise* in Sentences.   Number your paper 21–25. Read each of the following sentences, and determine whether it is correct. If it is correct, write a + after the proper number; if it is incorrect, write a 0.

21. You can sit the wastebasket in the corner, then set up the chairs.
22. Everyone rose when the judge entered the courtroom and sat when she was seated.
23. The grizzly bear suddenly raised up from the shadows.
24. I like to lay out under the stars and just think.
25. We had just lain out the blueprints for the architect.

USAGE

CHAPTER 21

Using Modifiers Correctly

COMPARISON; PLACEMENT OF MODIFIERS

DIAGNOSTIC TEST

A. Correcting Errors in the Use of the Comparative and Superlative Forms. Number your paper 1–10. After the proper number, write the incorrect word(s) from each sentence. Then write the correct form, adding words if necessary.

EXAMPLES   1. I was more hungrier than I thought, so I ordered three hamburgers.
   1. *more hungrier—hungrier*
   2. This storm was even badder than the last one.
   2. *badder—worse*

1. During the Middle Ages, Richard the Lion-Hearted of England was known as the most bravest champion of English chivalry as well as a noble Crusader.
2. Richard was the more able and intelligent of King Henry II's three sons.
3. John was Richard's youngest brother, and the favorite of their father.
4. While Richard was away fighting in one of the Crusades, John took over the reins of government and ruled in the disagreeablest manner his subjects had known.

513

5. After Diego had started lifting weights, he bragged that he was stronger than any man in town.
6. People who live along this road complain because it is the worstest in the entire township.
7. Floyd and his brother are landscape designers who are famous throughout the state, but Floyd is the best known in this area.
8. After the band had practiced, their music sounded more better.
9. When I had a choice of chocolate or vanilla, I took vanilla because I like it best.
10. Looking across the water at sunset, you can see the beautifullest view you can imagine.

B. Revising Sentences by Correcting Dangling and Misplaced Modifiers. Each of the following sentences contains a dangling or misplaced modifier. After the proper number, revise each sentence, arranging the words so that the meaning is logical and clear. You may have to add or delete some words.

EXAMPLE 1. The class sent a get-well message to their teacher on a balloon.
1. The class sent their teacher a get-well message on a balloon.

11. Running in circles, they saw that the dogs could herd the sheep into the pen.
12. The winners marched onto the stage carrying ribbons and trophies.
13. A police officer warned students who drive too fast about accidents during the defensive-driving class.
14. After walking through the park, a cold drink was needed.
15. A brightly colored watercolor was hanging on her wall depicting the four seasons.
16. Mother found a package outside our house tied with ribbons.
17. Maria took a close-up photograph of a lion with a telephoto lens.
18. Sitting in a tree outside my window, I see a small brown bird, apparently building a nest on one of the limbs.
19. A young woman knocked on the door wearing a suit and a hat.
20. Walking in the sunshine, it felt warm to the children.

Knowing when to use an adverb and when to use an adjective is not just a matter of form but of meaning. Notice the difference in meaning in the following two sentences:

Lisa does **strenuous** exercise. [adjective]
Lisa exercises **strenuously**. [adverb]

A modifier is a word or a group of words that makes the meaning of another word more definite. Two parts of speech are used as modifiers: the adjective, which modifies a noun or pronoun, and the adverb, which modifies a verb, an adjective, or another adverb.

ADJECTIVE AND ADVERB FORMS

Almost the only common problem in distinguishing an adverb from an adjective concerns the following three pairs: *bad—badly, good—well,* and *slow—slowly.* The problem is to learn when to use the adverb form and when to use the adjective form. Apply the following rule to the three troublesome pairs.

21a. If a word in the predicate modifies the subject of the verb, use the adjective form. If it modifies the verb, use the adverb form.[1]

EXAMPLES   The swimmer was **careful**. [The adjective *careful* modifies the noun *swimmer: careful swimmer*.]

He swims **carefully**. [The adverb *carefully* modifies the verb *swims: swims carefully*.]

Linking verbs are usually followed by a predicate adjective. The following are the most commonly used linking verbs: *be, become, seem, grow, appear, look, feel, smell, taste, remain, stay, sound.*

In general, a verb is a linking verb if you can substitute for it some form of the verb *seem.*

She **felt** happy. [She seemed happy.]
The car **appeared** abandoned. [The car seemed abandoned.]

Because many verbs may be used as either linking verbs or action verbs, you must be able to tell which way a verb is used in a particular sentence.

LINKING   The bell **sounded** loud. [verb followed by an adjective modifying the subject: The bell *seemed* loud.]

ACTION   The bell **sounded** loudly. [verb modified by an adverb]

---

[1] Most adjectives become adverbs by adding *-ly: nice—nicely, vague—vaguely, incidental—incidentally.* A few adjectives, however, also end in *-ly (lively, lonely, friendly)*, so you cannot always be sure that an *-ly* word is an adverb.

USAGE

LINKING   The calf **grows** fat. [verb followed by an adjective modifying the subject: The calf *seems* fat.]

ACTION   The calf **grows** quickly. [verb modified by an adverb]

Bad and Badly

Bad is an adjective; in most uses *badly* is an adverb.

EXAMPLES   The dog was **bad**. [bad dog]
The dog behaved **badly**. [adverb modifying the verb *behaved*]
The milk smelled **bad**. [After the linking verb *smelled,* the adjective *bad* modifies the subject *milk.*]
The old roof leaked **badly**. [The adverb *badly* modifies the verb *leaked.*]

With linking verbs the adjective form is used.

NONSTANDARD   The medicine tasted badly.

STANDARD   The medicine tasted **bad**. [The adjective *bad* modifies the subject *medicine.*]

☞ USAGE NOTE   One prominent exception to this rule is the use of *badly* after the sense verb *feel.* In informal English either *bad* or *badly* is acceptable after *feel.*

He feels **bad** about the accident.
He feels **badly** about the accident. [informal]

However, formal English calls for *bad* after *feel.*

He feels **bad** [not *badly*] about the accident.

Follow the rules for formal written English in doing the exercises in this book.

Well and Good

Well may be used as either an adjective or an adverb. As an adjective, *well* has three meanings:

1. To be in good health:

Fran is well.   She seems well.

2. To appear well dressed or well groomed:

> She looks well in red.

3. To be satisfactory:

> Everything is well.   That is well.

As an adverb, *well* means *capably:*

> The house was built well.

Good is always an adjective. It should not be used to modify a verb.

NONSTANDARD   She sings good.

STANDARD   She sings **well**.

NONSTANDARD   The car runs good.

STANDARD   The car runs **well**.

STANDARD   The color looks **good** on you. [adjective following linking verb]

USAGE

☞ USAGE NOTE   *Well* is also acceptable in sentences like the last example above: That color looks *well* on you.

Slow and Slowly

Slow is used as both an adjective and an adverb. *Slowly* is always an adverb.

EXAMPLES   Go **slow**. [*Slow* is an adverb modifying *go*.]
Go **slowly**. [*Slowly* is an adverb modifying *go*.]

In most adverb uses (other than *go slow* or *drive slow*), it is better to use the form *slowly* as an adverb instead of *slow*.

EXAMPLES   **Very slowly** the tiger crept forward.

☞ USAGE NOTE   Certain words like *loud, hard, deep,* and *fast* may be used as adverbs without changing their forms.

EXAMPLES   Samantha laughed **hard**.   The band played **loud**.

EXERCISE 1. Selecting Adjectives or Adverbs to Complete Sentences. Number your paper 1–10. Write the correct one of the two words in parentheses after the proper number.

1. I can't hear you (well, good) when the water is running.
2. The opening paragraph is written (well, good).
3. The situation looks (bad, badly).
4. Why does that ketchup always come out of the bottle so (slow, slowly)?
5. She certainly plays the marimba (well, good).
6. Can you dance as (well, good) as you sing?
7. These shoes don't fit (bad, badly) at all.
8. Our gym teacher told us today to do all of the exercises (slow, slowly).
9. Did you do (well, good) on the last algebra test?
10. The chef at the corner cafe cooks very (bad, badly).

EXERCISE 2. Using Adjective and Adverb Forms Correctly in Sentences. Number your paper 1–10. If the sentence is correct, write a + after the proper number; if it is incorrect, write a 0.

1. All went well at the interview.
2. Raising the camera slow, he tried not to startle the animal.
3. That new hair style looks well on Pat.
4. You had better start slow.
5. He was panting so bad that he had to sit down.
6. Marquita felt bad about her lost pet.
7. You sing so good that you could go on the stage.
8. He read slow, wanting to be careful.
9. This juice doesn't taste very well.
10. The train seemed slow, but it was actually ahead of schedule.

COMPARISON OF MODIFIERS

Adjectives state qualities of nouns or pronouns:

an **expensive** jacket   **fluffy** clouds   **shiny** metal

You can show the degree or extent to which one noun has a quality by comparing it with another noun that has the same quality. For instance:

This jacket is **larger** than the other.

Similarly, you can show degree or extent by using adverbs to make comparisons:

> I ran well, but you ran **better.**

21b. The forms of modifiers change as they are used in comparison.

There are three degrees of comparison: *positive, comparative,* and *superlative.* Notice how the following forms of modifiers change to show comparison:

POSITIVE	COMPARATIVE	SUPERLATIVE
low	lower	lowest
fearful	more fearful	most fearful
promptly	more promptly	most promptly
bad	worse	worst
good	better	best

Regular Comparison

(1) A modifier of one syllable regularly forms its comparative and superlative by adding -er and -est.

POSITIVE	COMPARATIVE	SUPERLATIVE
thin	thinner	thinnest
small	smaller	smallest
short	shorter	shortest

(2) Some modifiers of two syllables form comparative and superlative degrees by adding -er and -est; other modifiers of two syllables form comparative and superlative degrees with *more* and *most*.

In general, the *-er* and *-est* forms are used with two-syllable modifiers unless they make the word sound awkward. The *more* and *most* forms are used with adverbs ending in *-ly.*

POSITIVE	COMPARATIVE	SUPERLATIVE
lovely	lovelier	loveliest
tricky	trickier	trickiest
awkward	more awkward	most awkward
quickly	more quickly	most quickly

Some two-syllable modifiers may use either *-er* and *-est* or *more* and *most: able, abler, ablest,* or *able, more able, most able.*

(3) Modifiers of more than two syllables form their comparative and superlative degrees by means of *more* and *most*.

POSITIVE	COMPARATIVE	SUPERLATIVE
catastrophic	more catastrophic	most catastrophic
predictably	more predictably	most predictably

(4) Comparison to indicate less or least of a quality is accomplished by using the words *less* and *least* before the modifier.

POSITIVE	COMPARATIVE	SUPERLATIVE
frequent	less frequent	least frequent
helpful	less helpful	least helpful

Irregular Comparison

Adjectives and adverbs that do not follow the regular methods of forming their comparative and superlative degrees are said to be compared irregularly.

POSITIVE	COMPARATIVE	SUPERLATIVE
bad	worse	worst
good } well	better	best
little	less	least
many } much	more	most

Caution: Do not add -*er*, -*est*, or *more, most* to irregular forms: *worse*, not *worser* or *more worse*.

EXERCISE 3. Writing the Comparative and Superlative Forms of Modifiers. Write the comparative and superlative forms of the following modifiers:

1. little
2. fundamental
3. humid
4. smart
5. silly
6. good
7. likely
8. congenial
9. bad
10. well

Use of Comparative and Superlative Forms

21c. Use the comparative degree when comparing two things; use the superlative degree when comparing more than two.

USAGE

The comparative form of a modifier is used for comparing two things, as these examples indicate.

EXAMPLES   Our old house was **larger** than this one.
           Omaha is **nearer** than Joplin.
           Roberto studies **harder** than Dick.

The superlative form of a modifier is used for comparing three or more things.

EXAMPLES   The whale is the **largest** animal.
           Meg is the **worst** person in our family to try to awaken.
           Which of these four shirts costs the **least?**

In informal speech it is common to use the superlative for emphasis, even though only two things are being compared.

EXAMPLES   May the **best** person [of two] win.
           Put your **best** foot forward.

In writing, however, you will do well to observe the distinction stated in rule 21c.

EXERCISE 4. Writing Sentences Using the Comparative and Superlative Forms of Modifiers. Write five sentences using adjectives or adverbs to compare two things, and write five sentences using the same adjectives and adverbs to compare three or more things.

21d. Do not omit the word *other* **or** *else* **when comparing one thing with a group of which it is a part.**

It is absurd to say "Stan is taller than anyone in his class." Stan must obviously be a member of the class himself, and he can hardly be taller than himself. The word *else* should be supplied: "Stan is taller than anyone else in his class."

ABSURD   Our school is smaller than any in the county. [This would mean that the school is smaller than itself.]

ACCURATE   Our school is smaller than any **other** in the county.

ABSURD   Lucy is funnier than anybody in her group. [This means that Lucy, a member of her group, is funnier than herself.]

ACCURATE   Lucy is funnier than anybody **else** in her group.

USAGE

ABSURD   Rhode Island is smaller than any state in the Union.

ACCURATE   Rhode Island is smaller than any **other** state in the Union.

21e. Avoid double comparisons.

A double comparison is one in which the comparative or superlative is incorrectly formed by adding *-er* or *-est* in addition to using *more* or *most*.

NONSTANDARD   The second movie was more scarier than the first one.

STANDARD   The second movie was **scarier** [or *more scary*] than the first one.

NONSTANDARD   What is the most deadliest snake?

STANDARD   What is the **most deadly** [or *deadliest*] snake?

21f. Be sure your comparisons are clear.

In making comparisons, you should always state clearly what things are being compared. For example, in the sentence "The climate of Arizona is drier than South Carolina," the comparison is not clear. The climate of Arizona is not being compared to South Carolina, but rather to the climate of South Carolina. The sentence should read: "The climate of Arizona is drier than that of South Carolina."

AWKWARD   The Millers would rather plant and harvest their own vegetables than canned ones.

CLEAR   The Millers would rather plant and harvest their own vegetables than buy canned ones.

Often an incomplete clause is used in making comparisons. Both parts of the comparison should be fully stated if there is any danger of misunderstanding.

NOT CLEAR   We know her better than Dee.

BETTER   We know her better than we know Dee.
We know her better than Dee does.

EXERCISE 5. Using Modifiers Correctly in Sentences.   Number your paper 1–10. If the sentence is correct, write a +; if it is incorrect, write a 0. Be prepared to explain your answers.

1. Laurie is more friendlier than she used to be.
2. Which of the four seasons do you like better?
3. I never saw a countryside more flatter.
4. Margaret Mead was one of the world's most famous anthropologists.
5. Of the two albums that I wanted to purchase, this was the least expensive.
6. The cheetah is the world's most fastest running animal.
7. The muscles of the leg are stronger than the arm.
8. Denver has a higher elevation than any major city in the United States.
9. Which is largest, St. Louis or Pittsburgh?
10. This flood was much worser than the last.

REVIEW EXERCISE. Correcting Errors in the Use of Comparative and Superlative Forms. Number your paper 1–10. After the proper number, write the correct form of any incorrectly used modifier. If a sentence is correct, write *C*.

EXAMPLE 1. After we had heard the dog howling, we became fearfuller.
    1. *more fearful*
    2. The child was toddling so slow that his sister soon was far ahead.
    2. slowly

1. Ida Wells, who spoke out brave for civil rights from 1892 to 1931, was one of the founders of the National Association for the Advancement of Colored People.
2. In the Northern Hemisphere, days in June are warmer than November.
3. The governor considered our proposal more favorably than the one written by the other group.
4. She felt badly because she had not recovered from the illness and could not play with the team.
5. That blue suit looks good on Father, but I like the brown striped one best.
6. Coming in from the cold, they appreciated the fire that burned brightly in the old iron stove.
7. Finding that the new map was usefuller to me than my old one, I took it with me in the car.
8. I like Heather better than Carla.

USAGE

9. The red apples in that basket are more sweeter than the green ones you bought yesterday.
10. Because his old car ran so good, he decided that he did not need to buy a new one.

WRITING APPLICATION A:
Using Comparative and Superlative Degrees to Make Comparison Clear

Have you ever heard someone talk and talk and not seem to say anything? Meaningless chatter does not really give the listener anything to think about and respond to. Occasionally writers produce many words but say little because they omit details or reasons.

> I prefer to live in the city instead of the suburbs for many reasons. Cities are interesting. I really enjoy the things available in cities. Cities have lots of advantages.

Writing Assignment

Use one of the following ideas for a comparison. Be sure to support your opinion with clear reasons. Include each of the three degrees of comparison: positive, comparative, and superlative. Underline and label each when you use it.

EXAMPLE   Autumn is <u>more beautiful</u> than winter because of the colorful foliage. [comparative degree]

IDEAS   two sports   the beach versus the woods
        city and country   freshman year/sophomore year

DANGLING MODIFIERS

21g. A phrase or clause that does not clearly and sensibly modify a word in the sentence is á *dangling modifier*.

A modifier consisting of a phrase or a clause may be momentarily confusing to a reader if it appears to modify a word that it cannot sensibly modify. Verbal phrases are particularly likely to dangle, since they have only a loose grammatical relationship with the rest of the sentence.

CONFUSING Looking back over my shoulder, the team went into a huddle. [The participial phrase seems illogically to modify *team*.]
Towed away by the truck, I sadly watched my car. [The participial phrase seems to modify *I*.]

In both examples the participial phrase appears to modify a word that it cannot logically modify. The word that each phrase is supposed to modify has been omitted from the sentence. Compare the following correct examples.

CLEAR Looking back over my shoulder, I saw the team go into a huddle.
I sadly watched my car being towed away by the truck.

Dangling modifiers can be corrected by rearranging the words in the faulty sentence or by adding words that make the meaning clear.

CONFUSING Going to the store, a building was on fire.

CLEAR Going to the store, I saw a building on fire.

CONFUSING While frying the bacon, the eggs were scrambled.

CLEAR While frying the bacon, Cindy scrambled the eggs.

CLEAR While Jo was frying the bacon, Cindy scrambled the eggs.

CONFUSING To qualify for the Olympics, many trial heats must be won.

CLEAR To qualify for the Olympics, a runner must win many trial heats.

CLEAR Before a runner may qualify for the Olympics, he must win many trial heats.

EXERCISE 6. Revising Sentences by Correcting Dangling Modifiers. Revise each sentence so that the modifier *clearly* and *sensibly* modifies a word in the sentence. You may have to supply some words to fill out the sentence properly.

1. Sitting on the telephone wire, he saw a meadowlark.
2. Looking through the telescope, the moon seemed enormous.
3. While out running, his mouth got dry.
4. Going around the bend, the ocean came into view.
5. Doing a few tap dance steps, the floor got scratched.
6. Carefully cleaning her whiskers, we watched the mother cat.
7. To grow plants successfully, light, temperature, and humidity must be carefully controlled.

8. After doing the housework, the room almost sparkled.
9. To make manicotti, pasta must be stuffed with cheese.
10. Concluding her speech, the jury looked at her in awe.

MISPLACED MODIFIERS

21h. Modifying words, phrases, and clauses should be placed as near as possible to the words they modify.

Most of the errors in modification in the above examples resulted from the omission of the word that was supposed to be modified. Unclear sentences can also result from placing modifiers too far away from the words they modify.

Misplaced Phrase Modifiers

(1) Modifying phrases should be placed as near as possible to the words they modify.

The following sentences will indicate the importance of observing this rule.

CONFUSING Who is the person with the dog in the sports jacket?

CLEAR Who is the person in the sports jacket with the dog? [The phrase *with the sports jacket* obviously modifies *person*. Otherwise it appears to modify *dog* and gives the impression that the dog was wearing the sports jacket.]

CONFUSING We learned that Pearl Buck wrote *The Good Earth* in our English class.

CLEAR In our English class we learned that Pearl Buck wrote *The Good Earth*.

EXERCISE 7. Revising Sentences by Correcting Misplaced Phrase Modifiers. In each of the following sentences, pick out the misplaced phrase, and revise the sentence, placing the phrase near the word it should modify.

1. Mrs. Barry drove downtown after her husband had left for the factory to do some shopping.
2. I found a huge boulder taking a shortcut through the woods.

3. Mr. Tate noticed some caterpillars pruning his fruit tree.
4. We saw a woman with her elkhound in high-heeled shoes.
5. Missie saw a heron driving over the bridge.
6. We noticed several signs riding down the highway.
7. We could see corn growing from our car window.
8. Barking wildly and straining at the chain, the letter carrier was forced to retreat from the dog.
9. I met a woman on the plane in a mink coat.
10. He recounted an incident about a nuclear chain reaction during his chemistry lecture.

Misplaced Clause Modifiers

In using modifying clauses, follow the rule for phrases.

(2) Place the clause as near as possible to the word it modifies.

The following sentences will show you how a misplaced clause may make a sentence ridiculous.

AWKWARD   There was a building in the city that was condemned.

CLEAR   There was a building that was condemned in the city.

The modifying clause *that was condemned* modifies *building,* not *city.* In the second sentence the clause has been put next to the word it modifies.

AWKWARD   The letter was in the mailbox that bore a foreign stamp.

CLEAR   The letter, which bore a foreign stamp, was in the mailbox.

AWKWARD   Lyn got a package from one of the stores we visited that she hadn't ordered.

CLEAR   From one of the stores we visited, Lyn got a package that she hadn't ordered.

EXERCISE 8. Revising Sentences by Correcting Misplaced Clause Modifiers.
In each of the following sentences, take out the misplaced clause and revise the sentence, placing the clause near the word it modifies. If you find a misplaced phrase, correct it.

1. We put the clothing in the cellar that we had outgrown.
2. I gave olives to my friend that I had stabbed with my fork.

3. The plane landed safely on the airport runway that had the engine trouble.
4. The picture was hanging on the wall that we bought in Canada.
5. I ignored any topics in the book that we covered in class.
6. They showed us a camera on the bus that works underwater.
7. We washed the dishes with sudsy water that had been stacked in the sink all day.
8. They took the cat to the manager's office that had been lost.
9. Jan showed the rooms to her visitors that she had painted.
10. We ran after the dog into the street that had escaped.

WRITING APPLICATION B:
Using Modifiers to Make Your Writing Clear

Dangling or misplaced modifiers do not belong where they are placed. Notice how the misplaced modifier in the following sentence makes the meaning unclear.

EXAMPLE   While studying for biology, the ice cream tasted good.

Think about the meaning of this sentence. Can ice cream study? How would you correct this sentence?

Writing Assignment

Complete each of the following sentences. If the modifier does not start with a capital letter, place it at the end of your sentence. Make sure you review your sentences for dangling or misplaced modifiers.

1. wandering around the school grounds
2. Hoping my parents wouldn't be angry
3. after taking the test
4. Placing the assignment on her desk

CHAPTER 21 REVIEW: POSTTEST

Revising Sentences by Correcting Errors in the Use of Modifiers.
Most of the following sentences contain errors in the use of modifiers

(words, phrases, clauses). Revise such sentence, correcting the faulty modifiers. If a sentence is correct, write *C* after its number on your paper.

1. While riding my motorcycle, the neighbor's dog chased me.
2. I bought these clothes with my birthday money that I'm wearing.
3. Adrianne is better at chemistry than anybody in her class.
4. Grading all the papers, the teacher was pleased to see that the students had done better than they had on any previous assignment.
5. I think that kale is more tastier than spinach, but some people don't like either one very good.
6. Food may cause an upset stomach that is very spicy.
7. Hank worked rather hasty so he could catch up with Clay and Nina.
8. We bought this cat from a farmer that really catches mice good.
9. Although Mitzi Akira is shorter than any player on her volleyball team, she's the best of the top two scorers.
10. Although Marian felt bad about losing the game, she knew things could be worser.
11. Millie can dance as well as Scott, but of the two, his singing is best.
12. By playing carefully, the game was won.
13. To economize during cold months, weatherstripping should be used for all loose-fitting windows with an adhesive backing.
14. Wearily struggling into my boots and parka, a sudden cold wind out of the northeast was faced grimly.
15. I found a seashell on the beach with beautiful scalloped edges.
16. To develop photographic prints, a source of water and a room that can be darkened completely are needed.
17. Because one carton of chemicals smelled badly, it was examined for contamination before being used in the laboratory.
18. Although Helen is the better actress, Wenona will probably get the leading part because she is more reliable.
19. Requiring a previous course in drawing, I could not enroll in the museum's advanced art course.
20. Nero earned the reputation of being one of Rome's worstest rulers.

USAGE

CHAPTER 22

Glossary of Usage

COMMON USAGE PROBLEMS

This chapter contains a short glossary of English usage intended mainly for reference. Get in the habit of referring to it whenever you are uncertain about a point of usage.

Several kinds of usage problems are treated here. In some, a choice is described between standard and nonstandard ways of phrasing things. Other choices are between formal and informal usages. (Follow the formal practice in doing the exercises.) Problems arising from the confusion of similarly spelled words are treated in Chapter 28.

DIAGNOSTIC TEST

Revising Expressions by Correcting Errors in Usage. In each of the following sets of expressions, one expression contains an error in usage. After the proper number, rewrite this expression correctly, using standard formal usage.

EXAMPLE 1. (a) She taught me to sing. (b) fewer letters in the box (c) Set down in the shade and rest.

  1. *(c) Sit down in the shade and rest.*

1. (a) anywheres you travel (b) as fast as sound travels (c) Learn French cooking from him.
2. (a) affect the outcome (b) candidate implied in his speech (c) among his two opponents

3. (a) made illusions to the Bible (b) fewer participants in the contest (c) replied to her grandmother respectfully

4. (a) family emigrated from Germany (b) should of gone yesterday (c) discovered a new planet

5. (a) Try and win the game. (b) draw as well as her mother (c) that kind of car

6. (a) Let the dog out. (b) an effect of cold weather (c) books, pencils, papers, and etc.

7. (a) not excepted by the club (b) older than you (c) Bring your records with you.

8. (a) I heard nothing. (b) can't hardly tell the difference (c) Lay the book on the shelf.

9. (a) picture fell off the wall (b) What kind of a dog is that? (c) larger than he

10. (a) sitting beside the tree (b) going a little ways (c) not reality but illusion

11. (a) coat doesn't fit well (b) an immigrant to this country (c) inside of the cabinet

12. (a) car looks like it had been wrecked (b) chair that was blue (c) water jug that burst

13. (a) She effected an improvement. (b) a problem which must be resolved (c) Less students joined the club this year.

14. (a) Take the package to the mailroom immediately. (b) Apples fell off of the tree. (c) This will scarcely be enough food for all of them at the picnic.

15. (a) invented a better safety device (b) No one beside my aunt knows. (c) played well in the tournament

16. (a) Funds were allotted among six counties. (b) Where is my hammer at? (c) This is as far as the fence extends.

17. (a) going nowheres (b) Doesn't he know the way? (c) She finished reading; then she wrote her essay.

18. (a) Read the book and report on same. (b) Try to learn this poem. (c) Leave the green grapes on the vine.

19. (a) Set the brake on the car. (b) The fog will rise from the lake. (c) One of them glasses broke.

20. (a) It was an illusion caused by light on the surface. (b) Their report implies a need for funds. (c) That dog he limps.

21. (a) no exception to this rule (b) being that she is the oldest (c) Bring

your own tools with you.
22. (a) Set a good example. (b) looked like it had been burned (c) They ought to study before the test.
23. (a) The ice bursted a pipe. (b) Lie on the couch and rest. (c) emigrate from their birthplace
24. (a) Leave me have my turn. (b) Ellen, Jose, and Kim, respectively (c) somewhat cold for swimming
25. (a) haven't only three days of vacation (b) the effect of smoking on the lungs (c) learned that the winner had been announced

---

a, an   These short words are called *indefinite articles.* They refer to one of a general group.

EXAMPLES   **A** salesperson walked to the counter.
The tourists are looking for **a** hotel.
June has **an** appointment next week.

Use *a* before words beginning with a consonant sound; use *an* before words beginning with a vowel sound. In the examples above, *a* is used before *hotel* because *hotel* begins with a consonant sound. *An* is used before *hour* because *hour,* which has a silent "h", begins with a vowel sound.

accept, except   *Accept* is a verb; it means "to receive." *Except* may be either a verb or a preposition. As a verb it means "to leave out"; as a preposition it means "excluding."

EXAMPLES   Gary could not **accept** that he had lost.
If you were absent, you will be **excepted** from this test.
Everybody knew **except** Chrissie.

affect, effect   *Affect* is usually a verb; it means "to influence." *Effect* used as a verb means "to accomplish" or "to bring about." Used as a noun, *effect* means "the result of some action."

EXAMPLES   The heat did not seem to **affect** them.
Did the drug **effect** a cure?
The director wanted to create a special **effect.**

all the farther, all the faster   These expressions are used informally in some parts of the country to mean "as far as" and "as fast as." In formal English, *as far as* and *as fast as* are the correct expressions.

USAGE

NONSTANDARD   This is all the farther we can go.

STANDARD   This is **as far as** we can go.

allusion, illusion   An *allusion* is a reference to something. An *illusion* is a "false, misleading, or overly optimistic idea."

EXAMPLES   She made an **allusion** to the poem.
The magician was a master of **illusion.**

and etc.   Since *etc.* is an abbreviation of the Latin *et cetera,* which means "and other things," you are using *and* twice when you write "and etc." The *etc.* is sufficient.

anywheres, everywheres, nowheres   Use these words and others like them without the *s.*

EXAMPLE   **Anywhere** [not *anywheres*] you travel, you see the same hotels.

at   Do not use *at* after *where.*

NONSTANDARD   Where's the main office located at?

STANDARD   Where's the main office **located**?

being as, being that   Avoid each; use *since* or *because.*

NONSTANDARD   Being that he was late, he had to stand.

STANDARD   **Since** he was late, he had to stand.

NONSTANDARD   Being as her grades were so high, she got a scholarship.

STANDARD   **Because** her grades were so high, she got a scholarship.

beside, besides   *Beside* means "by the side of"; *besides* means "in addition to."

EXAMPLES   He nervously glanced at the person **beside** him.
Did anybody **besides** you see what happened?

between, among   *Between* implies two people or things; *among* implies more than two. This distinction in meaning is usually observed in formal English; however, use *between* when you are thinking of two items at a time, regardless of whether they are part of a group of more than two. (See third and fourth examples below.)

EXAMPLES   The twins had a strong bond **between** them.
The basketball team talked **among** themselves.
There were differences **between** Massachusetts, Vermont, and Connecticut. [*Between* is correct because the speaker is thinking of differences between *two* states at a time.]

USAGE

There was a friendly agreement **between** the people of our town and those of the neighboring town. [Although more than two people are involved, the agreement is between two groups.]

bring, take   *Bring* means "to come carrying something." *Take* means "to go away carrying something." The situation is complicated by the fact that a speaker, out of politeness, sometimes adopts the point of view of the person being spoken to: "Shall I bring you something to eat?" Usually it is helpful to think of *bring* as related to *come* and *take* as related to *go.*

EXAMPLES   **Bring** your radio when you come.
Don't forget to **take** your coat when you go.

bust, busted   Avoid using these words as verbs. Use a form of either *burst* or *break.*

NONSTANDARD   I busted the switch on the stereo.
STANDARD   I **broke** the switch on the stereo.

NONSTANDARD   The water main busted.
STANDARD   The water main **burst.**

EXERCISE 1. Identifying Correct Expressions. Number your paper 1–20. Choose the correct one of the two words in parentheses, and write it after the proper number on your paper.

1. The tasks were divided (among, between) the two scouts.
2. He didn't seem to be (affected, effected) by the news.
3. Penicillin has (affected, effected) some remarkable recoveries.
4. No one (accept, except) the sophomores is supposed to attend.
5. Is that (all the faster, as fast as) you can walk?
6. Please (bring, take) these papers when you leave.
7. A clown distributed treats (between, among) the many children.
8. We were afraid that the bull had (busted, broken) loose.
9. Ask Ginny to (bring, take) me her new record album.
10. (Being that, Since) everyone is here, let's begin.
11. They graciously (accepted, excepted) my halting apology.
12. I wonder where the mustard (is, is at).
13. Your sock has (a, an) hole in it.
14. (Everywhere, Everywheres) in Hot Springs there are interesting old buildings.
15. I couldn't find the cat (anywhere, anywheres).

16. The crosslike rays radiating from the moon were an (allusion, illusion) caused by the screen door.
17. The excessive humidity (affected, effected) all of us.
18. (Bring, Take) your radio with you when you come to my house.
19. Somebody (beside, besides) Julie must have picked up the tickets.
20. The speaker made an (allusion, illusion) to a statement in Ralph Ellison's book.

can't hardly, can't scarcely   See **The Double Negative** (page 543).

could of   *Could have* sounds like *could of.* Do not erroneously write *of* with the helping verb *could.* Use *could have.* Also avoid *ought to of, should of, would of, might of,* and *must of.*

EXAMPLE   Muriel could **have** [not *of*] gone with us.

discover, invent   *To discover* means "to find something that already exists." *To invent* is "to be the first to make something not known before."

EXAMPLES   Sarah Boone **invented** the ironing board.
Columbus **discovered** America by accident.

don't   A contraction of *do not, don't* should not be used with a singular noun or a third person singular pronoun (*he, she, it*). Use *doesn't.* See page 458.

NONSTANDARD   He don't like to eat parsnips.

STANDARD   He **doesn't** like to eat parsnips.

NONSTANDARD   It don't matter at all.

STANDARD   It **doesn't** matter at all.

effect   See **affect, effect.**

emigrate, immigrate   *Emigrate* means "to go from a country to settle elsewhere." *Immigrate* means "to come into a country to settle there."

EXAMPLES   My great-grandfather **emigrated** from Norway.

Much of Australia's population is composed of people who **immigrated** there.

everywheres   See **anywheres.**

except   See **accept, except.**

USAGE

fewer, less In standard formal English, *fewer* (not *less*) is used before a plural noun. *Less* is used before a singular noun.

EXAMPLES There are **fewer** [not **less**] whales than there used to be.
We should have bought **less** meat [but **fewer** eggs].

good, well *Good* is an adjective. Do not use it to modify a verb.

NONSTANDARD They skate **good.**

STANDARD They skate **well.**

Well is an adverb except in three uses: (1) when used to mean "healthy," (2) when used to mean "neatly groomed" or "attractively dressed," and (3) when used to mean "satisfactory." In all of these instances, *well* is an adjective.

EXAMPLES The car ran **well.** [adverb]
I didn't feel **well.** [adjective]
They looked **well** in their new outfits. [adjective]
All seems **well.** [adjective]

had of See **of.**

had ought See **ought.**

hardly See **The Double Negative** (page 543).

he, she, they Do not use unnecessary pronouns. This error is sometimes called the *double subject.*

NONSTANDARD My father he works downtown.

STANDARD My **father works** downtown.

illusion See **allusion, illusion.**

immigrate See **emigrate, immigrate.**

imply, infer *Imply* means "to suggest something." *Infer* means "to interpret" or "to derive a certain meaning from a remark or an action."

EXAMPLES In her speech, the candidate **implied** that she was for tax reform. From other remarks that she has made, I **infer** that she feels that certain taxes are unfair.

EXERCISE 2. Identifying Correct Expressions. Number your paper 1–15. Write the correct form in parentheses.

1. My sister's statement (implied, inferred) that she was displeased with the cut in her allowance.
2. Was it George Washington Carver or Thomas Edison who (invented, discovered) all those uses for peanuts?
3. From his letter I (implied, inferred) he would be away all summer.
4. He (don't, doesn't) always say what he means.
5. She read the poem aloud, interpreting it very (good, well).
6. (My aunt, My aunt she) lived a year in San Juan.
7. (Emigration, Immigration) to Alaska was spurred by the gold rush.
8. Explorer Jedediah Smith (discovered, invented) the first overland route to California.
9. The heat has affected the growing season; we'll harvest (fewer, less) crops this year.
10. Many French Canadians (emigrated, immigrated) from Quebec to work in the industries of New England.
11. In spite of losing our best player, we played (good, well) and won.
12. Mary Beth Stearns (discovered, invented) a device to study electrons.
13. You could (have, of) borrowed the books from me.
14. To prevent cavities, one should eat (fewer, less) sugar.
15. Audrey must (have, of) taken my jacket by mistake.

invent See **discover, invent.**

kind of, sort of These expressions, used in informal English, mean "rather" or "somewhat." Avoid them in formal written English.

INFORMAL She seemed kind of bored.

FORMAL She seemed **rather** bored.

INFORMAL The waves were sort of rough.

FORMAL The waves were **rather** [or *somewhat*] rough.

kind of a, sort of a The *a* is unnecessary. Leave it out.

EXAMPLE This job takes a special **kind of** screwdriver.

learn, teach *Learn* means "to acquire information." *Teach* means "to instruct" or "to give out knowledge."

EXAMPLES She **learned** how to saddle the horse.
The stable owner **taught** her how.

USAGE

leave, let *Leave* means "to go away." *Let* means "to allow" or "to permit."

EXAMPLES **Let** [not *leave*] them find their own way.
We **let** [not *left*] the trapped bird go free.

lie, lay See page 504.

like, as *Like* is usually a preposition. *As* is usually a conjunction.

EXAMPLES The animal looked **like** a fox. [prepositional phrase]
The animal ran and dodged **as** a fox might. [This is a subordinate clause introduced by a conjunction. In this construction, *like* is often used informally, but *as* is preferred in formal English.]

like, as if Phrases such as *as if* and *as though* are used as conjunctions to introduce a subordinate clause. In writing, avoid using *like* in place of these conjunctions.

INFORMAL This looks like it might be the right place.

FORMAL This looks **as if** [or **as though**] it might be the right place.

might of, must of See **could of.**

nowheres See **anywheres.**

of Do not use *of* with prepositions such as, *inside, off,* and *outside.*

EXAMPLES **Outside** [not *outside of*] the building was a patio.
The diver jumped **off** [not *off of*] the board.

Of is also unnecessary with *had.*

EXAMPLE If **I had** [not *had of*] remembered my keys, I would have been able to open this locker.

off of See **of.**

ought The verb *ought* should never be used with *had.*

NONSTANDARD Nikki had ought not to say such things.

STANDARD Nikki **ought** not to say such things.

NONSTANDARD They had ought to have thought of that sooner.

STANDARD They **ought** to have thought of that sooner.

respectfully, respectively *Respectfully* means "with respect or full of respect." *Respectively* means "each in the order given."

EXAMPLES   The reporters listened **respectfully** to the senator's request.

Nick, Margo, and Ted are nineteen, seventeen, and fifteen, **respectively.**

EXERCISE 3. Identifying Correct Expressions. Number your paper 1–15. Write the correct form in parentheses.

1. Will your parents (leave, let) you go to the game?
2. This is a powerful machine, so treat it (respectfully, respectively).
3. Hilary jumped down (off, off of) the horse.
4. We went to the hardware store for a special (sort of, sort of a) wrench.
5. You can do (like, as) you like, but you should do (like, as) you think best.
6. Rachel Carson (learned, taught) me to care about ecology.
7. (Leave, Let) us listen without any interruptions.
8. Adelita stayed (inside, inside of) the building until the rain stopped.
9. The muskrat slipped (off, off of) the bank smoothly and swam away.
10. We could (of, have) left earlier, I suppose.
11. Why did she feel (like, as if) she'd said something wrong?
12. T. J. (ought, had ought) to see this program.
13. We should mind our own business and (leave, let) that porcupine mind his.
14. John was trying in vain to (learn, teach) me some new dance steps.
15. We didn't want to take the boat out because the waves looked (sort of, rather) choppy.

rise, raise   See page 508.

same   *Same* is used as an adjective (the *same* day, the *same* person) and as a pronoun (more of the *same*). In the latter use, *same* should always be used with *the*. Such uses as the following ones should be avoided:

EXAMPLE   We located the plant known as the Lousewort and photographed same. [In this sentence, *it* is preferable.]

shall, will   There was a time when careful speakers and writers used *shall* in the first person (*I shall, we shall*) and *will* in second and third persons (*you will, he will, they will*). Today, however, *will* is considered as correct as *shall* in the first person.

USAGE

STANDARD I **shall** return. I **will** return.

sit, set See page 506.

so In writing, avoid using this overworked word as a conjunction meaning "therefore."

POOR The meeting was over at noon, so Karen came home early.

BETTER Since the meeting was over at noon, Karen came home early.

some In writing, do not use *some* for *somewhat* as an adverb.

NONSTANDARD This medicine will help your cough some.

STANDARD This medicine will help your cough **somewhat.**

sort of See **kind of, sort of.**

take, bring See **bring, take.**

than, then Do not use *then* in the place of *than. Than* is a conjunction used in comparisons. *Then* is an adverb telling when.

EXAMPLES She is younger **than** you.
Jake swept the floor; **then** he emptied the trash.

them *Them* is not an adjective. Use *these* or *those.*

NONSTANDARD It's one of them fancy show dogs.

STANDARD It's one of **those** fancy show dogs.

this here, that there *Here* and *there* are unnecessary.

NONSTANDARD This here fooling around has got to stop.

STANDARD **This** fooling around has got to stop.

try and In writing and in formal speaking, the correct form is *try to.*

INFORMAL When you're at bat, you must try and concentrate.

FORMAL When you're at bat, you must **try to** concentrate.

way, ways Use *way,* not *ways,* in referring to distance.

EXAMPLE She lives quite a **way** [not *ways*] from here.

what Do not use *what* to mean *that.*

EXAMPLE This is the book **that** [not *what*] I told you about.

when, where Do not use *when* or *where* incorrectly in writing a definition.

NONSTANDARD S.R.O. is when all tickets have been sold, and there is standing room only.

STANDARD S.R.O. means that all tickets have been sold and there is standing room only.

where Do not use *where* for *that*.

EXAMPLE I read **that** [not *where*] the renovation of the town hall was turned down by the voters.

where . . . at See **at**.

which, that, who *Which* is used to refer only to *things*. *That* is used to refer to either *people* or *things*. *Who* is used to refer only to *people*.

EXAMPLES The hat **which** I want is now on sale.
There is the tube **that** needs replacing.
There is the woman **that** won the medal.
There is the woman **who** won the medal.

who, whom See pages 479–82.

EXERCISE 4. Revising Sentences by Correcting Errors in Usage.
The following sentences contain examples of the errors listed after Exercise 3. Revise each sentence, correcting errors in usage. Then practice saying aloud the corrected form.

1. A solar eclipse is when the moon comes between the earth and the sun.
2. The workers which put up this building were certainly fast.
3. I found the right equipment in the catalog and ordered same.
4. I really like them science fiction movies.
5. A run-on sentence is where two sentences are erroneously joined as one.
6. When the bell finally rang, I felt relieved some.
7. Them mosquitoes can drive a person nearly crazy.
8. They were the very ones which complained about the achievement test.
9. Betty heard on the radio where the mayor is going to Washington about the redevelopment project.

10. I'm tired of trying to cut the grass with this here old lawn mower that should be in an antique exhibit.

REVIEW EXERCISE A. Identifying Correct Expressions. Number your paper 1–10. Choose the correct form in parentheses, and write it after the proper number.

1. Thanks to modern medicine, there are (fewer, less) cases of tetanus and diphtheria nowadays.
2. I tried to (learn, teach) my dog to do tricks, but he just sits and stares at me.
3. I see (where, that) pandas are an endangered species.
4. Cape Porpoise is (somewhere, somewheres) near Portsmouth.
5. Priscilla wrote a much longer paper (than, then) Tammy.
6. I have to go home and feed the cats, dust the furniture, take out the garbage, load the dishwasher, defrost the chicken, (and etc., etc.)
7. We (hadn't ought to, ought not) decide until we know more facts.
8. It (don't, doesn't) make any difference if we finish today or tomorrow.
9. Someone must (of, have) left the door unlocked.
10. Was it Benjamin Franklin who (discovered, invented) electricity?

REVIEW EXERCISE B. Selecting Appropriate Expressions. Number your paper 1–20. For each sentence, write the correct form or forms shown in parentheses.

1. When E. E. Cummings published his strangely punctuated poetry, many readers were not sure what (kind of, kind of an) experiment he was up to.
2. (Inside, Inside of) the box was (a, an) heap of glittering gems.
3. After our slumber party, my room looked (like, as if) a tornado had swept through it.
4. The five hikers divided the camping equipment (between, among) themselves and loaded their packs.
5. She shouldn't (have, of) driven all by herself when she could (of, have) joined our car pool.
6. Linda (doesn't, don't) enjoy doing (them, those, that) sort of exercise.

7. May I (imply, infer) from your yawns that you are bored?
8. My great-grandmother (emigrated, immigrated) from Italy as a young woman.
9. (Being that, Because) school was canceled today, we are going out sledding.
10. Those events happened in 1949 and 1952, (respectfully, respectively).
11. (Beside, Besides) speaking Spanish, Vera can speak Portuguese, and she speaks both very (good, well).
12. (My uncle, My uncle he) wanted to be (learned, taught) to fly helicopters.
13. Far before us on the desert, a lake seemed to sparkle, but it was only an (allusion, illusion).
14. Please leave at once, and (bring, take) your pet skunk with you.
15. This water shortage will (affect, effect) the whole state (accept, except) for two counties.
16. I don't think my parents will (leave, let) me borrow the car in this kind of weather.
17. She was taught to speak to all of her elders (respectfully, respectively).
18. We made (this, this here) maple syrup on our own farm.
19. San Diego is quite a (way, ways) from here, but we (ought, had ought) to get there by 4:00.
20. Because of the indiscriminate slaughter, each year there were (fewer, less) buffalos.

The Double Negative

A *double negative* is a construction in which two negative words are used when one is sufficient. Before the eighteenth century, two or more negatives were often used in the same sentence to make the meaning more emphatic. Today this method of gaining emphasis is no longer used, and a double negative is considered nonstandard.

can't hardly, can't scarcely The words *hardly* and *scarcely* should not be used with *not* (or the contraction of *not, n't*).

EXAMPLES You **can** [not *can't*] **hardly** see ten feet in front of you.
We **had** (not *hadn't*) **scarcely** enough time to finish our essay test.

haven't but, haven't only In certain uses, *but* and *only* convey a negative meaning and should not be used with *not*.

EXAMPLES   We **have** [not *haven't*] **but** three more days.
            We **have** [not *haven't*] **only** a dollar between us.

no, nothing, none Do not use these negative words with another negative.

NONSTANDARD   There isn't no reason to be nervous.

STANDARD   There **is no** reason to be nervous.

STANDARD   There **isn't any** reason to be nervous.

NONSTANDARD   I didn't hear nothing.

STANDARD   I **heard nothing.**

STANDARD   I **didn't hear anything.**

NONSTANDARD   We searched the playground for clues but didn't find none.

STANDARD   We searched the playground for clues but **found none.**

STANDARD   We searched the playground for clues but **didn't find any.**

EXERCISE 5. Revising Sentences by Correcting Errors in Usage.
Rewrite each sentence, correcting its errors in usage. Practice saying *aloud* the correct sentences.

1. They haven't only one more chance to score before the buzzer sounds; the situation looks sort of hopeless.
2. Mother told us we hadn't ought to have played our radio so loudly.
3. I might of gone to the concert if I'd of heard about it earlier.
4. Pam and her sister Stacey look so much alike that you can't hardly tell them apart.
5. My cousins didn't hardly know how to swim, but they wouldn't of missed going to the lake.
6. We told the usher which handed out the programs that we didn't need but two more.
7. Them reference books in the library are kept in some kind of a special section.
8. This here is the car what I told you about.
9. Hadn't you ought to try and help them?
10. I wonder where them fishing poles are at.

USAGE

11. We don't live in that there neighborhood no more.
12. We might of gone on the tour, but we wouldn't of had no camera to take pictures.
13. A foot fault in tennis is when the server steps over the base line before hitting the ball.
14. Since there wasn't scarcely any rain last spring, there are less mosquitoes this summer.
15. When the play was over, the audience seemed sort of subdued.
16. I saw on the news where manufacturers will start putting them air bags into all the new cars.
17. She don't know nothing about football, and she don't like nothing about football.
18. Miss Kim she likes to give those kind of surprise quizzes.
19. Let's try and finish early so we can relax some.
20. Leave us work a while longer on the motor; we can't hardly leave it this way.

USAGE

WRITING APPLICATION
Using Standard English to Make Your Writing Acceptable to the Audience

In writing, you make many choices. You may choose between the word *buy* and the word *purchase*, for example. One of the choices you do *not* have in writing, however, is whether to use standard or nonstandard English. Although nonstandard English might be all right in casual conversation, it is not acceptable in writing except when imitating dialect.

Writing Assignment

Using standard English, write an original sentence with each of the following words or phrases. Underline the word or phrase in your sentence.

1.	can hardly	6.	somewhat
2.	have only	7.	ought not
3.	burst	8.	nowhere
4.	where is	9.	than
5.	respectively	10.	set

CHAPTER 22 REVIEW: POSTTEST

Revising Expressions by Correcting Errors in Usage. In each set of expressions, one expression contains an error in usage. Write the expression correctly, after its number, using standard formal usage.

EXAMPLE 1. (a) Her speech implies that a change is needed. (b) Leave me have some oranges too. (c) This house is somewhat larger than our old one.
1. (b) *Let me have some oranges too.*

1. (a) wasn't no reason (b) words had no effect (c) can hardly wait
2. (a) families immigrated from Europe (b) sail as far as the channel marker (c) made allusions to classical literature
3. (a) being that he was alone (b) The people accepted new ways. (c) the woman who was elected
4. (a) From the newspaper article you may infer his reasons. (b) acts like a child (c) can't hardly hear the music
5. (a) what kind of gloves (b) There is overtime besides the regular work. (c) an historic moment
6. (a) Listen respectfully to the sermon. (b) her head raised from the pillow (c) the chair that you repaired
7. (a) the man for whom you voted (b) the police officer which is on duty (c) the house beside the church
8. (a) those lockers beside the gym (b) Leave him have his own way. (c) Leave the door open when you go.
9. (a) To return, take the same road. (b) Their gifts were the same. (c) Buy this pen and write your lessons with same.
10. (a) Teach your dog this trick. (b) I'm feeling kind of ill. (c) might have been too late
11. (a) the winners of first and second prizes, respectively (b) Take the books off of that shelf. (c) The bag burst, spilling nuts.
12. (a) invented less expensive fuel (b) had ought to try harder (c) raised the heavy timbers
13. (a) This is all the farther he had gone. (b) creating an optical illusion (c) His coaching effected a change.
14. (a) fewer stamps in the collection (b) Bring the tray to the kitchen when you come. (c) He works like he will never tire.
15. (a) saw on TV where the strike ended (b) made no exceptions to his terms (c) proudly accepted the blue ribbon

16. (a) They took all the peaches, besides taking the pears. (b) The seller he said that the car had low mileage. (c) It costs less to drive a small car.

17. (a) Strong rivalry grew among the two athletes. (b) He doesn't want to go. (c) They should have called.

18. (a) After his vacation he looked good. (b) Children can't hardly reach that bookshelf. (c) The rule takes effect soon.

19. (a) Paintings, photographs, drawings, and etc. will be displayed. (b) The blue dress is somewhat more expensive than the black one. (c) "The golden touch" is an allusion to King Midas.

20. (a) a rabbit hiding among the bushes (b) a rose growing beside the cabin door (c) a stack of busted bicycles

21. (a) It could of been worse. (b) Hardly any money was taken. (c) That kind of house suits me.

22. (a) The mayor inferred that he would run for reelection. (b) made fewer mistakes on the final exam (c) Clothes lay on the floor.

23. (a) Let me go with you. (b) The dog is walking like its leg is broken. (c) He might win first place this time.

24. (a) taller than her sister (b) Dough will rise in a warm place. (c) We read where the damage was extensive.

25. (a) Try to be on time. (b) They walked a long way. (c) Them stairs are dangerous and need repairs.

USAGE

Capitalization

STANDARD USES OF CAPITALIZATION

Capital letters are used mainly to individualize what you are writing about. When you capitalize a word, you serve notice to the reader that you are referring to some *particular* person, place, or thing rather than to the general class. Custom determines the use of capital letters, and it is the wisest course to conform to customary or standard usage.

This chapter contains the basic rules for capitalization. In your reading of books, magazines, and newspapers, you may very well find examples of capitalization or cases of a lack of capitalization that do not agree with the rules stated here. This is often a matter of the style of the piece in which the word appears. Fortunately, most writers follow the basic rules that are given here; it is only occasionally that one encounters variations. Therefore, by understanding and learning these rules, and by applying them correctly, you can avoid capitalization errors.

Take the following diagnostic test to see how much you have to review.

DIAGNOSTIC TEST

Correcting Sentences by Using Capitalization Correctly. Number your paper 1–20. Each of the following sentences contains an error in capitalization. After the proper number, write the word or words correctly, supplying capitals where they are needed or omitting capitals where they are unnecessary.

EXAMPLE   1. In the Fall the trees along Main Street are lovely.
            1. *fall*

1. This year my easiest classes are geometry, spanish, and American history.
2. We went to the City of Miami on vacation.
3. They bought a videotape from the Grand Video company.
4. Colorado is located West of the Great Plains.
5. Lansing, Michigan, is in Ingham county.
6. She lives at 321 Maple boulevard, which is south of here.
7. My RCA Stereo is ten years old and still works well.
8. Carla entered her St. Bernard in the Centerville Dog club's show.
9. They live half a block north of Twenty-First Street.
10. Our neighbors are alumni of Drake university in Des Moines, Iowa.
11. Last year my sister Lisa joined the National Audubon society.
12. We are holding a bake sale next Saturday to raise money for the junior Prom.
13. The club members celebrated bastille day by having dinner at a French restaurant.
14. Ms. Davis wrote to the U.S. department of Agriculture for information on soybean cultivation in the Midwest.
15. Mars was the Roman God of war.
16. The Biograph theater is a well-known site in Chicago because John Dillinger, a notorious gangster, was shot there.
17. Sean McShane is planning to take a cruise on the Caribbean sea over spring vacation.
18. Would you like to be the first student to ride in a Space Shuttle that orbits the earth?
19. That novel takes place in the Middle ages and highlights the problems of the feudal system.
20. Erica wants to be Secretary of the Shutterbug Club.

23a. Capitalize the first word in every sentence.

INCORRECT   Roald Amundsen and Robert Scott challenged each other in a race to reach the South Pole, with careful planning Amundsen easily won.

CORRECT   Roald Amundsen and Robert Scott challenged each other in a race to reach the South Pole. With careful planning Amundsen easily won.

INCORRECT After studying reports on new cars, Mother said, "the models with front-wheel drive have improved."

CORRECT   After studying reports on new cars, Mother said, "The models with front-wheel drive have improved."

☞ NOTE   The first word in a line of poetry is often capitalized.

EXAMPLE   Good friend, for Jesus' sake forbear
          To dig the dust enclosed here;
          Blest be the man that spares these stones,
          And curst be he that moves my bones.

                                        WILLIAM SHAKESPEARE

23b. Capitalize the pronoun *I* and the interjection *O*.

INCORRECT The line i translated was "Hear us, o Zeus."

CORRECT   The line **I** translated was "Hear us, **O** Zeus."

The common interjection *oh* (as in *Oh, yes!*) is capitalized only when it appears at the beginning of a sentence.

23c. Capitalize proper nouns and proper adjectives.

A *proper noun* is the name of a particular person, place, or thing. How a proper noun differs from an ordinary, common noun, which is not capitalized, can be seen from the following lists:

COMMON NOUN	PROPER NOUN
county	Wayne County
author	Shirley Jackson
lake	Crater Lake
ocean	Atlantic Ocean

Do not confuse proper nouns, which are *names,* with nouns which merely state kind or type. For instance, *subcompact* is not the name of a particular automobile company (like Ford or General Motors) or of a particular automobile model (like Sentra, Thunderbird, Model T). The word *subcompact* is merely a general name for a type of automobile, one that is smaller than a compact.

INCORRECT   On her birthday, Joy received a Ford Subcompact.

CORRECT   On her birthday, Joy received a Ford subcompact.

INCORRECT   Chris's favorite snack is a box of Sun-Maid Raisins.

CORRECT   Chris's favorite snack is a box of Sun-Maid raisins.

A *proper adjective* is an adjective formed from a proper noun.

PROPER NOUN	PROPER ADJECTIVE
France	French pastry
Arabia	Arabian horses
Scotland	Scottish terrier

Compound adjectives are frequently a source of trouble. In most cases, only the part of a compound adjective that is itself a proper noun or adjective is capitalized.

EXAMPLES   Spanish-speaking Americans, northern-Italian cuisine

Study the list that follows carefully. It classifies the most frequently used kinds of proper nouns and adjectives into seven categories.

(1) Capitalize the names of persons.

GIVEN NAMES   Matthew, Jennifer, Kathryn

SURNAMES   Bowman, Kantor, Cruz, Ryan

In some surnames, more than one letter should be capitalized. This practice varies; to be sure you are right, check a reference source.

EXAMPLES   McEnroe, O'Shea, MacCartney, LeCroy

The abbreviations *Jr.* and *Sr.* (*junior* and *senior*) should always be capitalized when they follow a name.

EXAMPLES   Robert W. Wilson, Jr.   Simon L. Snyder, Sr.

(2) Capitalize geographical names.

Cities and towns: Chicago, Wooster, San Diego
Counties and townships: Orange County, Franklin Township
States: Virginia, Minnesota, Texas
Countries: Italy, United States of America, Brazil

MECHANICS

Continents: Australia, North America, Europe
Islands: South Bass Island, Captiva
Bodies of water: Hudson Bay, Lake Erie, Rio Grande
Mountains: Allegheny Mountains, Mt. Saint Helens, Sierra Madre
Streets: Blair Boulevard, Sunshine State Parkway, Elm Drive, Fifty-first Street
   [In a hyphenated number, the second word begins with a small letter.]
Parks: Stone Mountain Memorial Park, Humboldt Redwood State Park,
   Gettysburg National Military Park
Sections of the country: the South, the Northeast, the Mississippi Delta

---

☞ NOTE Do not capitalize *east, west, north,* and *south* when they merely indicate direction. Do capitalize them when they refer to commonly recognized sections of the country. The modern tendency is to write nouns and adjectives derived from capitalized *East, West, North,* and *South* without capital letters (an *easterner, western boots*).

EXAMPLES We entered on the east ramp and headed north.
          We are looking forward to our vacation in the South.

When an adjective indicating direction is *part of the name* of a recognized region or political unit, capitalize it. When such an adjective merely indicates some portion of a region or political unit, do *not* capitalize it.

EXAMPLES North Dakota, South Korea, southern California, western Missouri

EXERCISE 1. Correcting Phrases by Using Capitalization Correctly.
Write the following phrases, using capital letters wherever they are required. Some phrases do not need capital letters.

EXAMPLE 1. atop granite peak
          1. *atop Granite Peak*

1. zion national park
2. bering sea
3. pro-canadian
4. an irish linen handkerchief
5. at moon lake
6. a house on starve island
7. beside the ohio river
8. in lancaster county
9. the illinois oil fields
10. near baffin bay
11. a southerner
12. french vanilla ice cream
13. texas cowboys
14. forty-fifth street
15. william watson, jr.
16. the west side of the river

17. the north
18. near dundee mountain
19. colombian coffee
20. japanese-american

EXERCISE 2. Correcting Paragraphs by Using Capitalization Correctly. Number your paper according to the numbers of the sentences in the paragraphs. After the proper number, write the words that should be capitalized. Do not write words already capitalized.

EXAMPLES
1. We got lost when Dad turned north on pennington parkway, and we never did find wilshire square.
1. *Pennington Parkway, Wilshire Square*
2. We chose, instead, a restaurant on fifty-second street near kenton boulevard.
2. *Fifty-second Street, Kenton Boulevard*

1. Our choir in lawrenceburg, tennessee, decided to have an international fair to raise money for a bus trip to washington, d.c.
2. Colleen O'Roark said that the fair would feature crafts and food from many european and asian countries.
3. Juana Santiago said we should include countries of central and south america, since she is particularly familiar with venezuelan cooking.
4. Julian, who recently returned from a trip to italy, planned a display of venetian glass.
5. Karen suggested that we include items from quebec, our french-speaking neighbor to the north.
6. Erin McCall, whose family moved to lexington avenue from phoenix, arizona, decided to bring rock samples from the petrified forest.
7. Since Maxine was born in tokyo, she offered to demonstrate japanese paper folding.
8. Some of us met at Paula's house at the corner of columbus street and hickory lane in the east end of town to choose the items to represent the united states.
9. We chose american indian artifacts from the southwest, country crafts from the appalachian mountains, and shell gifts from the southern states along the gulf of mexico.
10. When the fair is over, I hope we will have raised enough money to include a special tour of mammoth cave national park in kentucky in our bus trip to the nation's capital.

(3) Capitalize the names of organizations, business firms, institutions, and government bodies.

Organizations and clubs: Longboat Key Club, Kiwanis Club, National Organization for Women, National Honor Society

☞ NOTE   Do not capitalize such words as *democratic, republican,* and *socialist* when these words refer only to types of societies rather than to specific parties. The word *party* in the name of a political party may be capitalized or not; either way is correct: *Republican party, Republican Party.*

EXAMPLES   Although Marie worked for the **D**emocratic party in college, she has now become **R**epublican.
Many foreign students are amazed by the **d**emocratic process.
Allen read a **s**ocialist newspaper for his history report.

Business firms: **E**astern **A**irlines, **X**erox **C**orporation, **I**nternational **B**usiness **M**achines, **N**ational **B**roadcasting **C**ompany, **M**otorola, **I**nc.
Institutions and buildings: **S**tanford **U**niversity, **S**ears **T**ower, **G**ood **S**amaritan **H**ospital, **F**ox **T**heater, **B**oone **H**igh **S**chool, **W**aldorf **A**storia **H**otel

☞ NOTE   Do not capitalize such words as *hotel, theater, college, high school* unless they are part of a proper name.

EXAMPLES   a **h**otel in New Orleans   the **R**oosevelt **H**otel
a **c**ollege in Ohio   **M**arietta **C**ollege
a **t**heater in San Francisco   **C**urran **T**heater
a **h**igh school in Virginia   **B**ayside **H**igh **S**chool

Government bodies: the **S**enate, **P**arliament, the **N**uclear **R**egulatory **C**ommission, **C**ongress

(4) Capitalize the names of historical events and periods, special events, and calendar items.

Historical events and periods: the **R**evolutionary **W**ar, the **I**ndustrial **R**evolution, the **Y**alta **C**onference, the **D**ark **A**ges, the **B**attle of **G**ettysburg
Special events: the **O**lympics, **B**oston **M**arathon, the **S**uper **B**owl, **I**naugural **B**all, the **S**enior **P**rom
Calendar items: **F**riday, **C**hristmas, **M**arch, **S**t. **V**alentine's **D**ay, **C**hanukah

☞ NOTE   Do not capitalize the names of the seasons: summer, winter, spring, fall.

MECHANICS

(5) Capitalize the names of nationalities, races, and religions.

EXAMPLES   Jewish, Italian, Lutheran, Presbyterian, Canadian, Indian

(6) Capitalize the brand names of business products.

EXAMPLES   Häagen-Dazs ice cream, Ritz crackers, a Nikon camera

> ☞ NOTE Do not capitalize the nouns that often follow a brand name.

EXAMPLES   Luden's cough drops, Sharp microwave oven, Timex watch, Apple computer

(7) Capitalize the names of ships, planes, trains, monuments, awards, heavenly bodies, and any other particular places, things, or events.

EXAMPLES   the *Titanic* (a ship), the *Enterprise* (a fictional spaceship), the Lincoln Memorial (a monument), the Congressional Medal of Honor (a medal), the Pulitzer Prize (an award), the *Orient Express* (a train), Saturn (a planet)

> ☞ NOTE The names of planets, constellations, asteroids, stars, and groups of stars are capitalized. However, do not capitalize *sun, moon,* or *earth* unless they are used in conjunction with other heavenly bodies that are capitalized.

23d. Do *not* capitalize the names of school subjects, except names of languages and course names followed by a number.

EXAMPLES   English, Latin, German, geography, mathematics, history, music, Mathematics II, Chemistry I

> ☞ NOTE Do not capitalize *senior, junior, sophomore,* and *freshman* unless these words are part of a proper noun or are used to designate a *specific* organization.

EXAMPLES   Only juniors and seniors attended the Junior Prom.
The Sophomore Class held a party for the freshmen.

MECHANICS

EXERCISE 3. Correcting Sentences by Using Capitalization Correctly. After the proper number, write the words that should be capitalized. Do not write words already capitalized.

EXAMPLE 1. The united states abounds in exciting vacation spots, from the coast of maine to the pacific shoreline.
1. *United States, Maine, Pacific*

1. The state of florida, one of the most popular vacation areas in the United States, has thousands of kilometers of coastline. The state is bounded by the atlantic ocean, the gulf of mexico, and the straits of florida.
2. Whether you travel on a daily nonstop flight aboard a delta airlines jet, on a cruise ship such as the *queen elizabeth 2,* or on a train such as the *silver bullet,* the florida bureau of visitor services will be delighted to welcome you.
3. Central florida abounds in lakes, with lake okeechobee being the largest.
4. In florida history, an important role belongs to osceola, a powerful leader of the seminole indians who guided his people through a long and costly war from 1835 to 1837. An important battle of the war occurred in the everglades, a huge wilderness region.
5. The everglades national park, which includes big cypress swamp, is today a major tourist attraction. Beautiful beaches, such as those at daytona, miami, and fort lauderdale, also draw large crowds of visitors.
6. The second-largest city in the state is miami, the seat of dade county and one of the most famous resort areas in the eastern united states. Miami beach is on an island between biscayne bay and the atlantic and is connected to the city of miami by four causeways.
7. Visitors to miami may be interested in biscayne boulevard, the route to miami beach, or they may be interested in the orange bowl, the home of the city's football team.
8. Thousands of students each year attend the university of florida, located in gainesville. The university offers degrees in engineering, french, english, and many other fields.
9. Many space flights, including some to the moon, have been launched from cape canaveral, the site of the john f. kennedy space center.

MECHANICS

10. Florida has one of the fastest-growing populations in the country. Many retired persons have settled in the state, particularly in the area near st. petersburg.

REVIEW EXERCISE. Correcting Paragraphs by Using Capitalization Correctly. As you did in Exercise 2, write all words requiring capitals in the following sentences. Do not list words that are already capitalized.

EXAMPLE 1. Even though I enjoy trivia games, I need to learn more about american inventors, the korean war, and the history of the united states.
1. *American*
Korean War
United States

1. Last saturday night, may 18, marks the momentous occasion when my brother Ted and I won our first trivia match against our parents. 2. This semester Ted is studying history, political science, and french, while I am taking world literature I and geography II. 3. We surged into the lead when our parents couldn't remember that the first u.s. satellite, *explorer I*, followed the u.s.s.r.'s *sputnik I* into space. 4. From geography class I remembered that mount mckinley and death valley are the highest and lowest points on the north american continent.

5. Our parents rallied for the lead by knowing that the name of the boy on the cracker jack box is jack and that his dog is bingo. 6. Then Ted knew that the steel framework of the statue of liberty was designed by frenchman alexandre gustave eiffel, who also designed the eiffel tower in paris. 7. None of us knew that john wilkes booth was only twenty-six years old when he shot president lincoln at ford's theatre on good friday in 1865. 8. Because Mom has always been a staunch democrat, she knew that *engine 1401*—the southern railways locomotive that carried franklin d. roosevelt's body from warm springs, georgia, to washington, d.c.—can now be seen in the smithsonian institution.

9. Ted and I lost some points because I didn't know that kleenex tissues were first used as gas mask filters during world war I. 10. However, Ted won the game for us because he knew that the white house was originally called the executive mansion before it was painted white to cover the damage inflicted by the british during the war of 1812.

23e. Capitalize titles.

(1) Capitalize the title of a person when it comes before a name.

EXAMPLES   General MacArthur, Dr. Quigley, President Kennedy

(2) Capitalize a title used alone or following a person's name only if it refers to a high official or someone to whom you wish to show special respect.

EXAMPLES   The President spent the weekend at Camp David. [When it refers to the highest official of the United States, *President* is capitalized.]

Earl Warren, Chief Justice of the United States from 1953 to 1969, may be best remembered for his work on the Warren Report. [The office of Chief Justice is a high one.]

Alice was elected president of the organization.
Talk to the guidance counselor about your test scores.
Ms. Larsen was promoted to manager of the department.

☞ NOTE   When an official is directly addressed by title, it is customary to capitalize the title.

EXAMPLES   Mr. Mayor, will you please test the microphone?
Do you intend, Governor, to visit the disaster area?

(3) Capitalize words showing family relationship when used with a person's name but *not* when preceded by a possessive.

EXAMPLES   Aunt Edith, Uncle Fred, my brother Bob, Grandmother Bechtel

☞ NOTE   When family-relationship words like *uncle, cousin,* and *grandmother* are customarily used before a name, capitalize them even after a possessive noun or pronoun.

EXAMPLES   My Grandmother Nilsson was born in Sweden.
Did you take swimming lessons from your Uncle Wayne? [You customarily call these persons *Grandmother Nilsson* and *Uncle Wayne.*]
My sister Jeri takes riding lessons. [You do not customarily call her *Sister Jeri.*]

MECHANICS

☞ NOTE   Words of family relationship may be capitalized or not when used *in place of* a person's name.

EXAMPLE   "Hello, Father" *or* "Hello, father." [*Father* is used in place of the man's name.]

(4) Capitalize the first and last word and all important words in titles of books, periodicals, poems, stories, movies, television series, paintings, and other works of art.

Unimportant words in a title are *a, an,* and *the,* prepositions (of fewer than five letters long), and coordinating conjunctions.

EXAMPLES   *Harper's Bazaar* (magazine), Turner's *Crossing the Brook* (painting), *Pride and Prejudice* (novel), Treaty of Versailles, the Charter of the United Nations, the *Talmud,* "Under the Lion's Paw" (short story), "The Tuft of Flowers" (poem)

The words *a, an,* and *the* written before a title are capitalized only when they are part of the title. In a composition they are usually not capitalized before the names of magazines and newspapers.

EXAMPLES   *The Outsiders* (book), *A Day in the Life of President Kennedy* (book)
Joan buys the *Atlantic Monthly* (magazine) and the *Rocky Mountain News* (newspaper).

(5) Capitalize the word *God* except when it refers to the gods of ancient mythology.

☞ NOTE   Other words referring to God are usually capitalized as well.

EXAMPLES   Father   Lord God   His will

EXERCISE 4. Correcting Sentences by Using Capitalization Correctly.

Write all words requiring capitals after the proper number. Do not list words already capitalized.

MECHANICS

EXAMPLE 1. The names of norse and roman gods always stump me when I do
the sunday paper's crossword puzzle.
1. *Norse, Roman, Sunday*

1. One of georgia o'keeffe's finest paintings, *cow's skull, red, white and blue,* hung in the hirshhorn museum in washington, d.c.
2. In *people* magazine, Kim read details of bill cosby's television series *the cosby show.*
3. Did you recite robert frost's poem "fire and ice" to grandma Stone when you visited her at Sparrow Hospital?
4. In 1908 mary baker eddy founded the *christian science monitor.*
5. My cousin Judy's favorite statue is the *indian hunter* by manship.
6. I enjoyed reading annie dillard's *pilgrim at tinker creek,* particularly the chapter "the horns of the altar."
7. For a time, general alexander haig served as deputy to henry kissinger on the National Security council.
8. The president addressed the american people in a television news broadcast after he had met with the president of France.
9. mayor johnson and the county commissioners came to the groundbreaking ceremony.
10. Jane White, president of our latin club, showed us a print of the movie *julius caesar.*

WRITING APPLICATION:
Using Capitalization to Make
Your Writing Easier to Understand

By using a capital letter, you can signal the beginning of a sentence or the particular name of a person, place, or thing. Notice that the second group of sentences is easier to understand than the first.

i saw stuart yesterday. he told me he had bought an olds cutlass.
I saw Stuart yesterday. He told me he had bought an Olds Cutlass.

Writing Assignment

Write a paragraph giving information about a particular historical society, located in a specific town and state, that is directed by a person who is planning a parade for a national holiday. Capitalize where necessary and proofread.

MECHANICS

CHAPTER 23 REVIEW: POSTTEST

Correcting Sentences by Using Capitalization Correctly. Number your list according to the numbers of the sentences. Next to the proper number, write the words that should be capitalized.

EXAMPLE 1. Renée searched every store in concord, new hampshire, until she found a gift at j. c. penney for her grandparents.
1. *Concord, New Hampshire, J. C. Penney*

1. Katy and Heather study ballet at the academy of dance on mills avenue.
2. "One in a million" is the title song of her new album, which was recorded at carnegie hall in new york city.
3. Both ernest hemingway and walt disney once worked for the *kansas city star.*
4. Every thanksgiving before we sit down to dinner, grandma penny sings "the battle hymn of the republic," which was written by julia ward howe.
5. The winner of the first kentucky derby, the annual race at churchill downs in louisville, was a horse named aristides.
6. The movie *gone with the wind* premiered at the loew's grand theater in atlanta, georgia, on december 15, 1939.
7. I cannot name five of the signers of the declaration of independence, but I do know that the document was first signed at independence hall in philadelphia.
8. Charles lindbergh made the first solo flight across the atlantic ocean in his plane *the spirit of st. louis* in 1927.
9. The mystery of amelia earhart's disappearance between new guinea and howland island on her round-the-world flight has never been solved.
10. *The harvesters* is a painting by pieter brueghel, a sixteenth-century artist.
11. One of the cities of the incas, machu picchu, lay hidden among the peaks of the andes in peru and was never discovered by the spanish conquerors.
12. The nobel prize was established by alfred nobel, the swedish inventor of dynamite.

MECHANICS

13. My aunt elsie, who lives in salt lake city, showed us pioneer trails state park and the mormon temple in temple square.
14. Some historians trace the origin of valentine's day to an ancient roman festival; others believe it is connected with one or more saints of the early christian church.
15. I have seen the white mountains, which are in the northeastern corner of new hampshire, but I have not seen the green mountains in central vermont.
16. We crossed the connecticut river, which divides vermont and new hampshire.
17. Virginia's house of burgesses was the first representative legislature in america.
18. If Beth passes english and history II, she intends to ask her parents if they will let her apply for a job at the 7-eleven store on twenty-third street.
19. Our debate team argued in favor of pro-american economic policies as the best way to foster democracy in the socialist countries of africa and south america.
20. While Shirley Chisholm served in the u.s. house of representatives, she fought for help for the nation's poor and also for an end to the vietnam war.

SUMMARY STYLE REVIEW

Names of Persons

Mrs. Andrew D. McCall, Jr.	a family friend
Sean O'Farrell	the boy next door
Mr. Hank McNalley	a guidance counselor

Geographical Names

Kansas City	a city in Missouri
Canyonlands National Park	a national park in Utah
Great Smoky Mountains	mountains in Tennessee
Arctic Ocean	a voyage on the ocean
Monongahela River	river in Pennsylvania
a vacation in the South	the south side of town
Baltic Sea	the sea north of Poland
Marblehead Peninsula	a peninsula in Lake Erie

Organizations, Business Firms and Products, Institutions, Government Bodies

Eastman Kodak Company	a film company
Cavalier Hotel	a restored hotel
Chrysler	an automobile
Litchfield High School	a small high school
National Association of Home Builders	a national organization
the Supreme Court	a court of law

Historical Events and Periods, Special Events, Calendar Items

World War I	a war in Europe
the Ice Age	a prehistoric age
the Chicago World's Fair	a fair in our city
Groundhog Day	a day in February

Nationalities, Races, Religions, Languages

German	a nationality
Caucasian	a race
Hinduism	a religion
Spanish	a language

Ships, Planes, Trains, Monuments, Awards, Heavenly Bodies, and Particular Places, Things, or Events

the *Mary Deere*	a famous ship
the Nobel Prize	an award
the *Silver Streak*	a train in a movie
Saturn's rings	a full moon
the Lincoln Memorial	a memorial in Washington, D.C.
Discovery	a space shuttle

Titles

Mayor Taylor	Ms. Taylor, the mayor
the President, the Prime Minister (high government officials)	the president of the club, the senator's duties
Praise God for His blessings	the gods of the ancient Greeks
Uncle Jim	her uncle
Last of the Mohicans	a novel
"The City in the Sea"	a poem
"America the Beautiful"	a song

MECHANICS

Punctuation

END MARKS AND COMMAS

The main purpose of punctuation is to make the meaning of what you write clear. When you speak, a number of factors—the sound of your voice, the rise and fall of your inflections, your pauses and hesitations, your gestures and expressions—do this for you by supplying a kind of verbal punctuation.

When you write, however, you do not have these hints to rely on, so you use punctuation to group your words and make their meaning clear. If you heard the following sentences spoken, you might know exactly what was meant; but as they stand, with no punctuation to show where one thought ends and another begins, they are confusing.

> For breakfast Jim ordered bacon and eggs and Jill asked for half a grapefruit and whole-wheat toast.

> The marathon course ran along the beach across the highway through the tunnel and into the stadium.

Don't overpunctuate. Use a mark of punctuation for only two reasons: (1) because the meaning demands it or (2) because conventional usage requires it.

DIAGNOSTIC TEST

Correcting Sentences by Using End Marks and Commas Correctly. Rewrite the following sentences, inserting end marks and commas as needed.

EXAMPLE   1. Well what do you want me to say
           1. *Well, what do you want me to say?*

1. Although scholars are not certain of the first European printer to use movable type Johann Gutenberg is usually credited
2. The students who have signed up for the field trip may leave at noon but all others must attend classes
3. Gloria did you see where I left my bowling ball
4. Willa Cather who was born in Virginia but moved to Nebraska at the age of eight wrote most of her stories about people living on the western plains
5. The Great Pyramid of Cheops in Egypt dates back to 2680 BC
6. Vendors sold T-shirts buttons caps and pennants to the sports fans outside the stadium
7. Standing in the pouring rain I waited over an hour for you
8. We munched on unsalted roasted sunflower seeds and quenched our thirst with cold refreshing spring water
9. Their address is I think 1042 Cleveland Avenue Enid Oklahoma 73703
10. My cousin a mail carrier does not like jokes about postal workers
11. Rita did not call me this morning nor did she call in the afternoon
12. We rushed to the airport stood in line bought our tickets and then heard that the flight would be delayed for three hours
13. Norm has had an incredible run of bad luck yet he still says that tomorrow will be a better day for he prides himself on being an optimist
14. The Ming vase wrapped carefully in cotton and packed in a crate was delivered to the museum today
15. Of course if we arrive late for practice one more time Ms. Stubbs will kick us off the team
16. Thank goodness my sister had taught me how to swim for I could have drowned when the boat tipped over
17. On the sidelines near the home fans the coach watched the downcast discouraged team trudge off the field
18. The advertisement for toothpaste was in my opinion clearly misleading
19. In 1883 Jan Matzeliger an inventor in Lynn Massachusetts revolutionized the shoe industry with his machine that mechanically joined the top of the shoe to the sole

MECHANICS

20. The following people should report to the auditorium after lunch hour: Bob Wilcox Amalia Gibson Phil Assad and Cora Mall

The rules for the correct use of end punctuation and commas are listed on the following pages. Study the rules; do the exercises; and above all, apply what you learn about punctuation to everything you write.

PERIODS, QUESTION MARKS, AND EXCLAMATION POINTS

24a. A statement is followed by a period.

EXAMPLES   Margaret Walker has written many beautiful poems.
"I'm going to stay after school," said Barb.
Underneath the waterfall floated an ivory swan.

24b. A question is followed by a question mark.

EXAMPLES   What do you want for lunch?
Who bought the pizza?
When are you leaving?

Sometimes the way in which a writer intends a sentence to be read determines whether it is a statement or a question.

STATEMENT   You're angry with me. [Read with falling inflection.]

QUESTION   You're angry with me? [Read with rising inflection.]

Be sure to distinguish between a declarative sentence that contains an indirect question and an interrogative sentence, which asks a direct question.

INDIRECT QUESTION   She asked me **why I left so early.** [declarative]

DIRECT QUESTION   When is the party? [interrogative]

24c. An exclamation is followed by an exclamation point.

EXAMPLES   Great shot!
I'm freezing!
Fantastic!

24d. An imperative sentence is followed by either a period or an exclamation point.

EXAMPLES   Open the door for me, please. [calmly]
Open the door! [with strong feeling]

EXERCISE 1. Correcting Sentences by Using End Marks.   In this exercise all end marks have been omitted. On your paper, write the final word of each sentence with the proper end mark, followed by the first word of the next sentence, if any.

EXAMPLE   1. Miriam Colón, a native of Puerto Rico, is an accomplished actress using her own experience, she wished to acquaint Americans with the art and culture of Puerto Rico to that end, she founded and directed the Puerto Rican Traveling Theatre
1. *actress. Using*
Puerto Rico. To
Theatre.

1. Gail was assigned a report on knighthood, and she undertook the assignment eagerly she knew from the stories she had read that knights were spotless champions of God and humanity she knew also that a long apprenticeship preceded the honor of knighthood and that young boys of the nobility started this training as soon as they were able to wield a sword or draw a bow

2. When a lad completed his training as a page, he was promoted to the rank of squire in this capacity he accompanied his lord into battle, fighting at his side and caring for the knight's horse and equipment at long last the squire himself was deemed fit to become a knight he was accorded this honor, however, only after several honorable wounds and some show of gallantry on his part had impressed the sovereign with the lad's readiness to uphold the code of chivalry

3. When the sovereign considered him ready, a day was appointed for the ceremony how long had the youth waited for this glorious hour how many times had he rehearsed in his fancy every step in the stately ceremony now that it was at last at hand, he could scarcely believe his good fortune he resolved to conduct himself always as a perfect knight—to bear true and faithful allegiance to his lord, to bow his head meekly before misfortune, to help the weak, to punish the wicked, and to answer any insult to his honor with terrible, swift power

MECHANICS

4. The chivalry of Europe arose from a simple economic circumstance the first chevaliers were those rich enough to afford horses *chevalier* in French and *Ritter* in German mean "knight," but these words also mean "rider" this fact suggests that the first knights were merely those Frankish warriors who rode into battle while their humbler fellows walked behind in the dust

5. When the cavalry of Charlemagne became the foremost military force in Europe, his way of ordering the forces was adopted by all other nations the class of soldiers comprising the calvary became, therefore, an elite class or an aristocracy with special privileges but also with special obligations they were supported in peacetime, for example, by the labor of the rest of the population however, when the state was in danger, they were obliged to rally immediately underneath the royal standard

24e. An abbreviation is usually followed by a period.

EXAMPLES   Maj.   Major
               Minn.   Minnesota
               A.D.   *anno Domini*
               Jan.   January
               lb.   pound
               O. J. Simpson   Orenthal James Simpson

> ☞ NOTE Abbreviations of government agencies, service organizations, and other groups are often written without periods.

NASA National Aeronautics and Space Administration
HUD Department of Housing and Urban Development
NCTE National Council of Teachers of English
AMA American Medical Association

Abbreviations in the metric system are often written without periods, especially in science books.

km   kilometer
ml   milliliter

Most abbreviations are capitalized only if the words they stand for are capitalized.

MECHANICS

WRITING APPLICATION A:
Using Periods, Question Marks, and
Exclamation Points Correctly in Your Writing

When you use periods, question marks, and exclamation points correctly in your writing, you make your purpose clear to your readers. As you read the following sentences, notice that the end punctuation makes the purpose of each clear.

You want me to leave the theater. [sentence making a statement]
Please leave the theater. [sentence making a request]
Do you want me to leave the theater? [sentence asking a question]
You want me to leave the theater? [sentence intended as a question]
Leave the theater! [sentence expressing strong feeling]

You should take care to use correct end punctuation. Refer to the rules on pages 566–67 whenever you are in doubt.

Writing Assignment

Write five sentences according to the following guidelines. Use correct punctuation.

1. Write an imperative sentence that expresses a mild emotion.
2. Write an imperative sentence that expresses a strong emotion.
3. Write a sentence that is intended as a question.
4. Write a sentence that asks a direct question.
5. Write an exclamatory sentence that begins with an interjection that expresses a strong emotion.

COMMAS

Commas are necessary for clear expression of ideas.

Items in a Series

24f. Use commas to separate items in a series.

WORDS IN SERIES   The counselor distributed baseballs, bats, volleyballs, tennis rackets, and bandages to the campers. [nouns]
The dog growled, snarled, and leaped at the intruder. [verbs]

MECHANICS

PHRASES IN SERIES   We have a government of the people, by the people, and for the people.

SUBORDINATE CLAUSES IN SERIES   I know I will pass the test if I take good notes, if I study hard, and if I get a good night's sleep.

> ☞ NOTE   When the last two items in a series are joined by *and,* you may omit the comma before the *and* if the comma is not necessary to make the meaning clear.

CLEAR   The entertainers sang, danced and juggled. [clear with comma omitted]

UNCLEAR   John, Sue and Mary went fishing. [Not clear with comma omitted. Is John part of the series, or is he being addressed?]

CLEAR   John, Sue, and Mary went fishing.

Some words appear so often paired with another that they may be set off in a series as one item.

EXAMPLES   peanut butter and jelly, bacon and eggs, pen and paper

(1) If all items in a series are joined by *and* or *or* (*nor*), you should not use commas to separate them.

EXAMPLES   We ran and walked and even limped to the finish line.
A volunteer addresses envelopes or answers phones or files correspondence.

(2) Independent clauses in a series are usually separated by semicolons. Short independent clauses, however, may be separated by commas.

EXAMPLES   For physical fitness we swam twenty-five laps in the pool; we jogged four miles around the lake; and we exercised with workout equipment in Pam's basement.
For physical fitness we swam, we jogged, and we exercised. [short clauses]

24g. Use a comma to separate two or more adjectives preceding a noun.

EXAMPLE   The accident was a frightening, horrible sight.

When the last adjective before the noun is thought of as part of the noun, the comma before the adjective is omitted.

EXAMPLE   The new elementary school will be completed in 1990.

Here the adjective *elementary* is so closely associated with the word *school* that the two words are considered a unit. The adjective *new* modifies not just *school,* but *elementary school.*

To determine whether it is right to put commas between two adjectives in a series of adjectives modifying a noun, substitute the word *and* for the doubtful comma. If the *and* sounds wrong, then you don't need a comma.

PROBLEM   I cautiously raised my broken right hand in response. [comma before *right*?]

USE *AND*   I cautiously raised my broken and right hand in response. [obviously wrong!]

SOLUTION   I cautiously raised my broken right hand in response. [no comma]

EXERCISE 2. Correcting Sentences by Using Commas.   Number your paper 1–10. Write each word after which a comma is needed and then add the comma. Some sentences will not need commas. If a sentence is correct without commas, write *no commas needed.*

EXAMPLE   1. The singer wore a red vest blue shoes and white jeans.
          1. *vest, shoes,*

1. My new alarm clock didn't go off my breakfast was cold and the school bus had a flat tire.
2. The river overflowed again and filled our basement and our neighbors' basements.
3. Alligators sharks and snakes are dangerous annoying nuisances in Florida.
4. I took a flashlight sleeping bag extra tennis shoes pocket knife and rain parka on our camping trip.
5. James Garfield Harry Truman and Gerald Ford were left-handed U.S. Presidents.
6. At the gymnastics meet Les performed on the parallel bars the rings and the high bar.
7. A little blond child in faded blue jeans emerged from the shrubbery to stare at the mail carrier.

MECHANICS

8. Catherine of Aragon, Anne Boleyn, Jane Seymour, Anne of Cleves, Catherine Howard, and Catherine Parr were wives of Henry VIII.
9. Sylvia admires the great women novelists: Jane Austen, the Brontë sisters, Virginia Woolf, Willa Cather, Elizabeth Bowen, George Eliot, and many others.
10. With a quick, powerful leap to the ground, the stuntman bounded over the burning balcony.

Commas Between Independent Clauses

24h. Use a comma before *and, but, or, nor, for, so,* **and** *yet* **when they join independent clauses.**

EXAMPLES   Patrick brought the hot dogs and buns, and Cindy brought the potato salad.
              We were there on time, but Jeff and Maria arrived late.

> ☞ .NOTE   Independent clauses joined by *and, but, or,* or *nor* need not be separated by a comma when they are very short. If the clauses are joined by the conjunctions *yet, so,* or *for,* they must be separated by a comma.

EXAMPLES   The poodle tensed and the German shepherd growled. [Clauses are too short to require commas.]
              We sprayed with insecticide, yet the bugs still found us. [Clauses are short but are separated by the conjunction *yet.* Therefore, a comma is required.]

SIMPLE SENTENCE   Bob brought charcoal and lighter fluid but forgot matches. [one independent clause with a compound verb]

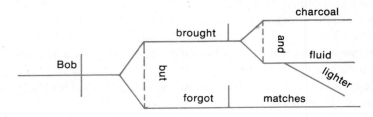

MECHANICS

TWO CLAUSES   Bob brought charcoal and lighter fluid, but he forgot matches.
[two independent clauses]

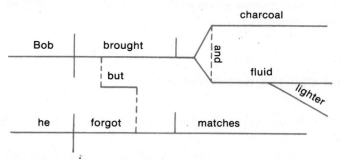

EXERCISE 3. Correcting Compound Sentences by Using Commas. The sentences in this exercise contain independent clauses joined by the conjunctions *and, but, or, for, nor,* or *yet.* After the sentence number, write the word preceding each needed comma. Add the comma and the conjunction following it. If a sentence is correct without commas, write *no commas needed* after the proper number.

EXAMPLE   1. Uncle Phil carefully maneuvered the boat through the narrow
channel and Lynn began baiting the hooks.
1. *channel, and*

1. All students must arrive on time for no one will be admitted late.
2. The newspaper review complimented every performance in the movie but the leading actress received the strongest praise.
3. A few spectators tried to climb over the fence but the police ordered them back.
4. Environmentalists who try to prevent the destruction of valuable land and water areas must stay alert or their efforts may be frustrated by their opponents.
5. In general, people today work fewer hours than their grandparents did yet for some the difference is not great.
6. The cost of living is rising for consumers must pay higher prices for gasoline and other products.
7. Our guide led and we followed closely.
8. Although the manager had signaled for a bunt, Patricia hit a home run and later the manager said nothing about disobeying instructions.

9. She said she did not like the story in the science fiction magazine nor did she enjoy the illustrations.
10. High-school graduates may go on to college or they may prefer to begin a career immediately.

Nonessential Clauses and Phrases

24i. Use commas to set off nonessential clauses and nonessential participial phrases.

A nonessential[1] clause is a subordinate clause that is not essential to the meaning of the sentence. Such clauses serve only to add some extra information or to explain something further; they could be omitted without altering the fundamental meaning of the sentence. An essential[2] clause, on the other hand, is one that cannot be omitted without changing the meaning of the sentence.

NONESSENTIAL Peter Lincoln, who works with my father, bought a new Corvette yesterday.

Since you know without the clause who it was that bought a new Corvette yesterday, the clause is not necessary to identify Peter Lincoln; it merely adds information about him. It is a nonessential clause and should be set off by commas. *Most adjective clauses that modify proper nouns are nonessential and require commas.*

ESSENTIAL All books **that are damaged** go in these boxes.

The clause *that are damaged* is essential because it tells which books go in these boxes. Omitting the clause would change the meaning of the sentence into something absurd. Since the clause is an integral, or essential, part of the sentence, it is not set off by commas. (Adjective clauses introduced by *that* are almost always essential.)

EXAMPLES The friend **whom I invited to the beach** could not come. [essential]
Kelly, whom I invited to the beach, could not come. [nonessential]
The U.S. President **who enjoyed turkey hash on waffles for breakfast** was Andrew Jackson. [essential]
Andrew Jackson, who was a U.S. President, enjoyed turkey hash on waffles for breakfast. [nonessential]

[1] A nonessential clause is sometimes called a nonrestrictive clause.
[2] An essential clause is sometimes called a restrictive clause.

The meal **that I like best** is spaghetti. [essential]
Spaghetti, which I like best, is our meal tonight. [nonessential]

At times the writer of a sentence is the only one who knows whether a clause is nonessential (commas) or essential (no commas). To make the meaning clear, the writer will either use commas to enclose the clause or abstain from their use.

NONESSENTIAL   My sister, who attends Duke University, sent me a college sweatshirt. [The clause is not needed to identify this sister. Since it is nonessential, it requires commas.]

ESSENTIAL   My sister **who attends Duke University** sent me a college sweatshirt. [I have more than one sister. The clause is necessary to tell which sister I am talking about. It should not be set off by commas.]

The same principles govern participial phrases. Recall the two kinds of participles: present participles ending in -*ing* and past participles usually ending in -*ed*. A participial phrase is a group of words in which a participle is the chief word. When such a phrase is nonessential—not necessary to the sentence—the phrase is set off by commas. When it is essential, no commas are used.

NONESSENTIAL   Esther, running at a slow, leisurely pace, easily finished the marathon.

ESSENTIAL   The woman **running at a slow, leisurely pace** easily finished the marathon.

NONESSENTIAL   Vicky's silk-screen, wrapped carefully inside a cardboard box, arrived today.

ESSENTIAL   The silk-screen **wrapped carefully inside a cardboard box** was not damaged.

EXERCISE 4. Correcting Sentences by Using Commas.

Number your paper 1–10. After the proper number, write all words in the sentence that should be followed by a comma, inserting the comma after each. Be prepared to explain your answers. If a sentence does not require commas, write *no commas needed* after its number.

EXAMPLE   1. The idea for supermarkets which we take for granted today developed in the nineteenth century.
    1. *supermarkets, today,*

MECHANICS

1. The stores which became the world's first supermarkets were designed by Clarence Saunders.
2. Mr. Saunders who lived in Memphis, Tennessee named his stores Piggly Wiggly.
3. He got the idea for the name when he saw a fat pig wiggling under a fence.
4. The Piggly Wiggly store that Saunders developed had only one long aisle.
5. Customers who were shopping there saw all the products before they came to the exit.
6. Albert Gerrard who noticed that people had difficulty finding products opened his own grocery store.
7. All items that were for sale were arranged alphabetically.
8. The name that Gerrard selected for his store was Alpha-Beta.
9. George Hartford who founded the Great Atlantic & Pacific Tea Company in 1859 nicknamed his stores A & P.
10. The model for today's huge supermarket complexes which was developed by Michael Cullen opened in an abandoned garage in Queens, New York, on August 30, 1930.

Introductory Elements

24j. Use a comma after certain introductory elements.

(1) Use a comma after words such as *well, yes, no,* and *why* when they begin a sentence. Exclamations like *wow, good grief,* and *gee whiz,* if not followed by an exclamation point, must also be set off by commas.

EXAMPLES **No,** I haven't taken the exam yet.
Why, I thought you left yesterday!
Wow, look at those wheels!

(2) Use a comma after an introductory participial phrase.

EXAMPLES **Calling for a timeout,** the referee began waving her arms.
Exhausted after three hours of continuous swimming, Diana emerged from the water.

(3) Use a comma after a succession of introductory prepositional phrases.

EXAMPLES **By the light of the silvery moon in autumn,** we went on an old-fashioned hayride. [Three prepositional phrases precede the comma.]

A single introductory prepositional phrase does not usually require a comma unless the comma is necessary to make the meaning of the sentence clear.

EXAMPLES **By noon** we had hiked four miles.
In our bank, checks are sorted automatically. [The comma is needed so that the reader does not read "our bank checks."]

(4) Use a comma after an introductory adverb clause.

An introductory adverb clause is a subordinate clause preceding an independent clause.

EXAMPLES **When you have gone to this school as long as we have,** you will know your way around.
The first game of the season is Friday; **after we claim our first victory,** we'll celebrate at Darcy's Pizza Parlor.
If you enter the lot from the west, you can usually find several empty parking spaces.

EXERCISE 5. Correcting Sentences by Using Commas. If a sentence requires a comma after an introductory clause or phrase, copy the word before the comma and add the comma. If a sentence does not require a comma, write *no commas needed* after the proper number.

EXAMPLE 1. During the morning classes will be shortened by ten minutes.
1. *morning,*

1. For many people in the world meat is not a daily food staple.
2. Serving as a primary source of nutrition whole grains such as corn, barley, oats, wheat, and rice feed millions.
3. In Mexico a favorite nutritious meal is a corn tortilla combined with beans.
4. Because it has been a principal crop for over 5,000 years the soybean, which is high in protein, is extensively used by people in Asian countries.
5. As an economic measure you may want to substitute unrefined whole grains for meat occasionally in your diet.

MECHANICS

6. As very healthy alternatives to meat whole grains contain nutrients such as vitamins, amino acids, proteins, and starches.
7. In order to make a spoilage-resistant product food manufacturers refine whole grains.
8. Refined for commercial use the grains lose most of their food value because the nutritious outer hulls are stripped away.
9. If you take time in the supermarket you should be able to find whole grains.
10. Since many cookbooks now include recipes for grains you can learn to prepare a variety of interesting snacks and meals.

REVIEW EXERCISE A. Correcting Sentences by Using Commas.
This exercise covers all uses of the comma that you have studied so far. Number your paper 1–10. In each sentence, write each word which should be followed by a comma, and add the comma.

EXAMPLE   1. In her lecture on cities Professor Gonzales who is an expert in her field suggested that the development of towns might have had as much to do with self-defense as with commerce.
       1. *cities, Gonzales, field,*

1. The English word *weapon* is related to the Old English *waepen* the Dutch *wapen* the German *Waffe* and some earlier common root.
2. Sticks stones and poisons were among the weapons used by primitive cultures.
3. Modern weapons which are produced by sophisticated people like ourselves are more fully developed.
4. Weapons that were produced in early times were not well developed nor were they distinct from each other in appearance function or design.
5. The cord sling which is easily the most familiar sling was used all over the world for it was easy to put together and not too difficult to master.
6. When he slew Goliath David used a simple sling.
7. Among the many kinds of weapons the stick thrown by hand became one of the most heavily specialized.
8. The dart the arrow the spear the lance and the javelin all developed from the plain stick thrown by hand.
9. Among the more unusual weapons *bolas* consist of weighted balls of stone wood or metal tied together with thongs.

MECHANICS

10. The purpose of the *bola* which is somewhat different from that of most other weapons is to entangle the victim without inflicting pain injury or death.

Interrupters

24k. Use commas to set off expressions that interrupt.

There are three kinds of "interrupters" that you should be able to recognize and punctuate properly.

(1) Appositives and appositive phrases are usually set off by commas.

An appositive follows a noun or pronoun and usually identifies or explains it.

EXAMPLES   Nancy Landon Kassebaum, the **senator** from Kansas, was the principal speaker.
I loved my gift, a pearl **ring**.

In these sentences *senator* and *ring* are appositives.

When you set off an appositive, you include with it all the words that modify it. Together, an appositive and its modifiers constitute an appositive phrase.

EXAMPLES   I enjoyed *At Home in India*, **a book by Cynthia Bowles.**
Neil Armstrong, **the first man to walk on the moon,** took his historic step on July 20, 1969.

Sometimes an appositive is so closely related to the word preceding it that it should not be set off by commas. Such an appositive is called a "restrictive appositive." It is usually a single word.

EXAMPLES   my brother **James**
the author **Herman Melville**
my cat **Bonkers**

EXERCISE 6. Correcting Sentences by Using Commas. Rewrite the following sentences containing appositives, and insert commas where needed.

1. The *Mona Lisa* a painting by Leonardo da Vinci is a prize possession of the Louvre.

MECHANICS

2. The painting a portrait of a young Florentine woman is slightly cracked as a result of temperature changes.
3. In 1911 an Italian house painter Vincenzo Perugia stole the painting from its frame.
4. For two years the Paris police some of the cleverest detectives in the world were baffled by the crime.
5. Since its recovery the painting one of the most valuable portraits in the world has been carefully protected.

(2) Words used in direct address are set off by commas.

EXAMPLES **David,** please close the door.
Did you call me**, mother?**
Yes**, Mr. Kirk,** I gave you the paper.

(3) Parenthetical expressions are set off by commas.

These expressions are often used parenthetically: *I believe (think, suppose, hope,* etc.*), on the contrary, on the other hand, of course, in my opinion, for example, however, to tell the truth, nevertheless, in fact, on the whole, also, too, in addition, thus.*

EXAMPLES You are**, I hope,** planning to come.
His new poems**, in fact,** are as inspiring as his earlier ones.

These expressions are not *always* used as interrupters.

EXAMPLES She wore her ring **on the other hand.** [not used as an interrupter]
Who**, on the other hand,** really knows which is proper? [used as an interrupter]
I believe today is my first absence. [not used as an interrupter]
It is**, I believe,** my first absence. [used as an interrupter]

> ☞ NOTE A contrasting expression introduced by *not* or *yet* is parenthetical and must be set off by commas.

EXAMPLE Emily Brontë**, not Charlotte,** was the author of *Wuthering Heights.*

EXERCISE 7. Correcting Sentences by Using Commas. Number your paper 1–10. After the proper number, write the words in each sentence that should be followed by a comma, and place a comma after each word.

1. In 1984 Geraldine Ferraro a New York congresswoman became the first female vice-presidential candidate on a major party ticket.
2. However she wasn't the first woman to seek high office for Victoria Woodhull was the presidential nominee of the Equal Rights party in 1872.
3. To send her daughter to a boarding school Antonetta Ferraro Geraldine's mother worked as a crochet beader a person who fastens beads and sequins on evening dresses.
4. Geraldine was very active in school and was in fact named most likely to succeed.
5. After she graduated from college Geraldine an ambitious woman felt that a job as an elementary-school teacher was not enough.
6. Consequently she began attending Fordham Law School at night.
7. Although she married John Zaccaro in 1960 she kept her maiden name professionally.
8. When her younger daughter was seven years old Geraldine became an assistant district attorney in Queens, New York.
9. Generally speaking that experience gave her many valuable insights into the criminal justice system and helped her to form strong feelings about the rights of victims.
10. Geraldine Ferraro credits her mother for helping her become a strong yet compassionate person.

Conventional Situations

24l. Use a comma in certain conventional situations.

(1) Use a comma to separate items in dates and addresses.

In addresses the street number and the name of the street are not separated from each other by a comma. Neither are the name of the state and the Zip code number that follows it. Similarly, in dates the day of the month and the month itself are considered one item. Commas do go between the date and the year and the city and the state.

EXAMPLES On June 15, 1985, my best friend Cary moved to 814 Georgia Avenue, Miami Beach, Florida 33139.

MECHANICS

My cousin moved to Jackson, Mississippi, last April.
The national exam will be given on Tuesday, February 1, at the high school.

(2) Use a comma after the salutation of a friendly letter and after the closing of any letter.

EXAMPLES Dear Marcus,   Dear Aunt Meg,
          Affectionately yours,   Sincerely yours,

(3) Use a comma after a name followed by *Jr., Sr., Ph.D.,* etc.

EXAMPLES Dr. Elena Moreno, Ph.D.
          Russell E. Davis, Jr.
          David Owens Knopp, M.D.

Unnecessary Commas

24m. Do not use unnecessary commas.

Too much punctuation can make a sentence as confusing as too little punctuation. Do not use a comma unless a rule specifically calls for it or unless the sentence would be unclear without it. When in doubt, leave it out.

EXERCISE 8. Correcting Sentences by Using Commas.   Number your paper 1–5. Write the words in each sentence that should be followed by a comma, and place a comma after each word.

EXAMPLE 1. On our way to Birmingham Alabama we stayed overnight in Chattanooga Tennessee.
         1. *Birmingham, Alabama, Chattanooga,*

1. On September 1 1985 we moved from Eureka California to 220 Tuxford Place Thousand Oaks California 91360.
2. We left Tampa Florida on Monday June 15 and arrived in Albuquerque New Mexico on June 17.
3. The hotel on Gulfport Road was destroyed by fire on Tuesday March 13 1984.
4. My brother received a letter that started, "Dear John There's something I've been meaning to tell you."
5. We interviewed Franklin R. Thomas M.D. at his emergency clinic on Wilson Road.

MECHANICS

REVIEW EXERCISE B. Correcting Sentences by Using Commas.
Number your paper 1–20. Write the words in each sentence that should
be followed by a comma, placing the comma after each.

EXAMPLE   1. It was to tell the truth really my mistake.
           1. *was, truth,*

1. John Adams John Quincy Adams Theodore Roosevelt Rutherford B. Hayes Franklin D. Roosevelt and John F. Kennedy were all graduates of Harvard University.
2. Many movie stars have left their footprints in cement outside Mann's Chinese Theater 6925 Hollywood Boulevard Hollywood California.
3. Yes Ms. Kim I remembered that a sonnet has fourteen lines.
4. On the other hand haiku I believe have only three lines.
5. Although Johnny Weissmuller was a champion swimmer most people remember him as Tarzan.
6. The Tony Award an annual award for theatrical excellence was named for Antoinette Perry an American theatrical producer.
7. *Steamboat Willie* Mickey Mouse's first sound cartoon debuted at the Colony Theatre in New York City on November 8 1928.
8. Sherlock Holmes a detective created by Sir Arthur Conan Doyle is I think the best-known fictional character in the world.
9. He lived at 221B Baker Street London England with Dr. John Watson.
10. Roy Rogers "King of the Cowboys" sang with the Sons of the Pioneers married Dale Evans and starred in many westerns.
11. The word *theater* comes from the Greek word *theatron* which means I believe "a place for seeing."
12. In fact Greek tragedy was the beginning of drama as we know it today.
13. On the slope below the Acropolis in Athens Greece early plays were performed at the Theater of Dionysus.
14. The actors wore masks to show which characters they portrayed and they often appeared in several roles.
15. Yes Gary men played all the roles.
16. Although the Greeks wrote hundreds of tragedies fewer than thirty-five survive.
17. Aeschylus the earliest Greek dramatist wrote the *Oresteia* a powerful story of murder revenge and divine mercy.

18. Aristophanes whom the ancient Greeks considered the greatest of comic dramatists wrote *The Clouds* and *The Frogs.*

19. Sophocles often regarded as the greatest dramatist of all times is credited with almost a hundred plays of which only eight have been recovered.

20. Although the play was acclaimed by the critics the public did not like it and thus refused to recommend it to their friends.

WRITING APPLICATION B:
Using Commas Correctly in Your Writing

When you use commas correctly, you are being a careful and considerate writer; you express your ideas clearly for your readers. In the following pairs of sentences, notice that the second sentence in each is clearer than the first because the writer has used commas correctly.

CONFUSING   In our high school students may participate in work-study programs.

CLEAR   In our high school, students may participate in work-study programs.

CONFUSING   I bought pots and pans trays and glasses for our apartment.

CLEAR   I bought pots and pans, trays, and glasses for our apartment.

Writing Assignment

Think about the sights and sounds on a street in your neighborhood or in an imagined neighborhood. Write a descriptive paragraph in which you list many of those sights and sounds. Be sure to use commas to separate the items in your sentence.

MECHANICS

CHAPTER 24 REVIEW: POSTTEST

Correcting Sentences by Using End Marks and Commas.   Rewrite the following sentences, inserting end marks and commas as needed. Remember to capitalize the first word of each sentence.

EXAMPLE 1. Stop the bus for I want to get off
        1. *Stop the bus, for I want to get off!*

1. My dad works for the Parker Pen Company 1 Parker Place Janesville Wisconsin 53545
2. Water transports nutrients throughout the body aids in digestion and helps regulate body temperature
3. Why Bill I didn't know you were born in Windsor Ontario too
4. Woodrow Wilson our twenty-eighth President was born in Staunton Virginia on December 28 1856
5. Did you know that Wilson was President during World War I and was awarded the Nobel Peace Prize in 1919
6. However the United States Senate rejected the League of Nations the project that Wilson sponsored
7. Trinidad is one of the most prosperous islands in the Caribbean but unemployment usually averages thirteen percent
8. Sugar coffee cocoa citrus fruits and bananas are Trinidad's chief crops
9. Located off the coast of Venezuela Trinidad has 1,100,000 people and 150,000 television sets
10. A group of kangaroos is called a mob but a group of geese on the other hand is a gaggle
11. If I finish my report if I do the laundry and if I promise to be home by eleven I can go to the concert
12. At the clambake on the beach George ate thirty clams four lobsters and a loaf of French bread
13. We were exhausted yet we couldn't fall asleep
14. Even though I miss Topeka I love our new home at 416 Lincoln Road Chicago Illinois 60606
15. If you could come home from your vacation a day early Janice you could come to my party on July 4
16. Of course I want you to come
17. Please address this letter to Phyllis M Saunders M D
18. The party which I have been planning for three months will celebrate our country's birthday my sister Megan's graduation and my parents' wedding anniversary
19. He believed things would turn out all right for he always carried his lucky charm a rabbit's foot in his pocket
20. I tell you Joseph no one not even our parents will believe that we were kidnapped

MECHANICS

SUMMARY OF THE USES OF THE COMMA

24f. Use commas to separate items in a series.
  (1) If all items in a series are joined by *and* or *or* (*nor*), do not use commas to separate them.
  (2) Independent clauses in a series are usually separated by semicolons. Short independent clauses may be separated by commas.

24g. Use commas to separate two or more adjectives preceding a noun.

24h. Use commas before *and, but, or, nor, for, so,* and *yet* when they join independent clauses.

24i. Use commas to set off nonessential clauses and nonessential participial phrases.

24j. Use commas after certain introductory elements.
  (1) Use a comma after such words as *well, yes, no,* and *why* when they begin a sentence.
  (2) Use a comma after an introductory participial phrase.
  (3) Use a comma after a succession of introductory prepositional phrases.
  (4) Use a comma after an introductory adverb clause.

24k. Use commas to set off expressions that interrupt the sentence.
  (1) Appositives and appositive phrases are usually set off by commas.
  (2) Words used in direct address are set off by commas.
  (3) Parenthetical expressions are set off by commas.

24l. Use commas in certain conventional situations.
  (1) Use a comma to separate items in dates and addresses.
  (2) Use a comma after the salutation of a friendly letter and after the closing of any letter.
  (3) Use a comma after a name followed by *Jr., Sr., Ph.D.,* etc.

24m. Do not use unnecessary commas.

MECHANICS

Punctuation

SEMICOLONS AND COLONS

DIAGNOSTIC TEST

Correcting Sentences by Using Semicolons and Colons. The following sentences contain a comma or no punctuation where there should be a semicolon or a colon. Number your paper 1–20. After the proper number, write each word that should be followed by a colon or semicolon. After the word, place the correct mark of punctuation.

EXAMPLE   1. The Arthurs are not home, they never are this time of day.
        1. *home;*

1. They phrased the petition carefully and presented it at the requested time, however, the governor ignored it.
2. The meeting is scheduled for 3 30 tomorrow afternoon please be prompt.
3. The following committees will report at that time budget, membership, awards, and programs.
4. As was his custom upon arising, he read a meditation on peace this morning he selected John 14 27.
5. We took some food to the stray dog it looked so forlorn standing in the doorway.
6. The modern literature class read these poems, "Incident" by Countee Cullen, "The Love Song of J. Alfred Prufrock" by T. S. Eliot, and "Ars Poetica" by Archibald MacLeish.

7. After she came to Barton Hall, Millie finished her work on time, learned her lessons, and kept her clothes mended and clean nevertheless, other girls received more attention and praise than she.

8. The social worker repeated the request, "We are in desperate need of the following items, canned food, powdered milk, and disinfectant. All contributions will be appreciated."

9. Conrad Aiken was, for a number of years, a correspondent for the *New Yorker* magazine and also wrote essays and short stories he is best known, however, for his poetry.

10. The Bering Strait links the Arctic Ocean with the Bering Sea, both the sea and the strait are named for Vitus Bering, a Danish explorer.

11. In the essay "Self Reliance," Ralph Waldo Emerson makes this statement "Whoso would be a man must be a nonconformist. He who would gather immortal palms must not be hindered by the name of goodness, but must explore if it be goodness."

12. Winners in the Douglas Fun Run last Saturday morning were Otis Williams, a sophomore, Janice Hicks, a senior, and Rodrigo Campas, a junior.

13. They opposed every motion that came before the meeting in addition, they said they would circulate petitions if any of the proposals were passed.

14. At first the children were afraid, believing that they were lost only after their teacher reassured them that she knew the way did they become calm and walk along the path.

15. This design will be applied to the following types of machines commercial, manufacturing, military, and agricultural.

16. Shirley Jackson, a promising author before her untimely death in 1965, lived in Vermont most of her life as a writer she was best known for the short story "The Lottery."

17. In addition to the imaginative, eerie tales for which Shirley Jackson is known, she wrote *Life Among the Savages* and *Raising Demons* these autobiographical novels are amusing accounts of her own household.

18. In his short life Justin has lived in Tulsa, Oklahoma Tucson, Arizona Dallas, Texas and Shreveport, Louisiana.

19. The tournament was badly organized because low-handicap players

were paired with partners who barely knew how to play golf consequently, the experienced players were frustrated and the novices were confused.

20. None of the entries that were submitted met the standard of quality the art museum expected for the contest therefore, no winner was named.

THE SEMICOLON

The semicolon [;] says to the reader, "Pause here a little longer than you do for a comma, but not as long as you do for a period."

25a. Use a semicolon between independent clauses in a sentence if they are not joined by *and, but, or, nor, for, so,* **or** *yet.*

EXAMPLES   Everyone else in my family excels in a particular sport; I seem to be the only exception.

When the thoughts of two short sentences are *very closely connected,* it is better to turn them into one sentence by means of a semicolon.

25b. Use a semicolon between independent clauses joined by such words as *for example, for instance, that is, besides, accordingly, moreover, nevertheless, furthermore, otherwise, therefore, however, consequently, instead,* **and** *hence.*

EXAMPLES   Only two people registered for the calligraphy lessons; **consequently,** the class was canceled.
I am planning to go shopping tomorrow; **however,** I could wait and go with you on Saturday.

When the connectives mentioned in this rule are placed at the beginning of a clause, the use of a comma after them is frequently a matter of taste. When they are clearly parenthetical (interrupters), they are followed by a comma. The words *for example, for instance,* and *that is* are always followed by a comma. The word *however* is usually followed by a comma.

25c. A semicolon (rather than a comma) may be needed to separate independent clauses joined by a coordinating conjunction if there are commas within the clauses.

MECHANICS

EXAMPLES   My birthday gift to Margaret is a surprise, and I think she will enjoy it. [A comma between the clauses is sufficient.]
My birthday gift to Margaret, a ticket to the rock concert next week, is a surprise; and, since she likes the group that will be performing, I think she will enjoy it. [Additional commas make the semicolon preferable.]

25d. Use a semicolon between items in a series if the items contain commas.

EXAMPLES   There are four home stations for the Goodyear blimps: Long Beach, California; Houston, Texas; Miami, Florida; and Rome, Italy.
You may turn in the reports on Thursday, September 14; Friday, September 15; or Monday, September 18.

EXERCISE 1. Correcting Sentences by Using Commas and Semicolons. Write (in the order in which they appear in the sentences below) all words that should be followed by a semicolon or a comma. After each word, place the needed mark of punctuation. Number your list by sentences.

EXAMPLE   1. The orchestra will perform on Thursday, May 5 Friday, May 6 and Saturday, May 7 all performances begin at 8:00 P.M.
1. *5; 6; 7;*

1. The instruments in a symphony orchestra are divided into families many musicians can easily play different instruments within one family.
2. One group is the woodwind family, which consists of instruments that once were made of wood but today are made of metal or plastic this group includes instruments such as the flute, saxophone, and clarinet.
3. When a musician blows air through the tube of a woodwind instrument, a reed vibrates this vibration produces the sound, a very distinctive tone.
4. The oboe, bassoon, and English horn have two reeds but the clarinet has only one.
5. Kettledrums or tympani are percussion instruments that can be tuned to a specific pitch on the other hand the cymbals, the triangle, and the other kinds of drums cannot change pitch.

MECHANICS

6. Brass instruments, such as the trumpet, cornet, and tuba, have valves that adjust the length of the tube to raise or lower the pitch but the trombone has a slide for this purpose.
7. The symphony conductor's job is to combine these diverse instruments into one harmonious sound however this responsibility is only part of the talent required for the job.
8. Conductors must study for many years furthermore they must be skilled in at least one instrument.
9. Most people see conductors in the limelight they do not realize that conductors must select the music, interpret the composer's meaning, and rehearse the orchestra.
10. The goal of every conductor is to lead a major symphony in London, England Berlin, Germany Boston, Massachusetts or Chicago, Illinois.

WRITING APPLICATION A:
Using Punctuation to Connect Ideas

In writing, one of the elements that joins ideas is the transition. Some useful transitional words are *besides, accordingly, however, therefore,* and so on. These transitional expressions connect two independent clauses that are closely related.

EXAMPLE The math portion of the PSAT was difficult for me; **nevertheless,** I did my best.

Writing Assignment

Write ten original sentences using transitional expressions (see pages 45–50). Use a semicolon in each sentence. Review your work carefully to make sure an independent clause follows the transitional expression.

MECHANICS

THE COLON

The usual purpose of the colon is to call the reader's attention to what comes next. A colon means "notice the following."

25e. Use a colon to mean "note what follows."

Use a colon before a list of items, especially after expressions such as *as follows* or *the following items.*

EXAMPLES We were allowed four articles in the examination area: pencils, compasses, rulers, and protractors.

We visited three major attractions in Washington, D.C.: the White House, the Washington Monument, and the Lincoln Memorial.

Over her summer vacation, Juanita read biographies of the following people: John Ross, Annie Wauneka, and Maria Martinez.

☞ NOTE When a list comes immediately after a verb or preposition, do not use a colon.

INCORRECT At the amusement park we rode: the roller coaster, the ferris wheel, the bumper cars, and the water ride.

CORRECT At the amusement park we rode the roller coaster, the ferris wheel, the bumper cars, and the water ride. [The list follows the verb *rode.*]

25f. Use a colon before a long, formal statement or quotation.

EXAMPLE Thomas Paine's first pamphlet in the series *The American Crisis* starts with these famous words: "These are the times that try men's souls. The summer soldier and the sunshine patriot will, in this crisis, shrink from the service of their country; but he that stands it *now* deserves the love and thanks of man and woman."[1]

25g. Use a colon in certain conventional situations.

(1) Use a colon between the hour and the minute when you are writing the time.

EXAMPLES 6:15 P.M.   9:55 tomorrow morning

(2) Use a colon between chapter and verse in referring to passages from the Bible.

EXAMPLES Psalms 8:9   Luke 10:27

[1] For further discussion of the use of long quotations in a composition, see pages 601–602.

(3) Use a colon after the salutation of a business letter.

EXAMPLES   Dear Ms. Weinberg**:**
              Dear Sir**:**

Use a comma after the salutation of a friendly letter.

EXAMPLE   Dear Suzanne**,**

EXERCISE 2. Correcting Sentences by Using Colons.

Number your paper 1–10. If a sentence needs no colon, write *C* for correct after its number. If a colon is lacking, write the word preceding the colon; then add the colon. Be able to explain your answers.

EXAMPLE   1. I began my acceptance speech as follows "Fellow students, thank you for your votes!"
               1. *follows:*

1. My family enjoys the talent of the following cartoonists Gary Trudeau, Charles Schulz, Cathy Guisewite, and Lynn Johnston.
2. Sometimes the paper comes at 6 15 A.M., but other times it doesn't hit the driveway until 9 00.
3. My little sister has several items embossed with Garfield's picture a poster, a nightgown, a notebook, and a clock.
4. Bruce Barton made this perceptive comment "Many a man who pays rent all his life owns his home, and many a family has successfully saved for a home only to find itself at last with nothing but a house."
5. Sherry's favorite spy novelists are Robert Ludlum, Helen MacInnes, and Frederick Forsyth.
6. The story of Moses and Pharaoh's daughter is told in Exodus 2 5–10.
7. The directions were as follows remove plastic wrap, place in oven, and bake for thirty minutes.
8. I prefer my bicycle to a car for three reasons I don't pay for gasoline, I don't pay for insurance, and it's all mine.
9. On our vacation in Florida, we visited Walt Disney World, Sea World, Cypress Gardens, Epcot Center, and the John F. Kennedy Space Center.
10. Mr. Wise asked us to bring the following items to science class for an experiment a deciduous leaf, a coniferous needle or branch, and wax paper.

MECHANICS

WRITING APPLICATION B:
Catching Your Audience's Interest by Using Colons

Two beachcombers, strolling along a deserted stretch of seacoast, came upon a sealed bottle at the water's edge. Peeling away the seal, they opened the bottle and extracted a note. It read:

> Help! I am stranded on a deserted isle. Please come get me and bring the following items: two dozen oranges, a pair of blue suede shoes, volumes six and seven of the *Oxford English Dictionary*, and three bagels.

Notice how the writer of the note used a colon to draw the beachcombers' attention to the rescue shopping list. A colon signals to your audience to notice what follows.

Writing Assignment

Imagine that you are stranded on a deserted isle. Write two different notes to place in sealed bottles, each directed to a different audience and each including a rescue shopping list. Be sure to use a colon to draw your audience's attention to your list.

CHAPTER 25 REVIEW: POSTTEST

Correcting Sentences by Using Semicolons and Colons. Rewrite the following sentences and punctuate them correctly, using semicolons and colons where necessary.

EXAMPLE   1. Please bring the following items books, pencils, and newspapers.
            1. *Please bring the following items: books, pencils, and newspapers.*

1. If you want to send fragile items through the mail, the post office recommends that you pack them in fiberboard containers use foam, plastic, or padding to cushion them and then seal the package carefully, reinforcing it with filament tape.
2. Mary McCleod Bethune, a forceful leader for black education in the 1930's and 1940's, founded a school for girls in Daytona Beach, Florida later she became a special adviser on minority affairs to President Franklin D. Roosevelt.

MECHANICS

3. One of the best-known passages in the Bible comes from Psalms 23 1–6.

4. Cheryl worked hard to improve her grades last semester she wanted a record that would help her enter college.

5. If I had a million dollars, I would visit London, England Cairo, Egypt Buenos Aires, Argentina and Tokyo, Japan.

6. We have to write reports for gym class on one of the following athletes Jesse Owens, Sonja Henie, Jim Brown, Althea Gibson, or Babe Didrikson Zaharias.

7. The neighbor's cocker spaniel barked all night long if it happens again, I will have to speak to the owner.

8. Candice, who has rehearsed for the role, will take Sandra's place in tonight's performance unfortunately, Sandra sprained her ankle and cannot walk.

9. My aunt loves to play games such as backgammon and chess however, I usually win when we play.

10. Asia has both the highest and the lowest points on earth Mount Everest, the highest, soars 29,028 feet the Dead Sea, a salt lake, lies 1,300 feet below sea level.

11. Instructed to be prompt, we arrived at the school at 7 15, but the doors were locked consequently, we waited until 8 30 before we could enter the building.

12. Indira Gandhi, who served for many years as the Prime Minister of India, was virtually raised in politics and government for her father was Jawaharlal Nehru, the first Prime Minister of India from 1947 to 1964.

13. My two friends, Ruth and Cindy, are not on speaking terms Ruth argued that people can become whatever they want, but Cindy insisted that people have no choice in their fate.

14. I really dislike writing outlines for reports nevertheless, the highest grade I ever received was for a report that I wrote from an outline.

15. Mrs. Kowalski has always regretted that she never learned to speak Polish when she was a little girl now she is taking Conversational Polish I and hopes to be able to talk with the older family friends.

16. The computer software industry is an enormous, growing business for instance, people can buy software for everything from balancing budgets to plotting astrological charts.

17. Every morning Esther rises at 5 00, jogs until 5 30, showers and eats

breakfast by 6:15, and catches the 6:35 bus.

18. Red Cloud, leader of the Oglala Sioux, was an inspired military genius he successfully defended Sioux lands against the whites, who wanted to build a trail from Laramie, Wyoming, to Bozeman, Montana.

19. Gates of the Arctic National Park, which is located in northern Alaska, is known for the many animals that live there caribou, grizzly bears, moose, and wolves.

20. I have ridden bicycles, horses, and motorcycles and I have traveled in trains, buses, and planes but someday I hope to ride in a hot-air balloon.

CHAPTER 26

Punctuation

UNDERLINING (ITALICS)
AND QUOTATION MARKS

DIAGNOSTIC TEST

Correcting Sentences by Adding Italics or Quotation Marks.   The following sentences contain words that should be in italics (underlined) or in quotation marks. Number your paper 1–20. After the proper number, write these words and punctuate them correctly.

EXAMPLE   1. Can you tell me the way to Logan Street? she asked.
   1. *"Can you tell me the way to Logan street?"*
   2. We attended the production of Twelfth Night by the Shakespeare Festival Players.
   2. *Twelfth Night*

1. Tchaikovsky wrote The Nutcracker in 1892.
2. We have subscribed to the Orlando Sentinel ever since we moved here.
3. Are you going to help me, he asked, or shall I get someone else?
4. James Dickey wrote the novel Deliverance, on which the movie was based.
5. After someone told her it looked less affected, she spelled her name with a y instead of an i.
6. Clarita served a delicious appetizer, called pulpo; hours later I asked her what it was, and she said it was octopus.

MECHANICS

597

7. For our homework assignment we have to define ionization, electrolyte, quark, and neutrino.

8. During the Civil War, two ironclad ships became famous: the Merrimack, a Confederate ship, and the Monitor, a Union ship.

9. I never should have agreed to be chairperson, wailed Ellie. When I asked Tina to help, she said, Not on your life. Now I'm doing all the work myself.

10. Where have you been, Ramon? asked Leroy. The bus leaves in three minutes!

11. When the principal announced the scholarship winners, she said that the following girls were, and she used these words, Elwood High's finest scholars: Daphne Johnson, Martha Lewis, Julia Perez, and Winsie Chung.

12. The poet Carl Sandburg called Chicago the Hog Butcher for the World.

13. It was difficult for me to understand Sam because he dropped all the r's from his words.

14. Although Abraham Lincoln said it many years ago, politicians still quote his phrase, government of the people, by the people, for the people.

15. During lunch we discussed the magazine article Michael Jackson's Perfect Universe.

16. Recalled to Life is the opening chapter in one of Charles Dickens' novels.

17. Susan looks cool in her new leather jacket.

18. In his composition, the critic of Emily Dickinson's poems explains the term paradox, that is, a statement that seems contradictory but is true.

19. When the players came onto the field, why did the fans shout, Who cares?

20. I could study the sculpture Young Shadows, by Louise Nevelson, for hours?

UNDERLINING (ITALICS)

Italics are printed letters that lean to the right, like this:

These words are printed in italics.

When you are writing or typing, indicate italics by underlining the words you want italicized. If your composition were to be printed, the typesetter would set the underlined words in italics. For instance, if you typed

All sophomores in our school read <u>The Good Earth,</u> by Pearl Buck.

your sentence would be printed like this:

All sophomores in our school read *The Good Earth,* by Pearl Buck.

26a. Use underlining (italics) for titles of books, periodicals, works of art (pictures, musical compositions, television programs, statues, etc.), planes, trains, and so on.

EXAMPLES   <u>The Red Badge of Courage</u> [book]
<u>The Three Musicians</u> [work of art (painting)]
<u>National Geographic</u> [magazine]
the <u>Lusitania</u> [ship]

☞ NOTE   The words *a, an,* and *the* before a magazine or newspaper title are not underlined. Notice, however, that in titles of books these words are underlined if they are part of the title.

EXAMPLES   the <u>Runner's World</u> [magazine]
the <u>Kansas City Times</u> [newspaper]
<u>The Sound and the Fury</u> [book]
<u>The Red Pony</u> [book]

26b. Use underlining (italics) for words, letters, and figures referred to as such and for foreign words not yet adopted into English.

EXAMPLES   John, what does the <u>L</u> in your name stand for?
Write five compound sentences without using the word <u>and</u>.
There are four <u>3</u>'s in my phone number.
Oh, I try to keep <u>au courant</u>.

EXERCISE 1. Correcting Sentences by Adding Italics. Number your paper 1–10. After the proper number, list all words and word groups that should be italicized. Underline each.

MECHANICS

1. Did you know that the B in Cecil B. deMille stands for Blount?
2. The first full-length movie cartoon, Walt Disney's Snow White and the Seven Dwarfs, used two million drawings.
3. Among the necessities of life brought by the Pilgrims on the Mayflower were apple seeds.
4. James Earle Fraser, famous for his painting End of the Trail, designed our Indian-head nickel.
5. Teddy Roosevelt, an avid reader, read Decline and Fall of the Roman Empire while on a trip in the jungles of Brazil.
6. The submarine Seaview was the ship commanded by Admiral Nelson in Voyage to the Bottom of the Sea, an old TV program.
7. Daktari is Swahili for the English word doctor.
8. Our first space shuttle was supposed to be named Constitution, but President Ford, who received 100,000 letters from Star Trek fans, changed the name to Enterprise.
9. Richard Sears met Alvah Roebuck through an ad in the Chicago Daily News.
10. The three M's in 3M Company stand for Minnesota Mining and Manufacturing.

QUOTATION MARKS

Quotation marks are used mainly to show the reader that someone's *exact words* are being reproduced. Thus, quotation marks come in pairs; one set marks the beginning of the quotation and the other the end.

26c. Use quotation marks to enclose a direct quotation—a person's exact words.

Do not use quotation marks to enclose an indirect quotation.

DIRECT QUOTATION   Joan said, "My legs are sore from the new exercise." [Joan's exact words]

INDIRECT QUOTATION   Joan said that her legs were sore from the new exercise. [not Joan's exact words]

> ☞ NOTE   Place quotation marks at both the beginning and the end of a direct quotation.

INCORRECT	"I'm getting my braces off tomorrow, said Reed.
CORRECT	"I'm getting my braces off tomorrow," said Reed.

26d. A direct quotation begins with a capital letter.

EXAMPLE   Bonnie asked, "When do we get our uniforms?"

☞ NOTE   If the quotation is only a fragment of a sentence, not intended to stand alone, do not begin it with a capital letter.

EXAMPLE   Christine promised that she would come "as soon as possible."

26e. When a quoted sentence is divided into two parts by an interrupting expression such as *he said* or *she replied*, the second part begins with a small letter.

EXAMPLES   "I hope," said Dave, "that it doesn't rain for the first part of the football game."
"I'm not sure," replied Ann, "if I can make it to the club's rummage sale."

If the second part of a broken quotation is a new sentence, it begins with a capital.

EXAMPLE   "The date has been set," said Greg. "We can't change it now."

26f. A direct quotation is set off from the rest of the sentence by commas or by a question mark or an exclamation point.

EXAMPLES   "Where will it all end?" asked Eileen.
"Let me do that!" exclaimed Helen.
"There is no specific homework assignment for this weekend," announced Mrs. Levitt, "but remember that your term papers are due next Friday."
"Has anyone in this class," asked Mrs. Lukas, "seen a performance of *A Raisin in the Sun*?"

☞ NOTE   A long quotation in your composition is usually introduced by a colon and is set off by itself from the text by wider margins and by single spacing instead of double spacing (unless your teacher instructs otherwise). This practice so clearly identifies the passage as a quotation that no quotation marks are needed.

MECHANICS

After the collapse of Europe and the tragedy of Dunkirk, the German dictator thought he had penned the British lion in its home islands and that, weakened as it was by its losses on the continent, it would easily succumb to an invasion. The British Prime Minister, voicing the grim resolve of the whole nation, warned him against such a move:

> We shall defend every village, every town and every city. The vast mass of London itself, fought street by street, could easily devour an entire hostile army; and we would rather see London laid in ruins and ashes than that it should be tamely and abjectly enslaved.

26g. Other marks of punctutation, when used with quotation marks, are placed according to the following rules.

(1) Commas and periods are always placed inside the closing quotation marks.

EXAMPLE "The concert tickets are sold out," Mary said, "and I had really hoped to go."

(2) Colons and semicolons are always placed outside the closing quotation marks.

EXAMPLES Ms. James said, "A stitch in time saves nine"; however, I'll admit I never really understood what that saying means.

The following students have been selected as, in Ms. Kovak's words, "honorary disc jockeys": Nick Paludo, Tom Weber, and Sally Ortega.

(3) Question marks and exclamation points are placed inside the closing quotation marks if the quotation is a question or an exclamation. Otherwise, they are placed outside.

EXAMPLES Maria asked, "What time is the game tomorrow?"
Why did you yell, "It doesn't matter"?
When Mark turned to leave, Kathy yelled, "Wait!"
Don't say "I don't know"!

EXERCISE 2. Correcting Sentences by Using Capitalization and Punctuation. Rewrite the following sentences, inserting the necessary punctuation. Watch carefully for the placement of commas and end marks in relation to quotation marks and for capital letters at the beginning of direct quotations.

1. Oh, I left the bibliography for my paper at home! exclaimed Beth.
2. Don't panic, replied Natalie. Perhaps it's just lost in your notebook.
3. No, sighed Beth, I see it now, lying on the typewriter.
4. Was it completed asked Natalie.
5. Natalie, asked Beth, did Mrs. Gwinn say that we could turn our papers in tomorrow?
6. The following students have, in the words of Coach Hatch, demonstrated leadership both academically and athletically: Steven Cline, Becky Dodge, Judith Lewis, and Fred Vine.
7. Why did Jennifer say, You ought to know?
8. Glaring at her opponent, Samantha replied, Do I look like a mind reader?
9. I turned on the television in time to hear the reporter saying, That ends the list of school closings; however, I didn't hear which schools were closed due to the blizzard.
10. In a crowded place, never shout fire! unless you mean it.

26h. When you write dialogue (two or more persons having a conversation), begin a new paragraph every time the speaker changes.

EXAMPLE

"And whom do we have here?" boomed Captain Jenkins.

"Actually, no one, sir," replied the young stowaway from the shadowed corner.

Captain Jenkins squinted as the anxious young man stepped forward. "I will have to turn you in to the police. Did you really think you could get away with this?" asked the captain.

"Well, sir," stammered the young man, "I just thought a kid should get a chance to fly on a space mission."

26i. When a quoted passage consists of more than one paragraph, put quotation marks at the beginning of each paragraph and at the end of the entire passage.

EXAMPLE

"Now, this car is one of the hottest sellers we have," explained the salesman to Dad and me. "It has bucket seats, a tape deck, and alloy wheels.

"This model is also one of the safest cars on the road because of the heavy suspension and front disc brakes. It gets good mileage, too. All in all, it would be the perfect car for you."

MECHANICS

26j. Use single quotation marks to enclose a quotation within a quotation.

EXAMPLES Ron said, "Dad shouted, 'A ski trip sounds great to me, too!'"
Val asked, "Did you like the new interpretation of 'America the Beautiful' that I arranged?"

26k. Use quotation marks to enclose titles of short works such as short stories, poems, articles, songs, chapters and other parts of books, individual episodes of television programs, and periodicals.

EXAMPLE "The Unicorn in the Garden" is my favorite Thurber story.

> ☞ NOTE The length of a written work determines whether the title should be italicized or enclosed in quotation marks. Book-length works are italicized; shorter works usually are not. However, the titles of poems long enough to be divided into books, cantos, or sections—like Longfellow's *Evangeline* and Coleridge's *The Rime of the Ancient Mariner*—are italicized.

WRITING APPLICATION A:
Using Italics and Quotation Marks as Signals

Think about the last time you wanted to select a movie to see or a record to buy. Perhaps a recommendation from a friend helped you make up your mind. You and your classmates can maintain an ongoing file of recommended books, stories, poems, plays, and songs. Just remember that when you are recommending titles to people, they want to know whether a title is for something as short as a story or as long as a novel. When you use italics and quotation marks correctly in titles, you will be sending the right signals to your audience.

Writing Assignment

Think about books, short stories, plays, poems, or songs you have enjoyed recently. In two separate paragraphs, write a recommendation for any two of these works. Be sure to use italics and quotation marks correctly.

MECHANICS

26l. Use quotation marks to enclose slang words, technical terms, and other expressions that are unusual in standard English.

EXAMPLE   We used to **"**hang out**"** at the bowling alley.

Putting slang expressions within quotation marks amounts to apologizing for them. If you are doubtful about a word's appropriateness, do not use it.

EXERCISE 3. Correcting Sentences by Adding Italics or Quotation Marks.   Number your paper 1–10. After the proper number, write all words that should be italicized (underlined) or placed in quotation marks, and punctuate them correctly.

EXAMPLE   1. He read aloud The Tell-Tale Heart from The Collected Stories of Edgar Allan Poe.
      1. *"The Tell-Tale Heart"* *The Collected Stories of Edgar Allan Poe*

1. Mr. Croce used the word denouement as we discussed A Tale of Two Cities.
2. The counselor tried to impress the young campers by saying things like cool and right on, but they were only faintly amused by the slang from another era.
3. While I was in the library, I read an article called El Niño, Global Weather Disaster.
4. Karen asked her teacher if there were two m's in the word accommodate.
5. Fannie Farmer, one of the first advocates of proper diets, published the Boston Cooking School Cookbook in 1891.
6. My favorite plant is the Saintpaulia ionantha, also called the African violet.
7. I cooked dinner for Tony, Barbara and Ira; we had risotto alla milanese.
8. At first glance, the short story Luke Baldwin's Vow is about a boy and a dog, but it also deals with conflicts in values.
9. By next Thursday I have to read the following works: A Visit of Charity, a short story by Eudora Welty; Miss Julie, a play by August Strindberg; and The Climatic Effects of Nuclear War, an article in Scientific American magazine.
10. She crossed the t with such a flourish that she obliterated the letters above it.

MECHANICS

WRITING APPLICATION B:
Using Quotation Marks in Dialogue

At some time, you may see a very curious sight. The person in the car next to yours may appear to be talking to herself. That is, she is alone in the car, and her lips are moving. It may be that she is just singing along with her radio or tape player, but it still looks a little peculiar, doesn't it? Actually, you "talk to yourself" frequently. In the thinking process, you often carry on an "internal dialogue," especially if you are trying to come to a decision or think through a serious problem that has several sides.

Writing Assignment

Use an idea or significant issue of your own to write an "internal dialogue." Pretend that your thinking is divided on the issue, and that a debate is going on between two "parts" of you. Use your first initial and a raised one or two for each speaker. Be sure to use quotation marks correctly.

EXAMPLE
H¹ asked, "Are you going to go out for football or not?"
H² answered, "I don't think I'll have time if I take five hard academic subjects."
"But listen," said H¹, "you have a good chance of making the varsity team this year!"
"Sure, but what good is it if I'm so buried in homework I can't move?" H² asked, disheartened.

CHAPTER 26 REVIEW: POSTTEST

Correcting Sentences by Adding Italics or Quotation Marks.
Number your paper 1–20. After the proper number, write the words or phrases that should be in italics (underlined) or in quotation marks, and punctuate them correctly. If a sentence is correct as written, write *no punctuation necessary.*

1. Why did you buy another sleeping bag? she asked.
2. Mrs. Smith said that she would be at the club by 7:00 P.M.
3. Susan drove one hundred miles, he replied, to see you on your birthday.

4. Anita asked, Why did he say, I will not be in the play?

5. Charles Dickens' A Christmas Carol is the perfect gift for her.

6. How many but's did you use in the paragraph?

7. There is an article in Newsweek that I would like you to read, said Joan.

8. Why do you want to read Shakespeare's play Romeo and Juliet again? asked Patricia.

9. His street address has four 4's in it said Rose. Did you know that?

10. The dance company is performing Swan Lake, a ballet by Tchaikovsky.

11. My teacher subscribes to English Journal, a professional magazine.

12. Please write to me, Joyce requested. I want to keep in touch with you.

13. Mr. Shore said, This nail will hold the picture in place; however, I knew that it would not.

14. While I ran, Charles said, Keep running!

15. Sally said, John just whispered, I'll be at the game tonight.

16. Our assignment for history is Chapter 14, Great Ideals in the Constitution.

17. Did you read the article The Costs of College Today?

18. You looked cool in your new glasses, said Joy.

19. The Novelist, by W. H. Auden is in a collection of his shorter poems.

20. You often use the French expression au revoir, said Hannah.

Punctuation

APOSTROPHES, HYPHENS, DASHES, PARENTHESES

DIAGNOSTIC TEST

A. Correcting Sentences by Using Apostrophes and Hyphens.
Each of the following sentences contains a word that needs an apostrophe or a hyphen. Number your paper 1–10. After the proper number, write the word, adding the apostrophe or hyphen.

EXAMPLE 1. The childrens boots were placed in a row outside the door.
1. *children's*

1. The towns record on supporting youth projects and local activities is good.
2. Teresa and I are looking forward to our three weeks vacation in the Rockies.
3. The police officer said that everyones house should be searched for the missing child.
4. Only fifty three people went to our ballet recital, and thirty of them were our relatives.
5. I bought four pairs of gloves as my two younger sisters birthday presents.
6. The team members showed their self control when the fans threw empty cups and crumpled programs on the field.

MECHANICS

7. The womens basketball team, which is coached by an ex-Laker, has run up an impressive string of victories.

8. Were going on a field trip to the art museum to see the exhibit of post-Impressionist art.

9. Christopher's writing is difficult to read because he never crosses his *t*s.

10. Sampson and Smiths Bakery, which displays its pastries in the window, is around the corner from my house.

B. Correcting Sentences by Using Dashes and Parentheses.

Rewrite each of the following sentences, inserting dashes or parentheses where they are needed. (Do not add commas or colons.)

EXAMPLE 1. The school's volunteers freshmen, sophomores, and juniors were honored during the assembly.

1. *The school's volunteers—freshmen, sophomores, and juniors —were honored during the assembly.*

11. The flowers looked beautiful but were expensive and impractical they only lasted two days before the petals turned brown.

12. When we met my chemistry teacher at the mall, my little sister's question "Why doesn't that man have hair on his head?" embarrassed me so much I wanted to hide.

13. This report contains information about agriculture in three South American countries Brazil, Argentina, and Colombia.

14. Mr. Franklin works all day in his garden he retired last year and is always weeding, mulching, and pruning.

15. Last night I read the wrong chapter for history class a disastrous mistake!

16. Mary Ellen Jeter, a former State's attorney, will speak at next Thursday's assembly I'll miss gym class then and will address the topic of student rights.

17. Our newspaper, the *Sexton High Chronicle* it used to be called the *Weekly Warrior* won the highest award in the state.

18. The new principal, Ms. Lawrence, is the nicest she really cares about the students and the best we've ever had.

19. Rushing to catch the bus, I dropped my books in the mud I should never have overslept! and then lost the heel of my shoe.

20. Crystal's time for the fifty-yard dash the best time of anyone on the team qualified her for the regional track meet.

MECHANICS

APOSTROPHES

The possessive case of a noun or a pronoun is used to indicate ownership or relationship.

OWNERSHIP   The **boy's** calculator
her bracelet [The bracelet is *hers.*]

RELATIONSHIP   one **day's** notice   **his** mother

The possessive case of nouns is formed by adding an apostrophe and an *s*—or, with some words, merely an apostrophe—to the noun.

EXAMPLES   John's jacket   two girls' cars

Making a word possessive is easy. *Remembering* to do so, however, may be hard. When you are in doubt whether or not to use an apostrophe, try an "of" phrase in place of the word. If the "of" phrase makes good sense, then an apostrophe is called for.

EXAMPLE   yesterdays news [Should there be an apostrophe in *yesterdays?*] news "of yesterday" [This makes good sense; therefore . . .] yesterday's news

27a. To form the possessive case of a singular noun, add an apostrophe and an *s*.

EXAMPLES   Barbara's house   tonight's dinner

☞ NOTE   A proper name ending in *s* may add only an apostrophe if the name consists of two or more syllables and if the addition of 's would make the name difficult to pronounce (*Artemis' death, Themistocles' oration*). Some singular nouns ending in *s* need the apostrophe and the *s* if the added *s* must be pronounced as a separate syllable to make the meaning clear (*waitress's uniform*). In general, adding an apostrophe and an *s* is a correct way to make any singular noun possessive.

27b. To form the possessive case of a plural noun ending in *s*, add only the apostrophe.

EXAMPLES   teachers' desks   cities' problems

☞ NOTE   The few plural nouns that do not end in *s* form the possessive by adding an apostrophe and an *s*.

EXAMPLES   men's lockers   children's stories

Take care not to use an apostrophe to form the *plural* of a noun.

INCORRECT   The four horse's performed perfectly.
CORRECT   The four horses performed perfectly.

Study the following examples of the application of these rules for forming the singular and plural possessives of nouns. Be able to explain how each possessive was formed.

SINGULAR	SINGULAR POSSESSIVE	PLURAL	PLURAL POSSESSIVE
coach	coach's order	coaches	coaches' orders
doctor	doctor's office	doctors	doctors' offices
ox	ox's hooves	oxen	oxen's hooves
car	car's motor	cars	cars' motors
Mr. Jones	Mr. Jones's house	the Joneses	the Joneses' house
woman	woman's shoes	women	women's shoes

EXERCISE 1. Writing the Singular, Singular Possessive, Plural, and Plural Possessive of Nouns. On your paper, make a four-column chart, and write the singular, singular possessive, plural, and plural possessive of the following words:

1. man   3. governor   5. pencil   7. class   9. chief
2. secretary   4. deer   6. bird   8. picture   10. mouse

Pronouns in the Possessive Case

27c. Possessive personal and relative pronouns do not require an apostrophe.

The lists below show the nominative and possessive forms of personal and relative pronouns. Note that there are no apostrophes.

NOMINATIVE CASE	POSSESSIVE CASE	NOMINATIVE CASE	POSSESSIVE CASE
I	my, mine	it	its[1]
you	your, yours	we	our, ours
he	his	they	their, theirs
she	her, hers	who	whose

[1] The common form *it's* is not possessive; it is a contraction meaning *it is* or *it has*. See page 635.

MECHANICS

27d. Indefinite pronouns in the possessive case require an apostrophe and an *s*.

EXAMPLES   anyone's choice
someone's breakfast

If you need to review indefinite pronouns, see Chapter 18.

Compounds in the Possessive Case

27e. In compound words, names of organizations and business firms, and words showing joint possession, only the last word is possessive in form.

COMPOUND WORDS   sister-in-**law's** office
board of **directors'** report

BUSINESS FIRMS   Hardy and **Hudson's** Sport Shop
Billings and **Randolf's** office

JOINT POSSESSION   Bob and **Jim's** canoe
Susan and **Samantha's** house
Sean's and her car [exception: noun and possessive pronoun]

27f. When two or more persons possess something individually, each of their names is possessive in form.

EXAMPLES   **Michael's** and **Mark's** wallets
Denise's and **Lila's** hairbrushes
Beth's and **Jim's** ideas.

EXERCISE 2. Correcting Expressions by Using Apostrophes.

Some of the following expressions need apostrophes; some do not. Number your paper 1–20. After the proper number, write each expression, inserting apostrophes where needed. If the expression is correct, write *C* after the proper number.

EXAMPLE   1. the cameras lens
1. *the camera's lens*

1. the jets wing
2. six years of study
3. the boys gym
4. two weeks pay
5. Anns and my project
6. a months vacation
7. two pairs of tennis shoes
8. a counselors advice

MECHANICS

9. the dishes in the sink
10. a mayors reception
11. a good nights sleep
12. Demosthenes oration
13. Lynns and Mikes shoes
14. the seconds ticking by

15. my father-in-laws boat
16. waitress uniform
17. the two balloonists feats
18. plants in the lobby
19. a citizens rights
20. Black and Deckers products

EXERCISE 3. Correcting Sentences by Using Apostrophes. List on your paper, in the order in which they appear in the numbered sentences, the words that require apostrophes. After each word with an apostrophe, write the thing possessed. Remember that plural nouns ending in *s* require an apostrophe only.

EXAMPLES
1. We drove Bettys car to last nights exciting game.
1. *Betty's car   night's game*

2. The cars battery died and we missed the games beginning.
2. *car's battery   game's beginning*

1. Last week I followed my parents suggestion and enrolled in an amateur photography class offered by our citys art center. 2. I had shared my mom and dads exasperation when once again, I had spent a whole weeks allowance on disappointing pictures. 3. I had borrowed Uncle Freds expensive camera; but even with all that cameras extra features, my photographs looked like childrens smudged finger paintings.

4. My pictures of Bob and Ruths wedding reception, our familys social event of the year, were destroyed when, in search of a perfect angle, I fell into the country clubs pool with my camera. 5. Last summer I also took pictures during our months vacation in Arizonas famous Painted Desert. 6. Unfortunately, I did not understand enough about the suns strong light at midday, and my photographs had that washed-out look.

7. My lifes most embarrassing moment occurred when I took my class picture for the schools yearbook and discovered that I had forgotten to put film in the camera. 8. Another time, I took my camera to Toms party but could not get anyones attention long enough to pose the shots that I wanted. 9. As a result, I gave up on people and tried to take my pets pictures; however, a dogs will and a parakeets wings are hard to control. 10. After all these discouraging experiences, I knew that I needed a professionals advice.

Contractions

Contractions are shortened forms of certain words or certain word groups that commonly go together. The apostrophes in contractions are to indicate that letters have been left out.

27g. Use an apostrophe to show where letters or numbers have been omitted in a contraction.

EXAMPLES you have   you've
we are   we're
it is   it's

What words or figures have been contracted, and what letters or numbers have been omitted from the following?

Rock 'n' roll is still our favorite music.
The summer Olympics of '84 were held in Los Angeles.
It's time to go.
They're almost ready for you.

EXERCISE 4. Writing Contractions. Study the following contractions. Be able to write them when your teacher dictates the uncontracted expressions to you.

1. shouldn't   should not
2. they've   they have
3. o'clock   of the clock
4. they'd   they would
5. weren't   were not
6. she'll   she will
7. he's   he is
8. let's   let us
9. who's   who is
10. doesn't   does not

REVIEW EXERCISE A. Correcting Sentences by Using Apostrophes. Rewrite the following sentences, inserting apostrophes wherever necessary.

EXAMPLE 1. Werent you the one who didnt like eggplant?
1. *Weren't you the one who didn't like eggplant?*

1. Whos going to be at Leon and Joshs party?
2. Lets hide and see if theyll look for us.
3. I cant find them; they werent in the girls gym.
4. Is her doctors appointment at nine oclock?
5. Cleve doesnt have time to mow both his and Rays lawns this weekend.
6. Thats the best idea youve had in two days.

7. Were lucky that that dogs barking didnt awaken them.
8. Im trying to follow Pauls map to Jeans house.
9. Its hailing; therefore, I dont think you should go skiing.
10. Roberta couldnt remember the last time shed taken her cat to the vets.

Do not confuse possessive pronouns with contractions.

POSSESSIVE PRONOUNS	CONTRACTIONS
its roof	it's = it is or it has
your house	you're = you are
their house	they're = they are
whose house	who's = who is

EXERCISE 5. Using Possessive Pronouns and Contractions Correctly. Number your paper 1–10. After each number, write the correct word from each pair in parentheses.

EXAMPLE 1. (It's, Its) never too late to learn something new.
1. *It's*

1. (You're, Your) sure that (you're, your) allowed to bring (you're, your) book to the exam?
2. (Whose, Who's) ring is that on (you're, your) finger?
3. (They're, Their) trying to sell (they're, their) house.
4. (It's, Its) the best choice.
5. Do you know (who's, whose) responsible for (they're, their) leaving?
6. I hope the dog can find (it's, its) way home.
7. (It's, Its) Philip (who's, whose) always late.
8. Although (it's, its) been snowing all day, (they're, their) still planning to go.
9. (Who's, Whose) the girl knocking at (they're, their) front door?
10. I know (you're, your) upset with the plan, but (it's, its) the only way to solve the problem.

27h. Use an apostrophe and an *s* to form the plural of letters, numbers, signs, and words referred to as words.

EXAMPLES There are four *s*'s and four *i*'s in *Mississippi*.
You use too many *if*'s in your writing.
Put *X*'s by all incorrect answers.

REVIEW EXERCISE B. List all items needing apostrophes in each sentence, and add the needed apostrophes.

EXAMPLE 1. You agree with the school boards decision, but I dont.
1. *school board's   don't*

1. Arent you familiar with the expression "Threes a crowd"?
2. Youve forgotten that there are two *l*s in *llama.*
3. My grandmothers favorite acting group, the Dead End Kids, broke up in 39, the year she entered high school.
4. Lewis Carrolls novel *Alices Adventures in Wonderland* was originally called *Alices Adventures Underground.*
5. Whos going to cook the babies dinner?
6. After school were going to visit Pams brother; hes in St. Marys Hospital.
7. Youre required to write a report on one of classical musics three *B*s: Bach, Beethoven, and Brahms.
8. Its been six weeks since I checked the cars oil and its tires.
9. Your story would be better if youd remove about thirty *and*s.
10. There are five *2*s in my telephone number.

HYPHENS

27i. Use a hyphen to divide a word at the end of a line.

Division of words at the end of a line in order to maintain an even margin should be avoided but is sometimes necessary. A hyphen is used between parts of words divided in this way. Never divide one-syllable words. When you divide a word of more than one syllable, follow these rules:

1. Divide a word between its syllables.

INCORRECT Jenny wants to be a corporate la-
          wyer like her father.

CORRECT Jenny wants to be a corporate law-
        yer like her father.

2. Words containing double consonants should be divided between the double consonants.

cor-rect, begin-ning

See rule 3 for exceptions like *tell-ing* and *call-ing*.

3. Words with a prefix or suffix should usually be divided between the prefix and root or the root and suffix.

   pro-mote, peace-ful, tell-ing, depend-able

4. Divide a word that is already hyphenated only at the hyphen.

| INCORRECT | She raised her arm in self-de-fense. |
| CORRECT | She raised her arm in self-defense. |

| INCORRECT | Ms. Malamud is hap-py-go-lucky. |
| CORRECT | Ms. Malamud is happy-go-lucky. |

5. Divide a word so that at least two of its letters are carried forward to the next line.

| INCORRECT | We caught a momentar-y glimpse of them. |
| CORRECT | We caught a momen-tary glimpse of them. |

6. Do not hyphenate a proper name or separate a title, initials, or first name from a surname.

| INCORRECT | Before signing the contract, Mrs. David-son read the contents carefully. |
| CORRECT | Before signing the contract, Mrs. Davidson read the contents carefully. |

EXERCISE 6. Using the Hyphen to Divide Words. Assume that the following words come at the end of a line and have to be divided. Write each word, indicating by the use of hyphens how it might be divided.

EXAMPLE 1. intentional
         1. *in-ten-tion-al*

1. private
2. responsible
3. message
4. merry-go-round
5. kettledrum
6. hyphen
7. serious
8. everyone
9. difference
10. excellent

Compound Words

Hyphens are used to join the parts of some compound words. There are three kinds of compound words in our language: solid compounds (*stopwatch*), hyphenated compounds (*self-conscious*), and open compounds (*ginger ale*). Every year a great number of new compound words come into the language.

In recent years the trend has been to spell compound words solid or open. For example, notice that *data base* and *car pool*—two new compounds—are spelled without hyphens.

Only dictionary makers can keep track of the present-day forms of compound words. Consult an up-to-date dictionary.

27j. Use a hyphen with compound numbers from *twenty-one* to *ninety-nine* and with fractions used as modifiers.

EXAMPLES   forty-four bicycles
a two-thirds majority [*Two-thirds* is an adjective modifying *majority*.]
three fourths of the class [*Three fourths* is used as a noun.]

27k. Use a hyphen with the prefixes *ex-, self-,* and *all-,* with the suffix *-elect,* and with all prefixes before a proper noun or proper adjective.

EXAMPLES   self-control, ex-president, all-American, secretary-elect
mid-December, post-Olympic, pro-Japanese

27l. Hyphenate a compound adjective when it precedes the noun it modifies. Do not use a hyphen if one of the modifiers is an adverb ending in *-ly.*

EXAMPLES   a well-organized trip (But *The campaign was well planned.*)
an after-school job
a desperately rash move

EXERCISE 7. Using Hyphens in Compound Words.   Number your paper 1–10. In the following sentences, find the compound words that should be hyphenated; write them, correctly punctuated, after the proper number.

1. Ex students were not allowed at the festively decorated post prom party.
2. His self confidence faded quickly when he forgot his well planned speech.

3. Ninety eight girls tried out for the fast paced varsity cheerleading squad.
4. Two thirds of the class voted, but the proposal was defeated by a seven tenths majority.
5. The governor elect was once an all American football player in college.
6. In our debate some students were pro United Nations, but others were anti UN.
7. The state's new senator elect, an ex teacher of politics, is a self made man.
8. We had to memorize a list of twenty five well known writers and their works.
9. You must turn in your reports by mid November.
10. Jack's achievement test scores ranked in the eighty eighth percentile.

DASHES

27m. Use a dash to indicate an abrupt break in thought.

EXAMPLES   The party—I'm sorry I forgot to tell you—was changed to next week.
            When Jimbo was born—he was the last puppy—we weren't sure if he would make it.

27n. Use a dash to mean *namely, that is, in other words,* or the like before an explanation.

EXAMPLES   The weather was unseasonably warm—eighty-degree temperatures—which was a welcome change. [*in other words* or *that is*]
            We need three vehicles for our family—a business car, a station wagon, and a four-wheel drive. [*namely*]

☞ NOTE   The dash and the colon are frequently interchangeable in this type of construction.

In typewritten work, you indicate a dash by striking the hyphen key twice. Do not leave a space before or after the hyphens.

MECHANICS

PARENTHESES

27o. Use parentheses to enclose matter that is added to a sentence but is not considered of major importance.

EXAMPLES   The pyramids loomed before me (I had only seen pictures of them until now) and rose majestically against the purple sky.
My grandmother (she's very superstitious) avoids ladders and stays inside every Friday the thirteenth.

Put punctuation marks within the parentheses when they belong to the parenthetical matter but outside the parentheses when they belong to the sentence as a whole.

EXAMPLES   Marsha's comment upon seeing the mummy ("Is it really dead?") convulsed the whole class.
After we drove to Shaker Heights (it's just outside Cleveland), we met our parents for dinner.

> ☞ NOTE   Commas, dashes, and parentheses may all be used to enclose incidental words or phrases that interrupt the sentence and are not considered of major importance. Commas are much more commonly used in this way than dashes or parentheses.

EXAMPLES   We rehearsed for the show, a wonderful musical comedy. [a slight pause]
We rehearsed for the show—the musical event of the year! [a stronger break in the sentence]
We rehearsed (or should I say forgot our lines?) for the show. [a strong interruption]

EXERCISE 8. Correcting Sentences by Inserting Dashes and Parentheses.
Dashes and parentheses have been omitted in many of the following sentences. If a sentence is correctly punctuated as written, write *C* after the proper number. If a sentence is incorrectly punctuated, rewrite it with correct punctuation.

EXAMPLE   1. The Oak Ridge Boys and Alabama I have every one of their albums have won many awards.
     1. *The Oak Ridge Boys and Alabama (I have every one of their albums) have won many awards.*

1. Anne Murray I love her songs! has a degree in physical education.
2. "Yankee Doodle" it was the unofficial national anthem at the time was played after the signing of the Treaty of Ghent.
3. While standing at the top of Pikes Peak, Katherine Lee Bates wrote the words to "America the Beautiful."
4. There were three original members of the Sons of the Pioneers Roy Rogers his real name is Leonard Slye, Bob Nolan, and Tim Spencer.
5. A recording and a television appearance by Chubby Checker started the twist dance craze in the 1960's.
6. The Beatles used several names Foreverly Brothers, the Cavemen, the Moondogs, and the Quarrymen before they finally settled on Beatles.
7. Liberace's full name Wladziu Valentino Liberace is certainly a mouthful of words.
8. Cathy agreed to listen to Mozart's concertos what a surprise! if her parents would listen to one of David Bowie's albums.
9. Last night's concert was about average the beat was good, but the singers were uninspired.
10. Loretta Lynn remember the movie *Coal Miner's Daughter*? was married when she was fifteen years old.

WRITING APPLICATION:
Using the Dash Appropriately in Your Writing

Sometimes people use dashes ineffectively as a substitute for other punctuation. On the other hand, many good writers use the dash effectively to indicate an abrupt break in thought or to take the place of such words as *that is, in other words*, etc.

EXAMPLES   The village was stunned by the news—the plant was closing down.

My sister's dog—the one that chews holes in my socks—needs his annual vaccination.

Writing Assignment

Write ten sentences in which you use the dash to indicate an abrupt break in thought or to take the place of such words as *that is, in other words*, etc. Keep in mind that except for this assignment, the dash is used only occasionally.

MECHANICS

CHAPTER 27 REVIEW: POSTTEST

A. Correcting Sentences by Using Apostrophes or Hyphens.
Each of the following sentences contains an item that needs an apostrophe or a hyphen. Number your paper 1–15. After the proper number, write the word, and add the apostrophe or hyphen in the correct place.

EXAMPLE 1. This stamp collection contains thirty two rare stamps.
       1. *thirty-two*

1. Because of the sudden blizzard, the armies supplies were cut off.
2. Its frustrating when the car won't start because its battery is dead.
3. After hours of discussion, the decision is that we need a two thirds majority to pass new rules in the student council.
4. I was very pleased with my grades, which were mostly Bs, but I plan to study even harder next time.
5. If you attend the game on Saturday, whos going to watch the children?
6. Miranda had the flu this week, and now she has five days worth of homework to do this weekend.
7. Rodney interviewed the treasurer elect of the Honor Society for his "Personality Plus" column in the school newspaper.
8. They were greatly disappointed in the quality of the videotape which had been produced by a well respected company.
9. One of my aunts favorite expressions is "Never let the sun set on your anger."
10. After his car ran over a nail, my brother in law had a flat tire.
11. If we return the tape recorder by five oclock, the store clerk said she would return our deposit.
12. The alarm clock hasnt worked since the day I knocked it off the night stand.
13. The senator presented as evidence the anti American pamphlets distributed by the terrorist group.
14. You have such a lovely singing voice, I am sure youll get a part in the school musical.
15. Don't be alarmed; the red +s on your paper indicate correct answers.

MECHANICS

B. Correcting Sentences by Using Dashes and Parentheses.

Number your paper 16–20. Rewrite the following sentences, and insert dashes or parentheses where they are needed. (Do not add commas or colons to these sentences.)

EXAMPLE 1. The books on that table they are all nonfiction are on sale today.
1. *The books on that table—they are all nonfiction—are on sale today.*

16. The discovery of gold at Sutter's Mill brought floods of people settlers, miners, and prospectors to California in their covered wagons.
17. The old white house on Tenth Street it was once a governor's mansion is a landmark in our town.
18. Answer the questions on this English quiz be careful, they're tricky! and then write a couplet or a limerick for extra credit.
19. The dance music if you could call it that was furnished by Swinging Eddie and the Accordionettes.
20. The Atacama Desert the driest region on earth receives so little rainfall that it cannot be measured.

CHAPTER 28

Spelling

IMPROVING YOUR SPELLING

Naturally good spellers are rare people. If you belong to this group, you are indeed fortunate. If you do not and know you have difficulty, you can improve your spelling if you want to and if you are willing to make the effort. No one else can be of much help to you. *Learning to spell is your responsibility*.

GOOD SPELLING HABITS

There is no one way to learn to spell. What works for one person may not work for you, but careful observation and good visual memory will help, no matter what method you adopt. By using a combination of several methods, you can become a good speller. Some of the following ways have helped others to spell. Read them over; put them into practice.

1. *In your notebook, keep a list of the words you misspell.* Set aside a few pages in your notebook and jot down all the words you misspell in your written work for all subjects. At first, this job of entering word after word will seem wearisome and never-ending. Nevertheless, as the therapy takes effect, fewer and fewer words will need to be added to the list, and eventually weeks will pass before another mistake forces you to check your notebook.

A three-column spelling sheet is best. In the first column, correctly spell the word you have missed and circle the troublesome part. In the second column, divide the word into syllables. This insures against misspelling the word by first mispronouncing it. In the third column, jot down any little counsel to yourself, or trick of association that may help you to spell the word.

1.	February	Feb-ru-ar-y	Pronounce correctly.
2.	disapproval	dis-ap-prov-al	Study Rule 28c.
3.	candidate	can-di-date	Word has three small words in it: *can, did, ate.*

2. Get the dictionary habit. Don't guess at the spelling of a word. Actually opening the dictionary and searching down the page until you come upon your word fortifies your memory with its correct spelling and reduces the chances of misspelling it again. In addition, you can come across some of the cognate forms of the word you are looking for. By making the acquaintance of these "cousins" to the word in question, you deepen your knowledge of the word itself. It is much harder to misspell *denomination* after you know its kinship with such words as *nominate, nominal, denominator,* etc.

3. Learn to spell words by syllables. When you divide a word into small parts that can be pronounced by themselves, you divide a word into syllables. For example, the word *pul'sate* has two syllables; the word *bul'le tin* has three syllables; the word *en vi'ron ment* has four syllables.

4. Avoid mispronunciations that lead to spelling problems. Careful pronunciation will help you to spell many words. The person who says *sup rise* for *surprise* will probably spell the word incorrectly, leaving out the first *r.* The person who says *mod ren* for *modern* will also probably misspell the word.

Study the pronunciation of the words in the following list. Notice how incorrect pronunciation leads to incorrect spelling.

escape	(*not* excape)
ridiculous	(*not* rediculous)
entrance	(*not* enterance)
temperament	(*not* tempermant)
athletic	(*not* athaletic)
recognize	(*not* reconize)
height	(*not* heighth)
perspiration	(*not* prespiration)

MECHANICS

5. *Proofread your papers before handing them in. Proofreading* is the process of carefully rereading for inaccuracies whatever you have written. Proofreading is the best cure for carelessness in punctuation, capitalization, spelling, and grammar. It takes only a few minutes, yet it makes a great difference in the correctness of your work.

SPELLING RULES

The English language owes its richness to the vast number of words it has borrowed from other languages. The cost of this richness, however, is wide variety in spelling. Words that sound alike are, all too often, not spelled alike. Nevertheless, there are strong family likenesses among many words, and the simple rules describing them are easy to learn.

ie and *ei*

28a. Write *ie* when the sound is long *e,* except after *c.*

EXAMPLES   piece, belief, niece, deceive, receive, conceive

EXCEPTIONS   either, seize, neither, weird, leisure

Write *ei* when the sound is not long *e,* especially when the sound is long *a.*

EXAMPLES   neighbor, weigh, veil, freight, forfeit, height

EXCEPTIONS   friend, mischief

EXERCISE 1. Spelling *ie* and *ei* Words.   Write the following words, supplying the missing letters (*e* and *i*) in the correct order.

1. ach . . . ve	6. w . . . ld	11. conc . . . ve
2. rec . . . pt	7. y . . . ld	12. sl . . . gh
3. p . . . rce	8. c . . . ling	13. v . . . l
4. bes . . . ge	9. dec . . . t	14. th . . . r
5. rel . . . f	10. rec . . . ve	15. h . . . ght

-cede, -ceed, and -sede

28b. Only one English word ends in *-sede: supersede.* Only three words end in *-ceed: exceed, proceed,* and *succeed.* All other words of similar sound end in *-cede.*

EXAMPLES recede, concede, precede

Adding Prefixes

A prefix is one or more than one letter or syllable added to the beginning of a word to change its meaning.

28c. When a prefix is added to a word, the spelling of the word itself remains the same.

il + legible = **il**legible	dis + advantage = **dis**advantage
in + sensitive = **in**sensitive	dis + similar = **dis**similar
im + partial = **im**partial	mis + lead = **mis**lead
un + necessary = **un**necessary	mis + spell = **mis**spell
re + capture = **re**capture	over + run = **over**run

Adding Suffixes

A suffix is one or more than one letter or syllable added to the end of a word to change its meaning.

28d. When the suffixes *-ness* and *-ly* are added to a word, the spelling of the word itself is not changed.

EXAMPLES usual + ly = usual**ly**   mean + ness = mean**ness**
EXCEPTIONS Words ending in *y* change the *y* to *i* before *-ness* and *-ly*: *steady—steadily, sloppy—sloppiness.* One-syllable adjectives ending in *y*, however, generally follow Rule 28d: *shy—shyness, dry—dryly.*

EXERCISE 2. Spelling Words with Prefixes and Suffixes. Spell correctly the words indicated.

1. *heavy* with the suffix *ness*
2. *satisfied* with the prefix *dis*
3. *mean* with the suffix *ness*
4. *legal* with the prefix *il*
5. *spell* with the prefix *mis*
6. *sincere* with the suffix *ly*
7. *nerve* with the prefix *un*
8. *qualified* with the prefix *un*
9. *literate* with the prefix *il*
10. *ordinary* with the suffix *ly*
11. *ability* with the prefix *in*
12. *mature* with the prefix *im*
13. *consider* with the prefix *re*
14. *adequate* with the prefix *in*
15. *appoint* with the prefix *dis*
16. *sudden* with the suffix *ness*
17. *use* with the prefix *mis*
18. *stated* with the prefix *mis*
19. *special* with the suffix *ly*
20. *rate* with the prefix *over*

MECHANICS

28e. Drop the final *e* before a suffix beginning with a vowel.

EXAMPLES   dine + ing = dining
sense + ible = sensible
use + able = usable

EXCEPTIONS   Keep the final *e* before a suffix beginning with *a* or *o* if necessary to retain the soft sound of *c* or *g* preceding the *e*.
serviceable, advantageous, manageable
dye + ing = dyeing [to prevent confusion with *dying*]

28f. Keep the final *e* before a suffix beginning with a consonant.

EXAMPLES   use + ful = useful
advertise + ment = advertisement

EXCEPTIONS   true + ly = truly
argue + ment = argument

EXERCISE 3. Spelling Words with Suffixes. Correctly write the words formed as indicated.

1. guide + ance
2. courage + ous
3. approve + al
4. nine + ty
5. taste + less
6. advance + ing
7. compare + able
8. hope + ful
9. whole + ly
10. achieve + ment

28g. With words ending in *y* preceded by a consonant, change the *y* to *i* before any suffix not beginning with an *i*.

EXAMPLES   lively + ness = liveliness
bury + ing = burying
bury + al = burial

EXERCISE 4. Spelling Words with Suffixes. Correctly write the words formed as indicated.

1. happy + est
2. friendly + est
3. merry + est
4. marry + ing
5. marry + ed
6. prophesy + ing
7. prophesy + ed
8. carry + er
9. beauty + ful
10. spy + ing
11. pity + ful
12. pity + ing
13. mercy + ful
14. satisfy + ed
15. try + ed
16. pretty + ness
17. busy + ly
18. busy + ing
19. gory + ness
20. glory + fied

MECHANICS

28h. Double the final consonant before a suffix that begins with a vowel if both of the following conditions exist:

(1) The word has only one syllable or is accented on the last syllable.

(2) The word ends in a single consonant preceded by a single vowel.

EXAMPLES   win + ing = winning [one-syllable word]
omit + ed = omitted [accent on the last syllable]
begin + er = beginner [accent on the last syllable]
differ + ence = difference [accent on the first syllable]
droop + ed = drooped [single consonant ending preceded by
a *double* vowel]

EXERCISE 5. Spelling Words with Suffixes. Correctly write the words formed as indicated.

1. hit + er
2. propel + er
3. shovel + ing
4. refer + al
5. beg + ing
6. refer + ed
7. deter + ent
8. repel + ent
9. confer + ed
10. suffer + ance
11. develop + ed
12. pin + ing
13. deep + en
14. big + est
15. hop + ing
16. shop + ed
17. remit + ance
18. rebel + ion
19. stop + ing
20. control + ed

The Plural of Nouns

28i. Observe the rules for spelling the plural of nouns.

(1) The regular way to form the plural of a noun is to add an *s*.

EXAMPLES   dog, dogs   pencil, pencils

(2) The plural of some nouns is formed by adding *es*. Words ending in *s, x, z, sh*, and *ch* form the plural by adding *es*.

The *e* is necessary to make the plural form pronounceable.

EXAMPLES   waltz, waltzes   trench, trenches
bush, bushes   glass, glasses

(3) The plural of nouns ending in *y* following a consonant is formed by changing the *y* to *i* and adding *es*.

EXAMPLES   city, cit**ies**   spy, sp**ies**
                  enemy, enem**ies**   penny, penn**ies**

(4) The plural of nouns ending in *y* following a vowel is formed by adding an *s*.

EXAMPLES   turkey, turkey**s**   essay, essay**s**

(5) The plural of most nouns ending in *f* or *fe* is formed by adding *s*. The plural of some nouns ending in *f* or *fe* is formed by changing the *f* or *fe* to *v* and adding *es*.

EXAMPLES   Add *s:*
              belief, belief**s**   chief, chief**s**
              roof, roof**s**   cliff, cliff**s**
           Change *f* or *fe* to *v* and add *es:*
              wife, wi**ves**   wolf, wol**ves**
              knife, kni**ves**   thief, thie**ves**
              leaf, lea**ves**

(6) The plural of nouns ending in *o* preceded by a vowel is formed by adding *s*. The plural of most nouns ending in *o* preceded by a consonant is formed by adding *es*.

EXAMPLES   *o* preceded by a vowel:
              patio, patio**s**   radio, radio**s**
         o preceded by a consonant:
              tomato, tomato**es**   hero, hero**es**

EXCEPTIONS   Words ending in *o* that refer to music form the plural by adding *s:*
              alto, alto**s**   piano, piano**s**
              soprano, soprano**s**   solo, solo**s**

(7) The plural of a few nouns is formed in irregular ways.

EXAMPLES   child, children   woman, women
              ox, oxen   tooth, teeth
              mouse, mice

(8) The plural of compound nouns consisting of a noun plus a modifier is formed by making the noun plural.

In the following examples, the phrases *in chief* and *in-law,* and the words *on* and *up,* are all modifiers. The nouns modified by them are made plural.

EXAMPLES editor in chief, editors in chief
son-in-law, sons-in-law
looker-on, lookers-on
runner-up, runners-up

(9) The plural of a few compound nouns is formed in irregular ways.

EXAMPLES drive-in, drive-ins
lean-to, lean-tos
two-year-old, two-year-olds

(10) Some nouns are the same in the singular and the plural.

EXAMPLES Chinese, Chinese   trout, trout   sheep, sheep
deer, deer   salmon, salmon

(11) The plural of foreign words is sometimes formed as in the original language.

EXAMPLES alumnus [man], alumni [men]
alumna [woman], alumnae [women]
vertebra, vertebrae
parenthesis, parentheses
datum, data
monsieur, messieurs

> ☞ NOTE The plural of other foreign words may be formed either as in the foreign language or in the regular way in English by adding *s* or *es*. Sometimes the English plural is preferred: For such words, consult the dictionary.

EXAMPLES formula, formulae or formulas [preferred]
index, indices or indexes [preferred]
concerto, concerti or concertos [preferred]

(12) The plural of numbers, letters, signs, and words considered as words is formed by adding an apostrophe and *s*.

EXAMPLES In the equation are two *t*'s.
There are three *7*'s in my address.
Please don't use so many *and*'s.

MECHANICS

EXERCISE 6. Spelling the Plural of Nouns. Write the plural form of each of the following nouns and the number of the rule that applies.

1. dish
2. girl
3. valley
4. oasis
5. calf
6. porch
7. sky

8. goose
9. coach
10. monkey
11. Japanese
12. ox
13. father-in-law
14. deer

15. solo
16. self
17. board of education
18. alumnus
19. loaf
20. hero

EXERCISE 7. Following Rules for Spelling Words Correctly. By referring to the rules you have learned, explain orally the spelling of each of the following words:

1. crises
2. deceive
3. writing
4. believe

5. sopranos
6. misstep
7. meanness
8. noticeable

9. relief
10. cities

WORDS FREQUENTLY CONFUSED

Some of the following words are confusing because they are homonyms —their pronunciation is the same. Others are confusing because their spelling is the same or similar.

affect	[verb] *Affect* is usually a verb meaning *to influence.* Did that tearful movie *affect* you?
effect	[noun or verb] As a verb, *effect* means *to accomplish.* New glasses *effected* a remarkable change in his vision. As a noun, *effect* means the *result of some action.* What *effect* did the rain have on the garden?
all right	[This is the acceptable spelling. *Alright* is not acceptable.]
already	*previously* We have *already* painted the sets.
all ready	*all are ready* We were *all ready* to leave.

MECHANICS

all together   *everyone in the same place*
The teammates were *all together* in the gym.

altogether   *entirely*
I am not *altogether* convinced.

brake   [noun or verb] *to slow yourself down* or the device you use to do so
At the curve, Georgia *braked* the speeding car.
The driver applied the *brakes* abruptly.

break   [noun or verb] *to fracture* or the fracture itself
Don't *break* the speed limit.
I studied for three hours before I took a *break*.

capital   [Correct spelling for all uses except when the word means a *government building*.]
What is the *capital* of Colorado?
You need *capital* to start a business.
Begin all sentences with *capital* letters.
Do you believe in *capital* punishment?

capitol   government building [frequently capitalized]
We could see the *capitol* from our hotel.

choose   [verb, present tense]
Alicia and Katherine, *choose* partners now.

chose   [verb, past tense]
When the signal was given, the girls *chose* two seniors.

coarse   *rough, crude*
When he spilled the *coarse* salt, he used *coarse* language.

course   *path of action;* also used with *of* to mean *as was to be expected*
Of course, you are always right.
She skipped the first *course* at dinner.
The *course* in speech helped my diction.
A new golf *course* opened last week.

complement   [noun or verb] *to make whole or complete* or *that which makes whole or complete*
The *complement,* or full crew, is six hundred people.
The *complement* of 60° is 30°.

compliment   [noun or verb] *respect, affection,* or *esteem*
Convey my *compliments* to the captain.
I *complimented* her on her success.

MECHANICS

consul	[noun] *a diplomat appointed by a government to reside in a foreign country and look after the interests of fellow citizens traveling or doing business there* The American *consul* in Rangoon arranged for my trip to the interior.
council, councilor	[noun] *a group meeting to discuss and take action on official matters; a member of such a group* The *councilors* on the Security *Council* voted for the Canadian resolution.
counsel, counselor	[noun or verb] *advice* or *to advise; an adviser* Sue's aunt *counseled* her to take judo lessons. Ask your guidance *counselor*.
des'ert	a dry region The car crossed the *desert* at night.
desert'	to leave The rats *deserted* the unlucky ship.
dessert	*the last part of a meal* For *dessert* we had custard.

EXERCISE 8. Completing Sentences with Words Frequently Confused. Number your paper 1-10. After the proper number, write the correct one of the words given in parentheses.

1. The illness had a strange (affect, effect) on Margie.
2. The soccer team was (all together, altogether) at one huge table in the dining room.
3. My cousin knows the (capitol, capital) city of every state in our country.
4. Of (course, coarse), you burned the (desert, dessert) again.
5. The British (council, consul) removed his pince-nez and (counciled, counseled) Marlowe to leave Stanleyville.
6. After all his worry, everything turned out (all right, alright).
7. The two fast guards on our basketball team are (complimented, complemented) perfectly by an exceedingly tall center.
8. The actors were (all ready, already) to audition for the play.
9. If you don't have your car's (brakes, breaks) inspected every year, you will be (braking, breaking) a state law.
10. Did you (choose, chose) a topic for your essay yet?

EXERCISE 9. Writing Sentences with Words Frequently Confused.
Write sentences in which you use correctly each of the words just studied.

---

formally

in a formal manner
For funerals, weddings, and christenings, one should dress *formally*.

formerly

previously
The high ridges of the Blue Ridge Mountains were *formerly* the bed of an ancient sea.

---

hear

use your ears
You will have to speak louder; I can't *hear* what you are saying.

here

this place
You can't sit *here;* this section is only for juniors.

---

its

possessive of it
The town hasn't raised *its* tax rate in three years.

it's

it is
It's not time to get up.

---

lead

[present tense] *to go first*
You *lead* us to the restaurant because you know the way.

led

[past tense of *lead*]
He *led* us five miles out of the way.

lead

[pronounced "led"] *a heavy metal;* also *graphite in a pencil*
These books are as heavy as *lead*.

---

loose

free, not close together
Put all the *loose* papers in the folder.
His little brother has two *loose* teeth.

lose

[pronounced "looz"] *to suffer loss*
Do not *lose* your tickets.

---

miner

[noun] *a collier* or *worker in a mine*
Miners' canaries told them when the air grew bad in the deep shafts.

minor

lesser or *under legal age*
In some states in our country, *minors* may not operate a vehicle after dark.

MECHANICS

| moral | good; also a lesson of conduct
We admire a *moral* person.
The *moral* of the story is to look before you leap. |
| morale | mental condition, spirit
After three defeats, the team's *morale* was low. |

| passed | [verb, past tense of *pass*]
We *passed* the papers to the front. |
| past | [noun or adjective or preposition]
To understand the present, you must study the *past*.
Adele read the minutes of the *past* meeting.
The dog walked right *past* the cat and never noticed it. |

EXERCISE 10. Completing Sentences with Words Frequently Confused. Number your paper 1-10. After the proper number, write the correct one of the words given in parentheses.

1. Where did you (here, hear) that story?
2. If you (lose, loose) the directions, we'll never get there.
3. The general spoke to the troops to improve their (moral, morale).
4. While the heir was a (minor, miner), the estate was held in trust.
5. Our horse (lead, led) all the others around the track.
6. In only a few minutes the guest speaker will be (hear, here).
7. After she went on a diet, her clothes were too (lose, loose).
8. (Formerly, Formally), California was part of New Spain.
9. (Its, It's) not every day that her parents let her use the car.
10. After two years of taking French I, Barney (passed, past) the course.

EXERCISE 11. Writing Sentences with Words Frequently Confused. Write sentences in which you correctly use each of the words just studied.

| personal | individual
The manager gave the customer his *personal* attention. |
| personnel | a group of people employed in the same place
The management added four new employees to the *personnel*. |

principal	*head of a school;* also an adjective, *main* or *most important* The *principal* of our school is Mr. Grebinar. The *principal* export of Brazil is coffee.
principle	*a rule of conduct;* also *a main fact* or *law* Her *principles* are very high. On what *principle* did you base your argument?
quiet	*silent, still* To study properly, one should make sure there is complete *quiet.*
quite	*wholly* or *rather* or *very* Are you *quite* sure the studio is soundproof?
shone	[past tense of *shine*] The star *shone* in the sky.
shown	*revealed* or *demonstrated* The slides were *shown* after dinner.
stationary	*in a fixed position* One of the desks is movable; the other is *stationary.*
stationery	*writing paper* That purple and perfumed *stationery* is in bad taste.
than	[a conjunction, used for comparisons] She is smarter *than* I.
then	[an adverb or conjunction] *at that time* or *next* We swam for an hour; *then* we went home. They didn't know me *then.*
their	[possessive of *they*] *Their* new apartment has a view of the river.
there	*a place:* also an expletive I haven't been *there* in ages. *There* is too much pepper in my soup.
they're	*they are* *They're* singing off-key.

MECHANICS

EXERCISE 12. Completing Sentences with Words Frequently Confused. Number your paper 1-10. After the proper number, write the correct one of the words given in parentheses.

1. Jonathan doesn't understand any of the (principals, principles) of physics.
2. The sun (shone, shown) all day.
3. He acts much older (than, then) he really is.
4. She spoke in a (quite, quiet) voice, (quite, quiet) out of keeping with her usually raucous manner.
5. You ask too many (personnel, personal) questions.
6. (Quite, Quiet) soon after the strange uproar, all became (quite, quiet) again.
7. The bookstore is having a big sale on (stationery, stationary).
8. We are going to (there, their, they're) house.
9. If you see the (principle, principal) in the hall, tell him he is wanted in the main office.
10. I don't care what (their, they're, there) parents let them do; you still aren't going to come in so late at night.

EXERCISE 13. Writing Sentences Using Words Frequently Confused. Write sentences in which you correctly use each of the words just studied.

to	[preposition; also part of the infinitive form of the verb] You must return the books *to* the library. He began *to* whistle.
too	[adverb] *also, too much* Vito plays the trumpet, and Carrie plays it *too*. You are *too* young to drive.
two	one plus one I will graduate in *two* years.
waist	*the midsection* She wore a sash around her *waist*.
waste	[noun or verb] *to spend foolishly* or *a needless expense* *Waste* not; want not.
weather	*conditions outdoors* The *weather* has been perfect all week.
whether	[as in *whether or not*] They didn't know *whether* or not their parents would let them go canoeing.

MECHANICS

who's	*who is, who has* *Who's* been using my socks? *Who's* there?
whose	[possessive of *who*] *Whose* book is that?

your	[possessive of *you*] *Your* coat is in the closet.
you're	*you are* *You're* never on time.

EXERCISE 14. Completing Sentences with Words Frequently Confused. Number your paper 1-10. After the proper number, write the correct one of the words given in parentheses.

1. Around his (waste, waist) he wore a handmade leather belt.
2. (You're, Your) guidance counselor wants to see you today.
3. There was (too, to, two) much traffic on the road (too, to, two) enjoy the ride.
4. (Whose, Who's) going to use her ticket now?
5. It really doesn't matter (whose, who's) fault it is.
6. You (to, two, too) can be a good speller if you really have the desire.
7. (Weather, Whether) or not it rains or snows, we will be there.
8. This is fine (whether, weather) for a softball game.
9. (Your, You're) sure that Miss Thompson wanted to see me?
10. I don't know (whose, who's) taller, Brad or you.

EXERCISE 15. Writing Sentences with Words Frequently Confused. Write sentences in which you correctly use each of the words just studied.

One Hundred Spelling Demons

ache	answer	believe
again	any	blue
always	been	break
among	beginning	built

MECHANICS

business
busy
buy
can't
choose
color
coming
cough
could
country
dear
doctor
does
done
don't
early
easy
enough
every
existence
February
forty
friend
grammar
guess
half
having
hear
here
hoarse

hour
instead
just
knew
know
laid
loose
lose
making
many
meant
minute
much
none
often
once
piece
raise
read
ready
said
says
seems
separate
shoes
similar
since
some
straight

sugar
sure
tear
their
there
they
though
through
tired
tonight
too
trouble
truly
Tuesday
two
very
wear
Wednesday
week
where
whether
which
whole
women
won't
would
write
writing
wrote

Three Hundred Spelling Words

absence
absorption
abundant
acceptable
accidentally
accommodation
accompaniment
accurate
accustomed
achievement

acquaintance
actuality
adequately
administration
adolescent
aggressive
agriculture
amateur
ambassador
analysis

analyze
angel
annual
answered
apparatus
appearance
appropriate
approximately
arousing
arrangement

ascend
association
athlete
bankruptcy
basically
beneficial
benefited
bicycle
breathe
brilliant

calendar
category
changeable
characteristic
chemistry
chief
circumstance
civilization
cocoon
commencement

commissioner
committed
comparative
comparison
competition
conceivable
confidential
confirmation
conscientious
consciousness

consequently
considerable
consistency
continuous
controlled
controversial
cordially
corps
correspondence
criticize

curiosity
curriculum
definition
delegate
denied
develop
difference
disastrous
disciple
dissatisfied

distinction
distinguished
dividend
dominant
dormitory
earnest
easily
ecstasy
eighth
eliminate

embroidery
endeavor
enemy
enormous
equipment
especially
essential
estimation
etiquette
exaggeration

examination
exceedingly
exceptional
excitable
executive
exercise
exhaustion
exhibition
expense
extension

extraordinary
fallacy
fantasies
favorably
fiery
financial
foreigner
forfeit
fragile
fulfill

fundamentally
gasoline
grammatically
grateful
guidance
gymnasium
handkerchief
happiness
heroic
hindrance

humorist
hygiene
hypocrisy
illustrate
imitation
immense
inability
incidentally
indispensable
influential

innocence
inquiry
institute
intellect
interference
interpretation
interruption
interval
irrelevant
irresistible

MECHANICS

island
jealousy
journal
laborious
liability
lightning
likelihood
liveliest
locally
luxury

magnificence
maintenance
maneuver
mansion
martyr
maturity
medical
merchandise
merit
miniature

mischievous
missile
misspelled
monotony
mortgage
municipal
narrative
naturally
neighbor
noticeable

nuisance
obstacle
occasionally
occupy
odor
offensive
omitted
opinion
opposition
optimism

ordinary
organization
ornament
pageant
pamphlet
parachute
parallel
pastime
peaceable
peasant

peril
permanent
persistent
perspiration
pertain
phase
picnic
pigeon
playwright
pleasant

poison
politician
positively
possibility
practically
practice
precede
precisely
predominant
preferred

prejudice
preliminary
preparation
primitive
priority
prisoner
procedure
proceedings
procession
prominent

proposition
prosperous
prove
psychology
publicity
purposes
qualities
quantities
questionnaire
readily

reference
referring
regard
register
rehearsal
religious
remembrance
representative
requirement
resistance

resolution
responsibility
restaurant
ridiculous
satisfactorily
security
senator
sensibility
sheer
sheriff

significance
simile
situated
solution
sophomore
souvenir
specific
specimen
spiritual
strenuous

stretch
studying
substantial
subtle
succession
summarize
superintendent
suppress
surgeon
suspense

syllable
symbol
symphony
technique
temperature
tendency
tournament
traffic
twelfth
tying

tyranny
unanimous
undoubtedly
unforgettable
unpleasant
unusually
vacancies
varies
vengeance
villain

MECHANICS

PART FOUR

RESOURCES FOR
WRITING AND STUDYING

CHAPTER 29

The Library

ACCESS TO INFORMATION

During the Renaissance, some scholars set themselves the task of mastering all knowledge. Today no one imagines that one person can know all there is to know. There is simply too much information. As a result, you are not expected to know all the answers, just how to find the answers that you need.

You can find the answers to a great number of questions in a library or media center. Books, pamphlets, and other sources of information record knowledge for you to use. To take advantage of these resources, however, you must know what your library contains and how it is arranged.

ARRANGEMENT OF THE LIBRARY

29a. Learn the arrangement of resources in your library.

When you are familiar with one library you can find your way in others.

Fiction

The fiction section contains novels and stories imagined by creative writers. Here the books are arranged alphabetically according to the author's last name. Jane Austen's novels, for example, will come near the beginning of the section. If the library has several of her novels, they will be arranged under *Austen* alphabetically by *title*. For example, *Pride and Prejudice* will come before *Sense and Sensibility*.

Nonfiction

Since nonfiction includes so many kinds of books on so many subjects, the simple method used for arranging fiction is not adequate. Instead, most libraries use a system invented by Melvil Dewey.[1]

The Dewey decimal system classifies all nonfiction under ten major subject areas. Each area is assigned an identifying number, which is printed on the spine of a book near the bottom.

The classifications and the numbers that stand for them are as follows:

000–099	General Works (encyclopedias, periodicals, etc.)
100–199	Philosophy (psychology, behavior, etc.)
200–299	Religion (including mythology)
300–399	Social Sciences (communication, economics, government, etc.)
400–499	Language (dictionaries, grammars, etc.)
500–599	Science (mathematics, chemistry, physics, etc.)
600–699	Technology (agriculture, engineering, aviation, etc.)
700–799	The Arts (sculpture, painting, music, etc.)
800–899	Literature (poetry, plays, orations, etc.)
900–999	History (geography, travel, etc.)

Within each of the ten major classifications, there are an unlimited number of subdivisions. A work of history, for example, bears a number in the 900's. Since, however, even a small library might contain several hundred books on history, the 900's must be further broken down.

The Dewey decimal system accomplishes this by creating many subdivisions within each major class. For example, it breaks down the general class *History* in the following way:

900–999	History
910–919	Geography, Travel
920–929	Biography (arranged alphabetically according to the name of the person written about)
930–939	Ancient History
940–949	European History
950–959	Asian History
960–969	African History
970–979	North American History
971.0–971.99	Canadian History
972.0–972.99	Mexican History
973.0–973.99	United States History

---

[1] Large libraries may use a somewhat different method of classification developed by the Library of Congress. This system is not described here; but if a library in your area uses this system, the librarian will tell you how it works.

974.0–974.99 History of the Northeastern States
975.0–975.99 History of the Southeastern States
976.0–976.99 History of the South Central States

Therefore, a book bearing the number 972 will be generally a work of history (900), specifically a work on North American history (970), and still more specifically a work on Mexican history (972). This number, the *call number,* may include a decimal point and additional identifying numbers to indicate a smaller division of the subject, such as a particular period of history. Large libraries necessarily use many numbers after the decimal point, but in smaller libraries the author's initial is usually printed under the call number to distinguish the book from other works on the same subject.

For example, the call number $\frac{972}{P}$ may be used to designate William Prescott's history, *The Conquest of Mexico;* it will appear not only on the spine of the book itself, but also on every card in the card catalog referring to it.

Once you know the call number, you may go directly to the proper shelf and pick out the book or, if the stacks are not open to the public, have the librarian get the book for you.

LOCATING INFORMATION IN THE LIBRARY

The Card Catalog

29b. Learn the uses of the card catalog.

In every library there is a cabinet of small drawers containing cards that list every book in the library alphabetically. In the average library there are three cards for each book: a *title card,* an *author card,* and at least one *subject card.*

1. *The author.* On the *author card,* the author's name appears on the top line, last name first. If you want a book by a particular writer, look it up under the author's last name. All books by an author are listed on similar cards and are arranged under the author's name in alphabetical order of their *titles.* All books *about* an author are listed on cards coming after the cards for the author's own books.

2. *The title.* The title of the book is printed at the top of the *title card.* Title cards are arranged alphabetically according to the first letter of the

title. However, if this first word is an article—*a, an,* or *the*—the card is filed according to the next word. Jack London's *The Call of the Wild* would come under the *C*'s, not the *T*'s.

3. *The subject.* The subject is printed at the top (usually in red) on the *subject card*. This card is a great timesaver when you go into the library to look up information on a topic with no particular book in mind. Among the subject cards, you frequently find still other subject cards dealing with different aspects of the main topic. For example, under the subject "Languages," you may find cards labeled "Linguists," "Orthography," "Composition," as well as "see" or "see also" cards. Under "Democracy," you might find a card saying, "See also Politics."

4. *The call number.* This Dewey decimal number appears on every catalog card referring to the book.

5. *The publisher and the date of publication.* This information is important to make sure you are consulting the latest information on any subject. A book on atomic physics published in 1980 would be vastly different from one published in 1930.

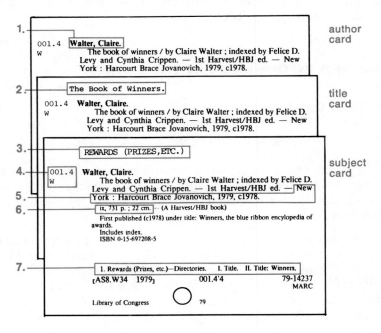

Sample Library Cards

6. *The description of the book.* Claire Walter's book, for example, has 9 pages of introductory material and 731 pages of text. It is not illustrated, nor does it have maps or charts, for these would be noted here. Twenty-two centimeters is the length of the book's spine.

7. *The subject headings in the card catalog under which the book is listed.*

EXERCISE 1. **Using the Card Catalog.** Remembering that books are cataloged by title, author, and subject, answer the following questions by using the card catalog in your library.

1. Does the library have these books?

   The Good Earth　　　*The Swiss Family Robinson*
   To Kill a Mockingbird　*Jane Eyre*

2. Does your library have any books written by Virginia Woolf, Marjorie Kinnan Rawlings, and John Dos Passos? If it does, write the title of one book by each.
3. Give the title, author, publisher, and publication date of a book about Martin Luther King, Jr.
4. Does your library have any books by Margaret Mead? If so, give the title and call number of one of them.
5. What is the most recent book about computers in your library? Give the call number.

The Parts of a Book

Once the card catalog has helped you find your book on the shelves, a quick glance at certain standard parts will tell you if it contains the information you seek.

29c. Learn the parts of a book.

Not every book has all the parts described here, but all books have some of them. Every careful reader should be familiar with them.

1. *The title page.* A page giving the complete title of the book, the complete name of the author (or authors), the name of the publisher, and the place of publication.

2. *The copyright page.* A page on the reverse side of the title page telling when the book was listed at the United States copyright office to protect the author's rights of ownership. The copyright page also tells by

whom the book was copyrighted (sometimes the author, sometimes the publisher).

The copyright date is important when you want to know if the book's information is up-to-date. A book may be many times reprinted (each time with a new publication date) and yet be unchanged in form and content. A new copyright date, on the other hand, informs you that new material has been added. Do not confuse the copyright date with a date of reprinting. Copyrights often appear as a list of dates.

EXAMPLE   Copyright © 1985, 1982, 1977, 1969

3. *The preface, foreword, or introduction.* A section at the beginning of a book in which the author may comment about the writing of the book, acknowledge help received from others, indicate the purpose of the book, and generally prepare the reader for what is to come.

4. *The table of contents.* A table giving the title of chapters or sections, their subdivisions, and the number of the page on which each begins. The table of contents enables you to determine whether the book contains the information you want without leafing through the entire book.

5. *List of illustrations.* A list telling what graphic materials (maps, pictures, diagrams, etc.) are provided in the book and where they are found.

6. *The appendix.* A section containing material not included in the body of the book, which the author nevertheless considers relevant. The appendix may include charts, maps, lists, statistics, or even long quotations from other works on the same subject. A text on American history might include the *Declaration of Independence* and the *Constitution* in the appendix.

7. *The glossary.* A dictionary section, usually at the end of the book, in which technical or difficult words and expressions are explained.

8. *The bibliography.* A list of books, periodicals, films, and other sources which the author has consulted in preparing the text. Bibliographies may appear as a list at the end of each chapter or at the end of the book.

9. *The index.* An alphabetical guide to all topics in the book. It is much more detailed than the table of contents and gives the exact page on which a topic is discussed. For those in search of specific information, it is the most important part of the book other than the text itself.

10. *The endpapers.* Pages pasted inside the front and back covers of the book. Maps, diagrams, charts, and illustrations are sometimes printed there. For example, the endpapers of a history of California might have a map of the state.

EXERCISE 2. Understanding the Parts of a Book. Write the answers to the questions that follow.

1. Explain the importance of the copyright date.
2. Why is a glossary more useful in a book about stagecraft than in a collection of modern plays?
3. What is the difference between a table of contents and an index?
4. By what company was this textbook published?
5. Skim the preface of this book, and briefly explain its main purpose.

The *Readers' Guide*

29d. Learn to use the *Readers' Guide to Periodical Literature.*

To find articles or topics published in a magazine, you will need to use the *Readers' Guide to Periodical Literature,* an index to the contents of more than one hundred and fifty magazines. The *Readers' Guide* is published eighteen times a year, and at regular intervals these booklets are combined into a cumulative volume.

Magazine stories are listed in the *Readers' Guide* by title and author; poems and plays are listed by author and under the headings POEMS and DRAMAS. A sample excerpt from the *Readers' Guide* is reproduced on page 654. You can probably figure out the meaning of the various abbreviations. If not, all of them are explained in the front of the *Readers' Guide* itself.

Information Files

29e. Learn the nature and proper use of the vertical file.

Useful information on current topics is often to be found in pamphlets. They are published by government agencies, industrial concerns, museums, colleges and universities, welfare organizations, etc. The librarian files pamphlets in a special cabinet, usually referred to as the vertical file, and can help you to find material on your subject, especially if it is of contemporary interest.

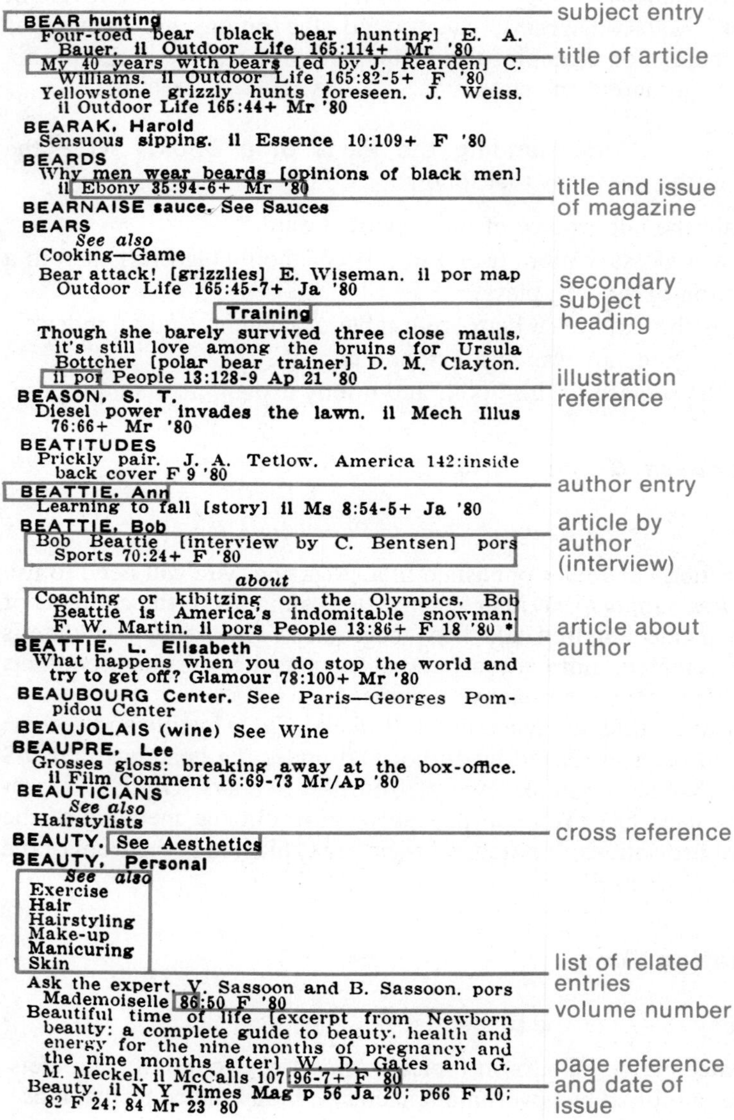

BEAR hunting
  Four-toed bear [black bear hunting] E. A.
    Bauer. il Outdoor Life 165:114+ Mr '80
  My 40 years with bears [ed by J. Rearden] C.
    Williams. il Outdoor Life 165:82-5+ F '80
  Yellowstone grizzly hunts foreseen. J. Weiss.
    il Outdoor Life 165:44+ Mr '80
BEARAK, Harold
  Sensuous sipping. il Essence 10:109+ F '80
BEARDS
  Why men wear beards [opinions of black men]
    il Ebony 35:94-6+ Mr '80
BEARNAISE sauce. See Sauces
BEARS
    See also
  Cooking—Game
  Bear attack! [grizzlies] E. Wiseman. il por map
    Outdoor Life 165:45-7+ Ja '80
      Training
  Though she barely survived three close mauls,
    it's still love among the bruins for Ursula
    Bottcher [polar bear trainer] D. M. Clayton.
    il por People 13:128-9 Ap 21 '80
BEASON, S. T.
  Diesel power invades the lawn. il Mech Illus
    76:66+ Mr '80
BEATITUDES
  Prickly pair. J. A. Tetlow. America 142:inside
    back cover F 9 '80
BEATTIE, Ann
  Learning to fall [story] il Ms 8:54-5+ Ja '80
BEATTIE, Bob
  Bob Beattie [interview by C. Bentsen] pors
    Sports 70:24+ F '80
      about
  Coaching or kibitzing on the Olympics. Bob
  Beattie is America's indomitable snowman.
  F. W. Martin. il pors People 13:86+ F 18 '80 *
BEATTIE, L. Elisabeth
  What happens when you do stop the world and
    try to get off? Glamour 78:100+ Mr '80
BEAUBOURG Center. See Paris—Georges Pom-
    pidou Center
BEAUJOLAIS (wine) See Wine
BEAUPRE, Lee
  Grosses gloss: breaking away at the box-office.
    il Film Comment 16:69-73 Mr/Ap '80
BEAUTICIANS
    See also
  Hairstylists
BEAUTY. See Aesthetics
BEAUTY, Personal
    See also
  Exercise
  Hair
  Hairstyling
  Make-up
  Manicuring
  Skin
  Ask the expert. V. Sassoon and B. Sassoon. pors
    Mademoiselle 86:50 F '80
  Beautiful time of life [excerpt from Newborn
    beauty: a complete guide to beauty, health and
    energy for the nine months of pregnancy and
    the nine months after] W. D. Gates and G.
    M. Meckel. il McCalls 107:96-7+ F '80
  Beauty. il N Y Times Mag p 56 Ja 20; p66 F 10;
    82 F 24; 84 Mr 23 '80

Annotations (right margin):
- subject entry
- title of article
- title and issue of magazine
- secondary subject heading
- illustration reference
- author entry
- article by author (interview)
- article about author
- cross reference
- list of related entries
- volume number
- page reference and date of issue

In the vertical file the librarian also stores interesting pictures and important clippings from newspapers.

29f. Use microfilm and microfiche to find information.

To save space, many libraries store some publications or documents on microfilm and microfiche. *Microfilm* is a roll or reel of film containing photographically reduced publications. You view the film through a projector that enlarges each microscopic image to a size suitable for reading. *Microfiche* is a sheet of film, rather than a roll or reel, containing photographically reduced publications. To read the microfiche, you use a machine that, like the microfilm projector, enlarges the microscopic images to a readable size. Your librarian can tell you which publications are stored on microfilm or microfiche, where they are located in the library, and how to use the appropriate projectors.

29g. Use computers to find information.

Many libraries and media centers are replacing their present book lists, catalogs, and periodical lists with a computerized system. Instead of looking through the card catalog or the *Readers' Guide,* you type the information you need into the computer. Then the computer searches for the titles and locations of the publications on that subject and prints a list. Depending on the type of computer, you might have to read the list from the screen, or you might be able to get a printout of the list of books or periodicals. The librarian will be able to tell you how to use the computers.

REFERENCE BOOKS IN THE LIBRARY

29h. Acquaint yourself with the reference books in your library.

In every media center there is an area known as the reference section. Here the librarian keeps together those ready-reference volumes that are designed to help you look up brief articles giving various kinds of information.

Special Dictionaries

Various dictionaries of the English language, such as those described on pages 662–64, are in the reference sections of libraries. In addition, there are many special dictionaries to help you with specific problems of word choice, correct usage, etc. Very often a writer has trouble thinking of the exact word to express a certain meaning. Often, too, a writer has used the same word so many times in a composition that he would like to find a synonym for it to avoid monotonous repetition. The following two books will help you to find the right words.

Roget's Thesaurus of English Words and Phrases

The word *thesaurus* derives from a Latin word meaning "treasure," so that literally a thesaurus is a storehouse or treasury. The contents of this storehouse are synonyms and antonyms. While the thesaurus can be useful, you should use it with care. Since the synonyms are listed without definitions or other indication of differences in meaning, it is easy to choose an inappropriate word. For example, the following synonyms are given for the verb *change: alter, modulate, veer, swerve,* and *deviate.* All of these synonyms have something to do with the general idea of change, but each has a specific shade of meaning that would make it unsuitable for most of the contexts in which *change* appears.

Make it a rule to use a thesaurus only as a memory aid—a reminder of words you already know. Do *not* use an unfamiliar synonym you find in a thesaurus without checking its meaning in a reliable dictionary.

Webster's New Dictionary of Synonyms

Much safer to use because of its detailed distinctions between synonyms, *Webster's New Dictionary of Synonyms* can be a great help to a writer in search of a word.

Encyclopedias

Any encyclopedia offers information on a wide range of subjects. The articles in an encyclopedia are arranged alphabetically, but many facts and references can be found only by using the index. For example, the *Encyclopedia Americana* has a long entry on the "Olympic Games," but by using the index, you can find references to this topic elsewhere in the encyclopedia.

Encyclopedias are designed for quick reference. Because they give a general background on a subject, they are a good place to begin research on an unfamiliar subject. Remember, however, that encyclopedias should be the starting point, not the end, of research. A report based entirely on encyclopedia entries is likely to be too general to be of any real merit.

Most reliable encyclopedias are kept up-to-date through frequent revisions. In addition, yearbooks are published to supply information on important developments of the preceding year.

The following general encyclopedias are well known and widely used:

Collier's Encyclopedia
> 24 volumes
> Bibliography and Index in Volume 24
> Publishes *Collier's Yearbook*

Encyclopædia Britannica
> 30 volumes
> Cross-referencing throughout *Micropædia*
> Publishes the *Britannica Book of the Year*

Encyclopedia Americana
> 30 volumes
> Index in Volume 30
> Publishes the *Americana Annual*

World Book Encyclopedia
> 22 volumes
> Research Guide and Index in Volume 22
> Publishes an annual supplement

Biographical Reference Books

Besides the standard encyclopedias there are many reference books that give biographies of famous persons.

Webster's Biographical Dictionary

A one-volume work with very short entries giving the basic facts of the person's life.

The New Century Cyclopedia of Names

A three-volume work, the *Century Cyclopedia* contains short biographies as well as information about all sorts of proper names: people, places, works of art, events, literary and mythological characters.

Current Biography

Published monthly, *Current Biography* is the best source of information about prominent people in the news. A picture of the subject usually heads the biography. The monthly pamphlets are bound together into a book each year with a cumulative index. Using these indexes, the student can often follow the career of an important person from early issues of *Current Biography,* at which time the celebrity first attracted public attention, to the latest issues of the magazine, in which later achievements are reported. A separate index covers the years 1940 through 1970. The cumulative index runs from 1971 on.

Who's Who and *Who's Who in America*

These volumes give data about prominent *living* persons. *Who's Who* is a British publication dealing mainly with famous English people; *Who's Who in America* provides similar information about famous Americans. In both works the biographical entries are fairly short, giving such data as parentage, date of birth, positions held and honors received, principal achievements, names of immediate family, and present address. *Who's Who* is published annually; *Who's Who in America,* every two years.

Reference Books About Authors

Some books are devoted exclusively to literary men and women. In the "author" books by Stanley Kunitz, the biographies are headed with a picture of the subject. *The Writers Directory,* which comes out every two years, lists about 18,000 writers living today.

> *British Authors of the Nineteenth Century* by Kunitz and Haycraft
> *British Authors Before 1800* by Kunitz and Haycraft
> *Twentieth Century Authors* by Kunitz and Haycraft
> *American Authors 1600–1900* by Kunitz and Haycraft
> *European Authors 1000–1900* by Kunitz and Colby
> *The Writers Directory,* St. Martin's Press, N.Y.
> *Contemporary Authors,* and *Contemporary Authors, First Revision,*
>   Gale Research Company
> *World Authors* by Wakeman
> *Dictionary of Literary Biography,* Gale Research Company
> *American Writers* by Unger
> Magill's *Cyclopedia of World Authors*

Atlases

An atlas is chiefly a collection of maps, but it may contain a wealth of statistical material about industries, raw materials, trade routes, rainfall, air and sea currents, and many other kinds of information. Any of the following atlases are good and are likely to be found on the shelves of your library.

Goode's World Atlas
Hammond Contemporary World Atlas
New York Times Atlas of the World
National Geographic Atlas of the World

Four historical atlases of particular interest to students of world history are listed below. These atlases represent graphically historical changes from earlier times, showing the rise and fall of empires, the movement of peoples, and the spread of culture.

Heyden's *Atlas of the Classical World*
The American Heritage Pictorial Atlas of United States History
Rand McNally Atlas of World History
Shepherd's *Historical Atlas*

Almanacs and Yearbooks

For factual information on the world today, the most useful of all reference books are the almanacs. Two popular ones are the *World Almanac and Book of Facts* and the *Information Please Almanac*. All are usually published annually and are full of information and statistics about current events—sports, industry, agriculture, science, entertainment, and census information. In addition, almanacs contain articles on significant events and issues of the past year.

The Statesman's Yearbook

This large volume is published annually and contains a compilation of statistical information about the world and its nations. Most of the information is in quantitative form (e.g., number of bales of cotton produced, balance of foreign payments, etc.), and can be understood without much knowledge of economics. It begins with information about international organizations, like the United Nations and the World Council of Churches, and goes on to cover individual nations and other more limited organizations.

Literature Reference Books

Bartlett's *Familiar Quotations*

Occasionally you will need to know a quotation or the author of a quotation. In such a case, the place to look is the famous Bartlett's *Familiar Quotations*.

The quotations in Bartlett's are arranged chronologically by author; that is, Emily Dickinson comes before Robert Frost. At the end of the work, there is a huge index in which every quotation is listed alphabetically by its first (and every important) word.

Stevenson's *The Home Book of Quotations*

Used for somewhat the same purpose as Bartlett's, Stevenson's *The Home Book of Quotations* is, however, arranged differently. The quotations in this book are arranged by subjects.

Magill's *Quotations in Context*

This book of quotations includes the contexts of the quotations.

Granger's *Index to Poetry*

Granger's *Index* contains no poems. It tells you in what books you can find almost any poem or recitation (popular prose passage) you wish. If you know the title of a poem or its author, yet do not know in what books you will find the poem, look it up in Granger's.

Stevenson's *The Home Book of Verse* and Stevenson's *The Home Book of Modern Verse*

These anthologies, containing well-known poems, are so large that you are almost certain to find the poem you wish in any one of them. They are indexed in three ways—by title, by author, and by first word.

EXERCISE 3. **Selecting Reference Books.** Name the reference books best suited as sources for the following information. You may include dictionaries and encyclopedias. Be prepared to explain your choice.

1. A list of words meaning *knowledge*
2. An account of the construction of the Panama Canal

3. A very short biographical sketch of Coretta Scott King
4. An explanation of the difference in meaning between two common words often used interchangeably—*pretty* and *beautiful*
5. The years American tennis teams won the Davis Cup
6. The site in Asia Minor of ancient Troy
7. The average annual precipitation in Ghana
8. A clear explanation of Johann Kepler's laws of planetary motion
9. The principal exports of Argentina
10. A detailed map of Israel

CHAPTER 30

The Dictionary

ARRANGEMENT AND CONTENT OF DICTIONARIES

A good dictionary contains a wealth of information—the present spelling and meaning of a word, how a word is pronounced, what it has meant in the past, how it came to be a part of English, what other words it is related to, and other useful facts. Being able to find a word is an essential dictionary skill, but it is not the only one. It is equally important to know how to interpret the information.

KINDS OF DICTIONARIES

30a. Know the kinds of dictionaries.

Dictionaries have been prepared for many special purposes: for specialists in history, the sciences, and other special studies; for crossword puzzle enthusiasts; for poets and others with special interests. This chapter deals only with two main kinds of general dictionaries: *unabridged* and *college* dictionaries.

The Unabridged Dictionary

An unabridged dictionary is one that is not based on a still larger dictionary. The best known unabridged dictionary is *Webster's Third New International Dictionary,* which has been kept up to date through recent revisions. The newest unabridged dictionary is the *Random House Dictionary of the English Language, Unabridged Edition.*

An unabridged dictionary may contain almost a half-million words. For many words, it gives uncommon or historical meanings. It clarifies some meanings of a word by quoting examples of its use, and it contains fuller discussions of distinctions in meaning between words with similar meanings.

The College Dictionary

A college dictionary is a shorter work, designed for quick, convenient reference. Such a dictionary may contain from 125,000 to 150,000 words, as well as special sections giving abbreviations, biographical information of famous people, articles on spelling and punctuation, and other useful information. As the sample entries (page 664) suggest, a college dictionary does not report as fully on a word as an unabridged dictionary does. On the other hand, college dictionaries are likely to be revised more frequently and thus often have more up-to-date information on the meanings and uses of words.

Since all dictionaries must pack a great deal of information into relatively little space, they make extensive use of abbreviations, special signs and symbols, and other shortcuts. Each dictionary has its own system of abbreviations and symbols that is explained in the front part of the book. Compare the following two entries.

Unabridged Dictionary

¹ten·sion \'tenchən\ *n* -s *often attrib* [MF or L; MF *tension,* fr. L *tension-, tensio,* fr. *tensus* (past part. of *tendere* to stretch) + *-ion-, -io* -ion — more at THIN] **1 a :** the act or action of stretching or the condition or degree of being stretched to stiffness **:** TAUTNESS ⟨to install the belt, slip it over the pulleys and adjust its ∼ —H.F.Blanchard & Ralph Ritchen⟩ **b :** STRESS ⟨arterial ∼⟩ ⟨muscular ∼⟩ **c :** a momentary state of muscular tautness in dance technique that inevitably resolves into relaxation **2 a :** either of two balancing forces causing or tending to cause extension **b :** the stress resulting from the elongation of an elastic body — contrasted with *compressive stress* **c** *archaic* **:** PRESSURE **3 a :** inner unrest, striving, or imbalance **:** a feeling of psychological stress often manifested by increased muscular tonus and by other physiological indicators of emotion ⟨went back to bed and dropped asleep suddenly with the release of ∼ —Mary Austin⟩ ⟨∼s distort personality —Bruce Bliven b. 1889⟩ **b :** a state of latent hostility or opposition between individuals or groups (as classes, races, nations) ⟨there is bitter ∼ between them —Bernard De Voto⟩ ⟨a lessening of minority-group ∼s —J.A.Morris b. 1904⟩ ⟨mob insanity explodes when ∼ reaches the flash point —*New Republic*⟩ **c :** a balance maintained in an artistic work (as a poem, painting, musical composition) between opposing forces or elements **:** a controlled dramatic or dynamic quality ⟨the ∼ which makes his sonata . . . so compelling —Stephen Spender⟩ ⟨the poetry of Dryden and Pope is characterized by the ∼ between its constituent elements —F.W.Bateson⟩ **4 :** ELECTRIC POTENTIAL **5 :** any of various devices in textile manufacturing machines or sewing machines that are used to control the tautness and movement of thread or material passing through **syn** see BALANCE, STRESS

College
Dictionary

¹ten·sion \'ten-chən\ *n* [MF or L; MF, fr. L *tension-, tensio,* fr. *tensus,* pp.] **1 a :** the act or action of stretching or the condition or degree of being stretched to stiffness : TAUTNESS **b :** STRESS 1b **2 a :** either of two balancing forces causing or tending to cause extension **b :** the stress resulting from the elongation of an elastic body **c** *archaic* : PRESSURE **3 a :** inner striving, unrest, or imbalance often with physiological indication of emotion **b :** a state of latent hostility or opposition between individuals or groups **c** : a balance maintained in an artistic work between opposing forces or elements **4 :** electrical potential **5 :** a device to produce a desired tension (as in a loom) — **ten·sion·al** \'tench-nəl, -ən- l\ *adj* — **ten·sion·less** \'ten-chən-ləs\ *adj*

From *Webster's Ninth New Collegiate Dictionary.* © 1986 by Merriam-Webster Inc., publisher of the Merriam Webster ® Dictionaries. Reprinted by permission of Merriam-Webster Inc.

EXERCISE 1. Using the Dictionary to Find Information. Open to the table of contents at the front of your own dictionary. Notice where to find the introductory notes, the beginning of the definitions, and the special tables, charts, and illustrations. Then, on your paper, write down the page numbers on which each of the following items of information can be found.

1. An explanation of the way syllables are divided in the dictionary entries
2. The meaning of the abbreviation *SALT*
3. The population of Tampa
4. The capital of Uruguay
5. The dates (birth and death) of Jane Addams
6. An explanation of the metric system
7. The meaning of the abbreviations *n., adv., v.t.,* and *v.i.*
8. The meaning of the word *slalom*
9. A guide to capitalization
10. An explanation of the treatment of prefixes

KINDS OF INFORMATION IN DICTIONARIES

30b. Become familiar with the kinds of information in your dictionary and the method by which the information is presented.

As you study the following information that dictionaries contain, examine the sample column from a college dictionary on page 666.

Spelling

The boldfaced word at the beginning of a dictionary entry gives you the spelling. If there are other accepted spellings for a word, the various spellings are given. If one spelling is more common than another, the common one is given first. When in doubt, you will always be safe in using the first spelling.

EXAMPLES   judgment, judgement   theater, theatre

If a grammatical change in the form of a word is likely to create a spelling problem, this form is given. For example, a dictionary gives the plural of a word if the word is spelled irregularly—*hero—heroes*; it gives the present and past participle forms of *refer*, showing that the final *r* is doubled—*referring, referred*; it gives the comparative form of *funny*, with the *y* changed to *i—funnier*.

Capital Letters

Proper nouns and proper adjectives are given with capital letters in college dictionaries. If a word is capitalized in certain meanings only, a dictionary labels these meanings *cap.*

EXAMPLE   **pres·i·dent** (prĕz′ə-dənt, -dĕnt′) *n. Abbr.* **p., P., pres., Pres.**
1. One appointed or elected to preside over an organized body of people, as an assembly or meeting. **2.** *Often capital* **P.** The chief executive of a republic, especially of the United States. **3.** The chief officer of a branch of government, a corporation, a board of trustees, a university, or any similar body.   [Middle English, from Old French, from Latin *praesidens*, present participle of *praesidēre*, PRESIDE.] **—pres′i·dent·ship′** *n.*

Division of Words into Syllables

When it is necessary to divide a word at the end of a line, the word should be divided between syllables. Most dictionaries indicate a break between syllables with a centered dot (el·e·va·tor) Syllable division is indicated in the boldfaced entry word.

Pronunciation

Dictionaries indicate the pronunciation of words by means of accent marks and respellings which show clearly how the words should sound. The respellings are necessary because our alphabet uses more than two hundred combinations of letters to represent the forty-two or -three sounds. Each letter or special symbol used in the respellings always stands for the same sound. The sounds represented by the various letters and other symbols in the respellings are shown in a key that

in·fec·tive (in fek′tiv) *adj.* [ME. *infectif* < OFr. < L. *infectivus*] likely to cause infection; infectious ——————— main entry

in·fe·cund (in fē′kənd, -fek′ənd) *adj.* [ME. *infecunde* < L. *infecundus*] not fecund; not fertile; barren —**in·fe·cun·di·ty** (in′fi kun′də tē) *n.* ——————— pronunciation respelling

in·fe·lic·i·tous (in′fə lis′ə təs) *adj.* not felicitous; unfortunate or unsuitable —**in′fe·lic′i·tous·ly** *adv.* ——————— part of speech

in·fe·lic·i·ty (-tē) *n.* [L. *infelicitas* < *infelix,* unfortunate: see IN-² & FELICITY] **1.** the quality or condition of being infelicitous **2.** *pl.* **-ties** something infelicitous; unsuitable or inapt remark, action, etc.

in·fer (in fur′) *vt.* **-ferred′, -fer′ring** [L. *inferre,* to bring or carry in, infer < *in-,* in + *ferre,* to carry, BEAR¹] **1.** orig., to bring on or about; cause; induce **2.** to conclude or decide from something known or assumed; derive by reasoning; draw as a conclusion **3.** *a)* to lead to as a conclusion; indicate *b)* to indicate indirectly; imply: in this sense, still sometimes regarded as a loose usage —*vi.* to draw inferences —**in·fer′a·ble** *adj.* —**in·fer′a·bly** *adv.* —**in·fer′rer** *n.* ——————— spelling of verb forms ——————— numbered definitions

SYN.—infer suggests the arriving at a decision or opinion by reasoning from known facts or evidence [*from your smile,* I *infer* that you're pleased]; **deduce,** in strict discrimination, implies inference from a general principle by logical reasoning [*the method was* deduced *from earlier experiments*]; **conclude** strictly implies an inference that is the final logical result in a process of reasoning [*I must, therefore,* conclude *that you are wrong*]; **judge** stresses the careful checking and weighing of premises, etc. in arriving at a conclusion; **gather** is an informal substitute for **infer** or **conclude** [*I* gather *that you don't care*] ——————— synonyms with illustrative examples of usage and meaning

in·fer·ence (in′fər əns) *n.* [ML. *inferentia*] **1.** the act or process of inferring; specif., the deriving of a conclusion in logic by either induction or deduction **2.** something inferred; specif., a conclusion arrived at in logic

in·fer·en·tial (in′fə ren′shəl) *adj.* [< ML. *inferentia* + -AL] based on or having to do with inference —**in′fer·en′tial·ly** *adv.*

in·fe·ri·or (in fir′ē ər) *adj.* [ME. < L., compar. of *inferus,* low, below < IE. *ndheros,* whence UNDER] **1.** lower in space; placed lower down **2.** low or lower in order, status, rank, etc.; subordinate **3.** lower in quality or value than (with *to*) **4.** poor in quality; below average **5.** *Anat.* located below or directed downward **6.** *Astron.* between the earth and the sun [*Mercury and Venus are* inferior *planets*] **7.** *Bot.* having the sepals, petals, and stamens attached at the apex: said of the ovary of an epigynous flower **8.** *Printing* placed below the type line, as 2 in NO₂ —*n.* an inferior person or thing —**in·fe′ri·or′i·ty** (-ôr′ə tē, -är′-) *n.* ——————— etymology ——————— restrictive label ——————— illustrative example

inferiority complex 1. *Psychol.* a neurotic condition resulting from various feelings of inferiority, such as derive from real or imagined physical or social inadequacy and often manifested through overcompensation in excessive aggressiveness, a domineering attitude, etc. **2.** popularly, any feeling of inferiority, inadequacy, etc.: cf. SUPERIORITY COMPLEX ——————— cross reference

in·fer·nal (in fur′n'l) *adj.* [ME. < OFr. < LL. *infernalis* < L. *infernus,* underground, lower, infernal < *inferus:* see INFERIOR] **1.** *a)* of the ancient mythological world of the dead *b)* of hell **2.** hellish; diabolical; fiendish; inhuman **3.** [Colloq.] hateful; outrageous —**in·fer′nal·ly** *adv.* ——————— usage label ——————— derived form with label

infernal machine *earlier name for* a booby trap or time bomb

in·fer·no (in fur′nō) *n., pl.* **-nos** [It. < L. *infernus:* see INFERNAL] hell or any place suggesting hell, usually characterized by great heat or flames —[**I-**] that section of Dante's *Divine Comedy* which describes hell and the sufferings of the damned

usually appears at the front of the dictionary and at the bottom of every pair of facing pages. Since different dictionaries use different systems of indicating pronunciation, you should familiarize yourself with the key and notes on pronunciation in your own dictionary. The more detailed presentation of pronunciation that begins on page 671 of this book shows several different systems in wide use.

Part of Speech

After each word listed in the dictionary, an abbreviation tells what part of speech the word is.

noun *n.*	adjective *adj.*
verb *v.*	preposition *prep.*
adverb *adv.*	conjunction *conj.*
pronoun *pron.*	interjection *interj.*

Since many words may be used as more than one part of speech, some entries will contain several part-of-speech labels. In the sample column on page 666, for example, the first eight definitions for *inferior* are labeled *adj.* and the last one is labeled *n.* Verbs have, in addition to the label *v.*, the labels *v.i.* (intransitive verb) and *v.t.* (transitive verb). See the entry for *infer* on page 666.

Meaning

Since a single word may have many different meanings, many dictionary entries contain a number of different definitions, which are distinguished from one another by means of letters and numbers. Numbers usually indicate important differences in meaning, and letters indicate differences within the numbered definitions.

In some dictionaries, these separate meanings are listed in historical order—the earliest recorded meaning first, the latest last. Other dictionaries give meanings in order of the frequency of their use—from the most common meaning to the least common. The following definitions illustrate these two methods of ordering meanings. The first is in historical order, and the second in order of use.

hec·tic \'hek-tik\ *adj* [ME *etyk,* fr. MF *etique,* fr. LL *hecticus,* fr. Gk *hektikos* habitual, consumptive, fr. *echein* to have — more at SCHEME] **1** : of, relating to, or being a fluctuating but persistent fever (as in tuberculosis) **2** : having a hectic fever **3** : RED, FLUSHED **4** : filled with excitement or confusion <the ~ days before Christmas> — **hec·ti·cal·ly** \-ti-k(ə-)lē\ *adv*

hec·tic (hek′tĭk), *adj.* **1.** characterized by intense agitation, feverish excitement, confused and rapid movement, etc.: *The period preceding the trip was hectic and exhausting.* **2.** marking a particular habit or condition of body, as the fever of phthisis (**hec′tic fe′ver**) when this is attended by flushed cheeks (**hec′tic flush′**), hot skin, and emaciation. **3.** pertaining to or affected with such fever; consumptive. —*n.* **4.** a hectic fever. **5.** a hectic flush. **6.** a consumptive person. [< LL *hectic(us)* < Gk *hektikós* habitual, equiv. to *hekt-* (s. of *hēxis*) state, condition + *-ikos* -IC; r. ME *etyk* < MF] —**hec′ti·cal·ly,** **hec′tic·ly,** *adv.* —**hec′tic·ness,** *n.*

Derivation

Most dictionaries indicate the history of a word. They show by means of abbreviations what language the word originally came from and what its original meaning was. English is unusual among languages for the vast number of words it has taken from other languages. The source of newly coined words is also given. Knowing the source and original meaning of a word is often a great help to you in understanding the word's present meaning and correct use.

The abbreviations that are used to indicate the languages from which words are derived are explained in the front of your dictionary under the heading "Abbreviations Used in This Book" or another heading of essentially the same meaning. The following derivation of *curfew* is given in *Webster's New World Dictionary:*

cur·few (kʉr′fyōō) *n.* [ME. *curfeu* < OFr. *covrefeu,* lit., cover fire < *covrir* (see COVER) + *feu,* fire < L. *focus,* fireplace (see FOCUS)]

The symbol < means "from" (abbreviated *fr.* in some dictionaries). If this etymology were written out, it would read "derived from Middle English *curfeu* from Old French *covrefeu,* literally "cover fire," from *covrir* (see COVER) + *feu,* "fire," from Latin *focus,* "fireplace" (see FOCUS).

Restrictive Labels

Most words defined in a dictionary belong to the general vocabulary of standard English. Some words, as well as some special meanings of otherwise standard words, require special treatment, and these usually appear with a label. There are three main kinds of labels: *subject* labels, which specify that a word has a particular meaning in a certain field: *Law, Med., Aeron.* (Aeronautics), etc.; *geographical* labels, which indicate the area in which a particular word, meaning, or pronunciation is principally used: *Brit., SW U.S.* (Southwest U.S.); and *usage* labels, which characterize usage of a word: *informal, slang, nonstandard,* etc. As the following examples show, however, different dictionaries may not agree about giving a usage label:

glitch \'glich\ *n* [prob. fr. G *glitschen* to slide, slip; akin to OHG *glitan* to glide — more at GLIDE] **1 a** : an unwanted brief surge of electrical power **b** : a false or spurious electronic signal **2** : MALFUNCTION <a – in a spacecraft's fuel cell> **3** : MISHAP *also* : a minor technical problem

From *Webster's Ninth New Collegiate Dictionary.* © 1984 by Merriam-Webster Inc., publishers of the Merriam Webster ® Dictionaries. Reprinted by permission of Merriam-Webster Inc.

glitch (glich) *n.* [< G. colloq. *glitsche,* a slip < *glitschen,* to slip, slide, intens. of G. *gleiten:* see GLIDE] [Slang] a mishap, error, malfunctioning, etc.

Synonyms and Antonyms

For some entries in the dictionary, synonyms or antonyms, or both, are given. A synonym is a word having nearly the same meaning as the word being defined: *brave—courageous.* An antonym is a word having the opposite meaning: *brave—cowardly.* See the entry for *infer* on page 666.

Illustrations

If the meaning of a word can best be shown by a picture, the dictionary may give an illustration. In most cases, pictures will accompany definitions of objects that are difficult to describe.

OTHER INFORMATION IN THE DICTIONARY

Biographical Entries

Who was Clara Barton? When did Pablo Casals die? What was Chopin's nationality? What were the dates of Queen Elizabeth I's reign? For what is Thurgood Marshall famous? What was George Eliot's real name? The answers to such simple fact questions about famous persons can probably be found in your dictionary.

Some dictionaries have a special section called *Biographical Names.* Others give names of persons and places in a section called *Proper Names.* Sometimes these names are included in the body of the book.

The following common pieces of biographical information are usually given in a dictionary:

1. *Name:* spelling, pronunciation, first name
2. *Dates:* of birth and death and of reign if a king or queen, or term of office if head of a government
3. *Nationality*
4. *Why famous*

The following is a typical dictionary entry for a famous name.

> **King** (kiṅg), *n.* **1. Ernest Joseph,** 1878–1956, U.S. naval officer. **2. Martin Luther,** 1929–68, U.S. Baptist minister: civil-rights leader; Nobel peace prize 1964. **3. Rufus,** 1755–1827, U.S. political leader and statesman. **4. William Lyon Mackenzie,** 1874–1950, Canadian statesman: prime minister 1921–26, 1926–30, 1935–48. **5. William Rufus De·Vane** (də vān′), 1786–1853, vice-president of the U.S. 1853.

Mythological and Biblical characters, as well as some literary characters, may be listed in the body of the dictionary: *Ruth, Lancelot, Scrooge, Juno,* etc.

Geographical Entries

Like the biographical entries in the dictionary, the geographical entries are sometimes given in the body of the book and sometimes in a special section. This section may be called a gazetteer—a geographical dictionary.

In general the following information is given about a place:

1. *Name:* spelling, pronunciation
2. *Location*
3. *Identification:* whether a city, country, lake, mountain, etc.
4. *Size:* population, if a city or country (often given in thousands: 225 = 225,000); area in square miles, if a country or territory or body of water; length, if a river; height, if a mountain, etc.
5. *Importance:* If a city is the capital of a state or country, this will be indicated by a star or an asterisk. The capital city of a country or state will also be given under the name of the country or state.
6. *Historical or other interesting information of importance:* For Lake Mead, formed by Hoover Dam in the Colorado River, one dictionary says "the largest artificial lake in the world."
7. *Governed or controlled by what country:* For Guam, the dictionary says "a possession of the U.S."

Miscellaneous Information

Most good dictionaries include the following kinds of information, either in separate sections or in the body of the dictionary itself.

1. *Foreign words and phrases:* spelling, pronunciation, meaning
2. *Abbreviations:* a list of abbreviations of all kinds, giving the words in full

An unabridged dictionary and some of the larger student dictionaries include

3. *Signs and symbols:* Not all dictionaries include this section.
4. *Spelling rules*
5. *Punctuation rules*
6. *New words*

REVIEW EXERCISE A. Finding Information in the Dictionary.
Use your dictionary to help you write answers to the following questions.

1. Who was Ann Lee and for what is she famous?
2. Give the meaning of the abbreviation UNESCO.
3. What is the derivation of *hippopotamus*?
4. What is the height of Mont Blanc and where is it?
5. What is the capital of Mali?

REVIEW EXERCISE B. Finding Information in the Dictionary.
Look up in your dictionary the answers to the following questions:

1. Give the pronunciation and meaning of *dolce far niente*.
2. Give the more usual pronunciation of *apparatus*.
3. What country governs the Falkland Islands?
4. Who was Mrs. Malaprop? For what is she famous?
5. What is the meaning of the abbreviation CIF?

PRONUNCIATION

30c. Use your dictionary for pronunciation.

Because the actual spelling of many English words does not clearly indicate how they are pronounced, dictionaries use simplified respellings and special symbols called *diacritical marks* to show pronunciation.

The following pair of words illustrates both respelling and the use of diacritical marks.

knit (nit)   knife (nīf)

Notice that in both respellings the silent letters are dropped—both silent *k's* and the *e*. Notice also that the *i* in *knit* is unmarked, and the *i* in *knife* is written with a straight line above it.

You need to know how to interpret the pronunciation given in your own dictionary. Check the explanatory notes dealing with pronunciation and with the pronunciation key. Most dictionaries explain in the introductory pages the system they use. A full key is usually given inside the front cover. Many dictionaries print a shorter key on each page or each set of facing pages. The key illustrates the use of each letter and symbol used, giving simple examples that everyone knows how to pronounce.

The Schwa

Modern dictionaries use an *e* printed upside down (ə) to represent the indistinct sound of vowels. This symbol, called the *schwa* (shwa), is used in such words as:

against	(ə·genst')	correct	(kə'rekt')
banal	(bə nal')	serpent	(sûr'pənt)

EXERCISE 2. Finding the Pronunciation of Words in the Dictionary. Using the pronunciation key of your dictionary, pronounce each of the following words.

1. consummate
2. cultural
3. genuine
4. hog
5. hypothetical
6. irrevocable
7. Themistocles
8. thistle
9. those
10. Worcester

Accent

In words of more than one syllable, one syllable is pronounced louder than the others or other. The syllable stressed in this way is said to be *accented* and is marked with an *accent mark*. Dictionaries mark accents in two main ways: with a heavy accent mark (') after the accented syllable or with a mark (') before the syllable.

KEY WORD	WNC[1]	RHC[2]
compete	kəm-'pēt	kəm pēt'
pony	'pō-nē	pō'nē

Some longer words have two accented syllables—one receiving a heavy, or primary, stress and the other receiving a light, or secondary, stress. The following example illustrates ways of showing this difference in accent.

KEY WORD	WNC[1]	RHC[2]
elevator	'el-ə-vāt-ər	el'ə-vā' tər

Sometimes the same word may be accented in different ways, depending upon how the word is used. The listed words are examples of how the accent shifts when the words are used as different parts of speech.

com'pact (noun)	com·pact' (adjective)
con'duct (noun)	con·duct' (verb)
con'tent (noun)	con·tent' (adjective)
pro'test (noun)	pro·test' (verb)

EXERCISE 3. Finding the Accented Syllables and Part of Speech of Words. Rewrite each italicized word, showing the accented syllables and the part of speech as given in your dictionary.

EXAMPLE   1. I **refuse** to carry out the **refuse**.
            1. (*re fuse'*) *v.*, (*ref'use*) *n.*

1. One cannot *object* to the *object* of trial by jury: to allow the guilt of an accused person to be judged by peers.
2. The new track *record* was duly *recorded* in the book.
3. To *console* her invalid sister, Victoria bought her a huge mahogany *console,* housing both a TV and a record player.
4. Although the police did not *suspect* him, the thief sensed that to Sherlock Holmes he was already a *suspect*.
5. The queen's *consort* was known to *consort* openly with enemies of the crown.

EXERCISE 4. Finding the Phonetic Spelling of Words. Using the pronunciation key in the front part of your dictionary, write the vowel markings above the vowels in the following common words. Place ac-

---

[1] The abbreviation stands for *Webster's New Collegiate Dictionary.*
[2] The abbreviation stands for *The Random House College Dictionary.*

cent marks in the words of more than one syllable. The final silent *e*, of course, should not be marked.

1. like
2. boil
3. fur nish
4. re make

5. pro tect
6. rob in
7. com ment

8. loop hole
9. un til
10. out cast

CHAPTER 31

Vocabulary

LEARNING AND USING NEW WORDS

Tests are playing an increasingly important role in our lives. They are used to measure success in school and often to decide who is accepted into a particular college or kind of job. These tests differ, but most of them place great importance upon vocabulary. To prepare for these tests, you will find it worthwhile to take stock of your vocabulary right now and to consider ways of improving it.

The best way to increase your vocabulary is to read widely and thoughtfully. There are ways in which you can add to your vocabulary more of the new words you encounter than you may be adding now. This chapter will give you experience in using these techniques of word study.

DIAGNOSTIC TEST

Selecting the Meanings of Words

A. Number your paper 1–5. From the list below, choose the definition for the underlined word in each sentence and write the letter by the proper number. Use context clues to find the best meaning.
  a. producing wealth or profit
  b. to swing indecisively from one opinion to another
  c. characterized by graciousness

d. briefness of duration
e. to make impossible; prevent
f. vague; indistinct
g. to push or thrust out

1. The popular speaker was known for his humor and *brevity*.
2. Selling popcorn at the basketball game became a *lucrative* project.
3. Although it looked like an easy bookcase to assemble, the project was difficult because the instructions were very *nebulous*.
4. The community's failure to support the fund-raiser *precluded* the band from sponsoring another talent night.
5. As the prom approaches, Mike *vacillates* between going and staying home.

B. Number your paper 1–5. After the proper number, write the letter of the synonym for the underlined word. Use context clues to find the best synonym.

1. After a grueling track practice, Kelly needed something to *assuage* her thirst.
   a. relieve   b. rub   c. brighten
2. The hikers walked for two days before finding a *denizen* who could lead them out of the swamp.
   a. bear   b. tower   c. inhabitant
3. An *indolent* typist refuses to correct his mistakes.
   a. sorrowful   b. lazy   c. unpredictable
4. A rabid raccoon was the *miscreant* that attacked the children.
   a. friend   b. visitor   c. villain
5. When the play was canceled, the cast assumed the *onerous* job of notifying everyone who had purchased tickets.
   a. burdensome   b. rich   c. frequent

WAYS TO LEARN NEW WORDS

You have learned some of the words you know by looking them up in the dictionary, but the number of words you can learn this way is limited. Most of the words that you have in your vocabulary have come to you in other ways. You are constantly meeting new expressions in the course of your schoolwork and your conversations, but you will never be able to make them a part of your own word list unless you become *word conscious*. Be alert for new words, and when you meet them, you will be able to add them to your collection.

Context

31a. Learn new words from their contexts.

If your teacher asks you what *cumulative* or *exotic* means, or if your younger brother looks up from a book and asks if you know what *grotesque* means, you won't be able to answer their questions unless the words are already in your vocabulary. However, most of the words you encounter will not be isolated; instead, you will find them surrounded by other words and used in specific situations that will help you guess their meaning. The total situation in which a word is found is called its *context.* Often you can find clues in the context which help you discover the meaning of a new word. The most common context clues are **definition, synonym, example,** and **comparison** or **contrast.**

Definition

To ensure complete understanding, a writer may define or restate a word in a different way in the same sentence. Sometimes wording such as *that is, in other words,* or *or* will be there to indicate a definition. Read the following sentence.

> The nomenclature, or system of naming, now used in botany is in part the work of Linnaeus.

In this sentence *nomenclature* is defined by the phrase *system of naming.*

Sometimes a definition will be in the form of an appositive or appositive phrase (see pages 406–407). Read the next example.

> The opprobrium, the deep public disgrace, of this treason stayed with him for the rest of his life.

The word *opprobrium* is defined by the appositive phrase *the deep public disgrace.*

Synonym

A writer may use a familiar synonym for an unfamiliar word in the same sentence. For example, in the following sentence, the writer uses the familiar word *treasury* as a synonym for the unfamiliar word *coffer.*

> The club's coffer was so low that the members had to solicit donations to fill the treasury.

Example

By reading the context carefully, you may find an example of a word that is new to you. Words and phrases such as *for example, for instance, such as, especially,* and *other* are often used with examples. If you did not know the meaning of the word *espionage*, you could probably guess the meaning from the two examples in the following sentence.

> The scientist was accused of several acts of espionage such as photographing secret documents and taping private conversations.

Comparison and Contrast

A writer may compare or contrast an unknown word with a more common word. For example, in the following sentence, *ornate edifice* is compared with *decorated building*, and the word *dilapidated* is contrasted with *stately*.

> The ornate edifice, like other decorated buildings of that era, now looked dilapidated rather than stately as it had in earlier years.

Look for words such as *like* or *as* to indicate a comparison and words such as *but, unlike, although,* and *rather than* to indicate contrast.

EXERCISE 1. Determining the Meanings of Words by Using Context Clues.

Copy the italicized word in each of the following sentences. Then examine the context clues, and write down what you think the word means. Check your answers in your dictionary.

EXAMPLE 1. The scientific report was so *abstruse* that even Professor Bowen had trouble comprehending it.
   1. *abstruse—difficult to understand*

1. This word is *ambiguous;* in other words, it can have two meanings.
2. They wanted no *remuneration* in money or gifts; their only reward would be the knowledge that they had saved the child.
3. The *epitaph* on her tombstone was brief: "Here lies one who died for her country."
4. After a *cursory* examination rather than a complete one, the doctor said that the child probably had not been seriously hurt.
5. The business had an extremely *lucrative* year; in fact, that year was their most profitable.
6. To drive home his accusation by repetition, he *reiterated* that he thought Smithers was a liar.

7. Smoking is likely to have a *pernicious* effect on one's health by contributing to a deadly disease.
8. Michael looked at the dead roach on the shelf without trying to conceal his *repugnance* or distaste.
9. She gave a *succinct,* or brief, account of her adventures.
10. The overpowering odor of roses spread from room to room, *permeating* the whole house.

EXERCISE 2. Determining the Meanings of Words by Using Context Clues. Number your paper 1–10. From the list of definitions below, choose the one that defines the underlined word in each sentence and write the letter by the proper number. Use context clues to help you learn the correct meaning.

a. to free from entanglement or difficulty
b. tediously long
c. keen in judgement
d. to forgive or overlook
e. to make less harsh or severe
f. careful in all details
g. unaware or forgetful
h. to discredit or disgrace
i. apprehension or fear
j. to pull out or extend
k. not inclined to speak
l. longing for the past or for home

1. *Oblivious* of the terrible danger threatening her, she sauntered along absent-mindedly.
2. Although he wanted to be part of the gang, Peter did not go because he knew his father would never *condone* his actions.
3. The *interminable* speech seemed endless to the children.
4. Before surgery, it is normal to have some signs of *trepidation* such as a nervous stomach or sweaty palms.
5. The trapped animal struggled for hours but could not *extricate* itself from the snare.
6. He was a *fastidious* dresser, always very neat and particular about what he wore.
7. The soothing ointment will *mitigate* the pain of the burn.
8. Cathy can be very chatty, unlike her sister, who is usually *reticent*.
9. The lonely explorers could not put aside their feelings of *nostalgia*.

10. An *astute* shopper will not be deceived by people on the street who sell expensive watches at ridiculously low prices.

Using the Dictionary

31b. Learn to find the meaning that fits the context.

To build up your vocabulary systematically, do not rely entirely on context clues. Track down the word further in the dictionary.

Very few nonscientific words in English have a single meaning. Most have many meanings, often entirely different when the context is different. Therefore, the first step in finding the meaning of any new word is always to determine how it is being used when you read it or hear it for the first time in conversation.

To help you, dictionaries often provide sample contexts. One dictionary, for example, lists twelve definitions of the word *bond* as a noun. The list begins with the most common use, "that which binds or holds together; a band; tie," and proceeds through more and more specialized contexts, for example, the meaning of *bond* in law, in finance, in insurance, in commerce, etc., and ends with its very specialized meaning in chemistry. This arrangement of definitions allows you to find quickly the one that best suits the context of your word.

Some dictionaries enter definitions in the order of frequency or importance. The first meaning given is the one considered the most common, and the one given last is considered the least common. Another type of order is historical order. A dictionary using historical order would give as the first definition of the word *forum* the notion of a Roman marketplace or other open public area and would list the idea of a public meeting much later. A dictionary that arranges its definitions in terms of contemporary importance would reverse this order.

EXERCISE 3. Finding the Meanings of Words in the Dictionary.

Number your paper 1–5. The italicized words in the following sentences all have a number of different meanings. Consult your dictionary to find the meaning that best fits the context of the word in the sentence. Then write the meaning after the proper number on your paper.

1. The pasture creek was fed by three tiny *affluents*.
2. Mr. Yamamoto was a teacher of high *caliber*.
3. The image on the screen *dissolved* from a tube of toothpaste to a panorama of giant cacti.
4. Joanne *executed* a series of elaborate dance steps on her skates.

5. To defend her interest in the suit, Ms. Jones *retained* a young attorney.

Finding the Right Word

31c. Select the right synonym, the word that conveys the precise meaning and impression you want to give.

You cannot use the dictionary for very long before discovering that there are many words meaning approximately the same thing. The distinctions in meaning between synonyms, though sometimes very slight, are important and are carefully preserved by people who want their speech to be as lively and expressive as possible. Consider, for example, the multiple ways a person can *say* something:

announce	descant	lisp	recite
answer	drawl	observe	reiterate
argue	enunciate	opine	respond
asseverate	expatiate	perorate	retort
aver	expostulate	plead	roar
comment	grate	preach	state
coo	hint	probe	threaten
declare	insinuate	proclaim	utter
deliver	insist	query	vociferate
demand	intimate	question	whisper

As you can see, none of these verbs are interchangeable, but some are nearly so. Remember that a useful vocabulary is one that for every common word has a good stock of synonyms.

EXERCISE 4. Using Synonyms to Complete Sentences. Number your paper 1–10. For each of the following sentences, choose from the preceding list the most appropriate synonym for the word *say*. Use a different synonym for every sentence, and change the tense of the verb to suit the context. Write the word next to the proper number on your paper.

1. Asked for the fifth time, Ted —— angrily that he had no more.
2. Endlessly, Mrs. Bronson —— the rule until the class knew it by heart.

3. Reminded of his oath, the witness —— that he had heard nothing that night.
4. Quick-witted Marie —— instantly to the cruel taunt by her older brother.
5. The subject was complex and difficult; accordingly, Mr. Ives —— on it slowly and methodically.
6. Told that promptly on February 2 the woodchuck comes out of its burrow to calculate the length of its shadow, Ms. Ranby, our biology teacher, removed her glasses and —— that there was more fancy than fact in that story.
7. Lucy was not bold enough to state her suspicions openly; she merely —— that our dog was guilty.
8. The President —— that henceforward the day would be dedicated to the memory of the war dead.
9. The civil authorities —— that the rioting stop.
10. Unwilling at first to announce her candidacy, Ms. Dixon —— that at a later date she would announce her intentions.

EXERCISE 5. Selecting the Synonyms of Words. Number your paper 1–10. After each number, write the letter of the synonym for the italicized word.

1. If we bought the property, our farm would *abut* the land of the famous author.
   a. ram   b. adjoin   c. hint
2. The doctor's announcement *allayed* the tension in the hospital waiting room.
   a. relieved   b. befriended   c. juggled
3. The little girl tried to *cajole* her grandfather into buying her another ice cream cone.
   a. calculate   b. heal   c. coax
4. The only way to make the back yard safe was to find the red ant pile and *decimate* it.
   a. operate   b. destroy   c. decide
5. The tired and lost hikers dropped the useless articles which *encumbered* them.
   a. hindered   b. consumed   c. undermined
6. Even though the parts were ready-made, it took us all day to *fabricate* my sister's dollhouse.
   a. brighten   b. make   c. descend

7. A new coat of paint would certainly *furbish* the old house.
   a. brighten   b. darken   c. sign
8. The reformed alcoholic promised to *imbibe* only nonalcoholic beverages.
   a. sponsor   b. bribe   c. drink
9. When all the facts were known, the suspect *recanted* his previous statement.
   a. retracted   b. argued   c. republished
10. Everyone waited while the guide *ruminated* over the situation of the lost trail markers.
    a. enlarged   b. pondered   c. belittled

PREFIXES AND ROOTS

Many words now part of the English language have been "borrowed" from another language. Latin has contributed more words to the English vocabulary than any other foreign language. Greek has also contributed a number.

Short elements that come before the main part of a word are called *prefixes; trans-* and *circum-* are common prefixes. The main part of the word is called the *root; -port-* and *-fer-* are roots. The part which is added at the end of the main part of the word is the *suffix; -ion* and *-ence* are suffixes. *Transportation* and *circumference* are words formed from these elements.

31d. Learn some of the common Latin and Greek prefixes.

Latin Prefixes

Learn the meaning of the following prefixes:

LATIN PREFIX	MEANING	LATIN PREFIX	MEANING
contra-	against	in-	in, into, not
de-	from	inter-	between, among
dis-	away, from, not	intra-	within
ex-	out of	non-	not

EXERCISE 6. Understanding Latin Prefixes. Using your dictionary, give the meaning of the prefix and the root word. Then show how the combination gives the meaning of the word.

EXAMPLE **ad**vent = ad (to) + (come) = arrive

1. **contra**band   3. **ex**cavate   5. **intra**mural
2. **dis**integrate   4. **inter**pose

Now learn the meanings of these prefixes:

LATIN PREFIX	MEANING	LATIN PREFIX	MEANING
per-	through	retro-	back
post-	after	semi-	half
pre-	before	sub-	under
pro-	before	super-	above
re-	back, again	trans-	across

EXERCISE 7. Understanding Latin Prefixes. Using the dictionary, write the meaning of each word in the following list, as you did in Exercise 6.

1. perennial   4. profane   7. semiannual   9. superhuman
2. posthumous   5. revoke   8. subjugate   10. translucent
3. preempt   6. retroactive

Greek Prefixes

The following Greek prefixes are found in many words in English as well as in other languages. Learn them for the exercise that follows.

GREEK PREFIX	MEANING
anti-	against
em-, en-	in
hemi-	half
hyper-	over, above

EXERCISE 8. Understanding Greek Prefixes. In a numbered list on your paper, write each prefix and, on the line below, each word. After each prefix, write its meaning. By referring to the dictionary, give a definition of each word.

1. antibiotic   3. embellish   5. hemisphere
2. hypercritical   4. encroach

EXERCISE 9. Understanding Greek Prefixes. By referring to the dictionary, define the following words by showing the relationship of the Greek prefix to the meaning.

1. hypo- (under) + dermic =
2. para- (beside) + phrase =
3. peri- (around) + meter =
4. pro- (before) + logue =
5. syn- (together) + thesis =

Changed Prefixes

English words sometimes use original forms of Latin and Greek prefixes, but those forms may have undergone change. The word *abbreviate,* despite its present form, does not illustrate an original *ab-* prefix but instead an original *ad-* prefix. The *d* of this prefix changed to *b* because it was much easier to say *abbreviate* than *adbreviate*. With the change in pronunciation came a change in spelling. The word now has two *b*'s in it. This kind of change is called *assimilation* and can be seen in many other prefixes besides *ad.*

ad	*com*
ad + peal = appeal	com + lect = collect
ad + tain = attain	com + rupt = corrupt
dis	*ex*
dis + ficult = difficult	ex + fort = effort
dis + lute = dilute	ex + lect= elect
sub	*in*
sub + ceed = succeed	in + legal = illegal
sub + pend = suspend	in + regular = irregular

As you can see, assimilation often disguises the original prefix. Despite this change, you can easily analyze words into their original components with the aid of any dictionary. It is a great aid to vocabulary building to do so.

EXERCISE 10. Writing the Original Forms of Prefixes. Number your paper 1–10. Write opposite each number the following words in order. Then, in a second column, write the original form of the prefix. Use your dictionary to find this. In a third column, write the root or base part of the word; this will be the remaining part of it.

EXAMPLE 1. divert
           1. *divert dis- vert*

1. allude		6. efface	
2. annex		7. elude	
3. appose		8. impart	
4. collide		9. succumb	
5. corrode		10. sympathy	

Latin and Greek Roots

It isn't hard to tell what beginning elements of words are prefixes. The *un-* of *unclear,* the *mis-* of *mistreat,* and the *re-* of *return* are obviously prefixes. It is somewhat more difficult, however, to identify a root.

A root is a base to which prefixes and suffixes may be added. Some roots, such as *clear* or *treat,* can appear by themselves. Many others, however, must have prefixes or suffixes added to them. One example is the root *-clude-,* which must have a prefix such as *con-* added to make *conclude.* Learning the meaning of some common roots will help you understand many new words.

31e. Learn some of the common Latin and Greek roots.

Learn the meaning of the following Latin roots in preparation for the exercise that follows.

LATIN ROOTS	MEANING	LATIN ROOTS	MEANING
-dic-, -dict-	say, speak	-spec-, -spic-	look, see
-fac-, -fact-	do, make	-tract-	draw, pull
-junct-	join	-vert-, -vers-	turn
-pon-, -pos-	place, put	-voc-	call
-scrib-, -script-	write	-volv-	roll, turn

EXERCISE 11. Writing the Meanings of Roots and Words.   Copy the words in boldfaced type. Referring to the dictionary, underline the root of each word, write the meaning of each root, and give the meaning of the word as it is used in the paragraph.

The governor read the letter that the secretary handed her and began to dictate an answer in faultless **diction.** Her **facile** delivery was not marked by any hesitation for thought as she explained her **position.** "At this critical **juncture** in the affairs of our state," she said, "we place confidence in the integrity of our legislators. We do not all **subscribe** to the same party policies, but we rely on one another's **perspicuity** to see the issues clearly. These **distractions,** designed to **subvert** the public welfare, are bound to fail, and in the face of the public outrage which has been **provoked,** we will do the duty that **devolves** upon us."

EXERCISE 12. Understanding Greek Roots. Learn the following Greek roots and their meanings. Then, using a dictionary, write the meanings of the words in the third column.

GREEK ROOT	GENERAL MEANING	WORD
1. -anthrop-	man	anthropology
2. -chron-	time	chronometer
3. -gen-	birth	genealogy
4. -geo-	earth	geology
5. -hetero-	different	heterogeneous

Study the meaning of these Greek roots.

GREEK ROOT	MEANING	GREEK ROOT	MEANING
-bio-	life	-log-	word, science
-homo-	same	-mon-, -mono-	one
-hydr-	water	-morph-	form

EXERCISE 13. Using Greek Roots to Define Words. Using the Greek roots above, define the following words by dividing each word into its proper parts. Refer to a dictionary.

EXAMPLE 1. monogamy
   1. *mono (one) + gamy (marriage) = one marriage*

1. homogeneous   3. monologue '   5. biology
2. hydrophyte   4. metamorphosis

Now study the meanings of these Greek roots.

GREEK ROOT	MEANING	GREEK ROOT	MEANING
-neo-	new	-psych-	mind
-ortho-	straight	-scop-	seeing
-pan-	all	-tech-	skill
-phon-	sound	-tele-	far

EXERCISE 14. Writing the Meanings of Roots and Words. Using the previous lists of Greek roots, copy the elements which are in boldfaced type, and write their meanings in relation to the following words. Then, by referring to the dictionary, write the meaning of the entire word.

EXAMPLE 1. live in a **demo**cracy
   1. *demo—people; democracy—rule of the people*

1. **anthrop**oid ape
2. **psych**osomatic ailment
3. a **hydr**aulic jack
4. an a**morph**ous substance
5. a **pan**demic disease
6. the science of eu**gen**ics
7. **phon**etic symbols
8. mental **tele**pathy
9. the **chron**ology of history
10. a **neo**phyte in a convent

EXERCISE 15. Selecting Vocabulary Words to Complete Sentences. Number your paper 1–10. Look up the following words in the dictionary, select the appropriate word for each blank in the sentences that follow, and write it after the proper number. Be prepared in class to identify and explain the prefixes and roots or bases.

anagram   epitome   lithograph   neolithic   philanthropist
epilogue   homophones   metabolism   orthodontist   protozoan

1. A concluding section added to a literary work is called an ——— .
2. The later Stone Age is referred to as the ——— age.
3. A dentist who specializes in straightening and adjusting teeth is called an ——— .
4. Two or more letters or groups of letters that have the same pronunciation are called ——— .
5. A microscopic, one-celled animal is called a ——— .
6. A word formed from another by transposing the letters is called an ——— .
7. A person who loves to help mankind and does good for humanity is called a ——— .
8. A picture made from a stone or a plate is called a ——— .
9. The chemical process by which cells derive energy from food and get rid of wastes is called ——— .
10. A condensed account or summary is called an ——— .

REVIEW EXERCISE. Using Prefixes and Roots to Define Words. Divide each of the following words into prefixes and roots, and explain how these parts make up the meaning of the word.

EXAMPLE   1. predict
          1. *pre (before)* + *dict (say)* = *to say beforehand*

1. circumspect
2. repose
3. subordinate
4. diverge
5. symbiosis
6. permeate

7. adjacent   9. posthumous
8. bipartisan   10. homonym

WORD ETYMOLOGIES

31f. Learn the *etymologies,* or origins and histories, of words as an aid to developing vocabulary.

Often, learning the etymology of a new word will help you remember it and use it well. The study of word etymologies may also provide some surprising information about words you have known for a long time.

Words with Interesting Etymologies

Many words have very interesting etymologies. Often our modern English words conceal within themselves references to romantic persons and places or to old, well-known stories. We all know the word *tantalize,* but few of us know that this word goes back to the Greek name *Tantalus.* Tantalus was a mythical figure who repeated the secrets told him by Zeus. He was punished by being placed in water that he could never drink because it always receded away from him and by having above him branches laden with fruit that always eluded his hungry grasp. Your dictionary is likely to give you short summaries of these histories.

EXERCISE 16. Writing the Etymologies of Words. Each of the following words in italics is derived from the name of a mythological or actual person. Number your paper 1–10. Referring to your dictionary, give the etymology of the words in italics below.

EXAMPLE   1. The outraged citizens resolved to *boycott* the store of the quarrel-
           some merchant.
        1. *boycott—refuse to do business with—from Captain Boycott, the*
           first person so treated

1. The *chauvinistic* politician made a warlike speech.
2. The winner said her *mentor* deserved more credit than she did.
3. The comedian kept us laughing by coming out with one *spoonerism* after another.
4. His *jovial* manner deserted him as he grew weary.
5. Rip Van Winkle's wife was a *termagant.*
6. The quiz contestant met her *nemesis.*

7. Only *herculean* strength could have accomplished the task that lay ahead.
8. It is sometimes difficult for a steady person to get along with one of *mercurial* disposition.
9. Faced by a *titanic* task, the man had the inclination to give up.
10. The quick thinking of the police officer prevented *panic*.

Recently Borrowed Words

English is filled with borrowed words. In fact, in the English language there are many more words borrowed from French, Latin, and Greek than there are from the original Anglo-Saxon or Old English phase of the language (the fifth to the eleventh centuries). Words given to illustrate Latin and Greek prefixes, bases, and roots in the preceding pages illustrate this. Many of these originally borrowed words are now so familiar to us that it comes as a surprise to think that they ever were foreign. But we have continued to borrow foreign words ever since early times, and we are still borrowing them. Sometimes we run across words borrowed rather recently, words that have been in the English language for so short a time that we still feel that they are foreign rather than English. These words may give us problems in determining their meanings (as well as their forms, spellings, and pronunciations).

EXERCISE 17. Learning the Meanings of Foreign Words or Phrases. Copy column A. After each item, write the language it comes from; then write the letter of the matching item from column B. You may refer to your dictionary.

A	B
1. nom de plume	a. noninterfering
2. junta	b. one's school or college
3. dilettante	c. a dabbler in the arts
4. denouement	d. slip in manners
5. hoi polloi	e. a secret council
6. coup d'etat	f. pen name
7. prima donna	g. an appetizer
8. faux pas	h. the masses
9. laissez-faire	i. outcome of a play or story
10. alma mater	j. sudden and decisive move
	k. false hope
	l. principal woman singer in opera

EXERCISE 18. **Writing Sentences Using Foreign Phrases.**

Consult your dictionary, write the meaning of the following words, and use them in a sentence.

EXAMPLE   1. à la carte
          1. *à la carte—with a stated price for each dish. Because he wanted a special combination of food, he ordered his meal à la carte.*

1. à la mode
2. entre nous
3. fait accompli
4. tour de force
5. gratis

Word List

You will find that many of the words in the following list contain familiar prefixes and roots. Make it a regular practice to learn new words from the list. Add them to the list in your notebook, giving the pronunciation, meaning, and etymology as you find them in the dictionary. Ten words a week will be as many as you can handle efficiently. After learning the words, use them as often as you can in your writing and speaking.

abdicate	assert	casement
abound	astute	caustic
acquittal	atrocious	censure
admirably	autonomy	charisma
aesthetic	axiom	clangor
affidavit	balmy	clemency
affiliate	bayou	cliché
amiable	bedlam	clientele
amnesty	beguile	closure
analogy	besiege	coffer
annihilate	bestride	coincidental
anthropology	bias	colloquial
antiquity	botch	commence
apex	bourgeois	commendable
appease	breach	compassion
apprehensive	buffet	compatible
aptitude	callous	compliance
arbiter	canine	composure
archaic	cant	conceive
ascertain	carp	concession

condescend
condole
conducive
consolidate
constituent
contemptuous
convene
crony
curtail
debase

debut
decimate
decrepit
defunct
delectable
demure
destitute
deteriorate
detonate
devastation

diminutive
disperse
diversion
documentary
ecstatic
edifice
edify
effervescent
eject
electorate

elite
emancipate
emphatically
encompass
encumber

enjoin
ensue
episode
equilibrium
erratic

espionage
ethical
evade
evolve
excerpt
expedient
explicate
exultant
fabricate
facilitate

facsimile
farce
flagrant
fluctuate
fortitude
gloat
grimace
harass
heresy
hieroglyphic

hors d'oeuvre
immaculate
impartial
impediment
imperceptible
implacable
imposition
inaccessible
inadvertent
inalienable

inanimate
inarticulate
incendiary
incentive
inclement
inconsistent
indestructible
indict
indignant
indomitable

ineffectual
inertia
infallible
influx
inhibition
innate
innovation
insipid
insolence
intermittent

intuition
invariably
invincible
irksome
irrational
irrelevant
itinerary
jargon
jostle
judicious

juncture
lament
lapse
latitude
legacy

lexicon
livid
loathe
malignant
malleable

mandatory
mannerism
martial
meager
mediocre
melancholy
melodramatic
mentor
merge
meticulous

mettle
mien
militant
momentum
mortify
mosque
mull
mutable
mystic
naive

negligible
notoriety
obligatory
obliterate
oblivious
odious
opportune
ornate
ossify
painstaking

palatable
pallid
paradox
paraphrase
parody
pastoral
patent
paternal
patriarch
pauper

perceive
perception
perseverance
personification
pertinent
pivotal
plausible
pompous
portly
posthumous

postulate
potency
precarious
prelude
pretext
prevalent
prolific
prophetic
protocol
protrude

proximity
purge
qualm
quantitative
quibble

rankle
ravage
reactionary
rebuke
recipient

recourse
rectify
recur
redundant
rejuvenate
reminiscent
rendezvous
repress
reprieve
requiem

requisite
resonant
retainer
retribution
rift
rivulet
sadistic
sardonic
scenario
seethe

sequel
simulate
sordid
sporadic
stamina
steppe
stimulant
stipulate
stratagem
stringent

submission
subsidiary
subsidize
substantially
succulent
succumb
synopsis
synthesis
tawny
theoretical

timorous
transcend
transition
transitory
translucent
ultimatum
unprecedented
vehement
verbatim
vigilant

visage
vulnerable
wan
wane
wheedle
whimsical
wreak
zealous
zenith
zephyr

CHAPTER 32

Studying and Test Taking

SKILLS AND STRATEGIES

Do you sometimes feel that you spend a lot of time doing homework but don't accomplish much? The time you take to develop good study habits will quickly be paid back.

A STUDY ROUTINE

32a. Establish an effective study routine.

Many students waste time and effort as they clear a place for their books, hunt for the scrap of paper the assignment was scribbled on, and then study while listening to the top twenty hits. Others end up working on a long-term project at the last minute or nodding over homework that they started too late in the evening.

All studying has two basic purposes. You study to acquire information and to apply this information. This chapter explains and illustrates skills and strategies that are effective means of achieving both of these purposes.

Follow these rules to cut down on your homework time and make the time you do spend much more effective.

1. *Establish a time and a place to do your homework.* You'll find you can do a better job if you have a place in your room or somewhere relatively quiet that you associate with work.

You may be reluctant to admit it, but "relatively quiet" means that you should not have your radio on. The mind cannot process two ideas simultaneously. If you pay any attention at all to the radio, you lose focus and spend more time getting through the material.

It is also important to schedule time each day for doing your assignments. While it is reasonable to take a break after a day of classes, do not wait until you are so tired that you cannot concentrate. In addition, make sure you plan a realistic amount of time for your work.

2. *Know your assignment.* Use an assignment book or a special page in each notebook to record your assignments precisely. Record pages, question numbers, and any special instructions. There is nothing more frustrating than discovering that you spent time doing the wrong thing.

It is also a good idea to set up some system for signaling long-term projects that are assigned in advance. Work out some kind of realistic schedule so you don't end up cramming everything in at the last minute.

Finally, make sure you follow directions *as they are given.* Know whether you are supposed to write single words or full sentences, to label a diagram or to give definitions, to prepare questions for class discussion or to write out the answers to be turned in. *Ask* if you are not sure what your teacher means or expects by an assignment.

3. *Review the assignment before beginning.* It is much easier to do a task when you know from the outset what is expected. When you are assigned a selection to read, begin by glancing through it to get a general sense of how the material is organized. Read the headings and glance at the study questions. They usually highlight the main points.

4. *Do study questions as a unit.* When you are actually doing the study questions, read them through before writing any answers. Very often the answer to one question serves as the basis for others.

Finally, when you have finished writing out an assignment, look over your answers. Be able to point to a specific place in the text that justifies each answer you wrote down.

32b. Use the SQ3R study method.

An educational psychologist, Francis Robinson, developed a method of study called *SQ3R*. The SQ3R study method is made up of the following five simple parts:

1. *S—Survey* the entire study assignment whether it is a chapter, a section, or a complete book. Look at the headings, the material in boldface and italics, the charts, outlines, and summaries. Get a general sense of the scope of the material.

2. *Q*—Make a list of *questions* to be answered after completing your reading. Sometimes the writer will have included questions; sometimes your teacher will provide them. At other times you will have to develop your own questions.

3. *R—Read* the material section by section; think of answers to your questions as you read.

4. *R—Recite* in your own words answers to each question.

5. *R—Review* the material by rereading quickly, looking over the questions, recalling the answers.

EXERCISE 1. Applying the SQ3R Study Method to a Homework Assignment. Select an assignment in any one of your subjects. Follow the five steps of the SQ3R study method to complete the assignment.

Reading Rate

32c. Adjust your reading rate.

You probably realize that you cannot zip through your science book at the same rate that you use to read the sports page or even a short story. Learn to recognize when you should switch to each of the major reading rates.

1. *Scan* material by glancing through it very quickly to find a particular point or reference. You scan to check answers, to study material, or to find a name, date, or detail.

2. *Skim* by looking quickly through the material, noting headnotes, italicized and boldfaced words, and other clues that help give you a general sense of the selection. This is a good rate to use when reviewing before a test.

3. Most reading is done at a *rapid* to *average* rate. The actual speed depends on conditions such as the difficulty of the material, the interest you have in learning details, or the number of distractions there are around.

4. Expect to read carefully at a *thoughtful* rate when you are dealing with technical material, when you are reading a selection that uses a

demanding vocabulary, or when you need to remember detail. Be aware of both thinking and reading when studying this kind of material. Make it a practice to stop regularly and mentally paraphrase what you have read.

Good readers not only know the different reading rates but also know how to switch from one to another in the course of reading a single selection. For example, you have just learned that it is a good idea to skim through an assigned reading before reading it more thoroughly. Sections in a difficult work should be read at an average rate while other parts will demand very thoughtful attention.

EXERCISE 2. Analyzing Reading Rates. Use the suggestions about good study routines as you complete the following exercise.

1. Read rapidly through all the questions in this exercise before writing any answers.
2. You need to know the name of the small town a short story was set in. What reading rate do you use to find it?
3. Find your thoughtful reading rate. Pick two passages you consider difficult, and find two you find easy; record how long it takes you to read each.
4. For an extra credit project you plan to read a Harlequin romance and compare it to the nineteenth-century novel *Jane Eyre.* What rate are you likely to use for each novel?
5. Skim through the previous five pages. Copy down all the sentences that begin with "For example."
6. List two situations in which you have skimmed material recently.
7. Record the author, title, and publisher of six books, and indicate the rate which you would expect to use for each.
8. You have to find and read an article from a professional journal or advanced history textbook on economic conditions in Victorian England. What rate or rates are you likely to use for the assignment?
9. List and define the major reading rates, and give an example of when each is likely to be used.
10. Do only the even-numbered questions in this exercise, beginning with question 2. After you have completed the questions, check your paper to see how well you followed the directions.

Visual Aids

32d. Take advantage of visual aids.

Don't skip over the charts, graphs, maps, and diagrams in material you study. They have been carefully designed to provide information, and they visually clarify material. It is essential to read the information on visual aids to understand exactly what is being shown.

STUDY SKILLS

In studying it is necessary to learn facts such as names, dates, places, and definitions—all categories of specific knowledge. It is just as necessary to know and remember the patterns of organization, the classification systems, and the criteria that make it possible to organize and relate these various facts.

Patterns of Organization

32e. Recognize the major patterns of organization and the kinds of information each is likely to present.

You can find random lists of facts in trivia games, but most of the time you are presented with and expected to know information that is related in some way. As you read and study, look for these four major patterns of organization; learn the kinds of information each is likely to include.

1. *Organization in terms of cause and effect.* Information that is organized to answer *How?* or *Why?* questions is usually presented in terms of cause and effect. In science you read about the consequences of certain controlled actions. English classes study the motives of characters or the events of the plot that lead to the outcome of a story. You, too, may be asked to read about influences that explain certain effects.

When you read a selection that is organized in terms of cause and effect, be sure that you can identify which factors are causes and which are effects. You should know that the cause must occur before the effect.

2. *Organization in terms of chronology, sequence, or placement.* Events that take place one after another or next to each other do not have to be related in terms of cause and effect. In fact, information is

regularly presented in this way simply to indicate the order in which events occurred or items were placed.

When you see information presented in terms of a *When?* or a *Where?* question, notice and remember the proper sequence of the details. For example, if you are learning about the development of the American colonies, you should know that Jamestown was settled before Philadelphia. You should learn the correct order of steps in a process and be able to tell what happened as when you recount a movie or a story. When location is important, expect to learn how to trace a route on a map or how to identify where parts or features should be located in relation to one another.

3. *Organization in terms of description.* Many selections are organized to answer simple *What?* questions. Such selections could include a description of a painting, the titles of the works by a certain artist, or the requirements to run for public office.

When studying a description that answers a *What?* question, be able to tell the difference between the most important points and the less important details.

4. *Organization in terms of comparison and contrast.* Sometimes the best way to explain a certain point is to show that it is similar to or different from something else. Thus a geography lesson may contrast the characteristics of a coastal and an interior desert, and a chemistry lesson might compare the properties of two different hydrocarbon chains. In literature classes, you might study the similarities and differences between several characters or, for that matter, between several poems or authors.

Whenever information is organized as a comparison that discusses "to what extent" or "in what way," look for the factors and the specific ways in which they are said to be similar or different.

Although these four patterns of organization can be distinguished, they are very often mixed. For example, a cause-and-effect discussion will be organized to some extent in terms of sequence. A description of an author's style might involve comparisons or discuss how the style developed over time. A comparison may be made between events that were separated by a time period or that are related as cause and effect. Learn to look for the main way in which the selection is organized.

EXERCISE 3. Identifying Patterns of Organization.   Write the main pattern of organization (cause and effect, sequence or placement, comparison/contrast, description) that you would expect to find in each of the following reading selections. Then briefly explain the kind of information the selection would include.

EXAMPLE 1. How to tell an elm from an oak
   1. *Comparison/contrast; would identify main ways an elm is similar to or different from an oak tree*

1. A short biography of Martin Luther King, Jr.
2. The major characteristics of Hemingway's style
3. Why drinking and driving don't mix
4. What to do in a medical emergency
5. How a computer works
6. Nogales, Arizona–Nogales, Mexico: the two different worlds of a border town
7. Why America got out of Vietnam
8. The motives of Lady Macbeth
9. Steps in writing a research paper
10. Major tourist attractions in California

Classification Systems

32f. Identify the classification systems of the subjects you are studying.

In each subject area, experts have agreed on a specific system for classifying things in terms of shared characteristics. This kind of grouping is necessary for describing, comparing, and relating material.

Some of these systems are part of your daily life. For example, American cash is classified as penny, nickel, dime, quarter, half dollar, and dollar; communities are identified as rural, village, town, county, suburb, city, state, etc.

When you study a subject, you are responsible for learning the classification system or systems involved in that area. Learn the *category,* that is, the name of the grouping, and learn what kind of shared characteristic the name indicates. Very often a category is *subclassified,* that is, divided into smaller categories.

Here are some of the major classification systems.

1. *Literary genre.* You should be able to recognize the difference between major types of writing, such as poetry, prose, drama, fiction, and nonfiction. In addition, you will often be required to identify subcategories within each form. For example, poetry can be classified as

lyrics, ballads, narrative poems, or sonnets; nonfiction might be divided into expository essays, light essays, persuasive essays, etc.

2. *Scientific classification systems.* One classification system is based on the structure of units that are building blocks for the next higher category: subatomic particle, atom, compound, molecule, cell, system, organism, etc. Another gives a specific order for classifying organisms into kingdom, order, genus, species, etc.; that classification can be used further to classify living things in terms of their complexity of life form: animal, plant, invertebrate, vertebrate, mammal, etc.

3. *Social science classification systems.* Among the common systems are those that identify political organizational units: republic, monarchy, dictatorship, territory, colony, protectorate, etc. At the same time, rulers are also classified: for example, a republic may be headed by a president, prime minister, or premier; a monarchy by a king, czar, emperor, etc. Several related systems are based on geographical units, such as continent, island, ocean, sea, mountain, volcano, archipelago, strait, and peninsula.

Notice that there are many ways of classifying things—by size, by function, by structure, or by content. It will be easier to remember the system if you remember the classifying principles.

EXERCISE 4. Classifying Items. After each of the following lists, write the general classification for the specific categories in the list. Choose one set, and give subclassifications for each item.

1. bank, savings and loan, money market, stocks, bonds
2. science fiction, historical fiction, fantasy, romance, myth
3. Buddhists, Hindus, Christians, Jews, Moslems
4. leaves, stems, roots, branches, flowers
5. folk, rock, classical, dance, jazz

Criteria for Evaluation

32g. Know the criteria applied in each field that you are studying.

Learning information also requires a knowledge of evaluation standards in particular fields.

You need to know these criteria to be able to improve your own performance and to be able to make evaluations. When you are asked to revise a theme you have written, the teacher may expect you to recognize the ways in which you failed to meet criteria relating to grammar, usage, spelling, or clarity. To take another case, you cannot analyze a poem if you don't realize that you should look for things like how well the poet handles rhyme and meter or how concrete and vivid the images are. If you have ever taken part in a science fair, you probably were given a set of standards to keep in mind from the time you began designing your experiment.

Knowing the standards or criteria for a field is not the same as being able to apply them. For example, most people watching a baseball game know that a pitched strike must cross the plate within a certain area, but many will not be able to throw a strike or act as umpire.

EXERCISE 5. Researching Criteria. Write the answers to the following questions, or be prepared to discuss them in class.

1. Think of a sport you enjoy or of an item that you collect. List at least three criteria used in judging performance in the sport or that are used to judge the most valuable items in your collection.
2. Following your teacher's directions, find either rules for a contest of skill or directions for an assignment that include some of the criteria that will be used in deciding the winner or the grade. List those criteria.

Paraphrasing

32h. Demonstrate that you understood the material by paraphrasing it.

Memorizing is not the same as understanding. The best check to test your level of understanding of what you read is to see if you can *paraphrase* it, that is, express the idea in your own words.

When you are studying, pause after each section and put the important terms or facts into your own words. If you can't seem to do anything but repeat the book word for word, go back and reread the passage until you can rephrase the meaning.

When you are reading very difficult material, you may need to paraphrase every two or three paragraphs. If you are reading a literature selection from another time period, check that you understand the vocabulary and style by paraphrasing sentences into simpler, more modern English.

At times you may decide or be asked to paraphrase in writing. Whether you are doing it orally or in writing, remember that the paraphrase should be very close to the original in terms of length and amount of detail.

A good paraphrase should meet these two criteria:

1. Although you should include important terminology (special vocabulary), try to use synonyms and your own sentence structure, instead of the author's.

2. Be sure that your paraphrase accurately reflects the *content* of the original. Do not confuse the content with your personal reactions or evaluations.

EXAMPLE   *Original:* Down through the centuries, surgery had been a desperate measure, always painful and often fatal. Only operations that could be completed in a few minutes, such as tooth extractions and limb amputations, were attempted. Patients were forcibly held down, or their senses were dulled with liquor or opium.

Paraphrase: In the past, surgery was only done when necessary. Since the patient often died and always felt pain, surgeons tended to do only quick jobs like pulling teeth or cutting off arms and legs. Patients had to be held still by force or were given drugs or liquor to make them less aware of what was happening.

EXERCISE 6. Demonstrating Understanding by Paraphrasing. Follow the numbered directions.

1. Read through and then paraphrase the following two sentences from Jonathan Swift's "A Voyage to Lilliput."

    My gentleness and good behavior had gained so far on the emperor and his court, and indeed upon the army and people in general, that I began to conceive hopes of getting my liberty in a short time.

    The natives came by degrees to be less apprehensive of any danger from me.

2. Choose one paragraph that you have already read in this chapter, and paraphrase it.

Summarizing

32i. Show that you understand what is most important in a selection by summarizing it.

You have seen how to use paraphrasing to check your understanding of a paragraph. However, learning often calls for more than understanding the meaning. You have to know the point of the selection as a whole. In other words, you must summarize what you learned.

You can do a mental summary as a review of the material you just read and studied. Sometimes the summary is written out as study notes or a précis. In either case, follow these steps:

1. Look quickly through the selection, including any headings and study questions, to get a general idea of the material's focus.

2. Read through the selection carefully, making sure you understand each part.

3. Without looking back at the text, identify the central idea, the main points that develop that idea, and the most important supporting details. Then try the mental summary.

Sometimes you can pinpoint a topic sentence to paraphrase. However, in many selections the topic sentence is not stated directly but is implied. Critical thinking calls on your ability to distinguish what is most important about what is being said.

Writing a Précis

32j. Be able to summarize an article or chapter in a précis.

When you are asked to write a summary, follow these procedures:

1. Go through the steps for summarizing under rule 32i.

2. Jot down notes about the main points of the selection. Paraphrase rather than quote. Avoid putting in too many supporting details.

3. Use your notes to write a first draft of your précis. Keep in mind that your finished summary should be about one third the length of the original.

4. Include all the essential points and leave out examples, repetitions, or conversations.

5. Revise the précis, taking out all unnecessary words. Try to be as concise and as clear as possible.

As you gain practice, you will find yourself writing a précis more quickly. Remember that when you make changes, you are not correcting mistakes; you are applying critical thinking and improving your understanding of exactly what the author meant to say.

Study the following example carefully. It includes the paragraph to be summarized, the summary notes, and the completed précis.

EXAMPLE   The earth is the mother of all people, and all people should have equal rights upon it. You might as well expect the rivers to run backward as that any man who was born a free man should be contented when penned up and denied liberty to go where he pleases. If you tie a horse to a stake do you expect he will go far? If you pen an Indian up on a small spot of earth and compel him to stay there, he will not be contented, nor will he grow and prosper. I have asked some of the great white chiefs where they get their authority to say to the Indian that he shall stay in one place, while he sees white men go where they please. They cannot tell me. (134 words)

CHIEF JOSEPH

Notes: Main points
1. All people have equal rights to the earth.
2. All are unhappy when they cannot move freely.
3. It's not right for Indians to be limited to one area while whites can be free.

Précis: The land belongs equally to all, and any restriction in one's right to move about freely is painful. Whites have no right to make Indians stay in one place while whites go where they like. (35 words)

EXERCISE 7. **Writing a Précis.**

Follow instructions to write a précis for each of the following items. In each case, list the number of words in your précis to show that you have kept it to one third of the original length. Ask your teacher if you should include the notes you took in preparing to write.

1. Write a précis of the forty-eight-word paragraph on page 704 that begins with "Down through the centuries, . . ." Your summary should not be more than sixteen words long. Be prepared to discuss the difference between the précis and the paraphrase.

2. Write a précis of the following paragraphs, taken from *Adventures in American Literature.*

> Among the forms of fiction the short story is perhaps the one to which American writers have made the most significant contributions. Edgar Allen Poë, more than anyone, furthered the craft of the short story by insisting that the short story is a distinct form with special rules of composition: a short story must have "a certain unique or single *effect.* . . . In the whole composition there should be no word written, of which the tendency, direct or indirect, is not to the one preestablished design." Around the turn of the century, Henry James pursued his ideal of the "art

of fiction" in creating many masterly short stories which were always unified, organic compositions, and which remain exemplars of the art.

As the United States approached the twentieth century, however, some writers felt that the short story was in danger of becoming an empty form. A fresh style seemed necessary to express the complexities and uncertainties of modern life. Sherwood Anderson, the most impressive of the early experimentalists, argued against "wrapping life up into neat little packages," and began to create stories with an "open form," in which plot development was less important than the expression of mood and character. The modern American short story can be said to begin with Anderson's "open form," which influenced several important later writers, including Ernest Hemingway and William Faulkner. (230 words)

Writing in Other Courses

32k. Use writing to explore concepts and topics in history or social studies.

By writing about concepts and topics in courses like history or social studies, you can understand the course better. Most often, writing in these subjects takes the form of reports and research papers (see Chapter 8). It is also possible to use other forms of writing to illustrate concepts or explore topics in history or social studies.

One way to use writing in history or social studies is to write book reviews about literary works dealing with historical figures, events, or periods. You might, for example, review *The Massacre at Fall Creek,* Jessamyn West's account of events in Indiana in 1824. Writing a book review combines your knowledge of history or social studies with your evaluation of how the literary work treats a historical event, period, or figure. Prepare to write this book review by referring to encyclopedias and other reference works for historical facts about the person or event in the book. Then do a close reading of the literary work, taking careful notes about the events it discusses, the author's attitude toward the topic, and any striking or essential details.

When you write your book review, be sure to answer one of the following questions: How does the literary work expand your understanding of this event, period, or figure? Is the work's portrayal of history accurate? Does the work present a biased, or slanted, view of the topic—and if so, how does the author support this perspective? When you write your review, include supporting details from reference works and from the literary work to develop your ideas. See also

Chapter 5, pages 146–156, on writing critical reviews and essays of literary analysis.)

You can also keep a writer's journal to record your reactions to the people, events, and concepts you are studying in social studies or history. This writer's notebook can be a source of subjects to write about, just as it is in an English class. It is also a way for you to discover and explore your own ideas about the course material, by recording your reactions as they occur to you and as you respond to specific questions your teacher may give you. Your history or social studies teacher, for example, might ask you to complete a journal entry about questions like the following ones:

1. Identify the primary effects of Reconstruction on the United States after the Civil War.
2. Trace the development of the Industrial Revolution in England.
3. Explain how scientific achievements and political change are related in modern society.

By writing about questions like these from your own perspective, or point of view, you will develop a deeper understanding of the material you are studying.

You can also learn through writing in history and social studies by using fictional forms—such as dialogues, personal narratives, short stories, plays, and poems—based on historical figures, events, or periods. To do so, you must apply your historical knowledge to represent the point of view of a historical figure or to convey the key events or mood of the time.

For example, you might write a narrative poem about the sequence of events that triggered World War I. You might also develop a dialogue between General George Armstrong Custer and his aides as they discuss the events unfolding at Little Big Horn. Or, you could use the dialogue format to interview a historical figure, with either you or a historical figure acting as interviewer—Benjamin Franklin interviewing Leonardo da Vinci about his inventions, for example. (See page 603 on writing dialogue.) You might also write character or biographical sketches in which you focus on a significant event in a historical figure's life, such as as Marie Antoinette and the fall of the Bastille in 1789 (see pages 212–228). Any historical event or person can also be the focus of a short story or play (pages 197–212). No matter which fictional form you use, you will take a more personal look at the content of your history or social studies class.

Whenever you write in history or social studies, or in any other course, be sure to apply your knowledge of narration, description, exposition, and persuasion (Chapters 4, 6, and 7), as well as your knowledge of the structure and development of paragraphs, compositions, and research papers (see Chapters 2, 3, 4, and 8). Also remember to apply your understanding of the writing process (Chapter 1) in all your content-area classes.

EXERCISE 8. Writing in History or Social Studies. Following the steps in the writing process, complete any one of the following writing activities:

1. Write a book review of a literary work about a historical period, event, or figure. In your review, answer one of the questions listed on page 707.
2. Using one of the questions on page 708, or a question your teacher provides, prepare a journal entry about a topic in history or social studies.
3. Write a dialogue, poem, character or biographical sketch, short story, or play about a historical figure, event, or period you are studying now.

Classifying Kinds of Statements

32l. Analyze and classify the different types of statements in a reading selection.

You have learned about the different patterns of organization. You also have seen how recognizing such patterns increases your ability to understand and think about the material. A good student is also able to analyze the kinds of statements included in reading and study assignments. Being able to recognize fact, opinion, assumptions, and nonliteral statements is an important skill.

Fact or Opinion

In order to understand and evaluate many statements, you need to recognize whether you are dealing with a fact or an opinion.

A statement of *fact* presents information that can be proved true or false. Check whether or not a given fact is accurate; that is, whether it can be shown to be true either by direct experience or by support from a reliable source such as an encyclopedia or a textbook.

A statement of *opinion*, on the other hand, expresses what someone feels or believes. Although they cannot be established in the same way as facts, statements of opinion should be well supported; that is, they should be reasonable conclusions in view of established facts.

EXAMPLE   *Statement of fact:* California is the third-largest state in the Union in terms of physical size. [This can be verified in an encyclopedia or an almanac.]

Statement of opinion: California's large, diverse population and many resources make it an important state to take into account when discussing the United States' economy and politics. [The opinion that California is an important state is supported by the facts given: It has a large, diverse population and many resources. These facts can be verified by sources such as an encyclopedia, Census Bureau figures, or textbooks.]

Assumptions

Facts and opinions can be based on hidden assumptions; that is, the speaker or writer takes for granted that the audience knows or agrees with something that is not expressed. For example, a description of a science project that states that "the agar culture was saturated with a glucose solution" assumes that the reader is familiar with such technical terms as *agar culture, saturated,* and *glucose solution.*

An editorial writer who declares that "Tom Jones, who openly admits he reads the newspaper comics daily, cannot expect to be considered a serious candidate for public office" makes a different kind of assumption. The implication is that everyone would agree that reading the comics in the newspaper is a sign of childishness, or lack of seriousness or intelligence.

It is important to recognize when assumptions are being made and to respond to them properly. You may need to do some background work to understand material that assumes you already know about the subject area. When you encounter assumptions about what you feel or believe, analyze whether or not the unstated fact or opinion is valid.

Nonliteral Statements

Finally, it is important to recognize and understand nonliteral statements. The meaning of such statements depends on a *comparison,* a *figurative expression,* or an *allusion* that the reader is expected to understand.

For example, "The deadly poison of fear filled the small room" does not mean that fear is a gas or liquid that can kill but that it is *like* such a substance in the effect it had on the people in the room.

If someone says, "I saw red when I saw what Gonzo had done to my room," you are not supposed to think the speaker actually saw the color red; you should recognize the expression "seeing red" as a figurative way of saying someone was very angry.

EXERCISE 9. Analyzing Statements. Complete the following items in writing or in group discussion.

A. For each item, first write whether the sentence is a fact (*F*) or an opinion (*O*). For a fact, list one place the fact could be checked; for an opinion, write *yes* or *no* to indicate whether it is supported as presented.

1. The giant dinosaur, *Tyrannosaurus rex,* lived in the late Cretaceous period.
2. Its huge size, strong jaws, and razor-sharp teeth made *Tyrannosaurus rex* one of the most fearsome creatures that ever prowled the earth.
3. Washington Irving's character Rip Van Winkle has great appeal for all people who feel that they can't keep up with changes.
4. Washington Irving published "The Legend of Sleepy Hollow" in 1819.
5. Unlike many writers, Washington Irving did not worry about being "original," because his best-known stories were based on legends and folk tales.

B. For each item, write whether the statement is based on an unstated assumption (*A*) or if it should be understood as a nonliteral statement (*NS*). Then identify each assumption and explain each comparison, figurative expression, or allusion.

1. The thousand days of John F. Kennedy's presidency have sometimes been described as a kind of American Camelot.
2. It would be easier to trap smoke in your hands than to get those kids to stay in one orderly group.
3. "Of course I did not ask him to sit with us," Lord Prowed said. "He doesn't even have a manservant."
4. According to the principles of quantum mechanics, the electron seems to have properties of both a wave and a particle.

5. The new mayor was horrified to discover how deeply the city's finances were in the red.

C. Look through textbooks, newspapers, or magazines to find one example of each of the following kinds of statements. Copy the statements, and label them as you did in parts A and B.

1. Statement of fact
2. Statement of opinion
3. A statement that assumes the reader knows and accepts a belief or point of view
4. A nonliteral statement that uses a comparison
5. A nonliteral statement that depends on an allusion

TEST-TAKING SKILLS

When a test is announced, find out exactly what kind it will be so that you can study for it effectively.

32m. Schedule your time and focus your attention when taking a test.

Knowing how to take a test can improve your grade. Learn and follow these strategies:

1. Skim rapidly through the test as soon as you get it. Note the number and type of questions. Get a sense of what sections seem manageable and which seem difficult. Then figure out how much time you should spend on each section of the test.

2. Work steadily and with concentration through the test. Read the instructions and each question carefully so that you do not lose points on careless errors. But try to keep to your schedule. Even if all the answers you put down are correct, you will fail if the test is only half complete.

It may be easier to say than do, but don't distract yourself and weaken your performance by putting energy into worrying. Take a deep breath and concentrate on doing the best you can.

Objective Tests

32n. Identify and review specific information likely to be included in an objective test.

Multiple-choice, true-or-false, fill-in-the-blank, and short-answer tests characteristically test how well you remember and understand information. As a rule, each question will have only one right answer.

Given these characteristics, preparing for an objective test is fairly straightforward.

1. Look through your textbook and study notes to identify the specific points on which you are likely to be tested. Master the important points. Many textbooks highlight key terms by putting them in boldface or italics or by including a glossary in the chapter review materials.

2. Use the list of likely points of information to test yourself. Try to remember the information in different forms. For example, work from a list of terms to see if you can define each of them. Then ask someone to quiz you by reading a definition and seeing if you can identify it.

Study and label any diagrams or maps that may be included. Do practice problems for your math and science classes. Redo ones you did for homework so that you can check the answers when you are done.

32o. Know the strategies that will help you take objective tests.

Do not spend too much time on any single question. Since you are drawing on your memory, the first answer you think of is usually correct. If you are not sure of one item, come back to it later.

Keep the following points in mind for objective tests.

1. *Multiple-choice questions.* As you look at the possible answers in a multiple-choice question, assume that one of the four will be obviously wrong and one will be less clearly wrong. The two remaining choices may both seem possible, but one will be either too general, too specific, or related to another part of the subject.

EXAMPLE Which of the following is the largest of the fifty states that borders another state in the U.S.A.? (a) California; (b) Alaska; (c) Texas; (d) Minnesota [The answer is c; Alaska is the largest state, but it does not border another U.S. state.]

2. *True-or-False Questions.* Pay careful attention to the wording of true-or-false questions. If any part of the statement is not true, mark the question false. Remember that words like *all, never, only,* and *always* suggest there are no exceptions. Don't worry about wild improbabilities, but be sure that the statement can be generalized before marking it as true. However, don't assume that statements that rule out exceptions are necessarily false.

EXAMPLES   1. There must always be someone who serves as Vice-President of the United States.[False]
             2. A sentence in standard English must always include a verb. [True]

3. *Fill-in-the-blank and short-answer questions.* Think of these two kinds of questions as the reverse of each other. For example, you might be given a definition and asked to fill in the word, or, alternatively, you might be given a word and told to define it. In all cases, use the vocabulary, definitions, or facts that are appropriate to the subject area.

EXAMPLES   1. Briefly identify one official who serves in the Judicial branch of the U.S. government. Include how the position is achieved, term of office, and function.
             1. *Supreme Court Justice, appointed by President for life to rule on constitutionality of cases brought before the Supreme Court*

             2. The secretaries of State, Defense, and the Treasury are several members of the President's —— .
             2. *Cabinet*

4. *Verbal analogy questions.* An analogy is a comparison. A verbal analogy question tests your ability to recognize the relationship between two words and to identify two other words that have a similar relationship. When answering an analogy question, be careful not to reverse the order of any pair of words. For example, *mile is to length* is not the same relationship as *length is to mile.*

EXAMPLE   *Shoe* is to *foot* as *pillowcase* is to   a. bed   b. head   c. sheet d. pillow [The answer is d; the shoe covers the foot and the pillowcase covers the pillow.]

EXERCISE 10. **Applying Test-Taking Skills.** Follow directions in writing answers to the questions.

1. Identify ten to twelve key terms or points that you might be tested on in an objective test on this chapter.
2. Using the terms and points you chose, prepare for a test on this chapter by writing sample questions. Include two of each of the following types:
    a. multiple-choice   c. fill-in-the-blank   e. analogy
    b. true-or-false   d. short-answer identification

Essay Tests

As you begin to take more advanced classes, you are likely to be asked to write longer, essay answers to questions. The best preparation for this kind of test is to think of several possible test questions and write their answers. Even if you do not come up with a question that is on the test, this preparation will help you review the material.

Every composition is different, so there can be no single correct answer to an essay question the way there can be to an objective test. However, keep in mind the following points about an essay test.

32p. Be sure to answer the question that is asked.

Essay test questions are often more than one sentence long; they also are likely to include several directions. Therefore, before beginning to answer, *read the entire question carefully and thoughtfully.*

1. Look for key terms that indicate which of the four patterns of organization you are expected to use.

EXAMPLE *Cause-and-effect approach:* analyze, explain, criticize, defend, show why, give factors that led to, tell the effect of
Comparison-and-contrast approach: compare, contrast, show the differences, find likenesses
Sequential or placement approach: list and discuss, trace, review, outline, give the steps, locate
Description approach: describe, identify, give examples of, tell the characteristics of

2. Note specific points that are to be included in your answer. It may be necessary to do more than one thing. For example, look at this essay question: "Show the difference between internal and external conflict. Include examples from at least three of the short stories studied in this unit." These directions specify three points that must be included for you to get full credit for your answer:

   a. Contrast internal and external conflict.
   b. Use examples.
   c. Draw the examples from three different stories.

32q. Think through and then answer essay questions.

Follow these steps in writing your answer.

1. Use the point value given for the question to estimate how detailed your answer should be.

2. Develop a thesis statement that will act as the basis for a very brief three- or four-point outline. Include points related to each part of the question.

3. Write the thesis statement as an introduction. Be sure you make some reference to the test question. Allow one paragraph for each main supporting point. Be sure to include specific details, examples, and references. Vague generalizations are a sign that you did not master the material.

4. End with a conclusion that summarizes your essay.

5. Allow a few minutes to proofread your essay for missing words, unclear statements, and spelling and usage errors.

The following material is a sample essay test question and answer. Carefully study how the test question is developed into an answer.

TOTAL TEST TIME   40 minutes

Question 1. (60 points) allow 24 minutes

Discuss the question: Who is the great tragic hero of *Julius Caesar* —Brutus or Caesar?

Thesis: Brutus is the real tragic hero.

OUTLINE   (1) Brutus in all five acts; Caesar dies in third.
(2) Brutus, not Caesar, is lamented at the end—"The noblest Roman of them all."
(3) Inner conflict occurs in Brutus, not in Caesar

There is room for much honest debate as to whether Caesar or Brutus is the real tragic hero of Shakespeare's *Julius Caesar.* In my close reading of the play, however, I found three compelling reasons for believing that Brutus is the protagonist. *(reference to the test question)* *(statement of answer)*

The first reason is that Brutus has a much bigger role than Caesar. Caesar dies in Act III; Brutus is present in every act. It has been argued that Caesar's ghost continues to make his presence and influence felt throughout the rest of the play. Such an influence is not evident in the number of lines reserved for the ghost, who speaks only three times, a total of sixteen words. Even a master dramatist like Shakespeare cannot build a success- *(first main point)* *(supporting facts)* ful final two acts with the hero offstage. By the mere reason of his presence on the stage, it is Brutus's play.

The second reason is also concerned with this matter of structure and presence. When the play ends, it is Brutus to whom Antony and Octavius pay tribute. Antony's final speech is especially significant here:

"This was the noblest Roman of them all. . . . Nature might stand up / And say to all the world, 'This was a man.'"

The most compelling reason of all is found in Brutus's own nature. *It is he in whom the moral issue of the play is fought out.* He is the person in the play who experiences the most intense inner conflict—and inner conflict in the tragic hero is the essence of all great tragedy. There is little of this in Caesar; he is a man with few doubts and uncertainties, a character who undergoes no change. Brutus, on the contrary, is torn with doubt and pulled apart by the moral issue. The tragedy is the chronicle of his rise and fall.

By reason of what happens on the stage and what takes place inside the characters, Brutus is the tragic hero of Julius Caesar.

Margin notes:
second main point
specific example
third main point
specific details
summary

EXERCISE 11. Writing Answers to Essay Test Questions. Follow the numbered directions.

1. Compare and contrast strategies used for preparing for an essay test, versus the strategies used for preparing for an objective test. Include a thesis statement, an outline, specific examples, and references.

2. Following your teacher's directions, compose your own essay question on a topic you are studying in one of your classes. Include its point value in a 40-minute test. Schedule the appropriate amount of time, and write a sample answer.

PART FIVE

SPEAKING AND LISTENING

CHAPTER 33

Speaking and Listening

SKILLS AND STRATEGIES

In high school you will often have to speak to groups of your fellow students and participate in group discussions. If you can speak clearly, easily, and forcefully, you will gain a skill that can help you later in your career. In the first part of this chapter, you will learn how to handle some of the most common speech situations you will meet in school.

The ability to speak before groups is a valuable asset, but an equally important talent is the ability to listen. By *listening* to what is said and not just *hearing* it, you can grasp the gist of a speaker's remarks without the need for repetition. In this chapter, you will learn how to listen carefully and evaluate what you hear.

PREPARING A SPEECH

A good speech requires careful preparation. This section will guide you through the necessary steps in preparing and delivering a speech. Note that preparing a speech is in many ways like preparing a paragraph or composition. Be sure to refer to the detailed suggestions for selecting and limiting a subject and organizing content in Chapter 1.

33a. Choose an appropriate subject.

Sometimes your teacher will suggest your subject; other times you will have to select your own subject. In the latter case, you should be guided by two principles:

1. *Choose a subject that you know well and that you find interesting.* Choosing a subject about which you know a great deal encourages you to talk about things you have had experience with—your hobbies, special talents, and jobs. It also ensures that you will speak with enthusiasm because the subject is close to you. If what you say engages your own interest powerfully, it will interest your audience as well. Choose your subject far in advance. Think about it daily—mulling over both what you will say and the way you will say it.

2. *Choose a subject that is interesting to your audience.* When thinking about your subject, you should also think about the needs, background, and interests of your audience. For example, work-study programs can be interesting to students because students are concerned about combining work with study. If your audience is made up of adults, you might change your focus—emphasizing, for example, your school's need for support of work-study programs.

EXERCISE 1. Choosing a Subject for a Speech. List five subjects you feel able to speak about. Submit the list to your teacher for comments and suggestions. When it is returned, put it in your notebook for future use.

33b. Limit your subject so that it can be adequately treated in your speech and so that it reflects a definite purpose.

In the few minutes allotted to you, you may not be able to tell everything you know about your subject. You must therefore limit your subject so that you can cover it in the time allowed. For example:

BROAD SUBJECT   Modern aircraft

SUITABLE TOPIC   Vertical-takeoff aircraft

Refer to pages 10–13 of Chapter 1 for suggestions on limiting topics.

Another way in which you should limit your subject is by determining a definite purpose for your speech. If you have a purpose and keep it in mind, you can *calculate* the effect on your audience of the remarks or gestures you are thinking of using. You can then eliminate every feature that does not advance your purpose.

Almost every subject can be developed for a specific purpose. The purpose may be to *inform*, to *entertain*, or to *persuade*.

Suppose, for example, that the subject of your talk is "Western movies." If your purpose is to *inform,* you may decide to discuss the first

Westerns or the rise of the tradition from the dime novel. If your purpose is to *entertain,* you might tell the class about famous Hollywood stars and how they began their careers in the Westerns. And if your purpose is to *persuade,* you might urge the class to join in composing a letter to the moviemakers, accusing them of distorting the real traditions of the Old West.

Write your purpose in an explicit statement, or thesis.

TOPIC   Recycling bottles and cans

PURPOSE   To inform. I shall explain clearly what types of bottles and cans are best for recycling. I will give examples of successful neighborhood recycling projects.

EXERCISE 2. Developing Topics for Your Speech.   Choose one subject from the list approved by your teacher in Exercise 1. Decide on a purpose for your talk; then limit the subject to three topics. Compose an explicit statement of purpose, and submit it to your teacher for suggestions and comments.

33c. Gather material for your speech.

Where will you find material for a speech? Start with yourself. Consider the vast number of facts and opinions you already have in your head. The information-gathering strategies used in the writing process will also be helpful here. For specific suggestions, see pages 14–19 of Chapter 1.

If you cannot find enough material for a speech from your own experience, go to outside sources such as your friends and acquaintances, newspaper and magazine articles, radio and television programs, and books.

As you find material for your speech, take notes on note cards.

EXERCISE 3. Gathering Material for Your Speech.   Select a topic for a three-minute speech to your class. Make a list of the sources of information you intend to consult.

33d. Prepare an outline for your speech.

Outline the structure of your speech. You may write out and memorize the opening and concluding sentences, but no more than that.

The outline of an anecdote is just a reminder of the sequence of events you intend to tell. An outline of an argument or explanation is more detailed. Head the outline with the topic; then write out the statement of purpose. After this comes the outline itself. Here is a typical outline for a persuasive talk.

Sample Outline

Topic: Water pollution must be stopped!
Purpose: To persuade listeners to protect our water supply

I. Current supply of fresh water
  A. Increasing demand—100 billion liters used every day
  B. Decreasing supply—as a result of water pollution
II. Causes of water pollution
  A. Garbage dumped by cities and towns
  B. Chemicals dumped by industries
  C. Detergents containing phosphates
  D. Oil spills
  E. Pesticides
III. What the average citizen can do
  A. Use laundry detergents without phosphates
  B. Conserve water whenever possible
  C. Write letters to state and federal legislators
  D. Watch for sources of water pollution; report offenders to environmental authorities

EXERCISE 4. Preparing an Outline for Your Speech. Using the topic and the sources you chose for Exercise 3, prepare an outline for your three-minute speech.

33e. Make sure that your talk has a good introduction and conclusion.

In your introduction, try to arouse interest. Often you can do this with an arresting sentence or question.

EXAMPLE Pollution never seemed important until I canoed on Inky Creek.

For other specific suggestions about writing introductory paragraphs, see pages 124–26 in Chapter 4.

There are two disappointing ways for a talk to end: (1) to sputter to a stop like a motor out of gas and (2) to be checked in full course by the admonition, "Time's up." Do not allow your speech to end in this way. Conclude strongly by summing up what you have said or by leaving in the mind of your audience a dominant impression of your talk.

EXAMPLE   Rusty cans, discarded tires, and other garbage may destroy our water
in years to come. Let's join together and stop this pollution!

For other specific suggestions for writing conclusions see pages 130–31
in Chapter 4.

EXERCISE 5. Writing an Introduction and a Conclusion for Your Speech.
Write an attention-getting introduction and an emphatic
conclusion for the topic you worked on in Exercise 4.

GIVING THE SPEECH

So far we have been discussing the *content* of a good speech. This
section will discuss the *technique*.

Good public speakers know their audiences thoroughly. They understand the needs, background, and interests of their particular audience.
They look at the audience as they talk. They have friendly manners,
speak distinctly, and pitch their voices so that they are easily heard.
They always speak as naturally as if they were conversing with friends.

If you take every opportunity you can to speak in public, you will
notice yourself growing in self-confidence and skill.

33f. Conquer nervousness.

Feeling nervous is natural. Even veteran performers become tense.
Tension is merely the body's signal that it is ready for whatever demands
the next few minutes will make on it. Once you are "on stage," excess
tension usually disappears.

Here are the five best antidotes for nervousness:

1. *Know your topic.* Know your topic so thoroughly that it tells itself.

2. *Know your audience.* Know the needs and interests of your
particular audience.

3. *Keep your purpose in mind.* Think of what you want your listeners
to believe, feel, or do. Concentrate on *why* you are speaking.

4. *Practice.* Practice imprints on your memory the sequence of your
talk and makes it very hard to get "stuck."

5. *Relax.* Deep breathing helps. Inhale through your nose and exhale
through your mouth, forcing all the air out of your lungs and relaxing
your muscles.

33g. Develop a good speaking manner.

1. *Rehearse your presentation.* Using your outline as a guide, practice your speech aloud at home. Do not write out or memorize what you are going to say.

2. *Use descriptive language.* As you practice, search for images and accurate words and expressions that will make your talk more vivid. Look for words that have life and sparkle.

EXAMPLES   My little brother squirmed onto the chair and let his legs dangle.
She toppled track records like rows of dominoes.

3. *Enunciate clearly and accurately.* While practicing, be sure to speak distinctly. Slovenly speech is caused by laziness of the lips and tongue. Be overprecise in practice, but when you speak before your classmates, concentrate on *what* you are saying rather than on *how* you are saying it.

33h. Use nonverbal communication.

Your audience will certainly be watching you as you speak. How you stand, how you move about, and how you gesture can communicate nonverbal (unspoken) signals to them. Think of these unspoken signals as part of your speech.

Limit, or control, your movements for effective nonverbal communication.

1. *Watch your posture.* If you are standing, keep your weight evenly distributed on both feet. If you are sitting, place both feet squarely on the floor. Do not slouch.

2. *Establish eye contact with your listeners.* Good speakers move their glance around the room, focusing on the faces of listeners. This eye contact makes the talk more personal and it enables you to see how well your talk is being understood. Do not stare at the floor or at your notes or you may easily lose your audience's attention.

3. *Choose gestures with care.* Effective gestures are visual clues to meaning. Hands, for example, can indicate size, shape, or direction. Do not call more attention to your movements than to your speech.

EXERCISE 6. Delivering Your Speech.   Deliver the three-minute speech you prepared in Exercises 4 and 5.

Here are some hints for practicing your speech:

1. Practice at home in front of a mirror.
2. Ask a friend or family member to listen to and evaluate your speech.
3. Record your speech on audio- or videotape; then evaluate your tape.

THREE SPEAKING SITUATIONS

The most common speeches you will be called upon to deliver will probably be the narrative talk, the explanatory talk, and the persuasive talk.

The Narrative Talk

In the narrative talk, you tell about a personal experience or relate an anecdote. It is not difficult to find a subject for such a talk if you keep in mind that it is the *manner* and not just the subject matter that makes such talks interesting. A funny experience on the bus can be just as fascinating as the description of a Caribbean cruise. Note that the detailed suggestions for planning and developing a story in Chapter 7 will also help you prepare a narrative talk.

33i. Make your narrative talk vivid.

1. *Begin with action.* After you have decided on your purpose, arouse the interest and curiosity of the audience by plunging right into your story.

EXAMPLE How many of you have been in a completely strange place, yet you were unmistakably certain *that you had seen it all before*—perhaps in a dream? Eerie, isn't it? Well, it happened to me!

2. *Maintain suspense.* Lead your listeners up to the climax, giving them no inkling until the last moment of how the story will end. Then end it and take your seat. To linger after the end of the story weakens the dramatic effect. See pages 198–203 in Chapter 7 for information on developing action and conflict.

EXERCISE 7. Relating an Unusual Personal Experience. Relate an unusual personal experience to the class. If you can, select an incident that illustrates a point. Arouse and maintain suspense. Use descriptive language. Pay attention to your posture and your enunciation. Practice your talk and limit it to three minutes.

EXERCISE 8. Relating an Experience or Anecdote. Relate an experience or anecdote to illustrate a proverb. Remember to arouse the interest and curiosity of your audience. The following list contains suggestions.

1. A stitch in time saves nine.
2. An empty barrel makes the most noise.
3. A watched pot never boils.
4. Pride goes before a fall.
5. Spare the rod and spoil the child.

EXERCISE 9. Relating an Unusual Incident. Relate an unusual incident in the life of a famous man or woman. Arouse the interest and curiosity of your audience. A list of suggested persons follows.

1. John F. Kennedy
2. Maria Tallchief
3. Susan B. Anthony
4. Bessie Smith
5. Martin Luther King, Jr.
6. Roberto Clemente
7. I. M. Pei
8. Abraham Lincoln
9. Margaret Thatcher
10. Babe Zaharias

The Explanatory Talk

From time to time you will be called upon to explain how to make or do something. To explain so that your listeners will understand easily, you must plan carefully and observe certain principles of organization and delivery.

33j. Make your explanatory talk clear.

1. *Limit your subject to a topic that can be adequately treated in your speech and in such a way it reflects a definite purpose.* Limit your subject to a topic that you know (or can get to know) thoroughly and that is suitable for your purpose. The more limited the topic, the more completely you can treat it in the time allowed.

2. *Choose a subject that is interesting to your audience.* Be sure to consider your audience's needs, background, and interests when you choose your subject.

3. *Gather material for your speech.* Start with yourself. Then go to outside sources such as friends and acquaintances, newspaper and magazine articles, radio and television programs, and books.

4. *Organize your explanation.* Your outline is all-important in a talk of this kind. In it you determine the arrangement of ideas in a step-by-step progression from the simple to the complex, the familiar to the unfamiliar, or whatever order is most suitable.

5. *Master all technical terms.* If you choose a topic that ordinarily uses technical terms, master this vocabulary so that you can explain technical terms as you go along.

6. *Use visual aids.* If you can bring to class the object or device you are going to explain and then demonstrate how it works, it will make your explanation clearer. If you cannot bring an object or device, illustrate your talk by drawing a diagram.

While you talk, hold the object you are going to demonstrate in front of you so that everyone can see it. If you use a diagram, stand to one side and refer to it with a pointer.

EXERCISE 10. Giving an Explanatory Talk. Give an explanatory talk to the class. Your talk should last about five minutes. Use one of the topics from the following list or choose your own.

1. A science experiment that you can do at home
2. Balanced meals for good health
3. How our local government is organized
4. How to train a dog
5. How to drive safely

The Persuasive Talk

Speakers must plan carefully, arrange arguments thoughtfully, and speak forcefully if they want to persuade others or get them to act.

33k. Make your persuasive talk effective.

1. *Choose a controversial opinion.* Facts and personal opinions are not arguable, but controversial opinions are.

2. *Arrange your arguments carefully.* Reword your outline until the speech it represents is logical, well supported, and hard-hitting.

3. *Rehearse your talk.* Rehearsing your talk in front of your parents or friends gives them the opportunity to raise questions and objections that you may have overlooked. For help in planning and developing a persuasive talk, see pages 96–101 of Chapter 3 and pages 157–72 of Chapter 6.

EXERCISE 11. Giving a Persuasive Talk.   Give a persuasive talk to the class on some topic you think is important. Choose one of the topics listed here or select one of your own.

1. A free college education ought to be the right of all.
2. Networks should stop showing violence on television.
3. Put a woman in the White House!
4. All drivers should take a road test every five years.
5. High-school students should not have part-time jobs.

LISTENING WITH A PURPOSE

This section will help you to become a more skillful listener. You will be able to apply your full attention to understand what is said; to sift fact from opinion, the weighty from the trivial; and to evaluate what you hear.

33l. Listen courteously.

Good listening manners require that you listen and do nothing else. Do not let yourself be distracted. Be patient and quiet if a speaker experiences difficulty.

33m. Listen accurately.

The greatest enemy to accurate listening is a wandering mind. You can often force your attention to stick to the subject by giving it the following tasks:

1. *Listen to understand and recall what was said.* Of course we cannot recall everything, but memory can be trained. Pay close attention to what is said and review it immediately in your mind, rehearsing the main points and repeating them to yourself in the order given.

EXERCISE 12. Listening Accurately.   Compose five questions similar to those that follow. Read them aloud, pausing for about five seconds between questions to allow your classmates time to jot down their answers. When you have finished, your classmates will check their answers to determine how accurately they have listened.

1. In the series of numbers *8—9—4—3—1*, the third number is —— ?
2. In the list of words *on—off—at—or—in*, the fourth word is —— ?
3. In the list of words *but—can—stop—then—until*, the word beginning with *c* is —— ?
4. In the announcement "Send your replies to Box 665, Los Angeles, California 90047, before March 31, together with a box top from our product," the post office box number is —— ?
5. In the statement "Fran will keep the score, Lucy will be captain of one team and Rose of the other, and Lena and Pam will pitch," what is Fran's assignment?

    2. *Listen to understand the underlying structure of a talk or a lecture.* Train your powers of analysis so that you can understand and recall the gist of a complicated talk by knowing what its main arguments will probably be. Use the signals a speaker gives in the opening remarks indicating what the main ideas will be.

    For instance, of the following opening remarks, you might ask, "What is the speaker's topic?" and then "How will the argument proceed?" You might then jot down the notes that follow each set of remarks.

        This morning we pay tribute to Theodore Roosevelt as a conservationist, President, and advocate of the outdoor life.

NOTES   Theodore Roosevelt
      1. As conservationist
      2. As President
      3. As outdoor enthusiast

EXERCISE 13. Analyzing the Introduction of a Talk or Lecture. Cut out the introductory paragraph of a short magazine article. Read it to the class, asking them what they think the main points of the article will be. Then compare these versions with the actual article.

    3. *Listen to grasp the main ideas.* As the speaker finishes the introductory remarks and develops the subject, you ask, "What arguments support the speaker's main points?" and "What factors are offered as proof?"

A speaker's main points frequently stand out because of the emphasis given to them. Forceful speakers punctuate each main idea by tone, gesture, and expression. They restate the arguments frequently, illustrating them, citing statistics in their support, and bringing in authoritative opinion on their behalf.

The transitions from one point to the next are signaled by words like *therefore, consequently, on the other hand,* and *however.* Other clues to the development of an argument are expressions such as *for example* and *for instance,* which usually indicate that the ideas that follow illustrate a point. Still others show that the speaker is about to summarize: *in conclusion, finally, to sum up*.

EXERCISE 14. Listening to Understand the Underlying Structure of a Talk. Your teacher will read to you a brief magazine article for approximately five to ten minutes. As you listen, write an outline of the lecture or article; then compare it with the outline your teacher puts on the board.

33n. Listen critically.

A critical listener insists on evaluating what is said. Critical listening is the art of making distinctions.

1. *Weigh the evidence.* To do this, you must distinguish fact from opinion.

FACT   Abraham Lincoln was born on February 12, 1809.
OPINION   Abraham Lincoln was the greatest President this country ever had.

Distinguish between reliable and unreliable authority.

RELIABLE   The U.S. Department of Commerce reports that the rate of inflation increased last month.
UNRELIABLE   Wednesday Jones, the popular star, says that inflation statistics are never accurate.

Distinguish between generalizations based on sufficient evidence and those based on insufficient evidence.

SUFFICIENT   Decatur High's team won every game in our league; our team lost every game. Therefore, Decatur's team is better than ours this season.
INSUFFICIENT   I know three students from Decatur High School. Each has red hair. Therefore, most Decatur students have red hair.

Distinguish between proper and improper comparisons or analogies.

PROPER   Esme, whom I can usually beat at bowling, beats Ruth regularly. Therefore, I probably can beat Ruth too.

IMPROPER John, who lives next door, read *Sounder* and didn't like it. Therefore, I probably won't like it either.

2. Recognize and avoid unfair argument. Because it is always easy to let emotion rather than reason control our judgments, a critical listener must be on guard against propaganda devices that may deceive or misguide. The following are some of these propaganda devices:

Prejudice. Opinions based on prejudice are really not opinions at all, for in most cases they simply ignore the truth.

EXAMPLES Country resident: City dwellers are stuck-up, devious, and untrustworthy.
          City resident: Country folks are lazy, unimaginative, and suspicious.

Bandwagon appeals. These play on the fear of being "different."

EXAMPLE   All over the country people are switching to Warwick soup. It's the thing to do.

Name-calling. By labeling problems with simple and emotionally charged names and slogans, the propagandist avoids rational argument. Name-calling can also damage someone's reputation by repeating false charges.

EXAMPLE   Of federal safety guidelines: "This is just more government red tape."

Slogans. A favorite device of propagandists, catchy slogans are easily remembered, quickly shouted, and impossible to refute. Like name-calling, slogans are designed to take the place of sober reasoning.

EXAMPLES Our country right or wrong!
          Be the first to own one!

Snob appeal. Most people like to think of themselves as successful and deserving. Advertisers play on these feelings by trying to make their products status symbols—visible signs of success.

EXAMPLE   Move up to the Champion class in ten-speed bicycles!

Unproved assertions. Advertisers and speakers often make statements without proof. Unless a statement is supported by reasons, figures, examples, or the opinions of competent and unbiased authorities, it should be questioned. The following statements seem to prove a point but actually do not because no evidence is offered.

EXAMPLES   Cigarette smoking causes cancer. It injures body tissue. It irritates the lungs, poisons the blood, and affects digestion.

Cigarette smoking does not cause cancer. Smokers are not physically impaired. There is no danger to the throat, lungs, heart, or arteries. Smoking is harmless.

EXERCISE 15. Evaluating Arguments.   In the following statements you will find examples of invalid and unfair argument. Identify each type of unfair argument, and explain briefly how each violates the standards of good reasoning.

1. The wise merchant knows never to employ a teen-ager. As any newspaper shows, all teen-agers are undependable, dangerous, and larcenous.
2. My political opponent is a demagogue whose philosophy is "soak the rich." This kind of policy will surely kill the goose that lays the golden eggs.
3. Olaf, Niels, and Karen are all excellent skiers. They are Swedish. All Swedes are excellent skiers.
4. Oneonta High won all of their games right after adopting a new cheer. For heaven's sake, let's end our losing streak by adopting a new cheer, too!
5. The math test was terribly unfair! I spent three days reviewing for it and only got a C.
6. The representative was against space travel and exploration for this reason: "If humans were meant to fly, they would have been given wings."
7. General Smith is certain to make a fine governor for our state. After all, he had a brilliant military career and was decorated many times for heroism.
8. Let's end foreign aid at once. Foreigners don't deserve our help. They don't believe in the American way and are so slick in diplomatic dealings that we, who have been taught always to live up to our end of a deal, are certain to lose our shirts.
9. Never vote for a Democratic candidate, for it is well known that Democrats steal from the rich to pay the poor.

10. Senator Jones failed to vote for the nuclear arms treaty. That action shows that he is a hawk on defense issues.

EXERCISE 16. Listening Critically. From reading or television viewing, collect two examples each of the following items.

1. A statement by a reliable authority
2. A statement by an unreliable authority
3. A generalization from sufficient evidence
4. An unproved assertion
5. A bandwagon appeal
6. A slogan

EXERCISE 17. Writing and Listening Critically to Arguments. Compose a one-paragraph argument for or against some idea, in which you deliberately break the rules of fair and honest thinking. Try to make your argument somewhat subtle so that your classmates must exercise their ingenuity to discover the abuse. If you cannot compose one yourself, look through a magazine, and cut out an advertisement that makes obvious use of some propaganda device. Bring it to class for discussion.

SUMMARY OF LISTENING TECHNIQUES

1. Give the speaker your full attention.
2. Be patient, and do not interrupt the speaker.
3. Review the speaker's main points in your mind immediately after the speaker has finished speaking.
4. Pay attention to signals that the speaker may give during a talk to indicate the main points.
5. Weigh the evidence the speaker presents. Distinguish fact from opinion, reliable from unreliable authority, sufficient from insufficient generalization, and proper from improper comparisons or analogies.
6. Recognize and avoid unfair arguments, such as name calling, snob appeal, and unproved assertions.

EVALUATING A SPEECH

33o. Evaluate a speech critically, politely, and constructively.

In the classroom you will probably be asked to evaluate, or critique, other students' speeches, and they will be asked to evaluate yours. A good rule to follow is to evaluate others' speeches as constructively and politely as you would have them evaluate yours.

Whenever you evaluate a speech, use all the critical listening skills, making notes as the speech progresses and paying attention to the speaker's strong points as well as to areas or skills that need improvement. Use your notes to give specific examples when you make your evaluation.

WEAK "I thought the speech was good."

BETTER "His opening was strong. It made me feel as though I were in the hot-air balloon with him."

"She sustained my interest by using unusual facts and personal experiences in rock climbing."

WEAK "The speech was hard to follow."

BETTER "Her eye contact and gestures were effective, but near the end of the speech I could hardly hear her."

"His organization was clear, but he gave no examples or facts to support the need for neighborhood crime watches."

Establish an atmosphere of constructive evaluation:

1. Give praise sincerely.
2. Be objective in your evaluation: do not let your personal likes and dislikes influence you.
3. State specific strengths and weaknesses politely.
4. Be definite and constructive.

The evaluation sheet on the following page will help you focus on specific strengths and weaknesses of the speech and the effectiveness of the speaker's delivery.

EXERCISE 18. **Evaluating a Speech.** Listen to a speech on television or at a community or school meeting. Use the evaluation sheet on the following page as the basis for your evaluation and make notes of specific examples. Summarize your evaluation of the speech in a written paragraph.

EVALUATION SHEET

Speaker ——

Topic ——

Evaluator ——

	Very good	Good	Fair	Weak
Speech				
Introduction				
Organization				
Conclusion				
Delivery				
Use of notes				
Speaking manner				
Posture				
Gestures				
Eye contact				
Voice				
Pronunciation/ enunciation				

Comments:

GROUP DISCUSSION

Group discussion skills will help you participate effectively in college and in a career. Through discussion you will discover that persons with differing views can disagree in an atmosphere of mutual respect, can work together for the common good, can perceive the extent of a problem more clearly by exchanging opinions, and can become more willing to compromise.

Types of Group Discussion

There are four kinds of group discussion:

Social conversation is private and unplanned, and it touches lightly on many topics. It requires no leader, although a host or hostess may occasionally steer it. Its aim is enjoyment, persuasion, or instruction.

Informal group discussion resembles social conversation except that it is usually more purposeful and deals with a single topic or a limited number of topics decided beforehand by the participants. An informal group, such as a small committee, may or may not be guided by a discussion leader.

Formal group discussion is public and planned. It considers many aspects of a single topic, and its aim is to reach an agreement, solve a problem, or start action. It is directed and summarized by a leader.

A *debate* is public and planned, like formal group discussion, but considers only two sides of a question. The supporters of one side attempt to defeat their opponents by arguments. The victor is determined by a judge or group of judges.

A debate may grow out of a group discussion. The numerous solutions developed in a discussion may be narrowed to one, which is then offered to a wider public for acceptance or rejection.

33p. Learn the characteristics of the various forms of group discussion.

The *round table* is a group discussion in which the participants exchange views around a table (not necessarily round) under the guidance of a discussion leader. The number of people usually does not exceed a dozen. The discussion is informal. There is no audience.

The most common example of a round-table discussion is the committee meeting. Most organizations conduct a large part of their business through committees. A committee considers matters and then reports its findings and recommendations to the entire organization.

A *forum* is any speaking program that is followed by audience participation—for example, a lecture followed by questions from the audience. A forum is most successful when the audience is small; otherwise, people are reluctant to stand up and speak their minds.

A *symposium* consists of prepared talks by several speakers on different aspects of a single topic. When all the speakers have finished their presentations, the discussion leader invites the audience to ask questions, contribute additional information, or express agreement or disagreement with the speakers' views.

A *panel discussion* is like an overheard conversation. It consists of a leader and four to eight participants seated, usually in a semicircle, before an audience. The participants remain seated during the discussion. They speak in conversational style, generally not longer than one to two minutes at a time. They express opinions and disagree with and question one another. The leader acts as a moderator, stimulating, directing, and summarizing the discussion. The audience may also join in the conversation.

Preparation for Group Discussion

33q. Select a topic that lends itself to a profitable group discussion.

Before selecting a topic for discussion, ask the following questions:

1. Is it sufficiently limited for the time allowed?
2. Is it worthwhile?
3. Is it timely?
4. Is it related to the needs, experience, and interests of listeners and speakers?
5. Is it stimulating?
6. Is it many-sided?

What are good sources of topics for group discussion? Your own experience may suggest some: "Teen-age problems," "Trends in popular music," "Choosing a career," or "Why study mathematics and science?" Books, newspapers, magazine articles, movies, and television programs can often stimulate discussion. Current events, especially controversial matters, can also hold an audience's attention.

A discussion topic should be a question of policy rather than a question of fact. "Do we have a supply of gasoline?" is a question of fact, and the only appropriate reply is a factual answer. "Should we stop using gasoline in cars?" is a question of policy that stirs discussion.

Topics that are trivial or timeworn, have no audience appeal, do not evoke strong differences of opinion, or can be answered *yes* or *no* are not suitable.

Select an up-to-date controversial topic.

EXAMPLES   What's wrong with today's economy?
            How can we prevent food shortages?
            Who should pay for college?

For strategies for selecting and limiting subjects, see Chapter 1, pages 10–13.

33r. Prepare for a group discussion by thinking, talking, and reading about the topic.

Many discussions fail because of insufficient preparation. To prepare for a discussion, everyone must think, talk, and read about the topic before the discussion takes place. When the topic is announced, follow these three steps:

1. *Think about it.* What is your opinion? On what evidence is it based?

2. *Talk to others about it.* Discuss it with your friends and parents. Discuss it with an authority on the subject. Be ready to modify your previous opinion in the light of your new knowledge.

3. *Consult reference books, recent publications, magazine articles, and editorials.* Inform yourself as thoroughly as you can about the topic. Keep an open mind while you are learning.

33s. Learn the duties of the discussion leader, the speakers, and the members of the audience.

The discussion leader is responsible for knowing the background and special interests of each speaker. If possible, a preliminary meeting of all the speakers should be arranged to go over the topic and procedure of the discussion.

When the discussion begins, the leader should state the purpose of the discussion, introduce each speaker to the audience, and mention something about each speaker's background. While the discussion continues, the leader should ask questions of the speakers, try to prevent fruitless digressions, and ensure that everyone has a chance to speak. At the close of the discussion, the leader should summarize the major points and thank the audience and speakers.

Speakers invited to a discussion should be able to listen carefully and courteously to others, speak so that everyone can hear, and be sure that the comments they give are directly related to the topic.

Members of the audience should listen to the speakers attentively, take notes if necessary, and join in the discussion when the leader invites questions from the spectators. Questions should, of course, relate directly to the topic under discussion and be spoken in a clear voice that everyone can hear.

EXERCISE 19. Selecting Topics for a Group Discussion. List five topics suitable for a group discussion. Test them against the criteria listed in the previous sections. The topics may be related to school, community, state, national, or international affairs.

Taking Part in a Group Discussion

You can be more successful in communicating your ideas to others if you learn something about speaking and listening effectively in group discussions.

A group is made up of individuals who are attempting to achieve a common goal. For example, a photography club is a group of photographers who might want to organize an exhibition. Within every group, each individual must accept and work for the group's common goal. An individual, however, might have private goals not shared by the group. Psychologists call these private goals a "hidden agenda." As you enter a group discussion, be aware of the difference between the goal of the discussion and the private goals of individual members.

33t. Learn to speak effectively in a group discussion.

1. *Think before you speak.* Know what you are going to say before you begin. Take a few seconds to organize your ideas.

2. *Keep the other person in mind.* Try to understand the other person's point of view. Avoid sarcasm and ridicule. In the midst of heated discussion, remain calm.

3. *Be brief.* Omit long and unnecessary explanations. Know the point you want to make and go directly to it. Speak simply but naturally and enthusiastically.

33u. Learn to listen accurately and critically while taking part in a group discussion.

In a group discussion the interplay of personalities is often so interesting that your attention may wander. Focus your attention by taking notes. Jotting down the arguments will enable you to see the merits of each point. Follow these principles:

1. *Recognize and guard against your own prejudices.* Don't let emotions color your thinking. For example, your reactions to a speaker's appearance, accent, or gestures may affect your acceptance or rejection of what you hear. Think fairly, and test ideas on rational, not emotional, grounds.

2. *Recognize a speaker's bias and take it into account.* When a speaker has an ax to grind, a listener must be careful. The arguments may be valid, but they may also be one-sided and rooted in prejudice.

3. *Watch for words, phrases, and attitudes that are emotionally loaded.* Some words report a fact objectively; others are loaded with emotion.

Compare the following pairs of words. Notice how one member of each pair is relatively colorless, while the other arouses feelings.

house—shack   dwelling—mansion   work—drudgery
reply—rebuke   dog—mongrel   failure—fiasco

Loaded words carry positive or negative charges. A positively charged word creates a favorable reaction; a negatively charged word, an unfavorable one. Propagandists use positively charged words to sway you to their way of thinking and negatively charged words to make you reject what they oppose.

EXERCISE 20. Identifying Loaded Words. Number your paper 1–10. After the proper number, indicate by a plus or a minus sign whether each of the following words affects you positively or negatively.

1. adorable   5. glamorous   8. rebellious
2. skinny   6. fabulous   9. sympathy
3. generous   7. miserly   10. screech
4. crude

4. *Don't be misled by catchy slogans and generalized introductory statements.* Advertisers and political organizations often employ slogans to popularize ideas, candidates, or products. A complex argument cannot be summarized fairly in a capsule expression.

EXAMPLES   See America first. [slogan promoting travel in the United States, as opposed to foreign travel]
Put yourself in our shoes. [advertising slogan]

Generalized introductory statements often have no basis in fact, but they imply that disagreement is impossible.

EXAMPLES   It is common knowledge that . . .
Everybody knows that . . .

5. *Look for and weigh evidence for every important statement.* If a speaker offers no evidence, ask for it. If the evidence is insufficient, ask for more.

EXERCISE 21. Conducting a Round-Table Discussion. Conduct a round-table discussion on a topic that concerns all the participants. Appoint a discussion leader who will end the discussion after twenty minutes, summarize, and invite class discussion. You may use one of the following suggested topics.

1. The school yearbook
2. Improving the student organization
3. Building school spirit
4. Improving the school cafeteria
5. Assembly programs

EXERCISE 22. Conducting a Symposium. Conduct a symposium on discipline. The speakers should represent the viewpoints of a student, a parent, a law-enforcement officer, an educator, and a community leader.

EXERCISE 23. Conducting a Panel Discussion. Select a discussion leader, and present a panel discussion on any of the following topics or one of your own choosing. Each panel should meet beforehand to settle matters of procedure and scope.

1. Radio and television advertising
2. Comic books and their characters
3. Youthful crime
4. Violence on the screen
5. Prejudice—and how to overcome it
6. The impact of the young voter
7. The ideal school
8. Professional versus amateur sports
9. Our foreign policy
10. Ways to prevent war

EXERCISE 24. Listening Critically. Why should you be particularly careful in listening to each of the following speakers?

1. The president of a college fraternity speaking about the advantages of fraternity life
2. A movie actress advertising a cold cream
3. A candidate of a political party speaking about the party's platform
4. A disc jockey delivering a commercial
5. A parent of a failing student criticizing a school

Evaluation of a Group Discussion

33v. Evaluate a group discussion by asking key questions about it.

By considering the merits and faults of a group discussion after it is over, you can learn to improve future discussions. The following questions will help you evaluate a group discussion.

1. Was the discussion purposeful? Were the causes of the problem considered? Were various solutions proposed and analyzed? Did the discussion ramble, or did it proceed in an orderly fashion?

2. Were the outcomes worthwhile? A group discussion need not reach a solution or agreement. It may be successful if it brings areas of disagreement into the open.

3. Were the participants thoroughly familiar with the problem? Did they present facts, instances, statements of competent and unbiased authorities, and statistics to support their opinions?

4. Was the discussion lively and general? Was there a give-and-take of opinion in an atmosphere of mutual respect? Did all participate? Did anyone monopolize the meeting, or did everyone speak briefly and to the point?

5. Did the participants reach a solution justified by the evidence? Do you agree with the solution? Why?

6. Were the audience's questions thought-provoking? Did the speakers answer them directly and fully?

7. Was the discussion courteous? Did each speaker exercise self-control by refraining from interrupting when another was speaking? Were statements and objections phrased courteously?

8. Did the discussion leader's introductory remarks arouse interest? Did the discussion avoid valueless digressions? Was everyone encouraged to join in? Was there a summary?

EXERCISE 25. Evaluating a Radio or Television Discussion.
Evaluate a radio or television discussion you have heard. Consider such matters as choice of topic, the speakers' familiarity with the topic, the quality of the discussion, and audience participation. In what ways could the discussion have been improved?

THE INTERVIEW

In some forms of interview there is a give-and-take of opinion between the participants, and in other forms one person necessarily monopolizes the conversation; but always there is a dominating purpose that the interview tries to achieve. One common type of interview with which you should be familiar is the interview for gathering information.

The Interview for Gathering Information

While preparing a composition, you may wish to interview someone who is knowledgeable about your particular topic. Make arrangements for the interview well in advance. You may request the interview in a letter, by a telephone call, or through a personal visit. State who you are and the reason for your request. Mention in general terms what days and times are most acceptable to you for a meeting, but allow the other person to specify the exact time and place.

Preparing for the Interview

Plan your questions carefully in advance. Write each question on a separate card or page so that you will have enough room to jot down the replies. If you are using a tape recorder, of course, you need only write your questions in a list.

Give plenty of thought to each question. Your interview will be much more successful if you can focus on important issues. Ask questions that will elicit useful responses, and use the answers to ask follow-up questions.

Ask questions that require extended replies reather than *yes* or *no* answers. For example, rather than asking, "Do you think students should be required to study a foreign language?" ask, "Why should students be required to study a foreign language?"

Be sure that the questions you ask are clear and straightforward. If the other person seems confused by a question you ask, be prepared to restate it.

Conducting the Interview

Arrive on time. Allow for traffic delays in setting out for your appointment. It is better to be early than late. Lateness for an appointment is discourteous, and it may create a bad impression.

Try not to rush through the interview, asking questions in rapid-fire order. Allow yourself and the other person enough time to consider and respond thoughtfully to each question. During the interview, remain tactful and courteous. Do not try to provoke argument, although you may disagree with some of the points being made.

Using a Tape Recorder

Before recording the interview, be sure to ask permission of the person whom you are interviewing. At the end of the interview, agree to play back the recording if you are asked to do so. Permit the person to modify any statements you have recorded.

Concluding the Interview

Before concluding the interview, ask whether you have omitted any aspect of the topic that the other person would like to discuss. When the interview has run its course, express appreciation for the privilege extended to you, and take your leave.

Whatever the purpose of the interview, it is always a good policy to send a thank-you note.

EXERCISE 26. **Conducting an Interview.** Conduct an interview to gather information for a composition. Get your teacher's approval of the topic of your interview, and be prepared to report on it in class.

CHAPTER 34

Understanding Mass Media

ELECTRONIC AND PRINT

The *mass media* are forms of communication that reach and influence you and millions of other people every day. The mass media include television and radio, which bring you information about what is going on in the world almost as it happens, and newspapers and magazines, which bring you detailed accounts and analyses of worldwide political developments, natural disasters, and scientific discoveries. Through the mass media, you have the means to know more about the world than people have ever known before.

THE NEW MEDIA ENVIRONMENT

A century ago news traveled very slowly, frequently by word of mouth. Printed news was also distributed slowly. The people who received the printed news read it and then shared and discussed it with others.

Today the media environment is quite different. People who have time to read the news have access to it in several daily newspapers and dozens of weekly and monthly magazines. Those who do not have time to read the news have access to it instantly—at the touch of a television or radio dial. The mass media thus make the news available to just about everyone. Yet you may not discuss and analyze the news as much as people did a century ago. News correspondents and analysts are paid to report world events and, often, to interpret them for you as well. In a certain respect, turning to professionals for their analysis of the news can help you, because you are surrounded by so much information.

You might think that in a world where so much information is distributed quickly, the mass media have only one role—to inform. However, the mass media bring entertainment into your life as well. Only a few short decades ago, if you did not see or hear something in person, you did not see or hear it at all. Today you can see and hear live performances of your favorite music, television, and film stars even if you cannot attend their performances in person. You can see our nation's great cities, view its natural resources, and visit its landmarks without leaving home.

EXERCISE 1. Determining How the Media Environment Has Changed. Use one of the following sets of interview questions with a person who can discuss the mass media as they were in the 1930's, 1940's, or 1950's. Present your findings in a short, written report. Be prepared to discuss them in class.

1. How have the numbers and kinds of magazines available thirty, forty, or fifty years ago changed as compared to those available today?
2. What memories of radio as a source of information do you have? To what extent was radio thirty, forty, or fifty years ago seen and used as a medium[1] of entertainment as well as a medium of information?
3. Do newspapers feature the same balance of local and national news as they used to? In what other ways have newspapers changed? In what ways do newspapers today seem more standard and alike compared to newspapers a few decades ago?
4. How has television affected American family life? Sports? Leisure time? News? Politics?

CONSUMERS AND THE MASS MEDIA

Like almost all members of our society, you probably read a newspaper or magazine, watch television, or listen to the radio on occasion. These activities make you a mass media consumer. As such, you should understand the role of the mass media in your life.

---

[1] Note that *medium* is the singular of *media*.

Uses of the Mass Media

34a. Understand how you can use the mass media.

You, the consumer, have a choice in how you use the media: (1) you can use the media *passively* and (2) you can use the media *actively*.

Sometimes you just feel like watching television. It does not really matter what you watch. You turn on any program, pay little attention to it, and will probably not remember much of what you see. When you entertain yourself in this way, you are using television passively. Television does, however, provide challenging programs that require you to pay attention and think. When you watch and concentrate on this kind of program, you are using television differently—you are using it actively.

EXERCISE 2. Considering Active Uses of the Media. Each medium below can make you think. Work in small groups to make a list of broadcasts or publications for each category. Include only those that you agree are interesting and *worthwhile*. Discuss each choice.

TELEVISION   MAGAZINES   NEWSPAPERS   RADIO

EXERCISE 3. Considering Passive Uses of the Media. Give "entertainment and escape only" examples for each of the following media categories. Do not include those broadcasts or publications you would consider informative or intellectually challenging.

TELEVISION   MAGAZINES   NEWSPAPERS   RADIO

Goals of the Mass Media

34b. Understand the goals of the mass media.

You have seen how you can use the media, but you should also understand in what ways you are used by them. Remember that a primary goal of the broadcast and print media is to build a successful business. To do so, they must develop and maintain loyal audiences. Radio and television stations must find listeners and viewers. Magazines and newspapers must find readers.

The mass media compete for your attention and loyalty. In most areas, more than one radio station wants you as a listener, and more than one television station wants you as a viewer. The people who produce mass media products must figure out what you want and then give it to you. At the same time, though, mass media producers must figure out what thousands of other people want so that they can satisfy as many consumers as possible.

The mass media need your attention and loyalty to stay in business. The media sell the promise, prospect, or proof of your attention to advertisers. With the dollars provided by advertisers, the media are able to fund their broadcasts or publications and become successful businesses. Advertisers, who want you to purchase their products, are eager to purchase your attention from the media. Your attention is an important *commodity*—something that is bought and sold—because it helps make advertisers, as well as the media, successful.

For example, a company that manufactures blue jeans buys advertising time on television, providing some of the money for a program that potential consumers of its product like. You watch that program—it draws your attention to the television—which is exactly what the company wants. Since you will probably see the company's advertisement as you watch the program, the chance that you will buy that company's blue jeans increases. Your attention thus becomes a commodity sold by television and bought by an advertiser.

EXERCISE 4. Understanding How the Mass Media Attract Consumers. Select one of the following activities. Prepare a five-minute oral report on your choice.

1. Review a recent copy of the most successful newspaper in your area. Identify five popular features or services provided by the paper that you feel readers would not want to do without. Compare your list to those of your classmates. In what ways are your lists alike? Study your lists and discuss what people who read the paper want.

2. Listen carefully to one hour of broadcasting on your favorite radio station. Write a description of what that station's listeners want. Consider the variety of music, the type of information, and the nature of the commentary. What does the radio station manager know about your radio tastes and needs—and about the needs of many people like you?

3. Each night for one week, watch a different hour of programming on a different television network. Take notes on what you view. What does your viewing experience suggest about what television producers must know? What does it tell you about what you "want" from television? Compare your observations with those of classmates. Do

you see many similarities? Does television give you what you want, or have you learned to want what television gives you? Is there a difference?

MASS MEDIA ADVERTISING

As you have already seen, your attention is a commodity being bought and sold as you use the mass media. The media do the selling and advertisers do the buying. Advertising in the mass media is very expensive. It is also very effective. If that were not the case, people with products to sell would not spend so much money on advertising to reach and influence you.

Knowing about the general art of persuasion (pages 96–101) and types of persuasive appeals (pages 732–34) can help you understand what advertisers try to do and how they try to do it. In addition to the types of appeals upon which much advertising is based, there are other important points about mass media advertising that you should understand.

34c. Advertising is designed to make you desire both products and life styles.

When you watch television, listen to the radio, or read a newspaper or magazine, you may feel that you gloss over the advertisements, paying little attention to them. That may be, but advertising has a subtle impact.

Suppose that you like to bake bread every week. However, baking bread is a time-consuming process. When you bake bread, you have to take time away from the other things you like to do. What do you really value—using your time to bake bread or saving time so you can do something else?

One day you see an advertisement on television for quick-rising frozen bread dough. The advertisement convinces you that you *need* to have some of that dough the next time you bake bread. You would not have to mix and knead the dough or wait so long for it to rise, which would allow you to save time and perhaps go to a friend's home to visit. Advertising is shaping your values by encouraging you to save time.

Imagine that soon afterward you see an advertisement in a magazine for a microwave oven—the person using it is dressed in casual clothes.

You realize that you could save even more time if you had a microwave and did not have to wait so long for the bread to bake. This advertisement also reinforces the value you place on saving time. In addition, it is suggesting that a casual and relaxed *life style* is desirable.

The efforts of advertisers thus shape you into the kind of consumer they want you to be. Understanding how mass media advertising can influence your consumer needs, values, and desired life style is crucial.

EXERCISE 5. Exploring How the Media Shape You. Select one of the following activities.

1. Clip ten full-page advertisements from magazines. Study each advertisement, paying as little attention as possible to the product being advertised. Focus your attention on what is *around* the product—the kind of people, the setting, the symbols and language used. What need does the advertiser try to create or reinforce? What value does the advertiser try to shape? What life style does the advertiser want you to seek? Discuss your findings in small groups.
2. Radio advertising must rely on language and music alone to form images in your mind. Tape record three minutes of radio advertising. Listen to the advertisements with a small group of classmates. What does the advertiser want you to feel? To desire? To value? Describe the "you" a particular advertiser wants you to become.

34d. Through advertising, mass media create consumer audiences for one another.

Since your attention is a valuable commodity, you might think the various mass media compete with each other for it. It is true that companies in the same medium are very competitive. Major television networks are the best examples; they all want you to view only *their* shows.

On the other hand, different media can create consumer audiences for one another. Those major television networks provide information about music by advertising record albums, radio stations, and special radio broadcasts. In this way, television can lead you into becoming a more frequent radio listener than you may already be. Media producers and advertisers want you to be highly dependent on media *in general*. The more often you are a consumer (whether a reading, viewing, or listening consumer), the easier it is for advertising to reach you—to create new needs and to shape your values and life style.

EXERCISE 6. Exploring Interdependence of the Media. Select a favorite musical group or performer, or a favorite television personality. Look and listen for that group's or performer's name in the media for one week. Make a list of all the places you see and hear the name. Do you see how the media rely on each other? Discuss your observations of the media in class.

DIFFERENCES AMONG THE MASS MEDIA

With so many different mass media products available to today's consumers, it is not always easy to decide which medium to use and when to use it. You need to analyze media products in terms of their *purposes, quality,* and *appropriateness* in order to make good consumer decisions.

Multiple Purposes

34e. The mass media have the potential to offer products that entertain, inform, and/or persuade.

In seeking readers, listeners, and viewers, mass media producers create products that will serve one or more purposes. For instance, a media product may be meant only to entertain you, or it may be intended to inform *and* persuade you.

The mass media convey what people decide to put into them. For example, magazine editors decide that there will be several cartoons in an issue of their publication, and then they decide which particular cartoons to use. It is likely that the cartoons are meant both to entertain and persuade you. The editors also decide whether to include features such as stock market reports, which are purely informational. Editorials may be clearly persuasive, or perhaps only entertaining; again, the editors decide. Similarly, the other media have the potential to offer products that serve several purposes at once.

EXERCISE 7. Identifying Multiple Purposes in a Mass Medium.

Work in small groups to analyze a copy of your local newspaper. First, list the major sections of the paper. Then, list examples of regular features or columns in each major section. Which features in a section are primarily for entertainment? For information? For persuasion? Prepare a brief group report, and be ready to compare your conclusions with those of other groups in class.

Standards of Quality

34f. Determine mass media quality using both subjective and objective standards.

Can you remember ever having said, "That was a good article" or "That was really a poor article"? What exactly did you mean? The difference between a good, informative magazine story and another article on the same topic that practically puts you to sleep is a question of quality. Since the quality of mass media products varies, it is important that you know how to evaluate it.

One way you can judge the quality of mass media products is by using *subjective* standards. They are the result of your personal feelings and beliefs. Your preferences come into play each time you think about what you find satisfying or disappointing in the media. Subjective standards are not based on logical criteria. They reflect your *individual* response to a media product.

Another way you can evaluate the quality of mass media products is by using *objective* standards. They are the result of group consensus. Suppose a number of consumers agree that a particular nature magazine uses the most original photography they have ever seen. Since no other magazine possesses that characteristic to the same degree, the objective standard for originality is established. Consumers can then compare other nature magazines with this objective standard of quality. If these magazines stand up relatively well against the standard, they are products of good quality. If they do not, then they are products of poor quality.

You can apply both subjective and objective judgments to what the media offer. Keep the following questions in mind as you evaluate the quality of a mass media product.

1. Why do I (or do I not) find this satisfying? Worthwhile? Informative? Enjoyable? Significant?

2. Are the reasons for my judgments mostly subjective or objective in nature?

EXERCISE 8. Developing Objective Standards to Evaluate Media Products. Determine by vote the two favorite television situation comedies of your classmates. List six to eight specific achievements, features, or attributes that you agree are common to both series. Summarize by writing statements of your objective standards. Begin with the words, "An enjoyable situation comedy . . ."; then, follow with a verb and a characteristic of a good situation comedy.

EXERCISE 9. Using Subjective Standards to Evaluate Mass Media. Select and read several editorials from your local newspaper. Then, choose the one editorial that you found least persuasive, least informative, and least interesting. Write a short essay explaining why you feel as you do.

Appropriate Uses

34g. Recognize that each of the mass media has strengths and weaknesses.

As a mass media consumer, you may prefer to use one medium over the others. Whatever the basis for your preference, you should be aware that each medium has strengths and weaknesses. For this reason, one medium may be more appropriate in a situation than another would be. There are four factors that determine which medium would be appropriate: (1) what the medium *can do,* (2) what its *purpose* is, (3) what role *time* plays, and (4) what the *event* is.

In reporting the results of nationwide legislative elections, for example, all the media could somehow be involved. Television and radio could provide up-to-the-minute coverage on which candidate was leading the race for each office. The purpose of the broadcasts would be to inform the audience of the most recent election developments. Once all the votes and results were in, the broadcast media would continue to inform the audience by providing the final outcomes of the elections. At this stage, the rate at which information was being created would slow, giving the media time to begin analyzing the election results as well.

It would be appropriate for newspapers and magazines to become involved in reporting once time was no longer so crucial. They could obviously not have offered the same up-to-the-minute coverage provided by the broadcast media, but they could certainly inform audiences of the final election results. In addition, they could provide thorough analyses of the election outcomes. It is likely that their analyses would be more complete than those of the broadcast media, because the print media would have more time to study the consequences and implications of the final election results.

Suppose the event was not nationwide elections, but perhaps a New Orleans jazz festival. How could all the media be involved in that situation?

EXERCISE 10. Determining Which Mass Medium Is Appropriate. Work in small groups. Discuss the strengths and weaknesses that radio, television, newspapers, and magazines would have in reporting one of the following situations. Share your conclusions with other groups.

1. You wish to provide first reports of an earthquake in South America.
2. You wish to expose a government's negligence in providing aid to earthquake victims.
3. You wish to provide technical, scientific information about measuring earthquakes to an audience of geophysicists.
4. You wish to tell the story of a person who was trapped for days, survives, and then becomes an advocate for a national earthquake recovery program.
5. You wish to provide information to people in earthquake regions about what to do in the event of an earthquake.

BECOMING ACTIVE MEDIA CONSUMERS

34h. Take active, personal responsibility for shaping mass media content and products by responding to the media.

Critical consumers learn that every medium has the potential to deliver high-quality content, to be accurate, and to be truthful. These are, in fact, among what you should hold as the responsibilities of the mass media.

However, mass media producers must make money. If they do not, they go out of business. As they seek to increase the size of their audiences, mass media producers may sacrifice the quality of their products. Producing high-quality broadcasts and publications is more expensive and time consuming than providing average or inferior ones. Without media responsibility for quality *and* accuracy, the result can be aimless, dangerous diversion. It is up to you to make the mass media responsible. You can do this by viewing, listening, and reading critically and then responding to the media.

The mass media must be sensitive to what you will tolerate, what you will support with your attention, and what you will demand. For example, if you and many other people refuse to listen to a radio broadcast, it will be taken off the air. If your local newspaper inaccurately reports a story about your school, you can respond by writing a letter to the editor. Good editors are interested in accuracy and work hard to provide it; they will be responsive to your letter. The degree to which you respond actively to the mass media will determine the quality of mass media products you consume.

EXERCISE 11. Responding to Radio. As you listen to your favorite radio station this week, make note of the services, features, approaches, or personalities that you appreciate. At the end of the week, compare your notes to those of classmates who have listened to the same radio station. Then, together, write a letter to the station's general manager, explaining what you and your classmates have appreciated, and why.

EXERCISE 12. Influencing a Magazine. Think of a feature or idea for an article you would like to see appear in a magazine you regularly enjoy reading. Write a letter to the magazine's editor. Explain who you are and include specific details about what you would like to see. State why you think your suggestion would be appealing to other readers of the same magazine.

EXERCISE 13. Writing a Letter to a Newspaper Editor. Find an article in a recent issue of your local newspaper with which you strongly agree or disagree. Write a letter to the editor, explaining your reaction and the reasons behind it.

EXERCISE 14. Becoming Involved in Television. Write a class letter to the program manager, public affairs director, or station manager of your local television stations. Invite a representative from each station to visit your class. Let them know in advance what you wish to discuss.

34i. Monitor, evaluate, and direct your use of the mass media.

To *monitor* your use of the mass media means simply that you should be aware of when and how you use the media. You may not realize which media you use most often, or how, or why. Keep a media log or diary to help you become aware of your use of the media.

Once you learn to monitor your use of the mass media, you should be able to *evaluate* that use. For instance, does one medium dominate most of your attention? At the same time, you can develop the skill of evaluating what the media bring to you. Here are a few general guidelines you can use to evaluate the media.

1. Publications and broadcasts should show *fairness and balance in telling you about issues.*

2. Publications and broadcasts should show *accuracy in reporting facts.*

3. Publications and broadcasts should show *respect for the dignity and freedom of individuals.*

4. Publications and broadcasts should show *freshness and originality in addressing issues.*

Once you evaluate the mass media—that is, once you are able to distinguish the good from the not-so-good products they offer—and can identify your strengths and weaknesses in using the media, you should *direct* your attention to particular media products. For example, to be informed about the world, you may need more than television. Direct your attention to what newspapers and magazines say about national and world events. This will add to what you know from television. Learn to direct your attention to new sources of information and to look for new and significant uses for the mass media in your life.

EXERCISE 15. Developing a Plan for Improving How You Use Mass Media. Think about how you use the media. Consider how you could use the media in more critical, balanced ways. Write a brief personal essay, including ideas on how you might monitor, evaluate, and direct your use of mass media. Discuss your essay with two or three classmates.

INDEX

Index

INDEX

INDEX

in critical review, 146
in expository paragraph, 77–79
in persuasive paragraph, 96–97
Fall, principal parts of, 491
Fallacies, 184–86
Familiar Quotations, Bartlett's, 659
Few, number of, 450
Fewer, less, 536
Fiction, arrangement of in library, 647–48
Figurative language
hazards of, 286–89
in creative writing, 195–96
metaphor, 284–85
mixed metaphor, 286–87
personification, 285
simile, 285
understanding, as aid in studying, 708
Figure of speech, 196
Fill-in-the-blank questions, strategies for answering, 712
First-person narrator, 201–202
5 W-How? questions, 18, 59
Folding a business letter, 265–66
Footnotes, 245
Foreign words
meaning of, 683–85
spelling of, 631
underlining for, 599
See also Etymology of words; English, history of
Formal English, 6–7, 441–42. *See also* Tone
Formally, formerly, 635
Forms, completing, 271–76
Fractions, hyphen with, 618
Fragment = Sentence fragment
Freeze, principal parts of, 491
Future perfect tense, 499
Future tense, 498
"Fuzzy language." *See* Jargon

G

Gathering information, techniques for, 14–20. *See also* specific types of writing
Gender, 434, 461–62
Generalization
defined, 63
forming, 63–64
hasty, 63, 185
topic sentence as, 64
Geographical names, capitalization of, 551–52

Gerund
defined, 399
diagramed, 404–405
Gerund phrase
defined, 400
diagramed, 404–405
Give, principal parts of, 491
Glittering generalities, 183
Glossary, 652
Go, principal parts of, 491
Good, comparison of, 516, 520
Good, well, 516–18, 520
Goode's World Atlas, 659
Grammar, English, influences on, 128–38
Granger's *Index to Poetry,* 660
Greek prefixes and roots, 684, 686–91
Guidelines for Evaluating
an argument, 168
business letters and forms, 276
character sketches and biographical sketches, 224
critical reviews, 150–51
descriptive paragraphs, 90
essays of literary analysis, 156
expository compositions, 134–35
expository paragraphs, 86–87
general, 25
narrative paragraphs, 94
paragraphs, general, 68
persuasive compositions, 175
persuasive paragraphs, 99
process explanations, 145
research papers, 249
short stories, 209
Guidelines for Proofreading, 32–33
Guidelines for Writing
expository compositions, 140–41
research papers, 260

H

Had of, 536
Had ought, 536
Hammond Contemporary World Atlas, 659
Hasty generalization, 63–64, 185
Haven't but, haven't only, 543–44
He, she, they, as double subject, 536
Heading, in business letter, 263
Hear, here, 635
Helping verbs, 344
Here, beginning a sentence, diagramed, 380
Here is, number of subject after, 457

INDEX

NOTES

NOTES

NOTES

NOTES

NOTES

NOTES

NOTES

NOTES

NOTES

NOTES

NOTES